A S U R V E Y O F

WESTERN CIVILIZATION VOLUME ONE

A SURVEY OF

WESTERN CIVILIZATION VOLUME ONE

RICHARD D. GOFF
GEORGE H. CASSAR
ANTHONY ESLER
JAMES P. HOLOKA
JAMES C. WALTZ

WEST PUBLISHING COMPANY
St. Paul   New York   Los Angeles   San Francisco

LIBRARY OF CONGRESS CATALOGING-IN-
PUBLICATION DATA

A Survey of Western Civilization.

   Includes bibliographies and index.
   1. Civilization, Occidental—
History.   2. Civilization—History.   I.
Goff, Richard D.
CB245.S95   1987   909'.09821
86-24601
ISBN 0-314-26135-4 (v. 1)
ISBN 0-314-26137-0 (v. 2)

Copyediting: Elaine Linden
Design: Janet Bollow
Illustrations: Asterisk Group
Cartographic Research and
Compilation: Robert Ward, James
Vaughn
Cartographic Design and
Production: Patricia Isaacs, assisted by
Rebecca Miller and Julie L. Mortenson
Photo Research: Monica Suder, assisted
by Linsay Kefauver
Composition: Parkwood Composition
Service, Inc.
Cover Design: Imagesmyth, Inc.
Cover Art: Michelangelo, The Creation
of Adam, detail of the ceiling of the
Sistine Chapel, the Vatican, Vatican
City, 1508–12. Scala/Art Resource,
N.Y.

ACKNOWLEDGMENTS

(The following list contains sources for all chapter-opening paragraphs.)

5 C. J., "Assyrian and Babylonian Beast Fables," American Journal of Semitic Languages and Literatures, Vol. 28 (1912), pp. 86–87, 100, as adapted in S. Moscati, The Face of the Ancient Orient (Garden City, N.Y.: Doubleday, 1962), pp. 85–86.

23 Hesiod, Works and Days, lines 156–73 (translated by J. P. Holoka).

30 Hesiod, Works and Days, from Hesiod: Theogony, Works and Days, Theognis: Elegies, translated by D. Wender (Harmondsworth: Penguin Classics, 1973), page 74, lines 458–462, 468–472, copyright © Dorothea Wender, 1973. Reproduced by permission of Penguin Books Ltd.

38 Homer, The Iliad of Homer, translated by R. Lattimore. (Chicago: University of Chicago Press, 1951), Book 12, lines 309–316, 326–328. Copyright © 1951 by the University of Chicago. Reprinted with permission.

38 R. Lattimore, translator, Greek Lyrics, 2nd ed. (Chicago: University of Chicago Press, 1960), lines 9–14 of Sappho 2; Archilochus 3; lines 71–73 of Semonides 1. Copyright © 1960 Richard Lattimore. Reprinted with permission.

41 Thucydides, History of the Peloponnesian War, translated by R. Warner (Harmondsworth: Penguin Books, 1954; rev. 1972), 2.41.

57 Plato, Protagoras, translated by W. K. C. Guthrie, in The Collected Dialogues of Plato, ed. E. Hamilton and H. Cairns (Princeton N.J.: Princeton University Press, 1961), p. 322.

64 Sophocles, Antigone, translated by E. Wyckoff in The Complete Greek Tragedies, D. Grene and R. Lattimore, eds. (Chicago: University of Chicago Press, 1954), lines 499–525. Copyright © 1954 by the University of Chicago. Reprinted with permission.

75 Isocrates, "Philip," in Greek Political Oratory, translated by A. N. W. Saunders (Harmondsworth: Penguin Books, 1970), pp. 164–165.

91 Livy, The Early History of Rome, translated by A. de Sélincourt (Harmondsworth: Penguin Books, 1960), 5.48.

107 Plutarch, Life of Caesar, translated by N. Lewis and M. Reinhold, in Roman Civilization: Sourcebook, I: The Republic (1951; reprinted New York: Harper, 1966), p. 291.

123 Vergil, The Aeneid, 2nd ed., translated by F. O. Copley (New York: Macmillan Publishing Company, 1975), Book 1, lines 276–279, 286–296.

125 Lucretius, The Nature of Things. Reprinted from The Nature of Things, Lucretius, translated by F. O. Copley, with permission of W. W. Norton & Company, Inc. Copyright © 1977 by W. W. Norton & Company, Inc.

127 Vergil, The Aeneid, translated by R. Fitzgerald (New York: Random House, Inc., 1983), Book 6, lines 847–853. Copyright © 1983 by Random House, Inc. Reprinted with permission.

143 Saint Augustine, The City of God, translated by M. Dods (New York: Random House, Inc., 1950), 14.28.

163 Procopius, Buildings, translated by H. B. Dewing in collaboration with G. Downey (London: Heinemann, 1940) Loeb Classical Library, Vol. 7 of Procopius, with an English translation, pp. 11–17, 25–29.

181 Annales Laureshameuses, year 801, edited by G. H. Pertz, Monumenta Germaniae Historica, Scriptores (Hanover, 1826) Vol. 1, p. 38; Annales regni Francorum, year 801, in Quellen zur karolingischen Reichsgeschichte, edited by R. Rau (Berlin: Rütten and Loening, n.d.), 1 Teil, p. 74; The Coronation of Charlemagne: What Did It Signify? (Boston: D. C. Heath, 1959), p. 2.

197 Adalberon, Carmen ad Rotbertum regem, in R. Boutruche, Seigneurie et feodalite (Paris: Aubier, 1959), pp. 371–372; The Medieval Pageant, N. Downs, ed. (Princeton, N.J.: D. Van Nostrand Company, 1964), p. 93.

215 Robert the Monk, "The Speech of Pope Urban II at Clermont," translated by D. C. Munro, Translations and Reprints from the Original Sources of European History, rev. ed., Series I, Vol. I, no. 2 (Philadelphia: University of Pennsylvania Press, 1902), pp. 5–8.

233 L. Thorndike, University Records and Life in the Middle Ages, Records of Civilization, Vol. 38 (New York: Columbia University Press, 1944), pp. 34–35.

251 Letter of Pope Innocent III to the prefect Acerbus and the nobles of Tuscany, 1198, in The Crisis of Church and State, 1050–1300, edited and translated by B. Tierney (Englewood Cliffs, N.J.: Prentice-Hall, 1964), p. 32.

273 Life and Letters of Ogier Ghiselin de Busbecq, C. T. Forster and F. H. Blackburne Daniell, eds. (London: C. Kegan, Paul & Co., 1881), pp. 153–155.

(continued following index)

CONTENTS

LIST OF MAPS

PREFACE

We have designed this textbook to promote interest in and comprehension of western civilization among students attending two- and four-year colleges and universities. Most of these students are majors in other disciplines who are fulfilling distributional requirements for graduation and are unlikely to take additional courses in history.

Our textbook provides a unique combination of characteristics designed to work effectively in this situation. The overall format—moderate length, color, boxed inserts, maps, section time charts, and chapter-opening vignettes—will attract these students to the subject matter. The relative brevity of the text gives the instructor the opportunity to assign supplementary readings. An instructor's guide and a set of map transparencies provide additional aid for the instructor.

In creating this text, we have particularly concentrated on pedagogical elements that will enable average students to apprehend and retain the principal historical points in each chapter. These elements include short chapters that keep the amount of information under control, a clear expository style, an introductory transition from the opening vignette to the body of the chapter, short subtopics to facilitate notetaking, time bars to reinforce a sense of chronology, and a summary to fix the impression of salient points. A short list of sources at the end of each chapter includes well written monographs, as well as engaging novels and drama, and relevant television programs and films from which students might also profit. A student study guide is also available at the professor's discretion.

We have had four governing principles in presenting the subject matter. First, we wish to help American students from diverse backgrounds to appreciate more clearly their place in western civilization, including the role played by their ethnic forebears and the rising importance of their nation. Therefore, in addition to the traditional comprehensive survey of western civilization in the Mediterranean lands and west-central Europe, we have treated eastern Europe, the Muslim role in transmitting and influencing western culture, the Jewish experience, the impact of western societies on the nonwestern world, and especially the modifications of western civilization in the Americas.

Second, our presentation stresses the last two centuries, when most of the technology, institutions, and ideology that directly affect the modern student took shape. Such an approach is more apt to hold the student's interest.

Third, we have selected for emphasis those elements that best encapsulate the western experience in a text of moderate length. We have concentrated on economic, institutional, and political history, while also treating social, cultural, and intellectual developments.

Finally, we have stressed concepts and causal forces rather than a parade of details. Although average students initially find it more difficult to grasp ideas than to remember discrete facts, with help from their professors they can understand causation and accommodate competing ideological stances. They will, as a result, gain more insight into the subject and retain a more meaningful understanding of western civilization.

Acknowledgments

An enterprise of this magnitude and complexity depends on the dedication and perspiration of many people. We were fortunate that West Publishing Company secured the services of many reviewers, whose insights and information materially strengthened this book. They include

Frank Holt,
University of Houston

Richard Golden,
Clemson University

Jerry Brookshire,
Middle Tennessee State University

Nancy Rachels,
Hillsborough Community College

Donald Higgins,
Glendale Community College

Nelson Diebel,
Moraine Valley Community College

Patrick Foley,
Tarrant County Junior College

Manuel Gonzales,
Diablo Valley College

Charles Bussey,
Western Kentucky University

Jack Censer,
George Mason University

Rizalino Oades,
San Diego State University

Karl Roider,
Louisiana State University

Marshall True,
University of Vermont

Glenn Bugh,
Virginia Polytechnic Institute

Richard Huch,
University of Minnesota-Duluth

Janet Polasky,
University of New Hampshire

Orazio Ciccarelli,
University of Southern Mississippi

Gary Ferngren,
Oregon State University

Patricia Bradley,
Auburn University-Montgomery

Arthur Smith,
California State University-Los Angeles

Frederick Dumin,
Washington State University

Stuart Persell,
California State University-San Bernardino

Bullitt Lowry,
North Texas State University

Rev. Charles E. Ronan, S.J.,
Loyola University of Chicago

Merle Rife,
Indiana University of Pennsylvania

Marc Cooper,
Southwest Missouri State University

Andrew Mikus,
Glendale Community College

Alfred Cornebise,
University of Northern Colorado

Julius Ruff,
Marquette University

Sandra Dresbeck,
Western Washington University

Thomas Kennedy,
University of Arkansas

Paul Devendittis,
Nassau Community College

Robert Linder,
Kansas State University

Marcus Orr,
Memphis State University

Henry Steffens,
University of Vermont

Our colleagues at Eastern Michigan University, Della Flusche, Walter Moss, Ira Wheatley, and Reinhard Wittke were generous with information and advice. We are particularly indebted to Lester Scherer, who read and improved significant portions of the manuscript. Robert Ward and James Vaughn provided the initial cartographic sketches. Jo Ann Holoka materially assisted her husband on the myriad tasks he undertook during this project. We are also especially indebted to Nancy Snyder, who not only put the entire text on the computer and entered the masses of revisions and corrections, but took care of innumerable practical chores to bring our project to fruition.

Finally, we wish to gratefully acknowledge the wizardry of the West Publishing Company staff, who transformed a proposal by five professors into an attractive textbook. Clark Baxter, with the assistance of Nancy Crochiere and Maureen Rosener, was the guiding and sustaining spirit. With assistance by cartographer Patricia Isaacs, our production editor, Mark Jacobsen, with patience and resourcefulness pulled the whole project together.

A S U R V E Y O F

WESTERN CIVILIZATION VOLUME ONE

THE ANCIENT WORLD

The first section of this book outlines the history of the human species from the Old Stone Age down through the civilizations of the ancient Near East and Greece to the fall of the western Roman Empire. The immensity and distance of the period of time covered unfortunately have a distorting effect. Because our perspective compresses the expanses of time during which humans learned their capacities and limitations, made discoveries, perfected tools, and won thousands of battles against the environment, we often underestimate the significance of such triumphs. This foreshortening effect on our view of ancient history is a problem for the Greek and Roman eras as well. The stretch of time between the death of Alexander the Great and the birth of Julius Caesar, for example, is longer than the entire history of the United States.

The problem of distance in time is compounded by lack of informa-tion. Despite such limitations, the inquiry into origins holds a peculiar fascination and excitement.

The history of the societies of the Stone Age and the ancient Near East highlights two points of acceleration: the agricultural revolution that divided the Old from the New Stone Age and the urban revolution that saw the emergence of the first city-states. In addition to material developments, humankind also began its continuing effort to fathom the nature of the universe by scientific thinking and varied systems of religious belief. Civilization, by any definition, would not exist without such momentous physical and spiritual changes.

Though the ancient Greeks built on foundations laid by Near Eastern peoples, they far surpassed their predecessors and contemporaries in philosophy, literature, and politics. At Athens, experimentation with democratic institutions accom-panied stunning advances in the plastic arts and such extraordinary cultural creations as tragic and comic drama and formal history. Greek thinkers broke new ground intellectually by their logical and rational inquiries into the nature of things, setting an indelible stamp on western ways of shaping and ex-pressing the human experience.

The great achievement of the Roman Republic was the fashioning of a new, more expansive and in-clusive political organization in the west. In addition, by the Roman imperial period, a large-scale adop-tion of earlier, Greek intellectual patterns resulted in a Greco-Roman culture. This was especially impor-tant because, at least until the Ren-aissance, it was via Roman litera-ture, history, philosophy, and art that western culture absorbed the ancient traditions of the Near East and Greece. However, the Roman Empire was also fertile ground for the growth of new ideas and beliefs, as the story of the rise of Christian-ity demonstrates. By the end of the empire, the new faith had sup-planted obsolescent political and spiritual frameworks of life and pro-vided an important bridge between the ancient world and subsequent epochs of western civilization.

4000 B.C. 3000 B.C. 2000 B.C. 1000 B.C. 800 B.C. 600 B.C. 400 B.C.

Politics

Above timeline:
- King Menes unites upper and lower Egypt
- Mycenaean period in Greece
- Assyrian Empire
- Founding of Rome
- Persian War; Athenian Empire
- Punic Wars

Below timeline:
- Sumerians settle in lower Mesopotamia
- Old Babylonian Empire
- Neo-Babylonian Empire
- Peloponnesian War
- Philip II, Alexander the Great, Hellenistic kingdoms

Economics & Society

Above timeline:
- Earliest cities
- Code of Hammurabi
- Solon's reforms
- Struggle for equality between patricians and plebeians at Rome

Below timeline:
- End of Neolithic Era
- Flourishing agricultural economy in Sumeria
- Phoenicians predominant trading power in Mediterranean
- Cleisthenes's democratic reforms at Athens

Science & Technology

Above timeline:
- First use of numerals
- Phoenician alphabet
- Thales begins Greek natural philosophy and science
- Pythagoras
- Euclid's *Elements*

Below timeline:
- Copper alloys used in Egypt and Sumeria
- First wheeled vehicles (Sumeria)
- Discovery of papyrus, irrigation, potter's wheel
- Etruscans introduce horse-drawn chariots in Italy
- Atomists

Religion & Thought

Above timeline:
- Akhenaton and Nefertiti abandon polytheism in Egypt
- Age of prophets in Israel
- Greek philosophy: Sophists, Socrates
- Epicureanism and Stoicism

Below timeline:
- Emergence of polytheistic religions in Egypt and Sumeria
- Israelite exodus from Egypt into Canaan, led by Moses
- Zoroaster in Persia
- Plato, Aristotle

Arts & Literature

Above timeline:
- Gilgamesh epic
- Minoan palaces at Knossos on Crete
- Greek lyric: Sappho, Archilochus

Below timeline:
- Sumerian cuneiform writing developed
- Pyramid of Khufu and Great Sphinx at Giza
- Babylonian Hanging Gardens, Ishtar Gate
- Homer's *Iliad* and *Odyssey*
- Greek drama: Aeschylus, Sophocles, Euripides, Aristophanes

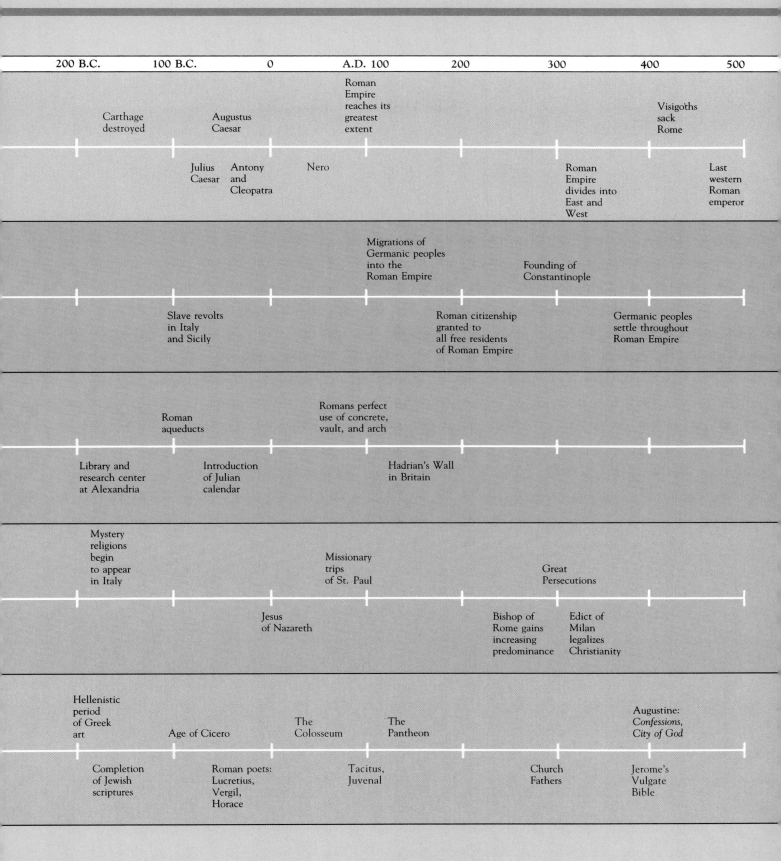

200 B.C.	100 B.C.	0	A.D. 100	200	300	400	500

Row 1 (above line)

Carthage destroyed

Augustus Caesar

Roman Empire reaches its greatest extent

Visigoths sack Rome

Row 1 (below line)

Julius Caesar

Antony and Cleopatra

Nero

Roman Empire divides into East and West

Last western Roman emperor

Row 2 (above line)

Migrations of Germanic peoples into the Roman Empire

Founding of Constantinople

Row 2 (below line)

Slave revolts in Italy and Sicily

Roman citizenship granted to all free residents of Roman Empire

Germanic peoples settle throughout Roman Empire

Row 3 (above line)

Roman aqueducts

Romans perfect use of concrete, vault, and arch

Row 3 (below line)

Library and research center at Alexandria

Introduction of Julian calendar

Hadrian's Wall in Britain

Row 4 (above line)

Mystery religions begin to appear in Italy

Missionary trips of St. Paul

Great Persecutions

Row 4 (below line)

Jesus of Nazareth

Bishop of Rome gains increasing predominance

Edict of Milan legalizes Christianity

Row 5 (above line)

Hellenistic period of Greek art

Age of Cicero

The Colosseum

The Pantheon

Augustine: *Confessions, City of God*

Row 5 (below line)

Completion of Jewish scriptures

Roman poets: Lucretius, Vergil, Horace

Tacitus, Juvenal

Church Fathers

Jerome's Vulgate Bible

THE STONE AGE AND THE ORIGINS OF CIVILIZATION IN THE NEAR EAST

The fenlands are in bloom, the fields are green;
The uplands are drenched, the dykes are watered;
Ravine and slope carry down the mountain-torrents
That rush into the dykes, watering the fields.
The soil . . . becomes a plantation,
The grass grows in wood and in meadow,
The bountiful womb of the earth is opened,
Giving plenteous food for cattle and abundance for the homes of men.

An ox and a horse struck up a friendship.
The rich pasture had sated their bellies,
And glad of heart they lay resting.
The ox opened his mouth to speak, and said to the horse, glorious in battle:
"I seem to have been born under a lucky star:
From beginning to end of the year I find food;
I have fodder in abundance and spring water in profusion. . . .
Change thy way of life and come away with me!"

[Said the horse:] "Strong brass to cover my body
Have they put upon me, and I wear it as a garment.
Without me, the fiery steed,
Nor king nor prince nor lord nor noble fares upon his way. . . .
The horse is like a god, stately of step,
Whilst thou and the calves wear the cap of servitude."

This passage from an Assyrian beast fable is a parable of the contrasting conditions of civilized life. The ox speaks for the good things, the creature comforts, of civilization: It relishes an idyllic life in a land made lush and fertile by the efforts of men and women who build dikes, divert water, sow seeds, reap the harvest, and raise the animals. The ox loves the settled and orderly life of peace. The horse, by contrast, scorns the slavish life of its bovine friend and glories in armor and the magnificence of great warriors,

Altamira Wall Painting. A section of the famous Paleolithic wall paintings in the caves at Altamira, Spain, showing bison. Paintings and carvings of this type have been found in caves throughout Europe, from southern Spain and France in the west to the Ural Mountains in the east. They are striking testimony to the extensive spread of Paleolithic culture in the whole region.

kings, and lords who depend on it for success in battle. The horse speaks for the ambition of the mighty, the love of power, the pride of conquest. The horse speaks for war.

This chapter surveys both peace and war in several ancient Near Eastern civilizations that provided the earliest models for the Greek and Roman societies from which western civilization grew. However, before turning to these, we shall first consider human development in the vast expanse of time, commonly called the Stone Age, that preceded civilized life.

FROM THE STONE AGE TO THE BEGINNING OF CIVILIZATION

The Stone Ages of human existence embrace 99 percent of our species' life on the planet, but cannot be described with much confidence or detail because no written records exist to illumine them. We must rely entirely on information, and conjectures based on that information, obtained from archaeological digs, as analyzed by anthropologists and other scientists studying humanity's cultural development. Although such information is increasing and ever more accurately understood, the geological formations of many millennia have yielded no fossil remains or are distinguished only by small changes in the techniques of fashioning tools. Exactly when, where, or how humans first appeared is not known, and dates assigned to events before 10,000 B.C. may be imprecise by thousands of years.

Hunter-Gatherers in the Old Stone Age

The story of humankind's achievement began in the Paleolithic or Old Stone Age, which extended from about 2,000,000 years ago to about 10,000 B.C. (in geological terminology, equivalent to the Pleistocene epoch). Over this vast expanse of time, in response to changes in the natural environment, Old Stone Age people made physical and cultural adaptations fundamental for subsequent human development. Crucial physiological refinements included the ability to stand and walk easily in an upright position, changes in the position and size of the teeth, especially the canines, the evolution and increasing dexterity of an opposable thumb, and changes in the size and configuration of the skull. Particularly dramatic was the doubling of brain size which gave humans a mental superiority over other species, demonstrated in the devising and use of various artifacts, particularly tools.

A series of four major glaciations or ice ages, marked by the movement of ice sheets hundreds of feet thick over vast areas of the Earth, changed land formations, sea levels, and plant and animal life and habitats. Survival in such conditions required people to be innovative and able to modify their patterns of living. Other animals, solely dependent on physical equipment for their survival, were often unable to adjust to changing Pleistocene environmental conditions and became extinct. Humans, however, with their enlarged brains could both expand and perfect their cultural equipment and transmit knowledge of the expert use of that equipment through language, the most flexible and finely calibrated tool of all.

By the end of the Paleolithic era, human beings had (1) manufactured a range of stone or bone implements (knives, scrapers, borers) and weapons (blades, bows and arrows, spears and spear throwers), (2) controlled fire for cooking and for giving heat and light, (3) developed spoken language in addition to the nonverbal gestures used by all primates, (4) formulated an artistic tradition, seen for example in the famous cave paintings at Lascaux in France, (5) created ritual practices connected chiefly with fertility and with burial of the dead, and (6) organized themselves into social groups for more efficient collection and sharing of food.

Because Paleolithic humans lived by hunting animals and by gathering wild fruits, nuts, and grains, they needed several thousand acres to support even a single family. This severely restricted the size of human communities and made settled life in one area impossible, since the group had to follow its food supply and move in conjunction with animal migrations and vegetation cycles. Only if people could shift from the random collection of food to its regular cultivation could they overcome these limitations.

The Food-Producing Revolution in the New Stone Age

With the retreat of the last ice age, beginning around 10,000 B.C., climatic conditions in that part of the Near East (see Map 1) called the Fertile Crescent became well-suited to raising cereal crops and domesticating animals. During a transitional period, the Mesolithic or Middle Stone Age (10,000 to 7000 B.C.), at places like Mount Carmel in Palestine, humans

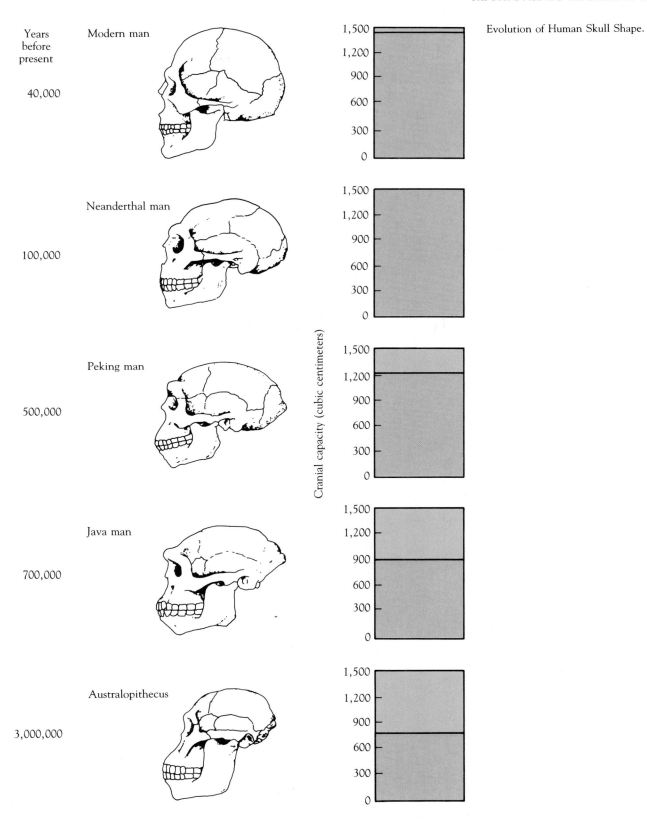

Evolution of Human Skull Shape.

made tentative efforts to move from hunting-gathering subsistence methods to the systematic harvesting of grain. But they did not develop true farming villages till the Neolithic or New Stone Age (7000 to 3500 B.C.). This transformation in the human condition is equalled in importance only by the related urban revolution beginning around 3500 B.C. and by the modern Industrial Revolution. Humans derived an assured food supply by developing agricultural techniques and domesticating food-producing animals. Stable food supplies in turn produced a rapid increase in population and in the number of permanent settlements, which later became centers for more complex social structures and more dynamic technologies.

Farming villages and towns in the Near East consisted of at most a few thousand inhabitants engaged in the cultivation of wheat, barley, peas, beans, and lentils and in the raising of goats, sheep, pigs, and cattle. These early farmers continued to supplement their diet with wild fruits, nuts, and grains. They lived in caves or pit

MAP 1
The Ancient Near East.

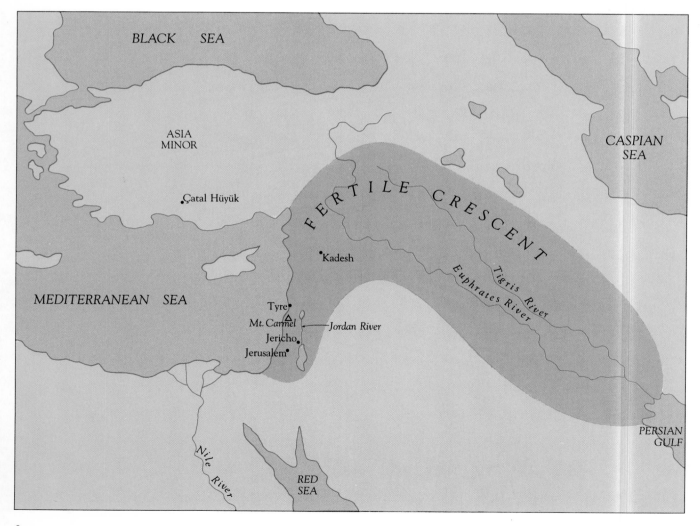

End of the
Neolithic
Era

Early Sumerian
Cities

Old
Babylonian
Empire

Assyrian
Empire

Polytheistic
Religion

Gilgamesh
Epic

Code of
Hammurabi

Neo-
Babylonian
Empire

houses or huts made of mud, reeds, logs, or stones, grouped in small open communities or in larger fortified towns like Jericho, in the Jordan Valley near the Dead Sea, or Çatal Hüyük in south central Asia Minor (the Anatolian Peninsula, or modern Turkey). They developed ovens for cooking and, later, for firing pottery, and discovered techniques for making porridge, bread, and beer. They devised and perfected the weaving of baskets and textiles from wool and flax, and began to work metals like gold, silver, and copper. Finally, they discovered the wheel and made wagons and pottery wheels and also invented the plow, superseding digging sticks and hoes. Food surpluses freed some members of the community to become at least part-time specialists: smiths, potters, weavers, artists, and perhaps priests. Humankind was now poised for the next major step toward civilization, from village to city.

MESOPOTAMIAN CIVILIZATION

No definition of "civilization" applies equally to all societies. For the ancient Near East, specifically, Egypt, Palestine, and Mesopotamia, however, the common characteristics of civilized life included (1) city-centered states of 5,000 or more inhabitants administered by a specific political leadership; (2) social class stratification of some sort (for example, ruling elite/small landowners/slaves); (3) complex division of labor, with full-time administrators, tradesmen, craftsmen, farmers, soldiers, priests, and scribes; (4) a relatively high level of artistic and intellectual development, large-scale architecture, sculptural and pictorial representations of human activities, and written materials. These elements appeared first in Mesopotamia (see Map 2), an extremely fertile alluvial plain in that part of the Fertile Crescent

MAP 2
Ancient Mesopotamia.

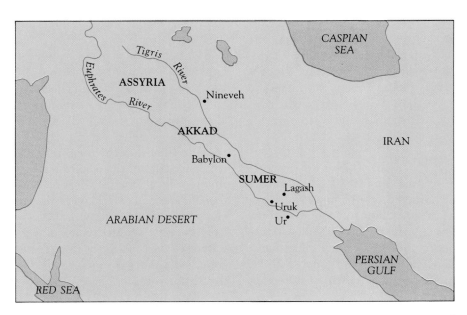

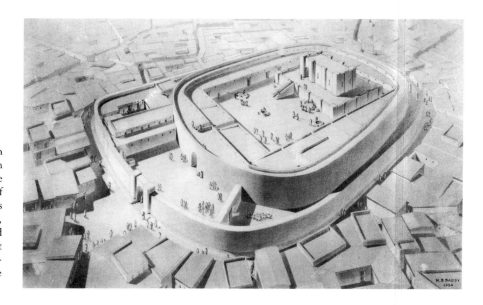

Temple at Khafajah. A reconstruction of an early dynastic temple at Khafajah in Iraq. Such elevated buildings dominated the vista of the city as the gods dominated the worldview of the Sumerians. However, since the Sumerians worked principally with sun-baked mud bricks, the resulting architecture, both originally and as excavated ruins, was less imposing than that of Egypt or Greece, where the use of limestone, granite, and marble made possible more elaborate and durable structures.

embraced by the Tigris and Euphrates rivers. Indeed, ancient records show as high as a hundredfold return on seed planted in the valley. This land, properly irrigated and cultivated, could support a much larger population than could those regions outside Mesopotamia where agriculture had first been practiced in Neolithic times. However, the climate of Mesopotamia created at certain seasons a hot, arid dust bowl and at others unpredictable flooding and unhealthful swamps. The valley dwellers had to mobilize a large, well-organized labor force to construct and maintain the necessary water control system of canals, dikes, drainage ditches, and reservoirs.

Sumerians

Sometime after 3500 B.C., the Sumerians, a people of unknown origin, began to exploit the potential of the lower Tigris-Euphrates Valley to support civilized urban life. The Sumerians built several city-states of 10,000 to 50,000 inhabitants, including Ur,

Uruk, and Lagash, and sustained themselves both by the agricultural produce of the land they controlled and by various imported goods and materials acquired in exchange for surplus crops. On this rudimentary economic basis, the Sumerians erected in the next 1,500 years a civilization of great sophistication and durability. Because the Sumerians were the model for later Mesopotamian civilization, they receive the greatest attention here.

The Sumerian city-state's physical appearance showed a striking advance in architecture, engineering, and technology over the attainments of the Neolithic farming village. The Sumerians parceled out the land in tracts of almost geometrical regularity, and efficiently watered them through an elaborate irrigation system of dams and canals, with smaller channels supplying individual plots. They built a network of roads and waterways and used packasses, wagons, boats, and barges to carry goods to the urban center.

The appearance of a Sumerian city was quite impressive. Fortifications were common. The city wall at Uruk, for example, nearly six miles in circuit, enclosed about 1,000 acres and contained some 900 defense towers. Within the walls were thousands of humble farmers' hovels and the more elaborate homes of civic and priestly officials and other members of the upper class. Though one could find some broad and straight avenues, the city as a whole gave the impression of a densely packed hive. Most conspicuous were the temples, set apart in walled-off enclosures and often raised on distinctive, stepped artificial mountains called ziggurats (the probable source of the biblical Tower of Babel).

The framework of Sumerian social, economic, and political life corresponded to the structure imposed on the natural surroundings. Perhaps 80 to 90 percent of the inhabitants of a city constituted human agricultural machinery. Most were slaves or tenant farmers who went out from the city to their plots or to the water control works and, by ceaseless toil, produced the abundant crops that sustained their society. They exchanged part of their produce for the wares of the city's craftsmen: metal workers (including now bronzesmiths), weavers, potters, and others. They also bartered for the foods available from fishermen, bakers, and brewers and for the merchandise brought from outside Mesopotamia by a host of traders.

Much of the peasants' produce went to support the temples and their many religious and civic activities. Increas-

ingly in the Sumerian period, the secular leadership of the state became identical with the religious hierarchy. The *ensi* (city ruler) was considered the agent of the city god and acted on his behalf. He coordinated the various temple communities within the city and assigned work on public buildings and on the water control installations. He imposed taxes and made legal decisions of various kinds. The city ruler also dictated the foreign policy of the state, including its defense policy and trade relations. The soldiers were under his direct command. Recognized by his subjects as

the supreme earthly authority, the *ensi* was given gifts and shown other signs of deference.

Writing is arguably the most significant achievement of the Sumerians. Archaeologists have found many thousands of cuneiform-inscribed clay tablets dating from nearly all periods of Mesopotamian civilization. These record mainly business transactions, inventories of supplies, production and taxation figures, or wage payments. They show too that the Mesopotamians employed such mathematical functions as multiplication and division, had devised a twelve-base sys-

Original pictograph	Pictograph in position of later cuneiform	Early Babylonian	Assyrian	Original or derived meaning
				Bird
				Fish
				Donkey
				Ox
				Sun Day
				Grain
				Orchard
				To plow To till
				Boomerang To throw To throw down
				To stand To go

The Evolution of Sumerian Writing. After earlier experimentation with picture writing, the Sumerians devised and perfected a script called cuneiform (wedge shaped). Since this system of signs transcribed sounds rather than pictures or ideas, it could be used to set down not only their own language but other languages as well. Cuneiform writing was later used by the Babylonians and Assyrians.

"FILL YOUR BELLY WITH GOOD THINGS"

Gilgamesh, where are you hurrying to? You will never find that life for which you are looking. When the gods created man they allotted him death, but life they retained in their own keeping. As for you, Gilgamesh, fill your belly with good things; day and night, night and day, dance and be merry, feast and rejoice. Let your clothes be fresh, bathe yourself in water, cherish the little child that holds your hand, and make your wife happy in your embrace; for this too is the lot of man.*

*The attractive and nubile Siduri, barmaid and vintner to the gods, gives this con-*soling advice to the hero Gilgamesh during his unsuccessful quest for eternal life in the great Sumerian Epic of Gilgamesh. This heroic poem was composed in the third millennium B.C., some 1,500 years before the earliest European literature (Homer). It was known to the Babylonians, Hittites, Assyrians, and perhaps to the Greeks. A seventh-century B.C. copy inscribed in cuneiform on clay tablets was found by excavators at Nineveh in 1853.*

*N. K. Sandars, trans., The Epic of Gilgamesh (Baltimore: Penguin, 1960; rev. ed. 1972), p. 102.

tem of numerical computation, and had formulated a calendar based on phases of the moon.

Cuneiform gives invaluable insights into the Sumerians' view of the world, including their religion, with its vision of a universe populated by all-powerful and often fickle deities. The gods were chiefly personifications of natural forces: Inanna, goddess of fertility; Enlil, storm god of earth, wind and air; Ereshkigal, queen of the underworld; Utu, sun god and lawgiver; Dumuzi, dying god of vegetation, beloved of Inanna. Humans were subject to these and a whole host of lesser but still awe-inspiring divine forces.

Sumerian religion offered no comforting theology of love and salvation and no clearly defined ethical code by which men and women might order their individual lives. Humans might only hope to ensure the security of their society by the proper ob-servance of the rituals demanded by imperious gods, and after death to experience a shadowy, limbolike existence in the underworld. The outlook here is in striking contrast to the more optimistic expectations of Egyptian religion. Still, there was a time for laughter and dancing as well as for weeping and mourning.

Babylonians

Mesopotamian civilization after its first 1,200 years experienced periodic upheavals and shifts in power centers. New peoples came to prominence in the region by gradual infiltration or conquest. The Sargonid rulers (2350–2150 B.C.) in Akkad, to the north of Sumer, conducted an early experiment in imperialism by subjugating the city-states of Sumer and forcing them into a federation under their direction. However, this first historical instance of empire building was terminated by the violent incursion of semibarbaric groups. A subsequent reassertion of Sumerian control, the Third Dynasty of Ur (2150–1950), was cut short by an invasion of a Semitic people, the Amorites, who organized the city-states of Sumer and Akkad into an empire with its administrative center at Babylon.

This Old Babylonian state lasted four centuries. The Babylonians assimiliated and refined many of the elements of the Sumerians, just as Rome later built on Greek cultural foundations. To cite only one example, the law code of Hammurabi (1792–1750 B.C.), Babylon's most famous dynast, set out in an orderly way, in some 280 articles, the body of law as it had evolved over 1,500 years of Mesopotamian history. The laws deal with a wide variety of actionable offenses, primarily indebtedness and breach of business contracts, but there are also regulations on marriage, adultery, and divorce, legitimacy and inheritance, incest, treatment of slaves, personal injury and property damage, and even medical malpractice. The Babylonians also improved on Sumerian innovations in mathematics and science, especially astronomy. In religion, their deity Marduk became the new president of a pantheon of Sumerian gods with Babylonian names: for example, Babylonian Ishtar was equivalent to Sumerian Inanna.

The sudden arrival around 1550 B.C. of the Kassites from the neighboring Iranian highlands to the east brought another transition in the sequence of Mesopotamian civilizations. The Kassites in their turn melded with existing Babylonian civilization and remained dominant in Sumer and Akkad for some 400 years.

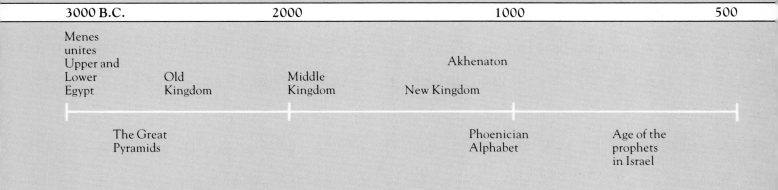

Menes unites Upper and Lower Egypt

Old Kingdom

Middle Kingdom

Akhenaton

New Kingdom

The Great Pyramids

Phoenician Alphabet

Age of the prophets in Israel

But during that period, the focus of Mesopotamian development shifted northward.

Assyrians and Chaldeans

Between about 1300 and 900 B.C., the Assyrians rose to prominence in northern Mesopotamia. Although the Kassites for a time prevented their consolidation of the entire Tigris-Euphrates Valley, ruthless Assyrian militarism won out after 900 and reached its peak in the careers of such warrior kings as Tiglath-Pileser III (744–727), Sargon II (721–705), and Ashurbanipal (668–630). Nearly all the lands of the Fertile Crescent (Asia Minor, Mesopotamia, Syria, Palestine, and Egypt) were at one time or another under Assyrian domination by the seventh century B.C.

In 612 B.C., however, another Iranian people, the Medes, allied with resurgent Babylon, succeeded in destroying Assyrian power at its very capital of Nineveh. The Neo-Babylonian or Chaldean era that followed was a time of foreign conquests, though not on the Assyrian scale. The most famous Neo-Babylonian king, Nebuchadnezzar (605–562), beautified Babylon with such adornments as the Hanging Gardens and the Ishtar Gate; he also sought to reanimate Babylonian religious devotion. The Persian ruler Cyrus conquered Babylon in 539 B.C. and ended the long story of Mesopotamian civilization by incorporating its territory into his empire.

EGYPTIAN CIVILIZATION

Because of the topographical uniformity of its location, Egyptian civilization (see Map 3) was more homogeneous, both geographically and politically, than was the case in Mesopotamia, with its numerous, densely populated city-states. Cities in Egypt, such as Memphis and Thebes, were comparatively few and tended to be purely administrative centers for governmental and religious activities. The mass of people lived in thousands of villages more or less evenly distributed in the 12,000 square miles of arable land in the valley and delta of the mighty Nile, where the dependable pulse of the river's yearly cycle of flood and subsidence regulated Egyptian life. The arid land was fertile only where its waters reached or could be made to reach. Besides bringing water during its annual flood stage, June to October, the Nile brought deposits of some 200 million tons of soil and minerals per year. Egyptians, by diverting floodwaters and draining swamplands in the Nile Valley, made their country the most productive agricultural land of the ancient world.

The Old Kingdom: A God-Ruled Society

Menes, the first king of Egypt's First Dynasty (royal family line), is credited with unifying upper and lower Egypt around 3000 B.C. The next two thousand years of Egyptian history are customarily divided into three periods of strong political unity, the Old, Middle, and New Kingdoms, separated by two intermediate periods of weak central government, social unrest, and foreign invasions.

The preeminent central authority in the Old Kingdom was the pharaoh, a god-king, variously son or manifestation of certain deities. He exercised his supreme will through a simple but rigid hierarchy ranging from royal agents and elite nobles to local officials who ruled some forty administrative districts. This political superstructure and the many building projects and other activities it supervised were supported by the tremendous agricultural surplus produced by the mass of peasants. This god-governed state engaged in exploration of and trade with neighboring lands, including Nubia, Ethiopia, the Sinai Peninsula, and Phoenicia. To build monuments or flood control installations, the pharaohs dictated the enlistment and provisioning of a large, skilled labor force: masons and stonecutters, sculptors, carpenters, and painters, as well as construction managers, surveyors, draftsmen, scribes, and others. These worked chiefly during the inundation phase of the Nile's cycle, when transport by water was easiest and farm workers were free to quarry, haul, and position stone building materials.

The pharaoh wielded such extensive powers because service to him on any state project was a religious as well as a civic duty. Egyptian religion was, like the Sumerian, a thoroughgoing polytheism (belief in many gods), in which most major and minor divinities were associated with the agrarian rhythms of fertility and germination, death and regeneration. The gods were mainly anthropomorphic (having human shapes and personalities), but could also have the

MAP 3
Ancient Egypt.

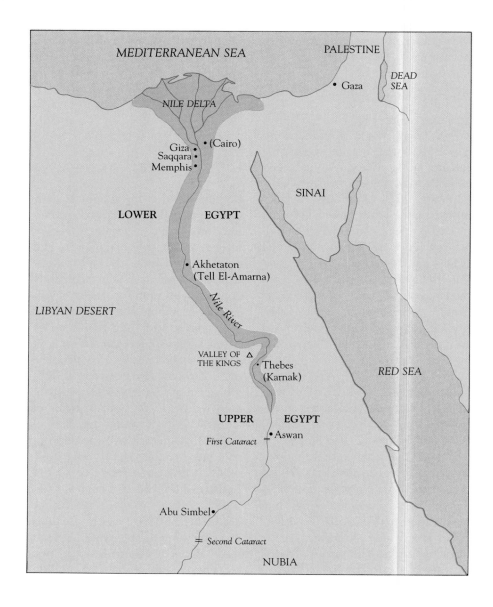

form of a beast, such as a beetle, bull, or snake, or a half-beast, human torso with the head of a jackal, crocodile, or cow. Perhaps the most dignified and universal Egyptian myths concerned the dying god Osiris, slain by the evil Set but reborn through the efforts of his sister/wife Isis. Osiris was the father of Horus, and Horus was, at least in most periods, embodied in the person of the king. After death, the pharaoh was equated with Osiris, however, and so thought to influence the life cycles that governed the natural world. Thus the security not only of the state but also of the whole universe was directly linked to the well-being of the king. He had to be accorded all due honors and signs of deference in this life as well as in the next. This accounts for the practice of mummification, which was an attempt to ensure the continued comfort and good will of the deceased king in the afterworld. Hence, too, the fantastic expenditure of time and resources on funeral monuments, temples, and tombs, of which the pyramids are the most notable.

During the Third and Fourth dynasties of the Old Kingdom, the Egyptians evolved and perfected the pyramid, the architectural form that has ever after been the distinguishing mark of their civilization. In the Third Dynasty, Imhotep, the first architect known by name, built for king Zoser (c. 2700 B.C.) the "step pyramid" at Saqqara. This marks the beginning of large-scale stone construction. The structure itself is a halfway development between ziggurat and true pyramid. Of the great pyramids built at Giza during the Fourth Dynasty, the largest is that of Khufu (or "Cheops"), c. 2600 B.C. It was 460 feet high and 755 feet on each side and was

made from some 2,300,000 stone blocks averaging 2.5 tons each. The whole was sheathed with limestone casing blocks, stripped in modern times to supply building stone for Cairo, that gave the pyramid the appearance of being one massive unit. The complex at Giza—the three great pyramids and the famous Sphinx—was only one of many Old Kingdom burial places in the region of Memphis; some eighty of the tombs are marked by pyramids.

The buildings at Giza are the best of Egyptian architecture, not only in scale, but also in the precision of their construction. This is particularly remarkable considering the lack of sophisticated hoisting equipment. Earthen ramps were used to haul the stones up and into position. Moreover, the tombs and temples, here and elsewhere in Egypt, were adorned with magnificent sculptures (full-figure and relief), paintings, and hieroglyphic inscriptions. The last were perhaps inspired by a knowledge of cuneiform, but they differ from that script by combining pictographs with syllable signs and letter signs. However, the Egyptians did not develop true alphabetic writing.

Although the pyramids were the eternal homes of royalty, the possibility of life after death was open to others besides the pharaoh, as the evidence of nobles' tombs indicates. (The tombs of common folk have left no traces.) Moreover, Egyptian religion had a slight ethical emphasis, a concern for justice that we do not see so consistently in Mesopotamia. The gods ruled a cosmos based on the Egyptian notion of moral right. Pharaoh was expected to treat his subjects equitably and those subjects were required to be fair in their dealings with

one another. Those with the means to do so were to assist those less well off, such as widows and orphans.

The Middle Kingdom

As Sumerian archetypes gave an enduring pattern to Mesopotamian civilization, the Old Kingdom originated many aspects of the political, religious, and artistic world view of the Egyptians. In Mesopotamia, change often came as a result of intrusions from the Iranian uplands to the east and north or from Arabian desert regions to the west and south. Egypt, by contrast, was better protected from invasion by vast tracts of uninhabitable desert wasteland. Internal social and political upheavals, however, occasionally led to weakness and disunity.

During the first intermediate period (2150 to 2050 B.C.), the central administration, already losing its grip in the Sixth and Seventh dynasties of the Old Kingdom, was replaced by a fragmented system of hereditary local leadership. The succeeding Middle Kingdom (2050 to 1750) was ushered in by the kings of the Eleventh Dynasty, whose capital was at Thebes, some 400 miles up the Nile from Memphis. Upper and lower Egypt were reunited. But toward the end of the Twelfth Dynasty (about 1750), another fateful erosion of the central authority occurred, perhaps owing to a succession of weak kings or stiffer competition from local nobility with royal aspirations. Consequently, Egypt, vulnerable because of its domestic disarray, suffered what has been called "The Great Humiliation," a successful invasion by an Asiatic people called the Hyksos, probably from the region of and near Palestine. Un-

EGYPTIAN HIEROGLYPHIC WRITING

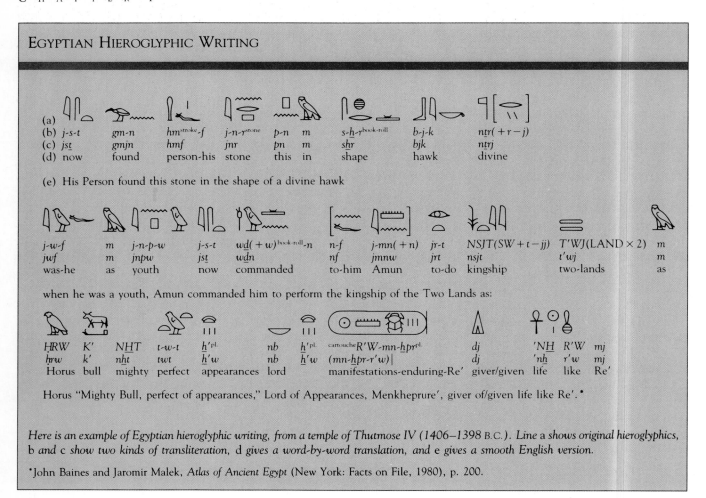

(a)
(b) *j-s-t*   *gm-n*   *hm*stroke-*f*   *j-n-r*stone   *p-n*   *m*   *s-ḥ-r*book-roll   *b-j-k*   *ntr(+r−j)*
(c) *jst*   *gmjn*   *hmf*   *jnr*   *pn*   *m*   *shr*   *bjk*   *ntrj*
(d) now   found   person-his   stone   this   in   shape   hawk   divine

(e) His Person found this stone in the shape of a divine hawk

j-w-f   *m*   *j-n-p-w*   *j-s-t*   *wd(+w)*book-roll-*n*   *n-f*   *j-mn(+n)*   *jr-t*   NSJT(SW+*t*−*jj*)   T'WJ(LAND × 2)   *m*
jwf   *m*   *jnpw*   *jst*   *wdn*   *nf*   *jmnw*   *jrt*   *nsjt*   *t'wj*   *m*
was-he   as   youth   now   commanded   to-him   Amun   to-do   kingship   two-lands   as

when he was a youth, Amun commanded him to perform the kingship of the Two Lands as:

ḤRW   K'   NḤT   *t-w-t*   *ḥ'*pl.   *nb*   *ḥ'*pl.   cartouche R'W-*mn-ḫpr*pl.   *dj*   'NḤ R'W *mj*
ḥrw   *k'*   *nḥt*   *twt*   *ḥ'w*   *nb*   *ḥ'w*   (*mn-ḫpr-r'w*)| *dj*   *'nḥ*   *r'w*   *mj*
Horus   bull   mighty   perfect   appearances   lord   appearances   manifestations-enduring-Re'   giver/given   life   like   Re'

Horus "Mighty Bull, perfect of appearances," Lord of Appearances, Menkheprure', giver of/given life like Re'.*

Here is an example of Egyptian hieroglyphic writing, from a temple of Thutmose IV (1406–1398 B.C.). Line a shows original hieroglyphics, b and c show two kinds of transliteration, d gives a word-by-word translation, and e gives a smooth English version.

*John Baines and Jaromir Malek, *Atlas of Ancient Egypt* (New York: Facts on File, 1980), p. 200.

---

like the Amorites or the Kassites, who were ultimately absorbed by the civilizations they attacked in Mesopotamia, the Hyksos remained an alien force. They maintained themselves in lower Egypt only by superior military ability and technology, the horse-drawn chariot and improved bronze arms. After about 200 years they were ejected by Theban rulers of the Seventeenth Dynasty, who were in turn followed by Egypt's most ambitious and imperialistic dynasties (XVIII–XX), those of the New Kingdom.

The New Kingdom

The Egyptian Empire, as the New Kingdom is sometimes labeled, restored much of the prestige lost during the Hyksos occupation. Thutmose III (1490–1436 B.C.) extended Egyptian influence beyond the Sinai into Palestine, Syria, and even to the Euphrates. At home, foreign conquest meant peace and prosperity; tribute, slaves, and valuable materials poured into Egypt. The pride taken in these achievements can be seen in

the art and architecture sponsored by the conquering pharaohs of the New Kingdom. Amenhotep III (1398–1361) and Ramses II (1290–1224), in particular, engaged in massive building programs to honor the gods and to publicize and magnify their own accomplishments. The colossal temple complex of Amon at Karnak near Thebes is an especially noteworthy example, as are the huge, lavishly furnished temples and tombs built in the Valley of the Kings across the Nile from Thebes and at Abu Simbel above Aswan. The tomb of an unimportant king, Tutankhamon (1352–1344), which escaped grave robbers, gives us a tantalizing glimpse of the wealth of these kings and nobles of imperial Egypt.

Amenhotep IV (1369–1353 B.C.) interrupted the series of militaristic pharaohs. A rebel in his attitudes toward art and theology, he recognized as gods only himself and the solar disk, Aton. He changed his name to Akhenaton ("It pleases Aton") and founded a new capital called Akhetaton ("Place of the Glory of Aton") at present-day Tell el-Amarna. Compared with the polytheism prevalent in the ancient world, his religion closely approached monotheism. Akhenaton and his queen, Nefertiti, are familiar from artistic depictions. But this pharaoh's reform efforts were short-lived. His successor, Tutankhamon, reinstated the previous polytheism with Amon as chief deity, pleasing the numerous priests who derived wealth and prestige from the cult centers at the restored capital of Thebes and many other places. Indeed, the ever-rising power of the various priesthoods, which Akhenaton had tried to curb, was a principal symptom of yet another decaying of the central authority.

Egypt after 1100 B.C. was only intermittently a unified state. More common were fragment states ruled by local potentates, high priests, or foreign (for example, Ethiopian or Libyan) dynasts. In the last millennium B.C., Egypt was subjugated in turn by Assyrians, Babylonians, Persians, Macedonians, and finally, in 30 B.C., by Romans. Despite sporadic reassertions of autonomy, Egypt never regained the strong and confident in-

Temple at Abu Simbel. The facade of the great temple at Abu Simbel with its colossal figures of Ramses II, more than sixty feet in height. At a cost of $40 million, a UNESCO team of German, Italian, French, and Swedish engineers dismantled and moved the temple to higher ground to prevent its being submerged by the rising waters of Lake Nasser after the completion of the Aswan High Dam; the move took four years (1964–1968).

Akhenaton Worshipping Aton. This limestone sculptural relief (c. 1360 B.C.) shows Akhenaton with his queen, Nefertiti, and one of their children presenting gifts to Aton, the solar disk. Note that some of the hands at the ends of the solar rays hold the Egyptian emblem of life known as the *ankh.* Metropolitan Museum of Art, New York.

dependence of spirit that had characterized its glorious past.

HITTITES AND PHOENICIANS

In the ancient Near East, Mesopotamia and Egypt enjoyed the best natural resources and strongest political organizations, maintained with relatively few interruptions for more than two millennia. Although these two areas were the foci of cultural and geopolitical achievements, there were also very significant developments elsewhere in the region. For example, archaeologists have uncovered extensive remains of the Hittite Empire in Asia Minor. The Hittites came to this region sometime before 2000 B.C., as part of a general movement of Indo-European peoples into Greece, Iran, and the Indus Valley from an unknown homeland, possibly the steppes of southern Russia. Between 1600 and 1200 B.C., the Hittites played a major role in Near Eastern power politics. They successfully invaded Babylonia and fought a great battle against New Kingdom Egypt at Kadesh in Syria. Ramses II later decorated many temple walls with carved depictions of his exploits at Kadesh, though in fact the battle was a standoff. The Hittites themselves then fell to a new wave of Indo-European invaders, who upset the equilibrium in so many parts of the Near East shortly after 1200 B.C.

Another significant Near Eastern people, the Phoenicians, were notable for their commercial and linguistic achievements. A Semitic people flourishing in a small expanse of coastland roughly coextensive with modern Lebanon, the Phoenicians were the best seamen and traders of the ancient world. By the second millennium B.C., they had established major ports at Tyre, Sidon, and Byblos. By the eighth century B.C., they had made contacts as far away as Spain at the other end of the Mediterranean. In between, on the north coast of Africa, they had founded Carthage, a city that later challenged Rome for control of the western Mediterranean.

The most enduring Phoenician gift to civilization, however, was the alphabet. This script, consisting of a small number of easily learned consonant signs, enormously facilitated the spread of literacy and all it entailed for cultural development. The actual characters seem to have been adapted from the much more cumbersome and difficult Egyptian hieroglyphics sometime after 1500 B.C. Alphabetic writing spread through trade contacts, and by the eighth century the Greeks had borrowed it, adding signs to represent vowels. They in turn passed it on to the Romans via the Etruscans. These Greek and Roman alphabets were subsequently adopted by virtually all modern European languages.

THE HEBREWS AND JUDAISM

The significance of another small group in the Near East, the Hebrews, also a Semitic people, was mainly based on their religious concepts. From about 2000 B.C. onward, the Hebrews moved into the fertile regions of the Near East from the surrounding deserts of Syria and Arabia, where they had subsisted as nomads. One contingent, led by Abraham, migrated from Ur in Babylonia to Canaan (Palestine), in response to a divine command, according to Genesis 12:2.

It is also recorded that sometime before 1600 B.C., certain Israelites (from Israel, another name for Jacob, Abraham's grandson) went to Egypt to avoid famine in Palestine; there they suffered oppression and fled in a mass exodus around 1300 B.C., under the leadership of Moses, who united his followers in the worship of Yahweh (sometimes rendered "Jehovah" in English). Back in Palestine, they exchanged a nomadic for a settled, agricultural mode of existence and engaged in many military actions to acquire and defend territory.

During the period 1025–928 B.C., the twelve tribes of Israel were joined in a united monarchy under three successive king-generals: Saul, David, and Solomon. After Solomon's death, the kingdom split into two parts, Israel in the north and Judah in the south. In 722, the expanding Assyrian Empire absorbed the kingdom of Israel; its people were scattered, being remembered in history as the "ten lost tribes." Judah was conquered by Nebuchadnezzar in 597; when the capital, Jerusalem, was destroyed in 586, many of its leading citizens were deported to Babylon. Though the Persian ruler Cyrus allowed the Jews to return to Jerusalem after his conquest in 539, not all did. Palestine continued as a Persian subject state till the conquest of Alexander the Great in 332. It thereafter came under the successive control of various Hellenistic kingdoms. Finally, after a last period of independence, it succumbed to Rome in 63 B.C.

The religious history of ancient Israel is important out of all proportion to its political history. For this we have the evidence of a truly remarkable body of literature, the sacred scriptures, known to Jews as *Tenakh* and to Christians as the Old Testament. These writings comprise two-thirds of "The Book" or Bible (Greek *biblos*) that has codified Judaeo-Christian tradition throughout western civilization.

The Old Testament is both a religious text and a rich work of literature. It is unique among Near Eastern documents in giving so thorough a description of its composers' history and in relating that history to a particular system of religious beliefs. The most significant and distinctive aspect of those beliefs is monotheism (belief in only one God).

Hebrew monotheism was characterized by an elaborate code of moral behavior. Unlike the gods of the Near Eastern and later Greco-Roman polytheisms, Yahweh presented men and women with a consistent code of morality and dictated a covenant under which humans would be rewarded for abiding by that code. By contrast, the gods of Egypt and Mesopotamia set out no coherently formulated standards of behavior. Whatever ethical imperatives these deities stood for were vague and subject to suspension or cancellation. Thus mortals, even a hero like Gilgamesh, suffered from a deep-seated insecurity, often finding themselves in the double bind of being punished by one god for obeying another. Judaism furnished men and women with a comprehensive code of ethics by which to live their lives. It offered the assurance that the Supreme Creator looked on human beings as intrinsically valuable, not as mere playthings of the deities.

Hebrew religion, however, presented its own problems. Yahweh could be vengeful and jealous as well as paternally nurturing. His ways could be hard to fathom, as the Book of Job attests. In addition, the Law was very fully elaborated and touched virtually all aspects of life. The Ten Commandments are only its essence: Orthodox Judaism finds 613 commandments in the Law. Over and over in scripture accounts, the Jews, both as individuals and as a nation, broke the Law and disobeyed their God. Moreover, the Israelites were not insulated from the religious influences of their Near Eastern environment. Elijah, for example, had to prove to his people the superiority of Yahweh to the Canaanite god Baal. Other prophets, like Amos, chastised the Jews for their shortcomings and, like Jeremiah, foresaw the coming of divine punishment in the guise of Babylonian conquest. During the exile in Babylon (586–539 B.C.), however, the "second Isaiah" and Ezekiel sang the praises of the one God and of his chosen people, holding out hope for a return to the promised land and a restoration of the temple at Jerusalem.

The canonical (official) books of the Bible were assembled between 400 and about 150 B.C. and constitute one of the most influential legacies of the ancient Near East. In religious thought, the Hebrews far outstripped their materially more fortunate neighbors.

SUMMARY

The period covered in this chapter is longer by far than that of the remainder of this book. Recognizing that change was slow and that we view such remote times with the unavoidable distortion and foreshortening of a telescopic lens, we may nevertheless speak of two great revolutions in the human condition during this period: the introduction of agriculture and the appearance of civilization. These profound changes took place in the ancient Near East. Here the agricultural revolution for the first time made greater population densities possible; here these populations organized themselves in politically and socially complex groupings—cities and city-states—in which a more efficient division of labor could occur. Large-scale architecture and other works of art soon appeared, together with improved industrial and agricultural techniques and equipment. These achievements were an indispensable basis for future growth in Greek and Roman times and later. A concomitant creativity occurred in the development of military power; imperialism and warfare made their appearance.

Important changes in intellectual life also took place. Egyptians, Mesopotamians, Phoenicians, Hebrews, all attempted to grasp and explain and somehow control the workings of their world. They did this by developing mathematics and astronomy, by creating alphabetic writing, and especially by applying their religious insights. Whether magic or anthropomorphic polytheism or ethical monotheism, religious thought shaped the world view of the first civilizations. Judaism was to exert the most enduring influence on western civilization, but the religions of Egypt and Mesopotamia also sought to understand the nature of the forces governing the universe. The human need to penetrate mystery and to dispel the anxiety of ignorance has been active without interruption from the religious speculations of the Near East down to modern scientific inquiry.

Perhaps the most pervasive underlying factor in the human intellectual experience is the striving for order. The impulse to exploit the order of nature led to agriculture. The need to impose order on the relationships of men and women to the environment and to one another led to civilized communities. The attempt to detect order in the dispositions of the invisible powers that shape the destiny of humanity led to religion. In all these arenas, later participants in the evolution of western civilization, in particular the ancient Greeks, were heavily indebted to their ancient Near Eastern forebears.

SELECTED SOURCES

Annaud, Jean-Jacques, dir. *Quest for Fire.* 1982. This film depicts a variety of Stone Age discoveries, including fire starting and spoken language.

*Bronowski, Jacob. *The Ascent of Man.* 1973. Chapters 1 and 2 of this best-seller, based on the BBC television series, offer a lively account of Stone Age developments.

*Frankfort, Henri, H. A. Frankfort, John A. Wilson, and Thorkild Jacobsen. *Before Philosophy: The Intellectual Adventure of Ancient Man.* 1946. A thought-provoking and readable analysis of the mythic and religious world views of Egyptians and Mesopotamians.

Grant, Michael. *The History of Ancient Israel.* 1984. A good, recent, well-written survey of ancient Hebrew civilization down to the time of the Roman domination.

*Harris, James E., and Kent R. Weeks. *X-Raying the Pharaohs.* 1973. This description of a radiological examination of mummies in the Egyptian Museum in Cairo includes an astounding "Portfolio of Pictures."

Hawkes, Jacquetta. *King of the Two Lands.* 1966. A historical novel set in the time of Akhenaton and Nefertiti, by an eminent British archaeologist.

Howell, F. Clark. *Early Man.* Rev. ed. 1980. A clear and extremely well-illustrated account of primitive human beings, as studied by archaeologists and anthropologists.

*Pritchard, James B. *The Ancient Near East: An Anthology of Texts and Pictures.* 1958. A convenient, widely available collection of interesting and important materials.

*Sandars, Nancy K., trans. *The Epic of Gilgamesh.* Rev. ed. 1972. The best translation of the great epic; equipped with a long, very useful introduction.

*Wilson, John A. *The Culture of Ancient Egypt* (formerly, *The Burden of Egypt*). 1951; reprinted 1956. The single best book on the subject; it skillfully interrelates political, cultural, and intellectual history in a penetrating account.

*Available in paperback.

GREEK BEGINNINGS
(c. 3000–500 B.C.)

Zeus, son of Cronos, created on earth a noble and just race of heroes, demigods throughout the land, a race before our own. War and fatal conflict ruined many of them—some in seven-gated Thebes, land of Cadmus . . . some in Troy, where they had gone in ships for fair-haired Helen's sake. There the shroud of death covered many valiant men. Others, however, Zeus gave an afterlife at earth's edge. There the heroes live happily in the Blessed Islands on Ocean's shore where fertile land bears fruit thrice yearly for them.

Late in the eighth century B.C., the Greek poet Hesiod described the age of heroes in the passage quoted here. He believed these were great warriors with nearly superhuman endowments and abilities, living in a remote past. These heroes took part in the famous quest for the golden fleece and in the Trojan War fought for the fabulously beautiful but faithless Helen. They were immortalized in epic songs like Homer's *Iliad* and *Odyssey*. For Hesiod, they were gone forever. Although the great warriors were actually legendary, we now know that there did exist at that time a flourishing society that inspired later notions of a heroic age. Hesiod thought his own age of iron produced a much inferior race, struggling to grind a meager livelihood from the grudging soil of Greece. He was wrong to believe this, for the eighth century marked the beginning of a new and exciting epoch, the Archaic (primal) age. After a brief look at Minoan civilization, a culture transitional between the ancient Near East and Greece, this chapter depicts two early Greek cultures, Mycenaean and Archaic, separated by the great divide of the Dark Age.

CONTENTS

GEOGRAPHY OF THE GREEK WORLD

Greece was a collection of many territorially and politically distinct communities. Geographically, it encompassed the southern end of the Balkan Peninsula (see Map 4), the west coast of Asia Minor, the islands

Mycenaean Gold Death Mask. This is the most impressive of a number of gold masks found in the shaft graves in the citadel of Mycenae, though Heinrich Schliemann erred by three centuries when he identified the portrait as that of Agamemnon. The mask was made by the repoussé process: hammering a thin plate into a mold from the back; c. 1525 B.C. National Museum, Athens.

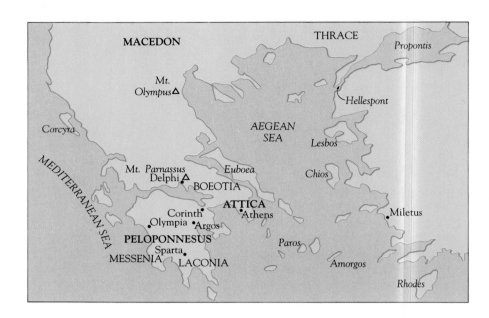

MAP 4
Greece and the Aegean Basin.

that dot both the Aegean Sea and the Ionian Sea, and the large islands of Crete and Cyprus.

Greece was not so blessed as Mesopotamia or Egypt with fertile soil or other natural resources. Its physical geography consisted of many mountains, small and scattered coastal plains and river valleys, and the ever-present sea. There were few places where one could not see mountains or the sea or both. These topographical features explained in part the political fragmentation of the Greek world as well as the scarcity of arable land; less than twenty percent was fit for cultivation, and even in antiquity that land was suffering from deforestation and generally poor soil management. The area was hot and arid in summer, in winter cool and moderately watered by rainfall. The grapevine and the olive tree were best suited to the soil and weather of the region, though wheat and barley were grown on virtually every acre of suitable land. There

was sufficient grazing land for sheep and goats, but not usually for cattle and horses. It was and is a beautiful country, a land of stunning contrasts, of crystalline skies and "wine-dark" seas, of brilliant, sun-drenched vistas of steep river valleys and mountain peaks.

THE FLOWERING OF MINOAN CIVILIZATION

Human beings had lived in Greece in the Neolithic era (7000–3000 B.C.) and, in a few places, even earlier. Around 3000, a change occurred, marked by new types of pottery and the introduction of metallurgy (hence the term *Bronze Age*). This break between Stone Age and Bronze Age may reflect the arrival of a new, but non-Greek-speaking people. In the next

1,500 years, down to about 1500 B.C., the most rapid cultural advances in the Greek area took place on the large island of Crete, on the southern edge of the Aegean Sea, where the civilization has been labeled Minoan after King Minos of Greek mythology.

The culture of the Minoans was unknown until modern times when Sir Arthur Evans excavated Knossos (see Map 5), beginning in 1899. He uncovered a vast, multistoried palace complex and eventually found that Minoan civilization had pervaded the whole island, some 150 by 35 miles. The Minoan culture that Evans unearthed was astonishingly rich and distinctive. The palace walls and floors were brightly decorated with fresco paintings showing plants and animals, aquatic and marine life. People were pictured in a wide variety of activities, including ritual sports such as the famous bull-jumping events. The style of this art was vivid and distinctively impressionistic.

Arrival of
Greek speakers
in Balkan
Peninsula

Mycenaean Period

Arrival
of
Dorians

Minoan palaces
at Knossos

Linear B

Trojan
War

Less is known about the people themselves who built and adorned the palaces. The architectural grandeur implies a strongly centralized administration, as does the evidence of two nonalphabetic forms of writing, called Linear A and Linear B. Inscribed clay tablets contain inventories of raw materials and manufactured goods, of agricultural production and stored goods,

MAP 5
The Greek World.

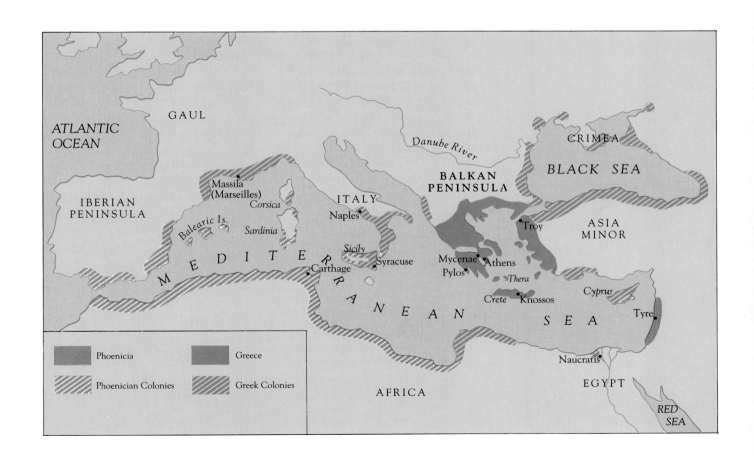

ATLANTIC
OCEAN

GAUL

Danube River

CRIMEA

BLACK SEA

BALKAN
PENINSULA

Massila
(Marseilles)

ITALY

IBERIAN
PENINSULA

Corsica

Balearic Is.

Sardinia

Naples

Troy

ASIA
MINOR

Sicily

Mycenae

Athens

M E D I T E R

Carthage

Syracuse

Pylos

Thera

R A N E A N

Crete

Knossos

Cyprus

S E A

Tyre

Phoenicia

Greece

Phoenician Colonies

Greek Colonies

Naucratis

AFRICA

EGYPT

RED
SEA

25

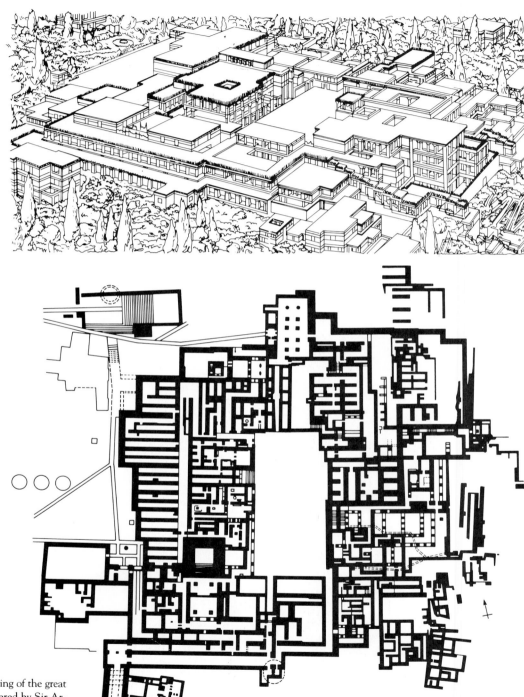

Knossos. Plan and artist's rendering of the great Minoan palace complex discovered by Sir Arthur Evans at Knossos on Crete. The palace's mazelike complexity may have inspired the myth of the labyrinth, in which the Greek hero Theseus slew the minotaur.

50 feet

suggesting that Crete was heavily populated and that the various palace centers controlled surrounding farmsteads, pastures, and villages.

A king called "Minos," perhaps an honorific title, controlled the palace complex, assisted by a corps of specially trained bureaucrats and scribes who supervised and recorded the activities of farmers, artisans, and slaves. Priests may have been in charge of religious observances, in which the bull figured prominently; whether the animal was a sacrificial offering or a god image is unclear, but it may have provided the kernel of the myth of the Minotaur, a monster usually depicted as a man with the head of a bull, who was slain by the Athenian hero Theseus. Snake-handling mother goddesses, sacred trees, and caves also figured in Minoan religion. As in Egypt and Mesopotamia, fertility, death, and regeneration were major concerns of this religion.

The people of Crete had learned from Egypt how to construct ships that could sail the Mediterranean. Though we have stories of Cretan naval domination of neighboring islands and even mainland sites, the influence of the Minoans appears to have been commercial and cultural rather than imperialistic. Unlike the Mycenaeans later, they neither protected their palaces by fortifications nor included military scenes and weapons in their art.

The Minoan civilization was dealt crippling blows by a devastating earthquake around 1700 B.C. and a huge volcanic eruption on the neighboring island of Thera around 1475. The Minoans seem not to have recovered fully from these disasters when, sometime after 1380, their palaces were again destroyed, this time

---

BRONZE AGE BUREAUCRATS

Astonishing and significant is the omniscience, the insatiable thirst for intimate detail [of Mycenaean officials]. Sheep may be counted up to a glittering total of twenty-five thousand: but there is still a purpose to be served by recording the fact that *one* animal was contributed by Komawens and another by Etewano. Restless officialdom notes the presence in Pesero's house of one woman and two children; the employment of two nurses, one girl, and one boy, in a Cretan village; the fattening of an insignificant number of hogs . . .; the existence somewhere of a single pair of brassbound chariot wheels labelled "useless,"—these things and hundreds more of the same type were duly recorded in the palaces of Pylos and Knossos. *

The records described in this passage come from thousands of clay tablets inscribed with a nonalphabetic script called Linear B. For a half century after their first discovery by archaeologists in 1900, it was thought that the language of the tablets was not Greek. Then, in 1952, a young British architect named Michael Ventris deciphered Linear B and showed it to be a primitive form of Greek. This amazing discovery forced researchers to rewrite the history of Greek civilization.

*Denys L. Page, *History and the Homeric Iliad* (Berkeley: University of California Press, 1959), p. 181.

---

by Mycenaean invaders. Minoan traditions, however, continued to live in the culture of the conquerors.

WARRIOR KINGS: MYCENAEAN CIVILIZATION

On the mainland, as on Crete, the Neolithic era ended with the arrival on the tip of the Balkan Peninsula (mainland Greece) of a new people, probably from Asia Minor, about 3000 B.C. Around 2000, the first Greek speakers arrived and founded powerful states centering on citadels at Athens, Pylos, Mycenae (from which the whole culture gets its name), and other sites. These were the heroes that Hesiod spoke of, people called "Achaeans" in Homer's epic poems. The uncovering of Mycenae by an eccentric amateur archaeologist, Heinrich Schliemann, in the 1870s sent shock waves through the scholarly world, for before Schliemann's discoveries historians believed that Homer's warriors, fabulous Troy, and "golden Mycenae" had never really existed.

Each Mycenaean site was a heavily fortified center from which a king governed surrounding territory. Administrative organization was quite intricate and, as on Crete, was overseen by a corps of bureaucrats and scribes who classified, counted, and recorded millions of bits of information in Linear B.

This civilization was wealthy and, at least in its art, quite cosmopolitan. It imported amber from the Baltic Sea coast, ivory from Syria, alabaster from Crete, lapis lazuli from Mesopotamia,

Mycenae. View of the grave circle just inside the Lion Gate and within the huge fortification walls. The site of the citadel was strategically located to dominate the large plain of Argolis, which was protected at its opposite end, near the sea, by the fortress at Tiryns.

and even ostrich eggs from Nubia in Africa. At Mycenae, excavation revealed royal graves exceedingly rich in gifts, including crowns and diadems, sword scabbards, pommels of ivory and gold, bronze daggers inlaid with lion hunt scenes, vases of gold, silver, bronze, and alabaster, numerous articles of jewelry, arrowheads, boars' tusks like those of a helmet in Homer's *Iliad*, axes, tridents, and many other valuables. The workmanship is very fine and points to influence from Asia Minor, Egypt, and especially Crete. Schliemann thought one of the gold masks he found was the death mask of Homer's King Agamemnon, and indeed the stern and angular features do give an impression of majesty and a will to power.

How did Mycenaean royalty acquire this wealth and power? A far-flung network of trade contacts and a firm agricultural base offer part of

the answer, but warfare played an important role too. The weapons buried with the warrior-kings show this, and so do the massive fortification walls later built to protect Mycenaean fortresses. The walls at Mycenae were adorned by the lion gate, the first large-scale sculpture in Europe. Indeed, the Mycenaeans engaged in one of the most famous military conflicts in ancient history. Around 1200 B.C., they attacked and destroyed Troy, located at the northwest corner of Asia Minor near the Hellespont. The Trojan War was celebrated in heroic song orally transmitted by epic poets down to the eighth century B.C., when the *Iliad* and the *Odyssey* of Homer were recorded in written form. These great poems are the earliest landmarks of European literature. Whatever the actual goal and the true scale of the Trojan War of legend, it was for the Greeks the earliest major event in their history.

DARKNESS BEFORE THE NEW DAWN

Starting around 1200 B.C., the influx of the Dorians, another Greek-speaking people, destroyed virtually all major Mycenaean centers. Raids by various roving warrior groups, internal strife in the Mycenaean world, and perhaps climatic changes may have contributed to the downfall of the culture. By 1050, a whole civilization had disappeared, with its royal ruling elite, administrative apparatus, writing system, monumental art and architecture, transport and trade networks, armed forces, fortifications and citadels, tombs and grave treasures. In the period that followed, the Greek Dark Age, down to 800, the population of Greece fell by about eighty percent. Many people had died in the times of trouble just before and during

Greeks adopt
Phoenician
alphabet

Beginnings of
Greek philosophy:
Thales

Cleisthenes

Homer's
Iliad and
Odyssey

Greek lyric
poetry:
Sappho,
Archilochus

Solon's
reforms

the Dorian invasion; others fled to new settlements on the west coast of Asia Minor. Trade contracts with lands outside the Aegean basin ceased, and in most cases loosely organized tribal groups replaced the former strongly centralized governments.

The Dorians both completed the ethnic picture of the Greek people and created a great divide in Greek history. For Greece in the Dark Age witnessed a transition between two quite distinct civilizations. The Mycenaean world was enshrined as a heroic age in the memory of poets.

ARCHAIC GREECE: THE GREAT REAWAKENING

The Archaic era, which began around 800 B.C., was one of dynamic change, expansion, and experimentation. By its conclusion around 500, Greeks had laid firm foundations for their later political, cultural, and intellectual achievements.

Trade and Colonization

In the Archaic period, renewed contact with Near Eastern cultures brought

Lion Gate at Mycenae. This limestone relief sculpture was probably erected during a rebuilding of the fortification walls around 1250 B.C. The motif of heraldic lions poised on either side of a central, Minoan-style column tapering toward the base symbolizes the power and authority of the Mycenaean royal family.

29

THE RIGORS OF FARM-LIFE IN GREECE

> *When ploughing-time arrives, make haste to plough,*
> *You and your slaves alike, on rainy days*
> *And dry ones, while the season lasts. At dawn*
> *Get to your fields, and one day they'll be full.*
> *Plough, too, in springtime; if you turn the earth*
> *In summer, too, you won't regret the work. . . .*
>
> *And strike the oxen as they tug the straps.*
> *A slave should follow after, with a stick*
> *To hide the seeds and disappoint the birds.*
> *Good habits are a man's finest friend, and bad*
> *Are his worst enemy.* *

Hesiod, a contemporary of Homer, worked a small farm in Boeotia. He recommended hard work, thrift, common sense, and vigilance as necessities for survival. Unfortunately, good work habits were often not enough to save the impoverished farmer toiling over his small plot of rocky land.

*Hesiod, *Works and Days*, trans. Dorothea Wender (New York: Penguin, 1973), lines 458–462, 468–472.

to Greece widespread manufacturing and artistic skills. Building construction, metallurgy, and pottery and textile production were again significant occupations, though farming remained the vocation of the great majority of people. A merchant class arose to import raw materials and to export finished goods. Sea routes linked Greece with trading depots and with sources of manufacturing supplies in, for example, Syria, the Nile Delta, the Crimean Peninsula in the Black Sea, and along the southern coasts of present day France and Italy. The Phoenician alphabet was adapted for use in transcribing the Greek language, and the practice of coining money was adopted from the Lydians in Asia Minor; both greatly expedited commercial activities.

At home, however, increasing population forced many smallholders to scratch a living from marginally productive soil. Many suffered near starvation, foreclosure, and debt-enslavement.

One solution to this problem was for Greeks to acquire new land in other Mediterranean regions. Between 750 and 550 B.C., and to a lesser extent thereafter, Greek city-states sent thousands of settlers to Sicily and southern Italy, eastern north Africa, Thrace, Macedon, and the coasts of the Black Sea. These new settlements were not true colonies but free and independent states, though bound to their mother cities by diplomatic courtesies and traditional ties of kinship. As a result, Greek cultural, political, and social institutions spread throughout much of the Mediterranean region. However, the Greeks were unable to create a unified empire such as the Romans later did.

The Evolution of the Greek City-State

The territory of ancient Greece was never united under one government but was divided into numerous independent states, each consisting of an urban center with its adjacent countryside. The Greek word for such a state was *polis* (the source of the English term *political*). The fully developed Greek city-state of the Classical era saw remarkable cultural achievements as well as the first democratic forms of government. Virtually all city-states allowed for some degree of citizen participation in policy making, both domestic and foreign. This set off the Greeks markedly from their Near Eastern predecessors and contemporaries, who in many other respects supplied the models and precedents for Greek cultural development. Politically, Near Eastern societies maintained strong monarchies with few rights or privileges for the common citizen.

The Greek city-states typically followed a sequence of governmental forms from monarchy through oligarchy and tyranny to democracy. Monarchy, the first of these stages, was characteristic of Mycenaean civilization. As we noted earlier, the powerful kingships commemorated in the archaeological record and in Homeric poetry were swept away by the cataclysms that ended the Mycenaean era. A restricted version of kingship persisted in the Dark Age when petty chieftains headed local tribes.

Oligarchy (government by a small group) began as weak kings were replaced by nobles, members of the major landowning families who had formerly served as advisers and military commanders under the king or chief man. These wealthy aristocrats sat in councils and held offices with defined powers and responsibilities. Already in the early eighth century, they monopolized civil and military authority. One reason for their monopoly was that cavalry, the principal arm of the military, was an exclusive preserve of the nobility because of the wealth needed to own and raise horses, as was true centuries later in the medieval period. This early aristocracy was essentially a tribal society, with heads of families and of clans in control of groups of blood relatives, usually living in close proximity.

Then, beginning about 675 B.C., changes in arms and in tactics increased the military importance of ordinary citizens, leading to the overthrow of oligarchies and the rise of tyrants. Pheidon of Argos introduced a new, standard outfit of armor and deployed carefully drilled men in a phalanx or mass formation of foot soldiers who were called hoplites. With this efficient new infantry, Pheidon inflicted a heavy defeat on the Spartans and temporarily controlled half of the Peloponnese. All city-states quickly realized that a force of hoplites—the larger the better—was indispensable for "national security."

Greek Hoplite Warrior. The hoplite warrior dates to the seventh century B.C. This red-figure vase of c. 480 B.C. shows the typical complete outfit of arms and armor: a circular shield with strap in the inside center and handgrip near the rim. Short sword under the left arm, spear, helmet, breast plate, and greaves. The warrior is pouring a libation to the gods, no doubt to ensure his success in battle. From Nola in southern Italy.

Small farmers, serving in the hoplite army, now displaced aristocratic cavalry as the backbone of the military.

This military innovation led to changes in the social and political fabric of Greek cities, for the hoplites desired a role in government appropriate to their new military importance. In this way, tyranny was established. The word *tyranny* did not yet have the negative flavor it later acquired. A tyrant was simply a ruler who gained power by nonconstitutional means; he was a usurper and often also a reformer. In general, the tyrant was a disgruntled noble who outmaneuvered his aristocratic political opponents with the help of a privately conscripted army supported by or composed of hoplite commoners. The tyrant then reshaped the constitution to improve the political and socioeconomic situation of the hoplite class. The more complex social and political arrangements of the city-state were replacing the patterns of tribal society.

In Greece, then, tyranny marked a step toward democracy, which arose when the citizens took control for themselves. This usually happened when the tyrant or his descendants abused their powers and oppressed their former supporters, thus becoming "tyrannical" in the familiar sense of the word.

In considering the various patterns of Greek government, we should note that "citizens" in the context of Greek or Roman society composed a more narrowly defined group than in modern times. By and large, full citizenship was confined to adult male landowners. Women could not vote or hold office, nor were they recognized without male representation in the law courts; they were citizens only by virtue of their relation to some male,

a father, husband, uncle, brother. Also, a very large part of the permanent labor force consisted of slaves, who had no legal standing even as human beings before the law. The Greeks and the Romans considered slavery, and all of the human degradation it could entail, a fact of life, and they regularly acquired slaves through both warfare and trade. Though they were much more liberal than later slaveowners in freeing individual slaves, they did not contemplate abolishing the institution of slavery itself; slaves could no more be given up than could tools. Finally, there were in most Greek states people of intermediate statuses, between slave and full citizen. Examples were the *perioikoi* in Sparta and the metics in Athens. Such individuals were offered certain protections under the law and were sometimes enlisted to serve the state as soldiers, but they were denied the right to vote or hold office or generally even to own land.

THE ATHENIAN EXPERIMENT BEGINS

The typical Greek political metamorphosis may be traced in detail in the history of Athens. Athens controlled the 1,000-square-mile peninsula of Attica and had the largest population of any Greek city-state. It underwent the usual sequence from Mycenaean kingship through Dark Age chieftainship to oligarchical rule by aristocrats. As in nearly all city-states, the government of Athens comprised three departments: managerial officials called archons, advisory councillors, and a ratificatory assembly of citizens. In the early part

of the Archaic era, aristocratic clans were politically dominant and competed with one another while excluding the common citizens from positions of authority. The lower classes did, however, make an important gain in the seventh century, when Draco, a man of whom little is known, supervised the first written codification of law at Athens. Though the "Draconian" law code was harsh, stipulating the death penalty for many offenses (people said it was "written in blood"), it did distinguish murder from manslaughter and prescribe penalties for each. It thus ended the bloody vendettas that such crimes often triggered by providing a peaceful method of settling blood feuds. Further, even if the code was as cruel as tradition held, it shielded the lower classes from altogether arbitrary judgments by aristocratic magistrates. The law, once recorded and made generally accessible by the new alphabetic script, was criticized, modified, and refined as judicial practices became more established and precedents accumulated.

Despite the codification of law, conflicts both between the social classes and within the upper class led to a crisis in the late seventh century. By the early sixth century, the indispensable hoplite infantrymen had little control over even their own personal destinies, let alone that of their city-state. Many, because their land was not very productive, were deeply in debt to wealthy, aristocratic creditors. Some were obligated to pay a sixth part of the yearly produce of their farms as loan retirement, making them still less able to support their families. They often forfeited their farms to the powerful landowners or, worse yet, were themselves sold into slavery, for at this time a man could place his own person as security for a loan. The situation grew critical and potentially explosive.

Solon

To head off violent revolution, aristocrats and commoners agreed to the appointment in 594 B.C. of a special arbitrator, Solon (c. 640-c. 560), a man of undisputed wisdom and moral probity, with extraordinary powers to reform the constitution, the laws, and the social system. Striving to treat equitably both the impoverished small farmers and the nobles, he canceled debts—a frequent demand of revolutionaries in all periods—and forbade debt bondage. Solon also took steps to recall citizens who had been sold into slavery and further guaranteed the personal freedoms of poorer citizens by revisions in the laws and in the judiciary. The wealthy, for their part, were spared the more radical measure of land redistribution; they kept what they had.

Solon also redefined the social classes, determining status by wealth measured in agricultural produce, rather than by birth. Eligibility for public office was keyed to this new classification. Any man by hard work and native intelligence might become upwardly mobile both politically and economically. The aristocratic monopoly of political authority was broken and the small farmers acquired a role in government. In addition, Solon encouraged foreign-born craftsmen and artisans to settle in Athens, even going so far as to offer citizenship as an inducement. Later Athenian leaders continued to encourage skilled foreigners to come to Athens, but stopped making them citizens. Such resident aliens, called metics, played a key role in the economic life of the Athenian state, but

were never entitled to the same rights as citizens. Solon also restricted the export of grain, so profitable for large landowners, because such crops were needed at home. He then selflessly relinquished his powers and left Athens for several years to give his reforms a chance to work. Later Athenians remembered him as a good and just man and a champion of democracy.

Peisistratus and Tyranny

Despite Solon's "shaking-up" of the Athenian constitution, the city-state continued to suffer from factional strife. A one-time cancellation of debts did not protect the small farmers from

future bankruptcy. The number of landless and dispossessed grew. Among the wealthy, power politics continued as usual. Finally, an aristocrat named Peisistratus became tyrant (546–527 B.C.) and brought many important changes to Athens. Unlike Solon, Peisistratus confiscated the land of his aristocratic opponents and redistributed it among his supporters, thus solidifying his popularity among the commoners. But he left intact nearly all of the Solonian constitution, going even further in his measures to improve the lot of all citizens. He built roads and public gardens, renovated the city's water supply system, introduced state pensions for vet-

---

SOLON, THE "WILY WOLF"

Did I stop then before I had accomplished
my task in gathering back the common people?
Great Olympian Mother Earth will swear before
time's court that I took from her breast
the mortgage-markers, freed her from bonds.
I repatriated many sons of Athens—slaves
(by law or not) or debt-exiles. Some had lost
our Attic tongue so far from home. Others,
fearfully cowed by masters here, I also freed.
Fitting might to right, I worked the deed
I'd promised, set straight laws alike
for lords and lowly. Another man, less sage,
less honest, could not have checked the mob.
Had I favored one side over the other,
our polis would have grieved many sons.
Like the wily wolf amid a pack of hounds,
I showed my strength toward all around. *

In addition to his many other impressive abilities, Solon was the first identifiable Athenian "man of letters." His poetry shows not only the sagacity one would expect in a wise social and political reformer, but also a high degree of literary artistry. Poems like the one quoted here, dealing with his role as mediator in difficult circumstances, helped enhance his image in the eyes of posterity.

*Solon, Poem 24.

erans, and greatly increased the size and splendor of state religious festivals.

Peisistratus particularly magnified the annual Panathenaic ("All-Athenian") festival, in honor of the birth of the goddess Athena, celebrated with special magnificence every fourth year. A large procession of sacrifice bearers, military contingents, and separate choirs of boys and girls wound its way through the marketplace along the Panathenaic Way and up the Acropolis ("upper city" or fortified height) to the Temple of Athena, the patroness of the city. This temple was later destroyed by the Persians and replaced by the Parthenon. Among the various ceremonies were games like those at Olympia, where prizes were awarded. Musicians and singers performed specially composed hymns, and rhapsodes (professional narrators) recited Homeric poetry from "authorized" versions perhaps commissioned by Peisistratus himself. Virtually all Athenians either participated in or enjoyed the spectacle of the celebration. At other seasonal festivals, in honor of the god Dionysus, the beginnings of Greek drama were seen in the performance of tragic choruses, which sang of the exploits of gods and heroes.

The psychological effect of all this was profound: Athenian citizens came to think of their city-state as particularly important and dear to the gods and of themselves as fortunate to be members of such a community. Peisistratus died in 527 B.C., and in 510 aristocratic opponents of the regime wrested control of Athens from his sons, with some help from Sparta.

Cleisthenes

After the removal of tyranny at Athens, there was a short period of governmental disorder, but in 508 B.C.

another reformer, Cleisthenes, emerged victorious. Solon had given Athenians judicial rights and personal freedoms; Cleisthenes increased their political privileges and ensured their more equal representation in the operations of the government. Cleisthenes ended the tribal pattern of aristocratic clan domination by reorganizing the state in ten large divisions, still called tribes but in fact each composed of wards or neighborhoods in three disparate areas: city, coast, and inland. Residence in a ward was the principal criterion of citizenship. From each tribe one archon was elected and fifty councillors were chosen by lot annually to serve in a Council of Five Hundred, which managed state finances and foreign policy and determined the agenda for the full assembly of citizens. The old, aristocratic Areopagus Council retained authority in certain court cases and especially in the supervision of the various government officeholders. Because serving in public office still carried no payment, the ten archons, who managed Athens on a day-to-day basis, were mostly aristocrats, who could afford to spare the time; and since the Areopagus Council consisted of ex-archons, it remained a conservative, oligarchic element in the system.

Cleisthenes also introduced a panel of ten annually elected military commanders, one from each tribe. Because its members could be elected repeatedly and thus serve for extended periods of time, this board eventually became the true executive branch of the government. The traditional officials, the archons, could serve only once and thus were unable to provide continuity of leadership. Cleisthenes may also have introduced the practice of ostracism, whereby the

citizenry could vote, using pottery fragments called *ostraca,* to send any dangerously powerful person into a ten-year exile.

THE SPARTAN PATTERN OF LIFE

Sparta never rivaled Athens in cultural or intellectual achievements, but a long, costly struggle between the two city-states gave it supremacy in the military sphere. Sparta was located in a large plain in that part of the Peloponnesian Peninsula known as Laconia. The non-Spartan inhabitants of Laconia, called *perioikoi* ("dwellers-around"), were free citizens of their own communities but subject to Spartan overlordship, being obliged to serve in the army and to abide by Spartan foreign policy decisions. The ruling Spartans called themselves *homoioi* ("equals").

The third and largest element of the population was the helots, state-owned slaves assigned to individual *homoioi* but not to *perioikoi.* The usual Greek practice in imposing slavery on a defeated enemy was to sell and disperse the inhabitants of the conquered territory. Sparta, by contrast, after defeating neighboring Messenia in the seventh century B.C., enslaved the Messenians, but did not export them. Instead, the whole population of helots was forced to farm Spartan controlled lands both in Laconia and in the annexed territories of Messenia. The Spartan poet Tyrtaeus described the helots as "worn down by great loads like asses, forced to bring their masters half of all their land's yield."

Freed by the helot system from

having to work the land, those of pure Spartan ancestry cultivated a highly developed military ethic. "Spartan" signified, then and now, a commitment to the most rigorous discipline in early education, in military training, and in all aspects of adult life. Males devoted their lives to the army and the state; indeed the two institutions were hardly distinguishable. This was essential for internal security in a territory inhabited by a vastly more numerous subject population. Moreover, the fear of revolt by helots at home made the Spartans hesitant to engage in lengthy campaigns away from their Peloponnesian homeland. Despite this, the Spartans carried the hoplite army to its most disciplined and successful level of operation. Though Spartans were generally outnumbered by their opponents in battle, they nearly always excelled their foes in fighting ability.

The political characteristics of the Spartan state were no less distinctive than its military characteristics. Not only was kingship not abolished as in other states but also there were two kings and two royal families. Though these kings remained the supreme military commanders throughout Sparta's history, civil authority was vested in five elected officials called ephors, who were similar to the Athenian archons in their responsibilities. An advisory council of thirty elders roughly corresponded to the Athenian Council or Roman Senate.

Sparta was the greatest military power in Greece until the fourth century, but it paid a high price for this supremacy. After promising early developments in art, especially vase painting and poetry, Sparta made little further cultural advance and devoted its energies exclusively to the code of the soldier.

THE GREEK DISCOVERY OF THE MIND

The Archaic period in Greek history was one of remarkable innovation in culture and the arts as well as in government and society. In religion, the personalities and exploits of the Greek gods, whose origins lay in the Mycenaean past, were now given distinctive formulations that would persist for centuries to come. Science and philosophy emerged as important intellectual investigations. The literature of the period included the first written record of an old form, epic poetry, and the creation of a new one, lyric poetry.

Greek Myth and Religion

Despite political fragmentation, ancient Greece had a common religious and cultural heritage, with roots in the Mycenaean age. Though no sacred book like the Bible or the Qur'an (Koran) appeared, hundreds of Greek gods and goddesses were portrayed in thousands of myths as distinct personalities with human intellects and emotions. The Olympians, so named from their mythical home on Mount Olympus, were already fully formed in the Homeric epics composed at the very beginning of the Archaic period: Zeus, the supreme deity, sky god, wielder of the thunderbolt; Poseidon, the god of the sea; Athena, the warrior goddess and patroness of intellectual endeavor; Aphrodite, the goddess of beauty and erotic love; Apollo, the god of music, prophecy, and medicine; Ares, the god of war, and so on. The gods were the principal figures in tales told by generations of poet-singers; they were de-

picted everywhere in art: vase paintings, sculptures, coins, and the like. The mythic stories served a variety of purposes. They were often explanatory: What caused thunder? Where did that strange black rock come from? They could convey a moral: Treat a guest as you would like to be treated were he your host; respect one's elders and one's kin. They could at the same time simply entertain, as good stories have done in every culture.

The worship of the Olympian gods involved all segments of society. It led to the development of the Greek temple, with its characteristic encircling colonnade, its relief sculpture, and its carefully worked out proportions, probably inspired by Egyptian models. Each temple was the home of a patron deity of a particular locality and the architectural focus of the city's life. The sculptural decorations of these temples furnish the first European examples of large-scale representation of the human form. Battles of gods and giants or of men and centaurs (creatures half man and half horse) were favorite themes in the sculpture.

Certain religious centers gained exceptional prestige among all Greeks. The city-states vied with one another in dedicating gifts and monuments in honor of Apollo at the breathtaking site of his Delphic temple on the slopes of Mount Parnassus. Here the oracle of Apollo served as adviser on a wide range of questions, both personal ("Who are my true parents?") and public ("Should we make war on city x?"). At Delphi, the Isthmus of Corinth, and especially Olympia in the western Peloponnese, the Greeks held athletic and other contests to honor the gods. The competitive spirit was deeply ingrained in Greek life, intel-

35

Bronze Statue of a Greek God. The magnificent bronze statue found in the sea off the island of Euboea. If the lost weapon was a trident, this is Poseidon; if a thunderbolt, Zeus. The statue was made by the lost wax method of casting. Slightly over life size, it is one of the finest surviving examples of original Greek bronze sculpture. National Museum, Athens.

lectual and artistic as well as military and athletic.

Philosophical and Scientific Thought

While some poets and artists were celebrating the traditional Olympian deities, early Greek philosopher-scientists were skeptically relying on human reason to provide new, non-mythological explanations of the origin and nature of the cosmos. At Miletus on the west coast of Asia Minor and later in other Greek areas, the first philosophical thinkers speculated about the relation of the supernatural power in the universe to the observable order of things on Earth and in the heavens. Thales, Anaximenes, Heracleitus, and others, believed that a controlling law underlay the rhythms of nature and that nature itself was arranged into its basic elements—earth, air, water, and fire. Philosopher-scientists also dared to inquire into the character of divine beings themselves and did not accept uncritically the poetic depictions of the Olympians. Xenophanes of Colophon, for example, criticized Homer and Hesiod because "they . . . attributed to the gods everything shameful and blameworthy among mankind: theft, adultery, and mutual deception." Pythagoras and his followers sought the hidden harmony of the universe in music and numbers. Not content with simplistic mythic resolutions of scientific problems, the philosophers put their theories to the test of rational criticism and debate in search of the most adequate explanations of natural phenomena. As Heracleitus said, "Men who love wisdom must be inquirers into very many things indeed," for "Nature loves to hide."

These earliest philosopher-scientists and, in direct line from them, Socrates, Plato, and Aristotle in the Classical period were "inquirers into very many things indeed." They handed on to western civilization a precious spirit of intellectual self-reliance and of faith in rational investigation.

Delphi. View of the sanctuary of Apollo at Delphi, the most important and celebrated oracle in the Greek world, with theater (foreground) and remains of the temple. Located on the steep slopes of Mount Parnassus on the north shore of the Gulf of Corinth in central Greece.

THE CODE OF THE HERO IN HOMER

And now [Sarpedon] spoke in address to Glaukos, son of Hippolochos:
"Glaukos, why is it you and I are honored before others
with pride of place, the choice meats and the filled wine cups
in Lykia, and all men look on us as if we were immortals,
and we are appointed a great piece of land by the banks of Xanthos,
good land, orchard and vineyard, and ploughland for the planting of wheat?
Therefore it is our duty in the forefront of the Lykians
to take our stand, and bear our part of the blazing of battle. . . .
Seeing that the spirits of death stand close about us
in their thousands, no man can turn aside nor escape them,
let us go on and win glory for ourselves, or yield it to others." •

Sarpedon, a son of Zeus and ally of the Trojans during their war against the Greeks, here summarizes the heroic code. The price of nobility and the material advantages it confers is to risk one's life on the battlefield. Humans are inescapably mortal. Death comes for us all, sooner or later. In Homer, the hero seeks to cheat death by winning glory, which will ensure both prestige in this life and continued life in the memories of men and women.

•Richmond Lattimore, trans., *The Iliad of Homer* (Chicago: Univ. of Chicago Press, 1951), 12.309–316, 326–328.

Literature

Greek literature from its beginning down through the Classical period was characterized by a chronological sequence of genres. At first, epic or heroic poetry was preeminent. The Homeric *Iliad* and *Odyssey*, though first in the written tradition of European literature, were in fact at the end of a long tradition of oral poetry. They provided the Greeks with a common heritage of heroic myth. Children learned their alphabet with the Homeric epics before their eyes and in their ears. Homer's answers to the great questions of human potential faced by Achilles on the battlefield at Troy and by Odysseus during his journey home to Ithaca influenced the mental outlook of every educated Greek. In particular, the aristocratic ideal of *arete* (moral and physical excellence) set a standard of heroic behavior for the whole society.

The Homeric versions of the heroic epic marked the end of a tradition extending back into Mycenaean times. The Archaic Greeks developed another poetic form, the lyric, which was a short composition sung to the accompaniment of a lyre. Lyric poems were less grand than epics, but also more personal, immediate, and flexible in both form and content. Lyric poetry gave way in turn to drama, the predominant genre of the Classical period.

The short lyric poem might recount virtually any human experience. The great poetess Sappho of Lesbos described in clinical detail the emotional and physiological responses ignited by love: ". . . my lips are stricken to silence, under-/ neath my skin the tenuous flame suffuses;/ nothing shows in front of my eyes, my ears are/ muted in thunder./ And the sweat breaks running upon me, fever/ shakes my body . . ." (trans. R. Lattimore). Archilochus of Paros wrote love and hate poetry and recalled with delightful self-deprecation his lack of expertise as a mercenary soldier: "Some barbarian is waving my shield, since I was obliged to/ leave that perfectly good piece of equipment behind/ under a bush. But I got away, so what does it matter?/ Let the shield go; I can buy another one equally good" (trans. R. Lattimore). Several of the philosopher-scientists discussed earlier also employed poetic forms to transmit their thoughts. As we have seen, Solon even wrote of his constitutional reforms in some of his lyrics. Satirical elements too appeared in early Greek lyric: Semonides of Amorgos, for example, wrote a tongue-in-cheek poem caricaturing women: "One was a monkey; and this is the very worst,/ most exquisite disaster Zeus has wished on men./ Hers is the ugliest face of all. . ." (trans. R. Lattimore).

Perhaps the single most distinctive aspect of these literary and philosophic developments, as compared with those of the ancient Near East, was the emergence of the self-aware individual, reporting his or her feelings on a wide range of topics and considering those reflections worthy of presentation to a larger audience. The inner life of the poet was for the first time appropriate subject matter for serious and not so serious writing.

38

SUMMARY

Greek civilization began about 2000 B.C. with the arrival of Greek speakers in the southern Balkan Peninsula. The Bronze Age culture that reached its peak at Mycenae drew on non-Greek civilizations in the Near East and especially on Crete, which was ultimately absorbed into the Mycenaean sphere of influence. By such borrowing, Greeks in the second millennium B.C. developed centralized governments with urban nuclei, monumental architecture, and a crude writing system. They established overseas trade networks and mounted major military expeditions. All of this came to an end in the great collapse that preceded the Dark Age. There survived only the memory of a mythic heroic age, including the Greek gods and legendary warriors who lived on in the poems of Homer.

The achievements of the Greeks in the Archaic period, which followed the Dark Age, were in many ways the most exciting in ancient history. Not only did the Greek world rebound materially from the deprived conditions of the Dark Age but it also nurtured new, increasingly equalitarian systems of government. No longer was the monarchical, palace-dominated state the norm for civilized societies. The Greek city-states innovated forms of governance that better reflected the needs and wishes of the governed. They were also the setting for artistic and intellectual advances. Men and women for the first time in the western experience acted as self-conscious, identifiable individuals. In the new literary form of lyric, in their sculpture and painting, and in the skeptical investigations of their philosophy, the Greeks examined their own nature and that of the world around them. They then presented their findings in new and enduring fashion, thereby paving the way for great achievements in the Classical period and in succeeding centuries of western civilization.

SELECTED SOURCES

*Boardman, John. *The Greeks Overseas: Their Early Colonies and Trade.* Rev. ed. 1980. A masterly examination of the evidence for the spread of Greek culture to all areas of the Mediterranean and Black seas. Superbly illustrated.

*Chadwick, John. *The Mycenaean World.* 1976. A well-written general account with helpful illustrations.

*Ehrenberg, Viktor. *From Solon to Socrates: Greek History and Civilization during the Sixth and Fifth Centuries B.C.* 2d ed. 1973. Especially valuable for its clear discussion of Solon and the impact of his reforms on the development of democracy at Athens.

*Finley, Moses I. *The World of Odysseus.* Rev. ed. 1978. A brilliant explication of the social and moral atmosphere of the Homeric epics; contains an appendix on "Schliemann's Troy—One Hundred Years After."

*Guthrie, W. K. C. *The Greeks and Their Gods.* 1950. A lively account of the ways in which the gods, both major and minor, permeated all aspects of ancient Greek life and culture.

*Hutchinson, R. W. *Prehistoric Crete.* 1962. A reliable overview of Minoan culture with useful bibliography and illustrations.

*Lattimore, Richmond, trans. *Greek Lyrics.* 2d ed. 1960. An excellent selection of work by some twenty early Greek poets.

*Lloyd, G. E. R. *Early Greek Science: Thales to Aristotle.* 1970. The first half of this book is especially valuable for its discussion of the achievements of early Greek philosophy, as contrasted with ancient Near Eastern precedents.

*Owen, E. T. *The Story of the Iliad.* 1946; reprinted 1966. Offers a sound, purely literary, book-by-book interpretation of the epic.

*Renault, Mary. *The Praise Singer.* 1978. A richly detailed recreation of the life of the lyric poet Simonides at the court of the sons of Peisistratus at Athens.

Starr, Chester G. *Individual and Community: The Rise of the Polis, 800–500 B.C.* 1986. A good, recent presentation of the cultural, economic, and political achievements of the citizens of the early Greek polis.

*Available in paperback.

CLASSICAL GREECE: THE FIFTH CENTURY B.C.

I declare that our city is an education to Greece, and I declare that in my opinion each single one of our citizens, in all the manifold aspects of life, is able to show himself the rightful lord and owner of his own person, and do this, moreover, with exceptional grace and exceptional versatility. . . . Athens, alone of the states we know, comes to her testing time in a greatness that surpasses what was imagined of her. . . . Mighty indeed are the marks and monuments of our empire which we have left. Future ages will wonder at us, as the present age wonders at us now. . . . For our adventurous spirit has forced an entry into every sea and into every land; and everywhere we have left behind us everlasting memorials of good done to our friends or suffering inflicted on our enemies.

Thus the great Athenian statesman and general, Pericles, patriotically celebrated the civil and military accomplishments of Athens at home and abroad, while assessing with prophetic insight their impression on posterity. The stage for these accomplishments had been set in the Archaic age, when the Greeks had enjoyed freedom from outside interference. At the beginning of the fifth century B.C., however, Greece faced a dire threat from the Persian Empire, which forced the Greek states for once to stand united. Greek victory in that conflict also inaugurated a period of specially brilliant cultural and political achievement, particularly at Athens. This chapter describes the Persian Wars and explains the rise of the Athenian Empire in the middle of the century, the era of Periclean Athens. It concludes with an account of the Peloponnesian War, which resulted in Spartan victory and Athenian defeat at the end of the century.

PERSIA AND THE GREEKS

After the destruction of its capital, Nineveh, in 612 B.C., the Assyrian Empire was succeeded by four smaller powers: Egypt; the Chaldean state in lower Mesopotamia; the warlike kingdom of the Medes, embracing upper

Pericles. A Roman copy of a bust of Pericles, originally made in the fifth century and dedicated on the Acropolis at Athens. It shows the Athenian statesman in a pose of somewhat idealized nobility; the helmet is a symbol of his service as *strategos* (general). Vatican Museum.

41

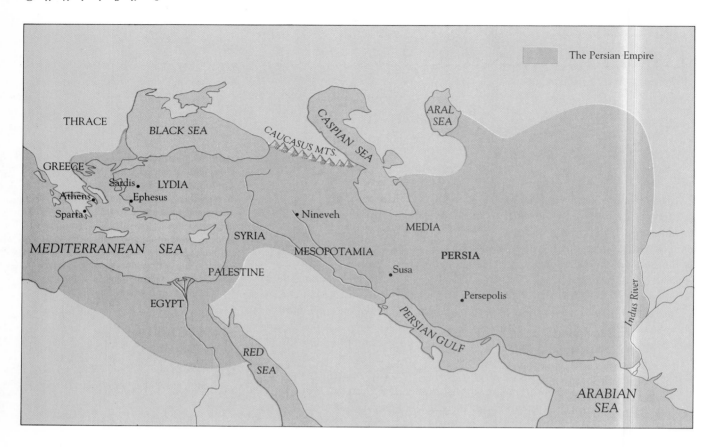

The Persian Empire

MAP 6
Greece and the Persian Empire.

Mesopotamia, Syria, and Iran; and the kingdom of Lydia in western Asia Minor. Of these, only Lydia was in direct contact with the Greek world. From these fragments of former Assyrian dominions, the Persian Empire was created and rose to become a major threat to the independence of the Greek city-states.

The Persian Empire: Its Extent and Character

The Persians, an Iranian tribe related to the Medes, established their empire in the sixth century B.C. (see Map 6). During the reign of Cyrus (559–530), they conquered the territories of the Medes, the Lydians, and the Chaldeans. Cyrus's son, Cambyses (529–522), added Egypt to the empire. After civil strife following the death of Cambyses, Darius I became king in 521 and reigned till 486. Darius enlarged the empire to the Indus River in the east, the Caucasus Mountains in the north, and upper Egypt in the south, while seizing a foothold in Europe in the west.

To rule this vast territory, Darius set up an administrative apparatus that lasted down to Alexander's conquest in 330 B.C. It consisted of military and civil officials drawn from the elite of the Iranian nobility. He organized the empire into tributary kingdoms and twenty provinces, but respected local forms of government and differences in religion and language. Darius solidified his authority by appointing provincial governors called satraps. They collected tribute, taxes, soldiers, and military provisions for delivery to the king, whose personal supervisors, called "Eyes and Ears," made regular rounds of the provinces. Communication and transport were facilitated by the world's first extensive network of good roads, including the Royal Road from Ephesus on the Aegean to Susa, some 1,600 miles away in Iran. Master of all this was the supreme autocrat, earthly viceroy of Ahura Mazda. To quote one inscription, he was "the great king, king of kings, king of the countries possessing many kinds of people, king of this great earth far and wide."

Persian Culture

Persia's artistic and intellectual accomplishments did not match its military and governmental performance. Little literature was produced, except for the *Avesta*, the collected sacred scriptures of Zoroastrianism. Science and mathematics did not advance beyond the substantial inheritance from Babylon and Egypt. In art and architecture, Greece and Egypt often provided the models and sometimes the expertise: Greek stonecutters and sculptors, for example, worked on the mammoth palace complexes at Susa and Persepolis.

The Persians showed great innovation in religion, however. Traditional Iranian religion was a typical Indo-European polytheism, whose chief officials were magi (priest-astrologers). In the early sixth century B.C., a reformer named Zoroaster ("Zarathustra" in Persian), removed the magical elements from the religion. In the new faith, Zoroastrianism, the world was ruled not by a horde of supernatural beings but by two only. Representing goodness, light, and truth was Ahura Mazda; opposing him was Ahriman, representing darkness and evil. The two gods were locked in a universal struggle, which Ahura Mazda was destined to win. On a future judgment day, all human beings, living and dead, would be consigned to heaven or hell. This notion of last judgment later appeared in Christianity and Islam. Men and women possessed free will and were expected to avoid sin and abide by the divine laws. The king of kings himself was a devotee and example to his people. Later, a new god, Mithras, supplanted Ahura Mazda and played a prominent part in the religious ferment of the Roman Empire.

In warfare, politics, religion, and material culture, the Persian Empire equalled or surpassed its Near Eastern predecessors. It brought lasting stability to a vast region of diverse peoples and cultures. In the ancient world, only the Roman Empire would match that achievement.

Greeks Against Persians

The Persians became a threat to Greece when Darius gained a foothold in Europe by establishing a satrapy, or province, in Thrace (see Map

Persepolis. A view of the east front of the royal palaces at Persepolis, showing the Gateway of Xerxes. The main buildings were erected on a vast rock terrace by Darius I and completed by Xerxes. The relief sculptures are among the finest surviving examples of Persian art of the period. Located in modern-day south central Iran.

7). Then, in 499 B.C., the Persians unsuccessfully attacked the island of Naxos along the sea route to mainland Greece. There immediately followed a revolt of the Ionian Greek cities that had been under Persian control since 544. Aristagoras of Miletus, the leader of the rebellion, asked mainland Greek cities for help, and Athens and Eretria responded by contributing warships. The rebels won some early victories and burned the Persian provincial capital of Sardis in 498, but overwhelmingly superior Persian forces crushed the revolt in 494.

The Persian assault on Greece intensified soon afterward. In 492 B.C., the Persians lost a fleet in a storm off Mount Athos, but in 490 a new attack force of 20,000–25,000 men was assembled and transported by sea. Its mission was limited to punishing Athens and Eretria for supporting the Ionian revolt and to securing bases for a full-scale expedition against Greece.

MAP 7

Major Battles of the Persian and Peloponnesian Wars and the Invasion Route of Xerxes in 480 B.C.

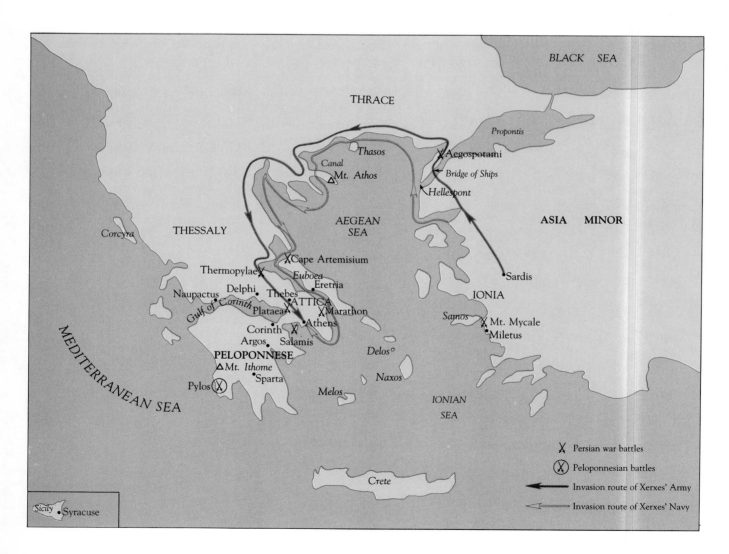

Burning
of
Sardis   Themistocles

Formation
of Delian
League

Pericles leader of
the democrats

Battle
of Marathon

Battle
of Salamis

Long Walls constructed

After defeating and enslaving the Eretrians, the Persians crossed from the island of Euboea to the plain of Marathon on the northeast coast of Attica. They were met by 10,000 Athenian hoplites. Reinforcements from Sparta, delayed by an important religious festival, arrived too late. Though outnumbered more than two to one, the Athenians, by their superior training, tactics, and armor, won a resounding victory at Marathon, driving the Persians back to their ships. Persian losses were 6,400, Athenian only 192. After the battle, the Persians sailed around the cape to Athens, hoping to take the city by surprise while the Greek army was still at Marathon. The hoplites made a forced march (the modern Olympic marathon race covers about the same distance) and were waiting when the fleet arrived. The Persians chose not to test these tough spearmen again and returned in defeat to Asia Minor.

The defeat at Marathon did not end Persia's designs on Greece. Darius began to gather men and materials for a much larger invasion, but he was delayed by a revolt in Egypt and died in 486 B.C. In the next year, Darius's son, Xerxes (486–465), resumed preparations, but this time for a coordinated movement of both land and sea forces along the northern shore of the Aegean, and then down into central Greece, Attica, and the Peloponnese. Fighting men were recruited from all parts of the empire. Xerxes even built a canal through the Mount Athos peninsula to avoid another devastating storm. Meanwhile, the Greek states had returned to their intercity rivalries. Many doubted the Persians would ever return.

Fortunately for Greece, persuasive leaders favored preparation for war. The Athenian statesman Themistocles (c. 528–462 B.C.) firmly believed the Persians would indeed come in force and that the survival of Greece depended on its control of the sea. First as archon and then as general, he expanded and fortified the excellent natural harbor at Piraeus, Athens' port city. Then, in 483, when a large new vein of silver was discovered in the state-owned mines at Laurium, Themistocles persuaded his fellow Athenians to use the bonanza to increase their fleet to 200 triremes. This decision, democratically adopted by free citizens, greatly affected the outcome of the Persian Wars and ultimately set Athens on a course toward preeminence among the Greek city-states.

By 481 B.C., a number of states,

Themistocles. A Roman copy of a portrait bust of Themistocles, originally done in his lifetime (c. 470–462 B.C.). It is a vivid representation of the tough-minded patriot-statesman, one of the principal figures in the Greek victory over Persia. Ostia Museum.

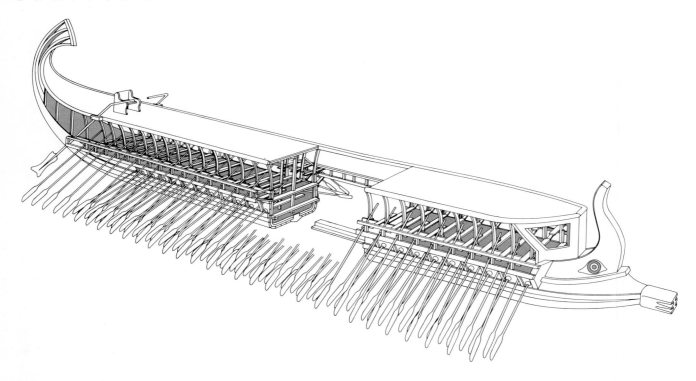

Greek Trireme. A cutaway view of a trireme, the standard Greek warship of the Classical period. Such vessels were about 120 feet long by 12 feet wide and were manned by some 150–175 men arranged in three tiers of rowing benches. The ram at the bow was the ship's main offensive weapon; note also the special steering oars at the stern.

including Athens and Sparta, had come to see that the survival of their distinctive social and religious institutions, indeed of Greek culture generally, depended on joint effort. They therefore formed a Greek league, with Spartan generals as supreme commanders. Many other states, however, chose to remain neutral or, in some cases, to cooperate with the Persians rather than be destroyed. Even Delphi predicted disaster for those who resisted the king of kings.

In the spring of 480 B.C., Xerxes led a force of about 150,000 troops across the Hellespont on a specially constructed ship bridge and began the 500-mile march to central Greece and Athens. After the destruction of a previous bridge in a gale, Xerxes is said to have executed its engineers and to have ordered the disobedient waters of the strait to be scourged, branded, and chained. Greek prop-

agandists depicted such acts as typical of an arrogant barbarian and foreign to their own more rational and enlightened intellects. Greek strategy, on both land and sea, was to minimize the Persians' advantage in numbers by meeting them only at bottlenecks. The Spartan high command favored the Isthmus of Corinth, which could most easily be held by land forces. This left states outside the Peloponnese, including Athens, undefended. Themistocles used the bargaining chip of the indispensable Athenian navy to persuade the Spartans to take a stand farther north, hoping to stop Persian forces by a combined land and sea defense at Thermopylae and Cape Artemisium. The Persian army could not take the long route around the mountains west and south of the narrow seaside pass at Thermopylae, because it needed the provisions carried by the fleet moving down the coast. The Greek navy held the Persians in a stalemate at Cape Artemisium, but the army could not hold the defile at Thermopylae. The Spartan king Leonidas and a suicide force of 300 Spartans fought fiercely to the end, while the bulk of the league troops retreated. After the final battle, Xerxes had Leonidas's head fixed on a stake. This was an uncharacteristically brutal act by the Persians, but the Spartan general had made them pay a high price in blood for a tiny piece of real estate.

The road to Athens was now clear, and the Persians soon took the hastily evacuated city and burned the temples on the Acropolis.

Despite these initial setbacks, the Greeks still possessed powerful military forces. Victory, however, de-

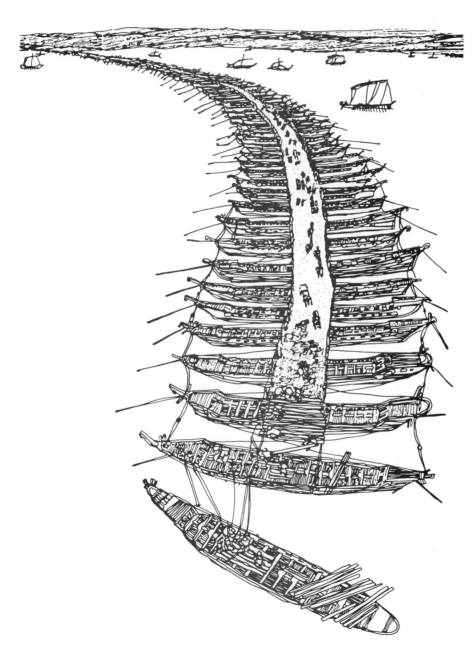

Xerxes' Ship Bridge. An artist's recreation of Xerxes' double ship bridge over the Hellespont narrows. The ships were anchored fore and aft and linked together by mile-long cables of linen and papyrus fiber; the Greeks later dedicated sections of these cables at Delphi as trophies of the war. A roadway of planks covered with earth was fitted with side screens so that horses, mules, and camels would not be startled at the sight of the water. Herodotus reports that the crossing took seven days and nights of continuous marching, an indication of the enormous size of Xerxes' army.

THE SPARTANS' LAST STAND AT THERMOPYLAE

Many of the invaders fell; behind them the company commanders plied their whips, driving the men remorselessly on. Many fell into the sea and were drowned, and still more were trampled to death by their friends. No one could count the number of the dead. The Greeks . . . fought with reckless desperation. . . . They resisted to the last, with their swords if they still had them, and, if not, with their hands and teeth, until the Persians, coming on from the front over the ruins of the wall and closing in from behind, finally overwhelmed them [with arrows and spears].•

For two days, Greek troops held the pass at Thermopylae against much larger Persian forces, including a special detachment of 10,000 men called the "Immortals" because the places of fallen members of the corps were immediately taken by replacements. On the third day, however, the Persians succeeded in bringing some of their troops around through the mountains and down to the coast behind Thermopylae. Leonidas and his men, specially chosen from those who had living sons, were thus caught in a slaughterous pincer movement.

•Herodotus, *The Histories*, trans. A. de Sélincourt (Harmondsworth: Penguin, 1954), 7.223–25.

manded coordination of the complementary military and naval strengths of Sparta and Athens, respectively. The Spartans again wanted to make a stand on the Isthmus of Corinth, but Themistocles convinced them that the strait between the island of Salamis and Attica was the best place to engage the Persian fleet. At Salamis, the Greeks used boarding parties of marines, superior oarsmanship, and effective ramming tactics to win a stunning victory. Xerxes, watching in bitter disappointment from high ground, saw his armada defeated by the triremes of the Greek league. In a fit of royal anger, he had a number of the defeated captains beheaded on the spot.

Salamis was the decisive victory of the war. Unable to provision his army by sea, Xerxes withdrew to Asia Mi-

nor but left a large force to winter in Thessaly, where supplies were sufficient. In the summer of 479 B.C., Greek troops led by the Spartan Pausanias destroyed this Persian army at Plataea, where the Spartans in particular distinguished themselves. At the same time, Greek forces destroyed the remnants of the Persian navy at Mycale in Asia Minor.

Victory over the Persians ensured the Greek city-states of the freedom essential to economic and cultural prosperity in the fifth century. But although they proudly commemorated the triumph of the thirty-one allied states on a special war memorial at Delphi, their experience in the Persian Wars did not teach them to prefer large-scale cooperation to the violence and divisiveness of intercity quarrels.

ATHENS BUILDS AN EMPIRE

The Persian Wars left Athens the strongest naval power in the Greek world. Though the fleet had been built to meet a specific and immediate challenge to the autonomy of the Greek city-states, its continued existence in the years after the war and after the threat of Persian aggression had disappeared gave Athens its chance for greatness. The Athenians used their naval strength to build an empire overseas and to carry further their experimentation with democratic rule at home.

The Delian League

After the Persian Wars, the Greek cities of Asia Minor and the neighboring islands wanted an alliance with Greek cities of the mainland against future Persian aggression. For leadership, they naturally turned to Athens, now the leading naval power in the Greek world. In 478 B.C., some 150 cities of Ionia and the Aegean Sea created by treaty an organization known as The Athenians and Their Allies, later called the Delian League because its treasury was on Apollo's sacred island of Delos.

Admission into the Delian League required that each state agree unilaterally to cooperate with Athens in defending the Aegean region against further Persian attacks and in harassing the Persians wherever possible. In proportion to their size and wealth, member states were obliged to contribute either men and ships or the monetary equivalent to an allied fleet under Athenian direction. Athenian treasurers were to oversee collection and disposition of these contributions. Aristides "the Just" drew up the first quotas. (According to one anecdote, Aristides was so honest that he once spelled out his name when asked to do so by an illiterate fellow citizen, who did not recognize him, during an ostracism vote.)

The Spartans did not join this new alliance. They lacked a navy and would not risk a revolt of helots by committing their troops outside the Peloponnese. Instead, they continued to cultivate their militaristic social system and gradually assumed leadership of a league of mainly Peloponnesian city-states.

The original purpose of the league —security from Persian aggression— was gradually replaced by the purely Athenian goal of domination within the Greek world. At first, the league's naval forces benefited all members by rooting out remaining Persian bases in the Aegean and Asia Minor. The fleet also suppressed piracy and thereby fostered seaborne mercantile activity. Over time, however, many league members switched from contributions of men and ships to the payment of annual tribute. Consequently, Athens' role in maintaining and manning the fleet became an increasingly prestigious and profitable one. When security in the Aegean was achieved and some states wished to dissolve their ties to the Delian League, Athens used the fleet to force them to remain; it even compelled some non-member cities to join.

Other city-states, especially Sparta, viewed the growth of Athenian power with increasing alarm. When the large northern Aegean island of Thasos seceded from the Delian League in 465 B.C. and was blockaded by the allied fleet, the Thasians secretly asked Sparta to relieve them by invading Attica. The Spartans agreed to do so, but in 464 a major earthquake in the Peloponnese killed more than 20,000 people, including many *homoioi*, and triggered a rebellion of helots, who fortified Mount Ithome in neighboring Messenia. When Sparta appealed for help to other Greek states, Cimon, a proponent of Spartan-Athenian balance of power, persuaded his fellow Athenians to send a force of hoplites to assist in quelling the revolt. Sparta, however, distrusted Athenian motives and sent the force back to Athens. Cimon was discredited and ostracized, losing his political influence to the extreme democrats Ephialtes and Pericles. Later, when the rebels on Mount Ithome were promised safe conduct so long as they left Spartan-controlled territory, Athens settled them at Naupactus at the western end of the Gulf of Corinth. This gave Athens a valuable station for its fleet on the route to Italy and Sicily and caused both Corinth and its ally Sparta to fear encirclement.

The transformation of the Delian League into Athenian Empire accelerated after 461 B.C., when Pericles became leader of the radical democrats in Athens. Elected *strategos* (general) frequently down to 443 and continuously thereafter until his death in 429, he strove to build an Athenian Empire. In 454, the treasury at Delos was removed to a less exposed location, the Acropolis at Athens. Henceforth, Pericles used league funds as he saw fit. Athens suppressed any attempt by member states to leave the alliance, even after the conclusion of a peace treaty with Persia in 449. Pericles also set up new colonies where groups of Athenians were settled on land seized in trouble spots in the Aegean, serving as reliable intelligence agents and on-the-spot security forces. Athens also interfered in the internal politics of member states by supporting or even imposing governments favorable to it. On the positive side, Athens, by eliminating piracy and establishing a uniform (Athenian) monetary system, improved trade opportunities and promoted economic prosperity.

Athens was supreme in the Aegean, but Pericles' attempt to extend Athenian control on the mainland brought war. Sparta and its allies, employing their superior infantry, inflicted several severe defeats on Athenian forces. As a result, Athens signed a Thirty Years' Peace with Sparta in 446 B.C. By its terms, each side was to respect the other's sphere of influence and retain its own allies. Nonaligned states could remain so or choose to join either side. Disputes were to be submitted to arbitration before resort to war. The peace would last only half the stipulated thirty years.

Periclean Athens

Pericles was the catalyst and symbol of Athenian achievement in this period. He loved Athens above all else and encouraged a similar love in his fellow citizens. Under his guidance, Athens, the richest and most powerful Greek city-state, became the capital of intellectual and artistic activity. The versatile Pericles led his people on the battlefield, developed further the democracy devised by Solon and Cleisthenes, and encouraged

THE ATHENIAN RATIONALE FOR DEMOCRACY

Some may say: "how could such a man find out what was advantageous to himself and the common people?" The Athenians realize that this man, despite his ignorance and badness, brings them more advantage because he is well disposed to them than the ill-disposed respectable man would, despite his virtue and wisdom. Such practices do not produce the best city, but they are the best way of preserving democracy. For the common people do not wish to be deprived of their rights in an admirably governed city, but to be free and to rule the city; they are not disturbed by inferior laws. If you are looking for an admirable code of laws, first you will find that the ablest draw them up in their own interest; secondly, the respectable will punish the masses, and will plan the city's affairs and will not allow men who are mad to take part in planning or discussion or even sit in the Assembly. As a result of this excellent system the common people would very soon lose all their political rights. *

The Constitution . . ., *a work by an anonymous writer traditionally called "The Old Oligarch," dates to about 425 B.C. Though firmly believing in the superiority of oligarchic government, the author attempts to make his fellow oligarchs see the logic of the Athenian practice of allowing a voice to members of even the lowest socioeconomic class.*

*J. M. Moore, trans., *The Constitution of the Athenians,* in *Aristotle and Xenophon on Democracy and Oligarchy* (Berkeley: University of California Press, 1975), pp. 38–39.

the arts by both public policy and personal example. He was the friend of the philosopher Anaxagoras; the chief sculptor of the Parthenon, Phidias; and the playwright Sophocles. His home, presided over by the beautiful and intelligent former courtesan Aspasia, was a meeting place for artists, men of letters, and thinkers. Athenians respected Pericles for his honesty and unswerving devotion to his city and called him "Olympian" because of the force and nobility of his speech and personal appearance. Though he had bitter political opponents, especially among the aristocrats, the masses admired him and heeded his call for patriotic fervor. The phrase "Periclean Athens" justly reflects his influence on the mental climate of his city.

Pericles' imperialistic foreign policy went hand in hand with the growth of democratic institutions in Athens. The empire, though it oppressed subject states, was a boon to the common free Athenian citizens, who rewarded Pericles by reelecting him to the generalship and by supporting his proposals in the assembly of citizens. Just

as the switch to hoplite infantry resulted in political change in the Archaic age, so now reliance on the fleet brought an extension of voting rights and other privileges to the thousands of rowers who manned that fleet. Many of these men were landless city dwellers previously excluded from political rights. Now, however, largely through the actions of Pericles, they began to share in the benefits of empire. (The majority of the population, including women, resident aliens, and of course slaves, still could not vote in the assembly, serve in office, or be recognized in courts of law.) Vast tribute from the empire enabled the state to pay public officials, jurors, and even those who simply attended meetings of the assembly; thus even the poorest citizen could participate. In addition, Pericles reduced eligibility requirements for higher offices and made selection by lot the rule. Because the *strategia* (generalship) alone remained elective, it came to be the true executive power in the state. It was this circumstance that allowed Pericles, despite his democratic reforms, to wield such enormous influence. The historian Thucydides wrote that "Pericles, by reason of his prestige, wisdom, and moral integrity, was able to respect the freedoms of the people but also to restrain them. . . . Though the system was democratic in name, power was actually vested in the leading citizen" (1.65).

The common people benefited from the empire in other ways too. Thousands earned a living as rowers and hoplites. Such empire-financed construction programs as the Parthenon and the defense works and harbor installations at Piraeus meant jobs for quarry workers, haulers, mule drivers, and an army of unskilled laborers, as well as for sculptors, architects, surveyors, engineers, stone cutters, carpenters, masons, and other craftsmen.

Some ancient Greek observers and political theorists considered this widening of enfranchisement and improvement in standard of living to be dangerous departures from traditional practices. In particular, many regarded the common free people as intellectually and morally inferior, incapable of the prudent decisions necessary to good government. The "respectable men" or aristocrats, after all, had been born and bred to leadership. But the oligarchic party resisted the equalization of opportunity without success, because Pericles was too powerful and influential.

THE PELOPONNESIAN WAR

While protecting Athenian democracy from opponents within the state, Pericles with remarkable foresight took steps to defend his city from external opponents, in particular, those of the Peloponnesian League. Realizing that Athens' best hopes for success rested with the navy, he built an impregnable corridor, the Long Walls (see Map 8), linking Athens to its harbor installations at Piraeus. These walls, 4.5 miles long and 200 yards apart, formed a key element in Periclean strategy. If invaders should destroy farms and crops, the Athenians would retreat within their walls and outlast their enemies by living on imported provisions from their invincible fleet and the merchant ships it protected.

CHRONOLOGY OF THE PELOPONNESIAN WAR

432	Conference at Sparta; Corinth voices grievances
431	Outbreak of the war
430	Pericles delivers Funeral Speech; plague strikes
429	Death of Pericles
425	Cleon victorious at Pylos
422	Cleon and Brasidas killed at Amphipolis
421	Peace of Nicias
416	Athenians victimize Melians
415	Beginning of the Sicilian expedition
413	Disaster at Syracuse
405	Athenian fleet destroyed at Aegospotami
404	Surrender of Athens; Spartan victory

Hoplites—even Spartan hoplites—could not sink triremes.

Causes

In the Peloponnesian War, the Athenian Empire clashed with the Peloponnesian League of Sparta and its allies. The "true cause" of the war, according to the historian Thucydides, was Spartan fear of ever-growing Athenian power. Pericles believed that Athens deserved the power it had acquired and must retain and expand it or be destroyed. From Sparta's viewpoint, the rise of Athens to dominance during the fifty years after the Persian Wars threatened the security of the city-states outside the Delian League. Athenian efforts to control supplies of grain, timber, and precious metals at their source was especially troubling to other Greek states.

The Peloponnesian War opened when Athenian actions against the interests of Corinth and Megara, allies of Sparta, brought the Peloponnesian League into emergency session. At the meeting in Sparta in 432 B.C., disgruntled members of the Peloponnesian League presented the case for war. The Corinthians bitterly contrasted Athenian opportunism with Spartan inactivity: "While you [Spartans] are hanging back, they [Athenians] never hesitate; while you stay at home, they are always abroad; for they think that the farther they go the more they will get, while you think that any movement will endanger what you already have" (Thucydides, 1.70). The Corinthians then threatened to abandon the Spartan-led alliance altogether.

Thus spurred to action, the Spartans declared war and prepared to march on Attica. First, however, they offered to refrain from open hostilities if Athens would rescind economic sanctions it had imposed against Megara. Pericles persuaded the Atheni-

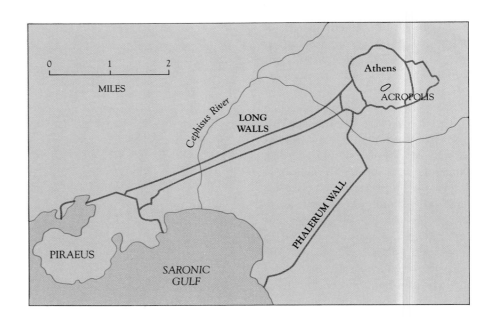

MAP 8
Long Walls Connecting Athens and Piraeus.

ans that to give in on this point would be a sign of weakness leading to further demands; the Athenian Empire itself was at stake. He stressed Athens' high state of military, naval, and financial readiness, and predicted victory if the people would do three things: first, avoid major land battles with the superior infantry of the Peloponnesian League; second, temporarily sacrifice their farms and live within the fortification walls on seaborne supplies; third, forego enlarging the empire till after the war. Pericles planned to rely on the economic resources of the empire and to use the mighty Athenian navy to harass the Spartans by quick strikes all around the Peloponnese.

Spartan resources at the outbreak of the war were less tangible than those of Athens. The Spartans lacked the financial resources of the Athenian Empire, nor did they possess naval forces to match their opponents. But they did possess tremendous discipline, patience, and courage, the

product of more than two centuries of cultivation of the "Spartan way." Their rigorous and constant military training starting in early childhood not only made them practically invincible on land (hence Pericles' strategy of avoiding land battles) but also equipped them with the moral stamina to endure a long and grueling struggle. Though the Spartans used severely repressive tactics in maintaining the enslavement of helots in their own country, they painted themselves as champions of Greek liberty in the struggle against Athenian imperialism.

Opening Phase

The state of preparedness of both sides, together with the large number of states involved as allies, made it likely that this war would be unusually long, hard fought, and costly. The opening phase of the Peloponnesian War, from 431 to 421 B.C., was marked by several shifts of fortune. The Athenians

at first followed Pericles' master plan for the war, though it was painful to allow the enemy to destroy crops and precious olive trees, which do not bear fruit plentifully until they are about twenty-five years old. Indeed, Pericles' chief task was maintaining good morale; his funeral speech for war casualties in 430 was as much an encouragement for the living as praise for the dead. A far greater crisis was caused by the outbreak of a virulent plague later that year. Athens lost perhaps one-fourth of its population, including Pericles himself in 429. Ironically, the overcrowding caused by Pericles' policy of having Athenians take refuge inside the walls was a major contributing factor in the epidemic.

Subsequent Athenian leaders lacked Pericles' essential qualities of restraint and perceptiveness. Cleon, for example, waged war much more aggressively, as did the Spartan general Brasidas. In 425 B.C., Cleon won a stunning victory at Pylos in the western Peloponnese, where he captured a force of 300 hoplites. He ignored subsequent Spartan peace overtures, however, and turned to the northern Aegean, where both he and Brasidas were killed in battle in 422. This opened the way for negotiation of the Peace of Nicias in 421.

Athenian Mistakes and Spartan Victory

The Peace of Nicias was soon ruined by the ambition of another Athenian politician as the volatile, high-living egotist Alcibiades (c. 450–404 B.C.) stirred up trouble in the Peloponnese by allying with Argos, an enemy and thorn in the side of Sparta. Then in 416, Athens cruelly punished the neutral island of Melos for refusing to become a tribute-paying member of the empire. After taking the city by siege, the Athenians slew the adult male population and sold the women and children into slavery.

In 415 B.C., mainly at the instigation of Alcibiades, Athens sent the finest Greek naval force ever assembled to attack the powerful city of Syracuse and add Sicily, with its rich grain production, to the empire. This was just the sort of endeavor that Pericles had advised against at the start of the war. The Athenians blundered badly by dividing leadership of the expedition among Alcibiades, Nicias, who had opposed the plan, and the career soldier Lamachus. Then, shortly after the great armada embarked, Alcibiades was recalled on charges of impiety and promptly defected to the Spartan side. After Lamachus was killed in the fighting, sole command fell to Nicias, who was suffering from kidney disease. In 413, the campaign ended in complete victory for Syracuse. Nicias and thousands of men were lost, along with the entire fleet. So great, however, was Athens' advantage in men and materials in the Peloponnesian War that it managed to build and man another navy, despite the disaster in Sicily.

The theater of the war now shifted to Attica and the Aegean Sea. The Spartans fortified a permanent position in Attica and increased the size of the Peloponnesian fleet, in part by borrowing funds from Persia. Alcibiades returned to the Athenian side and won several victories. In 405 B.C., however, the Peloponnesians caught the Athenian fleet off guard and destroyed it at Aegospotami in the Hellespont, severing the artery of Athens' grain supply route to the Black Sea.

In 404 B.C., the Athenians, besieged by land and sea and suffering from advanced starvation, surrendered unconditionally. Athens relinquished its empire and was stripped of its navy, except for a ten-ship coast guard. The Spartans also destroyed the Long Walls and the Piraeus fortifications. Thebes and Corinth would have imposed even harsher terms; indeed, the Athenians feared retaliation in kind for their treatment of the Melians in 416. Sparta, however, dictated milder terms, fearing that Thebes might grow too strong in central Greece without the counterweight of Athenian strength. Already the fluctuating alliances and foreign policies of the fourth century were being anticipated.

SUMMARY

At the beginning of the fifth century, Greece faced the threat of absorption into the neighboring empire that Persia had acquired and consolidated under the leadership of Cyrus and Darius I. The culturally advanced Persians controlled immense resources and diverse subject peoples. To repel them, the Greeks were forced, for once in their history, to stand together in defense of their own city-state societies and common ethnic and religious values. Sparta and Athens in particular led the successful struggle against the Persians, as the mighty invasion force of Xerxes was defeated both at sea and on land in 480–479 B.C.

Athens emerged from the Persian Wars as the preeminent naval power in the Greek world and therefore the natural leader of an anti-Persian alliance of Aegean states known as the Delian League. Athens capitalized on this situation to convert the league into an empire, reducing its allies to the status of tribute-paying subject states.

The statesman Pericles guided Athens on its course toward dominance. In the process, he increased and ensured the political rights of the lower classes of citizens, from whom came the thousands of rowers and marines of Athens' powerful fleet. At home he broadened the basis of Athenian democracy, carrying further the reforms of Solon and Cleisthenes. In its relations with subject states, however, Athens could be brutally tyrannical.

In the fifty years after the Persian Wars, Athens enjoyed fabulous prosperity as a result of its imperial holdings. Tribute-financed building proj-

ects meant beautification of the city and full employment for its residents. The city became a focus of economic and artistic activity.

The growth of Athenian power, however, brought friction with Corinth, Thebes, and Sparta. In 431 B.C., war broke out between the Peloponnesian League headed by Sparta and the Athenian Empire. The formidable strength of both sides, to-

gether with the varying fortunes of war and changes in leadership, led to a twenty-seven-year struggle. In the end, Sparta defeated Athens and dismantled its empire. There followed a widespread weakening of Greek city-states, which was to have dire consequences in the next century, when Macedon emerged from obscurity and took control of the Greek world.

SELECTED SOURCES

*Claster, Jill N., ed. *Athenian Democracy: Triumph or Travesty?* 1967. A collection of essays and excerpts dealing with issues of democracy and imperialism in fifth-century Athens.

Cook, J. M. *The Persian Empire.* 1983. A good, readable, up-to-date introduction to the political and cultural history of ancient Persia. Nicely illustrated.

*Freeman, Kathleen. *Greek City-States.* 1950; reprinted 1963. An interesting survey of nine diverse city-states in various parts of the Mediterranean region.

Green, Peter. *Armada from Athens* 1970. Easily the most exciting history of the Peloponnesian War, with special emphasis on the Sicilian expedition.

Green, Peter. *Xerxes at Salamis* 1970. A lively narrative of the Persian Wars, with emphasis on the campaigns of 480–479 B.C.

*Herodotus. *The Histories.* Translated by A. de Sélincourt. 1954; rev. ed. 1972. A good, current translation of the "father of history"; the revised edition has a helpful introduction and notes by A. R. Burn.

*Plutarch. *The Rise and Fall of Athens: Nine Greek Lives.* Translated by Ian Scott-Kilvert. 1960. Included are lives of Themistocles, Cimon, Pericles, and Alcibiades. Plutarch is more an entertaining journalist-storyteller than a serious historian.

*Renault, Mary. *The Last of the Wine.* 1956; reprinted 1975. Among the best

of Renault's excellent historical novels; set in the time of the Peloponnesian War.

*Robinson, Charles A. *Athens in the Age of Pericles.* 1959. A good, brief description of the era; especially useful for its many quotations of original sources.

*Thucydides. *History of the Peloponnesian War.* Translated by R. Warner. 1954; rev. ed. 1972. The best current translation of this historical masterpiece; with a particularly valuable introduction and notes by Moses I. Finley.

*Available in paperback.

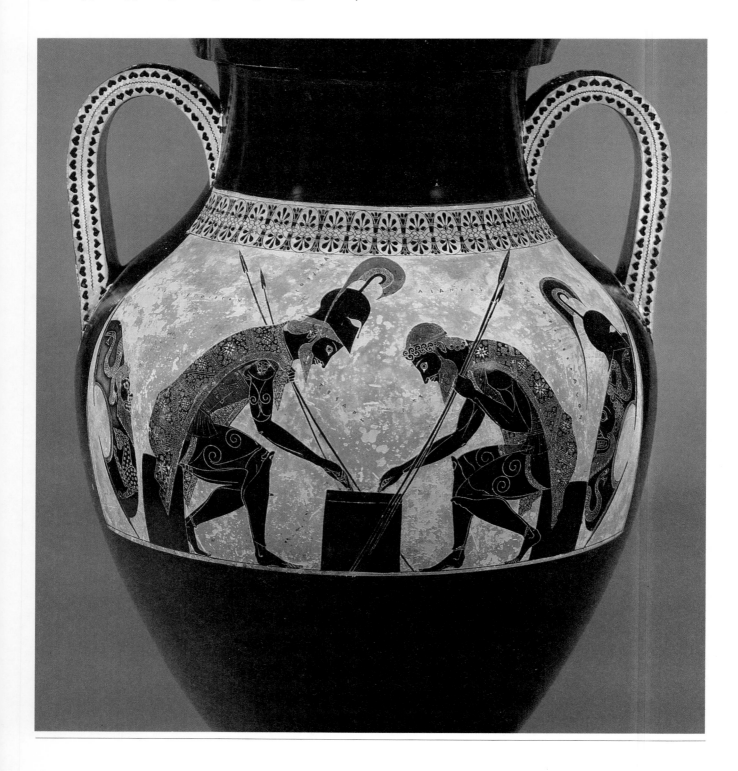

GREEK CULTURE IN THE FIFTH AND FOURTH CENTURIES B.C.

As soon as a child can understand what is said to him, nurse, mother, tutor, and the father himself vie with each other to make him as good as possible, . . . pointing out, "This is right and that is wrong, this honorable and that disgraceful, this holy, that impious; do this, don't do that." . . . Later on when they send the children to school, their instructions to the masters lay much more emphasis on good behavior than on letters or music. The teachers take good care of this and . . . set the works of good poets before them on their desks to read and make them learn by heart. . . . The music masters by analogous methods instill self-control and deter the young from evil-doing. . . . By this means they become more civilized, more balanced, and better adjusted in themselves and so more capable in whatever they say or do . . . . [And] they are sent to a trainer, so that a good mind may have a good body to serve it, and no one be forced by physical weakness to play the coward in war and other ordeals.

This passage from Plato's *Protagoras* well describes the ancient ideal of "a sound mind in a sound body," stressing the distinctively Greek notion that *arete* (moral and physical excellence) stemmed from proper education. The good citizen was the wise citizen. This outlook on the value of education led the Greeks, and the Athenians in particular, to value art, literature, and philosophy so highly that their achievements in these areas have seldom been equalled in the history of western civilization. The present chapter examines Greek intellectual and artistic history in the fifth and fourth centuries, first considering the various types of education available to the different social classes.

CONTENTS

EDUCATION AND PHILOSOPHY

The Greeks called the two bases of their education "music" and "gymnastic." Music embraced all that was sacred to the Muses, goddesses of

Black-Figure Vase. This magnificent black-figure amphora was painted by Exekias, c. 530 B.C. It shows the epic heroes Achilles (left) and Ajax (right) enjoying "R and R" between battles by playing dice; Achilles calls "four" and Ajax "three." Vatican Museum.

Red-Figure Drinking Cup. This cup depicts a lesson in lyre playing, with the balding white-haired master on the left and his adolescent pupil on the right. A larger instrument, the kithara, hangs in the background. Though the characters on this cup are mythological (the poet-musician Linos and Iphikles, the twin brother of Herakles), the scene itself was duplicated many times in the actual training of every educated Greek. From Cerveteri (c. 470 B.C.); Staatliches Museum, Schwerin.

all arts and sciences. Gymnastic was physical education conducted in an exercise ground called the gymnasium, a word that means "the naked place," since Greek exercises and sports were practiced in the nude.

Greek Educational Practices

At Sparta, education was state directed and designed exclusively to produce the best soldiers. Though boys learned to read and write, Spartans gave first priority to extremely rigorous training in wrestling, running, javelin throwing, and weapons drill. Girls too went through demanding physical training to become strong wives who would bear vigorous and healthy children.

At Athens, also, education was originally military, but later a much greater emphasis was placed on development of mental abilities. By the fifth century, formal education became nearly universal for freeborn Athenian boys, since most families could afford the modest fees of privately engaged teachers and trainers. Slaves often received training in the skilled trades to increase their usefulness.

The elementary curriculum at Athens included reading, writing, lyre playing, and physical education. Greek teachers emphasized memorizing and reciting passages from such poets as Homer and Hesiod. The fact that the Greeks and Romans always read aloud sensitized students to the beauties of their language. Instruction in arithmetic was minimal; students learned addition, subtraction, multiplication, division, and a bit about fractions.

Greek women had little opportunity to develop their minds through formal education. As girls, they might learn to read and write but spent little time in school, concentrating instead on the household chores that would form the daily round of their lives. As adults, they were virtually cloistered in their homes and were seldom regarded as sources of intellectual or spiritual companionship. Exceptions were the *hetairai* (female companions), as the better class of prostitutes was called. Such women, who were usually ex-slaves or resident aliens, often possessed and cultivated artistic and intellectual talents to complement their physical beauty. Though they lacked the respectability of wives, their stimulating companionship gained them entry to the parties and social gatherings held by Greek men. The most famous woman of fifth-century Greece, Pericles' mistress Aspasia, began her career as a *hetaira* in Miletus.

The closed male society of the educational, political, and military world of the Greeks fostered a specialized homosexuality known as pederasty or "boy-love." Greek religion, unlike Judaism or Christianity, neither sanctioned nor prohibited sexual behaviors, and pederasty was a part of normal social development. Because men devoted so much time and energy to essential civic and military duties of the city-state, familial ties, between both husband and wife and father and son, were often neglected. For the males in Greek society, pederasty often substituted for these atrophied relationships while satisfying the need for sexual gratification. It also served an educational purpose by its association with high standards of physical and intellectual excellence among males. The lover, usually more than twenty years of age, served as teacher and

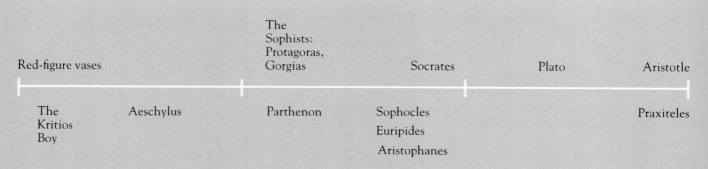

ennobling model; by his actions as citizen and his prowess as a warrior, he sought the affection and molded the character of his adolescent "pupil," usually aged twelve to nineteen. (At Sparta, the lover could even be held legally responsible for defects such as cowardice in the beloved.) The beloved in turn was expected to use worthily his attractive physical and mental attributes of strength, speed, devotion, and purposefulness. At adulthood, the young man became the equal and friend of his lover, fully initiated into the society of citizens and warriors. The sexual aspect of the relationship ended, as the new adult sought his own pupil on whom to lavish loving attention.

The Sophists

The scientific speculation begun in the Archaic period continued in the Classical. Parmenides and Empedocles argued about the concepts of Being and Becoming, about the precise nature of appearances and motion. In the atomic theory of Leucippus and Democritus, indivisible bits of matter were the basis of all reality. Anaxagoras, the friend of Pericles, maintained the sun was a lump of molten metal about the size of the Peloponnesian Peninsula. He was consequently tried on charges of atheism. There was little agreement among these philosophers as new physical theories proliferated.

By the second half of the fifth century, the inconclusiveness of the arguments of the natural philosophers had made men doubt the value of such speculation. Wisdom ought to be useful, have some practical application to human life. Such usefulness was promised by the Sophists (wise ones), who offered instruction, for a healthy fee, in everything from arts and crafts to medicine, philosophy, and oratory. These traveling professors gravitated to Athens, where young men who had completed primary education thirsted for new ideas and methods.

"Man is the measure of all things; of things that are, that they are, of things that are not, that they are not." This maxim of Protagoras typifies the skepticism and relativism of the Sophists. Just as human beings could not fathom the universe, "the things that are," as the disputes of the previous two centuries proved, neither could they ascertain absolute right and wrong or good and evil. What was "good" for one might be bad for another. Wisdom for the individual was to decide on and acquire one's own good without regard for any artificial code of morality. Sophist teachings had important educational implications, for the only subjects worth pursuing were those that gave the individual the means to acquire his own ends. In Athens, where public debate often shaped policy, Sophists stressed rhetoric—the theory and practice of persuasive oratory. Teachers like Gorgias trained their students to win arguments and persuade audiences, regardless of the merits of the position taken. Through skill in speaking, one could even make the worse case appear to be the better; indeed, *worse* and *better* became meaningless terms.

The Sophists were harshly criticized by comic poets and others for undermining traditional ethical values, but they attracted many students and raised vital questions about goodness and knowledge and the proper motives of the individual in society.

Socrates, Plato, and Aristotle

Socrates (469–399 B.C.), who is best known to us through the writings of his pupil Plato, extended this questioning of old values. As a young man, he dabbled in physical theories of the universe, but later shifted the focus of his inquiry to the right conduct of life: What is virtue and can it be taught? What is the just man or the just state? What is love? Is the soul immortal? What is the nature of the good? Of truth? Of beauty? Unlike his Sophist contemporaries, Socrates neither claimed to have the answers to these questions nor accepted fees from those who listened to him. He simply sought definitions from others and tested them by cross-questioning. Since the definitions nearly always crumbled under his questions, he sometimes made enemies, but never lapsed into the relativistic skepticism of the Sophists. Socrates thus left as his bequest to humanity a method of inquiry rather than a written body of doctrine. He believed the search for true knowledge, however frustrating, was a holy obligation that alone justified life.

Socrates' personal attributes impressed all who knew him. He performed the duties of a good citizen, served with distinction in the army, and met his religious obligations. He cared nothing for creature comforts and, though ugly and usually unkempt in his appearance, was admired for his courage and fabulous powers of endurance. Alcibiades reported that Socrates once stood for twenty-four hours on the same spot, lost in concentration on some problem, and then went about his business as if it had been twenty-four seconds.

In 399 B.C., at age seventy, Socrates was brought to trial by his enemies on capital charges of atheism and corruption of the young. In Plato's dialogue, *The Apology* ("explanation" or "defense"), Socrates portrays himself as a victim of old prejudices. His accusers lumped him together with the amoral Sophists rather than admit they disliked the difficult questions he asked and taught his young listeners to ask. Socrates stoutly re-

fused to stop his irksome inquiries, saying the unexamined life was not worth living. He was found guilty of the charges brought against him and sentenced to death. Though friends offered to help him escape into comfortable exile, he remained in prison and, as required, drank the lethal hemlock to show his respect for the laws of Athens, by which he had abided all his life. He spent his last day discussing the nature of the soul, as recorded in Plato's *Phaedo.*

Among the pupils of Socrates was a young Athenian aristocrat named Plato (c. 429–347 B.C.), who was to produce the philosophical masterpieces that have so profoundly shaped western intellectual history. (Socrates himself left no written works.) Indeed, in the twentieth century, the philosopher and mathematician Alfred North Whitehead claimed that "the European philosophical tradition . . . consists of a series of footnotes to Plato."

Plato's dialogues present philosophic conversations between Socrates and his pupil friends; they are dramatic, witty, and full of brilliant character portrayal. Besides illustrating the dialectic techniques of Socrates, they put forward important original concepts of Plato himself. Specifically, Plato makes a sharp distinction between the reality perceived by the five senses and the reality of the nonsensory world of ideas, which is, Plato says, the only proper source of knowledge, true and unchanging always and everywhere. Thus, for example, the idea of triangle or "triangularity" endures forever, regardless of inevitable changes in the world of sense impressions, whereas all earthly triangles come into being and pass away as mere appear-

ances, objects of opinion and not of knowledge. The true philosopher (lover of wisdom) must cultivate the soul, the seat of reason, and suppress the body and its misleading sensory experiences. Plato presented his theory of knowledge as it applied to such concepts as beauty, virtue, and justice in the trial and death dialogues mentioned previously, and especially in the *Republic,* in which the participants seek to define the just man. Under the guidance of Socrates, they decide that it will be easier to grasp the concept of justice if they consider it on a larger scale, that of the state. They therefore construct a detailed model of a perfect state, governed by philosopher-kings, whose education and responsibilities are described in detail. The result is an extraordinary mix of philosophy, political science, educational theory, sociology, psychology, and literary criticism.

Around 388 B.C., Plato founded at Athens a school called the Academy. His best student was Aristotle (384–322), the son of the physician to the Macedonian royal family. After leaving the Academy, where fellow pupils called him "the brain," Aristotle was for a time the tutor of Alexander the Great. He later returned to Athens to found his own philosophical school, the Lyceum, around 335.

Aristotle rejected Plato's notion that the only suitable subject of philosophy was a separately existing, unchanging reality and instead based his own general concepts on observation of the natural order. Aristotle took an interest in virtually every area of scientific and philosophical investigation. His systematizing of the departments of human knowledge was the most influential and enduring in the intellectual history of the West. His many writings, which are dry, technical, and scientifically objective, fall into the following categories: (1) logical works inquiring into the most efficient forms of reasoning, (2) metaphysical works dealing with questions of existence and the nature of true wisdom, (3) scientific works devoted to physics, biology, psychology, and astronomy, (4) ethical and political works seeking to define goodness and the good life for human beings both as individuals and as members of social groups, and (5) literary critical and aesthetic works treating questions of beauty and art. Aristotle's writings exerted a lasting influence. In the medieval period, for example, the scholastics, Thomas Aquinas in particular, revered him as an ultimate authority, and his biological works remained definitive until the eighteenth century. Dante rightly called Aristotle "the master of those who know."

HISTORY

Most Greeks of the Archaic period, like other peoples of that era, accepted as factual records the myths of epic poetry, with all their fairy-tale elements and heroic exaggerations. Beginning in the fifth century, however, the first true historians replaced the mythic tales with rational inquiries into the causes and course of human events.

Herodotus

Herodotus (c. 484–c. 425 B.C.), the "Father of History," was born in Asia Minor but lived at Athens and later at an Athenian colony in Italy. His History (from the Greek *historia*, meaning "inquiry" or "investigation"), though concentrating on the Persian Wars, is in addition a cultural survey of the Near East and Greece from the founding of the Persian Empire down to 478. Herodotus's accounts of his own eyewitness experiences and of oral reports collected on his travels throughout the Near East and Mediterranean enliven his narratives. A wealth of anthropological detail enriches his many comparisons of Greek with non-Greek cultures. The *History* is full of believe-it-or-not tales of amazing happenings, told in a leisurely and enjoyable style. It is also our best source of information about the Persian Wars. Herodotus combined the interests of cultural anthropologist, geographer, and naturalist with those of historian.

Although Herodotus's *History* marks a great advance in trustworthiness over the mythology of the epic poets, it is quite often unreliable. In particular, Herodotus naively accepted miracle stories, oracular pronouncements, omens, inspired dreams, and other instances of active divine interferences in human affairs. His chronology and statistics also are often faulty; for example, his number for the army of Xerxes— 5,283,220—is simply ridiculous.

Thucydides

Thucydides (c. 460–c. 400 B.C.) came much closer than his predecessor Herodotus to the critical standards of modern historiography. An Athenian by birth, he began his *History of the Peloponnesian War* immediately after its outbreak, "expecting it to be a great war and more worthy of recording than previous ones" (1.1).

> ## THUCYDIDES ON THE USEFULNESS OF HISTORY
>
> It may well be that my history will seem less easy to read because of the absence in it of a romantic element. It will be enough for me, however, if these words of mine are judged useful by those who want to understand clearly the events which happened in the past and which (human nature being what it is) will, at some time or other and in much the same ways, be repeated in the future. My work is not a piece of writing designed to meet the taste of an immediate public, but was done to last for ever.*
>
> *Thucydides recognized the appeal of Herodotean storytelling, but thought history should chiefly provide an accurate record and analysis of past events as a basis for intelligent decisions in later times. In this passage, he reflects the skepticism of the era by giving no place to the supernatural in human affairs. The narrative in the Peloponnesian War is tighter than in Herodotus, and its set speeches, though often reconstructed by Thucydides, are dramatic distillations of complex historical processes.*
>
> *Thucydides, History of the Peloponnesian War, trans. R. Warner (Harmondsworth: Penguin, 1954; rev. ed. 1972), 1.22.

He himself served as general in 424, but was stripped of command for failing to relieve the besieged city of Amphipolis and exiled until the end of the war in 404. This freed him to work exclusively on his *History*.

Thucydides picked up the thread of Greek history just where Herodotus left off, but differed from him by his greater concentration on political and military events and by his more responsible evaluation of documents and eyewitness accounts. In tune with the practicality of the Sophists, he believed history should offer real benefits and not merely entertainment. Thucydides believed history could teach about human nature and the hard realities of power. Individuals and states acted out of self-interest. Decency and morality counted for little. He admired Pericles and the Athenian Empire, but realized that growth in the power of any one state inevitably upset the balance between states. Further, because states with power either used it or ceased to be powerful, war with its unforeseeable turns and brutalizing effects on men was inevitable.

DRAMA

The invention of drama was one of the most important contributions of the Greeks to western civilization. As performed in the ancient world, tragedy and comedy were much more than entertainments. They fulfilled essential religious, civic, and educational functions, bringing the masses into contact with supreme artistic masterpieces and contributing to pride in the glory of Athens. The extensive involvement of citizens and the high level of state support indicate the prestige of public theater in classical Greece.

Greek Tragedy

Greek tragedy evolved from choral lyrics sung at Athenian state religious festivals. In the late sixth century B.C., one singer, Thespis, began to imper-sonate the god or hero whose praises were being sung and to interact with the chorus or chorus leader in dramatic dialogue (hence *Thespian* means "actor"). Later Aeschylus introduced a second and Sophocles a third actor; no Greek tragedy has more than three speaking actors on stage at once.

In the fifth century, tragedy formed part of the rituals in honor of the god Dionysus. At the religious festival called the City Dionysia held at Athens in early spring, three poets each presented three tragedies in competition for prizes. The plays consisted of set speeches, dialogue between characters, and choral odes. The actors and the chorus of twelve or fifteen singers wore costumes and masks.

The playwrights freely modified material from mythology for the plots of their dramas, which revolve around such perennially favorite themes as murder, incest, cannibalism, rape, insanity, parricide, fratricide, infanticide, and suicide. The plays sometimes include political references, praising Athens or criticizing Sparta, and Aeschylus's *Persians* recounts events from the Persian Wars. By comparison to, for example, Shakespeare, Greek tragedy presents a few episodes of limited complexity, focusing on one crucial problem and the interaction of several strongly delineated characters. (Although Athens was a male chauvinistic society, many of the strongest roles created by the three tragedians Aeschylus, Sophocles, and Euripides belong to female characters.) Aristotle said, in his *Poetics*, that in the best tragedies the crisis of the plot involved a simultaneous reversal of fortune and a moment of shocking recognition for the central character. He thought that an inexorable flow of dramatic events should arouse the emotions of fear and pity in the audience.

Productions were simple, having few props and little scenery. The theater itself was at first simply a convenient hillside (at Athens, the south slope of the Acropolis) at the base of which was a stage platform fronted by a circular orchestra in which the chorus danced and sang. Large stone theaters came later, in Hellenistic and Roman times.

The religious festivals, along with the dramas they featured, were community projects. The chief archon designated the poets who would be sponsored by wealthy private citizens. These sponsors volunteered or, if necessary, were nominated to provide financial backing at or above a stipulated minimum level. Pericles, for example, sponsored Aeschylus's *Persians* in 472 B.C. This private funding enabled the playwrights to hire and train chorus members and musicians and pay for costumes. The poets often acted in their own plays, but by the mid-fifth century the archon chose a lead actor from state-paid "stars" for each of the three competing authors. As in Shakespeare's day, all actors were men and played both male and female parts. Finally, critic-judges were selected from the ten tribes to award prizes to poets and actors. There were about 1,500 participants in the various religious activities and festival productions. Attendance at the performances was very large, perhaps 15,000–20,000, and included all social classes, women, and even slaves if their masters brought them. Admission fees were moderate and, in the time of Pericles, the state treasury paid for the seats of citizens. The funds went to private contractors who maintained and repaired the theaters.

Theater at Epidauros. The theater at the sanctuary of the healing god Asclepius at Epidauros is the largest and best preserved in Greece. It can accommodate eighteen thousand spectators and is still used for modern productions of ancient drama. Built c. 330 B.C.

Aeschylus

Aeschylus (525–456 B.C.) was the earliest of the great tragedians. In some ninety plays, of which seven written after the Persian Wars survive, he moved drama farther away from choral recitation by introducing a second actor. His chosen form was the trilogy, each play an act in a larger dramatic plot.

Aeschylean tragedy is concerned with major moral and theological issues. Aeschylus asserted that evil would breed evil unless vengeance was tempered by wise deliberation. Excessive behavior, especially *hubris* (prideful behavior), called down divine retribution. Moderation was best. Though the human predicament was often painful, wisdom resulting from suffering ennobled the individual. The Olympian gods of light and reason ensured ultimate triumph over the forces of darkness and madness.

The Oresteian trilogy, *Agamemnon, Libation Bearers,* and *Eumenides,* is an extended example of Aeschylus's interest in crime and appropriate punishment. In the first play, Clytemnestra avenges the sacrifice of her daughter, Iphigenia, by murdering the man responsible, her husband Agamemnon, the victorious commander in chief of the Greek forces at Troy. In the second play, Agamemnon's son, Orestes, avenges his father's death by killing Clytemnestra, thereby escaping the avenging spirits of his father but attracting the wrath of his mother's Furies (avenging spirits, or Eumenides). The divinely mandated cycle of vengeance puts Orestes in an appalling double bind, resolved in the third play of the trilogy. The benevolent Athena duly authorizes a law court to hear arguments on each side of the issue and, after rational deliberation, to hand down a binding decision. Orestes goes free and, more

important, vendetta has been eliminated, just as it had been historically under Draco.

Sophocles

Sophocles (c. 496–406 B.C.) was the most successful of the Greek tragedians, winning first prize with 96 of his 123 plays and second with the others. His seven surviving plays differ from those of Aeschylus by the addition of a third actor, a decrease in the role of the chorus, and the absence of the trilogy format. In Sophoclean tragedy, the dramatic action arises from the personalities of the major characters, who are often subjected to wrenching changes in outlook and fortune. Sophocles believed that fate was irresistible and placed human beings within certain limitations; to try to exceed them, especially by challenging the gods, was *hubris* and invited destruction. Life

63

ANTIGONE TAKES HER STAND

ANTIGONE: Why are you waiting? Nothing that you say fits with my thought. I pray it never will. . . . What greater glory could I find than giving my own brother funeral?

CREON: None of these others see the case this way.

ANTIGONE: They see, and do not say. You have them cowed.

CREON: And you are not ashamed to think alone?

ANTIGONE: No, I am not ashamed. When was it shame to serve the children of my mother's womb?

CREON: It was not your brother who died against him, then?

ANTIGONE: Full brother, on both sides, my parents' child.

CREON: Your act of grace, in his regard, is crime.

ANTIGONE: The corpse below would never say it was.

CREON: When you honor him and the criminal just alike?

ANTIGONE: It was a brother, not a slave, who died.

CREON: Died to destroy this land the other guarded.

ANTIGONE: Death yearns for equal law for all the dead.

CREON: Not that the good and bad draw equal shares.

. . .

ANTIGONE: I cannot share in hatred, but in love.

CREON: Then go down there, if you must love, and love the dead. No woman rules me while I live.*

Antigone believes, quite correctly in Greek religious practice, that the state's demands must give way to the higher allegiance she owes to the restless soul of Polyneices (Eteocles has received a funeral with full honors). The difference in sex between the central characters intensifies the collision between individual conscience and civic duty.

*Sophocles, *Antigone*, trans. Elizabeth Wyckoff, in *The Complete Greek Tragedies*, ed. D. Grene and R. Lattimore (Chicago: University of Chicago Press, 1954), lines 499–525.

was full of unforeseeable suffering, even for the innocent. Inborn character traits, whether despicable or admirable, often led to disastrous decisions. The proper attitude was resignation before the superior wisdom of inscrutable deities. As in Aeschylus, moderation in all things was essential.

In *Oedipus the King,* a man has unwittingly killed his father and married his mother. Oedipus is a conscientious ruler of Thebes, eager to rid the city of a terrible plague by apprehending the murderer of the previous king. Even after he suspects he is the guilty party, Oedipus doggedly pursues the truth. Others, including his wife, Jocasta, try to dissuade him, but he will not shirk his duty. His discovery of the truth destroys his wife/mother and drives him to blind himself. In a breathtaking turn of Sophoclean irony, the man who at first saw with his eyes but not with his mind later gains inner sight after losing his eyes. The man who loved his city more than himself is condemned by his own decree to leave it forever.

In the *Antigone,* two strong personalities—Creon, the new king of Thebes, and Antigone, the daughter/sister of Oedipus—clash in deadly conflict. Antigone's two brothers, Polyneices and Eteocles, have killed each other in combat over the throne vacated by their father/brother Oedipus. Creon has forbidden the burial of Antigone's brother Polyneices, whom he considers a traitor.

Antigone pays with her life for her convictions, but Creon suffers a worse fate as he alienates his son, Haemon, who kills himself in grief at the death of his fiancée, Antigone. Despondent at her son's death, Creon's wife Eurydice hangs herself. Creon is left alone and miserable to contemplate the error of his ways.

Euripides

Euripides (c. 485–c. 406 B.C.) was far more attuned to philosophic trends of the sophistic movement than was Sophocles. Some nineteen of his ninety plays survive and show a wide range of subjects and interests, focusing on political, religious, and especially psychological topics. In these dramas, Euripides questioned traditional social and moral values in the critical spirit of sophistic skepticism. In this regard, he was closer to the comic poet Aristophanes than to Aeschylus or Sophocles. Plays like the *Electra* and *Alcestis,* for instance, implicitly criticize the double standard inflicted on women. Others show Euripides' dislike of the ethics of exaggerated masculinity and aggressive war.

Euripides' most powerful works, however, deal with psychological abnormality, with the explosive emotions of men and, especially, women under stress. Euripides equated the traditional anthropomorphic gods with irrepressible compulsions within the human psyche. In the *Hippolytus*, for example, the goddesses Aphrodite and Artemis represent extremes of sexuality and chastity in Phaedra and her stepson, Hippolytus, respectively. Phaedra has a supercharged sexual appetite and cannot control her attraction to her stepson, who adheres to a personal cult of virginity and redirects his own sexual urges into obsessive hunting of wild animals. When Hippolytus learns of Phaedra's illicit infatuation and denounces her with maniacal bitterness, she hangs herself but leaves a note for her husband, Theseus, claiming she has been raped by Hippolytus. Theseus curses his son, who is trampled to death by his own horses before his father learns the truth.

Euripides' *Bacchant Women* is a study of mass hysteria caused by Dionysus, the vengeful god of intoxication, who represents primitive urges that may either exalt or destroy. Unless properly accommodated in the human personality, these impulses can disrupt civilized life. The *Medea* is a terrifying case history of a proud but, in Greek eyes, dangerously irrational barbarian mentality; in the play, Medea gets vengeance against her faithless Greek husband, the hero Jason, by murdering their children.

Comedy: Aristophanes

The Athenians also invented the other dramatic genre, comedy, which originated in processions of outlandishly dressed men behaving and singing in a humorously obscene fashion as part of religious festivals. In the fifth century, comedies were supported and produced in the same way as tragedies and were performed at the City Dionysia and certain other festivals. The "Old Comedy" of the Classical period was strongly satirical in tone and content.

Aristophanes (c. 450–c. 385 B.C.) is the only writer of Old Comedy whose works have survived. Most of his some forty plays, of which eleven survive, were produced during the Peloponnesian War. Aristophanic comedies are a delightful mix of serious satirical exposé and uproarious farce, often based on bodily function humor. Like musical comedies, they mingled social satire with burlesque slapstick. The twenty-four-member choruses often dressed as birds, frogs, wasps, or horses.

Old Comedy was distinctive in its irreverently critical attitude toward contemporary social, intellectual, and political issues. Interspersed with low comedy were deeply felt opinions on society and morality. In the *Clouds*, for example, Aristophanes parodied the Sophists and natural scientists by an outrageous caricature of Socrates, whose eccentric looks and behavior invited such attacks. In the *Knights*, Aristophanes mercilessly ridiculed the politician and general Cleon, who was then at the height of his success, as a contemptible demagogue and a blustering, vulgar, stupid upstart. Aristophanes' antiwar sentiments were given free rein in the *Acharnians*, in which the central character secures a separate peace, symbolized as a quantity of fine wine, with the Spartans. In the *Lysistrata*, Athenian women attempt to end the war by a sex strike against their soldier-husbands, who appear in humorously obvious states of agonizing sexual arousal. In the *Congresswomen*, the women disguise themselves as men to pack the assembly and legislate a transfer of political power to themselves; the sexual implications of this are humorously explored. That Aristophanes could heap such savage personal abuse on intellectual and political leaders of his day without fear of reprisal is a tribute to the remarkable freedom of speech in classical Athens.

THE VISUAL ARTS

The Greek achievement in literature and philosophy in the Classical period was matched by the progress made in the visual arts. In architecture, in sculpture, and in vase painting, we see in the fifth and fourth centuries a fulfillment of the promise of the Archaic period. As regards the marvelous sensitivity to symmetry and beauty in form, the work of this era has always typified "classic" perfection.

Architecture: The Parthenon

The Parthenon, temple of Athena Parthenos (the Maiden), is the finest architectural expression of the classical Greek love of symmetrical proportion. The Athenians used their great financial resources to build this impressive monument to their imperial strength and religious devotion. In its gleaming white brilliance, the building signifies the pride and power of the Periclean era. Unlike Roman temples or Gothic cathedrals, which were designed to be approached from one direction, the Parthenon and indeed all Greek temples were situated so as to dominate their surroundings

The Parthenon. The Parthenon was built by the architects Ictinus and Callicrates between 447 and 432 B.C. to replace an incomplete temple destroyed by the Persians in 481 and to symbolize Athenian imperial might and cultural superiority. The temple was nearly leveled in A.D. 1687, when Venetian bombardment set off gunpowder stored in it by the Turks. Though it was restored in the late nineteenth and early twentieth centuries, deterioration caused by atmospheric pollutants and rusting iron clamps has made necessary a complete disassembly and re-restoration, currently under way.

in all directions. The Doric columns of the Parthenon were (and are) visible even to ships miles out in the gulf. The material is fine marble hauled, at enormous state expense, from quarries on Mount Pentelicus a few miles from the city. The temple has eight, rather than the usual six, columns on its ends, seventeen on its sides. The inner chamber was in two parts. The smaller served as treasury of the Delian League; the larger housed a magnificent statue of Athena, the mighty warrior-protectress. The statue was thirty-three feet tall with face, arms, and feet sheathed in ivory, clothing plated in gold, and precious stones for eyes.

On the exterior, the sculptures in

the pediments represented the birth of Athena and her competition with Poseidon, the god of the sea, for the land of Athens. Other sculptures showed such scenes of warfare as men versus centaurs or amazons, gods versus giants, and Trojan War combat. Most interesting, however, is the immense Parthenon frieze, a continuous three-foot-high band of sculpture running along the top of the chamber and illustrating a Panathenaic procession. Horsemen and charioteers, boys carrying water jars or leading sacrificial animals, and girls with offering bowls proceed toward a central scene over the east entrance; there a group of gods and heroes presides as an official carries a sacred robe to be dedicated to Athena. A marvelously natural and noble serenity pervades all the sculptures in this building, which has set an enduring standard of architectural excellence in the West.

Sculpture

Ancient Greek sculpture idolizes beauty in the human form. In their representations of gods as well as humans, sculptors sought with ever-increasing sensitivity to portray an ideal of perfected human physique combining graceful muscularity with majestic sensuousness.

Free-standing, life-size, nonarchitectural sculpture in Greece began in the Archaic period. Maiden and youth statues, in rigidly solemn poses strongly reminiscent of monumental Egyptian sculpture, typify the period's style and level of accomplishment.

In the Classical era, a restrained realism produced a beautiful nobility in diverse renderings of the human figure. The handful of surviving fifth-century originals, like the Artemis-

Greek Architectural Orders. Of the two classical Greek architectural orders, the Doric columns are thicker in relation to their height and have no base and simple capitals. The frieze in the Ionic is continuous; in the Doric it is broken into metopes and triglyphs (tripartite decorative elements). The later Corinthian order, favored by Roman architects, differed from the Ionic only in having acanthus leaf rather than volute (spiral-shaped) capitals.

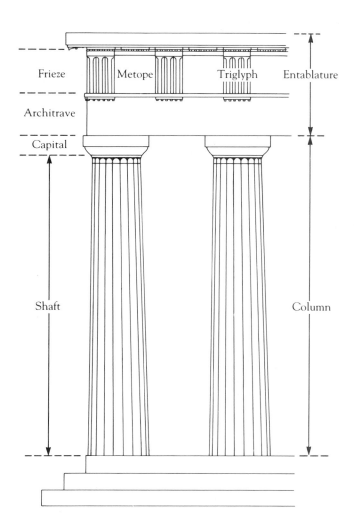

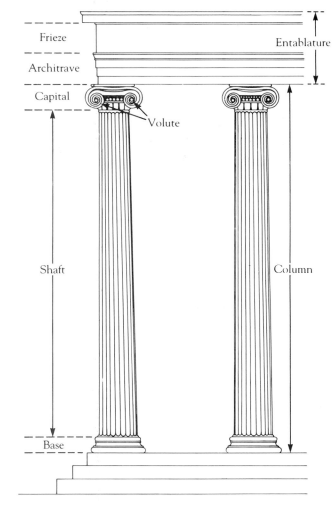

Pediment

Metopes

Frieze

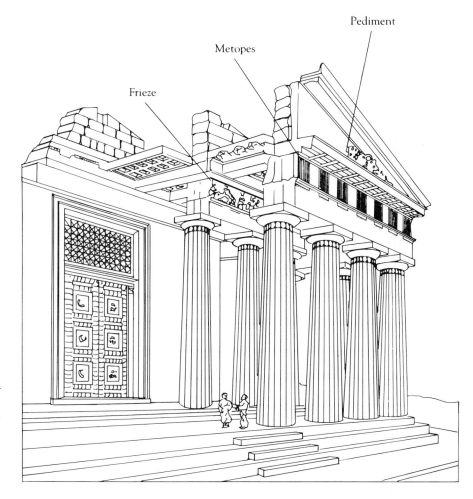

Schematic View of the Parthenon Exterior. This cutaway drawing shows the location of the various sculptures on the Parthenon. Pedimental and metope sculptures are usual for Doric-order buildings; the oddly positioned and probably very poorly lighted continuous frieze is an element borrowed from Ionic-order temples.

The Parthenon Frieze. This segment, from above the east entrance of the temple, shows the seated gods Poseidon (left), Apollo (center), and his twin sister, Artemis (right). Note the nobility of the heads, particularly the beautiful profile of the girl-goddess Artemis, and the treatment of the simple garments clinging or falling in response to the poses of the bodies. Acropolis Museum, Athens.

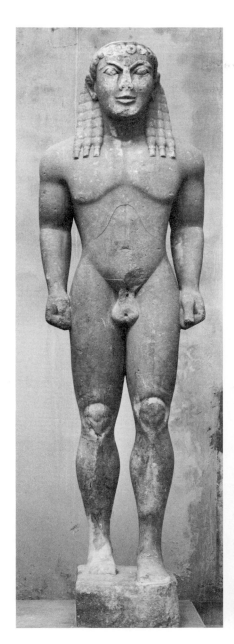

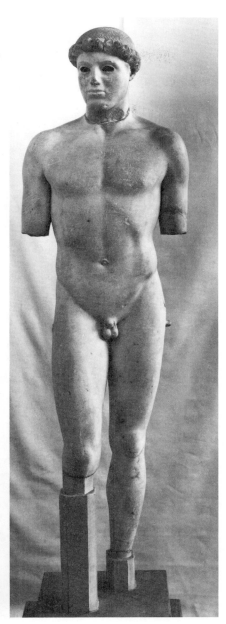

(Left) Archaic Youth Statue. Note the stiffly impassive frontal pose, left foot forward, arms at sides, hands clenched. These features, together with the broad shoulders, narrow waist, and small flanks, point to Egyptian or Mesopotamian inspiration; c. 600 B.C. Delphi Museum.   (Right) The Kritios Boy. This statue of c. 480 B.C. embodies the Greek pederastic ideal of physical perfection. The art historian Kenneth Clark called it "the first beautiful nude in art." The imbalance between tensed, weight-bearing left leg and free right leg and the sensual elasticity of the sculptor's rendering of flesh and skin mark a complete break from the four-square rigidity of the archaic youth figures. Acropolis Museum, Athens.

ium Zeus and the Kritios Boy, demonstrate this quality, as do copies of lost originals like Polycleitus's Spearbearer, which is a model of proportion and dynamism in its carefully balanced pose.

The great fourth-century sculptor Praxiteles (c. 370–c. 330 B.C.) exerted wide influence on contemporary and succeeding artists. His (lost) nude Aphrodite, commissioned by the city of Cnidus in Asia Minor, was one

of the most widely admired statues in antiquity. A surviving work shows Hermes teasing his little brother Dionysus. The delicate modeling and, to quote an ancient critic, the "melting gaze of the eyes" of such works

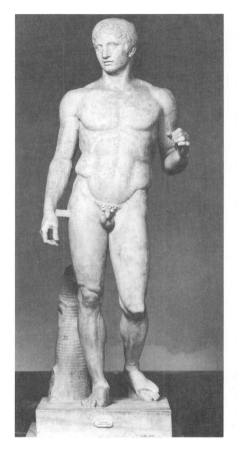 

(Left) The Spear Bearer. This Roman marble copy of a (lost) bronze original by Polycleitus illustrates the classic pattern of balanced contrasts. The straight, weight-bearing left leg is counterpoised to the bent left arm, which bears the (missing) spear; the free flexed left leg balances the free but straight right arm; the right-turned head contrasts with the left-turned hips and torso—all in perfect equilibrium; c. 450–440 B.C. Naples Museum. (Right) Hermes and the Infant Dionysus. This sculpture of c. 340 B.C. by Praxiteles marks a final step in the classical glorification of physical beauty. The subtly smiling Hermes holds a (missing) bunch of grapes just out of the reach of his little brother, whose taste for this fruit humorously foreshadows his adult love of wine. The work's strength, tenderness, and emotional lifelikeness prefigure much Hellenistic sculpture. Olympia Museum.

Red-Figure Wine Cup. Perhaps as a warning that "wine drinking may be dangerous to your health," the interior of this cup (c. 480 B.C.) depicts a youth suffering the effects of over-indulgence. He is being comforted by a young woman, probably a *hetaira*; Martin von Wagner Museum, Würzburg.

prefigured the intense emotional charge of much Hellenistic sculpture.

Vase Painting

Almost the only Greek painting that has come down to us is painting on vases. This relatively minor art form was carried to very high levels by potters and artists especially in workshops at Athens, which came to dominate the trade in both the vases and the olive oil they often held. The pleasing symmetry of Greek vases, with their skillfully balanced designs, has a clear affinity on a small scale with the classical ideals of the Parthenon.

The material of fired clay pots, whether intact or broken, is virtually indestructible. Because pottery was used throughout the ancient world to store and dispense wine, olive oil, and water, thousands of vases have survived. They show an evolution from black-figure style in the Archaic period to red-figure in the Classical.

The decorated vases are most interesting for the variety of their subject matter. They depict not only gods and heroes from epic mythology but also everyday life, for example, school scenes, athletic competitions, artisans' workshops, hunting and military scenes, and dinner parties. As with Greek sculpture, the artists delight in portraying the human form with great subtlety and attention to anatomical detail.

SUMMARY

The Classical period was one of unsurpassed cultural achievement. Particularly at Athens, there was a commitment to the highest intellectual ideals. Basic education for males was widely available and instilled a sensitivity to the language and thought of literary masterpieces. The Sophists made possible a more systematic pursuit of higher learning, whereas Socrates, Plato, and Aristotle laid the groundwork for subsequent philosophical inquiry in the West. In the area of inquiry into cultural and political institutions, the long-standing inclination of the Greeks to commemorate notable deeds led to the development of formal history. Herodotus by his diligent collection of information and Thucydides by his careful assessment of probabilities and patterns in human behavior set history on a sound basis.

The Greeks matched these achievements in intellectual endeavor with brilliant literary and artistic works. Drama was a uniquely Greek gift to western civilization. Within a century of their invention, both tragedy and comedy reached the highest levels of artistry in the works of Aeschylus, Sophocles, Euripides, and Aristophanes, thanks to the community's expenditure of time, energy, and money on the dramatic arts. Greek architecture and figural arts reached their height with the Parthenon and classical sculpture on one end of the scale and, on the other, with the small masterpieces of painted pottery. The Greeks' delight in balance and symmetry of structure is obvious in all their art forms, as is the central position of the human being and human society.

The Greeks were an extraordinarily articulate people; their thoughts and attitudes, as expressed in literature and art, demand and richly repay examination by students of history. By their unmatched cultural achievements in the Classical period, the ancient Greeks established models and pointed out paths for the future development of western civilization.

SELECTED SOURCES

*Aristophanes. *Four Comedies (Lysistrata, Acharnians, Congresswomen, Frogs)* and *Three Comedies (Birds, Clouds, Wasps)*. Ed. William Arrowsmith, 1969. Much the best translations available: plenty of verbal fireworks in a vivid American-English idiom. Good introductions and notes.
*Baldry, H. C. *The Greek Tragic Theater.* 1971. Especially valuable on the social context of the dramatic festivals and on the mechanics of mounting productions.
*Boardman, John. *Greek Art.* Rev. ed. 1973. A good basic introduction to

ancient Greek art and architecture from the Archaic period to the Hellenistic. Includes 249 illustrations.

*Doody, Margaret. *Aristotle Detective.* 1978. A highly entertaining detective story in which the great philosopher solves the mystery of the violent murder of a prominent Athenian citizen. Realistic background detail.

*Dover, K. J. *Greek Homosexuality.* 1978. An objective and authoritative account, scholarly in its thoroughness without being dry as dust; supersedes all previous studies of this important but often avoided subject.

Flacelière, Robert. *Daily Life in Greece at the Time of Pericles.* Translated by P. Green. 1965. Fascinating and highly informative survey of the quality and details of everyday life on all socio-economic levels. Best book on the topic.

*Grene, David, and Richmond Lattimore, eds. *The Complete Greek Tragedies.* 9 vols. 1953–1959. All of the plays of Aeschylus, Sophocles, and Euripides in superb translations.

*Guthrie, W. K. C. *The Greek Philosophers: From Thales to Aristotle.* 1950. A clear sketch of the history of Greek philosophy. Four (of eight) chapters on Plato and Aristotle.

*Lefkowitz, Mary R., and Maureen B. Fant. *Women's Life in Greece and Rome.* 1982. An invaluable sourcebook containing 269 items from original sources in English translation with helpful commentary and notes.

*Rouse, W. H. D., trans. *Great Dialogues of Plato.* 1956. A convenient one-volume translation of the trial and death dialogues, the *Republic,* the *Meno,* and the *Symposium.*

*Available in paperback.

MACEDONIAN CONQUEST AND THE SPREAD OF GREEK CULTURE
(400–30 B.C.)

You [Philip] are called to action . . . by your ancestors, by Persian effeminacy, by the famous men, true heroes, who fought against Persia, and most of all by the fitting hour which finds you in possession of greater strength than any previous European, and your adversary in deeper hatred and wider contempt than any monarch in history. . . . What will be the praises sung of you, when it is realized that in the political field you have been the benefactor of all Greek states, and in the military the conquerer of Persia? No achievement can ever be greater than to bring us all out of such warfare to unity of spirit.

In this passage from an open letter to Philip II, the Athenian orator Isocrates urges the Macedonian king to lead Greece in a crusade against the Persians, appealing to long-standing Greek prejudices: freedom-loving, rational, masculine Greeks are contrasted with enslaved, barbarian, effeminate Persians. As usual, however, the Greek states were fatally incapable of united action, and Philip was more interested in gaining supremacy for Macedon than in saving Greece from its chronic internal strife. This chapter describes how Philip, by 338 B.C., took advantage of weaknesses of the old city-state system to establish Macedon as the dominant political and military force in the Greek world and how his son, Alexander, capitalized on this military superiority to conquer vast territories in the east, leaving as his legacy a world divided into several very large kingdoms, which we designate Hellenistic (the word indicates post-Classical Greek civilization from the death of Alexander into the first century B.C.).

CONTENTS

Silver Tetradrachm. This four-drachma piece shows a divinized Alexander wearing the royal diadem and the ram's horns symbolic of Zeus Ammon, whose oracle he visited at the oasis of Siwah. For the first time in western civilization, coins bore the image of human rulers, rather than of gods. The coin, minted after Alexander's death, well demonstrates the continuing artistry of Greek coin designers and die cutters.

Epaminondas   Philip II   Conquests
                                                                   of Alexander
                                                                   the Great

Battle of   Demosthenes'   Battle of
Leuctra   *Philippics*   Chaeronea

THE DECLINE OF
THE GREEK POLIS SYSTEM

Though many city-states, especially
Athens, had ridden a crest of economic, cultural, and intellectual
achievement in the fifth century, they
never unified their world in a larger,
durable political organization. After
a brief time of glorious, though partial, unity in the Persian Wars, the
Greek states had fallen back into continual, mutually destructive conflict
that culminated in the disastrous Peloponnesian War. Thereafter, no
Greek state was powerful or persuasive enough to control or rally the
rest.

The division among the Greek
states did not change in the fourth
century. The principal powers aligned
and realigned themselves in complex
treaty arrangements. For about thirty
years the Spartans held a shaky predominance, but did not possess the
skills of diplomacy and finance that
the Athenians had demonstrated during their heyday. Athens itself re-
bounded for a time, even rebuilding
its fleet and organizing a new sea
league, this time of autonomous partners. Persia frequently interfered,
casting its support now with one, now
with another Greek state. The Persians temporarily settled internal
bickering in Greece by dictating the
"King's Peace" of 387 B.C. Among
other terms, the treaty required Athens to give up its new sea league and
Thebes to release the Boeotian cities
it was contolling. It also returned Cyprus and the Greek cities of Asia Minor to Persia.

MAP 9
Macedon and Mainland Greece.

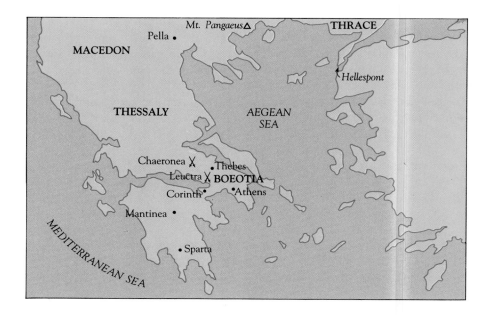

In 371, Thebes, under the leadership of a brilliant military tactician, Epaminondas, became preeminent for a time among the old city-state powers. Epaminondas had created a better-trained army than had previously existed, even at Sparta, and introduced a new, oblique or veer attack pattern for the phalanx, later adopted by the Macedonians. Using these new techniques, he soundly defeated a Spartan force at Leuctra (Map 9), killing the Spartan king and a large number of *homoioi*. However, when Epaminondas was killed at the battle of Mantinea in 362, Theban power outside central Greece died with him.

Thus, in the middle of the fourth century B.C., Greece remained splintered into many city-states. Could the polis ever achieve wider political union? Philosophers and political theorists debated the merits of democracy versus oligarchy, but seldom tackled the issue of interstate cooperation. Plato's *Republic*, for example, is essentially a blueprint for a perfectly just city-state ruled by enlightened philosopher-kings; it does not propose a system whereby all Greeks, regardless of city-state allegiance might live in harmony. The common folk, for their part, were disenchanted with endless warfare and lost their patriotic enthusiasm for the polis. Greek soldiers now often sold their services as mercenaries to the highest bidders, whether Greek or not.

PHILIP II AND THE RISE OF MACEDON

Before the fourth century B.C., Macedon was an underdeveloped region north of Thessaly and west of Thrace.

ALEXANDER ON HIS FATHER'S SERVICE TO THE MACEDONIAN PEOPLE

Philip found you a tribe of impoverished vagabonds, most of you dressed in skins, feeding a few sheep on the hills and fighting, feebly enough, to keep them from your neighbors. . . . He gave you cloaks to wear instead of skins; he brought you down from the hills into the plains; he taught you to fight on equal terms with the enemy on your borders, till you knew that your safety lay not, as once, in your mountain strongholds, but in your own valor. He made you city-dwellers; he brought you law; he civilized you. He rescued you from subjection and slavery, and made you masters of the wild tribes who harried and plundered you. . . . The men of Athens and Thebes, who for years had kept watching for their moment to strike us down, he brought so low . . . that they who once exacted from us either our money or our obedience, now, in their turn, looked to us as the means of their salvation. . . . When he was made supreme commander of all the rest of Greece for the war against Persia, he claimed the glory of it not for himself alone, but for the Macedonian people. *

These words, spoken by Alexander the Great near the end of his career, are a succinct and mostly accurate summary of the achievements of his father, Philip II.

* Arrian, *The Campaigns of Alexander*, trans. A. de Sélincourt (Harmondsworth: Penguin, 1958; rev. ed. 1971), pp. 360–361.

Its territory was very much larger than that of any classical city-state, but was distant from the cultural centers of the Greek world. Although many Greeks thought of Macedonians as hard-drinking, backward, and uncivilized, Macedon was in fact a sleeping giant, with valuable natural resources and huge manpower reserves.

Before Philip II, Macedon suffered from the lack of an efficient central organization, a situation that invited persistent damaging attacks by its Balkan neighbors. Macedon had not followed the path of city-state political development and instead retained its ancient hereditary kingship. Macedonian kings had cooperated with the Persians during the Persian Wars and often switched alliances during the Peloponnesian War.

Members of the royal families engaged in sensational and murderous intrigues in their quest for power.

Two men, Philip II (359–336 B.C.) and his son, Alexander (336–323), unified Macedon and brought it to political supremacy, first in the Greek world and later throughout the Near East as well. When Philip came to the throne after the death of his brother in a frontier war, Greece was in great political disarray. Though Macedon was as yet unable to take advantage of this circumstance, its new, twenty-three-year-old king took prompt measures to change that.

Philip began by remaking the army. As an adolescent, he had been a hostage at Thebes, where he learned the methods of Epaminondas. As king, he now reformed the Macedonian

Macedonian Phalanx. An artist's conception of the mighty Macedonian phalanx. Note the length of the thrusting spear; the protective armor is similar to that of the hoplite infantryman of classical times. Despite the intimidating size and solidarity of the phalanx formation, it was, under the direction of Philip and Alexander, a highly versatile and mobile fighting unit.

army along similar lines, making it fully professional, raising its standards of discipline and drill, and creating special elite units called "companions." He trained this army to carry its own equipment and supplies rather than relying on slow-moving pack animals and baggage trains. He increased the total striking force to more than 25,000 men diversified among infantry, light-armed skirmishers, archers, slingers, and cavalry. He also introduced a new weapon, the sarissa (a thirteen-foot thrusting spear), improved siege machinery, and perfected Epaminondas' offensive maneuvers. Tactically, he adopted the policy of total annihilation, using cavalry to run defeated opponents into the ground and not contenting himself with possession of the field of battle.

Philip secured the money needed to maintain this standing army by forcibly seizing the Mount Pangaeus gold and silver mines, which produced 1,000 talents yearly, as much as the largest annual tribute in the days of the Athenian Empire. He then defeated the Balkan neighbors who had long plagued Macedon.

With Macedon now secure, Philip next unified and modernized his country. In particular, he redistributed population to produce more urban centers and to make better use of cultivable land. He also fostered cultural development, guiding Macedon toward the mainstream of Greek civilization by promoting education and encouraging artists and intellectuals to come to his court at the new royal capital at Pella, where Alexander was born.

Philip was not content to have consolidated Macedon; he now began to direct his efforts toward the political domination of Greece proper. He meddled in the internal affairs of his neighbor Thessaly and alarmed Athens by seizing positions on the northern Aegean coastlands and attacking cities on the Hellespont grain-supply route between Athens and the Black Sea.

The Greek city-states feared this growth of Macedonian power and influence. In a series of speeches called *Philippics*, the Athenian statesman Demosthenes, with good reason, depicted Philip as a menace, incurably addicted to power. As Philip moved south into central Greece, the Athenians and Thebans decided the time had finally come for a showdown and confronted the Macedonians at the battle of Chaeronea in 338 B.C. Philip and the eighteen-year-old Alexander crushed the allied force.

Chaeronea marked a major turning point in the political history of Greece. Philip emasculated the polis as a political entity by absorbing the city-states into a much larger organization. Though he maintained the fiction of polis autonomy by calling the new organization the Greek League, recalling the league of states that had fought the Persians in the fifth century, in fact Greece was merely the first of many territories to fall victim to the expanding power of Macedon. Chaeronea ended the tempestuous history of the city-state as the primary political unit in the Greek world. From now on, large empires would incorporate the Greek states into new political structures.

As *hegemon* (leader) of his newly formed Greek League, Philip announced his intention to avenge Persian offenses, especially Xerxes' burning of Greek temples, committed 150 years earlier. Having subjugated Greece, Philip now envisaged a campaign of glorious conquest in Persia, but in 336 B.C., with preparations for this expedition well under way, he was murdered by a disgruntled member of the royal bodyguard.

ALEXANDER THE GREAT

After the assassination of Philip, the troops proclaimed Alexander king amid rumors that his mother, Olympias, had engineered the king's death on her son's behalf. Although only circumstantial evidence implicates him and his mother in the assassination, Alexander clearly had most to gain from his father's death. In any case, the chance for glory in the Persian campaign would now go to the son, not the father.

Early Years

The records give a fairly clear picture of Alexander as he came to the throne. Not yet twenty years old, he was endowed with tremendous determination and an insatiable thirst for power. In this respect, he was the true son, not only of Philip, but also of Olympias, who was herself a passionate and domineering woman. In appearance, he was shorter than average but well-muscled. His light complexion was set off by oddly colored eyes, one blue-gray, the other dark brown. Though his voice was rather harsh and high-pitched, he was an effective speaker. As a youth, Alexander had been well trained in athletics and the use of weapons; he was a fast runner and rode a horse almost before he walked. At the age of ten or twelve, to the amazement of his elders, he broke the mighty Thessalian stallion, Bucephalas, which he subsequently rode in every major battle of his career. His military training culminated in his command of the attacking wing of the Macedonian forces at Chaeronea. By the time his father was assassinated, Alexander was a favorite among the troops.

Philip carefully supervised his son's intellectual development, even hiring the philosopher Aristotle to be Alexander's tutor. His education gave Alexander a scientific curiosity about

Demosthenes. This forceful life-size portrait statue of Demosthenes shows the Athenian statesman-orator in a pensive mood, reflecting perhaps on the troubled times in which he played so important a role. This is a Roman marble copy of a (lost) bronze original set up around 280 B.C. in the agora at Athens. Vatican Museum.

79

the natural world, a pro-Greek ethnic bias, and a deep love for literature, especially the poetry of Homer and Pindar. The *Iliad* was Alexander's favorite book, partly because he believed himself to be descended through his mother from the Homeric hero Achilles. Aristotle also stressed the pursuit of *arete* and the superiority of enlightened monarchy over other forms of government.

In 336 B.C., as earlier in Macedon's history, change of leadership sparked invasions by its unfriendly neighbors. While Alexander was quelling these, the Greek city-states saw a chance to regain the freedom they had lost at Chaeronea. A rumor went about that Alexander had been killed in battle. When Thebes, with Athenian encouragement, revolted from the Greek League, Alexander marched swiftly into Greece and destroyed the city (except for the house Pindar had lived in) as a terrible example. He treated Athens much more leniently, out of respect for its cultural history and especially its naval power.

Years of Conquest

Alexander was now ready to begin his great campaign against Persia. Leaving in Macedon an army of 12,000 to maintain control in Greece, he crossed the Hellespont in 334 B.C., at precisely the place Xerxes had crossed to attack Greece in 480—the symbolism was obvious. His expeditionary army, initially 65,000 men, was the same highly mobile and diversified force developed by Philip. Accompanying it were technicians, road builders and engineers, surveyors, administrators, financial officers, and secretary-journalists. In addition,

geographers, botanists, zoologists, astronomers, and mathematicians collected information that formed the basis of western knowledge of the Near East and India for many centuries afterward. Thanks to Aristotle's influence, Alexander meant to satisfy his intellectual curiosity as well as his thirst for power.

In the next decade, Alexander's army marched more than 20,000 miles and conquered the whole Persian Empire (see Map 10). Macedon and Greece were already under Alexander's control in 336 B.C. However, conquering Asia Minor and Syria-Palestine presented difficulties because the Persian navy dominated the Aegean and eastern Mediterranean. Alexander did not have the money to build a comparable Macedonian fleet, nor did he trust the navy of the unreliable Athenians. He thus ran the risk that the Persian navy might attack Greece or cut his supply lines at the Hellespont, forcing him to withdraw from Asia. The Persians, however, unwisely decided not to capitalize on their naval strength and gave battle on land. They opposed Alexander first at the Granicus River in 334 and then, under King Darius III himself, at Issus in 333. Alexander won both battles and began to turn his attention to neutralizing the Persian fleet.

After Issus, Alexander continued the Mediterranean portion of his conquests. Darius tried to buy him off by offering him Asia Minor, which Alexander already held, and large sums of money. Alexander refused, advising the Persian king to address him in future as "King of all Asia." He then marched into Syria and Palestine, where he took Tyre, a key Persian naval base, after a costly and difficult six-month siege. Afterward he

crucified 2,000 Tyrians and sold another 30,000 into slavery. Alexander then advanced toward Egypt, where he met little resistance because the Persians had been harsh and unpopular overlords. The Egyptians proclaimed him pharaoh. While in Egypt, Alexander founded the city of Alexandria in 331 B.C. This later became the principal center of Hellenistic cultural development, the most important port in the eastern Mediterranean, and the second most populous city, after Rome, in the history of the ancient world.

While in Egypt, Alexander underwent a decisively important religious experience when he made a 300-mile pilgrimage through burning wasteland to consult the oracle of Ammon, whom the Greeks equated with Zeus, at the oasis of Siwah. At one point, a sandstorm obliterated the trail and Alexander and his party were saved by following two ravens believed to have been sent by the god. Though he never revealed the oracle's message to him, it marked a psychological turning point for Alexander. Henceforth, he believed himself akin to the gods themselves and marked out for even greater achievements than merely gaining vengeance against the Persians.

Made confident by his earlier successes and by the experience at Siwah, Alexander next set out to conquer the heartland of the Persian Empire (modern Iraq and Iran). Darius assembled a huge and unwieldy army and gave battle at Gaugamela (see Map 11) near the Tigris in 331 B.C. Hoping to neutralize Alexander's superior infantry, Darius had protruding blades attached to the axles of his war chariots. Alexander's superbly drilled infantrymen coolly opened their ranks, allowing

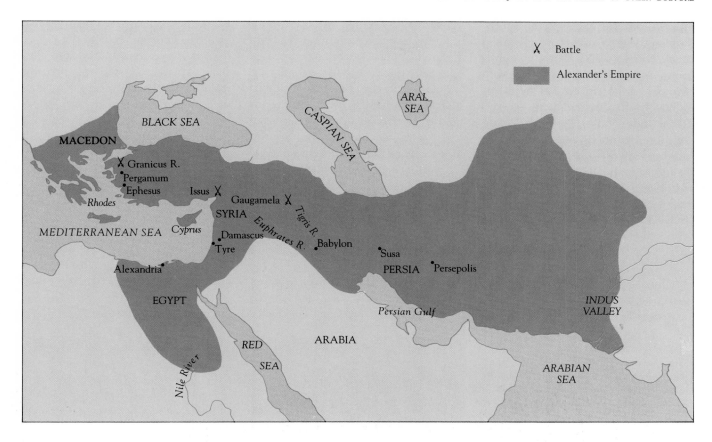

the onrushing chariots to pass harm-lessly through the army. A brilliantly coordinated attack of infantry and cavalry put Darius to flight. The beaten king escaped despite a furious sixty-mile pursuit by Macedonian cavalry, but he was now a mere fugitive. Alexander then marched triumphantly into Babylon, Susa, and Persepolis, seizing massive booty in gold and silver. At Persepolis, he burned the great royal palaces and temples, fulfilling his pledge to avenge Persian destruction of Greek temples.

Alexander had far exceeded his father's goals but meant to go farther still. Philip had probably hoped only to gain control of the Greek cities in Asia Minor, at the western edge of

the Persian Empire. Alexander had penetrated the heart of the empire and delivered a horrendous punishment. Now he wanted nothing less than to become emperor of Persia, king of kings. In 330 B.C., he marched north in pursuit of the fleeing king, but in the meantime Darius was assassinated by dissatisfied allies. Alexander assumed the king's titles and treated Darius's body with great respect, placing it in the royal tombs at Persepolis.

As king of kings, Alexander meant to bring under contol the remainder of the old Persian Empire, stretching eastward to the Indus Valley in present-day Pakistan. During this phase of the campaign, Alexander repelled

MAP 10
Conquests of Alexander the Great.

hit-and-run surprise attacks by enlarging the army and then splitting it into several independently operating divisions. His troops had to cope with winter weather in mountainous terrain and with torrential monsoon rains in the Indus Valley. In the only conventional pitched battle of this part of the expedition, Alexander defeated the Indian potentate Porus. Afterward he allowed Porus to control a large territory as a vassal-ally.

Reluctantly yielding to the wishes of his weary troops, Alexander abandoned his plan to march even farther east. The journey back to Persia proved perilous. Alexander encountered heavy fighting, and an arrow through his lung nearly killed him. The route to the Persian Gulf ran through a large desert region. Alexander planned to provision his forces from ships that would sail in the Indian Ocean, but the fleet was held up by contrary winds and did not link up with the army until after the journey through the desert. Alexander lost some 60,000 of the 85,000 infantrymen and virtually all of the 50,000 noncombatants who accompanied him during this horrible trek. Nature had dealt him his only defeat.

Back in Persia, Alexander's vision of himself as the godlike head of a new Greco-Persian empire posed problems. In particular, his men disliked Alexander's attempts to create an elite class of civil and military leaders by marrying Greeks to Persians. They also bitterly resented his training "barbarian" recruits for service in the army and his own adoption of Persian customs. Especially grating, for example, was Alexander's insistence on the ritual of prostration before the great king, a gesture reserved in the Greek world for the gods alone. Once, in a fit of drunken rage, Alexander ran a spear through a trusty lieutenant, known as Cleitus the Black, for criticizing this policy, even though Cleitus had saved his life years before at the battle of the Granicus River.

MAP 11
The Battle of Gaugamela. At this battle, Alexander again used the oblique battle line to advantage. While Parmenio stood firm in a holding action against the attacking Persians, Alexander's right wing deployed to hold off the outflanking efforts of Persian calvary under Bessus. At precisely the right moment—when the Persian line had begun to stretch thin at the center—Alexander delivered his decisive assault, smashing through at the weak point.

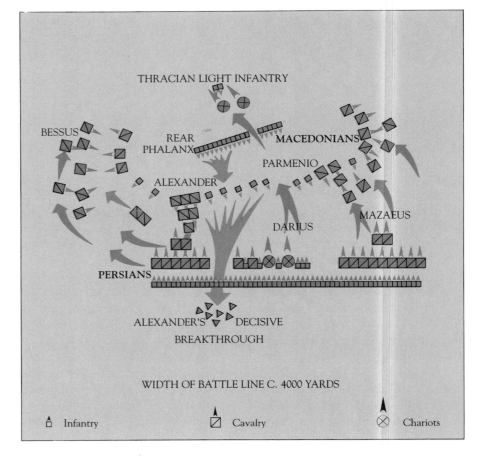

Menander

Euclid's
Elements

Hellenistic Kingdoms

Eratosthenes

Philosophy:
Epicurus,
Zeno and
Stoicism

Library at
Alexandria:
Callimachus

Archimedes

Unfortunately, Alexander was not content to devote his life to achieving political and social stability in already conquered lands. Instead he was planning new expeditions to other lands: the Arabian Peninsula, Africa, and perhaps the western Mediterranean. However, in June of 323 B.C., shortly before his thirty-third birthday, he died at Babylon of a fever of unknown origin, possibly malaria. The long journey, his many wounds, and probably advanced alcoholism had finally exhausted the marvelous stamina of Alexander.

THE HELLENISTIC PERIOD

When Alexander was asked on his deathbed to whom he wished to leave his empire, he answered, "To the strongest." In the half century or so after Alexander's death, several of his best generals fought a complex series of wars to determine who was strongest. The result was a division of the empire into three Hellenistic kingdoms: Macedon and Greece; the Seleucid Empire, extending from Asia Minor eastward all the way to India; and the Ptolemaic kingdom, embracing Egypt and, at times, parts of Pal-

estine. These endured till the arrival of Roman power in the eastern Mediterranean in the second and first centuries B.C. Other Greek settlements in the west, especially on Sicily and in southern Italy, continued to be important.

Society, Politics, and Economics

The Hellenistic kingdoms differed markedly from the classical city-states. Much larger in territory and ethnically more diverse, they were administered by an elaborate hierarchy headed by a remote, godlike king of Macedonian descent who made the laws, owned much of the land, and was deified after death. Private citizens counted for much less politically than had their fifth-century ancestors, and consequently felt little patriotic fervor. The individual was a tiny, voiceless component within a vast political organism.

Although wars between the Hellenistic kingdoms did occur, in general, there was an unprecedented level of cooperation among both the cities within a kingdom and the kingdoms themselves. This brought stability and prosperity. Greek educators, artisans, craftsmen, merchants, and soldiers moved into recently conquered re-

gions, as new cities arose and old ones expanded. Trade relations were more secure and extensive, thanks to Alexander's conquests, and Greek language and culture suffused the newly formed kingdoms, at least among the upper classes, who enjoyed the traditional Greek gymnasium education.

Though farming, as always in the ancient world, occupied the great majority of the population, a remarkable growth in manufacturing and international commerce took place. Every city or region had special commodities, which were exchanged around the Mediterranean and southwestern Asia: grain from Egypt, the Black Sea, and Sicily, olive oil from Athens, wines from Ionia and Syria, salt fish from Byzantium, cheese from Bithynia, prunes from Damascus, glass from Sidon, parchment from Pergamum, bitumen (used in Egypt for embalming) from the Dead Sea, marble from Paros and Attica, timber from Macedon and Lebanon, precious purple dye from Tyre, ivory from India and Egypt, gemstones from India and Arabia, frankincense (used in every religion) from Arabia, balsam from Jericho, slaves from Thrace, Syria, and Asia Minor. To focus on the trading activity of only one Hellenistic city, Alexandria imported timber, silver, copper, iron, wool, dyes, marble, wine, spice, and horses; it exported wheat, papyrus, glass, linen and other textiles, perfumes and ointments, ivory, and various luxury items.

Hellenistic governments promoted and safeguarded these trade relations. Existing road networks, for example, that of the Persians, were maintained and expanded; water supply along caravan routes was ensured; efforts were made to suppress piracy; and standard monetary systems were adopted. Certain cities, Rhodes, Delos, Corinth, and Ephesus, in particular, grew wealthy as transit depots. With the rise of Rome in the third century and after, new Italian markets further stimulated commerce.

Manufacturing enterprises, some of them state run, were another distinctive feature of the age. At Pergamum, for example, it was in state-owned factories that slaves produced the parchment for which the city was famous.

Science and Scholarship

In classical Athens, the money for cultural development had been milked from subject states. In the Hellenistic kingdoms, financial support for cultural enterprises came from revenues raised within the kingdoms themselves. The Ptolemies of Egypt, who exploited the fertile Nile Valley even more systematically than earlier dynasties had, built and supported two important facilities, the first of their kind in history: the great Library of Alexandria and the affiliated think tank known as the Museum, where scholars gathered to pursue their research. Eminent chief librarians, including Callimachus (c. 305–c. 240

B.C.) and Eratosthenes (c. 275–194), presided over the collection of some half-million volumes (papyrus rolls); here the world's first philologists or textual critics carefully edited the great works of Greek literature.

The scientific contributions of Alexandrian scholars were especially significant. Earlier, the physical and life sciences had been subcategories of philosophy; Hellenistic researchers pursued these studies as significant in and of themselves, apart from any philosophical view of nature. By 300 B.C., Euclid had clearly explained the principles of geometry in his *Elements,* which remained the basic textbook for the subject for the next 2,000 years. The brilliant inventor and mathematician Archimedes of Syracuse (c. 287–212) worked on the geometry of spheres and cones and established the value of pi. Astronomers made surprisingly accurate calculations about the dispositions and movements of the heavenly bodies. Aristarchus of Samos even proposed a Sun-centered theory of the universe, although the older, Earth-centered theory won out because it seemed to account better for the operation of gravity and gave less offense to religious beliefs. The Earth-centered theory, usually called Ptolemaic, after Claudius Ptolemy, a second-century A.D. astronomer influenced by Hellenistic predecessors, was not superseded until the sixteenth century. Eratosthenes accurately calculated the circumference of the Earth by comparing the angles of shadow at noon during the summer solstice at two widely separated locations on the same meridian. In biology and medicine, dissection of cadavers and even of living convicts (supplied by King Ptolemy for this purpose) advanced

understanding of anatomy. Investigators described the function of the brain and central nervous system and distinguished between veins and arteries.

Hellenistic thinkers showed little interest in applied science and engineering. However, under pressure from their rulers and patrons, they did produce some new military hardware, such as torsion-spring catapults and huge mechanical bows. Archimedes was as famous for his machines and weaponry as for his mathematical genius. He once boasted, "Give me a place to stand on and I will move the earth." One of his inventions was a giant catapult that could fire 200-pound missiles up to 200 yards. It was difficult to aim, but direct hits sank enemy ships immediately.

Religion and Philosophy

Hellenistic religions became oriented more toward individual human needs and less toward civic duty than earlier Greek religion. Formerly, because the gods were protectors of the city-states, the citizen's religious and civic duties were closely connected. By contrast, in the Hellenistic kingdoms, the individual was no longer an integral part of a civic group watched over by guardian deities, and the old state religion lost its meaning. Because people now needed more immediate emotional satisfaction and assurance of self-worth, they often turned to the impressive secret ceremonies of popular new sects known as mystery religions. Cults like those of Dionysus from Greece, Isis from Egypt, and Mithras from Persia offered a joyful hallucinatory experience of union with a god or goddess, an experience often induced or enhanced by alcohol, de-

Nike of Samothrace. The magnificent statue (c. 200 B.C.) of the winged goddess Nike (Victory) of Samothrace. She stands triumphant in her wind-blown garments, originally placed on the prow of a ship in a fountain basin, in memorial of a victory at sea. Louvre Museum.

lirious dancing, and sexual frenzy. In addition, the promise of future immortality also made these cults attractive alternatives to official state religion and the spiritual alienation it engendered. Mystery religions remained popular in the Roman Empire and helped pave the way for Christianity.

For many in the more educated classes, two new philosophical systems—Stoicism and Epicureanism—filled the vacuum left by the waning of the old religion and overshadowed the teachings of the Platonic and Aristotelian schools. Zeno of Citium (335–263 B.C.) taught in Athens at the Stoa Poikile (painted hall), and his doctrine is thus called "Stoic." Its principal tenets were as follows: First, goodness is based on knowledge. Only the wise man, understanding the true nature of reality, is really virtuous. Second, the truly wise man lives in harmony with nature by means of human reason, which is a part of the divine, universal reason (=God) that necessarily governs the natural world. It follows that, third, the only good is harmony with nature. External "accidents" like sickness, pain, and death cannot harm the truly good person, who is absolutely unfearing, passionless, and impartial. Stoicism, which also emphasized outwardly directed concepts like duty and civic responsibility, would later appeal to the Roman mind and become the most prevalent philosophical creed in the Roman Empire.

Competing with Stoicism, though in key ways similar to it, was Epicureanism. Epicurus (341–270 B.C.), who also taught at Athens about the same time as Zeno, preached the following principles: First, nothing exists but atoms and void. The soul, like all else, is material and disintegrates like the body; thus it cannot suffer after death. Second, the only good in this life is pleasure, a perfect equilibrium or inner tranquillity, defined as the absence of pain or stress. Third, all our actions should be directed toward the minimizing of pain, that is, toward pleasure. Though personal friendships were, in Epicurus's view, essential to happiness, his philosophical system was inwardly directed, recommending withdrawal from society and discouraging participation in public life.

Epicurus's emphasis on pleasure invited attacks by those who, ignorant of his special definition of pleasure, saw his doctrine as vulgar hedonism: "Eat, drink, and make merry, for tomorrow you die and will not be held accountable." Still, the Epicureans exerted great influence and found their most eloquent proponent in the Roman poet Lucretius.

Stoicism and Epicureanism both offered ethical systems suited to the conditions of life in the Hellenistic world. Rather than focusing exclusively on the search for knowledge about the nature of the universe, they stressed the ability of properly educated individuals to ensure their own happiness. In different ways, each promised release from the psychological and spiritual pain of life in a cosmopolitan world where traditional values were dying.

Literature and Art

Greek literature in the Hellenistic period is disappointing after the masterpieces of the Classical era. Alexandrian writers, obsessed with precision and detail, shunned epic and tragedy. Believing Callimachus's maxim, "big book, big evil," they concentrated on miniature forms like epigram, lyric, and elegy, written with excruciating attention to metrical pattern, mythological allusion, and high stylistic polish. An exception was the *Argonautica*, a Homeric-style epic written in the third century by Apollonius of Rhodes, describing the adventures of Jason and his companion heroes in pursuit of the golden fleece. The poem is interesting for the psychology of its characters, but has none of the sublimity of Homer's poetry.

The best poet of the era was Theo-critus (c. 300–c. 260 B.C.), a Greek native of Syracuse who invented pastoral poetry. Shepherds sing to each other of their love for beautiful girls against a lovingly detailed background of the meadows, trees, and flowers, the animals, wild and domestic, of the Sicilian landscape.

In drama, Menander (c. 342–c. 290 B.C.) perfected the New Comedy, so called to distinguish it from the Old Comedy of Aristophanes. Recent papyrus finds give a clearer impression of this comedy of manners, featuring young lovers, upstart slaves, crotchety old men, and so on. Mistaken identity, contrived or accidental, often motivates the plot. There is none of the sharp-witted satirical reference to current events typifying Aristophanic comedy. An immensely popular form, New Comedy influenced the Roman stage in the plays of Plautus and Terence and later Shakespeare's comedies. The situation comedies of television are modern analogies.

Hellenistic art, best represented in sculpture, is both more ornate and more realistic than classical art; it is particularly innovative in its representation of extreme emotion in the human face and figure. Artists could still capture classical Greek nobility and grandeur of form, as in the superb winged Nike of Samothrace, but they originated a new, supple sensuality, as in the Venus de Milo. Humbler subjects were chosen too; for instance, a gnarled old boxer with a broken nose and cauliflower ear waiting his turn to compete, or a little jockey, a mere boy of perhaps twelve, frozen in mid-gallop for all time. But the piece that most fully typifies the Hellenistic style is the Laocoön group. The grotesque extension of limbs, the

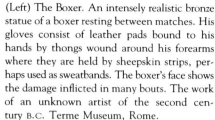

(Left) The Boxer. An intensely realistic bronze statue of a boxer resting between matches. His gloves consist of leather pads bound to his hands by thongs wound around his forearms where they are held by sheepskin strips, perhaps used as sweatbands. The boxer's face shows the damage inflicted in many bouts. The work of an unknown artist of the second century B.C. Terme Museum, Rome.

(Right) The Jockey. To judge from the unknown artist's rendering, the boy immortalized in this bronze statue was either a black or of mixed blood. Blacks (that is, Ethiopians) in antiquity often worked as grooms, jockeys, or charioteers. Made around 200 B.C. and recovered in this century from an ancient shipwreck. National Museum, Athens.

The Laocoön. The Trojan priest Laocoön and his two sons are attacked by two not very true-to-life sea serpents sent by angry gods as an omen of Troy's imminent destruction. The style of the sculpture group, completed in the first century B.C., differs radically from the restraint and serenity of most classical sculpture. The discovery of the Laocoön at Rome in 1506 was the most celebrated archaeological event of the Renaissance. This work profoundly influenced such artists and thinkers as Michelangelo (who viewed it within hours after its discovery), Titian, and Lessing. Vatican Museum.

agony etched in the faces of the victims, the treatment of curvilinear form in the serpents' coils, all are striking departures from classical norms. This horrifying portrait lifted from the story of Troy captures the essence of war's hellish human price.

Hellenistic artists practiced their art at the behest of the royal families or for wealthy private citizens. They did not, like their classical predecessors, create adornments for the greater glory of the beloved city-state or the gods who watched over it. In this regard, they followed the same trend toward individualism and escapism that can be seen in Hellenistic philosophy and literature.

SUMMARY

After the great convulsion of the Greek world in the Peloponnesian War, the fragmentation inherent in the city-state system prevented the emergence of any single dominant power or of a workable combination of powers in some larger federation. This fatal disunity allowed Macedon, which had previously been insignificant, to rise to ascendancy in the Greek world. Philip II engineered the internal cohesion of Macedon, the professionalism of its armed forces, and the subsequent conquest of Greece. Philip's son and successor, Alexander the Great, extended Macedonian dominance to vast regions outside the Greek homeland. By his brilliant and daring generalship and ruthless pursuit of personal glory, he conquered the mighty Persian Empire, which had once threatened Greece with annexation. This opened the way for the expansion and intensification of the influence of Greek culture throughout the Mediterranean and the Near East.

In the wake of Alexander's early death, his empire was ultimately divided into three major Hellenistic successor states: Greece and Macedon, Ptolemaic Egypt, and the extensive Seleucid kingdom. An elite of Macedonian and native civil and military administrators, under the direction of a supremely authoritative king, governed these new states. As Greek settlers migrated to the lands conquered by Alexander and interacted with native populations, a truly cosmopolitan atmosphere arose.

In an era of relative peace, commerce and manufacturing prospered, often subsidized by the government. The arts and sciences flourished as well, particularly at Alexandria in Egypt, where the Ptolemaic kings founded the world's first research facility. The size and complexity of the Hellenistic kingdoms and the changed circumstances of life they brought led many people to seek direction in new religious cults and philosophical systems. Mystery religions were popular, and the Stoic and Epicurean philosophies attracted many adherents. In the period to come, the expanding Roman Empire would supersede the Hellenistic kingdoms and through them become heir to the rich Greek cultural legacy.

SELECTED SOURCES

*Copleston, Frederick. *A History of Philosophy.* Vol. I: *Greece and Rome.* 1946; rev. ed. 1962. Part Five, "Post-Aristotelian Philosophy," provides a clear explanation of the various philosophical systems of the Hellenistic period, especially Stoicism and Epicureanism.

*Ehrenberg, Victor. *The Greek State.* 1960. Includes a concise overview of the political, socioeconomic, military, and cultural aspects of the Hellenistic state.

*Engels, Donald W. *Alexander the Great and the Logistics of the Macedonian Army.*

1978. A fascinating study of the problems of transport, manpower, supply, terrain, and climate confronted by the Macedonian army during its historic expedition.

Green, Peter. *Alexander the Great.* 1970. This engaging and superbly illustrated biography of Alexander is well-balanced in its assessment of his accomplishments. Covers the career of Philip II also.

*Lloyd, G. E. R. *Greek Science after Aristotle.* 1973. A well-written account of the advances in mathematics, astronomy, biology, medicine, mechanics, and technology during the Hellenistic era.

*Renault, Mary. *Funeral Games.* 1981. A typically vivid fictionalized treatment of an era of Greek history by Renault. She focuses on the bloody and chaotic stuggle for power by Alexander's successors after 323 B.C.

*Saunders, A. N. W., trans. *Greek Political Oratory.* 1970. Contains a good selection of speeches by Isocrates and particularly Demosthenes.

*Vellacott, Philip, trans. *Menander: Plays and Fragments.* 1967. Contains the one extant complete work, *The Bad-Tempered Man,* and seven other, fragmentary ones.

*Walbank, F. W. *The Hellenistic World.* 1982. A concise, accurate, up-to-date presentation of political and cultural developments of the era.

Webster, T. B. L. *Hellenistic Poetry and Art.* 1964. A good, quite thorough analysis of the distinctively Hellenistic traits of the poems and works of plastic art produced in this period.

*Available in paperback.

89

CHAPTER 6

THE ORIGINS AND GROWTH OF ROMAN POWER
(753–201 B.C.)

The Senate . . . met, and the military tribunes were authorized to arrange the terms [for the ransom of Rome]; Quintus Sulpicius conferred with the Gallic chieftain Brennus and together they agreed upon the price, one thousand pounds' weight of gold. . . . Insult was added to what was already sufficiently disgraceful, for the weights which the Gauls brought for weighing the metal were heavier than standard, and when the Roman commander objected the insolent barbarian flung his sword into the scale, saying "Woe to the vanquished!"—words intolerable to Roman ears.

Mention of ancient Rome calls to mind invincible soldiers conquering a vast empire and noble statesmen governing it, architects designing great buildings, artists and writers passing on Greek cultural values and adding to them. Rome had humble origins, however, and its people were not always masters of the world. The preceding passage by the Roman historian Livy is from an account of a devastating defeat inflicted by Gallic invaders in 387 B.C. Rome was forced to ransom itself. So close was the "eternal city" to extinction that its people thought of pulling up stakes and migrating to a neighboring town. Considering its early weakness, how did Rome rise to its later overlordship thoughout the Mediterranean world? In answering this question, the present chapter describes the origins of Rome, the social and political practices that gave it internal strength, and the military exploits by which it survived external threats and conquered great reaches of land in Italy and outside it. The resulting Greco-Roman civilization was the basis on which later ages of western civilization built.

Bronze She-Wolf. This bronze statue (fifth-century B.C.) represents the most famous city symbol ever devised. The wolf was a kind of Roman totem animal from earliest times: When Romulus and Remus were exposed on the banks of the Tiber by their evil great-uncle, a she-wolf rescued and suckled them. The statue is a fitting symbol of the Roman virtues of warrior prowess and unflinching dedication to family (the twins are a Renaissance addition). Palazzo dei Conservatori, Rome.

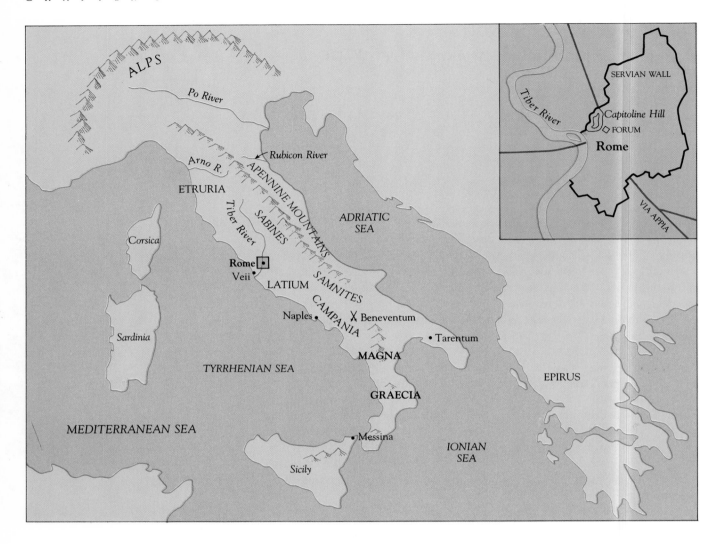

MAP 12
Ancient Italy and City of Rome (inset).

EARLY ITALY AND THE FOUNDATION OF ROME

The boot-shaped Italian Peninsula has the advantage of being centrally located in the Mediterranean region. It is similar to Greece in climate and topography. Summers are hot and dry, winters mild and marked by moderate rainfall. Only in the Po Valley and near the Alps (see Map 12) is weather more like that of northern European countries, with colder winters and greater rainfall. As in Greece, the mountainous character of the land separated the population into numerous city-states in valleys or coastal plains. The central spine of the Apennine range was a particular barrier to unification, both because it divided one half of the peninsula from the other and because its high valleys were homelands for mountain peoples who resisted assimilation and raided the more fertile low-lying lands. Unlike Greece, Italy had abundant timberland and comparatively greater tracts of cultivable land. The potential of the land to support large populations was a key element in Rome's rise to power. As usual in the ancient world, agriculture was the occupation of the majority.

The site of the city of Rome (Map 12, inset) embraced several readily defensible hills at an easily forded spot on the Tiber River in west-central Italy. It was on the intersecton of trade routes between coast and interior, as well as between fertile and productive Etruria to the north and the plains of Latium and Campania to the south. Rome had easy access to the sea down the navigable lower Tiber, but was far enough inland to be secure from pirate raids along the coast.

Early Italic Peoples

The history of Rome begins in the eighth century B.C., when three ma-

jor ethnic groups inhabited the Italian Peninsula. Two—the Etruscans and the Greeks—were recent arrivals. In addition, a Mediterranean people, perhaps from north Africa, had merged with Indo-Europeans from across the Alps to create the farming and iron-working cultures of the Latins, Sabines, Oscans, Umbrians, and other Italic peoples.

The Italic peoples on the eve of the historical period were a hardy peasant stock, primarily farmers and herdsmen. The tribe was the major social unit, with more powerful clans competing for the best land. Relgous belief focused on place-spirits and agrarian deities and emphasized magic, taboo, and rites of purification and atonement. No large political entities existed, and warfare consisted of land or cattle raids made by peasant soldiers armed with javelins, bows, and hide shields. The impulse to more urbanized forms of civilized life came

with immigrants from the eastern Mediterranean.

Greeks in Italy

Greek colonists of the Archaic period built towns along the coast from the Bay of Naples south to the toe of the Italian boot and along its instep to Tarentum. They also settled in Sicily, most thickly in the eastern half of the island. The whole region came to be called Magna Graecia (Greater Greece). The climate and topography here were similar to those of Greece, and timber and good farmland were added attractions. Some of these western Greek city-states became wealthier and more powerful than their mother cities.

The Greeks seized land for settlements from native Italian tribes, often enslaving their unorganized and less-well-armed victims in the process. The early Greek presence in Italy was

Tiber Island. Because two small streams are easier to cross, and two small bridges easier to build, than one large one, river crossings were often established at islands. Rome's location at Tiber Island put it at the convergence of many overland trade routes between Etruria to the north and Latium and Campania to the south.

largely beneficial, however, promoting urbanization and Mediterranean trade relations while introducing literacy and other cultural advances. Like their mother cities in Greece, the cities of Italy were unable to form large-scale political federations.

Etruscans

The third major group in early Italy, the Etruscans, occupied the territory between the Tiber and the Arno rivers. Little is known about their origins, because their undeciphered language, though written in an alphabet borrowed from the Greeks, belongs to no known language family. The Etruscans were Rome's chief early rivals for superiority in central Italy. They lived in about two dozen cities loosely joined by common religious rites and cultural values. They possessed rich resources of timber, minerals, and agricultural land. By about 500 B.C., Etruscan influence extended from the Po Valley to Campania, including the as-yet-insignificant city of Rome. But the lack of strong political cohesion subsequently led to setbacks at the hands of new Celtic invaders in the north and of Greeks and Italians in the south. By the third century B.C., their cities had fallen one by one to the growing power of Rome.

Archaeological exploration of Etruscan cities has revealed that they possessed a vigorous, highly developed material culture. For example, the tombs of rulers and aristocrats were equipped with gold and silver jewelry,

Etruscan Coffin Cover. Archaeologists have excavated many richly decorated Etruscan tombs, often adorned with imported Greek art works, in particular very fine vases. The sculpture pictured here exhibits a distinctively Etruscan style in the angular facial features and in the dignified yet vibrant bearing of the devoted husband and wife, who recline as if at a meal; c. 550 B.C. From Cerveteri; now in Villa Giulia Museum, Rome.

Etruscan Funerary Urn. This ash urn replicates a luxurious Etruscan house. Notable elements in this model are the arched door, gabled roof, and second story, all conforming to a style of house later described in detail by the Roman architectural writer, Vitruvius. From Chiusi; now in the Archaeological Museum, Florence.

excellent imported Greek vases, beautifully dyed clothing, and exquisite wall paintings and sculptures.

The Etruscans were the first civilized power in contact with early Rome and exerted a crucial influence on its development in many areas. Their cities and architectural styles, especially in temple building, shaped Roman practices. Livy called the Etruscans the most religious people on Earth, and the personal attributes of many of their gods were adopted by the Romans for their deities; for instance, the Etruscan triad of sky god Tinia, his wife Uni, and the city-patroness Menrva corresponded closely to Roman Jupiter, Juno, and Minerva. The practice of divining the will of the gods was an Etruscan specialty. Experts who interpreted the significance of all sorts of signs and omens in, say, the flight of birds or flashes of lightning or the entrails of sacrificial animals enjoyed consider-

able prestige throughout Roman history. A darker element of Etruscan religion, death combats as part of ceremonies in honor of the dead, gave rise to the Roman spectacle of gladiatorial contests.

THE ROMAN STATE

Since no contemporary written records of the first five centuries of Rome's history exist, we are often unable to reconstruct precisely what events took place at what specific times. Particularly for the period from the foundation of the city down to the First Punic War in 264 B.C., we are forced to rely on mythology and the findings of modern archaeology. For later periods, fortunately, there are fuller literary and historical documents available.

Rome under Kings

According to myth, Rome was founded in 753 B.C. by Romulus and Remus, twin sons of the god Mars and a vestal virgin (priestess of the goddess Vesta) descended from the Trojan hero Aeneas. Romulus became king of Rome after killing Remus, and was succeeded by six kings, the last three of whom were Etruscan. Monarchy ended in 509, when dissatisfied Romans, led by Junius Brutus, expelled King Tarquin the Proud.

The archaeological record, less colorful but more reliable, shows that Rome in the eighth century was inhabited by shepherd folk: Latins from Latium and Sabines from the central mountains. Under Etruscan influence in the next three centuries came progressive urbanization. Swampy areas were drained and a forum (business district) established in their place, and fortifications were built on the Cap-

King
Tarquin
expelled

Gauls
sack
Rome

First
Punic
War

Second
Punic
War

Republic
begins

XII
Tables

Hannibal,
P. Cornelius
Scipio

A Roman Noble. This sculpture (first-century B.C.), typifying the Roman noble-man's sense of family pride and tradition, shows a toga-clad patrician holding busts of two eminent ancestors. Such images were displayed with great pomp and ceremony at funerals as reminders of the glorious past of the clan and of the obligation to live up to the standards set by earlier family members. Palazzo dei Conservatori, Rome.

itoline Hill. The Tarquins of Roman myth likely reflect a historical period of Etruscan political and cultural domination. Rome's expulsion of its overlords was one chapter in the story of Etruscan decline starting in the late fifth century. With this act of revolution began the period of more democratic government by elected officials, the Roman Republic.

Patricians, Plebeians, and Slaves

In the early republic, the population of Rome was sharply divided into patricians and plebeians. The patricians were a hereditary aristocracy of wealthy, landowning families whose elders, called *patres* (fathers) had served the kings as councillors in a kind of pre-republican Senate. With the coming of the republic, this elite minority monopolized elective offices. The patricians had a political expertise that increased over the years until they were thought of as born to rule. As at Athens before the fifth century, public service in the various magistracies was unsalaried; only the wealthy could afford to run for office.

The patricians accepted high civic responsibility because of the dignity that public recognition of their ser-

vice conferred. This dignity was linked with the pride in family so ingrained in the Roman mentality. The chance of birth gave the patrician social advantages and political and military opportunities denied others. He was expected to use these in service to his fatherland and thereby to magnify the dignity of his entire family.

The great mass of Rome's free population consisted of plebeians, who made their livings as peasant farmers, shepherds, merchants, small tradesmen, and artisans. They were not only excluded from public office but also suffered poverty and fought a bitter struggle against oppression by aristocrats. By going on strike or threatening secession, however, the plebeians eventually succeeded in attaching essential individual rights and freedoms to Roman citizenship. The citizen's liberty, as opposed to the servitude of the slave, meant liberty to do what was allowed by law and social custom as well as to be secure from punishment beyond what the law provided for. To cite two examples, a citizen's marriage to another citizen was recognized as legal and conferred citizenship and the right to inherit on his children. A citizen could not be imprisoned or executed without due process of law and had the right to appeal to the judicial apparatus for redress of wrongs committed against him.

The plebeians were the basis of Roman military strength. Like the hoplite farmers in Greece, they wanted a share in the operations of the republic and assurances of fair treatment by the ruling elite. The nearly exclusive control of the offices of state by patricians had led to abuses of power, as unscrupulous officeholders victimized plebeians. Although the plebeians respected the political competence of the patricians, especially in matters of state finance and foreign policy, they successfully agitated for the right to intermarry with patricians and for a written codification of law. The Twelve Tables (449 B.C.), as this code was called, marked the beginning of a long and distinguished history of Roman law which extended down to Justinian's Code of the sixth century A.D. and formed one of the great Roman contributions to civilization. Though excluded by bloodline from patrician status, the plebeians were able to raise their social status to the rank of *equites* (knights), if they possessed the financial resources to raise horses and serve as cavalrymen in the army. They also eventually won the right to serve in the highest public offices, and decisions enacted by their own assembly were binding on all citizens, patrician and plebeian alike. A system of election that had given disproportionate weight to the votes of the aristocrats was modified over the centuries in the direction of a one-man, one-vote system. By the early third century B.C., such guarantees of fair play and opportunities for advancement, won by hard struggle, constituted the inalienable liberty of every Roman citizen.

THE PATRICIAN WAY OF DEATH

This image [of the deceased] consists of a mask, which is fashioned with extraordinary fidelity both in its modeling and its complexion to represent the features of the dead man. . . . And when any distinguished member of the family dies, the masks are taken to the funeral, and are there worn by men who are considered to bear the closest resemblance to the original, both in height and in their general appearance and bearing. These substitutes are dressed according to the rank of the deceased: a toga with purple border for a consul or praetor, a completely purple garment for a censor, and one embroidered with gold for a man who had celebrated a triumph or performed some similar exploit.

They all ride in chariots with the fasces, axes, and other insignia carried before them, according to the dignity of the offices of state which the dead man had held in his lifetime, and when they arrive at the Rostra [podium] they all seat themselves in a row upon chairs of ivory. It would be hard to imagine a more impressive scene for a young man who aspires to win fame and to practise virtue.*

This passage describes the Roman practice of fashioning imagines, *or wax masks of prominent deceased family members. When not being used in ceremonies such as that described here, the masks were displayed in the home in a family tree arrangement. Every Roman noble's home thus contained a "hall of fame" of notable ancestors who were paid religious homage; the effect was to instill deep family pride and to spur new generations to high achievement.*

*Polybius, *The Rise of the Roman Empire*, trans. Ian Scott-Kilvert (Harmondsworth: Penguin, 1979), 6.53.

Rome, like Greece, was a slave-owning society. Perhaps one-fourth of the population throughout antiquity consisted of persons who had been transformed into property, with no claim to any rights of citizenship or even to be treated with common human decency. Slaves were acquired in very large numbers through warfare, piracy, and trade. They provided an indispensable labor force, serving their masters in household tasks as well as in the heavy work of farming and mining.

Slavery in ancient Rome was also a mechanism for the assimilation of new peoples. The common practice of freeing slaves as a reward for loyal and competent service gave rise to a body of second-class citizens called freedmen. Freedmen remained attached to their former masters in a strong patron-client relationship but enjoyed some, though not all, of the liberties of full citizens. They could not, for instance, serve in public office. The children of freedmen, however, were free born and suffered none of the legal disadvantages of their ex-slave parents. Thus large populations of non-Romans imported through the slave trade were eventually integrated into the citizen body. As a result of this involuntary immigration, perhaps one-half of the citizenry of Rome by the late republic had slave ancestry.

The Republican Form of Government

Hatred of kingship led Romans to devise their republican government specifically to preclude control by a single individual. It never became so democratic as the Athenian system, but it did allow for representation of various elements of the society and was adjustable to the changing needs of the growing Roman empire. What follows is a description of the fully evolved republican system, the result of three centuries of hammering out by trial and error; the Roman Republic, unlike that of the United States, did not have the benefit of a carefully formulated constitution from its outset.

Two consuls were the chief civil authorities within the city and commanders of the armed forces. They were elected annually for a one-year term, ordinarily only once in a lifetime. The division of *imperium* (power) between two officials and the one-year tenure were checks against a return of monarchical rule and were the norm for most Roman magistracies. The consuls, however, were empowered to appoint a dictator in times of dire military emergency requiring swift action by a single supreme leader. This official ruled by virtual martial law for a limited period, usually no more than six months.

The praetors were next in importance among the elected officers. Their chief responsibility was to administer justice in the law courts of Rome. Their interpretations of the laws were final and set precedents by which the Roman legal system was shaped. The number of praetors elected each year increased from two to eight, as Rome grew.

The aediles (at first two, later four) were below the praetors. They supervised public construction, road building and repair, grain and water supply, waste disposal, markets, and the bureau of weights and measures. Aediles also had responsibility for producing public games, races, and contests.

The quaestors (at first two, eventually twenty) were financial aides to the consuls. These state-employed public accountants were in charge of the treasury department. They paid state contractors and soldiers and sometimes issued coins by the state mint.

Ten tribunes of the people, elected yearly by and from the plebeians, performed a watchdog function in the republic. They possessed absolute veto power to forbid any legislative or other governmental action judged harmful to the masses. They were an additional check against abuse by elected officials; the steady expansion of their powers was an important result of plebeian agitation for fair treatment by the aristocratic leadership.

Censors held an office of special importance and prestige. Every five years the citizens elected two of the most distinguished former consuls for an eighteen-month term to conduct a census and to draw up the official lists of senators. If the censors found an individual to be lacking in property qualifications or in moral character, they could change his citizenship status or strike him from membership in the Senate.

The Roman Senate was a 300-(later 600-) member advisory body consisting of ex-magistrates who normally held membership in it for life, assuming the censors found no act of misconduct. Though the Senate, unlike the U.S. Senate, lacked direct legislative powers, it was a valuable repository of collective wisdom, and its views on finance, foreign policy, war and peace, religion, and legislative issues were sought and carefully attended to by elected magistrates. The accumulated individual authority of its members and its permanence as an institution made the Senate the most stable and dominant element in a government whose elected officials changed each year. This dominance was symbolized in the phrase *Senatus Populusque Romanus* ("the Senate and Roman People"); indeed, the abbreviation SPQR was the universal mark of Roman authority.

In addition to the civic magistracies, the Romans elected (for life) the pontifex maximus (chief priest)—the Latin title of the pope in Christian times—who presided over the entire apparatus of the state religion, including other priests and the vestal virgins, six women specially chosen to tend the sacred eternal flame of the goddess Vesta at her temple in the forum. He supervised the proper observance of festivals in honor of the gods and regulated the calendar of religious events for each year.

Loyalty and the Cohesion of the State

Res publica, Latin for "republic," means literally "the public affair," or "the people's affair." Romans were an intensely patriotic people and expected each citizen to serve the state to the extent of his or her abilities. Patricians were solemnly obligated to care for the public interest as elected officials. Plebeians and knights were to respect and obey their governmental leaders and to answer the call to arms in times of need. Such behavior exemplified the Roman notion of loyalty: devotion to one's country and fellow citizens, even to the point of sacrificing one's life. The Roman equivalent of the U.S. Congressional Medal of Honor was awarded "on account of citizens saved."

An important institution—the patron-client relation—was also based on loyalty and honor. Aristocratic patrons looked out for less fortunate citizens called clients. The patron might give money or food or intercede to resolve a legal problem or to press a grievance in the law courts. By such favors, the patron placed his influence and dignity at the disposal of a disadvantaged fellow citizen, however briefly or slightly. In return, the client showed deference to the patron, thereby increasing the latter's dignity, sometimes by performing menial chores or errands, but especially by voting for his patron or for candidates approved by the patron. In this way, aristocratic families could evade the restrictions of a one-man, one-vote system and monopolize for their class the dignity derived from high office. Thus social strife that might have destroyed the republic from within was lessened by a widespread class cooperation not spelled out in legally binding terms but based on the distinctively Roman sense of loyalty.

Piety and Right Relations with the Gods

The Roman empire was also built on the bedrock of patriotism fostered by "piety," the value system that inter-

locked Roman religious and family life. Piety embraced devotion to the gods and to members of one's family, both living and dead. Though ancestor worship was not practiced, Romans honored the memory of their forefathers and held to their morality of hard work and self-discipline in service to god, family, and state. Reverence for and obedience to elders and unfailing concern for the welfare of children were the highest domestic virtues. The father was effectively king and chief priest of the miniature state of his family, with absolute power over all its citizens. Roman women were educationally and legally disadvantaged, like their Greek sisters, and always subject to male authority, but they could aspire to be *matronae* (mothers of families). The following epitaph of c. 125 B.C. illustrates the typical virtues of the Roman matron: "This unlovely tomb holds a beautiful woman. Her parents named her Claudia. She loved her husband with all her heart. She bore two sons; one she left on the earth, the other beneath it. She was pleasant in speech and proper in appearance. She kept house and worked in wool." In return for her fidelity, fertility, and domesticity, the Roman woman was revered within her family and greatly respected within her society. She was not segregated within her own home, as in Greece.

Roman religious practice was based on a combination of piety and the patron-client concept. Human beings were clients of supernatural patrons, and the loyalty cementing their relations was piety. Roman religion, like Greek, was polytheistic; the security of both the state and the individual depended on the good will of a host of anthropomorphic gods. Religion involved civic as well as personal duty,

and separation of church and state was unimaginable.

Roman religious beliefs were shaped by Etruscan and Greek influences. The old Italic gods were agricultural, outgrowths of nature-spirits who ensured or, if angered, withheld good weather, fertility, and fine harvests. Mars and Venus, for example, were originally gods of this type. Later, however, the Italic deities were modifed to parallel Etruscan and/or Greek gods. Venus was equated with Greek Aphrodite, Jupiter with Etruscan Tinia and Greek Zeus, and so through the pantheon.

The goal of Roman religion was right relations with the supernatural or *pax deorum* (peace with the gods). The underlying premise was summed up as *do ut des* ("I give so that you will give"). Prayers, vows, sacrifices, ritual acts of purification or atonement were all sacred transactions designed to appease gods who were easily angered and could inflict punishment on an entire group, guilty and innocent alike. In return for dutiful observance of religious rituals, Romans expected favorable answers to their requests for divine assistance. Everything was carefully spelled out in formulas resembling legal contracts more than devotional prayers.

THE ROAD TO EMPIRE

As a people, the Romans possessed social and cultural institutions that served them well in the republican era. They were sufficiently flexible to adapt their political system to new conditions as their power expanded. In their foreign policy, they learned from contact with other peoples even

Altar of Domitius Ahenobarbus. This late re-publican sculpture shows a typically Roman combination of religious and administrative ceremonies, probably a census. Soldiers dressed in parade armor and civilian officials in togas supervise the *suovetaurilia* or "pig-sheep-ox" sacrifice. The animals are oversize, probably to convey that many sacrificial victims were offered. Louvre Museum.

as they absorbed them within an emerging empire. These attributes stood the Romans in good stead as first Italy and then the western Mediterranean came under their control.

Roman Conquest of Italy

After 509 B.C., Rome joined, and later dominated, a league of Latin cities that adopted common policies and in wartime served under a dictator elected by member states. In the fifth century B.C., this league defended its fertile plains against the frequent incursions of neighboring hill peoples like the Sabines. Success against these enemies led ultimately to their political absorption and the replacement of Oscan language dialects by Latin.

In the early fourth century B.C., Rome won a great victory over the neighboring Etruscan city of Veii. Legend put the siege on a par with the Trojan War. Rome's heroic leader, the dictator Furius Camillus, was said to have persuaded the goddess Juno to abandon Veii in favor of Rome. This success, however, was followed in 387 by a shattering defeat at the hands of Gauls, fearsome Celtic invaders from across the Alps. The Roman army was soundly beaten and the city burned. The Gallic horde left only after payment of a large indemnity. This searing experience of defeat gave the Romans a fierce determination never to suffer such a humiliation

again. The five-and-a-half-mile-long Servian Wall they built around the city after the Gauls left was not penetrated by a foreign enemy for 800 years. In the latter half of the fourth century, Rome embarked on campaigns of conquest against Gauls and Etruscans to the north and against Samnites and Latins to the south. There were setbacks, but by 290 Rome controlled more than half of the Italian Peninsula from the Rubicon River in the north to the Bay of Naples in the south.

Further Roman expansion southward threatened the interests of the Greek cities in the region. Tarentum tried to stem the tide by enlisting the aid of Pyrrhus, the king of Epirus across the Adriatic. With a crack force of 25,000 and the new tactical advantage of twenty war elephants, Pyrrhus twice defeated Roman armies, but they were costly victories (thus the term *Pyrrhic victory*), and after a drawn battle at Beneventum in 275, he withdrew to Epirus having lost two-thirds of his men. Roman mastery of the southern part of the peninsula was complete.

Rome's conquests were achieved by an army of militiamen conscripted for each campaigning season according to their ability to furnish arms. The wealthy served as cavalry, small farmers as infantrymen, the poor as light-armed troops. The backbone of the army was the infantry, armed and trained along the lines of Greek hoplite warriors. The government introduced pay for military service in the fourth century, as longer and more frequent expeditions kept soldiers away from their farms. Discipline, obedience to authority, and endurance of adversity combined with first-rate training and drill to make the Roman soldier the best the world had yet seen.

Roman predominance in the Italian Peninsula at the beginning of the third century B.C. rested on a shrewdly conceived system of annexations and alliances. Typically, when Rome defeated a city, it annexed a third to a half of its territory and sometimes enslaved some of its citizens, but allowed the majority to continue living on their own land, to govern themselves as they saw fit, and even to share in certain rights of Roman citizenship, so long as they agreed to contribute forces to the Roman army when these were requested. The Latin cities in particular acquired a preferred status among Roman allies, which was sometimes extended to other peoples as "Latin rights." To control newly annexed territories and secure bases for further military actions, Rome established colonies of citizens or, more often, of allies with Latin status. Rome increased its territory, its available manpower, and its military strength by these complementary processes of alliance and annexation/colonization. The loyalty that bound Rome and its allies was a critical factor in the third-century struggle with Carthage.

The First Punic War

In the third century B.C., Carthage was the major power in the western Mediterranean. Founded as a colony

---

BARGAINING WITH THE GODS

Father Mars, I pray and beseech thee that thou mayest be propitious and of good will to me, our house and household, for which cause I have ordered the offering of pig, sheep, and ox to be led round my field, my land, and my farm, that thou mightest prevent, ward off and avert diseases, visible and invisible, barrenness and waste, accidents and bad weather; that thou wouldst suffer the crops and fruits of the earth, the vines and shrubs to wax great and prosper, that thou wouldst preserve the shepherds and their flocks in safety and give prosperity and health to me and our house and household; for all these causes, for the lustration [cleansing] and purification of my farm, land, and field, as I have said, be enriched by the sacrifice of this offering of sucking pig, lamb, and calf. *

This farmer's prayer well illustrates the careful legalistic quality of Romans' dealings with their divinities. The god is invoked by name and informed both of the exact nature of the farmer's offering and of the favor expected in return. The many repetitions ("prevent, ward off, avert . . .," and so on) are to ensure correct understanding of the terms of the contract.

*Cato, De Agri Cultura, 141, trans. C. Bailey, in Phases in the Religion of Ancient Rome (Berkeley: University of California Press, 1932), p. 74.

---

of Phoenician settlers (called *Poeni* in Latin, giving the adjective "Punic") from Tyre in the eighth century B.C., its geographical position, near modern Tunis, and its excellent harbor made it a preeminent trading city. It directed the exchange of gold, silver, and tin from Spain and Africa for wine, textiles, and manufactured goods of its own or from the Hellenistic east. By the third century, Carthage, with a population of perhaps 400,000, had a massive, twenty-two-mile-long fortification wall and improved harbor installations. It monopolized trade in the area from Sicily to Gibraltar by sinking the ships of competitors. The rise of Rome to a rival first-class power imperiled that advantage.

By 264 B.C., Rome had a strong interest in both the commercial and military security of allied or subject cities in southern Italy, with their valuable trading networks and agricultural holdings. Thus when Carthage began to expand its presence on Sicily and to endanger the flow of Roman trade through the Straits of Messina (see Map 13), Rome decided in 264, by a vote of the assembly of citizens, to send troops to Sicily. For the coming showdown of superpowers, Carthage could rely on the supremacy of its ships and sailors for control of the seas; for land engagements it hired north African, Spanish, Gallic, Greek, and even some Italian mercenary troops. Although it had no fleet, Rome did have the advantage of a strong system of alliances and a military machine finely tuned in the centuries-long struggle for supremacy in Italy. Hiero, tyrant of Syracuse, joined Rome, which had

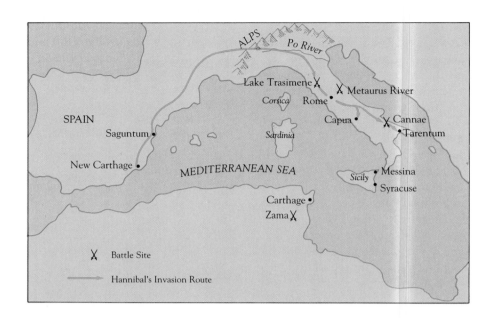

MAP 13
The Western Mediterranean.

some initial successes in battle, but the Carthaginian fleet provisioned its coastal cities and made raids on the Italian Peninsula. To counter this, Rome built a fleet of 120 heavy galleys, with which it won a series of naval battles and, in 256, landed an army near Carthage. The consul Marcus Atilius Regulus routed the enemy, but proposed such harsh terms that the Carthaginians decided to continue resistance. The Spartan mercenary general Xanthippus defeated the Romans through skillful use of elephants and African cavalry. The theater shifted again to Sicily, where the war dragged on for another fifteen years. The stalemate was broken by a major Roman naval victory off the western tip of Sicily in 241. Carthage was unable to supply its forces in Sicily and sued for peace. Rome won the First Punic War, despite enormous losses of 200,000 men and 500 ships, because of the high quality of its citizen army and because its system of Italian alliances and colonies supplied vast reserves of manpower and material.

The fruits of the hard-earned triumph were sweet. Carthage paid an indemnity of 3,200 talents (200,000 pounds in weight) of silver over the next ten years and ceded its territory in Sicily. Not long after, it yielded control of Corsica and Sardinia. Rome had acquired its first overseas possessions, and the long process of adapting the republican government of a small, central Italian state to the requirements of a far-flung empire began in earnest. In the next 200 years, as more and more provinces were acquired, the number of elected magistrates was increased to handle military, financial, and judicial administration. Immediately after their term of office, consuls and praetors were assigned as "proconsuls" and "propraetors" to annual provincial governorships.

In the years after the war with Carthage, Rome repelled a Gallic invasion in the north and established new colonies in the Po Valley. It also stopped piracy in the Adriatic and carved out a 120-mile protectorate along the coast of Illyria opposite Italy.

The Second Punic War

As in the First Punic War, initial hostilities in the second were ignited by friction in a region, this time Spain, where both Rome and Carthage desired to extend their influence. Members of the Barca family—Hamilcar and later his son Hannibal (247–183 B.C.)—directed the creation of Carthaginian colonies in Spain to replace possessions lost in the First Punic War. In 219 Hannibal took by siege the Spanish town of Saguntum, which had contracted an alliance with Rome. War was declared in the following year.

The Roman war strategy was to mount a two-pronged attack, one pinning down Hannibal in Spain, the other challenging Carthage on its home soil. Hannibal was not one to wait for interception by Roman forces. He intended to win the war by boldly invading Italy before Rome could prepare itself. He mistakenly thought that the Italian allies were eager to revolt and that he could enlist their support for an offensive against Rome. He surprised the Romans by leading men, horses, and combat elephants across the Alps into the Po Valley, where he recruited large numbers of Gauls. By his tactical brilliance and his superior cavalry, Hannibal defeated Roman troops sent to stop his progress into central Italy. At the battle of Lake Trasimene in 217, he ambushed and obliterated two entire legions along with their consular commander.

But Hannibal could not follow up these successes by taking Rome itself, for the allied cities of central Italy held firm and would not open their gates to the Carthaginians. Further, Hannibal's strength was cavalry, not siege machinery. He marched farther south, where he enveloped and annihilated Roman armies at Cannae in 216. The outlook for Rome now seemed grim, and some important cities went over to Hannibal, including Syracuse, Tarentum, and Capua; the latter was the largest city in Campania and probably hoped to be capital of a great Punic province in Italy. Carthage also stepped up its attacks on Roman forces in Spain and signed an alliance with Philip V of Macedon, who declared war on Rome with the intent of seizing Rome's Illyrian protectorate.

Through all this, Roman government, in particular the Senate, did not panic. After Cannae had shown the folly of meeting Hannibal in a pitched battle, Quintus Fabius Maximus, consul in 215 and 214, outmaneuvered Hannibal by hit-and-run skirmishes and cut off his reinforcements, meanwhile recovering rebellious former allies. This policy of "Fabian" (delaying) tactics began to pay off by 211, when Rome recaptured Capua as well as Syracuse, despite the ingenious war machines of Archimedes. Philip V was kept at bay by the Roman fleet in the Adriatic, and Roman forces in Spain were increased. Rome now had some 250,000 men under arms.

The tide began to turn for good with the appointment of a brilliant twenty-five-year-old general, Publius Cornelius Scipio (236–183 B.C.), to the command of Roman forces in Spain. Scipio's father and uncle, the previous commanders, had died in action in 211. Scipio succeeded in taking the city of New Carthage, the nerve center of Punic power in Spain in 209. Hasdrubal, the brother of Hannibal, eluded Scipio and brought reinforcements into Italy in 207, but was defeated by Roman forces at the battle of the Metaurus River in northern Italy. Hannibal learned that the reinforcements would not be joining him when a Roman cavalryman threw Hasdrubal's severed head into his camp.

In 204 B.C., Scipio took the war home to the Carthaginians. He landed in Africa and negotiated an armistice on the condition that Hannibal be recalled. Thus the great Carthaginian general, for fifteen years undefeated in Italy, returned without having won the war. The Romans found a pretext to break the armistice in 202, and Scipio, who bolstered Roman cavalry with African contingents, defeated Hannibal at Zama. In 201, Carthage capitulated, dismantling its military power, surrendering Spain, and agreeing to pay an indemnity of 10,000 talents over the next fifty years. The once mighty city survived only to be razed in 146 after the Third Punic War.

Hannibal gave the Roman Republic its last great external threat. The firm loyalty of Italian allies, the resilience of the Roman people, and the resourcefulness of Roman senatorial and military leadership withstood the test. Rome, now the foremost military and naval power in the western Mediterranean, was ready to turn to the Hellenistic east.

SUMMARY

Rome's rise to greatness could not have been predicted in the eighth century B.C. Indeed, until the fifth century, the culturally advanced cities of the Etruscans or of the Greeks in southern Italy were better candidates to gain control of the peninsula. Rome, however, enjoyed topographical advantages of defensible hills and an easy river crossing and possessed crucial sociopolitical and religious values and traditions.

After ousting the last of their Etruscan monarchs, Romans of all classes engaged in hammering out a new governmental system. Rule by a public-spirited aristocracy was moderated by the assurance of individual liberties for all citizens. The system of interlocking human and religious loyalties that typified the Roman people gave their state a cohesion unmatched by any of their enemies.

The first two phases of Rome's rise to power ended with conquest of Italy and victory over the Carthaginians. In Italy, Rome's preferred method was to strengthen itself by strategically placed colonies and by the addition of former enemies to a network of alliances that benefited all but gave ultimate authority to Rome. In this way, Rome moved from the mere defense of territory against hostile neighbors to offensives that steadily enlarged its influence in Italy. The Etruscan and Latin cities were absorbed in the fourth century, despite the setback Rome suffered at the hands of Gauls. By the early third century, Rome controlled virtually the entire peninsula.

Two long, life-or-death struggles with the Carthaginian Empire in the third century raised Roman power beyond that of any previous Mediterranean people. In these Punic Wars, Rome maintained the confederation of allies that gave it almost inexhaustible manpower. It acquired provinces—Sicily, Sardinia/Corsica, Spain—and made needed modifications in its government to rule them ably. It also became a first-rate naval power, something indispensable to leadership in the Mediterranean and, given Carthage's overwhelming initial advantage in this area, a tribute to Roman geopolitical sagacity.

Rome achieved all this within three centuries of its liberation from Etruscan political domination. The next two hundred years witnessed further conquests, especially in the eastern Mediterranean, and important internal changes stemming from them. Among these changes was the unforeseen disintegration of the republican form of government.

SELECTED SOURCES

Adcock, Frank E. *The Roman Art of War under the Republic.* 1940. A good, succinct account of Roman military training and strategy.

*Adcock, Frank E. *Roman Political Ideas and Practice.* 1959. An extremely clear, short explanation of the social and ethical attitudes that underlay Roman politics.

Bailey, Cyril. *Phases in the Religion of Ancient Rome.* 1932. An older work still valuable especially for its lucid discrimination of magical, animistic, and polytheistic stages in Roman religion.

Bloch, Raymond. *The Origins of Rome.* 1960. This useful introduction to the prehistory of Italy and Rome's early centuries expertly incorporates archaeological evidence. Well illustrated.

*Bryher, Winifred. *The Coin of Carthage.* 1963. An entertaining historical novel about the fortunes of two Greek traders trying to make their way in a world convulsed by the Second Punic War.

*Crawford, Michael. *The Roman Republic.* 1978. The best brief recent treatment of the whole period.

*Lewis, Naphtali, and Meyer Reinhold, eds. *Roman Civilization, Sourcebook,* I: *The Republic.* 1951; rev. ed. 1966. An extremely useful and thorough collection of source materials of all sorts. The selections are equipped with helpful introductions and notes.

*Livy. *The Early History of Rome.* Translated by A. de Sélincourt. 1960; reprinted 1971. Books I–V of Livy's *History;* the classic formulation of the inspiring legends of earliest Roman history.

Scullard, Howard H. *Scipio Africanus: Soldier and Politician.* 1970. An engrossing and lively biography of this brilliant general, the only Roman to defeat the magnificent Hannibal.

*Von Vacano, Otto-Wilhelm. *The Etruscans in the Ancient World.* Translated by Sheila A. Ogilvie. 1960. A concise political and cultural history of the Etruscans, carefully tracing their interaction with other ancient peoples.

*Available in paperback.

ROMAN REVOLUTION: FROM REPUBLIC TO EMPIRE
(201 B.C.–A.D. 14)

Those who had come prepared for the murder bared each of them his dagger and closed in on Caesar in a circle. Whichever way he turned he encountered blows and weapons leveled at his face and eyes, and driven hither and thither like a wild beast he was entangled in the hands of all; for it had been agreed that they should all strike him and taste of the slaughter, for which reason Brutus also gave him one stab in the groin. Some say that he fought and resisted all the rest, tossing this way and that and crying aloud, but when he saw that Brutus had drawn his dagger he pulled his toga over his head and sank . . . against the pedestal on which Pompey's statue stood. And the pedestal was drenched with his blood.

By an irony of history, the Roman Republic began to succumb to an enemy within as soon as it had defeated all serious threats from outside. The assassination of Julius Caesar on the Ides (fifteenth) of March 44 B.C., described in this passage by Plutarch, was only the most electrifying in a series of acts of political violence, military coercion, and civil war that destroyed the republican system of government. The present chapter describes the completion of Roman conquest of the Mediterranean world and the profound social, economic, and cultural effects of Rome's expansion in the republican era. It then examines the period of bloody revolution between 133 and 31 and Augustus's subsequent inauguration of the imperial era of Roman history.

ROME AND THE GREEK EAST

Shortly after the Second Punic War, Rome began to turn its attention to the eastern Mediterranean (see Map 14). Its conquests in this region were as rapid as those in the west had been, but they brought dramatic social and cultural changes as well as new territorial gains.

Julius Caesar. A portrait bust of Julius Caesar. Shrewd politician, military genius, skilled orator and writer, Caesar also found time to mingle in high society and had the reputation of a ladies' man. In physical appearance, he was tall, lean, somewhat balding, and a careful dresser. Perhaps to control a tendency to epilepsy, Caesar was precautious in diet and rather Spartan in his personal habits. Naples Museum.

Military Conquests

Rome undertook many of its military expeditions initially to protect current holdings or support the interests of friends. As Cicero put it, "Our people, by defending allies, have become masters of the entire world" (*Republic* 3.23.35). Beginning with the acquisition of Sicily after the First Punic War, the fruits of imperialist expansion became a major additional incentive.

As we have seen, the limited initial goal of securing the Straits of Messina had led to the First Punic War. The Second Punic War raised Rome to a major power, but it required a number of follow-up actions. The provinces in Spain had to be protected from fierce native tribes, and Gauls had to be subjugated in Cisalpine Gaul (northern Italy).

The Romans also attacked Macedon, the homeland of Philip V (221–179 B.C.), who had cooperated with Hannibal against Rome. When the states of Rhodes and Pergamum appealed to Rome to stop Philip's conquest of Greece, Roman armies defeated the Macedonian king in 197. Rome left Macedon independent, declared freedom for Greece, and annexed no territory for itself.

Unfortunately, matters were not so easily settled in the complicated world of Hellenistic power politics. The Seleucid king Antiochus III (223–187 B.C.) of Syria sought to become master of Greece. Rome defeated him in 189, after crossing into Asia Minor for the first time. His guest Hannibal committed suicide in 183 rather than fall into Roman hands. Again, Rome annexed no territory, and Pergamum and Rhodes gained most from the war.

Roman patience with Greek political intrigues now began to wear thin. After crushing a new challenge by the ambitious Macedonian king Perseus (179–168 B.C.), son of Philip

MAP 14
The Eastern Mediterranean.

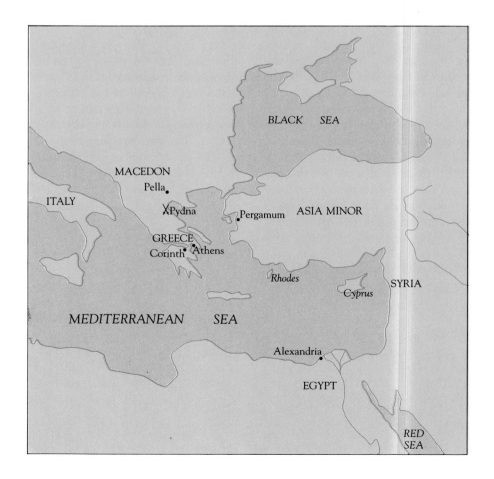

Rome defeats Philip V		Battle of Pydna	Third Punic War: Carthage destroyed	Slave revolt in Sicily
	Marcus Porcius Cato	Scipionic Circle	Corinth destroyed	Attalus III bequeaths Pergamum to Rome

V, at Pydna in 168, Rome annexed Macedon as a province in 147. Many Greek states, discontent with Roman efforts to impose "freedom" in their region, had created a new confederation called the Achaean League. In 146, the consul Lucius Mummius dissolved the league after savagely destroying Corinth, its leading city and a hotbed of resistance to Roman interference. Now only technically independent, Greece was henceforth under the supervision of the Roman governor of Macedon. In addition, Attalus III (138–133 B.C.), the last king of Pergamum (present-day western Turkey), bequeathed his kingdom to Rome and it became the province of Asia.

Rome also tightened its grip outside the Greek east. Some conservative politicians feared a rebirth of Carthaginian power. Among them was Marcus Porcius Cato (234–149 B.C.), called Cato the Elder, who had fought in the Hannibalic war and who habitually ended his speeches in the Senate with the phrase *delenda est Carthago* ("Carthage must be destroyed"). A suitable pretext for war arose when Carthage resisted the attacks of a neighboring north African kingdom that was allied with Rome. At the end of the Third Punic War (149–146), Roman legions thoroughly plundered and destroyed the city of Carthage. No second Hannibal would rise from those ruins. An area roughly coextensive with modern Tunisia became the province of Africa.

In Spain, with its coveted resources of gold and silver, Scipio Aemilianus (185–129 B.C.) used a force of 60,000 to break organized resistance to Roman authority by forcing the surrender of the strategic town of Numantia in 133. Four thousand defenders had even resorted to cannibalism in their efforts to hold out during the eight-month siege.

Between 264 and 133, Rome won important victories because of the bravery and discipline of the loyal legionary soldier. It was also able to find competent, and sometimes brilliant, generals when it most needed them. Rome's military success cost its opponents dearly. Barbarian Spaniards, Gauls, and Sardinians were hunted down and butchered. Nor were civilized adversaries spared plunder, enslavement, rape, and extortion. Cities were destroyed, and vast populations were displaced. For example, 150,000 allies of the defeated Perseus were sold into slavery on a single day.

Roman Legionary Soldier. A reconstruction of a Roman legionary soldier equipped with crested helmet, a coat of mail to protect the torso, and a four-foot oval shield; offensive weapons are the throwing spear and the double-edged cut-and-thrust Spanish sword.

SLAVES: ILL-TREATMENT AND REBELLION

a) Slave miners in Spain:

As a result of their underground excavations day and night they become physical wrecks, and because of their extremely bad conditions, the mortality rate is high; they are not allowed to give up working or have a rest, but are forced by the beatings of their supervisors to stay at their places and throw away their wretched lives as a result of these horrible hardships. Some of them survive to endure their misery for a long time because of their physical stamina or sheer will-power; but because of the extent of their suffering, they prefer dying to surviving. [*]

b) Slave rebels in Sicily:

The Sicilians, being grown very rich and elegant in their manner of living, bought up large numbers of slaves. They brought them in droves from the places where they were reared, and immediately branded them with marks on their bodies. . . . Oppressed by the grinding toil and beatings, maltreated for the most part beyond all reason, the slaves could endure it no longer. . . . Those who were thus cruelly abused were enraged like wild beasts and plotted together to rise in arms and kill their masters. . . . They stole into the houses and wrought great slaughter. They were joined by a large throng of the slaves in the city, who first visited the extreme penalty upon their masters and then turned to murdering others. [**]

Although household slaves of wealthy Romans received good treatment and could even expect the reward of manumission (emancipation) for loyal service, most slaves had bleak lives of endless toil. The domestic slaves of comic drama are threatened, when they misbehave, with transfer to the grinding mills or the mines. Miners had very short life expectancies. Roman courts sometimes sentenced criminals to mine work virtually as a form of capital punishment. As a slave-owning society, Rome lived with the endemic fear of revolt and imposed extremely harsh penalties to discourage insurrections. For example, all the slaves in a household, guilty and innocent alike, could be executed when a master was murdered by a slave. After putting down the Spartacus revolt in 71 B.C., Roman troops crucified 6,000 men along the Appian Way as a hideously effective deterrent to rebellion.

[*]Diodorus of Sicily, *Library of History* 5.36.3 and 38.1, trans. C. H. Oldfather (Cambridge, Mass.: Harvard University Press, 1939).

[**]Diodorus of Sicily, *Library of History* 34.2, trans. N. Lewis and M. Reinhold, *Roman Civilization*, rev. ed., vol. 1 (New York: Harper, 1966), pp. 231–232.

Social and Economic Change

By 133 B.C., empire building had become Rome's chief industry. Military victories became an intoxicating source of glory for the Roman nobility. War also proved profitable. To the traditional spoils of land, booty, and slaves, Rome added tribute and tax revenues from the provinces, with which it paid soldiers and reduced the tax burden of citizens. Particularly enterprising members of the *equites* grew fabulously wealthy as entrepreneurs, businessmen, publicans (tax collectors), and provisioners of the army; they benefited also by the opening of new trade routes and markets throughout the Mediterranean.

Many had little share in these profits of empire, however. The small farmer who had been the mainstay of the early republican state began to disappear. Devastation by Hannibal's army and nearly continuous warfare in the second century B.C. forced many off their farms. Wealthy senatorial aristocrats bought up the holdings of failed farmers and combined them into vast estates worked by the plentiful slaves obtained through foreign conquests. Dispossessed free men drifted to Rome in search of work or handouts, swelling the ranks of a restless urban rabble.

The greatly enlarged slave labor force, though an economic advantage, brought the threat of revolt. Although many literate and skilled slaves from the Greek east found a comfortable life in the homes of wealthy Romans, the great majority of slaves were consigned to hard labor in the fields and mines under conditions of extreme brutality. Runaway slaves often turned to banditry in the Italian countryside and posed a problem of national security: An army as large as 70,000 slaves terrorized Sicily in 135–132 B.C. and again in 104–100; 100,000 rebellious slaves led by the gladiator Spartacus were crushed in 73–71 after inflicting several defeats on Roman legions.

Provincials were another group that did not necessarily benefit from the increasingly aggressive imperialism that, by the late second century B.C., had brought Rome control of seven overseas provinces: Sicily, Sardinia/Corsica, two in Spain, Macedon, Africa, and Asia (see Map 15). Inhabitants of provinces had none of the guarantees of citizenship and were under the absolute authority of Roman governors, who were often less interested in fair administration than in enriching themselves through excessive taxation. Inclusion in the empire was thus a mixed blessing.

Cultural Change

Roman military conquest of the Greek east was paralleled by Greek cultural conquest of Rome. The events of the third and second centuries B.C. irreversibly altered Roman civilization. Greek ways of living and thinking so penetrated Roman society that we may properly speak of a Greco-Roman culture. As the poet Horace put it, "Captive Greece captured its crude conqueror and brought the arts to

MAP 15
Roman Empire in the Late Republic.

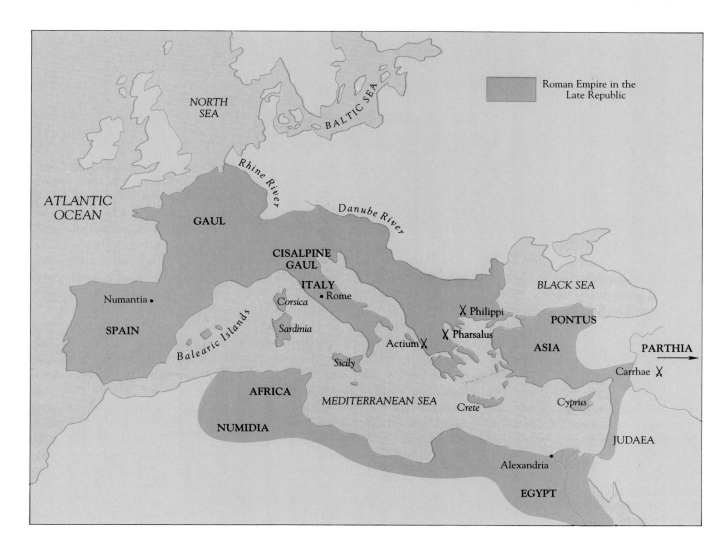

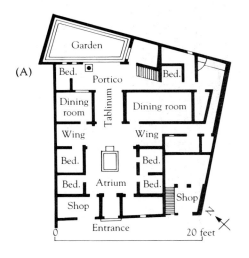

(A)

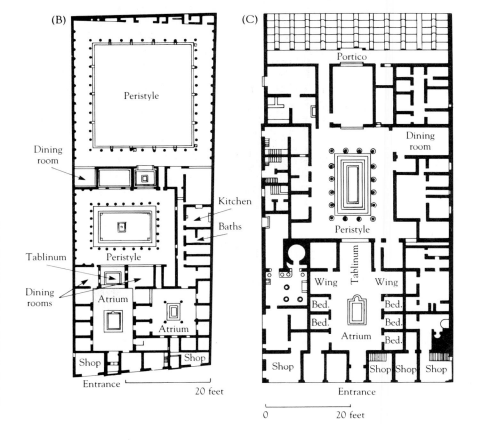

(B)

(C)

Pompeian House Plans. Plans of three houses excavated at Pompeii. "A," the House of the Surgeon, dating before 200 B.C., shows the basic residence, with open atrium to admit light and air, surrounded by a number of small side rooms, dining rooms, and a small garden. "B" and "C" show two second-century houses of a size and elaboration that outdo even their Hellenistic models. Both have amenities like heated baths and huge peristyles (colonnaded gardens) suited to the gracious living cultivated by affluent Roman aristocrats. The House of the Faun (B) has two atriums and two peristyles, one larger in area than the entire House of the Surgeon.

hayseed Latium" (*Epistles* 2.1.156–57).

In the course of campaigns in Campania, Sicily, Greece, and the Hellenistic kingdoms, Roman armies acquired a taste for things Greek. They admired magnificent temples and elaborate festivals, enjoyed dramatic performances in splendid theaters and athletic exercises in palestras. They indulged in the creature comforts of public baths (including *hot* baths!), of luxurious mansions richly furnished and adorned with refined works of art, of sumptuous meals with exotic foods skillfully prepared by master chefs. In imitation, Roman aristocrats beautified their homes with sculptures and vases and their bodies with jewelry and fabrics from cities of the Greek east. Slaves trained as barbers, masseurs, doctors, painters, personal secretaries, scribes, and tutors for children of nobles all brought high prices on the slave market. Romans now went to bakeries for bread made from fine-ground flour in preference to the solidified grain porridge called *polenta* that was a staple of the poor man's diet. *Thermopolia* (taverns) began to dot the streets and served imported wines as well as domestic varieties. Dates, peaches, apricots, lemons, plums, cherries, and spices were introduced to Italy from the east.

The Roman love of spectacle had brought gladiatorial contests from Etruria in 264, and theatrical productions from Greece in the late third and early second centuries. Livius Andronicus (c. 284–c. 204 B.C.) and Quintus Ennius (239–169 B.C.) wrote tragedies, and Plautus (c. 254–184 B.C.) and Terence (c. 190–159 B.C.) produced the first masterpieces of Roman literature by their adaptations of the Greek comic drama of social

THE BACCHIC CULT AND ATTEMPTS TO SUPPRESS IT

To the religious content were added the pleasures of wine and feasting, to attract a greater number. When they were heated with wine, and all sense of modesty had been extinguished by the darkness of night and the commingling of males with females, tender youths with elders, then debaucheries of every kind commenced: each had pleasures at hand to satisfy the lust to which he was most inclined. . . . False witnesses and evidence, forged seals and wills, all issued from this same workshop; also poisonings and murders of kin, so that sometimes the bodies could not even be found for burial. . . . This pestilential evil spread . . . to Rome like a contagious disease. At first the size of the city, with room and tolerance for such evils, concealed it, but information at length reached the consul Postumius. . . . The consuls ordered the curule aediles to search out all the priests of this cult, apprehend them, and keep them under house arrest for the inquiry; the plebeian aediles were to see that no rites were performed in secret. Three commissioners were instructed to post watches throughout the city, to see to it that no nocturnal gatherings took place, and to take precautions against fires. [*]

Livy's account of the Bacchic cult in Italy is sensationalistic, especially in its attribution of sexual impropriety to worshippers (repeated later in the case of Christianity), but bespeaks a real fear on the part of the Roman establishment. Foreign cults seemed to threaten not only the moral fiber of Romans but also the very security of the state. Those who joined in allegiance to a new deity might be tempted to participate in revolt against the Roman government too. A surviving copy of the official senatorial decree regarding the Bacchic cult (186 B.C.) reveals virtual paranoia on the subject. As with other attempts at suppression, persecution only fanned the fires of religious fervor.

[*]Livy, *History of Rome*, 38.8 ff., trans. N. Lewis and M. Reinhold, *Roman Civilization*, rev. ed., vol. 1 (New York: Harper, 1966), pp. 469–470.

mores. The treasure house of Greek literature, from Homer on, entered the Roman school curriculum, and aristocrats employed highly educated Greeks as tutors and schoolmasters. Soon every educated Roman was bilingual and well versed in Greek literature. Andronicus wrote a Latin version of Homer's *Odyssey*, which replaced the Twelve Tables as primer for youngsters learning their mother tongue.

Also in the second century B.C., Epicurean and Stoic philosophers brought their teachings to Rome. Mystery cults too first began to make inroads in the traditional beliefs. Romans indulged in bizarre practices surrounding the worship of the mother-goddess Cybele, imported from Asia Minor in 205, and participated in the orgiastic rites of Bacchus, the god of intoxication. These cults alarmed Roman authorities because of their particularly strong appeal to the downtrodden members of society. Bacchus's worshippers, like those of his Greek equivalent, Dionysus, were

113

POLITICAL CHRONOLOGY OF THE LATE ROMAN REPUBLIC

133	Tribuneship of Tiberius Gracchus
123–122	Tribuneships of Gaius Gracchus
105	Marius ends war with Jugurtha
104–100	Consecutive consulships of Marius
90–88	Social War
82–81	Dictatorship of Sulla
71	Crassus ends revolt of Spartacus
70	Consulship of Pompey and Crassus
63	Consulship of Cicero
60	First Triumvirate
59	Consulship of Caesar; Pompey marries Julia
58	Caesar begins conquest of Gaul
53	Crassus killed at Carrhae
49	Caesar crosses the Rubicon
48	Battle of Pharsalus; Pompey assassinated
44	Assassination of Caesar
43	Second Triumvirate; Cicero proscribed and killed
42	Deaths of Brutus and Cassius at Philippi
36	Octavian defeats Sextus Pompeius, deposes Lepidus
31	Battle of Actium
30	Suicides of Antony and Cleopatra
27	Imperator Caesar Augustus

often groups of women who participated not only to satisfy religious feelings but perhaps also to register a disguised protest against male social dominance.

Many aristocrats admired Greek culture and fostered philosophy and the arts at Rome. Scipio Aemilianus, victor at Carthage in 146 and Numantia in 133, was joined by a number of his friends in sponsoring thinkers, writers, and artists. This "Scipionic Circle" included the comic poet Terence, a man of Libyan origin; the philosopher Panaetius (c. 185–109 B.C.), who adapted the tenets of Stoicism to Roman traditional values; the poet Lucilius (c. 180–102 B.C.), inventor of satire; and the first-rate Greek historian Polybius (c. 200–c. 117 B.C.), who had come to Rome as an Achaean hostage after the defeat of Perseus in 168. A friend and mentor of Scipio Aemilianus, Polybius wrote an honest and lucid history of Rome's rise to power from the Second Punic War to 146; it is our most reliable source for the period.

What some Romans saw as cultural and intellectual advance, others, like the strict moralist Cato, saw as corruption. A canny politician with a reputation for unshakable honesty, Cato opposed the Scipio family and, while disguising his wide knowledge of Greek literature, played the role of curmudgeon-patriot, champion of traditional mores. Cato's failure to stem the tide of "un-Roman" social and intellectual values helped ensure the transmission of Greek culture to later ages of western civilization.

STRONGMEN AND THE BREAKDOWN OF REPUBLICAN GOVERNMENT

From 133 B.C. onward, the ambitions and methods of overly powerful leaders weakened the framework of Roman republican government. Unconstitutional political tactics, mob violence, and assassination began to alter the course of Roman history. Republican political institutions, designed to suit the needs of a geographically limited city-state, proved to be inadequate to the task of governing an extensive empire. The political atmosphere was one of tension between two factions. The *populares* consisted of strong individualists, both patrician and plebeian, whose political policies generally favored the common people. These were opposed by the *optimates*, who consisted of politicians, again both patrician and plebeian, whose policies generally favored the entrenched senatorial elite.

The Brothers Gracchus

The brothers Tiberius (163–133 B.C.) and Gaius (153–121 B.C.) Gracchus were the first in a series of political strongmen whose efforts to shore up the republican system in fact further undermined it. As *populares*, they were concerned about the plight of the small citizen farmer, whose disappearance presented grave difficulties for military conscription, since service in the Roman army was contingent upon land ownership. Further, eligible men often chose not to enlist in fear of hazardous and unrewarding combat duty. As tribune in 133, Tiberius Gracchus sought to replenish the population of small landowners by enforcing a long-ignored law restricting possession of state land to a maximum of 600 acres. All excess land would be confiscated and distributed in small plots to the landless poor. Aristocratic landowners, of course, opposed this measure vigorously. When they persuaded another tribune, Marcus Octavius, to veto the bill, Gracchus took the unconstitutional step of turning Octavius out of office by a vote of the people; he then established a land commission, including himself and his brother, to supervise the redistribution. When Tiberius sought reelection to the tribunate for the very next year—another unconstitutional act—he alienated even some of his own supporters. A mob composed of senatorial opponents and armed bands of their clients murdered Tiberius and 300 of his associates.

Gaius Gracchus, elected tribune in 123 B.C., reactivated the land commission and promoted legislation to lower grain prices and to found colonies to relocate the landless poor. But when he tried to extend full citizenship to the Italian allies, who had served Rome so loyally in the third and second centuries, he offended many plebeians, who were protective of their civic rights. When he resorted to violence in order to defend his policies, the Senate declared a state of emergency and Gaius Gracchus was slain with 3,000 of his men in the ensuing civil disorder.

Marius and Sulla

The murders of the brothers Gracchus taught later reformers the need for superior force as an instrument of political change in their own favor. The first to accumulate and use force was Gaius Marius (157–86 B.C.), an ambitious equestrian *popularis*. Marius solved Rome's recruitment problem and acquired a private army by ignoring property qualifications; he attracted volunteers from the poorest social classes by the prospect of regular pay, booty, and land grants upon discharge. When the *optimates* mismanaged a war against Jugurtha, the upstart ruler of Numidia, equestrian and plebeian support for Marius secured him both the consulship and the command in Africa. Marius was successful when his subordinate, Lucius Cornelius Sulla (138–78 B.C.), arranged for an ally of Jugurtha to betray him.

Marius was chosen to handle a new crisis in 105 B.C., when fearsome hordes of Germanic barbarians defeated Roman forces in southern Gaul (modern France). The Gallic sack of the city in 387 had been indelibly etched in the national memory, and the Roman people, rightly considering Marius their best hope, elected him to an unprecedented five consulships between 104 and 100. Marius responded by crushing the invaders.

Marius professionalized the Roman army. No longer a farmer-militiaman, the new soldier was a career man, methodically trained, often by techniques developed in gladiatorial schools, in the use of short sword and javelin, as well as in entrenchment and camp construction procedures. *Esprit de corps* was stimulated by identification with a particular legion, for which a silver eagle surmounting a standard served as a rallying point. Citizens made up the infantry, and auxiliaries recruited in Crete, Spain, the Balearic Islands, and other pacified regions served as light-armed troops, archers, and slingers.

Marius's military innovations accelerated Romanization of outlying parts of the empire. Discharged veterans settled on land granted them outside Italy in north Africa, Gaul, and elsewhere. These same innovations also shifted soldiers' allegiance from the civil authorities to the military commander. Marius chose not to use his privately raised army against his political competitors for power and sank into obscurity in the nineties. There was no guarantee, however, that another powerful leader would be content to do the same.

In 90 B.C., many of the Italian *socii* (allies), whose help had been so instrumental in Rome's rise to power, were disgruntled at the failure of efforts to secure their full citizenship. They combined in a strong confederation and rebelled against Roman authority. In the ensuing Social War (90–88), the rebels won a number of victories, whereupon Rome defused the revolt by extending citizenship to all Italians south of the Po River. The common bond of citizenship in the peninsula brought a greater uniformity of culture evidenced, for example, in the replacement of local dialects by the Latin language.

Marius's former subordinate Sulla now rose to power and set the precedent, ultimately fatal to the republic, of using military force to achieve his own political ends. A member of the *optimates* faction, he was elected consul in 88 B.C. and received an important command against Mithridates VI of Pontus, who had stirred up an anti-Roman revolt in Asia Minor and Greece. When Marius contested Sulla's command of this eastern campaign, Sulla used his legions to put down opposition. After defeating Mithridates, he returned to Italy in 83, fought a bloody civil war against *populares* opponents, and had himself appointed dictator in 82. He then rooted out his political opponents by creating a new terror. He set forth proscriptions, lists of public enemies (eventually thousands of them) who could be murdered for a reward. The lists included many whose only offense was wealth, for Sulla needed land and money to reward 120,000 faithful troops. Proscribed senators were replaced by supportive equestrians and wealthy Italians. Sulla weakened the authority of tribunes and censors and otherwise strengthened the hand of the Senate. After settling his veterans on confiscated land in Etruria and Campania, he laid down his offices and retired to Campania, where he died in 78.

TWO TRIUMVIRATES AND CONTINUED CIVIL WAR

After Sulla, between 78 and 48 B.C., three new strongmen appeared, accumulating fantastic military and political power. Gnaeus Pompeius (106–48 B.C.), called Pompey the Great, Marcus Licinius Crassus (c. 112–53 B.C.), and Gaius Julius Caesar (100–44 B.C.) cooperated for a time to subvert the republican system in favor of their own personal goals. But finally, the uneasy balance of mighty egos collapsed, to be replaced by the dictatorship of Caesar.

Pompey's early career in the army of Sulla earned him a successful command in Spain between 78 and 72 B.C. Crassus, who had amassed enormous wealth in the Sullan proscriptions, quelled the slave revolt of Spartacus in 71. Seeing the advantage of combining their military and financial resources to control the government, the two men collaborated in gaining the consulships for themselves in 70, and in unraveling Sulla's prosenatorial changes. Pompey was given an extraordinary command, with 120,000 men, 500 ships, and jurisdiction over coastal land for fifty miles inland throughout the Mediterranean, to halt the piracy that had long plagued traders and travelers. After succeeding in that mission, Pompey marched against Mithridates, who was again making trouble in Asia Minor. The old king was driven out of his land and committed suicide in 63. Pompey annexed former Seleucid territories in the east, making Syria (including Palestine) a Roman province and establishing client relationships with a number of kingdoms in a protective buffer zone between Roman territory and that of the strong new Parthian kingdom centered in Persia. Crassus, meanwhile, built up a strong political machine. He increased his immense wealth by astute business deals and mining and real estate investments, and used it to back potentially useful new political supporters.

When Pompey returned from his eastern campaigns in 62 B.C., some feared he might use his military strength to seize power as Sulla had. Pompey, however, disbanded his troops, expecting due recognition of his military achievements and of the arrangements that had greatly increased Rome's revenues from booty and taxation. But Pompey faced resistance from senatorial conservatives who, fearing his prestige, refused to grant land for his veterans. This prompted Pompey to conspire with Crassus and Caesar in 60.

The First Triumvirate

The first triumvirate (three-man group) was an illegal cabal designed to subvert the existing government while advancing the goals of Pompey, Crassus, and a new strongman on the rise, Julius Caesar. The latter had family connections to important *populares* (his paternal aunt was the wife of Marius). Caesar served as quaestor in Spain in 69 B.C. and then as aedile in 65, when he put on lavish public games by borrowing heavily from Crassus. He was praetor in 62 and propraetor in Spain in 61, where he gained more military experience. By the first triumvirate's secret pacts of 60 and 56, each member received consulships, special appointments, and legislative actions. Caesar got a command in Gaul; Pompey got land grants for his loyal veterans and ratification of his administrative settlements in the east; Crassus got a command against the Parthians and concessions for the equestrian businessmen in whose enterprises he had invested heavily. In 59, a politically convenient marriage temporarily sealed the partnership when Pompey wed Caesar's only child, Julia, who died in childbirth five years later.

The phenomenal success of Caesar

in the Gallic Wars of 58–50 B.C. upset this tripartite balance of power. Caesar defeated Germanic invaders from across the Rhine, conquered the Celtic peoples of Gaul, and made forays into Germany and even across the English Channel to the island of Britain. By 51, he had added to the Roman Empire the territory from the Alps to the Atlantic and the North Sea and from the Rhine to the Pyrenees, opening lands outside the Mediterranean basin to Romanization. More immediately, Caesar enriched himself by tremendous booty, shared liberally with his soldiers, and the sale of hundreds of thousands of slaves. His army grew from two to thirteen legions, fanatically devoted to their openhanded and brilliantly successful general.

Meanwhile, Crassus's dream of similar military glory died with him and most of his seven legions on the plains of Mesopotamia, near Carrhae in 53 B.C. The Parthians had developed special horses to carry cataphracts (mailed knights) armed with heavy lances. These hemmed in the Romans, who were then cut down by highly mobile mounted archers supplied by a train of 1,000 camels carrying an inexhaustible quantity of arrows. The Parthians proudly displayed the captured legionary eagle standards (and Crassus's head on a pike) as trophies.

Events now swiftly brought Caesar to supreme power. By 52 B.C., Cato the Younger (95–46 B.C.) had attracted Pompey to the *optimates*. To check mob violence in Rome, a problem throughout the fifties, Pompey was made sole consul with special powers. Then, early in 49, the Senate voted that Caesar should lay down his command before returning to Italy. Since this would open him to

political attacks by the conservative elite at Rome, Caesar chose rebellion and marched across the Rubicon River separating his province from Italy. As he himself put it, the die was cast. By a lightning strike into the peninsula, he forced Pompey to withdraw to Greece with an army loyal to the Senate. Caesar then followed and defeated him in 48 at Pharsalus, where Caesar's veterans courageously withstood cavalry attacks to defeat Pompey's larger army, inflicting heavy losses. Escaping to Alexandria, Pompey was stabbed to death by an agent of the Egyptian king, Ptolemy XIII, who hoped to ingratiate himself with the victor.

Caesar Dictator

Caesar now settled matters from one end of the Mediterranean to the other. He defeated Ptolemy and established the king's sister, Cleopatra (69–30 B.C.), as queen. The charms of this ambitious and intelligent young woman kept him in Egypt nearly a year, seeing the sights and fathering a son, Caesarion. Of his next campaign, in Asia Minor, Caesar proclaimed *veni, vidi, vici* ("I came, I saw, I conquered"). Finally, he defeated remnants of Pompeian forces in north Africa, where Cato committed suicide, and in Spain.

At Rome, Caesar reduced the number of grain dole recipients and founded new colonies and settlements for veterans. He carried out extensive public works and revised the calendar, making it solar rather than lunar. This Julian calendar, with minor refinements, remains to our own day, its authorship commemorated by the name of the seventh month. Caesar also improved tax collection

and liberally extended citizenship, enfranchising the whole of Cisalpine Gaul and admitting many supporters, including non-Italians, into the Senate.

Caesar did not envisage a military autocracy. He discharged most of his veterans after 46 B.C. and did not retain a personal bodyguard. He spared Roman citizens who had fought him in the civil war and tried to heal wounds by securing offices for former aristocratic opponents, including Gaius Cassius and Marcus Brutus (85–42 B.C.), who claimed to be a descendant of the Brutus who expelled Tarquin the Proud.

Despite these conciliatory gestures, Caesar intended to rule in the manner of a Hellenistic monarch. He was successively consul, dictator, and in 44 *dictator perpetuus* (dictator for life); he had been pontifex maximus since 63. This monopoly of authority angered jealous aristocrats and alarmed others, who feared a return to monarchy and naively hoped to revive the republic. A group of such individuals led by Brutus and Cassius murdered Caesar at a meeting of the Senate on the Ides of March 44 B.C.

The Second Triumvirate

The organizers of Caesar's assassination expected Roman citizens to rejoice at their liberation from a tyrant, but the only citizens "liberated" were the aristocrats. The plebeians knew Caesar to be a merciful and generous leader, the Senate was full of new members who owed their position to him, and the armies cherished his name in death as they had in life. Indeed, Caesar was eventually granted divine honors and joined the pantheon of Roman gods.

Silver Denarius. Ancient leaders publicized their achievements and programs on coins. This coin shows the name and likeness of Julius Caesar with his title of dictator for life. It is his earliest known portrait (44 B.C.). British Museum.

Marcus Tullius Cicero. This bust of Cicero is a first-century copy of an original done when the orator was about sixty (c. 46 B.C.). It shows him as a distinguished senior senator, a role he relished. Cicero was a vain man, proud of his oratorical powers but insecure because of his nonaristocratic origins. In the end, the force of his words—in the *Philippics*—cost him his life. Capitoline Museum, Rome.

Once again, powerful men chose their own advantage over constitutionality. Mark Antony (c. 83–30 B.C.), consul with Caesar in 44, soon gained control at Rome. Caesar's will revealed his unexpected adoption of his eighteen-year-old grandnephew, Gaius Octavius (63 B.C.–A.D. 14), who now assumed the magically prestigious name and became Gaius Julius Caesar Octavianus (Octavian). This surprisingly mature and politically cunning young man used his vast inherited riches to raise armies and buy influence. Cicero (106–43 B.C.), who wanted to restore the prestige of the Senate and reinstate the old republican order of things, hoped to play off Octavian against Antony. He delivered scathing speeches against the latter, entitled *Philippics* after Demosthenes' attacks on Philip II of Macedon. In 43, however, Octavian joined Antony and another senior Caesarian officer, Marcus Aemilius Lepidus, in becoming "Triumvirs for the Reordering of the Republic." The triumvirs were legally invested with extraordinary powers; as dictators in all but name, they ruthlessly followed the grim example of Sulla and pro-

scribed some 300 senators and 2,000 *equites*, eliminating enemies and acquiring money to pay some forty-five legions under their command. Antony, stung by the *Philippics*, insisted on Cicero's inclusion and had the murdered orator's head and hands nailed to the rostra (speaking platform) in the forum. Antony and Octavian went to the east and, at the battle of Philippi in 42 B.C., defeated Cassius and Brutus, who both committed suicide rather than be captured. Julius Caesar had been avenged.

As in the earlier case, the new triumvirate turned into a dictatorship of one man. After Philippi, the triumvirs divided the Roman world: Spain and Gaul went to Octavian, Africa to Lepidus, and the east to Antony. Italy was to be held in common. But the second triumvirate was even less stable than the first, and soon began to collapse.

Octavian rapidly became a skillful political and military leader. In 36 B.C., he defeated the son of Pompey, Sextus Pompeius (c. 67–36 B.C.), who had troubled the seas as a pirate-king in Sicily and Sardinia after Julius Caesar's death. When Lepidus then tried to lay claim to Sicily, Octavian simply deposed him and absorbed his armies. It was a case of a political nonentity unable to take advantage of the chances that Julius Caesar's favor had provided him.

Antony, meanwhile, allied himself, politically and romantically, with the still-alluring Cleopatra, prompting Octavian to depict him in his propaganda as a man driven by delusions of grandeur and by obsession with the Egyptian *femme fatale.* Octavian eventually persuaded the western provinces, Italy, and most of the surviving Roman aristocracy that Antony meant to shift the center of empire to Alexandria. In 31 B.C., after receiving an oath of allegiance from the entire west, Octavian crossed to Greece and defeated Antony and Cleopatra at the naval battle of Actium. When he took Alexandria the following year, Antony committed suicide to avoid capture, as did Cleopatra, last Hellenistic ruler in the Ptolemaic line from Alexander's day.

THE PRINCIPATE

Octavian's triumph inaugurated a new era in Roman history called the empire, which lasted some five centuries. *Empire* and *imperial* in this context refer to the period of rule by emperors; the territorial empire of Rome already existed in the period of republican government. This epoch witnessed a fusing of cultural traditions—Near Eastern, Greek, and Roman—that together shaped western civilization. As uncontested master of the whole Roman world, Octavian learned from the mistakes of Julius Caesar, shunned the names and external trappings of monarchy or dic-

tatorship, and adopted instead the inoffensive title of *princeps* (first citizen). Thus the first stage of Roman imperial history is often called the principate. In 27 B.C., he accepted the name Imperator Caesar Augustus (in Latin, *augustus* means "venerable" or "majestic") and announced his intention to restore republican institutions. Even the title *imperator,* from which the word *emperor* derives, had traditional overtones, since it was customarily given to victorious military commanders during the republic. However, the next forty-one years brought not a restoration of old ways of governance but the steady, calculated implementation of a new monarchy, which veiled naked absolute power in the garments of moderation and traditional values.

The transition to imperial rule was successful in large part because of the perceptiveness and talents of the first emperor. Augustus never tired of reminding the world that he had brought peace after the traumas of civil war and political chaos that had wrecked the republic. This cherished peace, the Pax Augusta, and Augustus's shrewd outward show of respect for republican institutions together made his monopoly of power tolerable to those who might still yearn for the old republic. Augustus, a master of the techniques of propaganda, used every available means to shape public opinion. Poets and historians were encouraged to give a patriotic cast to their writings. Monumental art and architecture celebrated Roman civic pride. Coins and their inscriptions promoted the policies and achievements of the regime. The emperor engaged in displays of religious piety and made direct public benefactions. He became pontifex maximus in 13 B.C., after the death of his predeces-

Octavian. This bust shows Octavian at about age thirty, not long before the battle of Actium. He appears as a determined leader, his brow furrowed in concentration. In fact, Octavian suffered fragile health throughout his life. His greatest skills were administrative, and he wisely surrounded himself with men who possessed the kinds of expertise he himself lacked. Capitoline Museum, Rome.

sor in that office, the former triumvir Lepidus. His purposes were to gloss over atrocities he had committed on the road to domination, to conceal his own dictatorial position, and to avoid the fate of Julius Caesar.

Beyond his propaganda measures, Augustus had a genuine respect for old-fashioned Roman traditions and a desire to reinvigorate a society demoralized by civil strife. He posed as the religious leader and arbiter of moral values for the Roman people. In this capacity, he passed legislation designed to encourage marriage and strengthen the family, the chief value-generating institution of Roman life. This legislation was often unsuccessful, and Augustus later exiled his own daughter for adultery.

On the emperor's powers and prerogatives there were no curbs other than his own sense of propriety and duty. All citizens took an oath of personal loyalty to the emperor, not to the state. Augustus maintained the fiction of republicanism by allowing citizens to fill the various magistracies at public elections, but accepted tribunician power that enabled him to veto whatever legislative actions displeased him. He made a show of sharing control of provinces with the Senate, but kept jurisdiction in those provinces where legions were stationed. Despite the lip service paid to republican forms, the consulship was an utterly hollow office. Thus

Augustus possessed ultimate civil and military authority.

The tremendous personal prestige of the emperor gave a focus to the world he ruled, but also retarded the independence of those aristocrats who had survived proscriptions and civil war. It was natural that ambitious and talented men increasingly sought advancement and rewards by subservience to the individual from whom all power derived. A cult of the divinity of the ruler grew up first in the areas of the Hellenistic east accustomed to pay such homage to kings. In Italy, Augustus and many of his successors were voted divine honors after their deaths.

Augustus's stupendous personal wealth allowed him to win and maintain the people's favor. He built new forum areas, renovated temples, and improved roads and the sewer system. He also financed public games, including gladiator shows, and kept grain prices artificially low. He set the precedent for later emperors in his skillful use of such methods.

The long duration of the emperor's rule had very practical advantages over the short tenure of the republican magistracies. Augustus created a badly needed civil service by training and employing both his own highly skilled slaves and freedmen and knowledgeable *equites* to oversee the functioning of the central administration and the provincial governments. The result

was greater stability, fairness, and efficiency. To cite one very practical improvement, Augustus divided the city of Rome itself into fourteen districts and stationed fire brigades and police in each.

Augustus's foreign policy was essentially defensive. Unlike Alexander, he engaged in conquest, not for for its own sake, but to secure borders. He regained the standards Crassus had lost to the Parthians by negotiation rather than warfare. Judaea now became a separate province, Gaul was reorganized, and the final pacification of Spain was achieved. The Rhine-Danube border became a natural dividing line between the increasingly Romanized west and the Germanic tribes of central and eastern Europe. Augustus encouraged the growth and local self-government of towns and planted many new colonies. Tranquillity within the empire and stable central government stimulated commercial and manufacturing activity throughout the Mediterranean.

So long as the emperor was competent and assisted by men of similar qualities, all was well, but a potential for abuse was inherent in the system. Not all emperors had the dedication and talent for administration of Augustus. In the years after his death in A.D. 14, Augustus's successors sometimes strained the imperial system of government by their eccentricities and whimsical brutalities.

SUMMARY

The second century B.C. saw the extension of Roman dominance to the Hellenistic world. One by one, Macedon, Syria, and Greece were defeated by the legions of Rome, which added these large territories to its provincial administration. By 146 B.C., the Romans were able to speak with pride of the Mediterranean Sea as *mare nostrum* ("our sea").

Conquest in the east spelled irreversible changes for Roman social, economic, and intellectual life. The more developed and refined tastes in physical comforts that Roman soldiers brought back from their campaigns affected all levels of society. Its new affluence enabled Rome to import cooks and philosophers, barbers and tutors, athletes and poets, the entertainments of the arena and those of the theater.

In particular, Greek cultural ideas and practices penetrated deeply into the lives of the Roman conquerors. Aware of the marvelous achievements of the classical and Hellenistic Greeks, the Roman upper classes borrowed from Greek literary, artistic, and philosophical traditions. They educated themselves in high culture to signal their worthiness of the political dominance to which they had risen.

The nearly incessant warfare of the second century and the enslavement of hundreds of thousands caused dislocations in the old agricultural society of Rome and jeopardized military preparedness. When the brothers Gracchus tried to correct this, the senatorial oligarchy responded with violence, damaging republican governmental machinery and opening the door to political violence and assassination. Marius solved the military recruitment problem by professionalizing the Roman army, but he and Sulla also set the dangerous precedent of diverting the allegiance of the soldiers away from the civilian government to themselves.

Increasing civil unrest in the first century B.C. paved the way for dictatorship. Pompey, Crassus, and Julius Caesar vied for supreme power and dug the grave of the dying republic. Caesar emerged triumphant from civil war; his assassination, however, set off one final power struggle. Octavian's victory over Antony and virtually every other opponent, military or political, left the Roman people exhausted and the republic a bloody and mangled corpse.

Octavian became Augustus and brought about a reconstruction and redirection that sustained Rome through another 500 years. The full development of the Roman cultural life that so strongly influenced western civilization took place in the context of an imperial political system.

SELECTED SOURCES

Africa, Thomas W. *The Immense Majesty: A History of Rome and the Roman Empire*. 1974. A recent, reliable, and well-written history of Rome. It provides a balanced assessment of the good and the evil resulting from Rome's rise to empire.

*Brunt, P. A. *Social Conflicts in the Roman Republic*. 1971. Particularly valuable on economic conditions, patricians versus plebeians, and the disintegration of the political system from the brothers Gracchus down to Octavian.

*Caesar, Julius. *The Battle for Gaul*. Translated by Anne and Peter Wiseman. 1980. An excellent new translation of Caesar's fascinating commentaries on his campaigns in Gaul, including useful illustrations and superb topographical maps.

*Copley, Frank O., and Moses Hadas, trans. *Roman Drama*. 1965. Includes three comedies by Plautus (*Menaechmi*, *The Haunted House*, and *The Rope*) and three by Terence (*Andria*, *Phormio*, and *The Brothers*).

Grant, Michael. *Julius Caesar*. 1969. A good biography of the Roman general and dictator, with plentiful illustrations.

Grant, Michael. *Cleopatra*. 1972. A lively companion biography to the author's *Julius Caesar*. It carries the story of the intriguing queen through her liaison and marriage with Mark Antony to her suicide by snakebite in 30 B.C..

*Jones, A. H. M. *Augustus*. 1970. The best recent account of the life and times of the first Roman emperor and of the system of government he instituted.

Kubrick, Stanley, dir. *Spartacus* 1960. An epic film (192 minutes) romanticizing the life of the gladiator rebel; Kirk Douglas (as Spartacus), Charles Laughton, Laurence Olivier, Peter Ustinov, and literally "a cast of thousands."

*Shackleton Bailey, D. R. *Cicero*. 1971. A biography based mainly on the 900 surviving letters of Cicero's correspondence, in which "we see a Roman Consular, . . . one of the most remarkable men of his eventful time, without his toga" (p. xii).

*Wiedemann, Thomas. *Greek and Roman Slavery*. 1981. An extremely helpful and thorough sourcebook of 243 selections from ancient inscriptions, literature, and legal documents on the subject.

*Available in paperback.

ROMAN CULTURAL ACHIEVEMENTS
(c. 70 B.C.–c. A.D. 130)

King Romulus shall found the walls of Mars,
and name his people "Romans" for himself.
For them I set no bounds of place or time;
rule without end I grant them. . . .
A Caesar shall spring of noble Trojan line
(Ocean shall bound his power, the stars his fame)—
Julius, a name come down from great Iulus.
Laden one day with spoil of the East, he'll have
welcome to heaven, and men will pray to him.
Hard hearts will soften then and wars will cease;
old Faith and Vesta, Romulus and Remus
will rule the world; tight bands of steel will close
the terrible temple of War, where Blood-Lust caged
will crouch on barbarous spears, bound hundredfold
with chains of bronze, screaming and slavering blood.

In this passage near the opening of his *Aeneid,* the epic poet Vergil
represents Jupiter granting unlimited and eternal power to Rome.
Prominently mentioned by the king of gods are the founding father,
Romulus, and his descendant Julius Caesar, whose accomplishments earn
him a place among the gods. Then comes the culmination of Roman rule
in the Augustan era of peace, so memorably celebrated in the *Aeneid,* the
greatest masterpiece of Latin literature.

These lines typify a primary motivation of Roman literature, art, and
architecture—the celebration of achievements in government and
conquest. Augustus, in particular, wished his people to think with pride of
their glorious history and to accept the image of himself as a generous,
fatherly, and wise leader. Whether or not they agreed with the emperor's
self-portrayal, the inhabitants of the Roman Empire did enjoy a remarkably
long period of freedom from the fiendish god Blood-Lust, who had plagued
the late republic. And in that context of security, Roman culture came to
full flower, not only in the "high" art forms—literature, art, architecture—
but also in the improvements of daily life by Roman technology and

The Emperor Augustus. This statue shows Augustus the supreme commander standing in the
pose of the heroic warrior familiar from Greek sculpture. His elaborately carved breastplate
depicts a noteworthy diplomatic triumph: The Parthian king submissively returns the standards
lost by Crassus at the Battle of Carrhae. By Augustus's right leg is the god Cupid, a reminder
that the Julian family traced its ancestry back to Iulus and his father Aeneas, who was, like
Cupid, a son of the goddess Venus. The intimation of divine right of kings is obvious. From
the villa of Augustus's wife Livia at Prima Porta, north of Rome; Vatican Museum.

123

Cicero: oratory, essays, letters

Augustan publicity program

Seneca: tragedies, essays

Lucretius: *On the Nature of Things*

Maecenas: Vergil, *Aeneid;* Horace, *Odes*

Petronius, *Satyricon*

Juvenal, *Satires*

engineering. Spiritual life also flourished in the early imperial period, as important new patterns of religious belief emerged. The present chapter examines these cultural developments.

THE GLORIES OF LATIN LITERATURE

Despite the political chaos of the time, Roman literature came of age in the late republic. It subsequently reached its zenith in the age of Augustus and in the century or so after his death.

The Age of Cicero

The first truly great master of Latin language and style was Cicero (106–43 B.C.). In 70, his speeches against a corrupt governor of Sicily established his reputation, not only as a lawyer and politician, but also as a man of letters, worthy of comparison with Demosthenes. Among the best known of Cicero's surviving speeches are those against the disgruntled nobleman Catiline, who attempted a *coup d'état* during Cicero's consulship in 63 B.C., and the verbal cannon blasts of the *Philippics*, which he directed against Mark Antony. He also wrote authoritative rhetorical and political treatises whose emphasis on civic responsibility formed an ideal of patriotism for later ages, especially the fifteenth-century Italian Renaissance. In a lighter vein are the treatises *On Friendship* and *On Old Age,* delightful reflections on ethical living by a man wise in experience. The 900 extant letters of Cicero's correspondence with friends and relations, because they were written without any idea of future publication, give us unparalleled insights into the character of an ancient author with all his human insecurities and vanities.

The balanced rhythms of Cicero's long sentences and his forceful word choice and arrangement made him the model of all who aspired to write Latin correctly from antiquity right through the Renaissance. So great was the Roman orator's stylistic authority that, centuries later, one Christian prelate found himself unable to refer to the Holy Spirit in a Latin sermon because there was no word for it in Cicero.

Another major participant in the politics of the late republic, Julius Caesar, was also a man of letters. His speeches, said to be second only to Cicero's in quality, are lost, but we do have the *Commentaries*, extensive reports of the events of the Gallic and civil wars. Stylistically spare and free from rhetorical flourishes, they are a great general's masterly and exciting descriptions of the nature of warfare. Caesar, however, like nearly every politician-autobiographer, sometimes amplified his successes while concealing his failures, for example, during the invasion of Britain. He portrayed himself always as a loyal patriot serving his country and his adversaries as petty and unpatriotic. Despite this element of propaganda, Caesar wrote about his role in history as brilliantly as he acted it. Napoleon said the education of every general should include careful reading of Caesar.

The greatest Roman poet of the republic, Lucretius (c. 94–c. 55 B.C.), produced a single masterpiece, the *De Rerum Natura (The Nature of Things)*, published posthumously, probably in the late fifties, after final editing by Cicero himself. In this long poem, Lucretius presented the central axioms of Epicurean philosophy with consummate artistry and fervent commitment. He believed unswervingly that poetry should teach as well as delight and that, in particular, a grasp of atomic theory would free his readers from superstitious anxieties about the role of gods in the universe. Lucretius became the most eloquent and inspired apostle of Epicurus, whom he especially admired for the intellectual integrity he showed in bravely dispelling the terrors of conventional Greco-Roman religious belief.

The great achievement of Lucretius in his philosophical poem was to enliven the dry expositions of Epicurus by presenting keen observations of the natural world. Particularly ingenious are the images used to prove the existence of atoms: "Consider when sunlight enters a darkened room how tiny specks intermix in space within the rays. . . . Thus invisible movements of colliding atoms little by little impinge on our senses as the specks we see in the sun's rays are impelled by imperceptible blows" (2.114–17, 138–141). Lucretian poetic language is strikingly musical and marked by the coining of words, both for poetic effect and to circumvent the lack of a Latin scientific vocabulary. Although little appreciated in antiquity, Lucretius found avid admirers in the modern era among poets such as Percy Bysshe Shelley and Alfred Tennyson, and philosophers and political theorists, including Voltaire and Jean Jacques Rousseau.

Another great Roman writer speaks with a distinctively modern voice. Gaius Valerius Catullus (c. 84–c. 54 B.C.) lived most of his adult life at Rome, as a member of a chic group of avant-garde writers called "New Poets." Many of his poems were inspired by his love for the woman he called Lesbia, in reality one Clodia, by birth and marriage a member of the highest aristocracy. According to various sources, especially Cicero, who attacked her in a speech on behalf of one of her former lovers, Clodia was beautiful, ultrafashionable, witty, nymphomaniacal, adulterous, and

THE TRUE NATURE OF THE SOUL

Come now and learn that mind and soul (slight things)
are born in living creatures and must die. . . .
To begin, since I have proved [soul] delicate
and made of tiny atoms—particles
much smaller than those of clear and fluid water,
or fog or smoke, for it is far more mobile
and moved by impulse far more delicate.
Why! it is moved by the image of smoke and fog!
Just as when asleep and deep in dreams, we see
altars breathing out vapors and making smoke,
these come to us, no doubt, as images.
Now since, from jars all badly cracked, you see
water leak out and liquids flow away,
since fog and smoke, too, scatter to the winds,
be sure that soul disperses even faster
and dies more quickly, dissolving into atoms
once it has gone and left our human frame.
Now since the body—the soul's jar, so to speak—
when somehow badly damaged and left porous
by drainage of blood, cannot contain the soul,
how do you think a thing like air could hold it,
a substance much more porous than our flesh?*

Much of Lucretius's Epicurean poem propounds an atomic theory of nature. According to that theory, all the things humans describe as "existing" are simply particular arrangements of atoms. The "death" of any existing thing is merely a change in the arrangement of atoms, which are indestructible and continue to exist for all time. This is of pivotal importance in Epicureanism, for it ultimately leads to the conclusion that souls must "die." This seemingly bitter realization is essential to the attainment of the inner tranquillity aimed at by the philosophy, for it frees the mind from oppressive anxieties about an afterlife where souls are judged and punished or, at best, suffer the anguish of separation from the good things of earthly life.

*Lucretius, The Nature of Things, trans. Frank O. Copley (New York: Norton, 1977), Book 3, lines 417–418, 425–444.

perhaps murderous. Catullus's Lesbia cycle, comprising about one-fourth of his surviving 113 poems, traces his progress from first infatuation,

Let's do some living, my Lesbia, and loving,
and not give a damn for the gossip
of all those stern old moralists . . .
(Poem 5.1-3)

through uneasy consummation,

My woman says there's nobody she'd rather marry
than me, not even if Jupiter himself were to ask.
She says . . . , but whatever a woman tells an eager lover
should be written on wind and rushing water (Poem 70)

to prolonged and hurtful realization,

> Catullus, you damned fool, stop being ridiculous,
> and what you see is lost, count lost . . .
> (Poem 8.1-2)

and finally bitter renunciation,

> Let her live and thrive with lewd lovers,
> embracing three hundred at a time,
> loving none truly, busting their humps over and over. (Poem 11)

Other poems transcribe such diverse experiences as practical jokes, a visit to the distant grave of a beloved brother, a mock funeral lament for a pet sparrow, and the delight of homecoming after a long absence.

Catullus's is the art that conceals art. His words appear simply to pour forth strongly felt emotions, but they fall into rhythmic cadences borrowed from the Greek lyrics of Sappho and others. Catullus is an engagingly experimental poet, both in poetic craftsmanship and in candid exploration of emotional responses.

The great writers of the republican era often had to look for support from wealthy aristocratic patrons with a taste for literature and the arts, since they could not expect profits from sales of large printings or multiple editions. Indeed, "publication" in ancient times meant the production of a few manuscripts by teams of slaves owned and supervised by wealthy businessmen. Cicero's friend Atticus was one such "publisher."

The Golden Age of Augustus

During his reign, Augustus, who had first shown his ability to channel public opinion during the struggle with Antony, monopolized the patronage of the very best literary talents. His intent was to restore the morale of educated Romans by means of poetry and history advocating nationalistic ideals of patriotism and morality. With his wealthy chief administrator, Maecenas (c. 70–8 B.C.), who was a connoisseur of the arts and generous sponsor of poets, he fostered a literature worthy of comparison with that of classical Greece. The writings of the Augustan "Golden Age" not only gave aesthetic pleasure but also promoted civic virtues and pride in the fatherland.

Vergil (70–19 B.C.) was born near the small town of Mantua in northern Italy. As a young man, he came to Rome to complete his education in rhetoric. By 30, he had attracted the attention and the patronage of Maecenas by two collections of poems, the pastoral *Eclogues* and the *Georgics*, poetic celebrations of the cycles of nature and of the lives of those who raised the animals and cultivated the good earth of Italy. These poems are of the very highest technical virtuosity. Vergil took seven years to compose the *Georgics*, a rate of less than a line per day. Influenced by Hellenistic standards of poetic craftsmanship as well as by Catullus and Lucretius, Vergil's work shows greater polish in its metrical rhythms and verbal music than any Latin poetry before or after.

Between 30 B.C. and his death in 19, Vergil created the *Aeneid*, one of the greatest poems of world literature. It describes the exploits of the Trojan hero Aeneas, familiar from Homer's *Iliad*, after the fall of his city. The gods choose Aeneas to lead a band of Trojan refugees on a long, perilous journey to the shores of Italy, where his descendants are to mingle with native Italians and found Rome. Since the gods in the epic gradually disclose the manifest destiny of the Roman Empire, the poem was both foundation myth and mission statement for the Roman people.

Vergil on his deathbed is said to have left instructions that the *Aeneid* be burned rather than published without the final touches he had wanted to give it. Fortunately, Augustus countermanded those orders.

The *Aeneid* succeeds for three reasons. First, without being jingoistic, it gave Augustus and the Roman world a national epic. The emperor may have wanted a poem about his own triumphs and the glory of his empire, but the *Aeneid* instead describes a heroic past some four centuries before the foundation of Rome. Aeneas, however, prefigures the patriotic Roman; by persisting in his difficult mission and obeying the will of the gods, he earns the epithet "pious." Despite the loss of home, relatives, and the women he loves, and despite his own indecision and fear, Aeneas never fails in his duty. Such a self-sacrificing man, so unlike Homer's more egocentric heroes, was precisely the ideal Augustus wished to hold up as a model of patriotic devotion in troubled times.

Second, the *Aeneid* succeeds in challenging the preeminence of both Homeric poems as standards for the genre. In the first half of the *Aeneid*, we have Vergil's equivalent of the *Odyssey*, as Aeneas survives many adventures during his quest for Italy. In the second half, we have his *Iliad*, recounting warfare between the Trojans and the Italians over a woman. Though there are many Homeric reminiscences, Vergil consistently makes new what he has borrowed. No other epic poet in the 700 intervening years had done the same.

Third, the *Aeneid*, despite its 8,000-line length, maintains the exquisite line-by-line matching of sound and sense that is normally possible only in short poems. In its imagery and the complex interweaving of themes and motifs, the *Aeneid* exerted a powerful influence on epic tradition in European literature, an influence visible in the works of Dante Alighieri and John Milton, among others.

Another first-magnitude poet of the Augustan period was Horace (65–8 B.C.). After working for a time as a clerk in the treasury, he met Maecenas and impressed him by a series of amusing satires that genially poked fun at human misbehavior and espoused a sensible Epicureanism. Maecenas set him up with a small place in the country, and Horace found himself in the position of poet laureate after Vergil's death.

Horace's *Odes*, written between 30 and 13 B.C., are compact poems on such universal subjects as love, pleasure, the brevity of life, and art and nature. More studied in design than the poems of Catullus and showing an extremely high linguistic and metrical finish, they are filled with memorable gemlike phrases like *carpe diem* ("seize the day") and with patriotic sentiments ("sweet and fitting it is to die for one's country"). Horace declined to produce an epic but extolled in some odes the blessed security and social regeneration of the Augustan age. Horace was translated into Italian, French, German, and English as early as the sixteenth century and was later admired and imitated by such poets as William Wordsworth, Robert Browning, and Tennyson. Louis XIV thought, in-

ROME'S MISSION AMONG NATIONS

Others will cast more tenderly in bronze
Their breathing figures, I can well believe,
and bring more lifelike portraits out of marble;
Argue more eloquently, use the pointer
To trace the paths of heaven accurately
And accurately foretell the rising stars.
Roman, remember by your strength to rule
Earth's peoples—for your arts are to be these:
To pacify, to impose the rule of law,
To spare the conquered, battle down the proud. *

With these words, Aeneas's father, Anchises, forecasts a thousand years of Roman history, down to Vergil's own day. He singles out the art of government as the special contribution of the Roman people, whose manifest destiny was to unify Earth's peoples into a peaceable order. This was something to be proud of, something excelling even the achievements of "others" (that is, Greeks) in the arts and sciences. Aeneas needed to hear this message at this point in the epic, and Roman citizens needed to hear it in the post-civil-war times of Vergil.

*Vergil, The Aeneid, trans. R. Fitzgerald (New York: Random, 1983), Book 6, lines 847–853.

correctly, that the Horatian theme of the Golden Mean was an endorsement of tranquil acceptance of autocratic rule.

In these years as well, Livy (59 B.C.–A.D. 17) wrote his massive history of Rome from the founding of the city down to his own day. The *History*, like the *Aeneid*, furnished models of patriotic heroism and morality for Roman readers. Thirty-five of the original 142 books survive. The first five books, on the legendary early history of the city, and the books dealing with the Second Punic War have always been among the best loved. In his concentration on important Romans making momentous decisions, Livy often distorted for the sake of literary or moral effects; he was also less critical in his judgments

and handling of sources than, for example, Thucydides or Polybius. The *History* was both an immediate popular success and influential in later ages. Niccolò Machiavelli wrote a long commentary, the *Discourses*, on the first ten books; Shakespeare drew on Livy in his *Rape of Lucrece;* and the heroes of the *History* were very appealing to readers during the French Revolution of 1789–1799.

Not all Roman writers could accommodate literary genius to the Augustan publicity program. Ovid (43 B.C.–A.D. 17), for example, was the most gracefully fluent of all Roman poets, but his principal subject matter—erotic love—was not morally edifying. Ovid's advice about sexual flirtation, including makeup and body language, was often tongue in cheek, but Augustus failed to see the humor. In A.D. 8, Ovid was exiled to the distant shores of the Black Sea, where he died after writing plaintive poems appealing for repatriation. His most influential work is the *Metamorphoses*, a collection of some 250 delightfully narrated myths centering on miraculous transformation. These include, for example, the myths of Apollo and Daphne, captured in marble by the baroque sculptor Giovanni Bernini, and of Narcissus, used by Sigmund Freud in describing the psychology of infantile self-love. Arthur Golding's English version of 1567, a landmark of the art of translation, was well known to Shakespeare. The *Metamorphoses* has always been an intriguing source of inspiration for artists and writers.

The Imperial Silver Age

The era from A.D. 14 to c. 130 is often called the "silver age" to indicate that the writings of the time, though of great value, were not up to the standards of the Augustan age. Overly ornate rhetorical flourishes and lack of depth and originality in content were symptoms of the decline. A few silver age writers, however, must be placed in the first rank of world literature.

Seneca (c. 4 B.C.–A.D. 65) is known for his nine tragedies and a variety of letters and essays espousing the doctrines of Stoic philosophy. His versions of *Oedipus, Medea, Agamemnon*, and other Greek tragedies were not produced on stage, but fascinated readers by their rhetorical artistry and grotesquely horrific accounts of human cruelty and suffering. The plays exerted an influence on European literatures, notably the Elizabethan

drama of Shakespeare and Christopher Marlowe, out of proportion to their literary merit.

Seneca's philosophical essays are mainly guides to achieving Stoic equanimity in times of grief or anger or good fortune. One essay, *On Clemency*, instructed the Emperor Nero, whom Seneca served as tutor and adviser, in the advantages of mercy in an autocratic ruler. The most popular of his works were the 124 *Moral Epistles*, which temper official Stoic doctrine by the studied informality of their reflections on such topics as friendship, old age, slavery, suicide, and life after death. Unlike Cicero's, these are not true letters, but were intended for publication from the beginning. Christian writers, like Jerome and Augustine, admired their uplifting moral messages. In 65, Seneca was wrongly accused of participating in a plot against Nero, and accepted the emperor's invitation to commit suicide.

Petronius (?–A.D. 66), another courtier of Nero's, wrote a peculiar work entitled *Satyricon*, which combines elements of satire, mock epic (based on the *Odyssey*), and novel. The surviving fragment of the original work tells of three freeloaders who have bizarre and madcap adventures while wandering from port to port from the coast of southern France to the toe of the Italian boot. Prominent plot elements are con games designed to cadge money or a meal and often involving humorously deviant sexual antics. A strong element of traditional satire can be found in the portrayal of a self-made millionaire freedman living in luxury on the Bay of Naples: The character Trimalchio, with his riotously funny blend of fabulous wealth and boorish manners, is

an incisive stereotype of the new rich. The *Satyricon* was not influential among ancient writers, but has numbered such later authors as John Dryden, Voltaire, and T. S. Eliot among its devotees.

The greatest Roman historian was Tacitus (c. A.D. 56–c. 120), who, in his *Histories* and *Annals*, created our best and most extensive narrative of the period from 14 to 96. Written early in the second century in a distinctively direct and pointed style, these works present the early empire from the perspective of a man disgusted with both the emperors' abuses of power and the subservience of the aristocratic classes. Tacitus gave his readers unforgettable portraits: the mistrustful Tiberius listening to the charges of informers and indulging in sexual perversions at his villa on Capri; the genial but naive Claudius, manipulated by scheming wives and freedmen; and, of course, Nero with his uncontrolled passions and delusions of artistic grandeur. More than any other Roman historian, Tacitus shaped posterity's view of an important historical era. The cynicism with which Tacitus stripped bare the hypocrisy and brutality underlying the Roman Imperial Peace led Napoleon to call him a "traducer of humanity." Astute critics, however, including Machiavelli, Rousseau, and writers of the French Revolutionary period, have valued his judgments.

As Tacitus attacked the political impotence of the aristocratic class, Juvenal (c. A.D. 60–c. 135) trained the powerful weapon of his biting satire on the social and moral degeneration of the same class. The Emperor Domitian exiled Juvenal to a remote corner of Egypt for criticizing favoritism in the system of political ad-

The Altar of the Augustan Peace. The enclosing wall is decorated with very fine sculptural reliefs showing Augustus and his family piously leading a procession of senatorial aristocrats to the dedication ceremony. It was part of Augustus's publicity program after Actium to emphasize that he had brought enduring peace after civil strife. The panel to the right of the door shows Aeneas offering sacrifice to the gods in good Roman form. Completed in 9 B.C., excavated in the twentieth century, and now housed in a special exhibit building in Rome.

vancement. When he returned after the murder of the emperor in 96, Juvenal was destitute. It was a deeply humiliating experience: "the poor man is a constant occasion for cruel jokes, with his cheap thread-bare cloak, his dirty toga, and badly mended shoes. . . . The mockery it brings a man is poverty's worst curse" (*Satire* 3, lines 147–152). In the years between his return and his death, Juvenal produced sixteen satires filled with outraged portrayals of human misbehavior and injustice. He mercilessly denounced those he felt were corrupting Roman society, especially the oily eastern immigrants or "Greeklings" who succeeded by gladly taking the most unsavory jobs while seducing the wives and children of native Romans. Juvenal's longest satire is a scathingly obscene account of the sins of upperclass married women, including even the wives of past emperors. Other satires attack Egyptians, homosexuals, soldiers, hypocritical philos-

ophers, and, of course, the evil Domitian. In viewing the great parade of vice with his notebooks in hand, Juvenal turned the tables on those who asked why he wrote by remarking, "It is difficult not to write satire." Juvenal's transformation of painful moral indignation into literary art made him the archetypal satirist in western civilization. His more illustrious translators and adapters include Dryden and Samuel Johnson.

Among less important writers, two biographers may be mentioned. The gossipy Suetonius (c. A.D. 69–c. 140), in his *Lives of the Caesars* from Julius to Domitian anticipated modern popular tabloids and magazines in his emphasis on sensational details about the personal lives of his subjects. More uplifting are the famous *Lives* of Plutarch (c. A.D. 46–c. 126), a Greek who wrote about important figures of Greek and Roman history, often in a "parallel lives" format matching Greek and Roman figures. Demosthenes and

Cicero, for example, are paired and similarities in their careers and writings stressed. The strongly moralistic *Lives* has always been popular reading. Thomas North's stirring translation of 1579 powerfully influenced English literature and furnished the raw material for Shakespeare's plays on Roman themes.

ACCOMPLISHMENTS IN ART AND ARCHITECTURE

Roman sculpture and painting derived almost entirely from Greek models. Indeed, Romans made thousands of exact reproductions of Greek works of art. The innovations in their own original works were not in technical craftsmanship but in more realistic representation of form and in the practical functions of their art. One such function was commemorative—the ultrarealistic depiction of actual persons, particularly in busts of worthy Romans that adorned homes and tombs. Others were the self-magnification of the emperor, as in the statue of Augustus from Prima Porta, and the publicizing of favored social and religious programs, as in the "Altar of Peace." Military successes too were spotlighted in the sculptural decorations of public monuments. For example, reliefs on the Arch of Titus in the forum record Roman soldiers sacking Jerusalem.

Roman paintings and mosaics, well known from the houses at Pompeii and Herculaneum, colorfully depict various subjects, from landscapes and architectural vistas to portraits and scenes from classical mythology. Delightfully commonplace touches include a mosaic of a fearsome dog with

the warning "beware of the dog" in the entranceway of one home. Though it is hard to distinguish innovation from imitation and though many of the artists were Greeks, the plenitude of such works bespeaks an appreciation for art in Roman everyday life as well as on the level of state-commissioned major monuments.

Like commemorative art, Roman architecture too was often motivated by civic pride. Most state-financed structures served practical needs of society while fulfilling the propaganda goals of their official sponsors. In the late republic, great leaders beautified Rome and won favor by major construction projects. Pompey built the first stone theater in the city in 55 B.C. Julius Caesar renovated the old forum area and enlarged it by the

MAP 16

The Roman Imperial Fora. (1) temple of deified Trajan, (2) Greek library, (3) column of Trajan, (4) Latin library, (5) temple of Mars the Avenger, (6) temple of Venus, (7) Senate House.

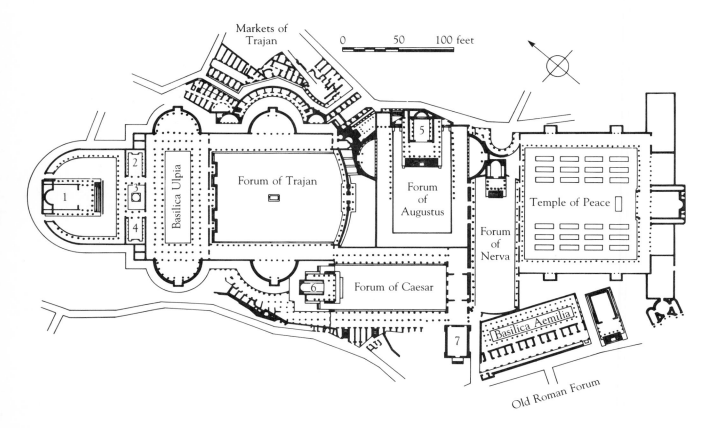

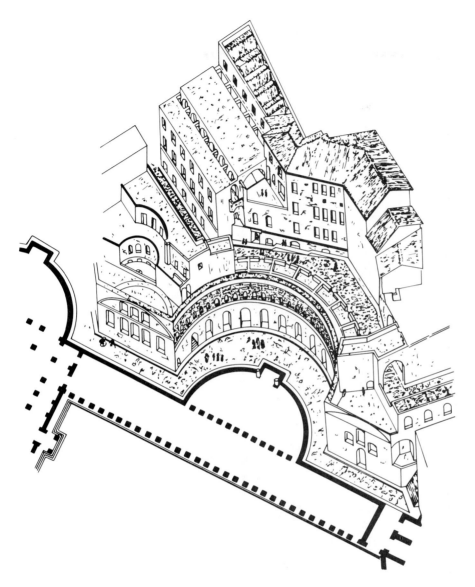

Trajan's Markets. This five-story commercial complex housed some 150 shops and offices, linked by stairways and streets, and a large, cross-vaulted market hall. The construction is brick-faced concrete. Curved forms are prominent in the barrel vaults of the shops, echoed in the round-headed windows, and in the conformity of the lowest street level to the hemicycle of the adjacent open forum area. Built c. 100–112.

addition of a new forum (see Map 16) containing a temple of Venus (he traced the Julian family back to Iulus, son of Aeneas and grandson of Venus). Augustus completed this work after Caesar's assassination and added one of his own, the first of the imperial forums, featuring the temple of Mars the Avenger that he had promised to the god in return for victory at the battle of Philippi years earlier.

Augustus's forum also housed a sculptural hall of fame, with life-size statues of many of the Roman heroes immortalized in Livy's *History,* including generals and statemen from Romulus onward and culminating in a statue of Augustus himself seven times life size.

The Romans' greatest contribution to architectural history was to use new construction materials and

techniques, specifically poured concrete, to alter in momentous ways the building types inherited from the Greeks. Augustus's tastes were conservative, and the architecture he sponsored tended to follow the colonnaded, rectilinear, post and lintel patterns of classical Greece. After his reign, however, Roman architects exploited the potentials of concrete to create curvilinear forms—the arch,

131

The Pantheon. The Pantheon, completed around 128, was built from sixty-five thousand tons of concrete. It is a colossal hemispherical dome, 142 feet in diameter, set on a cylindrical base with walls 20 feet thick. Entry is through a traditional colonnaded portico with sixteen monolithic granite columns in Corinthian style. Lighted only by a single 30-foot opening in its roof, the interior of the temple is a breathtaking allegory of the all-embracing Roman Empire: immense, solid, stable, and in right relation to the gods governing the universe.

the vault, the dome—while respecting Greek aesthetic norms of balance and symmetry. These distinctively Roman designs strongly influenced the architecture of later times, particularly the Romanesque.

Typical of the new imperial architecture were the huge public baths built by the emperors Nero, Trajan, Caracalla, and others. The biggest were larger than several football fields in area and accommodated thousands of patrons. They were actually athletic and social clubs, with swimming pools, hot, tepid, and cold rooms, exercise grounds, lecture halls and libraries, meeting rooms and food concessions. The American architect Charles McKim used the vast, cross-vaulted halls of the Baths of Caracalla as a model for Pennsylvania Station in New York City.

The amphitheater was a distinctively Roman innovation. It was essentially a 360-degree version of the Greek theater. The first examples appeared in southern Italy, but the most famous was commissioned by Vespa-

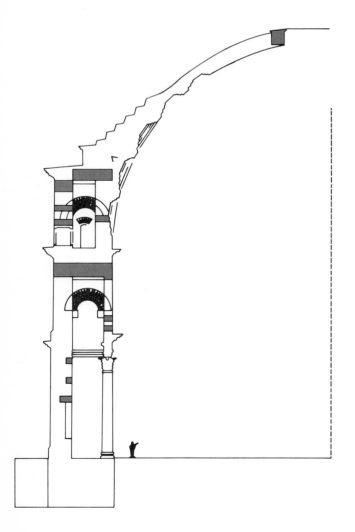

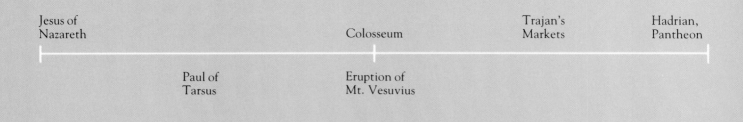

Jesus of Nazareth

Paul of Tarsus

Colosseum

Eruption of Mt. Vesuvius

Trajan's Markets

Hadrian, Pantheon

sian and dedicated by his son Titus in 80. Called the "Colosseum" because it was built near a colossal statue of Nero, it accommodated some 50,000 spectators and was the site of gladiatorial contests, wild animal "hunts," executions of Christians, and even mock sea battles.

The Emperor Trajan built the most spacious and elaborate of all imperial forums. Completed around 113, it included a large, cross-vaulted market, twin libraries for Greek and Latin texts, an enormous basilica, and a 125-foot column decorated with a continuous spiral relief sculpture illustrating scenes from Trajan's victories in Dacia (modern Rumania). Trajan appears more than fifty times on the column; his statue surmounted it and his ashes were later interred in its base. Spoils from the Dacian Wars had financed this immense complex of public facilities, and Trajan was not about to let his subjects forget his generosity.

The Emperor Hadrian, himself an amateur architect, built the most durable and impressive example of the new imperial architecture. The Pantheon (Temple of All Gods) replaced a previous structure destroyed by fire. Unlike Greek temples, which impress by stunning exterior views, the Pantheon depends on its huge enclosed space for its effect. Aside from tombs, it is the oldest unreconstructed roofed structure in the world, and was the largest dome until the building of St. Peter's in Vatican City. Partly because it so strongly influenced the Renaissance architect Andrea Palladio, the Pantheon has been the model for many buildings, including the library rotunda designed by Thomas Jefferson at the University of Virginia.

CIVIL ENGINEERING AND URBAN LIFE

In governing their empire, the Romans aimed at stability, order, and smooth practical function. In their cities and towns, their civil engineering skills secured the same goals on a wider scale and with greater uniformity than ever before. Every significant urban center in the Roman Empire possessed, in addition to private houses, the following: walls; paved streets; water supply/waste disposal systems; facilities for preparation, storage, and distribution of food; centers for political, administrative, and judicial functions; temples and associated structures; commercial shops; and recreational and cultural complexes.

Our best and fullest evidence for Roman urban life comes from two small towns on the Bay of Naples (see Map 17). In A.D. 79, Mount Vesuvius, dormant for centuries, burst into life in a major volcanic eruption. Nearby Pompeii and Herculaneum were buried within a few hours, preserved for the modern excavator as a frozen section of ancient Roman town life.

The two-mile-long walls at Pompeii enclosed 160 acres (see Map 18). Besides serving as a defense against attack, they permitted regulation of traffic through a small number of gates where the city street system was connected to the network of highways that linked town to town throughout the empire. They also facilitated the levying of duties on goods brought into the town and, at Rome, enabled authorities to restrict wheeled vehicles to certain hours of the day. Roman engineers built the most durable roads in the world, providing vital transportation and communication arteries throughout the empire and increasing military security by facilitating rapid troop movements. The huge Roman imperial highway system, some 50,000 miles in extent (longer than the interstate highway system in the United States), was a symbol of the linkage among distant

133

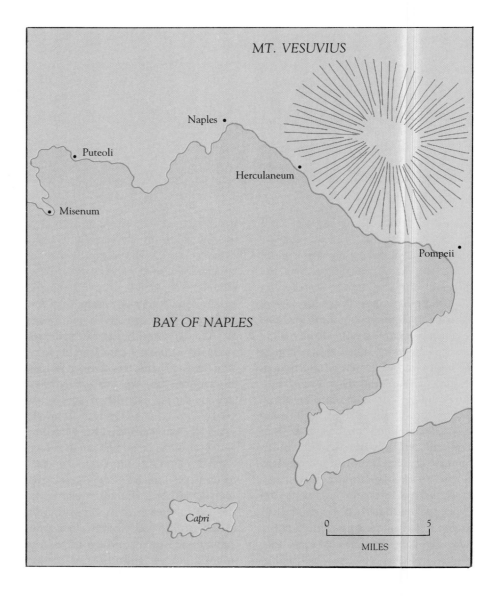

MAP 17
The Bay of Naples.

parts of a vast empire. The state-financed construction was done by soldiers or forced labor (slaves and prisoners of war). In Italy, special road commissioners supervised subsequent repair work and resurfacing; in the provinces, individual communities and wealthy landowners bore those expenses. Inside cities and towns too, there was always careful attention to good foundation, choice of material, smooth paving, and proper drainage. Except in the oldest quarter of town, the street plan at Pompeii is the rectilinear one favored by Greek city planners. City streets were lined with many shops and storefront businesses offering goods and services to a great throng of pedestrians. Given the cramped quarters in apartment buildings and the warm and sunny climate, ancient (and modern) city dwellers in Mediterranean regions spent most of their time outdoors, where the streets were the locus of many daily activities of life.

The Romans were excellent hydraulic engineers. The water system at Pompeii is typical: A large reservoir situated on high ground fed, in order of priority, public fountains, public baths, and private residences. In addition, a constant flow of water

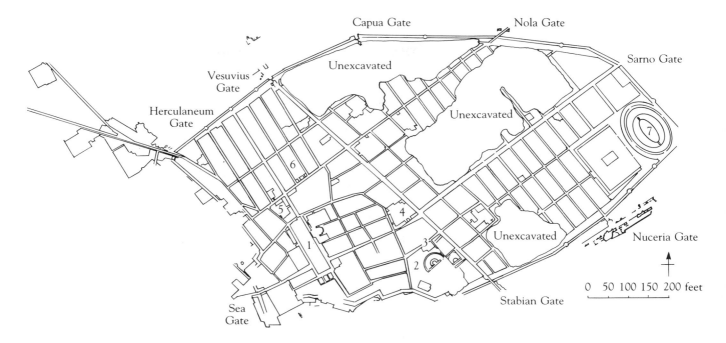

Capua Gate

Nola Gate

Sarno Gate

Vesuvius
Gate

Unexcavated

Herculaneum
Gate

Unexcavated

7

6

Unexcavated

Nuceria Gate

5

4

0 50 100 150 200 feet

1

2

3

2

Sea
Gate

Stabian Gate

through public latrines carried waste out to the sea through the sewer system. When sources were lacking nearby, water was diverted, sometimes over long distances, by aqueducts. At Rome, more than a dozen aqueducts kept 1,000,000 people plentifully supplied, and an extensive underground drainage system emptied into the Tiber.

In the forum at Pompeii (see Map 19), a large market for the sale of fresh fruits, vegetables, and meats had covered stalls facing north to minimize spoilage. A small, shaded pool kept fish fresh. Though some foods could be preserved by salting or pickling, the lack of refrigeration made necessary daily provisioning of the markets. In addition, one could buy prepared foods at streetside bakeries and "fast-food" shops.

Also in the forum at Pompeii were a polling place and municipal offices

for elected officials, town councillors, and public archives. Most imposing was the basilica, a large rectangular structure with a large central aisle bounded by massive columns to support the roof and two lateral ones. The building was used as a judicial tribunal and for various business activities. The name *basilica* apparently indicates "hall of the king" (from the Greek *basileus*) and may derive from Hellenistic buildings. The Roman basilica is important in the history of architecture, having influenced the design of Christian churches.

The Pompeian forum was a center of religious life as well. A large temple of Jupiter dominated the whole area from its high podium on the north end. There were also temples to Apollo and to the deified Vespasian.

Entertainment facilities at Pompeii included a large theater and a smaller adjacent one, perhaps a music

MAP 18
The City of Pompeii. (1) forum, (2) theater area, (3) temple of Isis, (4) Stabian baths, (5) forum baths, (6) House of the Faun, (7) amphitheater.

hall. Also an amphitheater had space for 20,000 spectators, roughly the entire population of the city. Both large, well-maintained public baths and small, private establishments abounded. Prostitutes were available in some twenty brothels.

At Pompeii, modern visitors can walk the streets of a typical Roman town. There they may feel the physical texture of daily life in the early empire more vividly than in the ruins of the city of Rome, which are islands of antiquity surrounded by a great modern city.

CHANGES IN ROMAN RELIGIOUS LIFE

By the late republic, a conglomeration of religions had begun to replace the traditional Roman religion, though the old Greco-Roman polytheism continued to be the official creed of the state, and the ruler cult increased the population of Olympus, beginning with Julius Caesar. By the time of Augustus, however, state religion was a matter of perfunctory observance rather than deeply felt spiritual experience. Augustus tried to counteract the decay in traditional religion; as he reminded the world in his official memoirs, "In my sixth consulship [28 B.C.] I restored eighty-two temples of the gods in the city on the authority of the senate, neglecting none that required restoration at that time" (*Res Gestae* 20.4, trans. P. A. Brunt and J. M. Moore). The number of temples fallen into disrepair suggests the extent of erosion in belief among the Roman people.

THE ERUPTION OF VESUVIUS

My uncle was stationed at Misenum, in active command of the fleet. On 24 August, in the early afternoon, my mother drew his attention to a cloud of unusual size and appearance. He had been out in the sun, had taken a cold bath, and lunched while lying down, and was then working at his books. He called for his shoes and climbed up to a place which would give him the best view of the phenomenon. It was not clear at that distance from which mountain the cloud was rising (it was afterwards known to be Vesuvius); its general appearance can best be expressed as being like an umbrella pine, for it rose to a great height on a sort of trunk and then split off into branches, I imagine because it was thrust upwards by the first blast and then left unsupported as the pressure subsided, or else it was borne down by its own weight so that it spread out and gradually dispersed. Sometimes it looked white, sometimes blotched and dirty, according to the amount of soil and ashes it carried with it. *

Pliny wrote the letter from which this excerpt is taken in answer to a request by the historian Tacitus for information about the death of the eminent administrator and encyclopedist, Pliny the Elder. This earliest eyewitness account of a natural disaster is so careful and detailed that modern volcanologists refer to similar eruptions, like that of Mount St. Helens in 1980, as "Plinian." The letter goes on to narrate the efforts of Pliny the Elder, who was admiral of the fleet stationed nearby, to rescue people from towns close to the volcano and his death by asphyxiation on the twenty-fifth.

*Betty Radice, trans., *The Letters of the Younger Pliny* (Harmondsworth: Penguin, 1963), Book 6, Letter 16.

Religious Ferment in the Early Empire

As we have seen, mystery religions in honor of Dionysus and Cybele had won enthusiastic followings in Italy by the second century B.C. By A.D. 100, the cults of the Persian god Mithras and the Egyptian goddess Isis, among others, had attracted many believers and begun to replace the old religion in the hearts of Roman citizens. Though new to the Roman world, these religions had roots in the distant past of the ancient Near East; they satisfied deep-seated desires for unity with the deity by their elaborate initiation rituals. Mithras attracted Roman soldiers by his militancy, for as a god of light he fought like a war-rior against Ahriman, representative of darkness and evil. Initiation involved baptism in the blood of a sacrificed bull. As "Savior from Death," Mithras also raised the universal human hope of happy immortality beyond the tomb.

The worship of Isis too offered new spiritual and sensuous excitements. Professional Egyptian priests presided over processions with dancing and singing, as well as ceremonies of penance and purification using sacred water from the Nile. The goal of eternal spiritual communion with the divinity seemed to come closer with each of the progressive steps of initiation. The worn-out rituals of Greco-Roman polytheism could not match such powerful inducements to belief. At

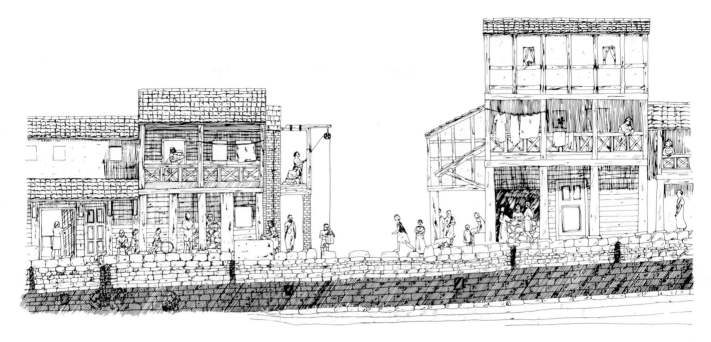

Pompeii, for example, although repairs on the Temple of Jupiter, damaged in an earthquake in A.D. 62, were unfinished when the city was buried seventeen years later, facilities at the sanctuary of Isis had been lavishly restored.

Judaism was another significant element in Rome's religious variety. After revolting against the Seleucid rulers, the Jews had enjoyed a century of independence until Pompey intervened in a disputed high priestly election and brought them under Roman authority in 63 B.C. In following centuries, Jews migrated to lands throughout the Roman Empire and even beyond its frontiers. Divergencies among the many Jewish groups and their uncompromising monotheism strained Roman–Jewish relations. The party of the Sadducees controlled the high priesthood and cooperated with Roman authorities, whereas the Pharisees advocated liberation from Roman dominance and

upheld Jewish identity by strict observance of Mosaic law. Another sect, the Essenes, pursued communal religious lives in desert isolation. A fourth group carried the Pharisaic freedom movement to militant extremes: the Zealots or, as the Romans called them, *Sicarii* (dagger men or assassins) urged armed revolt. The most extensive revolt, in A.D. 66–70, ended in destruction of the temple in Jerusalem (commemorated on the Arch of Titus in the Roman forum) and permanently embittered Jews against Romans.

The loss of their Temple as a central focus for their religion caused Jewish leaders called rabbis to place greater emphasis on observance of religious and social customs in whatever land the individual Jew was living. Of particular importance in preserving and teaching these customs was the *Talmud*, a multi-volume encyclopedia of Jewish religion. The lore contained in this authoritative

Pompeian Street Scene. This reconstruction shows a typical small-town street scene. The houses, some with upper stories and balconies, front directly on the street. There are also small shops and a public fountain. Workmen make repairs to the drainage channels beneath the street. Such buildings and activities could be found in virtually every town in the empire.

137

work accumulated orally over several centuries in Palestine and Babylonia and received final codification early in the sixth century.

Beginnings of Christianity

Amid Jewish religious fragmentation, an itinerant Jewish preacher named Jesus of Nazareth (c. 6 B.C.–c. A.D. 29) inaugurated a new world religion, Christianity. His teaching emphasized the imminent "coming" of the Kingdom of God, a new age of love and justice under God's reign. To prepare for God's kingly rule, men and women were enjoined to love God and their fellow human beings.

Although Jesus respected the Jewish scriptures, which Christians later adopted as the Old Testament, he was at odds with some Jewish leaders. Agreeing on some points with the Pharisees, Jesus opposed them on matters of Sabbath observance, food laws, and ritual purity. He also opposed the priestly Sadducees, who he believed had corrupted the Jerusalem Temple for personal gain. In a famous episode, he proclaimed the wickedness of the priests and assaulted money changers and other business people connected with the Temple. Furthermore, Jesus' popularity with the masses, who "heard him gladly," and his ties with some Zealots made him

Roman Aqueduct. A view of a half-mile-long stretch of the Roman aqueduct at Segovia, north of modern Madrid. The aqueduct, which worked by gravity feed, carried a water conduit along the top of 128 two-tiered arches reaching almost one hundred feet in height. The construction is in *opus quadratum* (carefully fitted square-cut masonry blocks). Roman structural engineers designed water supply systems, roads, bridges, and other public works to last for centuries. Built in the time of Augustus, the Segovia aqueduct is still used to carry the city's water.

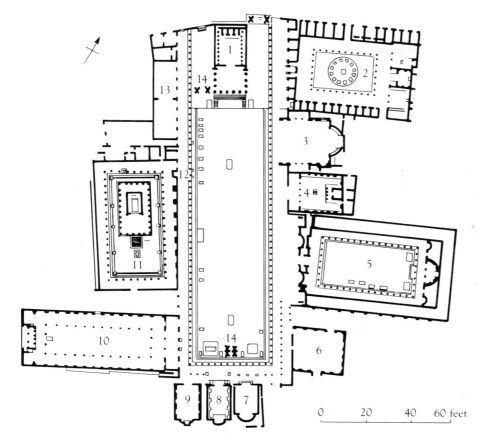

MAP 19
The Forum at Pompeii. (1) temple of Jupiter, (2) Market, (3) temple of Lares, (4) temple of deified Vespasian, (5) fullers' hall, (6) voting place, (7, 8, 9) municipal and archive offices, (10) basilica, (11) temple of Apollo, (12) bureau of weights and measures, (13) granary, (14) commemorative arches.

seem threatening to the Roman authorities in Judaea. While Jesus was in Jerusalem, Roman and Jewish officials arrested, tried, convicted, and crucified him as an agitator.

The death of Jesus led to the beginning of Christianity, as his followers announced he had risen from the dead and was the long-awaited Messiah (in Greek, *Christos*, "anointed one"). They met regularly and shared their experiences, their meals, and, for a time, their property. Empowered, as they asserted, by God's Holy Spirit, they added large numbers to their ranks by their dynamic preaching. Converts underwent ritual baptism; this rite and the common meal of bread and wine (the Eucharist or Lord's supper) became central ceremonies of Christian observance.

A Jewish convert to Christianity, Paul (c. A.D. 3–c. 67) of Tarsus carried the new faith to Greek-speaking non-Jews in a series of extensive missionary journeys. Educated in both Jewish law and Greek philosophy and mystery cults, Paul represented Jesus as a dying and rising savior God who taught that sin, human failure to satisfy God's law, so alienated humans from God that only God's initiative, called grace, could save them. God had taken that initiative, Paul maintained, in the life, death, and resurrection of Jesus the Christ, who was God become man. Traveling widely in eastern regions of the Roman Empire, Paul founded Christian churches and often wrote letters to them; some of these were included in the New Testament. By 100, there were Christian congregations in many cities of the eastern empire and in some in the west.

SUMMARY

The period from about 70 B.C. to about A.D. 130 was one of classic achievements in Roman cultural history. The speeches and other writings of Cicero and the war commentaries of Caesar, in their style as much as in their content, carried Latin literature to an unprecedented level of excellence. Lucretius's great philosophical epic and Catullus's vivid and engaging lyrics broke new ground in poetry. In the Augustan period, Vergil in his epic poem of Roman manifest destiny, the *Aeneid*, Horace in his gemlike *Odes*, and Livy in his monumental *History* accommodated their art to the emperor's program of national rebirth. They gave to Romans and to posterity a literature both aesthetically pleasing and patriotic. Although later Roman writers seldom reached such levels of artistry, the prose and drama of Seneca, the innovative protonovel of Petronius, the penetrating histories of Tacitus, and the caustic satires of Juvenal all marked new peaks in Latin literature.

In their sculpture and painting, Romans adapted Greek models and patterns to the publicity needs of a world state and of the aristocratic elite that governed it. In architecture, Rome built on Greek foundations, but created magnificent new designs. Curvilinear forms—the arch, the vault, and the dome—fostered a lasting emphasis on interior volumes. Hadrian's Pantheon most fully realized the potential of the new imperial architecture.

Roman culture was visible, not just in massive construction in the capital, but also throughout the far reaches of the huge empire. Every city and town benefited from Roman civil engineering. Transportation and communication, food and water supply, sanitation and entertainment, administration and commerce—in all these aspects of civilized life, Roman authority meant improved living conditions for millions.

In religion too, the assimilative powers of Roman culture led to experimentation. This sometimes displeased the administrative officials who supervised the moral health of the body politic, but it was a sure sign of the spiritual vitality and flexibility of a people searching for new meaning in religious belief. The old formal Greco-Roman religion was replaced by more vital faiths, the mystery cults, which promised immediate union with divine beings and rewards in the next life for those who endured the trials of this one. Though it could not have been anticipated in the first century, one of these new faiths, Christianity, was destined to sweep aside all competitors and long outlive the Roman Empire itself.

SELECTED SOURCES

Balsdon, J. P. V. D. *Life and Leisure in Ancient Rome.* 1969. The best recent book on Roman everyday life; based on a critical assessment of literary, inscriptional, and archaeological evidence.

*Brilliant, Richard. *Roman Art: From the Republic to Constantine.* 1974. A good, recent, well-illustrated survey of the subject. Includes chapters on Roman architecture.

Copley, Frank O. *Latin Literature: From the Beginnings to the Close of the Second Century* A.D. 1969. An extremely well-written treatment of Latin literature by its most successful American translator.

Fellini, Federico, dir. *Fellini's Satyricon.* 1970. This stunningly surreal film mixes remarkably faithful recreations of scenes from its Petronian prototype with large slices of Fellini's collective unconscious. Not for the fainthearted.

*Ferguson, John. *The Religions of the Roman Empire.* 1970. A clear guide to the varieties of (sought, tolerated, and persecuted) religious experience in the empire.

Grant, Michael. *Cities of Vesuvius: Pompeii and Herculaneum.* 1971. This engaging and detailed introduction to the archaeology of the buried cities is richly illustrated with plates, maps, plans, and drawings.

*Lucretius. *The Nature of Things.* Translated by Frank O. Copley. 1977. The lucid translation is accompanied by helpful notes and introduction.

Macaulay, David. *City: A Story of Roman*

ROMAN CULTURAL ACHIEVEMENTS

Planning and Construction. 1974. Especially valuable for its many detailed drawings of Roman construction.

* Petronius. *Satyricon.* Translated by William Arrowsmith. 1959. A masterpiece of translation, capturing the lively colloquial flavor of the original Latin. Includes notes and introduction.

* Virgil. *The Aeneid.* Translated by Robert Fitzgerald. 1983. This remarkable new version of the greatest Latin poem is, even considered simply as English poetry, a marvelous accomplishment.

* Available in paperback.

THE ROMAN EMPIRE FROM PROSPERITY TO COLLAPSE OF THE WEST
(A.D. 14–c. 500)

Two cities have been formed by two loves: the earthly by the love of self, even to the contempt of God; the heavenly by the love of God, even to the contempt of self. The former, in a word, glories in itself, the latter in the Lord. For the one seeks glory from men; but the greatest glory of the other is God, the witness of conscience. . . . In the one, the princes and the nations it subdues are ruled by the love of ruling; in the other the princes and the subjects serve one another in love. . . . The one delights in its own strength, represented in the persons of its rulers; the other says to its God, "I will love Thee, O Lord, my strength."

Augustine wrote these words in the final days of the Roman Empire, not long after the sack of Rome by the Visigoths in 410. From the vantage point of an eminent Christian man of learning, he contrasts the earthly city of humanity—most fully realized in Rome itself—with the heavenly city of the Christian God. As the ancient empire of Rome crumbled around them, many others as well turned their eyes toward visions of more enduring, timeless realms of spiritual truth and divine love. The history of ancient Rome, just then coming to its conclusion, was a long and marvelous one, full of mighty struggles, both physical and spiritual, within the empire itself and between it and its barbarian opponents. The present chapter describes Roman achievements at the zenith of the empire and the prolonged struggle for survival that ended in the final collapse of that empire in the west. It also focuses on the rise and ultimate victory of the Christian religion in the same periods.

CONTENTS

Constantine. This titanic marble head, eight and a half feet in height, remains along with a right hand and sundry other outsized limb fragments of a colossal seated statue of the emperor. The distant gaze of the eyes bespeaks a fixation on realms of power far beyond the ken of puny mortals. The statue (c. 313) graced the Basilica of Constantine in Rome; now in the Palazzo dei Conservatori.

Nero. Though the artists who designed coin portraits often tried to idealize their subject, the sensualist emperor is easily recognized on this coin by his thick-necked, bloated appearance. The wreath and longish neck locks are an effort to associate Nero with Apollo, patron of culture. British Museum.

PROSPERITY IN THE FIRST AND SECOND CENTURIES

The principate created by Augustus, in reality a disguised monarchy, functioned reasonably well during the first two imperial centuries. Its chief improvements over the old republican system were the creation of an administrative apparatus adequate to the needs of the empire and the elimination of frequent civil strife among military commanders competing for dictatorship.

By the time Augustus died and was formally deified by vote of the Senate in A.D. 14, any Romans who had lived during the republic remembered only the civil wars that tore it apart. After forty-one years of successful leadership by Augustus, no one seriously hoped for a return to that discredited system of government. But the question of succession remained. Augustus determined that his successor should be a member of his family, and in fact the next four emperors were Julio-Claudian (Augustus's wife, Livia, belonged to the aristocratic Claudian family).

The Emperors after Augustus

Tiberius (14–37) had been an excellent general and proved to be a capable administrator, preserving conscientiously the rights of the Senate. His later years, however, were marred by an excessive number of treason trials, a morbid fear of assassination, and various misunderstandings and suspicions arising after 26 from his long absence from Rome at his magnificent villa on Capri. In his reign, the Praetorian Guard became powerful. This was a corps of several thousand elite troops quartered at Rome and assigned to the protection of the emperor and his family. The guard and its commanders, called prefects, came to possess great influence in deciding imperial succession. The Emperor Claudius (41–54), for example, was a virtual appointee of the guard. Though rather eccentric and more a scholar than a man of action, Claudius proved to be a competent administrator; he also added Britain to the empire.

The reigns of Gaius (37–41), known as Caligula, and of Nero (54–68) showed the potential for abuse inherent in the imperial system. Both men were psychopaths. Not only did they commit incest, they also murdered family members. Nero, for example, murdered his mother. Further, both men were autocrats in their relations with the Senate and administrative officials as well as with the Roman people. Caligula, for example, insisted that divine honors be paid to him even before his death. Nero ruled well for a time, because of the influence of competent advisers, including his former tutor Seneca, but spent the last half of his reign obsessively cultivating the image of a performing artist. He offended Roman sensibilities by appearing in the theater as a singer and musician, often reciting his own poetry. Caligula's cruelty led to his assassination by an officer of the Praetorian Guard, and Nero, last of the Julio-Claudians, committed suicide to avoid a similar fate.

Despite problems of mismanagement at the top, the system Augustus installed was remarkably resilient and durable. A succession method based on the support of the army and the accident of birth into the imperial family sometimes brought incompetent and even deranged emperors to power, but this did not destroy the foundations of economic prosperity and military security in the empire at large.

It became clear in the period of the Julio-Claudians and its aftermath that force of arms, embodied in the Praetorian Guard or in the regular field armies, had become a necessity for imperial authority. No fewer than four emperors came to power in 68–69 in a rapid series of struggles waged by individual armies supporting their own preferred candidates for emperorship. Vespasian (69–79) emerged victorious and established the Flavian dynasty. He was followed by his sons, the short-lived and popular Titus (79–81) and the despotic Domitian (81–96). The *princeps* no longer had to be a Julio-Claudian. Vespasian and Titus restored the administrative and military efficiency of the principate, regained the respect for their position that Nero and others had damaged, and moved the principate toward absolute monarchy, though without committing the excesses of Caligula. Both were deified after death. Domitian was also an able manager, but in the end he alienated the Senate by persecuting many whom he suspected of disloyalty. He was assassinated in 96.

The short reign of Nerva (96–98), an elderly senatorial appointee, inaugurated what is often called an "era of good emperors" that lasted till 180. Problems of succession were solved in a more satisfactory way as each emperor selected and legally adopted his own successor, usually a capable and experienced administrator and/or

general. For the most part, the cultural and political currents of the first century carried on into the second. The bureaucracy of the central government increased, as the organization and institutions of the imperial system were more firmly established. Trajan (98–117) restored the good relations with the Senate that Domitian had damaged, and pleased the masses in Rome by his major building programs and gifts of money. He also enlarged the empire by the addition of Dacia (modern Rumania). Trajan's correspondence with Pliny the Younger (c. 61–c. 112), who was governor in Bithynia around 110, shows how deeply committed he was to efficient imperial administration in all its details.

Trajan's successor, Hadrian (117–138), was a multitalented ruler. He tirelessly traveled throughout the provinces of the empire, personally attending to military security along borders. In Britain, "Hadrian's Wall," a sixty-mile-long complex of ditches, stone walls, and forts, was built to defend against barbarians in Scotland. Hadrian also indulged his strong interest in the arts and architecture by beautifying Rome, Athens, and other cities through the construction and renovation of magnificent temples, markets, and other facilities. He thereby won the respect of both civilians and soldiers.

The general prosperity continued until the reign of Marcus Aurelius (161–180). Marcus was a Stoic philosopher who wrote a (posthumously published) collection of pithy and introspective *Meditations*. These random personal reflections touch on a wide range of subjects, from current events to the mysteries of life and death, from practical advice for self-

improvement to comments on passages in literature. They are marked by a moral enthusiasm for duty. Duty for the conscientious Marcus meant warfare. The emperor spent most of his time in the field directing armies that repelled Parthian attacks in the east and invasions by Germanic tribes along the Danube frontier and even into northern Italy. In 165 and following years, an epidemic (possibly smallpox) caused great loss of life, first among Roman soldiers in the east and then throughout the empire. These were ominous events, for decrease in Roman manpower and concurrent increases in Germanic pressure along the Rhine-Danube frontier overtaxed a defensive system designed to repel one border incursion at a time.

Socioeconomic and Cultural Characteristics

By the early imperial period, the Roman world was a vast cosmopolitan conglomerate of more than 5,000 towns and cities (see Map 20) and their surrounding hinterlands inhabited by a population of perhaps 50,000,000. The Roman "universal order" brought the benefits of civilization in a variety of ways, involving the material, intellectual, and spiritual life of the empire's population. Commercial activity flourished as the Roman government imposed a uniform currency system, suppressed piracy, and built and maintained roads. The emperors also kept harbors and dockyards well maintained. Particularly important were the port installations at Ostia by the mouth of the Tiber, Puteoli in the Bay of Naples, and outside Italy at such cities as Alexandria, Piraeus, and Ephesus, among others. A constant flow of textiles,

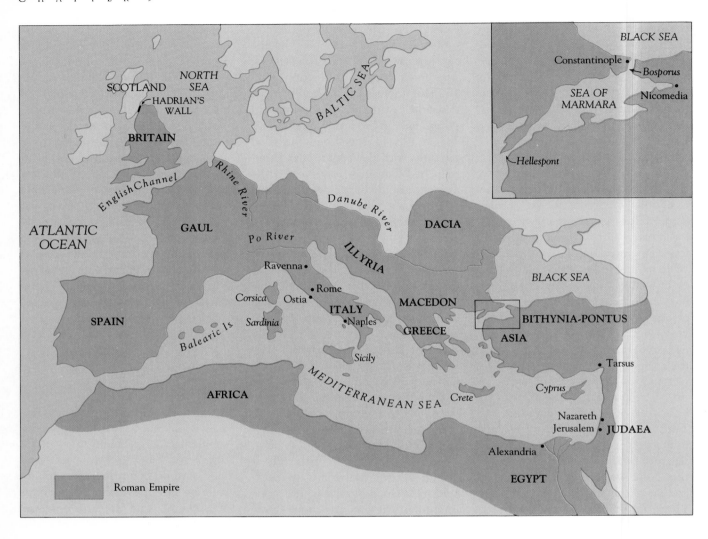

MAP 20
The Roman Empire.

foodstuffs, metals (gold, silver, copper, tin, lead, iron), manufactured goods (glass, pottery, jewelry, paper), and luxury items (silk, ivory, precious gems, spices) came into these harbors from all parts of the Mediterranean world. The imperial administration created a special corporation of shipowners to ensure an unfailing supply of grain, mainly from north Africa, to the city of Rome and to the armies.

The physical links between the cities of the empire, both by land and by sea, ensured greater speed of transport and security for travelers over long distances than had been possible previously in the ancient world. This contributed to a "melting pot" phenomenon observable, for example, in the ever-increasing proportion of immigrants in the city of Rome and in the eventual ascension of non-Italians to positions of authority in the Senate and in the imperial administration generally. Beginning with Trajan and Hadrian, who were born in Spain, the emperors themselves were often not from Italy.

Besides material advantages, a certain distinctively Roman intellectual culture also became widespread in the empire. The Latin language, for example, was learned (both formally and by word of mouth) by citizens in the western part of the empire. The modern Romance languages (French, Italian, Portuguese, Rumanian) are direct descendants of Latin. In the east, Greek persisted in preference to Latin as the language of educated people, and the schools focused on Greek literary masterpieces. In the west, by contrast, educated people were generally bilingual, as the literature and philosophy of both Greece and Rome were transmitted to succeeding generations. Although a true national education system never did develop and the literacy rate remained low, instruction was made widely available by the common practice in individual cities and towns of appointing teachers paid from public funds or by the benefactions of wealthy citizens. Students aged seven to eleven acquired elementary education in

THE ROMAN UNIVERSAL ORDER

Most noteworthy and marvelous is the grandeur of your concept of citizenship. There is nothing on earth like it. . . . Neither sea nor distance on land excludes one from citizenship. No distinction is made between Asia and Europe in this respect. Everything lies open to everybody; and no one fit for office or a position of trust is an alien. . . . You have made the word "Roman" apply not to a city but to a universal people. . . . You have re-divided mankind into Romans and non-Romans. . . . There is one pattern of government, embracing all. Under you, what was formerly thought incapable of conjunction has been united. . . .

You have surveyed the whole world, built bridges of all sorts across rivers, cut down mountains to make paths for chariots, filled the deserts with hostels, and civilized it all with system and order. . . .

Before your rule, things were all mixed up topsy-turvy, drifting at random. But with you in charge, turmoil and strife ceased, universal order and the bright light of life and government came in, laws were proclaimed, and the gods' altars acquired sanctity.[*]

This passage is from a speech delivered at Rome by Publius Aelius Aristides in the mid-second century A.D. It applauds the benefits of the "universal order" the Roman Empire had achieved throughout the Mediterranean world. The orator was a provincial, born in Asia Minor and educated in Greek culture. His very name bears witness to the fusion of peoples that he praises: "Publius" and "Aelius" are Latin, "Aristides" Greek. Though the speech is a flattering exaggeration, the Romans did succeed—where the Greeks had conspicuously failed—in unifying a world-state and endowing it with a culture that continued, modified, and sometimes even surpassed that of the Greeks.

[*]Aelius Aristides, To Rome (selections), trans. S. Levin, in N. Lewis and M. Reinhold, eds., Roman Civilization, Sourcebook, II: The Empire, rev. ed. (New York: Harper, 1966), pp. 135–138.

Ship Mosaic from Ostia. Located in one of the main squares in the port of Ostia were the offices of some seventy shipping companies. Mosaics in the pavement in the square identified the various companies. Seen here is the sign marking the establishment of the shippers from Narbo (modern Narbonne in southern France). The mosaic shows a ship loading cargo at its home port.

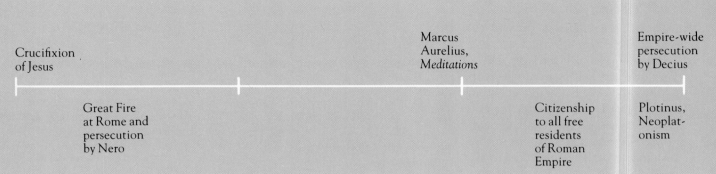

Crucifixion
of Jesus

Marcus
Aurelius,
Meditations

Empire-wide
persecution
by Decius

Great Fire
at Rome and
persecution
by Nero

Citizenship
to all free
residents
of Roman
Empire

Plotinus,
Neoplat-
onism

reading, writing, and arithmetic; girls were not excluded from this primary course as they had been in classical Greece. In the schools of grammar (for ages twelve to fifteen) and rhetoric (sixteen and over), males were trained in literature, philosophy, and especially oratory. The goal was to prepare promising young citizens for careers as lawyers, administrators, and civil servants, by equipping them with the means to speak and write effectively, gracefully, and persuasively.

Rome showed special originality in the field of education by creating law schools and recognizing medicine as an important specialization. A major figure in the history of medical education was Galen of Pergamum, the court physician of Marcus Aurelius. Galen possessed remarkable knowledge, both theoretical and practical, in all areas of medicine, but especially in anatomy and physiology. He showed, for example, that blood was carried by arteries as well as veins. Galen gathered and corrected the results of earlier research and exerted a dominant influence on medical science for centuries to come.

The Progress of Christianity

The most significant development in the cultural life of the Roman Empire was the rise of Christianity. In the first century and a half after the life of Jesus of Nazareth, this religion struggled through a difficult infancy but attracted large numbers of adherents among Gentiles (non-Jews). Perhaps partly because of this alarming growth, the Romans, who had at first viewed Christianity strictly as another Jewish sect, soon abandoned their usual policy of religious toleration. At least as early as the reign of Nero, they made Christianity illegal. The first recorded persecution of Christians took place after a terribly destructive fire in the city of Rome in 64, when Nero tried to curb rumors blaming him for the disaster by pinning responsibility on the Christians in the city. He imposed horrible penalties, including burning alive, a common punishment for arson.

This singling out and brutalizing of the Christians went against the more typical Roman tendency to tolerate foreign religions. Among possible reasons for that uncharacteristic approach was the seemingly treasonous refusal of many Christians to perform sacrifices to the goddess Roma and the divinized emperors or to serve in the Roman army. Furthermore, Roman authorities had always discouraged private associations in the belief that they might subvert citizens' primary allegiance to the Roman state. Before the third century, however, there was no consistent empirewide policy of persecution. Provincial governors only sporadically enforced the laws against Christianity. For instance, when Pliny the Younger wrote to ask Trajan what should be done about persons accused of being Christians in his province of Bithynia, the emperor answered, "No hard and fast rule may be set down. They are not to be hunted down; if they are brought before you and convicted, they should be punished. Nevertheless, anyone who denies he is Christian and verifies it by supplicating our gods should be pardoned accordingly, however suspicious his past life" (*Letter* 10.97). With few exceptions, this rather enlightened policy of Trajan's was adhered to until the mid-third century. Whatever persecutions did occur tended to enhance Christianity's appeal, prompting one writer to conclude that "the blood of the martyrs [those killed for their faith] is the seed of the church."

Despite its illegality, Christianity competed effectively with the mystery religions in the Roman Empire because of its superior literature and organization. In addition to the lives of Jesus and letters of missionaries such as Paul, Christian writers produced

Tomb of Galla Placidia. This fifth-century mosaic in Ravenna shows (left) bookshelves with texts of the four Gospels. Because Christianity emphasized the good word of Jesus' life and teachings, a new, more easily consulted and durable book form—the codex—replaced the older volumen (papyrus roll). The compact codex (about ten by seven inches) usually consisted of vellum (calfskin) or parchment (goatskin) sheets bound together as in a modern book. Constantine had fifty copies of the Christian scriptures written on vellum for the churches of Constantinople.

accounts of Christian teaching, traced the development of early church history, and composed vigorous arguments against rival religions and thought systems. From that rich and extensive body of written material, the Christians would eventually select twenty-seven items manifesting what they considered superior divine inspiration for inclusion in an official canon of holy scriptures. To affirm their belief that God had made a new covenant or agreement with them, they called that collection the New Testament and joined to it the body of Jewish scriptures, which they termed the Old Testament, to create the Christian Bible.

Christian organization early showed a remarkable diversity of specializations, including prophets, teachers, healers, and administrators. Committees composed of elders—members distinguished for their faith and maturity—regulated the activities of each local congregation, whereas its religious services were conducted by a presbyter (priest or minister). Where several congregations existed in the same city, they came to be supervised by a higher official, the bishop.

DECAY AND RECOVERY

After 180, a time of troubles set in for the Roman Empire. Instead of adopting a well-qualified man to follow him on the throne, Marcus Aurelius showed faulty judgment in designating his son, Commodus, as

Gold Coins. On the left is Marcus Aurelius; on the right, his son, Commodus. Marcus chose not to adopt a successor (as he himself had been by Antoninus Pius), instead allowing the crown to go to his son, who eventually became deranged by power and was assassinated. Seldom has a son been so unlike his father.

149

Valerian Captured by Persians. This rock carving shows the Emperor Valerian (on left) shackled and submissive before the mounted Persian king Shapur I, who is represented as a successor to Darius and Xerxes. The first emperor to be captured by enemy forces (in 260), Valerian died in captivity—a stunning catastrophe in Roman eyes. Naqsh-i-Rusta, Iran.

emperor. The brutally power-hungry Commodus (180–192) ruled tyrannically and was assassinated. The era of the principate and of peaceful Roman prosperity was over.

Third-Century Disintegration

Armed conflict among would-be successors effectively militarized the civil authority of the emperor in the third century. The Severan dynasty of emperors brought some stability between 193 and 235. One of its members, Caracalla, brought to its final conclusion a process begun early in the republican era, when he extended citizenship to virtually all inhabitants of the empire, partly to increase tax revenues.

Near anarchy reigned in the period from 235 to 284, when more than twenty emperors assumed power. They are sometimes called "barracks emperors" because they gained the throne thanks to the successes of the mutinous legions or Praetorian guardsmen who supported them. Some were later deposed and murdered by the same conspirators who had previously assisted them. Many were non-Italians, originating in Illyria, Africa, Gaul, and elsewhere; they often appointed non-Romans to positions of authority and ruled from the provinces, thus diminishing the central importance of the city of Rome.

In addition to this political instability, the Roman Empire in the third century faced increasing defense problems. In the east, the Persians, under the Sassanid dynasty, revived their empire by overthrowing the alien Parthians who had long dominated but never assimilated them, and pushed back Roman legions in the area. The capture of an emperor, Valerian (253–260), by Persian forces was a particularly conspicuous blow to Roman self-esteem. Elsewhere, Germanic tribes made incursions along the Rhine-Danube border and in Britain. The Dacians frequently broke into Roman territories in the Balkans.

Recovery under Diocletian and Constantine

The chaos of the third century was temporarily checked by the reforms of the Emperor Diocletian (284–305). An energetic and intelligent administrator, Diocletian staffed the imperial bureaucracy with the best available talent, promoting individuals on the basis of merit. He reorganized the imperial administration, in particular, by carving the prov-

Tetrarchy | Edict of Milan | Constantinople | Jerome and the Vulgate Bible

Galerius, the Great Persecution | Council of Nicaea | Julian attempts to restore paganism | Augustine, *City of God*

inces of the empire into smaller districts supervised by more officials. Especially important was the overall distribution of administrative responsibilities between eastern and western halves of the empire. In light of the frequency of barbarian invasions, Diocletian believed that the empire had become too large for one man to rule. Two men, both called "Augustus," split supreme authority, Diocletian in the east and Maximian in the west. Each was assisted by a "vice-emperor," called "Caesar," who would presumably succeed his superior when the time came. The system is sometimes called the tetrarchy (rule by four). Each tetrarch took up residence in a city in his own administrative quadrant of the empire. Diocletian, preoccupied with defensive operations against barbarian invasions in the eastern empire, set up his court at Nicomedia in Bithynia. Rome, which Diocletian visited only once, was not one of the four imperial capitals and thus faded farther into the background.

The defense needs of the empire, as it faced growing barbarian pressure along its frontiers, required a military reorganization as well. Diocletian responded as the competent military man he was and nearly doubled the size of the army from 300,000 to 500,000 troops, in part by enlisting barbarians. His new, smaller administrative units promoted better supervision of the forces charged with defense of the borders. Large, mobile reserve forces were formed to back up the frontier contingents where needed.

In 305, Diocletian, suffering from poor health, resigned from the emperorship. Without the backing of its strong-willed founder, who had ruled with absolute authority, the tetrarchy soon disintegrated in a complicated series of civil wars fueled by personal ambition and the reversion to dynastic inheritance. By 324, however, Constantine (306–337) emerged as the sole ruler of the Roman Empire.

In general, Constantine followed the governmental policies of Diocletian, ruling autocratically and consulting only a few trusted appointees. The emperor was a remote, divinely sanctioned, and nearly superhuman figure whose will was supreme. In recognition of this authority, he expected honorific titles ("our Lord," "eternal Victor") and acts of submission like kneeling and kissing the purple robe of the ruler. A gigantic statue of Constantine erected in a basilica in the forum at Rome depicts him as the embodiment of absolute earthly power. Such things were a final megalomaniacal outgrowth of a steady

Tetrarchs. This sculpture (c. 300), carved in porphyry, shows Diocletian and his fellow tetrarchs. Depicted in military garb and in rigid attitudes of mutual support, the monolithic figures symbolize the unity and symmetrical strength of the tetrarchy. The style looks forward to the Middle Ages rather than back to Greco-Roman forms. Indeed, the figures were once thought to represent Christian crusaders or St. George. On the southwest corner of the Basilica of San Marco in Venice.

151

process of self-magnification that began with the Julio-Claudians. By contrast, the Senate at Rome was fast becoming merely a town council with local jurisdiction only. Constantine further enlarged an already swollen bureaucracy by creating a second Senate (at Constantinople) and increasing the provincial subdivisions.

Though his sole leadership imposed a superficial unity on the empire, Constantine helped prepare the way for its ultimate split into eastern and western halves by founding a new imperial capital named after himself. Constantinople was built on the easily defensible site of the old Greek city of Byzantium (modern Istanbul). Located on a peninsula on the European shore of the Straits of Bosporus between the Black Sea and (through the Sea of Marmara and the Hellespont) the Aegean, the site was convenient for the direction of military operations along the Danube to the west and against Persia to the east. It was also on the main land route from Europe to Asia Minor. This "second Rome" soon surpassed the old capital as the control center of the empire. Dedicated in 330, it survived barbarian attacks and for more than 1,000 years preserved a residue of Greco-Roman civilization until its fall to Ottoman Turks in 1453.

Socioeconomic Characteristics

The troubles of the empire in the third and fourth centuries exerted a powerful disintegrative force on the society, economy, and culture of the Roman world. The populace was generally fearful of the constant threat of barbarian invasion. The increase in defense spending that this fear prompted, combined with the ex-penses of supporting the ever-growing imperial bureaucracy, led to dire economic difficulties. Prosperity came to an end as imperial tax collectors tightened the screws on a shrinking population of taxpayers. The emperors also tried to make revenues go farther by decreasing the ratio of silver to inferior metals in the coins issued by the imperial mints. This in turn led to rampant inflation. Diocletian unsuccessfully tried to solve the problem by a special Edict on Maximum Prices that fixed wages and prices throughout the Roman Empire.

Such problems had social consequences as well. Diocletian and Constantine reacted to the problem of decreasing manpower by requiring individuals and their descendants to remain in certain essential, but now much less profitable, occupations; these included soldiers, farmers, and grain shippers, among others. Among the elite classes of the society, the nobility now retained only honorific titles; the true power in the state was in the hands of thousands of petty bureaucrats. Well-to-do landowners in the towns of the empire, who had patriotically put their skills and funds at the disposal of the central or local governments in the early empire, were now taxed to their limit. They had to be forced to undertake public service. Many left the cities and towns for country estates in hopes of avoiding the tentacles of the imperial bureaucracy.

A further development of this era was the siphoning of wealth from the more prosperous eastern half of the empire to sustain the military and economic vitality of the overburdened society of the west. When the empire in the west finally did collapse, the eastern empire was thus released from a grievous economic burden.

CHRISTIANITY IN THE LATER ROMAN EMPIRE

By the third century, Christianity had become an increasingly divisive factor in the Roman world. Many were attracted to it for its apparent stability, order, and morality, whereas others blamed it for sapping the empire of its strength by diverting the interest and loyalty of its citizens away from their civic responsibilities.

From Persecution to Predominance

During his brief reign, the Emperor Decius (249–251) tried to stamp out Christianity entirely by instituting the first empirewide loyalty test. All citizens were required to demonstrate their faith in the Roman gods by offering sacrifice to them in the presence of officially authorized local commissioners. Those passing the test were issued loyalty certificates called *libelli*. Though Decius died before he could achieve his goal, other persecutions followed, most notably the Great Persecution begun by Diocletian in 303 and accelerated by his successor, Galerius (305–311). The aim of these programs was not only to crush a sect perceived as a subversive challenge to the state but also to seize its economic resources. For by 300 the Christian church had become virtually a state within a state, numbering perhaps ten percent of the empire's inhabitants among its membership. In this last great time of testing by hostile Roman civil authorities, churches were destroyed, Christians—especially bishops and other leaders—hunted out and executed, sacred scriptures burned, and church holdings seized.

The status of Christianity in the Roman Empire changed with startling suddenness during the fourth century from persecuted minority to dominant majority. While lying mortally ill, the arch-persecutor Galerius recognized the failure of his religious policy and issued an Edict of Toleration in 311, permitting Christians to practice their faith and rebuild their churches. Constantine, influenced by his mother's devout Christian faith and a prebattle vision of a Christian cross accompanied by a voice saying, "In this sign you will conquer," confirmed this toleration by his Edict of Milan in 313, restoring confiscated Christian properties. Moreover, he granted the Christians special favors such as lands and buildings, tax exemptions for their clergy, and permission for their bishops to act as imperial judges. That imperial patronage

greatly accelerated the spread of Christianity, which Constantine perhaps envisaged as a new imperial ideology that could provide unity to a sadly battered empire. This, combined with the missionary zeal so characteristic of Christianity, brought many new converts to the preferred religion of the emperor. Constantine's successors, except for Julian (361–363), who tried to revive the old pagan religion, followed and extended his pro-Christian policies, until by the end of the fourth century Christianity and Judaism were the only legal religions in the empire. Greco-Roman polytheism, though officially suppressed and sometimes vigorously persecuted, died a lingering death.

Besides the crucial factors of sincere belief in the Christian God and imperial encouragement of that belief, we may note four reasons for Christianity's final victory over competing faiths and fearsome persecution. First, it was simple in its demand for absolute allegiance, brushing aside the welter of alternative religions and requiring a single, irreversible com-

Christian Communal Meal. A third-century wall painting depicting the miracle of the loaves and fishes as a prefiguration of the Christian "love feast" or eucharistic meal. This communal Sunday meal commemorated the Last Supper and was an indispensable assertion of membership in the community of Christian believers. From the Catacombs of Saint Calixtus, Rome.

mitment to one creed. It offered permanent values at a time when political and spiritual absolutes were fast disappearing from the Roman horizon.

Second, Christianity was equalitarian, open to any and all, from the lowest slave (even female slave) to the emperor. Every individual mattered, every soul could be saved, regardless of ethnic origin or social status: "There is no question here of Greek and Jew, circumcised and uncircumcised, barbarian, Scythian, slave and freeman; but Christ is all, and is in all" (Colossians 3:11).

Third, Christianity held out the hope of a better life in the world of the heavenly city. This was a compelling enticement when the foundations of the earthly world of the Roman Empire were shaking. Though various mystery cults similarly promised immortality, in the case of Christianity the courage and equanimity of martyrs who endured torturous deaths lent credence to the notion that true believers would gain eternal bliss in the presence of their God. "I am the resurrection and I am the life. If a man has faith in me, even though he die, he shall come to life; and no one who is alive and has faith shall ever die" (John 11:25–26).

Finally, Christianity satisfied the universal need to belong. Founded on the injunction to "Love thy neighbor," the Christian community shared a value system and manner of living as well as a body of ritual. Persecution only strengthened this bond, as the church assumed the responsibility of caring for its own in a hostile environment, ministering to the indigent and sick, supporting orphans and widows, and supplying a source of self-respect in the lives of thousands of urban poor. Such activities, which were foreign to pagan religious expression, made the believer's earthly life more tolerable and meaningful, even in the face of adversity, quite apart from the prospect of a life after death.

The Church as an Institution

As the Christians became first legitimate and then preeminent, they devoted increasing attention to defining their beliefs. To do so, they employed the rich, profound, and precise vocabulary that Greeks had developed during a millennium of philosophical and religious discussions. The most vital ancient philosophical system from the mid-third century onward was Neoplatonism, which synthesized Platonic, Aristotelian, Pythagorean, and Stoic lines of thought. Though Neoplatonism offered a rival theology to Christianity, the writing of its best-known representative, Plotinus (205–270), exerted a great influence on Christian thinkers such as Augustine.

Christian efforts to make simple and clear statements of faith ironically often produced complexity, confusion, and conflict. Special councils were held, sometimes at the invitation of the emperor, to resolve such disagreements. During the fourth and fifth centuries, several councils produced the distinctive Christian doctrine of the Trinity, which stated that God was one essence in three distinct persons: Father, Son (Jesus the Christ), and Holy Spirit. The first ecumenical or world council, attended by 220 bishops, was held at Nicaea in 325; it formalized a statement of essential beliefs of Christian faith known as the Nicene Creed. Those Church leaders who were outvoted in those councils, however, often persisted in their variant beliefs and were labeled heretics by the victorious majority of leaders, who termed themselves orthodox. For the sake of unity, emperors and orthodox often used imperial military might against heretics, who sometimes fled to remote lands either within or outside the empire.

Besides the decisions of the church councils, the writings and works of theologians known as church fathers also helped to clarify Christian dogma during the fourth and fifth centuries. Jerome (c. 348–420) a Latin-speaking Christian, mastered Greek and Hebrew and produced a translation of the whole Bible known as the Vulgate (common or ordinary), because of its use of everyday Latin. His translation remained standard for 1,000 years and aided Christianity's spread throughout the Latin-speaking western empire. Ambrose (c. 339–397), a notable bishop, successfully challenged and limited imperial authority over the church by requiring the emperor of his day, Theodosius I (379–395), to do public penance for a massacre of many citizens before he was allowed to participate in the church's religious services. Basil (c. 330–379), another bishop, argued powerfully for retaining the study of pre-Christian and non-Christian writings in the Christian schools of the empire against those who wished to replace such works with exclusively Christian writings. The questions of whether and how to coordinate Christian thought with the wisdom of Greece and Rome troubled the minds of many church leaders. These were issues fraught with importance for the later existence and relevance of classical learning and culture, for it was the Christian church that preserved many of the treasures of ancient literature in centuries to come.

The greatest church father of this period was Augustine (354–430). A teacher of rhetoric by training and by inclination an experimenter in styles of thought and life, he had explored most Roman beliefs and enjoyed many of life's pleasures before embracing Christianity. In his autobiographical *Confessions,* he admitted the sinfulness of his earlier life and confessed that God's grace rather than his own abilities had made possible his triumph over that sinfulness. The work presented Christianity as the most satisfactory pattern for life and became a model for numerous saints' lives in subsequent centuries. In another work, the *City of God,* Augustine described how humans give their allegiance to one of two societies: the City of the World, including the Roman Empire, or the City of God, having its perfect form in heaven but present on Earth in the community of the church. Written in the period of stepped-up Germanic migrations, the book argues that destruction of the Roman Empire may be part of God's plan and that humans ought to give their permanent allegiance not to it but to the City of God. Augustine's interpretation of history quickly replaced those of classical thinkers and has remained influential down to the present day.

Contemporary with the church fathers, other Christians seeking the City of God on earth practiced a rigorously disciplined religious life called monasticism and formed communities of monks (men) and nuns (women). From the third century onward, some Christians withdrew from urbanized Roman life to pursue strict

---

CICERO OR CHRIST?

Suddenly I was caught up in the spirit and dragged before the judgment seat of the Judge. . . . Asked who and what I was I replied: "I am a Christian." But He who presided said: "You lie, you are a follower of Cicero and not of Christ. For 'where your treasure is, there will your heart be also.'" Instantly I became dumb, and amid the strokes of the lash—for He had ordered me to be scourged—I was tortured more severely still by the fire of conscience. . . . I began to cry and to bewail myself, saying: "Have mercy upon me, O Lord: have mercy upon me." . . . At last the bystanders . . . prayed that He would have pity on my youth, and that He would give me space to repent of my error. He might still, they urged, inflict torture on me, should I ever again read the works of the Gentiles. . . . Accordingly, I made an oath and called upon His name, saying: "Lord, if ever again I possess worldly books, or if ever again I read such, I have denied Thee."[*]

Around 374, during Lent, Jerome fell ill and had the nightmare described in this passage. Though he was deeply learned in classical Latin literature, Jerome worried about the compatibility of such interests with his devout Christian beliefs. This was a concern of many others too, and those who opposed the intermixture of classical and Christian cultures often referred to the lesson of Jerome's dream. But Jerome himself was not consistent and at other times spoke more favorably of using the classical legacy for Christian purposes.

[*]Jerome, *Letter* 23.30, trans. W. H. Fremantle, in *A Select Library of the Nicene and Post-Nicene Fathers of the Christian Church,* vol. 6 (New York: Christian Literature Company, 1893), pp. 35–36.

---

regimens of self-denial and spiritual discipline in wilderness areas. To check the excesses to which such zeal sometimes led and to channel the spiritual benefits from these activities to all Christians, thoughtful leaders urged these ascetics to live in communities, and composed rules of life for them. Typically, a society of monks or nuns vowed themselves to poverty, sexual abstinence, and obedience to superiors. Their day was divided into periods for physical needs such as eating and sleeping, prayer and meditation, study, and, in the Latin west, work. Such communities speeded the Christianization of the countryside, contributed new models for spiritual leadership, and preserved much of

classical civilization while transforming it to serve Christian purposes.

Another prominent Christian institution, the papacy, also developed during the period 300–500. As their members grew, the Christians recognized the bishop of a province's principal city as the chief or "arch-" bishop of that area, with supervisory responsibility over the province's other bishops. Archbishops in the empire's major cities became known as patriarchs. Although there were several patriarchs in the east, in the west there was only one, the patriarch of Rome, also called "pope" from his familiar Latin designation *papa* or "father." In contrast to the widely held view that all bishops were equal and each had

155

PETER AND HIS SUCCESSORS

The solidity of that faith which was praised in the chief of the Apostles [Peter] is perpetual: and as that remains which Peter believed in Christ, so that remains which Christ instituted in Peter. For when . . . the Lord asked the disciples whom they believed Him to be, amid the various opinions that were held, the blessed Peter replied, "You are the Christ, the Son of the living God." Then the Lord said, "blessed are you, Simon Bar-Jona! For flesh and blood has not revealed this to you, but my Father who is in heaven. And I tell you, you are Peter, and on this rock I will build my church, and the gates of Hades [power of death] shall not prevail against it. I will give you the keys of the kingdom of heaven, and whatever you bind on earth shall be bound in heaven, and whatever you loose on earth shall be loosed in heaven" [Matthew 16:16–19].

The dispensation of Truth therefore abides, and the blessed Peter, persevering in the strength of the Rock, which he has received, has not abandoned the helm of the Church which he undertook. . . . If anything is won from the mercy of God by our daily supplications, it is of his work and merits whose power lives and whose authority prevails in his See [official seat]. *

The Roman popes based their claim to authority over the whole church on the scriptural passage cited here by Pope Leo. The name Peter and the word for rock are spelled similarly in Greek and may represent a play on words. In any case, Pope Leo's formulation of the "Petrine Doctrine" remained authoritative for centuries and was used to support the claims of the popes to supremacy in Europe.

*Pope Leo I (440–461), Sermon III, trans. J. Barmby, in A Select Library of the Nicene and Post-Nicene Fathers of the Christian Church, vol. 12 (New York: Christian Literature Company, 1895), p. 117.

absolute authority in his own territory, the Roman popes asserted that Jesus had granted to the apostle Peter, the first bishop of the church at Rome, jurisdiction over the whole church, and claimed that they as Peter's successors were the bearers of that authority. The popes' insistence on their ascendancy over all patriarchs, bishops, and other Christians in the empire's Greek-speaking eastern portions later caused bitter conflicts. In the Latin-speaking west, however, where no other patriarch existed, papal claims to authority were readily accepted. As the Germanic migrations nullified the political power of the Roman emperor in the west, the papacy became a symbol of Christian unity in that area, focusing on Rome both religiously and politically.

THE COLLAPSE OF THE ROMAN EMPIRE IN THE WEST

The story of the Roman Empire after the death of Constantine in 337 is one of struggles for succession and of eventual submersion of the western half of the empire under ever-larger waves of Germanic and Asiatic immigrants and invaders (see Map 21). An ultimately fatal intensification of pressure on the empire's borders resulted from the movement of Huns into Europe and the consequent displacement of Germanic tribes, who desired a more settled existence in the fertile, cleared land within the borders of the Roman Empire. Emperors perished in battle, large tracts of the land were successively ceded or stripped away, and finally Rome itself was sacked in 410, for the first time since 387 B.C. The reigning emperor, Honorius, had already moved his court to the more secure city of Ravenna in northern Italy, and there in 476 the last western emperor, Romulus Augustulus, was deposed by the German leader Odoacer, who became the first barbarian king of Italy (476–493). The once brilliant light of Roman power in the west flickered out as Visigoths and Ostrogoths, Franks, Burgundians, Vandals, and others divided the territories of the old western empire.

The question of what caused the fall of Rome is endlessly fascinating and has prompted a wide variety of responses. Those who emphasize a decay from within point to economic crises caused in part by the bloated imperial bureaucracy and the financial strain it placed on an empire being depopulated by plagues, poverty, and declining birth rates. Some believe that Christianity, with its emphasis on the heavenly Kingdom of God, discouraged the patriotic virtues that had sustained Rome in earlier days. Others cite a loss of traditional Roman moral values as non-Italians and even barbarians gained precedence within the society, within the civil administration, and in the ranks and

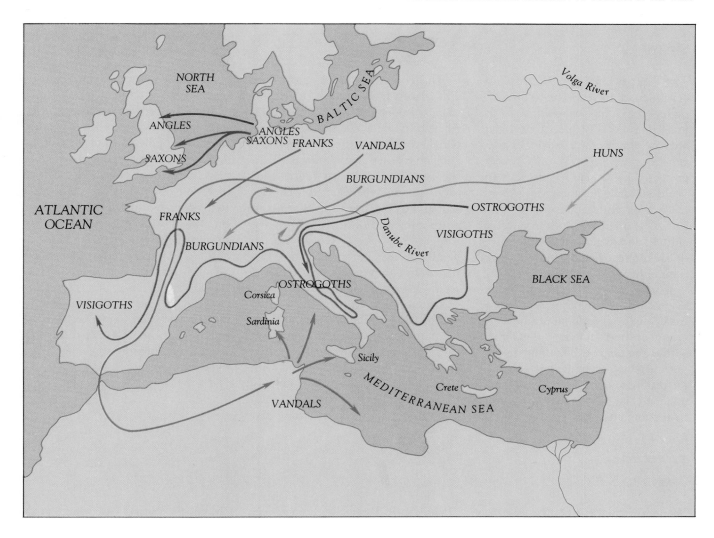

Map 21
Germanic Invasion Routes.

officer class of the army. Soil exhaustion, protracted drought, dysgenic lead poisoning among the aristocracy, and slavery as a disincentive to technological advance are still other suggested causes of decline. However, many of these weaknesses also affected the eastern half of the empire, which did not collapse.

The best explanation for the fall of the Roman Empire in the west is the intensified barbarian pressure directed against defense forces spread thin by the great length of the Rhine-Danube frontier. This pressure had been felt since the second century, and Rome had devised methods of coping with it. These included gradual assimilation of barbarians within the citizen population of the empire as well as strengthening of the defenses against invasion. But as Germanic migration steadily increased in the late fourth and throughout the fifth century, insupportable demands were placed on the military and financial resources of the western half of the empire, where the economic and social structure had long been crumbling.

SUMMARY

The Roman Empire in the first two centuries of its existence marked a high point of classical culture. In the material aspects of life, the inhabitants of the Roman world enjoyed general prosperity. Within borders protected by Roman legions, citizens could conduct business, raise crops, teach their children, enjoy the good things of material and intellectual culture, and in general live their lives in an unprecedented atmosphere of tranquillity.

The third century witnessed a dramatic change in the conditions of life. Invasions from without strained the resources, both human and material, within the empire. The imperial system of government underwent militarization and nearly disintegrated under the strain of civil strife among rival claimants to the throne.

The contemporaneous growth of Christianity both answered a need for stability among the anxious masses and triggered violent reaction by an imperial establishment that feared the challenge posed by the new faith. In the late third and early fourth centuries, strong-willed leaders—Diocletian and Constantine—succeeded in postponing the ultimate collapse of the political system, but at the expense of unity, as they promoted the division of the empire into east and west. Constantine also helped ensure the victory of Christianity in the competition of religions by embracing the faith. The Christian church in the late empire effectively replaced the collapsing political system with its own community and hierarchy of clergy. In addition to its doctrinal appeal, the church offered strong psychological and social inducements to membership.

In the fourth and fifth centuries, barbarian invasions finally overwhelmed the defenses of the western empire. Though internal deficiencies played a part in the collapse, the death of Rome resulted from assault more than from senility. From this point on, the destiny of western civilization, as begun and developed in the cultures of Greece and Rome, would be in the hands of Rome's heirs. These included, in a direct line, the Byzantine Empire and the Germanic kingdoms of western Europe, both already on the scene by 500. A third heir, the Islamic Empire, was looming just over the horizon.

SELECTED SOURCES

*Bonner, Stanley F. *Education in Ancient Rome.* 1977. A current, thorough, and authoritative presentation and interpretation of the available evidence on the subject.

*Brown, Peter. *Augustine of Hippo: A Biography.* 1967. The best recent biography of this important church father.

*Brown, Peter. *The World of Late Antiquity: A.D. 150–750.* 1971. Especially valuable for its coverage of religious and cultural developments and for discussion of the transition from antiquity to the Middle Ages.

*Chambers, Mortimer. *The Fall of Rome: Can It Be Explained?* 2d ed. 1970. A good anthology of essays constituting a brief survey of major theories.

*Dodds, E. R. *Pagan and Christian in an Age of Anxiety: Some Aspects of Religious Experience from Marcus Aurelius to Constantine.* 1965. Especially valuable for its placement of Christianity within the context of the intellectual history of the period.

*Eadie, John W., ed. *The Conversion of Constantine.* 1971. A handy collection of authoritative essays on a pivotal event in the history of western civilization.

*Grant, Michael. *The Climax of Rome: The Final Achievements of the Ancient World, A.D. 161–337.* 1968. A clear and detailed account of political, military, artistic, intellectual, and religious aspects of the period surveyed.

*Mattingly, Harold. *Christianity in the Roman Empire.* 1967. An extremely concise and cogent account of the subject; originally a series of lectures.

*Starr, Chester G. *The Roman Empire: 27 B.C.–A.D. 476.* 1982. A recent, brief, and lively history of the empire, by an eminent historian.

*Yourcenar, Marguerite. *Memoirs of Hadrian.* Translated by Grace Frick. 1963. A superb historical novel, written in the form of an autobiography addressed by Hadrian to the young Marcus Aurelius.

*Available in paperback.

THE EVOLUTION OF WESTERN CIVILIZATION

During the medieval period (500–1350), three cultures continued and modified the traditions of western civilization. The Byzantine Empire contributed significantly to the early development of eastern Europe. The Islamic civilization, which came to embrace the Middle East and parts of north Africa, preserved many features of Greco-Roman culture by assimilating non-Arab intellectual and cultural traditions.

In the lands of the third heir to Rome—western Europe—development was slow between 500 and 1000. Little trade existed, and people lived in farming settlements based on tribal social organizations. Weak monarchs and ineffective government institutions enabled strong individuals to seize land and power for themselves. Warfare was endemic, not only among powerful lords but also between Europeans and foreign invaders. Limited economic resources offered scanty support to educational, literary, and artistic activities.

The strongest institution in western civilization at this period was the Christian church. By 1000, missionaries had extended the faith to most Europeans. Monasteries developed improved agricultural methods and copied and preserved ancient manuscripts, as well as observing daily routines of prayer and devotion. Priests provided sacraments and spiritual guidance to their parishioners. The wealth of the church supported most of the cultural activities of the period.

After 1000, western civilization in Europe underwent considerable change. Commercial activity in the Mediterranean and northern seas increased, and trade and manufacturing became important options for many. Economic resources and political creativity centered on key trading points, which now became towns. Kings exploited feudal relations to control militarily powerful nobles and enhanced their royal positions by the effective administration of justice and the forming of strong ties with towns. England and France in particular developed healthy feudal monarchies. An artificial union of German and Italian regions, the Holy Roman Empire, was often weakened and split by conflicts between popes and emperors. The richer and politically more stable areas of Europe undertook a series of military expeditions, known as the Crusades, against Muslim neighbors.

A significant intellectual institution—the university—evolved from cathedral schools in the wealthier towns. The universities, which fostered the study of texts and exercise of reason, trained future leaders of church and state. The towns also supported large churches and cathedrals that became magnificent architectural showcases for their other arts. Although the church dominated medieval life, other influences gave western civilization in Europe a rich variety and stimulating cultural texture. The Crusades, for example, besides recovering formerly Christian territory, made Greek and Arabic literary and scientific works available to Europeans.

	400	500	600	700	800

Politics

496
Conversion
of Clovis

674
Arabs
besiege
Constantinople

751
Pepin III
establishes
Carolingian
dynasty

529
Justinian
collects
*Corpus Juris
Civilis*

711
Muslim
conquest
of Spain

800
Coronation
of Charlemagne

Economics & Society

Declining
trade in
Europe

Muslims
revive
Mediterranean
trade

German-
Roman
assimilation

Feudal
lords
gain
power

Growth of
manorial
agriculture

Science & Technology

Slavs
introduce
lightweight
plow

c. 770
Horseshoe,
three-field
system
introduced

Wider
use of
water
mills

Stirrup
introduced
to Europe

850
Arabs
perfect
the
astrolabe

Religion & Thought

529
Benedictine
order
established

610
Muhammad
begins
preaching
Islam

756
Papal states
established
by Pepin III

451
Council
of Chalcedon

590–604
Gregory I
claims
papal
absolutism

726–87
Iconoclasm
controversy

Arts & Literature

524
Boethius'
*The
Consolation
of Philosophy*

c. 699
Beowulf
legends
completed

831
Einhard's
*Life of
Charlemagne*

400
Augustine's
City of God

529
Hagia
Sophia
built

731
Bede's
*Ecclesiastical
History*

900	1000	1100	1200	1300	1400

c. 900
Alfonso III
begins
reconquest
of Spain

1066
Norman
conquest
of England

1152–90
Frederick I

1215
Magna
Carta

1328
End of
Capetian
dynasty

962
Otto I
crowned
Holy Roman
Emperor

1122
Concordat
of Worms

1204
Crusaders
sack
Constantinople

1226–70
"Saint"
Louis IX

Vikings
revive
Northern
sea trade

Growth
of
towns

Growing
prominence
of fairs
in Champagne

c. 1241
Hanseatic
League
founded

1350–1400
Peasant
revolts

Endemic
feudal
warfare

Beginnings
of money
economy in
western Europe

1193
Merchant
guild
established
in London

1347
"Black Death"
(bubonic plague)
begins

Shoulder
horse
collar
introduced

Iron
plows
replace
wooden

1125
Mariners'
compass

1214–94
Roger
Bacon

Mechanization
of fulling
of cloth

1050
Astrolabe
first
used by
Europeans

c. 1200
Windmill
use widespread

1289
First
block
printing
in Europe

910
Cluny
founded

1073–80
Gregory VII
initiates
reform

1122
Peter
Abelard's
Sic et Non

1309–77
Avignonese
papacy

Nadir of
medieval
papacy

1096
First
Crusade
launched by
Pope Urban II

1225–74
St. Thomas
Aquinas
Summa
Theologica

1387–1400
Geoffrey
Chaucer's
Canterbury
Tales

Romanesque
architecture

Chartres
cathedral;
Gothic architecture

c. 1170
Romances

Rosewitha
Drama

Chansons
de geste,
troubadours

1150
University
of Paris
founded

1307–21
Dante's
Divine
Comedy

Heirs of the Roman Empire (500–750)

As the inner part of the temple was seen, and the sun lit its glories, sorrow fled from the hearts of all. And when the first gleam of light, rosy-armed driving away the dark shadows, leaped from arch to arch, then all the princes and peoples with one voice hymned their songs of prayer and praise; and as they came to the sacred courts it seemed to them as if the mighty arches were set in heaven. Whenever anyone enters the church to pray, he realizes at once it is not by any human power or skill, but by the influence of God that it has been built. And so his mind is lifted up to God, and he feels that He cannot be far away, but must love to dwell in this place He has chosen.

Constantinople's magnificent church of Hagia Sophia (Holy Wisdom), described in these words by a contemporary writer, symbolized the Christian Roman or Byzantine Empire's glorious cultural achievement. In that empire, as in the building of Hagia Sophia, the Emperor Justinian I (527–565) combined cultural and political order of the classical period of Greece and Rome with the vital religious faith of Christianity. His successors and the rulers of the Latin west and Islamdom labored to do likewise. By their efforts, they and the many people they ruled began building a more impressive structure than Hagia Sophia—western civilization. This chapter examines what the three heirs of Rome accomplished during the period 500–750 and how they contributed to shaping and forming western civilization.

The East Roman or Byzantine Empire

By 500, Germanic peoples had destroyed the Roman Empire's Mediterranean unity and ruled large portions of its former territory in the west. The territory that remained under the emperor's control is called the Byzantine Empire after Byzantium, a Greek town incorporated in the imperial

Interior of the Church of Hagia Sophia (Holy Wisdom), Constantinople. By placing the dome atop two half-domes, the builders created a large open space, brightly lighted through the dome windows. The achievement astounded sixth-century contemporaries, who asserted that the dome had been let down from heaven.

163

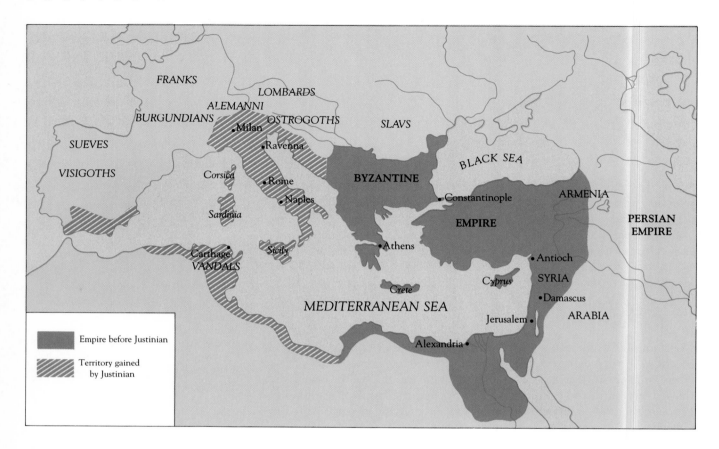

MAP 22
The Mediterranean in the Time of Justinian. The Byzantine Empire about 525, after the Germanic migrations into western Europe, occupied only the limited area shown. Justinian I enlarged it by recovering territories from Goths and Vandals, but some of those gains were lost soon after his death.

capital, Constantinople. The empire's inhabitants, however, considered themselves Romans.

The Empire in 500

The Byzantine Empire retained the Roman Empire's political and social structure and preserved its cultural heritage. Freed of heavy expenses for military defense and economic development of the west, the Byzantine Empire prospered economically. Socially, the empire remained diverse. In rural areas, aristocratic nobles held large landed estates, worked by slaves or by free tenant renters (sharecroppers) called *coloni*. Large numbers of merchants, artisans, educators, and administrators lived in the empire's numerous cities. Although members of the ruling elite lived comfortably and reaped the benefits of empire, most people lived on the margin of starvation in city tenements or village huts. Students learned classical Greek writings and followed classical educational traditions and techniques, but most of the empire's inhabitants spoke a different, common Greek. The New Testament was written in common Greek, and Greek-speaking church leaders dominated the fourth- and fifth-century councils, which defined Christian beliefs. Syria and Egypt, however, maintained rich cultural traditions in their own languages and scorned their Greek-speaking rulers.

Even though Christianity was the official religion of the empire, the

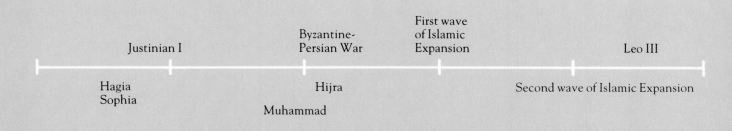

500	550	600	650	700	750

Justinian I

Byzantine-
Persian War

First wave
of Islamic
Expansion

Leo III

Hagia
Sophia

Hijra

Second wave of Islamic Expansion

Muhammad

empire's Christians were not united. The orthodox upheld the conclusions of the councils regarding the Trinity and the nature of Christ. There were also many nonorthodox churches in the empire. The most prominent heretical groups were the Arians, who held Jesus was not equal to God; the Nestorians, who held Christ had two separate natures; and the Monophysites, who taught that Christ's divine nature had absorbed his human nature. Heretics were especially numerous in Syria and Egypt, already alienated because these areas were not Greek speaking. The emperors, however, continued to pursue the ideal of Christian unity in belief and worship.

The emperor exercised absolute political control over the empire. He appointed and dismissed officials, issued edicts, sat as the final court of judicial appeal, and commanded the military and naval forces. He also conducted diplomacy with rulers and peoples outside the empire, preferring to negotiate rather than fight and restraining potential enemies by establishing agreements with their neighbors. Emperors were ordinarily chosen from the imperial family by the army and confirmed by the senate in Constantinople, but by the fifth century the patriarch of Constantinople, representing both the people and the church, crowned and consecrated the emperor.

Justinian I

Justinian I, the greatest Byzantine emperor, demonstrated the strengths and limitations of the empire. He regarded it as a Christian Roman state consisting of two parts, the ecclesiastical, which ministered to spiritual needs, and the political, which attended to earthly affairs. The emperor was responsible for keeping both parts in good order and harmony.

His able and courageous wife, Theodora (ca. 500–548), assisted in those tasks. She restrained his religious zeal and helped to maintain harmonious governmental relations with the heretics. When a riot early in his reign (532) prompted Justinian and his advisers to consider fleeing the capital, Theodora urged them instead to stay and fight; when they did, the riot was quelled and the throne secured.

Justinian was an active and effective ruler. He reformed the governmental administration and instituted a more efficient collection of revenues. The emperor made the beautification of Constantinople a special project and conducted a large-scale building program. He thus provided work for unemployed laborers and also for artists, who added mosaics, sculptures, and icons (pictures of religious figures) to many buildings. Byzantine art became nearly as important as the Greek language in defining Christian faith for peoples inside and outside the empire.

In addition to improving administration and rebuilding Constantinople, another of Justinian's enduring accomplishments was his compilation and systematizing of Roman law. He directed a committee to collect and edit all currently valid Roman legislation and legal commentaries of jurists on the civil law and to produce a standard textbook for the use of law students. He then centralized and controlled the teaching and interpretation of the law within the empire. Henceforth, Roman law meant the Corpus Juris Civilis (Collection of Civil Law); it remained extremely influential and became the basis for the civil law of many European and Latin American nations.

Justinian also sought to complete the Christianization of imperial society. He restricted the civil rights of heretics, Jews, Samaritans, and other

165

non-Christians and specifically prohibited them from holding public office or teaching. In 529, he closed the philosophical schools in Athens.

Justinian's reign promoted Byzantine literature and learning. Christian teachers stressed the best elements of classical moral training, philosophical thought, and literary craftsmanship. They taught the classical tradition from the Christian viewpoint and wrote on both classical and Christian topics, producing epigrams in the classical Greek manner, poems in elegant Homeric verse, and histories in the style of Herodotus and Thucydides.

The Empire's Neighbors

Although he devoted enormous energy to internal matters, Justinian spent most of his reign and much of the empire's wealth attempting to reconquer the German-occupied western territories. He quickly reestablished imperial control over north Africa and the southern coast of Spain, but regained Italy only after a protracted campaign (see Map 22). Following his death, however, the Visigoths reconquered southern Spain and a new Germanic group, the Lombards, moved from the Danube Valley to seize north and much of central Italy. Hence the Byzantine presence in the west was reduced to north Africa, Sicily, and some regions on the Italian coast, where the city of Ravenna served as an imperial administrative center.

Justinian's warfare in the west weakened the empire's defenses on its eastern and northern frontiers and created serious problems for his successors. To the north, the Slavs, an Indo-European agricultural people previously controlled by alien rulers,

surged southward through the Danube Valley, vacated by the Lombards. They entered Macedonia and Greece by 600 and soon after assaulted Constantinople. To counter the Lombards and Slavs, seventh-century emperors placed civil and military authority in the hands of regional military commanders, and the region's civilian population became the defending army. The plan was successful and the emperors thereby ensured the empire's survival, but it was changed into a society mobilized for continual warfare. The Byzantines also long enjoyed naval supremacy, thanks in part to "Greek fire," a petroleum-based incendiary substance whose exact composition remains unknown but which could be discharged from tubes and was not extinguishable with water.

Farther east, Justinian's successors discontinued his policy of buying peace through paying subsidies to Rome's longtime enemy Persia. War with Persia followed soon after 600. The Persians enjoyed early successes, quickly conquered Syria and Egypt, and then attacked Constantinople. However, the Byzantines countered by invading Persia and occupying its capital, Ctesiphon, and by 628 they had forced the Persians to seek peace.

The war with Persia brought the Byzantines no territorial gains; moreover, it exhausted the empire economically and damaged its ability to respond to attacks soon to be launched by new and vigorous foes. The Arabs, newly united under Islam, seized Syria and Egypt from the empire and Mesopotamia from the Persians shortly after 630. Two Arab sieges of Constantinople in 674–678 and 717–718 were unsuccessful; thereafter, the Taurus Mountains dividing the peninsula known as Asia Minor from Syria

became the Byzantine-Arab frontier. Another Asiatic people, the Bulgars, entered the Balkans late in the seventh century. They defeated a Byzantine force to gain control of the lower Danube Valley, and proceeded to integrate the local Slavic peoples into a Bulgar-dominated state.

Religious Issues

Because the Byzantines considered their state both Christian and Roman, their wars had religious as well as political dimensions. Justinian fought the Germans because of their Arianism as well as their occupation of imperial territory, and his seventh-century successors opposed Slavs and Bulgars as non-Christian pagans. Persians and Arabs followed rival religions, Zoroastrianism and Islam, respectively; each conquered Syria and Egypt easily in the seventh century, partly because of the hostility between heretic and orthodox Christians in those areas. Their conquests removed the important cities of Jerusalem, Alexandria, and Antioch, as well as many heretics, from the empire and left Constantinople and Rome as the major Christian centers.

Unfortunately, leaders in those two centers often disagreed on religious issues. The emperors considered it their duty to maintain orthodoxy in their dominions. Thus Justinian, and others after him, experimented with various formulas of faith in an effort to establish doctrinal unity. The bishops of Rome, or popes, however, claimed headship of the church and regarded the definition of Christian faith as their responsibility. Justinian and his successors found that a statement acceptable in the east often encountered papal opposition, whereas

Byzantine Icon of St. Andrew. Byzantine Christians extensively venerated icons, representations of religious personages such as saints. Icons were produced by monks according to standardized techniques. Artists stressed the subject's spiritual qualities by leaving the background blank and the gaze unfocused and exaggerating the size of eyes and hands. This icon dates from the thirteenth century. Museo Correr, Venice.

a statement the west could support met rejection in the east. Church councils in the sixth and seventh centuries failed to resolve such conflicts.

A new conflict, division among the Christians over iconoclasm, emerged in the eighth century. Emperor Leo III (717–741) thought people were worshiping religious images, angering God and bringing disasters to the empire, and believed that too many of the empire's bright and able men were entering monasteries rather than state service. Therefore, he sought to eliminate apparent idolatry from the empire and to discredit monasticism by attacking the use of icons. Monks made, sold, and promoted the use of icons, and exercised enormous economic and devotional influence in Byzantine life. The emperor's move sharply divided the empire's population into iconoclasts (image breakers) and iconodules (image users). Many of the latter fled to monasteries or to western imperial territories in south Italy and Sicily. Because the popes

167

opposed the iconoclasts, Leo retaliated by transferring many rich papal lands in Italy to the patriarch of Constantinople, greatly enhancing the patriarch's's prestige and enlarging his area of jurisdiction. Iconoclasm polarized Latin and Greek Christians and divided the Byzantine Empire even after the ecumenical Council of Nicaea in 787 restored relations between Rome and Constantinople.

THE ISLAMIC EMPIRE

During the seventh century, a group of southwest Asian people, the Arab Muslims, joined and in some areas replaced the Byzantines as heirs of Greco-Roman civilization. Already sharers of a common language, Arabic, and a seminomadic way of life, the Arab inhabitants of the Arabian Peninsula became united through the preaching of Muhammad (570–632) and the religion of Islam. They soon embarked on an astonishing career of military conquest and a remarkable process of religious expansion.

Arabia in 600

The Islamic movement began in the Arabian Peninsula, where many inhabitants migrated with their animals over large desert areas in search of water and grazing land. They typically lived in a tribe headed by an elected chief and were known for their love of independence, devotion to tribal gods, and contempt for urban life. Some Arabs practiced agriculture in scattered oases. Arabs in the rain-favored southern tip of the peninsula built dams and irrigation works to conserve and exploit available water

supplies and developed a flourishing state.

In addition to the Arabs who practiced nomadism or agriculture, still other Arabs engaged in trade. Arabs provided Mediterranean lands with spices and ointments such as frankincense and myrrh, either locally produced or imported from India and other eastern lands. Arab mariners crossed the Indian Ocean from India, bringing eastern cargoes to Arabia's rich southern tip. From there, other Arab merchants carried those goods to Mediterranean lands either via the Red Sea or along caravan routes in western Arabia.

An especially significant Arabian town at this time was Mecca. Its location midway along the west Arabian trade route made it a convenient stopping point for caravans, and growing trade attracted settlers to it. People throughout Arabia also came to Mecca on religious pilgrimage to venerate a black meteorite and worship various gods whose images were placed in the sanctuary that housed it.

Muhammad

Mecca became the chief center of one of the major world religions through the efforts of Muhammad, who united the Arabs in the religion of Islam. Muhammad, born poor and orphaned young, was reared by relatives, helped manage the family's caravans, and subsequently married a wealthy widow. He spent much time in thinking about his city and its people, and around 610 began to preach the oneness of God and transmit divine commands for moral living. It seems likely that he had some acquaintance with followers of Judaism, Zoroastrianism, and

Christianity, but the extent of that acquaintance and the influence of those religions on his thought and activity remain unclear although hotly debated. Although Muhammad gathered some followers from his family and clan, he also attracted opposition from the Meccan ruling aristocracy, who disliked his moral teaching, scorned his low birth, and feared a loss of the city's significance to pilgrims if Muhammad's teachings gained widespread acceptance. Opposition escalated from heckling to economic boycott and assassination attempts, prompting Muhammad to seek safety for himself and his followers. Invited to become arbiter of disputes in nearby Medina, he accepted and soon became Medina's chief leader. His followers, known as Muslims, those who submit to God, recognize the date of that migration (622) as the beginning of their religious calendar. During several years of war between Medina and Mecca, many desert tribes recognized Muhammad as both religious leader and paramount chief. In 630, Muhammad led a triumphant military force to Mecca, which then also adopted Islam.

Islam

Islam is a simple, direct religion in both faith and practice. Muhammad recited its holy book, the Qur'an (also spelled Koran), piecemeal as God's revelations came to him; pious Muslims compiled it in its present form within twenty-five years of his death. Muslims use the Qur'an as a spiritual resource, a language manual, a schoolbook, a code of law and ethics, a book of political theory, and a guide to conduct. They read it in Arabic, the language in which Muhammad

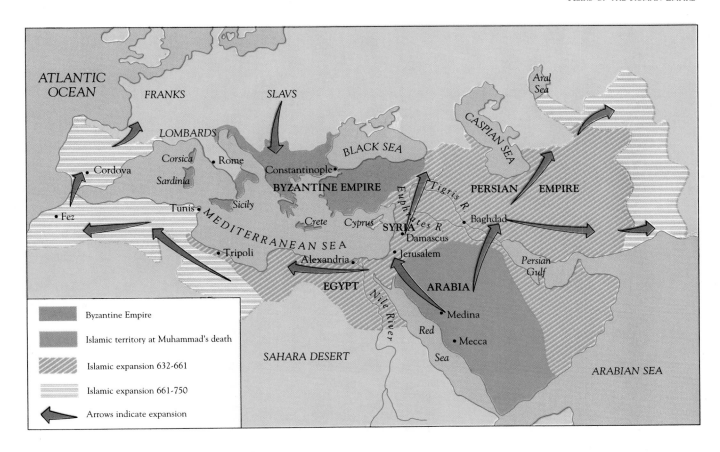

Byzantine Empire

Islamic territory at Muhammad's death

Islamic expansion 632-661

Islamic expansion 661-750

Arrows indicate expansion

recited it, although translations are now available. Islam teaches there is one God and Muhammad is his prophet. According to Islam's ethical law, Muslims must acknowledge these truths, perform ritual prayer five times daily (including joint public prayer at midday on Friday), fast daily from dawn to sunset during the month of Ramadan, give alms to aid the poor and unfortunate, and visit Mecca once in a lifetime if possible. Islam has no priests to mediate between humans and God and forbids the visual representation of living beings in religious art. It recognizes Moses and Jesus among its prophets, regarding Muhammad as the last and greatest of the prophets. Islam accepts Judaism and Christianity as religions based on divine revelation, but claims their holy books contain errors that God's revelation to Muhammad corrected.

Territorial Expansion

Muhammad understood part of his God-given task was to unite all people in a community in which Islam governed all aspects of life. When he died, the Islamic community's survival was in doubt, because many tribes thought his death ended their allegiance to that community. His followers, however, elected successors called *caliphs* to head the community and promptly restored the Islamic federation of the Arab tribes.

MAP 23
The Expansion of Islam. Most of Islam's early territorial gains were at the expense of the Persian and Byzantine Empires. The former was entirely absorbed, and the latter, already diminished by German gains, lost Syria, Egypt, and all its north African possessions. Arrows show the various directions of Islamic advance.

Detail of Tiled Dome of the Madrasah of Chahar Bagh, Isfahan. In addition to its religious and literary contributions, the Arabic language was artistically important. To avoid any semblance of usurping God's creative powers, Muslims did not depict living beings in religious art. Instead, they used geometric patterns, floral decorations, and, as in this seventeenth-century dome, calligraphy or artistic writing. Iran.

The Arabian tribes, which traditionally had raided and plundered their neighbors, could no longer attack fellow Muslims in an Islamically unified Arabia, so they directed their energies against non-Muslims. To bring such persons into submission to Islamic rule, the caliphs and their generals created a large, able, and dedicated army, making the Arabs a military aristocracy dedicated to fighting for the state, and promised them a place in paradise if they died in battle. To maintain that fighting readiness, the Arab leaders stationed the army in camps isolated from the

life of the cities in conquered territory. A campaign to protect the Islamic faith and community against opponents was called *jihad*, from an Arabic verb meaning "to strive."

The Islamic armies enjoyed astonishing successes. Within twenty years after Muhammad's death, Arab armies penetrated the bordering Byzantine and Persian empires, both of which were exhausted from their recent long war. They decisively defeated the Byzantine and Persian armies, and by 660 had conquered Palestine, Syria, Egypt, Persia, and north Africa as far as present-day Tunisia. Civil war for control of the caliphate interrupted Islamic expansion for some twenty years, but under the leadership of the Umayyad dynasty (661–750), the Islamic advance resumed (see Map 23). Between 680 and 750, the Umayyads conquered present-day Pakistan, central Asia, northwest Africa, and the Iberian Peninsula. They were not uniformly victorious, however: Two sieges of Constantinople proved unsuccessful, Chinese forces checked the Arab eastward advance in 751, and a Muslim raiding expedition was defeated by a Frankish force between Tours and Poitiers in 733.

The Muslims organized the conquered territories into wealthy, tribute-paying provinces ruled by the caliphs. At first, they lacked the experience and the bureaucracy needed to administer a huge empire. They employed Greeks and Syrians as government officials, but later replaced them with well-trained Muslims and made Arabic the language of government as well as of religion. Conquered Christians, Jews, and Zoroastrians became protected minorities who paid special although not excessive taxes and who remained free to practice their faiths and observe their own religious laws. Many descendants of the conquered peoples, however, adopted Islam, and the Arabs rapidly became a minority among their Islamicized subjects. Those non-Arab Muslims soon challenged the Arabs and overthrew the Umayyad dynasty in 750.

Cultural Activity

While they ruled, the wealthy, tolerant, and secular Umayyad caliphs promoted cultural life and encour-

---

ISLAMIC TOLERATION

The bishop [of Damascus] who had provided Khalid with food at the beginning of the siege of the city was wont to stand on its wall. Khalid would call him and when he came to him, Khalid would greet him and discuss matters with him. The bishop one day said to Khalid, "O abu-Sulayman, the prospects of your success are good, and you owe me a promise. Now therefore, offer me terms and I shall deliver the city." Thereupon Khalid requested an inkhorn and parchment and wrote:

"In the name of God, the merciful, the compassionate. This is what Khalid would grant the inhabitants of Damascus when he enters it. He shall grant them security for their lives, properties and churches. Their city wall shall not be demolished, neither shall any Moslem be quartered in their homes. Thereunto we give them the pact of God and the protection of His Messenger, upon whom be God's blessing and peace, the caliphs and the Believers. So long as they pay poll-tax nothing but good shall befall them."*

Religious toleration and generous terms to persons in conquered territories greatly facilitated Islamic expansion. Inhabitants of many areas, dissatisfied with their previous rulers, often welcomed and sometimes actively aided the conquering Muslims. That was especially true for heretical Christians, who had experienced oppression under Byzantine or Persian rulers.

*Philip K. Hitti, The Origins of the Islamic State, being a translation of Kitab Futuh al-Buldan by al-Baladhuri (New York: Columbia University Press, 1916), pp. 186–187.

---

aged the assimilation of both Arab and non-Arab intellectual, artistic, and cultural traditions. In so doing, they preserved many features of Greco-Roman civilization. They undertook an extensive building and decorative program in their capital, Damascus, and other east Mediterranean areas, constructing elaborate hunting palaces and summer houses for themselves and places of prayer, called mosques, for the Muslim faithful. The Umayyads employed Byzantine and Syrian artists to beautify mosques with mosaics and calligraphy and decorated those religious buildings with nonfigured art employing intricate geometric patterns. In nonreligious buildings, figurative art in painting and mosaics attractively blended Byzantine and Islamic artistic styles.

Under Umayyad rule, Muslims also began to translate and assimilate Greek philosophical and scientific thought. Christians, with centuries of practice in defining and discussing theological issues in precise Greek terminology, rigorously questioned and challenged Muslims about their beliefs. Muslims therefore learned the techniques of Greek philosophy to counter their opponents effectively. Scholars translated Greek scientific works into Arabic, expanding Muslim intellectual horizons and technical abilities. By 750, Muslims as well as Byzantines shared the inheritance of the richest

Dome of the Rock, Jerusalem. The oldest Islamic building, dating from the seventh century, it marks the place where Muhammad, according to Islamic tradition, ascended into heaven and directly encountered God. Consequently, Jerusalem is a holy city to Muslims as well as to Christians and Jews. Muslims employed Byzantine artists and architects in the building's construction.

and most cultured section of the old Roman Empire.

WESTERN EUROPE

By contrast with the Byzantine and Islamic empires, western Europe, divided among several Germanic peoples, appeared to be a much less promising region for inheriting the Roman culture (Map 24). Rulers of the modest Germanic states experienced difficulty in controlling their own territories and confronted warlike neighbors. Agriculture was mainly

carried out on large, landed estates, and as they sought economic self-sufficiency trade dwindled and towns shrank. The church was the only significant international institution, and it became the heir of much of the Roman cultural tradition. Creative individuals in those troubled times, however, made important contributions to the development of western civilization.

Social and Political Order in Germanic States

In England, formerly Britain, where Roman influences had almost disappeared, Angles, Jutes, and Saxons formed numerous small, free states. In Italy, the Ostrogoths who held Italy until Justinian's conquests acted as military protectors of the Roman population, but remained separate from them. Burgundians in Gaul and Visigoths in Spain prohibited intermarriage and retained separate Roman and German legal systems. In north Africa, the Vandals attacked Roman landowners and Christian clergy, confiscating property and exiling or forcibly converting the population to Arian Christianity. Justinian subsequently eradicated the Ostrogoths and Vandals, but the other Germanic states lasted longer. The Lombards, who overran Italy after Justinian's death, maintained dual systems of private law and ecclesiastical organization. The Franks, moving southward into Gaul from lands along the Rhine River during the fifth century, seemed almost untouched by Roman influences.

Instead of the Byzantine and Islamic institutions of imperial government and urban life, Germanic society featured family and tribal structures in a rural setting. German families owned or held land and were counted as free household units for military service or tax assessment pur-

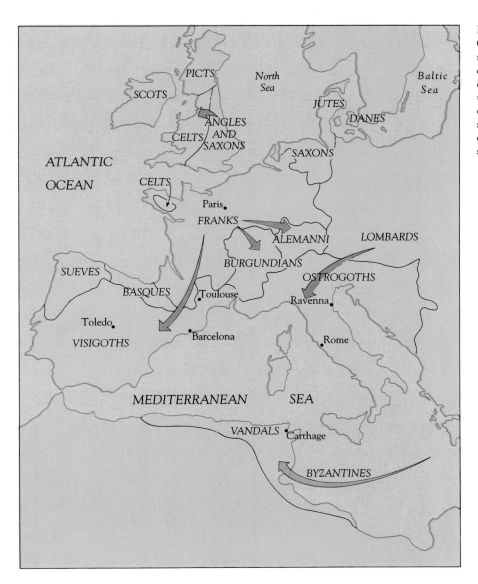

MAP 24
Germanic States in Europe. Major German states about 500 are shown here; arrows indicate important German advances after that date. Angles and Saxons pushed the Celts farther westward in England, the Lombards conquered much of Italy after Justinian I had destroyed the Ostrogoths, and the Franks expanded east and southward to become the strongest sixth-century Germanic state.

poses. They sometimes lived in isolated farmsteads, but were more often grouped together in villages. The tribe or people was the aggregate of all persons who lived under the same law, fought in the same army, and recognized a common king.

Tribes contained free persons, slaves, and half-free persons later known as serfs. Slaves became less common as settled life replaced migration and reduced slave-raiding activity. Depending on circumstances, many slaves rose out of slavery and free persons became half-free persons who lacked the full legal status of the free and were dependent on and protected by noble lords. The half-free persons had to remain on the land they worked, but were not another's personal property. Apart from the few merchants and the clergy, nobles gradually became the only fully free persons. Nobles retained their status

by intermarrying and collected benefits and privileges from Germanic kings.

Most Germans depended on agriculture for their livelihood. In the great plains of northern Europe, rainfall was generally plentiful, summers were cool and winters moderate, and the heavy, wet soil could produce two crops per year. However, farmers had only poor, locally made tools and little fertilizer, so crop yields remained low, until a heavy plow came into wider use after the sixth century. Because their only method of restoring soil fertility was to let land lie idle, the Germans required large areas to support relatively few people. They usually settled in small, densely populated communities widely separated from one another. Such communities produced great solidarity, with all members cooperating to perform the necessary agricultural activities.

The Germanic rulers of those scattered peoples retained and modified traditional features of Germanic kingship. Kings moved beyond the status of tribal chiefs by becoming successful war leaders who conquered and ruled territories, not merely people. They gave gifts to loyal followers, as war bands formerly divided booty. They maintained the tribal laws and settled disputes between free persons, whereas lords judged disputes among their serfs and slaves. The kings now embodied the tribe's common origin and history, and their succession came to depend on dynastic (family) right rather than individual right.

Germanic rulers also transformed traditional kingship by incorporating Christian and Roman elements. They began to use Latin for their royal documents and law codes and experimented with new conceptions of the king's role. Churchmen presented

The Baptism of Clovis. In this artistic recreation of the historic event, bishops on the left and nobles on the right witness the ritual. Above the king a dove, representing God's Holy Spirit, descends with oil for the ruler's anointing. Bibliothèque Nationale, Paris.

kings with biblical examples of good and evil royal behavior and adopted the biblical practice of anointing the king at accession. The king's activities now included the protection and patronage of the church; under the church's guidance he regarded his subjects as Christian people and defense of the Christian faith as one of his royal tasks.

The Rise of the Franks

Out of the preceding patterns of Germanic life, one people, the Franks, rose to prominence under the leadership of a dynamic ruler, King Clovis (481–511). Instead of separating Romans and Germans, Clovis chose to merge them by requiring both peoples to do military service and permitting intermarriage.

Clovis received baptism as a Roman Catholic Christian shortly before 500, separating the Franks from the other Germans, who were Arian Christians. The Franks promptly became champions of Roman Catholic orthodoxy against the Arians and won the support of the Christianized Roman aristocracy of Gaul and the Roman Catholic clergy, who supplied the Frankish kings with skilled and educated advisers and other benefits, such as the flattering legend that the Holy Spirit had descended directly from heaven for Clovis's baptism. Clovis and his successors greatly enlarged their realm by conquering territory held by Visigoths and Burgundians to the south. The Byzantine emperor recognized this achievement by designating Clovis an honorary consul.

Because the Germans customarily divided property equally among a father's surviving sons, Frankish unity

---

KING CLOVIS ADOPTS CHRISTIANITY

When . . . the army of Clovis was on the point of being completely destroyed . . . Clovis . . . lifted his eyes to heaven, . . . and . . . he spoke: "Jesus Christ . . . I ask you humbly for your mighty help. If you grant me now the victory over my enemies, and I thus experience that power which the people who honor your name claim to have proved, I will believe in you and have myself baptized in your name." . . . And as he was yet saying this, the Alemanni [another Germanic people] turned their backs and began to flee . . . [After receiving religious instruction] the king asked the bishop to be baptized. Then he stepped forward like a second Constantine to the baptismal font, . . . confessed God Almighty as the Trinity and was baptized in the name of the Father, of the Son, and of the Holy Spirit, and was anointed with the holy oil with the sign of the cross of Christ.*

This account of the baptism of Clovis shows many parallels to the conversion of the Emperor Constantine I. Moreover, it indicates the close connection of warfare, religion, and rulership in early medieval times. Clovis also commanded a number of his nobles to be baptized with him. Instruction in the beliefs and duties of the Christian faith would follow baptism.

*Gregory, Bishop of Tours, *History of the Franks*, edited by J. P. Migne, *Patrologiae cursus completus, series Latina* (1849), Vol 71, pp. 225–227. Joseph H. Dahmus, trans., *A History of Medieval Civilization* (New York: Odyssey Press, 1964), pp. 265–266.

---

did not long endure. Typically, a king's sons fought among themselves until only one survived to reunite the lands. Successive generations of the descendants of Clovis repeated the process, except for brief periods when a single ruler governed the whole Frankish kingdom. By the seventh century, however, three territories gained a sense of regional continuity and identity: Neustria in the west, Austrasia in the northeast, and Burgundy to the southeast.

Those dynastic conflicts not only weakened the Frankish monarchy but they also allowed nobles to assume political power and to assimilate royal lands and wealth to their holdings. Frankish kings had no centralized bureaucracy and few trained administrators and instead designated favorites as their representatives throughout

the realm. They appointed dukes to command armies and control large military districts and counts to administer smaller regions in accordance with local custom. Lacking money, the kings paid those officials with land grants or immunities, exempting these lands from royal taxation or visits by royal administrators. The kings also relied on such grants to obtain military service, especially from mounted warriors who required land to maintain themselves and their horses. As clan and tribal organizations deteriorated and ceased to provide customary protection and services, many people became personal and economic dependents of those noble landowners.

Some of the most powerful nobles became officials in the royal household and used their positions to in-

500	550	600	650	700	750

Clovis

Benedict Gregory I Charles Martel

Cassiodorus Isidore of Seville Synod of Whitby Bede of Jarrow

crease their families' wealth and power. The mayor of the palace was the most important official, serving as the king's chief adviser. In the late seventh and early eighth centuries, a series of kings who were not yet adults and could not rule in their own right weakened the monarchies of both Neustria and Austrasia. Successive mayors had exploited that situation and soon warred with one another. By 687, Pepin of Heristal, mayor of the palace of the Austrasian kings, had established his family in a dominant position in Frankish politics. His son Charles Martel (714–741) succeeded him as mayor of the palace in both Austrasia and Neustria. In 714, Charles, although still technically mayor of the palace, was virtually the undisputed ruler of the Franks and consolidated that position by defeating the Frisians to the north. He transmitted this position and his power to his son Pepin.

Religious and Cultural Activities

In an increasingly Germanized western Europe, the Christian church faced numerous problems as it assumed the moral, spiritual, and cultural leadership formerly exercised by the Roman Empire. Disappearance of Roman rule in the west deprived the church of imperial support, and the expansion of Islamdom reduced the territory of Christendom. Christendom became divided as Greek and Latin churches developed differences in belief, practice, and organization, and seemed likely to disintegrate into units coinciding with the Roman Empire's successor states. Superstition, violence, and immorality characterized popular life, and Christian beliefs and moral teachings were vaguely understood and rarely followed. Religious leadership was frequently entrusted to uneducated and morally lax priests and to bishops better qualified to wield political power than to provide spiritual guidance.

The church responded to those problems by undertaking a number of constructive activities. Christians attended to human needs by infusing their ideas of justice and mercy into codes of law, maintaining schools and hospitals, and assisting such neglected social groups as widows, orphans, and slaves. Moreover, Christianity expanded among the German peoples as well as to non-Germanic regions such as Ireland, bringing religious unity to western Europe.

The church also developed creative institutions in this troubled period. Monasticism, although introduced to the west before 500, was reformulated by Benedict of Nursia (480–547) near Spoleto in north central Italy. He wrote a moderate and human rule of life for monks that shaped devotional activity for a community devoted to study, prayer, and physical labor. To counter the evils of luxury, sexual laxity, and disregard for authority that afflicted clergy, he required monks to take vows of poverty, chastity, and obedience and to live under the absolute authority of an abbot. Benedict's Rule was also moderate and flexible, allowing monks to adapt to various situations they confronted. Pope Gregory I (590–604) wrote a life of Benedict and promoted the spread of Benedictine monasticism in Europe. Monks and nuns following the Benedictine rule won converts to Christianity and instructed those converts in basic Christian belief and practice. Consequently, Benedict's Rule became the basic guide for western Christian monastic life.

The other prominent Christian institution, the Roman papacy, was already established before 500 but gained increasing significance after that date, primarily through the efforts of Gregory I. By adroit land management and shrewd negotiations with Byzantines and Lombards, Gregory made the papacy financially and politically independent of the emperor and other rulers. He supplied significant spiritual leadership by his sermons, composed a *Book of Pastoral Care* to help clergy perform their duties effectively, and transmitted much theological information in his commentary on the biblical Book of Job. Moreover, he undertook dramatic initiatives, working to convert German kings from Arianism and sending missionaries to England in 597. Roman and Irish missionaries competed for England's religious allegiance for several decades, but the decision of the Synod of Whitby (664) definitely

Crucifixion of Christ. Attention to animals and use of curving lines for decoration typified much Germanic art. Here, the Greek letters alpha and omega hang suspended from the cross's arms to recall Jesus's words, "I am the beginning and the end." A bird representing the Holy Spirit perches atop the cross. Bibliothèque Nationale, Paris.

committed England to the Roman observance.

Although chaotic economic and political conditions during this period limited cultural activity, creative individuals worked to preserve and transmit classical culture. Boethius (480–524), an adviser to the Ostrogothic king Theodoric (493–526), created a Latin philosophical vocabulary and translated Greek philosophical works, especially those of Plato, into Latin. In *On the Consolation of Philosophy*, he also demonstrated how philosophical study led to Christian conclusions. Cassiodorus (490–585), who also advised Theodoric, wrote a *History of the Goths* to improve mutual understanding between Romans and Germans. His *Divine and Human Readings* organized and classified knowledge and established the seven liberal arts in European scholarship. He also formed a community of scribes and scholars to copy and transmit classical writings to succeeding generations. Isidore of Seville (560–636) in Spain collected much classical knowledge in his encyclopedic *Etymologies*.

Ireland was an important center of early medieval cultural and religious activity. Its conversion to Christianity, traditionally attributed to Patrick (389–461), a Roman citizen educated in Gaul, opened the island to continental influences. The absence of towns and the presence of tribal groupings in Ireland produced a church organization dominated by monks, monasteries, and abbots rather than priests, parishes (geographical units assigned to priests), and bishops. A rigorously ascetic hermit life became the religious ideal, and saintly Irish monks spread Christianity to Scotland, England, and central Europe during the sixth and seventh centuries. Irish monasteries were centers of intellectual and artistic activity, as well as spiritual life. Each monastery had its scriptorium (writing room), and copying both Christian and classical manuscripts was considered essential work. Skilled Irish copyists could produce both excellent, clear handwriting and elaborate, decorative calligraphy. They also developed the art of illumination (painting brightly colored pictures in manuscripts), which featured patterns of constantly recurring interlacing lines and emphasized symbolic allusions rather than realistic representations. Irish scribes produced similarly intricate repetitive and symbolic poetry.

England's conversion to Roman Catholic Christianity stimulated an outburst of literary productivity in that country. Theodore of Tarsus, sent to England in 668 to become archbishop of Canterbury and head of the English church, established monastic and cathedral schools to train English church leaders. These schools emphasized scriptural study and shaped devotional life while preserving much classical learning. Two prominent poets, Caedmon and Aldhelm, studied in the English schools and wrote on religious topics, the former in Old English and the latter in Latin. An unknown author composed the impressive Old English adventure epic *Beowulf*, which recounts the hero's slaying of monsters and a fire-breathing dragon. Although the themes of the poem are derived from the Germanic heroic tradition, the poem's spirit is altruistic, and it may have been intended as a Christian allegory. England's greatest scholar-writer of this period was Bede of Jarrow, who wrote many pedagogical works and biblical commentaries and an *Ecclesiastical History of the English People*, which presented a unified history of England within the framework of its conversion to Christianity. Bede's younger contemporary, Winfrid, later renamed Boniface, extended this English influence. He worked first as a missionary among the Germans and subsequently helped Charles Martel reform the Frankish church. He established higher standards of training for the Frankish clergy, developed an improved church organization, and forged closer ties with the popes.

SUMMARY

Despite the German conquest of the western portions of the Roman Empire, the eastern Roman or Byzantine Empire continued to prosper. Its rulers retained the Roman Empire's political and social structure and fostered both Christianity and Greek-based culture. Justinian I, the greatest Byzantine ruler, streamlined the government, codified the law, and promoted intellectual and artistic activity. However, his efforts to establish religious unity and to reconquer lost territories depleted the empire's finances and weakened its northern and eastern defenses. After his death, Slavs migrated into the Balkan Peninsula, Lombards seized parts of Italy, and Persians conquered the empire's eastern provinces. Conflict over religious issues such as iconoclasm also weakened the empire.

The Arab people became an important new force in Mediterranean affairs through the preaching and community building of the prophet Muhammad. United and energized by the religion of Islam, with its precise but moderate requirements, they rapidly conquered vast territories extending from the Atlantic Ocean to India. Arab Muslims promoted trade and cultural activities and became heirs of classical civilization.

In the Latin west, where Germanic peoples practiced subsistence agriculture in tribal societies under weak kings, one people, the Franks, became prominent. By adopting Roman Catholic Christianity and requiring Romans and Germans to work together, King Clovis gave the Franks a unique basis for further development. Succession struggles later weakened the Frankish monarchy and enabled nobles to seize greater power. There and elsewhere in the west, creative individuals preserved elements of the classical heritage, and creative religious leaders gave new directions to western European life.

SELECTED SOURCES

*Bark, William Carroll. *Origins of the Medieval World.* 1958. A brief and lucid examination of this much debated topic.

*Dawson, Christopher. *The Making of Europe.* 1945. An insightful survey by a noted Roman Catholic historian, stressing the role of the church.

*Decarreaux, Jean. *Monks and Civilization.* 1964. Traces the activity of monks in preserving the classical heritage and shaping Western civilization.

Downey, Glanville. *Constantinople in the Age of Justinian.* 1964. Introduces the reader to the various facets of life in this bustling metropolis.

*Gibb, Hamilton, A. R. *Mohammedanism: An Historical Survey.* 2nd ed. 1962. A classic presentation of the religion of Islam by a master scholar.

*Gregory of Tours, *The History of the Franks.* Translated by Lewis Thorpe. 1976. In this work, a sixth-century bishop describes the history and illuminates the life of his people.

*Lewis, Bernard. *The Arabs in History.* Rev. ed. 1962. This brief survey concentrates on the early centuries of Arab greatness.

Muhammed, Messenger of God. 1977. A stirring film portrayal of the career of the Islamic Prophet.

*Pirenne, Henri. *Mohammed and Charlemagne.* 1939. Pirenne's emphasis on the importance of Islam in the making of Europe turned historical investigation in new and fruitful directions.

*Runciman, Steven. *Byzantine Civilization.* 1948. A masterful presentation of the major features of Byzantine civilization by a scholar who lived many years in Turkey and southeastern Europe.

*Available in paperback.

THE CAROLINGIANS
AND THEIR NEIGHBORS
(750–1000)

*And because the name of emperor had now ceased to exist in the land of the
Greeks [the Byzantine Empire] and because they had a woman as emperor, it
was seen by the Pope, the holy fathers, and the rest of the people, that they ought
to name as emperor Charles, himself, king of the Franks.*

    *On the most holy day of the Lord's birth, when the king . . . rose up from
prayer, Pope Leo placed on his head a crown; and he was acclaimed by the
whole populace of Rome: 'To Charles, Augustus, crowned by God the great and
peaceful emperor of the Romans, life and victory!' After these praises he was
adored by the pope in the manner of ancient princes; and . . . he was called
emperor and augustus.* *

In those few words, contemporary writers recorded a momentous event: the
restoration of the Roman Empire in western Europe. The pope's actions on
Christmas Day 800 made Charles the Great, or Charlemagne (768–814),
king of the Franks and emperor of the Carolingian Empire (from Charles's
Latin name, *Carolus*). Pope and emperor deliberately used the Roman titles
emperor and augustus, together with the Byzantine procedures of
patriarchal coronation and popular acclamation. Charlemagne, rising from
prayer and crowned by God, probably reminded many of Constantine, the
first Christian Roman emperor, by whose authority the pope claimed to
act.

    The Carolingian Empire, however, was "Roman" only in the minds of
its rulers and of the popes in Rome. Nearly 300 years separated
Charlemagne's father, the founder of the Carolingian dynasty, from the last
emperor in Rome. The Carolingian Empire was, more realistically, a union
of Frankish kingdoms that had expanded to include most of what today is
central and western Europe. The present chapter examines the political
institutions and events, as well as the religious and cultural achievements,
of the Carolingian era, its position in relation to its powerful neighbors,
and its disintegration amid new waves of invaders.

The Coronation of Charlemagne. According to some contemporary writers, the coronation was
an unwelcome surprise to Charlemagne, although it clearly required advance preparation and
apparently had the monarch's approval. Bibliothèque Nationale, Paris.

181

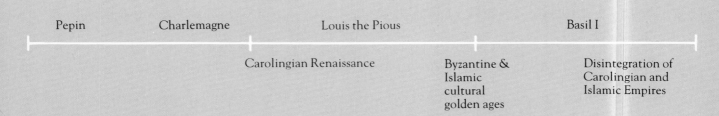

Pepin   Charlemagne   Louis the Pious   Basil I

Carolingian Renaissance   Byzantine & Islamic cultural golden ages   Disintegration of Carolingian and Islamic Empires

THE CAROLINGIAN DYNASTY AND ITS EMPIRE

The Carolingian family, which had been gaining power for more than half a century, took control of the Frankish Empire in 751, deposing the reigning king with the support of the Frankish church hierarchy and the pope, who agreed that the person who actually had power should be king. For nearly 250 years, the Carolingian dynasty remained a prominent force in European politics. The territory they ruled included most of present-day France, Belgium, the Netherlands and Luxemburg, and portions of Germany, Italy, Switzerland and Spain. The most significant Carolingian kings were Pepin (751–768), his son Charlemagne, and Charlemagne's son Louis (814–840) the Pious.

Structure of the Carolingian State

The Carolingians established an effective administration of their territory. At the center was a reorganized royal household that included officials accountable only to the king, supported by the extra lands held by the royal family. Outside the royal household, high nobles called counts, controlling territories called counties, became the essential personnel of Carolingian administration. Previously, counts had pursued their own family interests above the king's. By contrast, the Carolingian kings controlled these nobles much more effectively by granting them lifetime use of some of the lands, by requiring frequent public declarations of loyalty, and by making them live in areas where they had no personal connections. The monarchs spelled out the count's duties in a sequence of directives, and sent inspectors to review and when necessary correct their activities. The kings were especially vigilant in preventing the counts from passing on their offices to their children. Each count served as the king's governor and military commander in one province. He worked with a small staff of assistants, including a viscount and one or more judges. The large frontier areas known as marches were governed by other great nobles called dukes. They also repaid with extensive support the church's approval of their rule.

This system, however, was never fully effective. The rulers never had enough counts or supervisors, and long distances and slow communications hampered royal control. These problems were greater with dukes, who governed larger areas and commanded larger military forces. If kings were strong, they could crush rebellions of counts and dukes, but if kings were weak, the nobles sometimes became independent. Nevertheless, the Carolingians established a reasonably stable administration.

In addition to reforming their administration, the Carolingian rulers created the most effective armed forces in western Europe. They kept the march commanders on the multiple borders militarily prepared, and could in addition assemble every spring a large military force that would ordinarily enjoy a decisive advantage over any opponent. Their armies consisted primarily of well-armed and highly disciplined infantry, together with a smaller group of cavalry, wearing helmets and mailed coats and armed with swords and spears.

Expansion and Decline

The Carolingians used their armies to conduct many campaigns of conquest, adding large blocks of territories to the kingdom Pepin had seized. To the southwest, Pepin pushed the Muslims out of Gaul and south of the Pyrenees. In Italy, Pepin, in return for papal approval of his title to the

Frankish throne, campaigned against and defeated the Lombards, Arian heretics who threatened Rome, and added the Lombard crown to his Frankish one. He gave the popes greater independence from their Italian neighbors by granting them lands that the Lombards had previously wrested from the Byzantines. Pepin thereby created the Papal States, a large central Italian territory under papal control.

Charlemagne expanded Pepin's holdings. He invaded Spain, eventually capturing several northeastern towns and establishing a Spanish march, or border region, to protect the Carolingian frontier against the Muslims and to assist the survival of the Christian kingdoms of northwest Spain. To the southeast, Charlemagne defeated the rebellious duke of Bavaria and incorporated his lands into the kingdom. He next attacked the Avars, a group of Asiatic nomads who had conquered the middle Danube Valley in the sixth century, destroying their capital, seizing their great treasure, and eliminating them from history. In the northeast, Charlemagne fought almost annually against the Saxons in present-day Germany. By 804, he had added their territory to his domain and converted them to Christianity. Farther north, he conquered the Frisians and fought the Danes (see Map 25).

The Carolingians' rise to power, in close cooperation with the popes, culminated in Pope Leo III's imperial

MAP 25
The Carolingian Empire. Under Charlemagne, the Carolingian Empire reached its greatest extent. At war almost constantly throughout his reign, he acquired territories to the north, south, east, and west. Within thirty years of his death, however, as the inset map shows, his grandsons divided among themselves that vast territory he had painstakingly united.

DOCUMENTARY SUPPORT FOR PAPAL CLAIMS

To the extent of our earthly imperial power, we have decreed that [Peter's] holy Roman church shall be honored with veneration, and that more than our empire and earthly throne the most sacred seat of the Blessed Peter shall be gloriously exalted . . . And we ordain and decree that he shall have supremacy . . . over all the churches of God in the whole earth, and . . . shall be more exalted than, and chief over, all the priests of the whole world. . . . we give over and relinquish to the . . . Pope . . . the city of Rome, and all the provinces, places and cities of Italy and the western regions, and we decree . . . that they are to be controlled by him and by his successors, and we grant that they shall remain under the law of the holy Roman church . . .*

These words, from a document known as the Donation of Constantine, supposedly gave the pope authority over the Western Roman empire. Actually, however, the document was not from Constantine, it was written in the eighth century to persuade the Carolingian rulers to grant the popes the papal states. It also gave the popes a basis for claiming authority in temporal (this-worldly) as well as spiritual matters, and would later involve them deeply in European politics.

*The Treatise of Lorenzo Valla on the Donation of Constantine, Christopher B. Coleman, trans. (New Haven: Yale University Press, 1925), pp. 13, 17.

coronation of Charlemagne, as previously described. Hounded from Rome by his enemies, the pope had sought Charlemagne's aid. The king returned the pope to Rome and restored him to power. Gratefully, the pope welcomed the king to Rome with imperial ceremonies and, probably at the urging of Frankish clerics, crowned him emperor. Charlemagne now enjoyed greater prestige than any other German ruler.

Pepin and Charlemagne owed their successes to broad support from church leaders and laity, an effective army, and the weaknesses of their enemies. Still, the Carolingian monarchy lacked an effective institutional structure, and neither Christianity nor a central government unified it. Only a powerful ruler could enforce loyalty or obedience. Because he was able, vigorous, and fortunate, Charlemagne succeeded in ruling and expanding his realm. But his successors lacked those qualities, and during the ninth century the Carolingian Empire disintegrated.

Charlemagne's son and successor, Louis, although vigorous and well trained, lacked both his father's ability and his good fortune. Crowned by his father to free him from obligation to the papacy, Louis later permitted the pope to anoint him. Although he spent heavily on wars, he won few victories. Instead of expanding the realm, his armies were frequently on the defensive and had to protect or pacify different parts of the empire simultaneously. During his reign, he divided his empire and the crown lands among his sons, precipitating the civil wars that occupied his later years and continued after his death in 840.

The civil wars hastened the dis-integration of the old Carolingian Empire. Louis's sons concluded their struggle by the Treaty of Verdun, 843, which divided the realm into three parts: eastern, western, and central. The eastern and western rulers, whose lands later became the kingdoms of France and Germany, soon attacked and absorbed the central kingdom, but divided their lands among their sons. They in turn divided their lands among their sons. In their struggles against one another, Charlemagne's grandsons and great-grandsons tried to recruit support from the nobles within their little kingdoms and strengthened localism by ethnic appeals. But the nobles increasingly disregarded any central royal authority and enlarged their own power. By combining lands received from the king with lands they owned privately, something Charlemagne had prevented, and gaining the right to bequeath royal land grants to their heirs, nobles effectively divided the kingdoms into large territorial principalities and eroded what remained of Carolingian royal government.

CAROLINGIAN RELIGIOUS AND CULTURAL ACHIEVEMENTS

By establishing order and stability in his lands, Charlemagne prepared the basis for a ninth-century flowering of cultural activity often termed the Carolingian Renaissance. He sponsored schools and gathered a group of scholars to grace his palace school. Church leaders drew on late Roman materials, especially those of the Christian fathers, to improve the performance of religious ceremonies and

> ꝗ du m an nun ſo manac cuor
> for Xpi· for giꝑinir indino
> ganadæ ꝑæh ta ꝣalaupa.
> ꝗ cotan uuilleon. uuiſtom

Carolingian Minuscule Writing. Carolingian script was much clearer and more legible than the earlier Merovingian writing, and consequently became the basis for modern letters and typefaces.

the understanding of Christian teachings. Literature and art also exhibited an upsurge of creative endeavor.

Church Reform and Theological Activity

As part of their responsibility for the Christians in their realm, the Carolingian rulers undertook thoroughgoing church reform. Kings before 750 often left episcopal offices vacant for long periods or gave them to unqualified royal relatives or favorites. The Carolingians reorganized the administration of the Frankish church, restoring old bishoprics and archbishoprics and establishing new ones. They selected new bishops from the kingdom's greatest families, set up a clear hierarchy of archbishops, bishops, and priests, and held church councils frequently. Bishops and their noble relatives became strong supporters of the monarchs. Pepin and Charles enriched Frankish monasteries and restored them to compliance with the Benedictine rule. The monasteries in turn provided scribes and advisers for royal service and, like the bishops, firmly supported the Carolingian dynasty. Charlemagne also presented a broadly conceived program for peacefully introducing Christianity among the pagan Saxons and Slavs.

Besides administrative and mo-nastic reform, Charlemagne exerted Carolingian leadership in upholding Latin Christian theology against its challengers. At his instigation, Frankish religious leaders issued a statement criticizing the 787 Council of Nicea's refusal to permit the veneration of three-dimensional images and opposed Byzantine claims that church councils in Constantinople sponsored by the Byzantine emperor were binding on the Roman church. He affirmed that popes, rather than emperors or councils, should determine Christian beliefs. Later, Charlemagne and leading Frankish churchmen judged some of the Spanish clergy guilty of heresy for teaching the doctrine of adoptionism, which held that Jesus was adopted by God as a son, as a means to avoid offending Muslims, who denied Jesus's divinity.

Education, Literature, and Art

Believing that the quality of the clergy determined the quality of spiritual life, Charlemagne promoted both classical and Christian education. He looked for bishops with administrative skills, monks who understood theology, and priests capable of reading scripture well and conducting worship services properly. On Charlemagne's order, each cathedral had a teacher of grammar and each archbishop's cathedral had a teacher of theology. Cathedral schools, which trained young men for service in the church, emphasized practical or vocational education. Monastic schools, which concentrated on the liberal arts and the preservation of ancient knowledge, were also developed. Moreover, Charlemagne established a palace school for educating the sons of Frankish nobles for careers in the emperor's service. For that school, he recruited scholars from many lands both inside and outside the empire. The palace scholars gathered classical writings, making easier the discovery and assimilation of earlier knowledge. The school also developed improved teaching methods.

As another means of improving the quality of temporal life, Charlemagne stimulated monasteries to become active centers for producing hand-copied manuscript books. The monasteries made available many accurate text copies of such essential Christian books as the Bible, manuals for the conduct of worship services, and the Benedictine rule for monks. In special writing rooms, monks also produced manuscripts, including the works of classical writers as well as those of church fathers. Frankish copyists borrowed books from Spain, Italy, Ireland, and England, and in turn produced copies that went to other monastic and epis-

185

St. Matthew, from the Gospel Book of Archbishop Ebbo of Reims. This ninth-century product of the Carolingian Renaissance presents the Gospel writer in intense, frenzied, inspired activity. It forms a striking contrast to sedate, composed figures of the period based on Byzantine models. Bibliothèque Municipale, Epernay.

copal centers. More than 8,000 Carolingian manuscripts still exist, and more than 90 percent of Roman literature survived to later ages in Carolingian manuscript form.

By their copying activities, the monasteries provided the intellectual and literary complement to the administrative and disciplinary reform of the church, an outburst of activity sometimes termed the Carolingian Renaissance (meaning "rebirth"). The collection of ecclesiastical law Charlemagne obtained from the pope became the foundation for later collections of canon law, the copy of the Roman Sacramentary he received shaped subsequent continental worship practice, and the copy of Benedict's *Rule* Charlemagne secured became the basis for monastic reforms during the next several centuries.

Besides circulating and standardizing basic Christian literature, Carolingian copyists initiated significant changes in the techniques of book production. In addition to using book covers of jewels and precious metals to decorate and glorify the most important sacred writings, copyists wrote on durable materials and also developed a new and much clearer form of handwriting. The neatly formed letters and clearly separated words of that new script quickly became the standard way of writing Latin.

In addition to copying classical materials, scholars and writers of the Carolingian era produced original works. Rulers and monks kept historical records in the form of annals, brief accounts of each year's important events. Monastic scholars devised handbooks to explain to their German-speaking students the meaning of Latin words and Latin literary constructions and created commentaries to facilitate understanding of the biblical text. Others wrote biographies of rulers, such as Einhard's *Life of Charlemagne.* Also popular were biographies of saints, which reported miraculous events and virtuous traits to encourage readers and hearers to live more like those heroes of the faith. Some writers composed original and vividly expressive Latin poetry. The Irish monk Dicuil (760–835) composed a universal geography, and his countryman John Scotus Erigena (815–877) became western Europe's most prominent ninth-century philosopher.

The Carolingians also stimulated artistic activity. Carolingian art, like literature and education, evolved from religious activity and employed late Roman and contemporary Byzantine models and techniques. Artists decorated the books priests used to conduct the worship services to enhance their importance. Painters created pictures called illuminations in manuscript pages; these might be separate pictures, elaborately decorated book or chapter titles, or large initial letters using the traditional Germanic art forms of animals and interlaces. Carolingian painters followed late Roman techniques to present religious stories with a definite message. They were unconcerned with light and shade, modeling, and perspective, depicting abstract and formalized, rather than realistic, human figures, painting what they thought or felt, not what they saw. Builders of Carolingian churches usually followed the Roman basilica style. They occasionally roofed the basilica's atrium to form a porch or added an enclosed prayer room above the atrium. For Charlemagne's chapel at Aachen, however, builders copied Byzantine imperial architecture, constructing an octagonal building that symbolized and proclaimed the emperor's divinely aided joining together of earth and heaven, much as Justinian's Hagia Sophia did. Although artists painted church walls, they generally made little use of scriptural themes and human forms because they wished to avoid the appearance of idolatry.

Interior, Palace Chapel of Charlemagne, Aachen. Charlemagne's builders modeled the chapel after Byzantine structures in Italy built during Justinian's reign. Some aspects of the chapel also recall the Church of Hagia Sophia in Constantinople.

ROME'S OTHER HEIRS

East of the Carolingian territories, Byzantines and Muslims continued to develop their own distinctive adaptations of the Greco-Roman heritage. Byzantine cultural life flourished, and under the vigorous Macedonian dynasty (867–1025) Constantinople became a center for Christianizing and Byzantinizing Bulgars and Slavs. The

Muslims
raid Rome

Magyars
enter
Central
Europe

Vikings
occupy
Vinland

Alfred of England

Saxon Dynasty in Germany

Capetian Dynasty
begins in France

Viking Expansion

Vladimir, Prince
of Kiev, accepts
Christianity

Abbasid dynasty of caliphs (751–1258), although unable to maintain the political unity of the Islamic Empire, inaugurated a brilliant period of literary, intellectual, and artistic achievement.

The Byzantines

During the ninth century, as the Carolingian Empire declined, the Byzantine Empire was recovering from internal and external assaults. Good relations with the west were reestablished after the Council of Nicea in 787 reversed earlier imperial rulings against the use of icons. Ninth-century rulers finally reinstituted use of icons and restored the empire's financial and military resources. In 867, a transfer of political power occurred when an ambitious adventurer assassinated the emperor and seized the throne as Basil I (867–886), establishing the Macedonian dynasty (867–1054), which ably led the empire for nearly two centuries.

Byzantine cultural and religious life flourished under the early Macedonians. Literary output grew, educational activity revived, and contemporaries evidenced a renewed interest in classical authors. The patriarch of Constantinople, Photios (858–867,

877–885), renowned for his wide learning, energized religious studies. The imperial minister Bardas (842–866) revitalized the University of Constantinople by establishing one Leo, variously known as the Philosopher or the Mathematician, as its head, perhaps after learning of an Islamic caliph's bid to obtain Leo's services. Under Leo and his successors, the university became a focus for imperial learning and literature. Much literature emphasized religious themes in poems and hymns in praise of saints or accounts of their lives. Histories and lexicons were also produced, evidence of the Byzantine fascination with the classical past. The Emperor Constantine VII (912–959) patronized scholarly activity and stimulated the production of numerous compilations to preserve useful information. He authorized, if he did not actually compose, important works describing the administration of the empire and Byzantine court ceremonials. Out of the recurring border wars with Muslims came the *Epic of Digenes Akritas* ("the border warrior born of parents from different ethnic groups"), which closely resembles such later western European works as the *Song of Roland* and the *Song of the Cid*.

Byzantine art revived as well. The

iconoclastic controversy had turned the interests of artists to classical (Alexandrian) models, to historical and secular rather than ecclesiastical and spiritual topics, and to Islamic art and its use of ornament. Artists now employed those influences to achieve a Second Golden Age of Byzantine art, which exhibited dignity, grace, restraint, balance, and refinement. Artistic and literary developments were inspired by ancient models and by a tension between secular taste and religious sensitivity. Macedonian rulers stimulated production of a largely secular imperial art that made extensive use of classical models. That imperial style influenced both aristrocratic home decoration and monastic manuscript illumination, both of which emphasized classical themes and mythological or allegorical scenes. Byzantine superiority over western literary and artistic achievements in the ninth and tenth centuries may be attributed to that exploitation of the classical inheritance.

Relations between Greek and Latin Christians worsened during the late ninth century. Some Byzantine clergy, disliking Photios's elevation, appealed to Pope Nicholas I (858–867) to nullify it. They were also angered when the pope received an inquiry from the Bulgar rulers about liturgical and theological questions. Photios claimed that the pope lacked jurisdiction over both issues, and subsequently accused the Latins of heresy for making unilateral changes in the jointly accepted Nicene Creed. Although pope and patriarch later resolved their differences, the dispute increased the strains in their relationship, and the tendency of each to claim universal authority pointed to future conflicts.

Byzantine vitality contributed to cultural and religious expansion. Byzantine conquest in the late ninth century made the Serbians Eastern Orthodox Christians. The Bulgars negotiated during the late ninth century with both Latin and Byzantine Christians, but the effective work of Byzantine missionaries and the concerted diplomacy of Byzantine emperors and patriarchs persuaded the Bulgar ruler to adopt Eastern Orthodox Christianity. By the tenth century, the Bulgar capital of Preslav became a Slavic church-training center employing a literary language devised by Byzantine missionaries and known as Old Church Slavonic to infuse Byzantine culture into east and southeast Europe. Slavic tribes in Russia came under the domination of Viking warlords based in Kiev by 879 but moved during the next century into the Byzantine cultural orbit. As Kievan trade with the Byzantines grew during the tenth century, Kievan rulers sought closer ties with Constantinople. Olga (890–969, princess of Kiev ca. 910–955) was baptized by the patriarch of Constantinople and worked diligently to promote Christianity in Russia. Its success there was assured by the baptism of her grandson, Prince Vladimir (977–1015), in conjunction with his

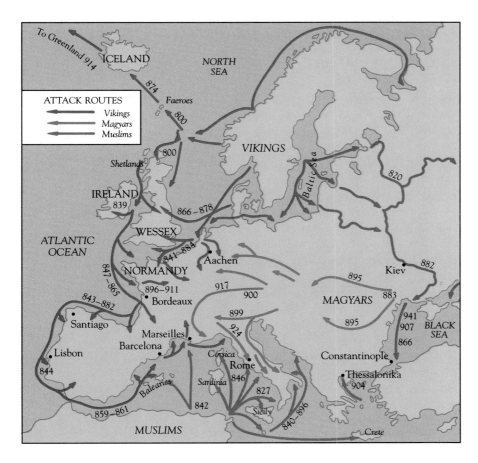

MAP 26
Ninth-Century Europe. During this period attacks from all directions threatened to overwhelm Europe. From the north, Vikings crossed the seas to plunder and sometimes settle western regions, and roamed along eastern rivers. In the south, Muslims from Africa dominated the western Mediterranean and raided its European coastlands. Meanwhile Magyar nomads from the east occupied the Hungarian basin and ravaged central Europe. Embattled Christian Europeans identified their various attackers as pagans and enemies of God.

marriage to Anna, sister of the Byzantine emperor Basil II (976–1025). The Bible, saints' lives, and religious service books translated at Preslav from Greek into Old Church Slavonic formed the earliest Russian Christian religious literature.

The Islamic Empire

Like the Carolingian Empire, the Islamic Empire began the period 750–1000 with a change of dynasty and later disintegrated. Conversions to Islam increased rapidly. Within a century after a territory's conquest, more than 90 percent of its population was usually Muslim. Non-Arab Muslims, especially the Persians, resented continued Arab control, and religiously conservative Muslims criticized the Umayyad caliphs for religious laxity. A new ruling dynasty, the Abbasids (750–1258), combined those discontented elements and overthrew the Umayyads. The Abbasids, relying heavily on Persian support, transferred the capital from Damascus to Baghdad and thus removed themselves farther from the Mediterranean. Islamic lands produced abundant food supplies and numerous manufactured articles, and Baghdad became the center of a trading network involving regions of Asia, Africa, and Europe. Traders, bankers, and landed nobles formed an affluent and powerful ruling class in the Islamic Empire.

Although the gradual conversion of large numbers of subject peoples to Islam made the Islamic Empire ethnically diverse, the Arabic language and the religion of Islam assured cultural unity. Muslims of every language recited the Qur'an in Arabic and observed the obligations of Islam. Islamic religious scholars developed a system of theology and a structure of religious law. Arabic gradually became the chief language of north Africa and southwestern Asian lands, and other languages such as Persian and Turkish adopted Arabic script and words. Arab and non-Arab Muslims wrote richly expressive Arabic poetry, studied law, history, and theology, and labored to explicate the Qur'an. Government-sponsored translators made Greek and Syriac versions of scientific and philosophical works available in Arabic, and so contributed to the vigor of Islamic thought, particularly in science and philosophy.

For more than a century, Abbasid rulers supervised a golden age in economic and cultural activity. Philosophers translated Greek works into Arabic and wrote commentaries to explain how Greek philosophy elucidated the Qur'an's teachings. The scientific knowledge acquired by earlier societies was compiled, augmented by the original contributions of Muslim scientists, and creatively applied to practical problems. Doctors studied diseases, conducted experiments, and dissected bodies; and mathematicians adopted the Indian numbering system (known to us as Arabic numerals), added the use of the zero, and created algebra. Several Islamic writers composed astronomical treatises, and Muslims perfected and introduced to Europe the astrolabe, an astronomical instrument invented by the ancient Greeks. Muslims used it for aligning mosques with Mecca and determining prayer times, but astrolabes were also used for nautical observations until the seventeenth century. Islamic literature was vigorous, colorful, and emotional; the famous stories of the *Arabian Nights* exhibit those qualities and suggest the diversity of cultural traditions the Muslims integrated. Islamic art exhibited Byzantine influence in the domes used to cover mosques (buildings for group prayer).

During the ninth century, the caliphs became more autocratic and their court more luxurious. Hence their resources dwindled and opposition to them increased. The caliphs also lost both wealth and power by awarding revenues and provincial governorships to favorites. Powerful local families and adroit military commanders in western and eastern Islamic regions exploited ethnic heritages or regional loyalties to obtain freedom from caliphal control and established independent states. Besides Spain and Morocco, already independent in the eighth century, Africa (approximately modern Tunisia) and Egypt separated themselves from caliphal control, and assorted Asian territories did likewise. By 900, the Islamic Empire was rapidly becoming a collection of independent states offering a nominal allegiance to a figurehead caliph.

EUROPE UNDER SIEGE

As the Carolingian Empire disintegrated in the late ninth century, Europe was besieged by new waves of invaders who contributed to the continent's further transformation. Muslims, Magyars, and Vikings produced widespread destruction and disrupted existing institutions and patterns of living (see Map 26). Amid the resulting disorder, successful resisters to those attackers began to establish new social, economic, and political patterns and to form new centers of European development.

Ninth-Century Invaders

One group of ninth-century invaders, the Muslims, attacked various areas of Mediterranean Europe. One band of adventurers established a base in southern Gaul from which they controlled Alpine passes, robbing merchants and holding dignitaries for ransom. Others served as mercenaries in Italy and established bases from which they raided the Italian countryside. Muslims from north Africa raided Rome in 846, greatly alarming Latin Christians, and conquered Sicily during the late ninth century. Egyptians raided the Greek coast and seized the island of Crete. These Muslim raids and conquests seriously interfered with trans-Mediterranean trade and communications, with the result that eastern and western Christians increasingly lost touch with each other, allowing the differences between them to deepen. Although popes prohibited Christian trade in war materials and the making of trade agreements or treaties with Muslims, many south Italian cities ignored such directives and engaged in lucrative trade with Sicilian and African Muslims.

Another group of invaders was the Magyars, nomadic ancestors of modern Hungarians who moved into central Europe. Invited from western Asia by the Byzantines to aid in war against the Bulgars, the Magyars occupied the Hungarian basin of the Danube by 900, and soon were raiding Italy, Burgundy, and other Frankish and Germanic territories. An early Magyar victim was the Slavic state of Moravia, which had emerged along the upper Danube in the early ninth century and sought to guarantee its independence from aggressive German neighbors by obtaining Christian missionaries from Constantinople. The missionaries developed a script for writing the Slavic language and produced a Slavic religious literature for the new converts' use. The Magyar conquest of Moravia in 906 terminated those developments.

A third group of invaders, Vikings from Scandinavia, raided widely throughout Europe in search of booty and captives during the early ninth century and later settled in some areas as royal dynasties at home began to assert authority and control over Viking bands. The reasons for Viking expansion are difficult to determine: In addition to desire for booty and dislike of royal centralization, population growth, climate change, and sheer love of adventure have been offered as explanations. Whatever the

Viking Ship. This ninth-century vessel could carry approximately forty men. Although shallow of draft, these ships were quite seaworthy, carrying Viking raiders across the seas, along the coasts, and up the rivers of Europe.

causes, the impulse to migrate spread through Scandinavia. Norwegians raided western England and Ireland and established settlements. Danish Vikings attacked lands on both sides of the English Channel. They settled in such numbers that eastern England was called the Danelaw. The Danes seized land at the mouth of the Seine River in Francia which became the nucleus of the later Duchy of Normandy. Well might western Europeans pray, "From the fury of the Northmen, O Lord deliver us." Swedish Vikings crossed the Baltic and worked their way southward across Russia on the extensive north-south river systems, reaching Persia and Constantinople via the Caspian and Black seas, respectively. They became so numerous that the name *Rus* ("ruddy") designating them became applied to the entire land.

The Vikings also traveled beyond Europe. Some sailed westward across the North Atlantic and in 874 settled Iceland, where they established the world's oldest continuously functioning democratic community. A century later, Erik the Red, an exile from Iceland, discovered the island of Greenland to the west, which attracted further settlements. In 1000, Erik's son Leif sailed farther west and briefly occupied Vinland, probably northern Newfoundland; other Vikings perhaps followed that westward route. As royal authority and Christianization increased in Scandinavian lands during the tenth century, the great age of Viking expansion ended.

Responses to the Invasions

The ninth-century invasions accelerated the already advanced disintegration of the Carolingian Empire, and

the absence of effective imperial power forced local leaders to develop their own responses to the invaders. Those responses varied in different parts of western Europe and contributed significantly to the development of European diversity.

Outside the Carolingian Empire, in England, Viking raids and English resistance combined to produce a united monarchy. The Danes destroyed all the Anglo-Saxon kingdoms except Wessex, whose King Alfred, later designated the Great (871–899), effectively opposed them. He organized a navy to combat the Vikings at sea and fortified and garrisoned towns to serve as defensive strongholds. Reviving the Germanic practice of summoning all adult males to military service, he developed an effective army to check the Danes. Gradually, he expanded his territory and consolidated his authority over those Anglo-Saxon lands in the west of England that had escaped Viking rule. By gathering scholars from various lands, he revived literature and learning in England. Alfred's achievements created a solid foundation for England's future development.

In Italy, independent towns attained prominence with the weakening of Carolingian authority and led the resistance to Magyar and Muslim invaders. Within these towns, bishops became the principal leaders, building town fortifications and collecting tolls and other monies to pay for them. They secured powers and privileges from kings and obtained and exercised control of urban defenses, revenues, and courts. Powerful bishops and strong, independent cities continued to play important roles in subsequent centuries.

In the eastern regions of the em-

pire, where Carolingian rule was recent and the county form of organization was imperfectly established, earlier German tribal divisions reemerged in five large duchies. The dukes, the former Carolingian administrators, seized royal lands and powers and exercised control over the churches in their districts. When the last Carolingian ruler died there in 911, the dukes chose one of their number as king to validate their rights and titles to land and to coordinate common defense measures. The dukes, however, failed to establish their political independence, and because they were unable to halt the Magyar invasions, an able, new dynasty of Saxon (919–1024) rulers soon emerged to reassert royal authority over the land, which became known as Germany.

In the Carolingian Empire's western areas, the invasions advanced the localization and decentralization of government, as counts and other nobles offered the only meaningful opposition to the invaders, acquired lands and goods, and usurped royal authority. Although Carolingian kings, with short interruptions, continued to rule until 987, when the last Carolingian king died without heirs, they lacked power to make their rule effective. In the absence of strong, central government, aggressive local lords exercised warfare and defense responsibilities and took control of royal courts and revenues. With increasing fragmentation of power, the number of territorial divisions in what became France doubled during the tenth century. The Capetian kings (987–1328) who followed the Carolingians had the formidable task of reasserting their usurped authority and reincorporating the numerous political divisions under their direct rule.

Feudal Relations

As Carolingian central government deteriorated during the ninth century, nobles resorted to personal agreements to provide protection and administer justice. They employed a combination of two well-established Carolingian practices: the personal relationship of vassalage and the landed relationship of benefice or fief to establish a new set of relationships called feudalism (from the Latin *feudum*, "fief"). In vassalage, a free man (the vassal) proclaimed his dependence on and faithfulness to another free man (the lord) and promised to give the lord service, usually of a military nature. The lord in return granted the vassal useful possession, but not ownership, of land called a benefice or fief to enable the vassal to maintain the horses, equipment, and training his military service required. By 900, the vassals, armed cavalrymen, were often termed knights.

The feudal relationship was a mutual contract having a number of reciprocal rights and obligations. By their mutual proclamation of loyalty and obligation, lords and vassals established a personal agreement that theoretically ended when one of them died, although in practice the sons of lords and vassals usually succeeded their fathers and continued it. However, either party might end the relationship if he thought the other was failing to fulfill his promises. In that case, the vassal's fief returned to the lord, who might grant it to another vassal. Typically, a vassal owed not only his own personal military service but often also that of additional knights from his own estates. In addition, he was expected to serve in the lord's court of justice and to feed and house

the lord and his traveling companions when required. Vassals also helped to raise a ransom if their lord was captured and gave the lord money on the occasion of the knighting of his eldest son, the marriage of his eldest daughter, and when a son succeeded to his father's fief. The lord provided the vassal with military protection and justice through his court and defended the vassal against enemy attacks. Vassal fiefs quickly became hereditary, but the lord regained them if the vassal died without heirs. The lord could also collect the revenues of a fief while training a deceased vassal's heir, and could veto the marriage of a deceased vassal's heiress.

These personal relationships extend through several levels of lordship. Counts and dukes held their lands as fiefs of the king, lesser nobles held their estates as vassals of counts or dukes, and they in turn granted smaller fiefs to their own vassals. Hence the same person might be the vassal of a greater lord and the lord of lesser vassals. Complications arose when vassals held fiefs from different lords who might become enemies; feudal relationship in such instances could become very involved.

Lesser lords and vassals were armed and trained as warriors to keep the peace, preserve the privileges of communities, and maintain the safety of the church, but most fought in the hope of conquering lands and acquiring wealth and some for the sheer joy of fighting. The armed and

---

SIX FEATURES OF FEUDAL RELATIONSHIPS

He who swears fealty to his lord ought always to have these words in mind: safe, secure, honest, useful, easy, possible. Safe, in that he do his lord no bodily harm. Secure, in that he do him no harm by betraying his secrets or the defenses by which he is able to be secure. Honest, in that he do no injury to his right of justice or in other matters that are seen to touch his honor. Useful, in that he do no harm to his possessions. Easy, in that he not make difficult that which his lord can do easily. Possible, in that he not make impossible what is possible.

Moreover, . . . he must . . . lend counsel and aid to his lord in these six things if he wishes to seem worthy of the fief and to be trustworthy in the fealty he has sworn. The lord ought to do likewise to his vassal in all these things. Should he not do so, he will justly be accused of bad faith just as the vassal, if he be found shirking or willing to shirk his obligations, will justly be accused of perfidy and perjury. *

This eleventh-century letter so aptly conveys the attitudes of the mutual feudal relationship and duties between lords and vassals that it was frequently cited by later writers. The tenor of the advice suggests the political disorder that made feudal relationships necessary. Unfortunately, lords and vassals often failed to realize the ideal behavior described here.

*Letter of Bishop Fulbert of Chartres to Duke William V of Aquitaine, 1020, in *Translations and Reprints from the Original Sources of European History* (Philadelphia: University of Pennsylvania Press, 1898), Vol. 4, no. 3, pp. 23–24.

---

mounted knight was a military machine comparable to a modern tank; he dominated offensive warfare. Defensive warfare centered on the castle, the noble's fortified home. Simple wooden towers set on a mound of earth encircled by a wooden stockade evolved by the twelfth century into stone-built structures. Castles gave great families a specific power center and a sense of family identity; families began to call themselves by the name of their castle, and as it passed through generations, family members developed their consciousness of family history.

Although at first nobles held large estates whereas knights held few if any lands—and led armies into battle whereas knights followed and obeyed—knights gradually gained extensive lands, privileges, and jurisdictional rights and married into old noble families, enabling nobles and knights to blend into a single aristocratic order. Because the aristocrats concentrated political and military power in their hands, kings who sought to rule effectively had to control such lords, especially those in their own royal domains. To do so, the kings attempted to exploit the system of feudal relations by creating new political structures known as feudal monarchies.

SUMMARY

During the period 750–1000, Carolingian rulers dominated European life. They created a workable governmental administration and used an effective army to expand their territories. Charlemagne, the greatest Carolingian ruler, was crowned emperor by the pope in 800. During the ninth century, however, Carolingian rulers engaged in civil wars, and the empire disintegrated into small, weak states.

The Carolingians produced notable religious and cultural achievements. They undertook reform of monasteries and reorganization of church administration and upheld Latin Christian theology against several challenges. They promoted education to improve the quality of clergy and to educate nobles' sons for imperial service. By encouraging the copying of manuscripts, the Carolingians enlarged their own cultural heritage and preserved many classical works for later generations. They also stimulated a modest, mostly religious, literary and artistic activity, sometimes called the Carolingian Renaissance.

Both the Byzantine and Islamic empires were economically and culturally vigorous during this period. The Byzantines enjoyed renewed activity in education and literature and spread a Greek version of classical culture and Eastern Orthodox Christianity to Slavs and Bulgars in east and southeast Europe. The Islamic Empire experienced a change of dynasties at the beginning of the period and a breakup into independent states toward its close. The Abbasid rulers presided over a remarkable age of intellectual, literary, and artistic productivity.

During the ninth century, Muslim, Magyar, and Viking invaders completed the breakup of the Carolingian Empire and caused local warlords to rise to prominence. Different European regions responded in various ways to the invasions, contributing to the development of feudal relationships and social and political diversity in different areas of Europe.

SELECTED SOURCES

Beowulf. Translated by David Wright. 1966. This remarkable Anglo-Saxon epic recounts a brave warrior's heroic adventures.

*Blair, Peter Hunter. *An Introduction to Anglo-Saxon England*. 1956. A well-written account of early English history.

*Bronsted, Johannes. *The Vikings*. 1965. A well-rounded treatment of Viking history, society, and culture.
*Boussard, Jacques. *The Civilization of*

Charlemagne. 1968. Text and illustrations provide a full picture of ninth-century life.

*Einhard, *The Life of Charlemagne*. Translated by S. E. Turner. 1960. Brief, readable biography of Charlemagne by a contemporary courtier; modeled after Suetonius' *Lives of the Caesars*.

*Fichtenau, Heinrich. *The Carolingian Empire*. 1957. Standard treatment of Carolingian economic, social, and political institutions.

*Hinks, Roger. *Carolingian Art*. 1962. Provides useful insight into the ideas and values of the period as expressed in painting and sculpture.

*Jenkins, Romilly J. H. *Byzantium, The Imperial Centuries: A.D. 610–1071*. A detailed and informative, popularly written account of an interesting period of history.

The Vikings. 1958. An adventure story film treatment of Viking activities.

*Winston, Richard. *Charlemagne: From the Hammer to the Cross*. 1954. Readable biography of the emperor by a modern popular writer.

*Available in paperback.

Social and Economic Developments (1000–1350)

Society is divided into three orders. The ecclesiastical order forms one body. The nobles are the warriors and the protectors of churches; they defend all the people, great and small. The unfree is the other class. This unfortunate group possesses nothing without suffering. Supplies and clothing are provided for everyone by the unfree because no free man can live without them.

Therefore the city of God which is believed to be one is divided into three; some pray, others fight, and the others work. These three groups live together and could not endure separation. The services of one of them allows the work of the other two. Each, by turn, lends its support to all.

This description of the three orders or estates of European society, written about 1000 and often repeated, ceased by 1300 to describe the increasingly complex realities of medieval social and economic activity. Although most workers remained directly involved in agricultural production, by the latter date many enjoyed their freedom. By 1300 a growing number of persons engaged in other occupations such as trade and manufacturing lived in towns rather than manorial villages. The growth of trade and the rise of towns produced economic and social changes that affected nobles and clergy and changed conditions for workers. The present chapter examines developments in the economic sectors of agriculture, trade, and manufacturing, in population patterns, and in the social contexts of village, city, and castle life.

CONTENTS

AGRICULTURE

During the period from 1000 to 1300, the economy of Europe developed and prospered owing mainly to increased agricultural production which enlarged and diversified the food supply. Technological developments also contributed to Europe's agricultural growth.

Detail from Andrea di Bonaiuto, the Church Militant and Triumphant. Members of the three orders of medieval society—clergy, nobility, and workers—appear in this Italian painting. Distinctive clothing permitted easy identification of a person's rank and occupation, making a medieval gathering a colorful sight. Santa Maria Novella, Capellone degli Spagnoli, Florence.

Increased Productivity

One factor that contributed to increased agricultural production was a great expansion of the amount of land under cultivation. Growing numbers of Europeans not only resettled lands depopulated by the ninth- and tenth-century invasions but also opened new lands for farming. Many people cleared forests, some drained swamps, and a few even reclaimed land from the sea. Crowded conditions in older farming regions and active efforts to bring additional lands under cultivation induced peasants to settle as colonists in frontier areas such as those east of the Elbe River in central Europe or those reconquered from the Muslims in the Iberian Peninsula. By such endeavors, Europeans doubled and possibly tripled the amounts of land they farmed and food they produced.

By making many separate im-provements, Europeans created the heavy compound plow, with wheels for easier movement, a coulter to cut the earth, a plowshare to cut it horizontally, and a moldboard to turn the earth and form a furrow, thereby facilitating soil drainage. The heavy plow made possible the cultivation of the thick, wet, and fertile north European soils. Medieval farmers learned to harness oxen with a neck yoke rather than one attached to the horns and developed a collar that permitted a horse to pull a load with its shoulders rather than its neck. Fitted with shoulder collars, horses worked more quickly and efficiently than oxen. Blacksmiths produced metal shoes for both oxen and horses, which improved traction and protected hooves against damage and excessive wear. Millers improved the water and windmills used to grind flour and operate wine and olive presses, freeing people for other tasks and enhancing productivity.

Medieval farmers also improved their methods of cultivation. By opening more land to tillage, the heavy plow promoted the spread of a new, three-field system of agricultural operations that enlarged productive capacity. Previously, farmers had divided plowlands into two fields, planted one in the fall, and left the other fallow, or unused, to renew fertility. Animals grazed the fallow fields and their manure partially replenished the soil. In the three-field system, farmers planted one field in the fall for early summer harvesting, a second in the spring for fall harvesting, and left the third fallow throughout the year. In the next year, the fields were rotated and the process repeated. The three-field system kept more land in production, increased food supplies by one-third, and ena-

Village Scene. Animals and agricultural workers led a busy existence in a medieval village. In the upper left, wood gathering is in process. At the bottom, horses fitted with shoulder collars unwillingly draw a heavy wheeled plow, mainstay of medieval agriculture, and a harrow is followed by a planter who spreads seeds from the bag slung over his shoulders.

1000	1100	1200	1300	1400

German Hansa
formed

Growth of agricultural
production

Serfdom weakens
in Western Europe

Black Death

Peasant
uprisings

Growth of trade
and towns

Champagne
fairs flourish

European
climate
grows colder

Double-entry bookkeeping

bled the work of plow teams to be spread more evenly over the year.

As medieval farmers cultivated more land with greater efficiency, they grew more grain, the traditional dietary staple. The grain supply began to exceed demand, and this permitted agricultural diversification. As grain production increased, farmers in some regions chose to increase the production of specialized crops such as grapes or dyestuffs, and others elected to raise cattle and sheep. As farmers diversified their agricultural activities, many Europeans became able to supplement their grain diet with peas and beans, butter and cheese, meat and fish.

Population Fluctuations

Largely as a result of the increased agricultural production, between 500 and 1300 Europe's population grew rapidly. It rose from 25 million persons in the sixth century to nearly 40 million in the eleventh and to more than 70 million in the thirteenth. This growing population was young; probably 40 percent of Europeans were under age fourteen and therefore became workers early in life.

Despite consuming a wider variety of foods, most Europeans still suffered from an unbalanced diet. Wealthy

persons typically ate too much animal protein and too few vegetables and suffered from gout and other ailments. Poor people normally had meat twice a year (Christmas and Easter) and consumed too many starches, developing dysentery as well as becoming vulnerable to various infections. Members of both classes experienced vitamin deficiency diseases such as scurvy and rickets. The foremost victims of malnutrition were the old and the sick, infant children, and nursing mothers. Although a wider variety of dietary choices made improved nutrition available to many, life expectancy remained low, approximately forty years for males and thirty-five for females, largely because of high infant mortality and the deaths of many women in childbirth.

As their numbers increased, Europeans spread over the landscape and brought new areas under cultivation, converting forests and waste areas into farmland. Moreover, they filled the countryside with agricultural villages and created numerous towns which provided cash-paying markets for agricultural produce. Increased food production met the needs of those markets, promoted the growth of trade, and freed people for nonagricultural occupations. The numbers of nobles, clergy, and town dwellers grew.

During the fourteenth century, however, Europeans experienced sharp changes in climate and population and a general economic recession. After 1300, Europe's climate became colder and rainier and its weather more unpredictable. Crops rotted from heavy rains or died from untimely frosts. Harvests shrank and prices soared. People in regions dependent on food imports especially suffered when food-exporting regions had poor harvests. Warfare intensified the food supply problem as ravaging armies destroyed crops, barns, and mills, and famine became a recurring European experience.

To add to the troubles of the fourteenth century, plague sharply reduced Europe's population. Rats accompanying European merchants trading in Asia brought fleas carrying bubonic plague back to Europe in 1348. During several years at mid-century (1348–1354) perhaps one-third of all Europeans died in a plague epidemic known as the Black Death because of the typically discolored bodies of its victims. The Black Death hit towns, particularly those in Italy, especially hard; many lost more than half their population, often the most enterprising and skilled individuals. Highly contagious, the plague spread rapidly, "like fire when it comes in

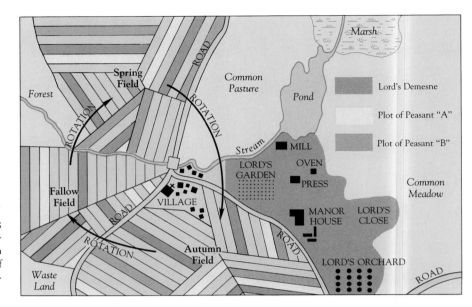

MAP 27
A Manor. The noble lord dominated the manor; he controlled good land and the essential services of oven, mill, and press. The operation of the three-field system and the division of land into strips prompted villagers to work together at common tasks.

contact with large masses of combustibles," according to one contemporary. Fear of the plague induced some persons to withdraw into country retreats and to live soberly, while prompting others to indulge in sensual pleasures. Only by the end of the fifteenth century did the European population recover from fourteenth-century dislocations.

Villages and Manors

The heavy plow and the two- or three-field system came into widespread use throughout western Europe and dictated the layout of the village, the basic unit of agricultural economy. Villages ranged in size from ten to several hundred peasant families, living in a cluster of huts surrounded by their fields. The villagers pooled their plows, draft animals, and labor, and to use them effectively arranged fields in long, narrow strips with spaces for turning the team at the ends of the strips. Each family was assigned several strips scattered throughout the village's fields to give it a share of both more fertile and less fertile soil (see Map 27). On its land, a family produced food for its consumption or for barter, as well as for payment of tithes to the church and dues to the lord. Beside their huts, families had gardens where they raised fruits and vegetables and kept poultry. The village included a pasture area where plow animals grazed and where sheep and cattle might be kept and a meadow that provided hay to maintain the animals during the winter. Most villages also had a wooded area from which the peasants gathered fuel and building materials and where pigs might forage, a stream or pond that supplied fish and powered the water mill, and an oven. However, they typically had no schools, hospitals, or other amenities sometimes found in medieval towns.

Villagers worked hard, lived close to nature, and enjoyed few creature comforts. The poorest lived in one-room huts with a timber framework, a thatched roof, roughly plastered walls, and an earthen floor. A villager's home ordinarily contained little furniture, few windows, no chimneys, and might be shared with their poultry, dogs, and other livestock as well as fleas and vermin. Meager straw bedding provided little protection against dampness, and many villagers suffered from rheumatism and arthritis. Bread and ale formed a typical breakfast; in addition to those items, evening meals ordinarily featured a meatless soup. Villagers worked from dawn until dark; while father and sons worked in the fields, mother and daughters did cooking and cleaning, made cheese and butter, spun and wove cloth, made clothing, milked cows, fed livestock, and tended the vegetable garden. All were vulnerable to the normal variations of nature such as heat, cold, drought, and excessive rain and to disasters like floods and epidemics of human, animal, or crop diseases, as well as famine and war.

The parish church, where one existed, was the center of village activity. Villagers celebrated baptisms and marriages there, and buried their dead in the churchyard. The churchyard was the site of village meetings and such buying and selling as the village engaged in. Celebrations of religious holidays, often including dancing and merrymaking, took place in the churchyard too. Church bells provided the only timekeeping most people knew, and religious festivals marked major portions of the agricultural year.

Most villages were included in manors, which were artificial units of political governance and economic exploitation granted to ecclesiastical establishments or secular nobles by other nobles or kings. A manor produced nearly everything needed for its inhabitants and its lord, who was ordinarily a vassal in the feudal system described in Chapter 11, so he could fulfill his promised services to his superior. Because the manor's output was primarily in the form of perishable agricultural products, lords traveled from one manor to another during the year to consume what the manors produced.

Although free men owning or renting their own small farms existed in many places, the work force on manors consisted primarily of serfs, semifree persons linked to the lord and to the land. Unlike slaves, serfs possessed certain rights. They could marry and have legitimate children, make legal contracts, and inherit property. Furthermore, they could not be sold away from their lands or farms. They retained about half of the produce of their fields and paid out the other half in charges. Serfs paid the lord a percentage of the crop for the use of the pasture and woods and fees for the use of the lord's mill and oven. The lord also collected payments when a serf's son inherited his father's holdings or when a serf's daughter married outside the manor. Moreover, the church collected a tithe (10 percent) of the serf's produce.

Serfs also performed labor services for the lord, both occasional services, such as road repair or carrying firewood, and regular services, usually three days of work per week on the lord's land, or demesne. The demesne consisted of strips scattered among those of the villagers, one-fourth to one-third of the manor's total lands.

The manorial lord had legal jurisdiction over the peasants, and his manor house was the local court. As most lords held several manors, a bailiff or steward usually supervised an individual manor, collected its dues, and conducted its court.

Changing Economic Conditions for Peasants and Lords

By 1300, increased agricultural productivity and population growth, coupled with the revival of trade and

Water Mill. Water power turns the wheels of a grain mill in this late medieval illustration. Such water-powered mills ground grain into flour throughout Europe. Note the grooved millstone beside the figure in the foreground.

A SERF IS FREED

Let all know that we have manumitted and liberated from all yoke of servitude William, the son of Richard of Wythington, whom previously we have held as our born bondman, so that neither we nor our successors shall be able to require or exact any right or claim in the said William. But the same William with his whole progeny and all his chattels shall remain free and quit and without disturbance, exaction or any claim on the part of us or our successors by reason of any servitude forever.

And if it shall happen that the said William or his heirs shall die at any time without an heir, the said buildings, land, rents, and meadows with their appurtenances shall return fully and completely to us and our successors.*

This thirteenth century document freed William, a reasonably prosperous peasant, from serfdom. It did not, however, make him the absolute owner of his property. Moreover, it left him with a cash rent to pay. Those conditions placed important limitations on his freedom. It was not easy for an individual to exchange the security of serfdom for the uncertainties of freedom, but many did so.

*Translations and Reprints from the Original Sources of European History, series I (Philadelphia: University of Pennsylvania Press, 1899), Vol. 3, no. 5, pp. 31–32.

ments of colonizers and the attractions of town life and to retain a labor force, lords began to improve the working conditions of their serfs. Some lords freed serfs from labor obligations in return for cash payments, and others allowed serfs to pay rent in money rather than crops and even leased demesne lands to peasants. In some cases, lords granted peasant communities charters that freed them from performing the obligations of serfs and permitted them to pay their dues collectively rather than individually. Many serfs thereby became tenant farmers, whose obligations were on a cash rather than a service basis. Such developments, however, occurred at different times in various parts of Europe. In France, the manorial system was prominent between the ninth and eleventh centuries, but it developed in Germany in the twelfth century as the French system underwent change. In eastern Europe, the twelfth and thirteenth centuries were periods of colonization, and serfdom was almost nonexistent there.

By the early fourteenth century, western European peasants found their situation deteriorating in a period of economic recession aggravated by the slowing of land reclamation. A surplus of peasants allowed lords to hire laborers at low wages or to enforce serf labor obligations strictly or to raise rents, taxes, and charges to serfs. The Black Death created a temporary shortage of labor and briefly permitted peasants to obtain lands at lower rents or to gain higher wages or more favorable conditions of manorial service. It also reduced the numbers of consumers for agricultural products, however, and as production satisfied demand, prices and wages fell. Landowning nobles also collaborated, either

informally or through legislative action, to hold down wages and fix prices at favorable levels.

During the fifteenth century, peasant conditions slowly improved in western Europe but worsened still further in eastern Europe. As wages and prices rose in the west, manorial lords sought to increase their cash incomes by raising cattle or sheep or commercial agricultural products such as dyestuffs, all of which required fewer laborers and gave high returns for low costs. Many other western lords now converted peasant labor services into money payments or rented or leased their lands. Peasants found either arrangement acceptable because the money economy allowed them to obtain cash for their labor and their products. Thus by 1500, most western European peasants were no longer serfs owing labor and goods to their lords but renters who traded the security of serfdom for the freedom to earn or to lose money and livelihood.

In contrast to product diversification and the money economy in western Europe, eastern European lords preferred to grow grain for export to western Europe and took advantage of fourteenth- and fifteenth-century wars and other upheavals to acquire large landholdings. To make those lands profitable, they enforced manorial obligations and imposed serfdom even on formerly free peasants. So while western European peasants enjoyed greater freedom by the fifteenth century, during that same period eastern European peasants lost what freedom they had.

Freedom, however, proved to be a mixed blessing. The manorial economy had furnished security for serfs, and lords often gave assistance in times of need. But renters rarely received

the growth of towns, had transformed the conditions of agricultural life. Seeking to bring new lands under cultivation, lords offered milder terms of service to encourage peasants to settle there. To counter both the induce-

such kindly treatment; instead, lords sought to collect the maximum rents possible from their tenants. Moreover, the ravages of war and the taxes of monarchs fell most heavily on peasants, as clergy and nobles were largely exempt from royal taxation.

As peasants increased their living standards, they also began to increasingly resent fees and other reminders of serf status. Lords now appeared to be exploiters rather than protectors. Taxation was another intensely held grievance of peasants, whose discontent sometimes exploded into rebellion, notably in the fourteenth century (Flanders, 1310; France, 1358; England, 1381). Although they burned and looted some castles and murdered their inhabitants, peasants were easily defeated and sometimes cruelly butchered by regular armies. Their grievances persisted, however, and would reappear to trouble later lords and rulers.

COMMERCE AND MANUFACTURING

Growing Trade

Like agricultural productivity and in close relationship with it, European commercial activity expanded dramatically during the medieval centuries. Improved agricultural production made food available for town dwellers, who in turn obtained leisure to produce and market other articles, increasing commercial activity. Early medieval trade, although modest, never entirely disappeared but persisted at two levels. Local merchants exchanged perishable items and commodities of everyday use, often by bartering salt, wine, and metals in village markets. Jews, Greeks, and Syrians controlled international trade and imported from lands east of the Mediterranean profitable luxury items to satisfy the demands of high churchmen and nobles for furs, silks, spices, and perfumes.

During the ninth and tenth centuries, Vikings in the north revived European commerce by making discoveries and settlements along the shores of the North Sea and the North Atlantic Ocean, using the proceeds of plunder to obtain necessary commodities. Their descendants traveled energetically across the northern seas, trading furs, timber, fish, and wax for textiles, grain, and wine. To the east, they established commercial relations with the Byzantine and Islamic empires via the Baltic Sea and the river routes of Russia, selling furs, timber, wax, and slaves for Islamic silver or Byzantine gold.

By the thirteenth century, Germans had replaced the Scandinavians as the primary merchants of northern Europe, and Lübeck, at the base of the Danish peninsula, was the foremost German trading city. The northern trade was primarily in staple commodities: grain, butter, cheese, fish, timber, metals, and salt; furs were the only luxury items exchanged, either for other furs or for other items. During the fourteenth century, German trading towns united in a Hansa (confederation) to preserve their dominant position in commerce against their Scandinavian opponents, especially Denmark. After defeating the Danes in 1370, the Hansa enjoyed a century of prosperity and contributed to north European economic development by opening new areas to economic activity. The lea-gue systematized weights and measures and built roads and canals.

At the same time that the Vikings were flourishing in the northern waters, Italian port cities, particularly Venice, revived the Mediterranean trade. Byzantine merchant citizens in some Italian port towns traded easily with both the Byzantine Empire and with the Muslims. They exported slaves, timber, iron, and tools and imported luxury items such as perfumes and textiles. During the eleventh century, Genoa and Pisa wrested control of the western Mediterranean from the Muslims. The crusades of the twelfth century made the Italians dominant in the lucrative commerce of the eastern Mediterranean. Pisa's and Genoa's moment of glory was relatively short-lived, however; the Venetian sponsors of the fourth crusade took control of Byzantine trade following the crusaders' sack of Constantinople in 1204 and obtained mastery of all Mediterranean trade by defeating Genoa, which had earlier overwhelmed Pisa, and capturing its fleet during the late fourteenth century.

The eastern Mediterranean trade that the Italians dominated by 1300 was the center of an extensive intercontinental commercial network. Venetian merchants bought luxury goods from the Byzantines and Muslims, who had brought them from India and China. The Venetians then carried the goods to western Europe, where they sold them to the upper classes. With the proceeds of those sales, merchants obtained raw materials or semimanufactured goods in Europe for Italian industry or for eastern customers.

From the northern and southern seas, trade quickly expanded inland,

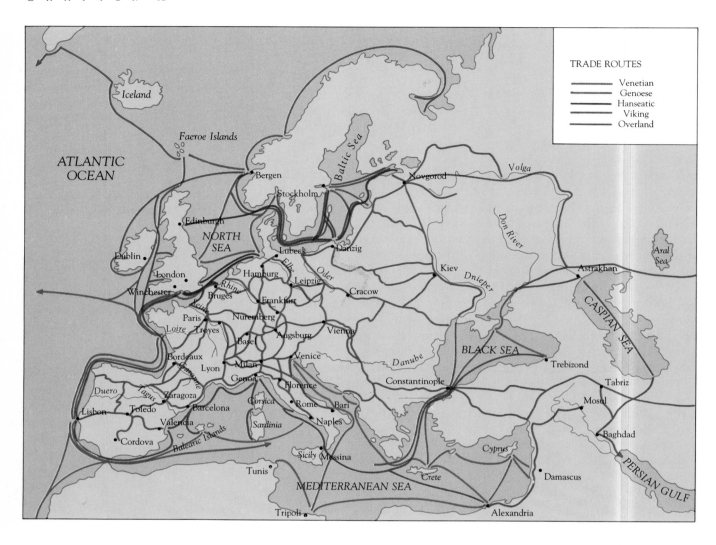

MAP 28
Medieval Trade Routes. By the end of the thirteenth century, trade routes covered most of western and central Europe. Vikings in early centuries and the German Hansa later controlled commerce in the northern seas. In the south, the Italian cities of Genoa and Venice dominated Mediterranean trade. Overland routes used rivers wherever possible to reduce transportation costs. In eastern Europe, however, trade routes were few and the economy remained primarily agricultural.

and by the late twelfth century merchants were moving continuously along Europe's rivers and roads, and commerce was fast displacing agriculture as the most dynamic force in European economic life (Map 28). Northern traders took their merchandise by river into England, France, and Germany, and Italian merchants began crossing the Alps to trade in northern lands. For much of the twelfth and thirteenth centuries, fairs, gatherings of buyers and sellers at a stated time and place for trade, became the exchange points between northern and southern trade. In the Champagne region of France, for example, a cycle of fairs permitted almost year-round transaction of business. As western European trade became an everyday activity, fairs, being only temporary, lost their importance. They remained important in central and eastern Europe, where commercial activity was less vigorous.

During the disastrous fourteenth century, European commercial activity diminished, as had agriculture. The population decline shrank available markets, and wars and a shortage of capital interfered with commerce. The Mongols had briefly permitted Europeans to bypass Islamic middlemen and to trade directly with east Asia. During the fourteenth century, however, the Mongol Empire broke up and the advancing Ottoman Turks blocked those connections, stimulating Europeans after 1400 to seek sea routes to east Asia.

Means for Facilitating Trade

Although merchants, a group not included in the traditional three medieval orders, grew in numbers and in prominence during the medieval centuries, they encountered many obstacles to commercial activity and sought ways and means to facilitate trade. Early European merchants lacked legal identity and confronted numerous tolls and charges and a variety of regional weights, measures, and coinages. Moreover, they were closely regulated, and their activities were confined to specific places, called markets, and specific times, known as fairs. To expedite trade, some authorities aided merchants by revising the structure of markets and fairs and establishing new legal procedures, gaining economic advantages for themselves. Moreover, as persons from many regions met at fairs, they began to standardize weights, measures, and coinage, to develop credit and banking procedures, and to spread mercantile law.

Transportation improvements also

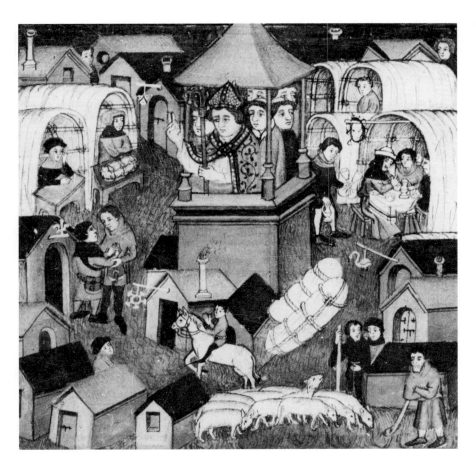

The Blessing of the Lendit Fair. This fifteenth-century illustration shows the activities of a medieval fair. In the center, the local bishop gives his blessing to the fair. Merchants in the booths await or assist customers. Below, additional merchandise, both packaged and on the hoof, arrives. Bibliothèque Nationale, Paris.

THE MAKING OF A MERCHANT

Aspiring to the merchant's trade, [Godric] began to follow the peddler's way of life, first learning how to gain in small bargains and things of insignificant price; and thence to buy and sell and gain from things of greater expense. At first he wandered with small wares around the villages and farmsteads of his own neighborhood, but in time he associated himself with city merchants. He traveled through towns, boroughs, fortresses, and cities, to fairs and to all the various booths of the marketplace in pursuit of his public trading.

Then he traveled abroad, and with men who were eager for merchandise, he began to coast frequently by sea to foreign lands. He traded in many diverse wares.

Eventually his great labors brought much worldly gain. In all lands he found certain rare and precious wares which he carried to other parts where he knew them to be least familiar, and coveted by the inhabitants. He ex-changed these wares for others coveted by men of other lands. Hence he made great profit in all his bargains, and gathered much wealth; for he sold dear in one place the wares which he had bought elsewhere at a small price. *

Many individuals undoubtedly followed Godric's progression from small peddler to large-scale trader and finally prosperous merchant. We know Godric's life story primarily because he later entered monastic life and became a saint. Because traders traveled so incessantly, courts to resolve their disputes were known in England as "piepowder" courts, from the French expression pieds poudres *("dusty feet"). Coasting was a trading practice in which a merchant ship stopped in every port along a coast and traders bought and sold whatever was available.*

*Reginald of Durham, "Life of St. Godric," in George C. Coulton, *Social Life in Britain from the Conquest to the Reformation* (Cambridge: Cambridge University Press, 1918), pp. 415–420.

facilitated trade. Merchants carrying goods over land benefited from more bridges and better road surfaces and the use of the horse collar to move heavy loads more effectively. In sea trade, the improved compass and the introduction of the astrolabe (a device for determining latitude by observing sun, moon, and stars) aided mariners in their navigation, and changes in ship design and sail arrangements made vessels more maneuverable. Because land transport was costly and time consuming, mer-chants preferred where possible to send goods by water.

In addition to benefiting from improved transportation, merchants developed organizations and institutions to assist them in their business enterprises. Traders formed merchant guilds to regulate their own activities and to protect themselves against kings, feudal lords, or rival merchants from other towns. Obtaining capital for business ventures was problematical, as Roman Catholic church councils opposed loaning money at interest, although some theologians were willing to permit interest-bearing loans under certain conditions. Jews, not subject to church law, provided some investment loans. Inventive Europeans devised other financing arrangements.

In Italy, new forms of business organization appeared to finance business enterprise. Partnerships were formed between investing partners who stayed at home and traveling partners who obtained rewards for their risks and who might also be investors. Insurance loans became common after 1300 to reduce liabilities for losses. A type of joint-stock arrangement also emerged in which several shipowners would hold a number of shares in several ships to limit their liability in the event of loss.

As money became an accepted measure of value and means of exchange, European businessmen developed more efficient banking and accounting methods. Deposits, loans, and credit transfers became standard procedures. To avoid conflict with the church's teaching limiting the taking of interest, banks gave depositors bonuses or collected penalties for nonpayment of loans by a specified time. Between 1250 and 1350, Italian entrepreneurs created double-entry bookkeeping, enabling businessmen to track their income and regulate expenditures more precisely. Such techniques became known only gradually in northern Europe, where commercial undertakings continued on a smaller scale.

During this period, several cities, such as Vienna and Bruges, Siena, and Florence, developed into prominent banking centers. Banking firms in Florence were responsible for collecting and transmitting papal taxes and Italian coinages became prominent in commerce. Banking remained a risky activity however; bankers loaned large sums to individuals, companies, and rulers, and were sometimes ruined when their debtors repudiated the loans and refused to repay them. Although some banks experimented with issuing paper money, most evaluated currencies according to the weight of gold or silver in coins. As a result, a region's economic activity often varied with its supply of precious metals, and a general scarcity of gold and silver within Europe prompted Europeans to seek new supplies of those metals from other sources.

Manufacturing and Mining

Manufacturing came later than trade in European economic development. Medieval "manufacturers" (the word comes from a Latin expression that means "to make by hand") were typically craftsmen who produced goods in their own shops and sold them directly to the public. Perhaps the first modern manufacturers employed individuals in building construction and textile making, which developed during the medieval period using complex systems of organization. Members of the building trades found employment erecting churches and public buildings in growing towns and cities. As many were wage earners and owned neither the materials nor the tools they used, they resembled factory laborers.

The textile industry developed in Flanders, Florence, and England and employed many workers to produce goods on a large scale. Work at first was done by hand, but technological developments introduced significant changes. The fulling mill replaced human treading of cloth with beating hammers driven by a revolving drum attached to a spindle of the water wheel. Other water-powered machines also entered textile production. To be near better sources of water power for the new machines and to escape guild and municipal regulations, producers sometimes moved cloth production to the countryside.

Some entrepreneurs used a 'domestic' system in which they distributed raw materials to and collected finished products from workers who labored in their homes rather than in a factory. They purchased the wool, distributed it to be carded and spun, collected the yarn and had it woven into cloth, then sent it out to be dyed and finished. This procedure, along with technological developments, allowed the manufacturer to reduce labor costs. Although the cloth makers thus helped to promote a vigorous rural craft industry in Europe's wool-producing areas, workers in older urban textile centers lost their employment.

Mine owners also made important use of technological innovations. Germans conducted most mining activities throughout Europe, extracting iron, lead, copper, and tin ores as well as gold and silver. By the fourteenth century, as surface and shallow seams became exhausted, miners had to sink deeper shafts to find the ores. The shafts in turn depended on better provision for drainage and better wall support and so required heavy capital investment. In the fifteenth century, new water-driven pumps, with improved wheels, axles, and gears, helped to drain tunnels and shafts. Manufacturers also used water power to operate crushers and bellows in blast furnaces to exploit formerly worthless low-grade ores.

TOWNS

Growth and Development

Enlarged agricultural productivity and increasing commercial activity sparked a growth of town life. Although towns continued to exist in western Europe after the Germanic invasions, by 1000 most were sparsely populated ecclesiastical, administrative, or defensive centers. Vigorous urban life continued only in Mediterranean lands, primarily in Italy. After 1000, many existing towns such as Cologne and Strasbourg grew in both area and population, and new towns appeared. As trade and population increased, some people left their rural communities and settled in towns.

Commercial activity revitalized older towns and brought new ones into existence. Where trade was active, merchants and traders developed markets and storage facilities or formed new suburbs in older towns. Artisans soon came to swell the populations of these settlements. Various forms of the German word for fortress, *burg*, such as burgh, bourg, or borough, came to apply to the town, and its inhabitants became known as burghers or burgesses and later as a social class, the bourgeoisie. Residents included, besides merchants and artisans, venturesome free peasants, runaway serfs, and ambitious younger sons of lesser nobles, and might also

CHAPTER 12

THE GROWTH OF A TOWN

After this, because of the work or needs of those living in the chateau, there began to stream in merchants—that is, dealers in precious goods—who set themselves up in front of the gate, at the chateau's bridge; then there followed tavern-keepers, then inn-keepers to provide the food and lodging for those who came to do business in the presence of the prince, who was often there. Houses began to be built and inns to be made ready, where those were to be lodged who could not be put up inside the chateau . . . . So many dwellings accumulated there that right away it became a large town.*

These words of a contemporary observer describe the beginnings of Bruges (originally Brugge, "the bridge"), one of

northern Europe's foremost medieval towns. In central and eastern Europe, outside the territories of the old Roman Empire, new towns were usually founded by colonies of merchants who settled around a fortified stronghold, such as a castle or monastery, strategically located on a major trade route or at the intersection of two or more routes. Such settlers needed services that others came to provide, and settlements quickly grew into towns.

Documents relatifs a l'historie de l'industrie et du commerce en France, ed. Gustave Fagniez, *Collection de textes pour servir a l'étude et l'enseignement de l'historie,* Vol. 1 (Paris: Alphonse Picard et Fils, 1898), pp. 54–55; tr. Carolly Erickson, *The Records of Medieval Europe* (Garden City: Doubleday, 1971), pp. 152–153.

include masters and students at a school or university. As European towns became economic centers, more and more of their residents earned their livelihood as merchants and artisans rather than being economically dependent on agriculture. Towns grew along with trade; they became markets for agricultural products, prompting lords and peasants to produce surpluses for sale in them. By such activity, villages became more integrated into regional trade networks.

Some of the earliest and largest commercial towns developed in north Italy. Merchants from those Italian cities, as already noted, dominated international trade in the Mediterranean and in much of Europe.

North of the Alps, towns were closely linked to the economic life of

the regions around them. For example, in Flanders, an important sheep-raising district, they became centers of woolen textile production. The wool trade was also important to England; to remind English nobles of that fact, the chancellor of the House of Lords sat on a woolsack, a cushion stuffed with wool. As demand for wool outstripped local supply, Flemish merchants imported wool from England, and Flanders increasingly stressed industrial rather than agricultural production. Flemish merchants, like their Italian counterparts, became active in maritime commerce, trading with regions along the North and Baltic seas.

Cities and towns were small by modern standards. A substantial eleventh-century trading city, such as Bruges, with a permanent settlement

of merchants and a fair attracting traders from other countries, might have only 5,000 inhabitants. Some people living there farmed land in the nearby countryside and pastured animals in the common fields surrounding the city. Towns grew with commerce during the medieval period, and by 1300 several Italian cities—such as Genoa, Milan, Florence, and Naples—had 100,000 inhabitants each, and Venice held 200,000 persons. North of the Alps, Paris had a population of 80,000, London and Bruges each half that amount, and other towns less.

Towns offered benefits not usually available in rural areas. Larger numbers of people provided a stimulating variety of social contacts and relationships. Schools were more accessible to town dwellers than to rural people. Large churches and better trained religious leaders contributed to the spiritual growth of individuals. Towns also offered avenues of upward social mobility through employment and education.

The physical appearance of towns was, to say the least, compact. Towns were fortified with walls and gates and the space within the walls was extremely crowded. Streets were intended to give pedestrians access to houses, hence few were wide enough to accommodate wheeled traffic. The burghers constructed most of their houses with two or three stories made of wood; in a craftsman's house, the ground floor would be the shop. To make maximum use of space, upper stories of houses sometimes projected two or three feet beyond lower ones, nearly meeting above the street and making it dark. The streets were unpaved and sloped toward the middle where gutters served as the town's sewer system. Townspeople threw waste materials from upper stories with the cry "Ware slops!" bespattering unwary pedestrians. Many towns had ordinances similar to those of Avignon, which decreed "that no one shall throw water, nor any steaming liquid, nor human filth, nor bath water, nor anything into the street under his house, nor allow his family to do so."

Good manners dictated that a man walk on the street side of a lady so that he rather than she would receive any spatterings. Towns were smelly, smoky, and dirty and vulnerable to

Medieval Town Street. This street in a town in southern France retains its medieval appearance. Note the adjoining houses and the narrowness of the cobblestoned street (slippery when wet!) with its gutter in the middle.

danger from fire as well as epidemics. Until the fourteenth century, churches were often the only stone buildings, and church towers and spires were the chief feature of the town as seen from a distance. Later, stone guild halls began to appear and some rich merchants began to build houses of stone.

The Black Death struck cities exceptionally hard; many recorded the deaths of approximately half their inhabitants during those few years, and plague outbreaks periodically recurred. Many persons left the countryside and migrated into towns, envisioning work opportunities created by Black Death losses, but often they lacked needed skills or otherwise failed to find jobs and joined a growing number of unemployed.

Charters

Because towns and town dwellers did not fit easily into the "three orders" social framework, but instead formed new elements in medieval society, they had to struggle to obtain acceptance for their activities. Moreover, they had needs that an agricultural society with its characteristic organization of manors and serfdom could not satisfy. Town dwellers especially needed freedom from the servile obligations and arbitrary taxation of the manorial system. To do their work and enjoy its rewards, they also needed freedom to move from place to place, to dispose of their property at will, and to take advantage of opportunities as they arose.

To obtain these freedoms, town dwellers strove to acquire charters from the lord of the land on which the town sat or from other authorities. A lord might grant a charter for a money payment or offer charter privileges to develop a town on his land but sometimes towns had to defeat lords in battle to obtain such documents. A charter gave town dwellers political privileges and enabled them to create institutions appropriate to their new way of life. Usually, it provided the town's inhabitants and anyone living there for a year and a day, freedom from servile obligations; thus a common proverb stated, "City air makes one free." A charter typically permitted inhabitants of a town to hold their land and buildings for a money rent and secured townspeople from the arbitrary seizure of their property. Furthermore, it restricted the lord's opportunities to raise money at will and might free a town from the jurisdiction of other courts. Charters also typically granted the town dwellers some rights and powers of self-government, such as allowing burghers to maintain their own courts and to make their own laws to regulate their affairs.

Where kings granted charters, as in France and England, towns remained subject to royal authority but free of lesser lords; in other areas, however, especially the Holy Roman Empire, charters granted by emperors or lords often permitted a town to administer its own affairs by establishing a commune. Generally, a commune elected its own officials, who had full rights within the town to govern and to dispense justice. Lords and their agents had no authority within the commune's territory, and obligations of the townspeople to the lord were specifically fixed and limited, usually involving a specified annual payment and a certain amount of military service. Gradually, over the next three or four centuries, kings favored the bourgeoisie with their increasing commerce and wealth over the nobility whose landed estates were no longer so important to the nation's economy.

Burghers in northern Italy whose towns were under the jurisdiction of the Holy Roman Emperor pushed beyond charter rights to become independent. There, kings had depended on city militias to repel ninth- and tenth-century invaders. They granted to the bishops who dominated the towns the rights to build walls and fortified towers and to collect tolls and public revenues to finance such defensive works. Rulers in Italy also exempted the cities from the jurisdiction of the local royal officials, the counts. In a series of struggles, townspeople seized control of the cities' defenses, revenues, and courts from the bishops and extended the cities' authority over the surrounding countryside. City leaders in the independent city-states of northern Italy thus were in the process of developing important aspects of a new political order: corporate authority, delegated power, and representative government.

Guilds

To regulate economic activity within towns, artisans and merchants formed guilds, which were associations of persons engaged in a common activity. Merchants in a town ordinarily formed a merchant guild to protect their interests within a town against outsiders. The guild also regulated the merchants' activities so that each could share proportionately in the trade available. Merchant guilds typically regulated prices and other trading conditions and practices to prevent anyone from gaining an unfair competitive advantage.

Like the merchants, artisans set up craft guilds that limited competition and maintained a livelihood for all. They regulated wages, prices, conditions of labor, standards of quality, methods of manufacture, and amounts of production. They also controlled conditions for admission to their trades. A person prepared to enter a craft by becoming an apprentice to a master and worked for perhaps seven years under the master's guidance, often living in his household. After this term, the former apprentice became a journeyman (from the French word for a day's work, *journée*) and worked for wages. A journeyman who obtained enough money and developed sufficient skill might open his own shop and become a master. To do so, his work (a masterpiece) had to survive rigorous examination by the guild. But as prosperity waned in the fourteenth century, heredity became the principal route to mastership, and many artisans spent their whole lives as wage earners and never became masters. The gap between rich and poor in towns consequently widened and social discontent increased, sometimes producing riots and revolts.

Guilds were also social organizations, conducting banquets to celebrate their activities and sponsoring religious festivals. The guild aided members in times of disaster, buried them when they died, and cared for their widows and orphans.

Women as well as men found economic opportunities in craft guilds. By 1300, at least 15 of 100 Paris guilds, including garment makers and workers in silk and embroidery, were entirely female. Widows of masters operated their deceased spouses' workshops and could retain guild membership by marrying another guild member. Still other women worked at crafts, as traders, or as teachers or medical practitioners. After 1300, however, economic activities for women were increasingly restricted or eliminated. Some scholars have attributed the economic decline of German towns in the period 1300–1500 to the suppression of flourishing female industries and the replacement of skilled women by unskilled men.

SUMMARY

During the medieval period, the social and economic bases of European civilization underwent remarkable transformations. Europe's population doubled and established new settlement patterns. The Black Death killed one-third of all Europeans in the fourteenth century, but the population recovered.

Europeans increased agricultural production by using the heavy compound plow and the three-field system, bringing much new land under cultivation. Villages, basic units of agricultural economy, were cooperative and largely self-sufficient communities. Many villages were included in manors, and their inhabitants became serfs, whose work benefited the manor's lord. By 1500, many serfs in western Europe had gained freedom, but conditions of serfdom had worsened for eastern Europeans.

Although some trade in luxuries and necessities existed before 1000, thereafter European commerce expanded rapidly and became the dominating force in European economic life. Italian cities conducted Mediterranean trade, whereas German towns controlled trade in northern Europe. Such forms of business organization as guilds, partnerships, banking, and accounting arose. Most manufacturing was done by members of craft guilds in small shops, but building and textile production developed factorylike systems of organization. Textile making and mining made use of several water-powered technological innovations.

Towns grew along with trade and became especially prominent in north Italy and Flanders, serving commercial and manufacturing functions. They eventually obtained freedom for their activities by means of charters. Merchant guilds usually dominated towns, but craft guilds were also important in regulating economic life. Although towns were dirty and crowded, people in them enjoyed freedom. Those solid economic and social foundations supported the predominant institution of medieval Europeans, the Christian church, as well as ambitious religious wars, conducted against their Muslim neighbors over centuries.

SELECTED SOURCES

A Description of the World: The Travels of Marco Polo. Translated by William Marsden. 1961. Vivid narrative by a thirteenth-century European who spent more than twenty years in Asia.

*Gies, Frances, and Joseph Gies. *Women in the Middle Ages.* 1980. Popular survey of a long-neglected topic.

*Gimpel, Jean. *The Medieval Machine: The Industrial Revolution of the Middle Ages.* 1976. Presents medieval technology in easily understood language, with provocative comparisons to the eighteenth-century Industrial Revolution and modern times.

*Hodgett, Gerald A. J. *A Social and Economic History of Medieval Europe.* 1972. Well-informed, nontechnical exposition of all facets of medieval economic activity.

*Holmes, Urban T. Jr. *Daily Living in the Twelfth Century.* 1962. A mine of information about medieval life, presented through the eyes of a university student in London and Paris.

*Lopez, Robert S. *The Commercial Revolution of the Middle Ages, 950–1350.* 1971. Vigorous treatment of the topic by a foremost economic historian.

*Pirenne, Henri. *Medieval Cities.* 1952. Eminently readable account of the medieval urban revolution, simple and scholarly, imaginative and accurate.

*Power, Eileen. *Medieval People,* 10th ed., 1964. Extensive sketches, drawn from source materials, of six medieval individuals, including two women.

*Southern, Robert W. *The Making of the Middle Ages.* 1962. A thoughtful investigation of obscure changes in European society, 1000–1200.

A Walk with Love and Death. 1969. A film by John Huston set in fourteenth-century France during the Peasants' Revolt.

*Available in paperback.

MEDIEVAL RELIGIOUS EXPRESSIONS

Oh race of Franks . . . race chosen and beloved by God . . . set apart from all nations by the situation of your country, as well as by your catholic faith and the honor of the holy church! . . . We wish you to know . . . that a race from the kingdom of the Persians, an accursed race, a race utterly alienated from God . . . has invaded the lands of [Eastern] Christians and has depopulated them by the sword, pillage, and fire . . .

The labor of avenging these wrongs [is placed] . . . upon you . . . .

Let the deeds of your ancestors move you and unite your minds to manly achievements . . . Enter upon the road to the Holy Sepulchre; wrest that land from the wicked race, and subject it to yourselves . . . .

When Pope Urban had said these . . . things, . . . all who were present . . . cried out "It is the will of God! It is the will of God!"

This eyewitness account of the origin of the first crusade (crusades were Christian military expeditions to retake Christian holy places held by Muslims, and participants wore a cross—Spanish *cruz*—as their insignia) attests to the confident and militant Christian faith Europeans shared by 1100.

The Crusades were but one manifestation of the pervasiveness of Christianity in European life. Church leaders were often prominent lords exercising political as well as spiritual influence. A church was usually the largest and most prominent building in a town. Portions of the day were identified by the ringing of church bells, while religious periods and holy days marked the passage of the year. The centrality of Christianity to European life in this period causes many to label it an "Age of Faith." The present chapter examines the organization of the medieval church, the efforts to reform it, and the beliefs and practices of Christians. It then discusses the Jews in medieval life and concludes with the crusades and reconquests as expressions of both militant Christianity and European expansion.

Pope Urban II Proclaims the Crusade. Using the occasion of a church council, the pope appealed for a military expedition to Jerusalem. Nobles and clergy, and even pious poor people, responded enthusiastically. Bibliothèque Nationale, Paris.

CHURCH ORGANIZATION AND REFORM

Like kings and princes who strove to create stable and effective governments, medieval religious leaders endeavored to centralize the organization and improve the quality of the medieval church. Reformers seeking to overcome the evils stemming from the church's involvement in feudal society sought to centralize the church's administrative structure and remove it from the control of lay rulers. Attempts to revitalize monastic discipline and life were paralleled by efforts to upgrade the intellectual preparation and the spiritual quality of secular clergy. As a result of such activities, the church became a more powerful institution and a more influential presence in European life.

Religious Abuses and the Need for Reform

Although by 1000, the rulers of most European peoples had adopted Christianity for themselves and their subjects, the problems of ordering Christian society remained formidable. The invasions of the ninth and tenth centuries by Vikings and Magyars had destroyed not only churches and monasteries but also ecclesiastical institutions. As clerics sought protection against invaders, lay lords assumed economic and political authority over church offices. They absorbed church lands into their fiefs or estates and diverted the resources of the church to private, family, and "state" purposes. Moreover, they controlled the appointment of abbots, bishops, priests, and occasionally during the tenth century, popes.

Significant religious abuses arose from this lay domination of church offices. Christians of the period frequently complained about the ineptitude and immorality of the clergy, shortcomings that were understandable, because few schools were available to train clergy and both priests and bishops were often appointed for political rather than spiritual reasons. Simony, the purchase of church positions, was another troublesome abuse. Not surprisingly, many clerics became preoccupied with controlling ecclesiastical property and obtaining personal advancement and demonstrated a shallow, mechanical attitude toward religious life. Many did not respect the church's prescription of celibacy and either married or had sexual partners, creating further possibilities for the diversion of church lands.

By 1000, efforts to reform the church to eliminate such abuses were under way. Reformers, often monks themselves, sought to make the traditional monastic vow of celibacy binding on all clergy. Popes issued decrees against clerical marriage, councils forbade it, and individual bishops were urged to combat it. The distaste for clerical marriage stemmed from an ideal of a pure clergy separated sexually and sacramentally from the laity. Moreover, reformers sought to eliminate simony and the lay appointment of church officials. Most reformers viewed marriage of clergy and simony as the major abuses needing reform, and blamed those abuses on lay control of the church. For the reformers, clerical marriage, lay control of church appointments, and a feudal attitude toward the holding of church offices were inextricably entwined and posed serious dangers for the church.

Centralization of Church Organization

As an alternative to local lords controlling the church, eleventh-century reformers created a centralized church organization under papal control. Building on allusions in scripture and the writings of church fathers, they conceived the church as a community of persons baptized into a common faith and pursuing the common goal of eternal salvation. Like contemporary political states, such a community needed its own head, law, and resources. Reformers with such views soon eliminated lay control of the papacy by restricting election of popes to the cardinals (1059). Some reformers became popes; one, Hildebrand, who became Pope Gregory VII (1073–1085) so dominated the enterprise that it is often termed the Gregorian reform. These reformist popes worked systematically to eliminate simony, clerical marriage, immorality, and lay control. They established a system of church courts in which the popes had final jurisdiction and ultimately improved the collection of papal revenues.

By the early thirteenth century, as successive popes pursued centralization, the organization of the medieval church became fully developed. The popes controlled an extensive bureaucracy, the Curia, which contained specialized departments handling correspondence and records, finances, judicial cases, and the application of church law. Well-trained

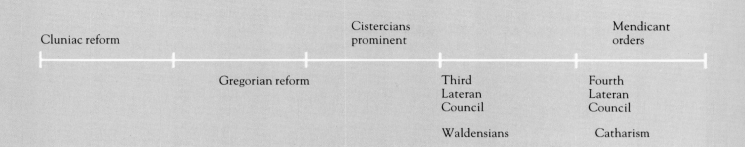

1000	1050	1100	1150	1200	1250

Cluniac reform

Cistercians prominent

Mendicant orders

Gregorian reform

Third Lateran Council

Fourth Lateran Council

Waldensians

Catharism

clerics who were career administrators staffed the Curia. Members of the College of Cardinals, a special body of churchmen from around Rome selected by the popes to provide advice and administrative expertise, directed the Curia. Popes directly asserted their authority in local areas either through correspondence or by means of legates, individual churchmen empowered to act on behalf of the popes. The financial support for that ecclesiastical organization came from papal property, assessments on clergy and laity, and numerous fees and gifts.

In addition to their own bureaucracy, the popes exercised authority over the hierarchy of archbishops, bishops, and priests below them. Archbishops and bishops administered their territories, called dioceses, through cathedral chapters, Curialike bodies staffed by canons. At the base of that ecclesiastical hierarchy, priests directed the religious life of the laity. As they exercised more direct control of the increasingly centralized and hierarchically organized church, the popes freed the church from lay control and furthered the development and implementation of reform within it. Unfortunately, the growth of pa-

pal centralization and the bureaucracy needed to implement it began to dull the reforming zeal of the church and by the thirteenth century produced a growing chorus of criticism.

Monastic Reform

Whereas some medieval reformers worked on centralizing church organization, others brought extensive changes within monasticism. The monastery of Cluny, France, which sought to restore the pure practice of the Benedictine rule, pioneered in monastic reform in both its organization and its worship services. Duke William of Aquitaine, who established the monastery in 910, made it directly subordinate to the pope and independent of all local ecclesiastical and lay authority. Its abbots provided remarkable continuity of leadership, traveled extensively, and became widely known in western Europe. In contrast to the traditional independence of each Benedictine monastery, the abbots of Cluny established a strongly centralized organization in which the abbot of Cluny was the abbot of the order and subordinate officials called priors governed the other Cluniac houses. Cluniac monks

followed a strict, godly life and worshiped God with an elaborate sequence of daily prayers and liturgical services that became a model for other monasteries and helped bring many of them under Cluny's direct control. Feudal nobles approved the Cluniac liturgy and supported the Cluniac monks. In return, the Cluniacs accepted the bodies of the nobles after death and prayed perpetually for their souls.

The monks' day was divided into periods for prayer, work, eating, and sleeping. Soon after midnight, they performed the day's first prayer service. After a few more hours of sleep, they awoke at sunrise and performed another service of prayer, after which they washed and celebrated the day's third prayer service. Then they attended chapter meeting and then worked for two to three hours. Some did farm or garden chores, others copied or illuminated manuscripts, and still others instructed beginning monks. At about noon came the fourth prayer service of the day, followed by an elaborate High Mass. The day's first, and in winter only, meal came at about 2 p.m.; in summer there was an evening meal in addition to the afternoon one. The day's fifth reli-

A SAINTLY MONK

The young boy [Bernard] advanced in his study of letters at a speed beyond his age. He began already to humble himself in the interest of his future perfection, for he exhibited the greatest simplicity, loved to be in solitude, fled from people, was extraordinarily thoughtful, submitted himself implicitly to his parents, had little desire to converse, was devoted to God, and applied himself to his studies as the means by which he should be able to learn of God through the Scriptures . . . .

God prepared him as a chosen vessel, not only to strengthen and extend the monastic order, but also to bear His name before kings and peoples to the ends of the earth . . . .

He prayed, read, or meditated continuously. If an opportunity for prayer in solitude offered itself, he seized it; but whether by himself or with companions, he preserved a solitude in his heart, and thus was everywhere alone. He read gladly, and always with faith and thoughtfulness, the Holy Scriptures.

And when he preaches, he renders so clear and agreeable that which he takes from Scripture, and he has such power to move men, that everybody marvels at his eloquent words. *

These excerpts come from a contemporary life of Bernard of Clairvaux, a Cistercian abbot and the foremost religious figure in the first half of the twelfth century. They indicate some of the qualities an "ideal" product of reformed monasticism exhibited. A desire for study and solitude marked a boy as unusual, then as now. As a monk, Bernard's individual Bible study and prayer contrasted with the Cluniacs' group performance of religious ceremonies involving Biblical readings. He was sharply critical of both the Cluniacs and Peter Abelard, the great exponent of the use of reason in theological investigation.

*William of Saint Thierry, *Life of St. Bernard*, book I, chapts. 1–4, trans. Frederic A. Ogg, *Source Book of Medieval History* (New York, American Book Company, 1907), pp. 252–256.

gious service followed the afternoon meal, and the monks then worked for another five hours before doing the evening prayer service. After washing, and in summer eating the day's second meal, the monks performed the day's final prayer service and went to bed soon after sunset, sleeping in their monks' robes on straw-filled pallets.

By the late eleventh century, the Cluniacs were becoming prosperous and complacent. They accepted novices, often as preadolescents, from aristocratic families on receipt of a gift, usually a landed estate, from the novice's family. Although some of these novices became outstanding monks, many never developed a serious commitment to the monastic life. The performance of religious ceremonies, especially memorial masses for deceased members of aristocratic families, became the focus of Cluniac activity, and their interest in transforming Christian society dwindled.

In contrast to the Cluniacs, other groups of monastic reformers sought

to make monasticism a means of achieving both personal perfection and social change and therefore built their monasteries in remote wilderness areas to avoid worldliness and contact with outside society. To assure commitment and spiritual intensity, they admitted to them only people who elected religious vocations as adults, after serious self-examination. Typically, such orders encouraged a severe and largely solitary life. Members wore simple clothing, ate vegetables but no meat, lived as hermits in individual cells, and spoke to others only when absolutely necessary, although they might meet for common meals and worship services.

The Cistercians were the most prominent of these new twelfth-century monastic orders. Founded in 1098 at Citeaux (Cistercium in Latin) in eastern France, the Cistercians had 500 houses in Europe within a century. Cistercian abbots regularly inspected one another's monasteries and met together annually at Citeaux to make collective decisions about the order. They accepted only gifts of undeveloped land, which they reclaimed, emphasized manual work, and developed improved techniques for stock breeding and for marketing agricultural products. The Cistercians admitted only adults, including peasant lay brothers, who took vows of chastity and obedience while following a less demanding form of the Cistercian life.

In contrast to Cluniac concern with liturgy, the Cistercians stressed the development of the monks' inner spiritual life and typically described spiritual growth by such images as following a path, conducting a quest, or climbing a ladder. They sought to regulate liturgical life and promote spiritual discipline by means of strict interpretation of the Benedictine rule. In devotional writings and scriptural commentaries, Cistercian writers placed new emphasis on God's sympathy and affection for humans, depicting Jesus Christ as an accessible, suffering figure and popularizing depictions of Mary and the child Jesus.

The Mendicant Orders

Monasticism's desire for greater separation from the world and the pressing religious needs of the expanding towns and cities prompted the development of mendicant (begging) orders during the early thirteenth century. Mendicants, familiarly known as friars or brothers, rejected life in monasteries and instead worked in the world while living under a spiritual rule. They followed a life of personal and corporate poverty, accepted no gifts of land, and relied on donations from the faithful to provide the necessities of life. By dedicating themselves to doing charitable deeds and preaching, they helped to make Christianity relevant, particularly to town dwellers. Mendicant orders drew their earliest members from the lower levels of society and also enrolled lay associates, who were not required to abandon their families and secular responsibilities.

The Dominicans, formally known as the Order of Preachers, were established in 1216 as one of the two major mendicant orders. Their founder, Dominic de Guzman (1170–1221), adapted the rule of the Augustinian canons for the order, which included communities of both women and men. Members belonged to the order rather than to a particular house and were assigned places of residence and spheres of activity. The order was to have no possessions (except churches and buildings to house members) and no fixed incomes, subsisting on charitable gifts. It grew rapidly during the thirteenth century, attracting religiously dedicated people challenged by the order's austerity and vitality. Dominic required members to gain broad educations as well as specific training in preaching; talented Dominicans subsequently joined university faculties. Moreover, Dominicans became energetic missionaries, evangelizing non-Christians in northern and eastern Europe and seeking conversions in eastern Mediterranean lands and India. Preaching remained a primary Dominican emphasis, with friars working diligently in southern France and among Jews and Muslims in Spain.

The other prominent mendicant order, the Franciscans, formally known as the Order of Friars Minor (Little Brothers) obtained papal approval in 1210. Its founder, Francis of Assisi (1182–1226), left his wealthy merchant family to associate with poor priests, lepers, and beggars. He rejected property ownership, and required those entering the order to sell all their goods and give to the poor. Members, who worked and served in return for food and necessities, demonstrated an attractive quality of world-embracing joyousness. A Franciscan order for women, known by its founder's name as the Poor Clares, also developed. Franciscans spread rapidly throughout Europe, and some became missionaries in Syria and north Africa. Able Franciscans pursued careers in scholarship and university teaching, forming noteworthy centers of theological study in Paris and Oxford.

Women as well as men found religious withdrawal from the world attractive and many daughters of the families of nobles or well-to-do townspeople became nuns. Numerous continental women followed the Cistercian rule of life, and several thousand women in England entered the houses of the Gilbertine order established by Gilbert of Sempringham (1083–1189). Besides professed nuns, many of whom possessed a good knowledge of church Latin, were lay sisters from peasant or artisan families who performed many menial tasks. Nunneries gave their residents self-respect, and they earned the respect of society. They also offered women the possibility of a good education and opportunities to use abilities, particularly in organization and management, that might otherwise be wasted. Unfortunately, nunneries were often poor and frequently in debt because they lacked endowments, suffered fire, flood, or attack damage, or were compelled to offer ruinously expensive hospitality to powerful persons.

Some religiously inclined women chose, instead of the ordered routine of the nunnery, the severer discipline of the hermitess. Hermitesses lived in crudely-built shacks whether in forests to attain isolation or along roadways to obtain donations. A twelfth-century guide for such women instructs them never to satisfy their hunger, to avoid delicate foods, and to wear coarse clothes. Such a routine was perhaps no harsher than the life of many peasants and involved less hard work.

Religious communities transferred the vitality of monastic reform to the parishes by living according to rules, like monks. Canons, clergy on the staff of large urban churches, often

St. Francis Preaching to the Birds. Francis's affinity with nature was as famous as his love for humanity. According to the story pictured in Giotto's painting, Francis delivered a sermon to a flock of birds, who listened attentively. Assisi.

led in such community formation, raising the standards of performance among secular parish clergy and improving the quality of ministry in areas where they worked. Most notable were the Augustinian canons, who organized their communal life in the twelfth century on the basis of a rule derived from the writings of Augustine, the fifth-century Christian father, and applied that rule to canons who took up teaching or hospital work in the towns.

BELIEFS AND PRACTICES

By the thirteenth century, Roman Catholic Christianity was the most obvious characteristic most Europeans shared. Nearly all accepted its beliefs and practices, as well as its ideals for living and its code of morals. Because not many persons read or owned books, scripture was interpreted only by the learned few under the direction of the church. From the Bible and tradition, which included the writings of the church fathers, decisions of councils, and papal statements, Catholic theologians derived their religious beliefs.

Formal Doctrine

The beliefs of medieval Christians formed a coherent and integrated system. They believed God was one, almighty and all-knowing, just and merciful. The universe, created by God, was orderly, and in it human beings had a special place and destiny. Humans, by sinning, had disobeyed God and thus had lost their original righteousness and God's supernatural grace, forfeiting their hope of heaven. Because of sin, humans were incapable of doing good by their own efforts. Therefore, God had sent Jesus Christ to redeem humans, and by his voluntary suffering, death, and resurrection, in obedience and love, he reconciled humans with God and enabled them to qualify for heaven. God also gave the church to aid humans in their quest for heaven and to permit them to share in his reconciliation and grace through the sacraments. As the custodian of God's grace through control of the sacraments, the church was an essential intermediary between God and humans. Moreover, by excommunication (barring an individual from the sacraments) and interdict (ceasing to perform sacraments in a region), it could enforce obedience on individuals and regions.

A system of dioceses administered by bishops and further divided into parishes, geographical units each having a church and a priest, brought the sacraments and Christian instruction to all. By the sacraments, whose number was fixed at seven early in the thirteenth century, the church claimed to bring God's grace to all

members at critical junctures of life. Sacraments were the outward and visible signs of inward and spiritual grace that God had instituted for human salvation. They conferred grace and provided all believers periodic communion with God. Baptism cleansed individuals of original sin and initiated them into the Christian fellowship. At puberty, Confirmation reaffirmed a person's membership in the church, and gave one additional grace for adult life. According to church teaching, two people might unite their lives in the sacrament of Holy Matrimony, or a person might "marry" the church in holy orders. At the point of death, the individual received Extreme Unction (anointing with consecrated oil) to prepare for events after death. Throughout their lives, Christians could receive forgiveness from sin's consequences through the sacrament of Penance, performed by confessing sins to a priest and receiving God's absolution. Persons might receive Jesus Christ's body into theirs by partaking of the Eucharist, the central sacrament of the church, in which bread and wine were changed by a miracle called transubstantiation into Christ's body and blood. The Fourth Lateran Council of 1215 required Roman Catholic Christians to confess their sins and to receive the Eucharist at least once yearly.

Popular Piety

People sought from religion not only the hope of eternal salvation from a harsh world but also the promise of a better life here and now. Throughout this period in art and in writing, we see a shift in emphasis from the awe and mystery of God and from the belief of Christ as judge to stress God's love and Jesus' suffering on the cross

for human sins. Christianity offered love, hope, and compassion, particularly in the person of Mary, who was regarded as an especially effective intercessor with God for sinful humans. As the beloved mother and protectress (mediatrix) of all, she would plead with her son on behalf of all sinners. The series of prayers known as the rosary, introduced from the east, deepened popular devotion to Mary.

Saints too were believed to intercede with God on behalf of humans. Each town, each trade, even each disease, had its appropriate saint, and prayers and devotion to them were supposed to be especially efficacious. People sought to own mementos of revered and powerful religious figures for protection and blessings, and churches needed relics, remains of saints, for their altars. Thus a lively traffic in holy relics developed. A pilgrim to Venice about 1400 reported seeing there the arm of one saint, the staff of another, the ear of St. Paul, and a tooth of Goliath, the biblical giant killed by King David.

Pilgrimage, although arduous and dangerous, also became increasingly popular. People became pilgrims partly from a desire to explore holy places and partly from a belief that visits to shrines could heal physical ills and provide spiritual benefits. Pilgrims usually traveled in groups, stopping at other shrines along the way to their final destination. Sometimes present or potential dangers from robbers and wars prompted pilgrims to travel with weapons; the crusades began as such armed pilgrimages. Geoffrey Chaucer's *Canterbury Tales* written in the 1390s vividly describes the members of such an expedition. A pilgrimage combined religious duty and holiday relaxation; hence pilgrimage routes came to be carefully arranged. Hos-

Mary with Jesus. Late thirteenth-century sculpture of painted wood. An important feature of popular religion after the twelfth century was the veneration of Mary. Embodying kindness and love, she forgave those who made an appeal to her and interceded with God to aid them. Many great churches and cathedrals honored her as Notre Dame (Our Lady). Metropolitan Museum of Art, New York.

tels were available at appropriate intervals, and larger churches were built to accommodate crowds of pilgrims. Rome and Jerusalem attracted pilgrims from throughout Christendom, and Santiago de Compostela in northwest Spain was, like Canterbury in England, a major regional pilgrimage destination.

Popular piety prompted criticism of the centralized institutional church and opposition to the growth of ecclesiastical wealth and power. Reformers and critics disliked the church's increasing bureaucracy and its burgeoning legal business. Town dwellers often viewed urban bishops as political oppressors and opponents of town independence, rather than as spiritual directors. Occasionally, pious lay persons formed sects that preached to the public, often denouncing ecclesiastical wealth.

The extent of popular piety, however, should not be exaggerated. Many people remained ill-informed about basic Christian beliefs and minimally involved in Christian religious observances. Pre-Christian religious practices persisted in many places. Demons and mysterious powers supposedly filled the world and had to be appeased or neutralized by any means available, Christian or non-Christian. Persons able to produce healing by judicious use of herbs and "home remedies" or able to "see" what the future had in store were in great demand.

Heresy

The church in earlier centuries had incorporated reform into the monastic orders, but by the thirteenth century its claim to be the sole repository of Christian truth brought it into conflict with popular efforts to practice Christianity more perfectly,

which the church judged to be heresies. One such reform movement so denounced, Waldensianism, was begun by a merchant of Lyons, Peter Waldo, who about 1173 distributed all his possessions to the poor and adopted a life of poverty. Waldensians opposed clerical corruption and urged the church to adopt poverty by disposing of its possessions. They claimed that only morally pure clergy should administer sacraments, did not believe the clergy were intermediaries between God and humans, and taught that all believers might act as priests. Furthermore Waldensians rejected or reinterpreted the Catholic sacraments, denied such practices as prayers for the dead, preached from selected portions of the biblical text and read scripture in local languages. When the Waldensians disregarded the archbishop of Lyons' limitations on their preaching, they were declared heretics and excommunicated. Fleeing from Lyons, they spread Waldensianism into Switzerland, Provence, Lombardy, and other areas of Europe.

Usually termed a major heresy, but more properly a rival religion, was Catharism, also known as Albigensianism because of its strength in the southern French town of Albi. The Cathars were dualists, recognizing two distinct realms of matter and spirit, each with its own god. A small, elite group of Cathars who sought to ascend to the realm of pure spirit vigorously rejected sensual and material things such as physical appetites and wealth, which kept spirits confined in the material body, and saw procreation as the greatest sin because it imprisoned another spirit in the material world. Most Cathars, however, continued to eat and make love and confined their rejection of the material world to criticizing the affluence of the church. Southern French nobles found Catharism an attractive justification for appropriating church lands for their own use, and the rapid spread of the belief soon alarmed church leaders. When efforts to eradicate it by reforming the clergy and promoting effective preaching of accepted doctrine (notably by the Order of Preachers, founded to counter the Cathars) proved ineffective, Pope Innocent III proclaimed a crusade. During a twenty-year campaign (1209–1229), a crusading army from northern France, impelled primarily by the French monarchy's desire to extend its authority over the South, eliminated the Cathars and also destroyed the distinctive culture of southern France. The French king incorporated the area into his realm.

In addition to employing military force to combat heresy, popes of this period developed a judicial process known as the Inquisition, which became a formidable instrument for detecting and eradicating heresy. Following precedents in German, Roman, and ecclesiastical law that authorized judges to make inquiries or hold inquests (examinations), twelfth-century popes ordered bishops to conduct inquests concerning heretics within their dioceses and to punish the guilty by excommunication. Pope Innocent III added confiscation of goods and property to the punishment of heretics, and Pope Gregory IX (1227–1241) established a central tribunal staffed by Dominicans and Franciscans to improve and standardize Inquisition procedures. The accused were denied legal counsel, subjected to torture as a means of obtaining information, and required to identify accomplices as a sign of repentance. They might be convicted on the testimony of only two witnesses, whose identity and testimony remained secret from the accused. Although some it found guilty were sentenced to penances or prison terms, the Inquisition was much less inclined to execute than has been presumed and most convicted heretics were put to death by governments, not by the church.

JEWS IN MEDIEVAL LIFE

Progressive Christian reconquest of Spain drastically changed the lives of the Jews, a significant European religious minority. They benefited from religious tolerance and economic freedom in Islamic lands to make im-

Execution of Heretics. Frequently, as in this thirteenth-century picture, heretics were executed by burning. At left, King Philip II of France sits on his horse. Note structure in upper right for mass hangings. Bibliothèque Nationale, Paris.

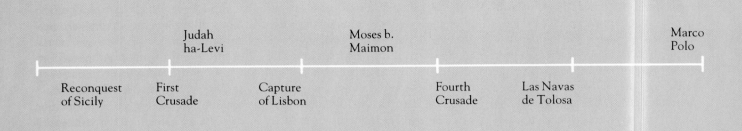

1050	1100	1150	1200	1250	1300

Judah
ha-Levi

Moses b.
Maimon

Marco
Polo

Reconquest
of Sicily

First
Crusade

Capture
of Lisbon

Fourth
Crusade

Las Navas
de Tolosa

portant intellectual, scientific, and cultural contributions, but endured harsh treatment and sharply restricted opportunities in Christian territories.

Contributors to Civilization in Islamic Lands

During the ninth and tenth centuries, large numbers of Jews moved westward from Mesopotamia as traders and settlers, making Umayyad Spain by the tenth century the dominant Jewish community. Instead of remaining separated from the Muslims like their coreligionists in Mesopotamia, Spanish Jews became Arabized. They adopted Arab names, used Arabic as their spoken and literary language, and immersed themselves in the activities of Islamic civilization.

Within Spanish Jewry, noteworthy individuals emerged to make important contributions both to Jewish life and to western civilization. Samuel ibn Nagdela (993–1055) was a capable poet and scholar, who also served as prime minister to the Islamic ruler of Granada. Judah ha-Levi (1086–1141) earned his living as a physician but was a masterful poet who composed passionate hymns to

the Holy Land and wrote a philosophical dialogue, *The Khuzari* (named for the Khazars, south Russian nomads whose rulers had recently adopted Judaism), which emphasized the rational basis of Judaism. The greatest medieval Jewish thinker, however, was Spanish-born Moses ben Maimon (1135–1204), inaccurately but popular known as Maimonides, who spent most of his adult life in Egypt. Employed as court physician to the Egyptian sultan Saladin (1169–1193), he wrote treatises on hygiene and a medical work entitled *Aphorisms* that criticized the authoritative opinions of Galen on the basis of empirical methods. He composed critical commentaries on major writings of the Jewish tradition and formulated a statement of Jewish faith, the Thirteen Articles, that many subsequently regarded as an authoritative creed. His codification of Jewish law, reducing a rich but bewilderingly confusing collection of material to an orderly and systematic structure, was quickly recognized as a brilliant work. Subsequently, he authored *The Guide for the Perplexed,* a philosophical interpretation of Judaism intended for persons seeking a rational basis for their faith. His openness to extra-Jewish influences, notably the thought

of Aristotle, provoked opposition from many Jews, but his analysis of the connection between revelation and reason attracted and was soon adopted by Christian thinkers such as Thomas Aquinas.

A Persecuted Minority in Christian Lands

Like Maimonides' family, many other Jews left Spain during the twelfth and thirteenth centuries, fleeing both Muslim and Christian persecution. To resist the Christians advancing from the north, Spanish Muslims summoned from Africa militant and rigorist coreligionists called Almohades. In contrast to the traditional Islamic tolerance practiced by Spanish Muslims, the Almohades required non-Muslims to adopt Islam, killing or expelling those who refused. Meanwhile, victorious Spanish Christians also became more religiously intolerant. Many Jews consequently fled northward into Christian lands to join meager groups of their coreligionists already there and to establish vigorous centers of Jewish life in southern and northeastern France and in the German Rhineland.

Life in Christian lands, however, was distinctly dangerous to Jews. They had only those legal rights that rulers granted them, and they were excluded from most occupations, with the notable exceptions of money-lending and trading. Although high church officials made strong statements guaranteeing the safety of Jews, anti-Jewish attitudes grew stronger among the masses and the lower clergy. Most Christians believed that Jews were collectively responsible for Christ's death, that they were active servants of Satan, that they murdered Christian boys and used their blood for secret rituals, and that they poisoned wells and spread disease through the land.

Because of such beliefs, Christians executed, lynched, and banished large numbers of Jews. An acceleration of violence and other harsh treatment began when the warriors of the first crusade paused on their way to the Holy Land to massacre the Jews in several Rhineland towns. The Third Lateran Council (1179) forbade Christians to live near Jews, spurring the growth of the ghetto, a walled section of a city in which Jews were compelled to live. Although Jews in ghettos were able to maintain their distinctive religious practices, they were overcrowded and isolated and forced into an embattled, defensive posture. This defensiveness became even more necessary as decrees of the Fourth Lateran Council (1215) required Jews to wear identifying marks on their clothing, making them easily visible targets of abuse. Rulers in need of money exploited popular feeling by expelling Jews from their domains and seizing their abandoned property (England, 1290; France, 1306; some German states at various times; Spain, 1492; Portugal, 1497). Iberian Jews found refuge in north Africa and Tur-key, and northern communities migrated eastward, especially into Poland and Lithuania, forming major new Jewish communities there.

THE CRUSADES

Besides reforms and monasticism, medieval European Christians also demonstrated their religious ardor by conducting warfare against the Muslims. Reformist popes adroitly joined the spiritual benefit of forgiveness of sins to the already established practice of an armed pilgrimage. The church promoted peace and reduced warfare within Europe by channeling the warlike energies of the European nobles against enemies of the faith, primarily the Muslims. The crusading movement also benefited from Europe's increased prosperity and stability. Wealth was available to finance crusading ventures, and younger sons in noble families unable to win fame and fortune at home sought to do so in foreign lands.

Islamic lands near the Mediterranean appeared to be especially vulnerable to Christian attack in the late eleventh century. Spain, united under independent caliphs from 919–1031, was divided into some twenty petty kingdoms, many mutually hostile and all relatively powerless. Muslims in north Africa and Sicily were also weak and ineffective. In the east, the caliphs of Baghdad effectively controlled only a small territory around that city and were confronted by a rival Egyptian caliphate. A new Muslim group, the Seljuk Turks ruled by Malik Shah (1072–1092), had gained control of most of southwest Asia dur-ing the century and seized most of Anatolia from the Byzantine Empire after crushingly defeating a Byzantine army in 1071 at Manzikent. The deaths of Malik Shah and the empire's architect and chief minister, Nizam al-Mulk (1018–1092) in the same year left the Seljuks leaderless.

Early Achievements

The crusading enterprise began in 1095 when the Byzantine emperor appealed for western European volunteers to augment his armies for offensives against the Muslims. Pope Urban II proposed a large armed pilgrimage to Jerusalem to an assembly of clergy and laity at Clermont, France, promising forgiveness of sins to those who participated (Map 29).

Many persons responded enthusiastically to this papal summons on the basis of intense and sincere religious convictions. As a result, four armies of western fighters departed for Constantinople in 1096. By his appeal, the pope made Christian knighthood a holy calling and allowed knights to win praise and salvation as soldiers of Christ fighting against infidels.

The first crusading armies enjoyed astonishing success. Allying with the Byzantine emperor Alexius, they seized Seljuk strongholds and defeated Seljuk armies in Anatolia. They then conquered the cities of Edessa and Antioch in Syria and finally entered Jerusalem in 1099, crying "God wills it!" To control their newly won territories, the crusaders established a feudal monarchy. They made one of their number the king of Jerusalem; as such he was overlord of the other crusader states and employed institutions and relationships already common in Europe.

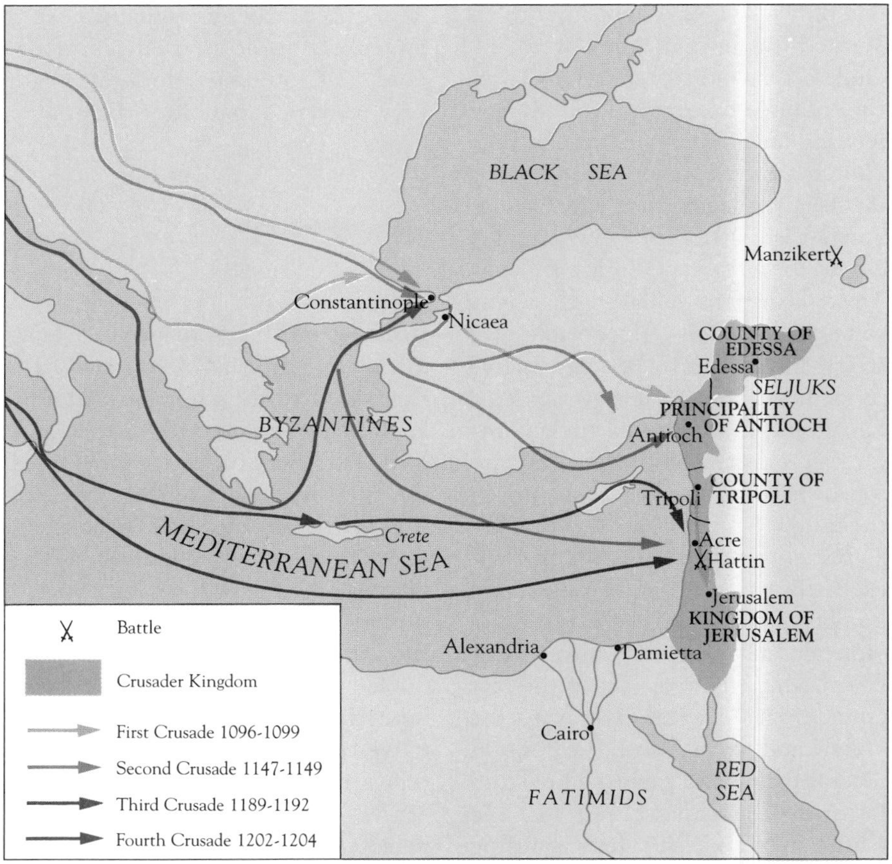

MAP 29
The Crusades. Although the first two crusades relied on overland routes, later crusaders traveled east primarily by sea. At their greatest extent, the crusaders' holdings formed only a small coastal strip amid extensive Islamic territories, and were rather easily retaken by the Muslims. Notice that the modern nations of Lebanon and Israel include much of the same territory the crusaders held.

Although the first crusade had been a marked success, the crusaders confronted several persistent problems in Palestine. They never received enough additional warriors from Europe to consolidate their position. They were forced to trade and make treaties with their Muslim neighbors to obtain money and to end conflicts, and so had to develop a tolerance toward Muslims. These circumstances antagonized later crusaders fresh from Europe.

Moreover, the crusaders' interest in seeking land and glory for themselves conflicted with Alexius' desire to restore his empire. For some time, the crusaders maintained their state despite those difficulties, and military religious orders, notably the Knights Templars (1119) and the Knights Hospitalers (1113) came into existence to assist them. However, an unsuccessful attempt in the 1140s to take Damascus, the major Islamic city in Syria, revived Islamic resistance. The Seljuks annihilated the Byzantine army in 1176 and reestablished Turkish control of Anatolia, depriving the crusaders of Byzantine aid. The dynamic Turkish military leader Saladin decisively defeated the crusaders in 1187 and recaptured most of the crusader territories except for a few seaports.

Loss of access to Jerusalem led the three greatest European monarchs of the time—Frederick I Barbarossa, Richard I of England, and Philip II of France—to organize the third crusade. But after Frederick drowned in Asia Minor in 1190, the other two quarreled and Philip soon returned to France. After military success at the port of Acre, Richard received a three-year truce in 1192 allowing Christians access to Jerusalem, but the power of the crusaders in the area began to decline.

Later Failures

As the Christian grip on the Holy Land weakened, Pope Innocent III organized new expeditions to aid the crusaders in the east. He hoped to regain control of the Christian holy places in and near Jerusalem, to increase papal power and prestige, and to reunite Eastern Orthodox and Roman Catholic Christians. The crusaders' objective was Egypt, the power base of Saladin's successors, and to reach it they sought sea transport from Venice. Unable to pay the Venetians' charges, the crusaders agreed to retake for Venice the Adriatic coast city of Zara, recently seized by Hungary. They did so in 1202 despite the pope's vehement objections against crusaders fighting Christians. When a recently deposed Byzantine emperor appeared and promised lavish payments for restoration to his throne, the crusaders went to Constantinople on his behalf. He failed to fulfill those promises, however, and the irate crusaders stormed and sacked the city (1204), gaining booty and establishing a short-lived Latin Empire of Constantinople (1204–1261). Although by their successes the crusaders ostensibly restored the unity of Christendom, in fact they thoroughly embittered the Eastern Orthodox Christians and made the schism (division) between them and the Roman Catholics permanent until it was ended by pope and patriarch in the twentieth century. This crusade discredited both the papacy and the crusading enterprise and by crippling the Byzantine Empire helped to facilitate later Turkish expansion into southeastern Europe. A later crusade launched by Innocent III landed in Egypt, but was soundly defeated and driven out.

Prominent rulers, rather than popes, conducted subsequent crusades. The Holy Roman Emperor

---

A CRUSADER CONFRONTS A MUSLIM

One day I entered this mosque [and faced southward toward Mecca] . . . and stood up in the act of praying, upon which one of the Franks rushed on me, got hold of me and turned my face eastward saying, "This is the way thou shouldst pray!" A group of Templars hastened to him, seized him and repelled him from me. I resumed my prayer. The same man, while the others were otherwise busy, rushed once more on me and turned my face eastward, saying, "This is the way thou shouldst pray!" The Templars again came in to him and expelled him. They apologized to me, saying "This is a stranger who has only recently arrived from the land of the Franks and he has never before seen anyone praying except eastward." Thereupon I said to myself, "I have had enough prayer."*

Christian ignorance of Islamic belief and practices was extensive, and the crusades provided eye-opening experiences, such as this encounter of a Muslim knight with a newly arrived crusader. Crusaders who had lived for some time in the East typically treated Muslims with tolerance and consideration and depended upon them for many goods and most services. Newly arrived crusaders, however, were full of zealous hatred against the "infidel" Muslims. Such hatred was fueled by misinformation. Many Christians believed Muslims were idolaters, or that they worshiped Mohammad as a god. Only gradually, by encounters such as this one, did Christians and Muslims come to know one another's religions more accurately.

*Memoirs of an Arab-Syrian Gentleman (Usamah ibn-Munqidh) and Warrior in the period of the Crusades, trans. Philip K. Hitti, (New York, Columbia University Press, 1927; Beirut: Khayats, 1964), p. 164.

Frederick II launched a crusade in 1228, and in the following year negotiated with the sultan of Egypt a treaty giving the Christians control of Nazareth, Bethlehem, Jerusalem, and a corridor from Jerusalem to the coast. Muslim recapture of Jerusalem in 1244 prompted King Louis IX of France to launch a crusade that also landed in Egypt, but his forces were routed and the king was captured and held for ransom. In 1270, Louis met his death by dysentery on a futile crusade against Tunis. Subsequent papal attempts to organize crusades were unavailing. As European crusading enthusiasm waned, Muslim capture

of Acre in 1291 ended the Latin presence in the Holy Land.

Impact of the Crusades

Although the crusader states in the east disappeared, the crusades had several lasting effects. Unification of many Europeans in a common effort and synthesizing of military and Christian life would recur often in Europe. European Christians, especially Italians, maintained important commercial relations with Islamic lands and peoples. Although hatred of Muslims continued to produce distorted views, some individuals at-

The Latin Capture of Constantinople, painted by Tintoretto. This event crippled the Byzantine Empire and enhanced the fortunes of Venice. It also destroyed many Byzantine literary and artistic treasures. Ducal Palace, Venice.

tempted peaceful Christian missionary activity among them, without, however, significant success.

Some European Christians saw in the Mongol conquests of Asia in the thirteenth century another opportunity to achieve victory over the Muslims. If the Mongols could be converted to Christianity, they and the Europeans would surround and could eliminate the Muslims. Embassies of diplomats and missionaries left Europe for various Mongol centers hoping to achieve such conversions, but failed; instead, many Mongols became Muslims. These efforts, however, indirectly opened Asia to European traders. Members of a prominent Venetian commercial family, the Polos, were especially active in Asia; Marco Polo (1254–1324) lived

and worked in Mongol lands for many years before returning to Europe. The account of his experiences stimulated other Europeans to go east, and Christian merchants in the eastern Mediterranean, Black Sea, and Baltic Sea brought money and merchandise from eastern lands into Europe, further stimulating economic growth. This activity directed European vision outward to a wider world.

RECONQUESTS

Instead of participating in crusading expeditions to the eastern Mediterranean, some European Christians fought against Muslims in the Italian and Iberian peninsulas, participating

in successful campaigns called reconquests (Map 30). By these campaigns, the Christians not only acquired additional territories, but also gained access to the intellectual and artistic riches of Islamic civilization.

South Italy and Sicily

In the Italian peninsula, Norman warriors who had participated as mercenaries in Italian wars won a series of victories against the Muslims after 1015, retaining the Muslim lands in southern Italy that they reconquered. Although at first opposed by the popes, the Normans overcame that hostility and obtained papal recognition of their authority over their conquests. In return for the title of duke, the Norman leader Robert Guiscard (1015–1085) pledged allegiance to the papacy and received permission to undertake the conquest of Sicily from the Muslims, a task the Normans completed in 1091.

In their south Italian-Sicilian lands, the Normans built one of the wealthiest and best-governed states in Europe. They joined Norman lord-vassal structures with sophisticated Byzantine and Islamic administrative techniques to unite an extremely diverse group of people into a cohesive realm. In 1130, Roger II (1130–1154) became, with papal approval, king of this land. A strong yet tolerant ruler, Roger drew heavily on Byzantine and Islamic experience to develop an efficient and centralized bureaucracy, staffed by nonnoble professionals, and incorporated Byzantine, Islamic, and Latin contributions in the kingdom's intellectual life and cultural activity.

The Iberian Peninsula

The reconquest of most of the Iberian Peninsula between 1050 and 1270 greatly enlarged the territorial area of Christian Europe. In addition, it provided major cultural gains by enriching Europe's knowledge with Indian, Greek, and Islamic learning. The small Christian kingdoms that survived in the peninsula's northern mountains after the Islamic conquest began advancing slowly southward during the ninth and tenth centuries, but rivalries among the Christian rulers limited their successes. The eleventh-century breakup of Islamic Spain into numerous petty kingdoms, however, offered the Christians enticing expansion opportunities.

By uniting the kingdoms of Leon and Castile, King Alfonso VI (1065–1109) gave the *reconquista* (reconquest) new impetus. He collected tribute and booty from the Islamic territories to the south and obtained warriors from Christian lands north of the Pyrenees to fight the Muslims. In 1085, he captured Toledo, the former capital and ecclesiastical center of Visigothic Christian Spain. Toledo's conquest deprived the Muslims of a key strong point in the center of the peninsula.

The capture of Toledo so weakened the position of the Spanish Muslims that they summoned from north Africa a puritanical sect of Islamic warriors, the Almoravids, as reinforcements. The newcomers briefly reunited the peninsular Islamic states and halted Alfonso's advance. However, one of his vassals, Rodrigo Diaz de Vivar, won Valencia for himself in 1099 and gained lasting fame as the hero of the Castilian epic, *The Song of the Cid* (*Cid* was a Spanish corruption of the Arabic term *sayyid*, meaning chief or lord).

While the reconquest efforts of Castile languished, those of other peninsular Christian powers quickened. In the east, Aragon was strengthened by the addition of the county of Barcelona in 1140 and gained several other important towns. In the west, adventurous nobles expanded the county of Portugal and

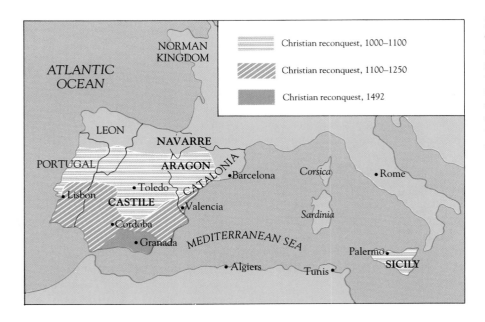

MAP 30
Christian Reconquests. In the western Mediterranean, Christians regained some territories previously taken by Muslims. Norman adventurers in Italy quickly wrested Sicily from its Muslim rulers in the eleventh century. The reconquest of Spain and Portugal, however, extended over six hundred years and permitted important Islamic cultural influences to penetrate Europe.

made it a kingdom in 1143. With the aid of a seaborne party of eastward-bound crusaders, the Portuguese captured the strong and strategically located city of Lisbon in 1147. After 1150, the Iberian Christians needed time and people to settle reconquered lands and money to finance further campaigning, and the reconquest slowed.

During the thirteenth century, the *reconquista* resumed. Pope Innocent III and the Spanish clergy assisted Castile in preparing a unified assault against the Muslims. The resulting victory of Las Navas de Tolosa in 1212 decisively established Christian superiority in the peninsula. Castilian forces thereafter took Cordoba and Seville extending Christian control into the Guadalquivir Valley, the major river basin of southern Iberia. Meanwhile, Jaime I (1213–1276) of Aragon captured the Balearic Islands in 1229 and subsequently conquered the major port cities of Valencia and Murcia. By 1270, the only Islamic presence in the peninsula was the small southeastern kingdom of Granada, whose ruler was a vassal of the Castilian king. Too weak to endanger the Christian kingdoms, but too difficult to attack easily because of its mountainous setting, Granada continued to exist as an Islamic stronghold for another two centuries until its capture in 1492, when the Spanish Christians consolidated their conquests and diverted their energies to dynastic contests and civil wars.

Spanish Christians also actively assimilated many Islamic intellectual and scientific achievements. Toledo became a vital center for the cultural transmission of the accomplishments of Muslims and the works of classical Greeks and medieval Jews from Islamic civilization to western Europe. A group of translators made available in Latin certain Arabic and Hebrew philosophical works and some Arabic versions of classical Greek writings. They also translated Islamic works on science and mathematics, including star catalogs and tables of planetary motion based on the work of Hellenistic astronomers such as Ptolemy but augmented by Arab observers. From the Muslims, Europeans learned the Arabic number system, derived originally from India. Its use of the zero or cipher (both Arabic words) and of positional notation, in which an individual number symbol, such as 1, takes a different value (that of a ten or a hundred or a thousand, for example) depending on its position in a numeral, speeded and simplified mathematical calculations. The English terms *algebra* and *alchemy*, derived from Arabic, indicate other aspects of European assimilation of Islamic achievements. Spanish Christians borrowed ideas and techniques from Islamic literature and art, which were incorporated into their works and those of other Europeans.

SUMMARY

Christianity was central to medieval European life and remained vigorous through recurrent reform. Reformers worked to eliminate abuses such as simony and clerical marriage, and Augustinian canons improved the quality of clergy. Reform popes established a strong, centralized Christian organization. In monastic reform, Cluniac monks emphasized extensive liturgical activity, whereas Cistercians sought to develop the monk's inner spiritual life. The mendicant orders of Dominicans and Franciscans effectively met the religious needs of town dwellers.

By the thirteenth century, Roman Catholic beliefs and practices were firmly established, and the sacramental system made God's grace available from cradle to grave. Popular piety emphasized Christian love and compassion and stimulated devotion to Mary, veneration of saints, and pilgrimages. Intensified popular piety produced criticism of the institutional church, occasionally leading to heresies. To eradicate heresy, the church employed military force and developed the procedures of the Inquisition.

Jews were Europe's most noticeable non-Christian inhabitants. In Islamic lands, Jews were tolerated and made important contributions to religious and scientific thought. However, in Christian Europe, Jews were despised, barred from most occupations, and frequently subjected to persecution.

Fervent Christian militancy produced the crusades, by which Christians conquered the Holy Land and adjacent territories from the Muslims, but lack of reinforcements and differences among the crusader states weakened the crusading effort. Later crusades permanently alienated Eastern Orthodox Christians but made no gains against Muslims, who ousted the crusaders by 1291. The crusades, however, enlarged European commercial relations with Islamic lands and awareness of Asia.

In crusading wars called reconquests, Italian and Iberian Christians regained much territory from Muslims. Benefiting from reconquest activities, Normans developed a well-governed state in south Italy and Sicily, and Castile and Portugal expanded at Muslim expense. By 1270, Muslim presence in the Iberian Peninsula was restricted to the small kingdom of Granada. Spanish Christians assimilated many Islamic intellectual and scientific achievements and transmitted that knowledge to other Europeans. Knowledge acquired from the Muslims was an important stimulus to subsequent medieval achievements in thought, literature, and art.

SELECTED SOURCES

*Barraclough, Geoffrey. *The Medieval Papacy.* 1968. A master scholar's illustrated, easy-to-read account of this dominant institution.

Lomax, Derek W. *The Reconquest of Spain.* 1978. Brief, readable account of this centuries-long enterprise.

*Mayer, Hans E. *The Crusades.* Translated by John Gillingham. 1972. The best one-volume survey of the crusading movement.

Oldenbourg, Zoe. *The Cornerstone.* 1955. A first-rate historical novel of medieval society and crusading life.

Packard, Sidney R. *Europe and the Church under Innocent III.* 1968. Excellent, brief treatment of papal government in operation under the most powerful medieval pope.

The Poem of the Cid. Translated by W. S. Merwin. 1959. Epic story of a Spanish noble's battles and adventures during the reconquest; also a film, *El Cid* 1961.

*Russell, Jeffrey B. *A History of Medieval Christianity: Prophecy and Order.* 1968. Provocative survey and interpretation of medieval church history by a leading modern scholar.

Sabatier, Paul. *Life of St. Francis of Assisi.* Translated by L. S. Houghton. 1924. The outstanding biography of this most winsome Christian figure. Also a film, *Francis of Assisi.* 1961.

The Seventh Seal. 1956. A returned crusader seeks life's meaning in this moving evocation of the medieval spirit by master Swedish filmmaker Ingmar Bergman.

*Workman, Herbert B. *The Evolution of the Monastic Ideal.* 1962. The only full-length treatment of this important aspect of medieval Christianity; also treats the friars.

*Available in paperback.

MEDIEVAL ACHIEVEMENTS IN THOUGHT, LITERATURE, AND ART

To masters and scholars studying in any land, the university of masters and scholars of Toulouse wish continued good life with a blessed end . . . This is the second land of promise flowing with milk and honey. Here theologians inform their disciples in pulpits and the people at the crossroads, logicians train the tyros [beginners] in the arts of Aristotle, grammarians fashion the tongues of the stammering on analogy, organists soothe the popular ears with the sweet-throated organ, law professors extol Justinian, and physicians teach Galen. Those who wish to scrutinize the bosom of nature to the inmost can hear here the books of Aristotle which were forbidden at Paris . . . If you wish to marvel at even more good things than we have mentioned, strap your knapsack on your back and leave home behind."

Many prospective students probably found this letter from the faculty at the newly established University of Toulouse (1229) in southern France enticing. It resembles modern university publicity brochures, both in tone and in its listing of graduate programs of study and components of the undergraduate curriculum. Although it suggests the vibrancy of intellectual life in the medieval period, it focuses on scholarly topics, which were studied in Latin. Other medieval writers, however, used vernacular (local) languages to write creative literature, and skilled artisans produced impressive buildings, sculptures, and other artistic works. The present chapter discusses the growth of universities and the development of scholarship and also examines European creativity in literature and art in the medieval period.

CONTENTS

THOUGHT

One important feature of medieval intellectual life was expanding interest in education, which culminated in a distinctive new institution, the university. Before 1000, most education in Europe took place in schools

Augustinian Hermit Henry the German Lectures on Ethics at Paris. Although clothing and furnishings differ, this medieval university scene, with attentive, talkative, and even dozing students, has many parallels in university life today. Staatliche Museum, Berlin.

233

Abelard

Thomas
Aquinas

Duns
Scotus

William
of Ockham

Gratian
Decretum

Rise of
universities

Grosseteste

Bacon

set up in monasteries. In addition, some cathedral schools existed, as well as semisecular municipal schools in Italy. However, during the eleventh and twelfth centuries, expanding royal bureaucracy, an increasingly complex ecclesiastical organization, and reviving commercial activity created a growing demand for educated persons who could perform a variety of clerical and administrative tasks. In response to that demand, cathedral and municipal schools grew larger and evolved into universities.

Education and the Rise of Universities

To meet the increased demands for educated persons, schools revised their curricula to include the intensified study of seven liberal arts. Derived from classical civilization and identified in writings of the late Roman Empire, those disciplines seemed suited to the new educational demands. Particularly important were the three disciplines of grammar, logic or dialectic, and rhetoric. Grammar taught people to read and write effectively, rhetoric contributed to both capable writing and competent speaking, and logic promoted clear thinking and careful reasoning. The other four liberal arts, arithmetic, geometry, astronomy, and music, although less central to contemporary needs, also enjoyed a revived and enlarged interest.

During the late twelfth century, several pressures transformed cathedral and municipal schools into universities. Masters and students wished to explore ideas and pursue truths that had no immediate practical or vocational application. Also, a flood of new knowledge had become available, primarily from the classical Greeks but transmitted and enlarged by Muslim and Jewish scholars. But it was the students themselves who directly established universities. Because students lacked legal status and the protection of citizenship, status, and privileges, they often experienced much hostility from townspeople or from ecclesiastical or secular authorities. In response to these pressures, scholars organized themselves, like artisans, into corporations or guilds, known as universities from the Latin word for guild, *universitas*.

Many universities began by emphasizing one area of learning, but the term *university* came to mean a group of scholars working in close proximity and providing a basic program of instruction in the seven liberal arts and in one or more of the higher disciplines of theology, law, or medicine. By completing the six- to eight-year program, a student obtained a master's degree and a license to teach. Bachelor's programs of four to five years' duration developed later, but did not authorize their holders to teach. Beyond the master's degree, some students pursued advanced degrees in one of the higher disciplines.

Although organized as self-governing bodies, the composition of universities varied. Paris stressed liberal arts and attracted younger students, some of whom needed supervision; hence it took the form of a corporation of masters and became a model for north European university organization. Bologna, begun as a center of higher studies for older professionals seeking further training, was a student corporation and became a model for the organization of southern European universities. Universities did not have buildings and campuses; instead, their classes met in rented rooms and students lived and learned in their masters' homes. Scholars sometimes chose to rent a house in which to live jointly. Such scholars' houses evolved into legally recognized corporations called colleges. Universities were highly mobile, and relations between them and towns were frequently strained and occasionally violent. Sometimes students and masters left town and established their university elsewhere. Gradually, wealthy patrons endowed colleges and universities with buildings and funds to pay for housing, feeding, and instructing students, and the universities settled in one place.

Philosophy and Theology

Many medieval scholars labored to improve their understanding of Christian faith, and during the eleventh century some investigated the value of human reason in comprehending religious truth. Anselm of Bec who became archbishop of Canterbury during the reign of William I (1066–1087) of England, considered logic an important dimension of human nature and emphasized the use of reason in theology. He even attempted to prove God's existence by reason. However, Anselm held that reason was subordinate to faith: "I do not seek to understand that I may believe, but I believe that I may understand; for this I also believe, that unless I believe I will not understand."

Anselm's younger contemporary Peter Abelard reversed that relationship, insisting that "by doubting we are led to question, and by questioning we arrive at the truth." Abelard maintained that proper use of logical method enabled a person to understand the relation between God and the self and the complexity of revelation. In his primary work, *Sic et Non (Yes and No)*, in 1122, he quoted acceptable but conflicting authorities on many important theological issues, demonstrating that authority alone was not a reliable guide to truth and arguing that only reason could resolve

the contradictions. His student Peter Lombard constructed a theological textbook entitled *Sentences* (1152), in which by the use of reason he resolved conflicting views on theological issues and formulated acceptable doctrinal positions based on the plan of *Sic et Non*.

As works of Jewish, Islamic, and Greek philosophy (especially Aristotle) were translated into Latin in the wake of Christian reconquest of formerly Islamic lands, studies in logic expanded. Aristotle became the leading authority on logic, but his thought presented problems for Christian thinkers. For example, Aristotle taught that nature was good and purposeful and that the earth is eternal. Such Aristotelian ideas contradicted accepted Christian views. Moreover, Aristotle's rationalism challenged scholars to harmonize the findings of natural knowledge and the conclusions of religious faith.

During the thirteenth century, numerous scholars (called scholastics because they worked in the medieval schools) responded to that challenge. A few attempted unsuccessfully to forbid the study and teaching of Aristotelianism. Two main groups were in opposition. One group wholeheartedly accepted Aristotelian rationalism and went on to the daring assertion that reason could delineate truth irrespective of religious faith. Another group rejected Aristotelianism and held that ultimate truth could not be discovered by reason, but was transmitted to humans via mystical illumination.

The most fruitful response to the challenge of Aristotelianism, however, was the attempt to reconcile faith and reason. Its foremost practitioner was Thomas Aquinas (1225–

1274). Starting from the position that God is the source of truth and that the world is created by God, Thomas recognized revelation and reason as two ways of knowing the truth and theology and philosophy as two realms of knowledge. Theology deals with supernatural truth, understood through revelation, and philosophy deals with natural truth, perceived by reason. Both realms of knowledge are compatible because both lead to the same faith and the same truth. Thus there can be no conflict between any two supposed truths; any such apparent conflict is the result of the limits of human reason. Reason operates competently and truthfully within the realm of its data, but beyond these limits, revelation operates with God-given authority. Because God chose to convey his one truth through two media, and because each medium is valid within its proper sphere, properly conducted rational inquiry will support the principles of revelation.

Thomas Aquinas set down his attempt to reconcile Aristotle's ideas and observation of the natural world with revealed truth in a massive work called the *Summa Theologica (Summary of Theology)*, which he left unfinished at his death in 1274. In it, he employed a rigorous analytic method, beginning with the statement of a truth, next considering all possible objections to that truth, then presenting the fallacies in those objections, and finally demonstrating the validity of the true position. He integrated all the individual truths into a comprehensive system of thought that related all knowledge to the perfect truth, God. Like the Gothic cathedral, Thomas unified religious aspiration and logical order.

In the fourteenth century, think-

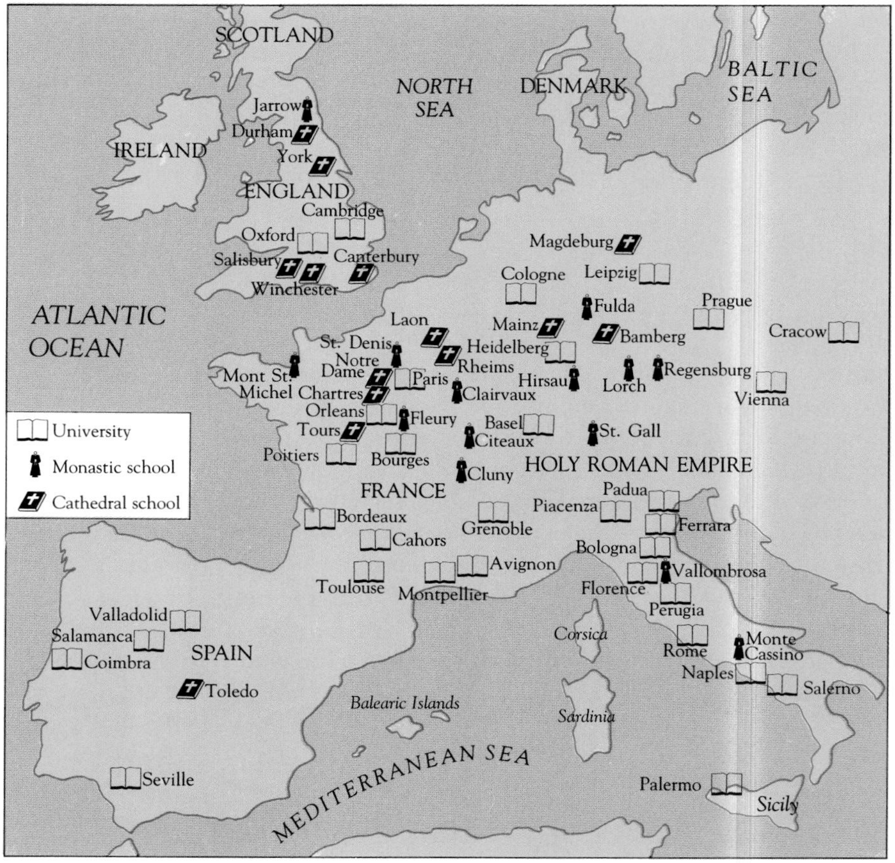

MAP 31
Cultural Centers of Medieval Europe. Monastic schools, although few, kept learning alive in Europe for several centuries. Cathedral schools subsequently provided instruction in many towns. However, universities proved to be the most enduring medieval educational establishments.

ers stressed analysis rather than synthesis. They separated the approaches of reason and revelation and the "sciences" of philosophy and theology that Thomas Aquinas had united. John Duns Scotus (1266–1308) argued through painstakingly thorough analysis that philosophy could not provide certain knowledge of God or anything else, and insisted that God is ultimately unknowable. He concluded that because reason was unable to supply reliable information about God, it was useless for theological investigation. William of Ockham (ca. 1285–1349) carried Duns Scotus's thought further. He ar-

gued that God was beyond the reach of reason and that many beliefs, such as the existence of God and the immortality of the soul, could not be demonstrated rationally. Humans could attain knowledge about God and other religious truths only by illumination, whereas human knowledge was derived only from sense perception of individual objects.

Such ideas propelled serious thinkers in new and profoundly consequential directions. Some abandoned the employment of reason to understand God and turned to mysticism or to propounding more radical theological interpretations and thus pre-

pared the way for a later religious reformation. Still others turned from the barrenness of contemporary philosophy to investigate the writings of classical civilization, inaugurating a renaissance in thought, literature, and art. A third group, following Ockham's insistence that reason must be limited to analysis of the observable world, intensified ongoing investigation of natural phenomena and prepared the way for a scientific revolution.

Law

Like theologians, legal scholars transformed their discipline by the appli-

236

cation of reason, and from the study of the Emperor Justinian's great rational legal work, the *Corpus Juris Civilis*, developed a method for the critical study of both civil and canon (church) law. Scholars of civil law used the coherent and logical tradition of Roman law with its emphasis upon centralized authority to rationalize, and sometimes even to replace, the often contradictory and sometimes chaotic Germanic custom-based law. Teachers and students of Roman law worked as scribes, agents, judges, lawyers, and consultants for towns, princes, and monasteries, and nonlawyers studied Roman law to acquire intellectual training and discipline. Lawyers trained in the Roman legal tradition of autocracy, centralization, and systematization became dominant in royal and imperial courts and devoted themselves to enhancing the power of their rulers. Europeans became accustomed to using Roman law to solve legal problems and to settle other disputes by collecting and analyzing evidence and reaching decisions based on rational procedures.

Scholars of canon law also employed Roman law and the methods of legal scholarship to systematize sources, explain obscurities, and ultimately to produce for canon law a single work comparable to the *Corpus Juris Civilis*. Gratian (ca. 1090–1186), a monk and canon lawyer from Bologna, advanced toward that goal by producing the *Decretum* in 1140. He collected statements from accepted authorities regarding the laws of the church, arranged them in logical sequence to solve specific problems, reconciled contradictions, and supplied his own commentary. The *Decretum* was thus the most comprehensive and convenient body of legal

principles available, and it quickly became the basic text for church courses and canon law schools. The *Decretum* and supplementary collections of decrees used after 1140 were termed the *Corpus Juris Canonici* and regarded as the canon law equivalent of the *Corpus Juris Civilis*. Like civil courts, ecclesiastical courts borrowed freely from Roman legal principles and procedures.

Science

Science was also prominent in medieval intellectual activity. The Latin Christian tradition preserved some scientific knowledge in early medieval encyclopedias, and scientific subjects—arithmetic, geometry, astronomy, music—were part of school and university curricula. Translators of Greek and Arabic scientific works during the eleventh and twelfth centuries enlarged Europe's store of scientific knowledge and gave new impetus to the study of science. Aquinas's teacher, a Dominican friar known as Albert the Great (1200–1280), examined scientific methodology and explored its philosophical basis, much of which derived from the work of Aristotle. Albert produced descriptive studies of plants and animals, attempted to develop a system of classification, and made several corrections and refinements of Aristotle's work. He was made a saint in 1931. In Latin, Albert the Great is Albertus Magnus.

During the thirteenth century, the basis of the rise of modern science was forged from a new combination of mathematical studies and direct observation of natural phenomena. The new approach found an especially congenial home at Oxford University

in England, where its chancellor, Robert Grosseteste (1168–1253), his Franciscan disciple Roger Bacon (1214–1294), and others made Oxford the center of scientific studies during the thirteenth century. Grosseteste translated Aristotle's scientific works and wrote commentaries on them. From Aristotle, he stressed the importance of observation and experiment as means of obtaining knowledge, but also maintained from Plato the importance of mathematics for understanding the physical universe. From his study of Islamic science, Grosseteste developed rigorous experimental procedures and offered new approaches to problems Aristotle had left unsolved. His emphasis on methodical and inductive use of observation and mathematics dominated English scientific thought for another two centuries.

Bacon carried Grosseteste's work farther. Bacon also criticized reliance on deductive logic and metaphysical speculations and urged scientists to adopt an inductive investigation method involving observation and experimentation with appropriate instruments and methods, rather than mere reasoning. Applying these techniques, he described the nerve system of the eye, made magnifying glasses, and proposed high-technology warfare employing gigantic mirrors to focus the sun's rays and incinerate opponents. His enthusiasm for the experimental method prompted him to observe, "Experimental science controls the conclusions of all other sciences. It reveals truths which reasoning from general principles would never have discovered. Finally it starts us on the way to marvelous inventions which will change the face of the world."

Medieval Scientist Working with an Armillary Sphere. Such objects assisted in the study of the heavens; the rings show the position of Sun, Moon, and important stars. An adaptation of the armillary sphere, the astrolabe, was widely used as an aid to navigation.

LITERATURE

In addition to numerous scholarly writings, medieval writers composed a great quantity and variety of imaginative literature, both in Latin and in the vernacular languages of everyday speech. Although some of that literature treated religious topics, much of it focused on the this-worldly interests of the nobility and the town dwellers. Writers employed classical models, but in time moved creatively beyond them.

Latin Poetry

Besides functioning as the international scholarly language for the university, Latin was a vehicle of lyric poetry. Religious writers used Latin for devotional works, particularly hymns expressing the intense religious feeling of love for God. Several hymns from this period, such as the Dias Irae ("Day of Wrath/Judgment") are still sung in churches today.

Secular writers also used Latin to treat nonreligious themes and produced poetry about all aspects of life. A group of students and churchmen called the Goliardic poets wrote poems for all occasions, including begging songs, drinking songs, and love songs. Opposed to contemporary conventions and irreverent toward established institutions, they satirized the follies and foibles of churchmen and parodied religious beliefs and institutions. In place of classical poetry techniques employing patterns of long and short syllables, they used accent and rhyme to express their deep feelings freshly and vigorously, making Latin sing.

Vernacular Literature for Nobles

In both quantity and artistic quality, poetry in vernacular languages such as French, German, and English became more important than Latin poetry. During the eleventh century, northern French minstrels began to compose epic poems known as *chansons de geste* (songs of great deeds) and to sing them for audiences of nobles. These action-packed songs realistically described battles, usually against non-Christian foes, and praised such noble virtues as physical prowess, bravery in battle, loyalty to the lord, and generosity to all (including the minstrel!). Foremost of these epics was the *Song of Roland*, which related a bloody but imaginary battle between Spanish Muslims and a detachment of Charlemagne's army commanded by Roland. The heroes of the *Song of Roland* soon became as well known as the figures from the *Iliad* and the *Aeneid*. Epics soon appeared in other languages. The Spanish *Song of the Cid* has already been noted, whereas the *Song of the Niebelungs* recounted in German the exploits of fifth-century German leaders in their warfare with the Huns. Scandinavian writers related in their *Sagas* and *Eddas* stories about ancient heroes and gods.

Meanwhile, minstrels known as troubadours composed lyric poetry in the Provençal dialect of southern

---

PIETY AND PLEASURE IN LATIN POETRY

Nigher still, and still more nigh
Draws the day of Prophecy,
Doom'd to melt the earth and sky

Oh, what trembling there shall be,
When the world its Judge shall see,
Coming in dread majesty!

Now the books are open spread;
Now the writing must be read,
Which condemns the quick and dead.

Now, before the Judge severe
Hidden things must all appear;
Nought can pass unpunish'd here.

In the third place, I
  will speak
Of the tavern's
  pleasure;
Nor shall I find it
  till I greet
Angels without
  measure,
Singing requiems
  for the souls
In eternal leisure
In the public-house
  to die
Is my resolution;
Let wine to my lips
  be nigh
At life's dissolution:
That will make the
  angels cry,
With glad elocution,
"Grant this toper,
  God on high,
Grace and absolution!"*

Both poems treat the theme of life's end, but in markedly different manners. The first, part of the majestic Dies Irae ("Day of Wrath") presents the somberness of the Last Judgment in words, meter, and rhyme. The second displays a very different attitude toward life, which the poet's technique helps to emphasize. Both moods were part of medieval life.

France, singing of their longing for love in vividly expressed verse. Troubadour lyrics typically tell of the poet's passionate love for a woman, but because some troubadours were women, the pattern was sometimes reversed, and in still other poems the idealized beloved is presented in sexually ambiguous terms. Poets in other lands soon imitated the Provençal troubadours in their own languages. Through her marriages, Eleanor of Aquitaine (1122–1204), whose grandfather was one of the first troubadours, spread Provençal lyric poetry to northern France and England.

The troubadours' emphasis on romantic love initiated important

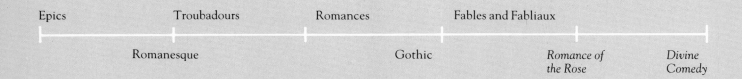

1050	1100	1150	1200	1250	1300

Epics   Troubadours   Romances   Fables and Fabliaux

Romanesque   Gothic   *Romance of the Rose*   *Divine Comedy*

changes in the social behavior of the nobility. In contrast to the epic's stress on loyalty to one's lord, the leading idea of troubadour poetry is love for one's lady. The troubadours elaborated an entire art of love that emphasized a lover's good manners and refinement, rather than skills in battle, and induced nobles to acquire some knowledge of music, poetry, and history. The idea of selecting a marriage partner on the basis of love made the marriages of some nobles more than business transactions. Such ideas also improved the status of women and brought them greater respect and consideration. Most nobles still married a woman for her dowry and expected her to produce male heirs and manage the household operations, however. The conflict between older people who emphasize family, status, and wealth as reasons for marriage and the young who seek to marry for love became a literary commonplace.

A third literary form, the romance, grew from the interaction of troubadour and *chanson de geste* traditions. Like *chansons de geste*, romances were long narratives with heroes, but like lyrics they were sentimental and emphasized love and adventure. Romances typically started from a theme or a person of the remote past, such as the Trojan War or Alexander the Great, but completely disregarded historical accuracy in their treatments. Especially prominent figures in the romances were Charlemagne, around whom many French romances developed, and Arthur, a semilegendary sixth-century English king who became an idealized twelfth-century monarch. Arthur's court at Camelot, full of charming ladies and chivalrous knights, became the imaginary setting for religious sentiment and romantic love. The French were the best romance writers of the twelfth century, but the Germans excelled in the thirteenth.

Writers of romances used idealized representations of feudal society to entertain their readers, but also depicted changing values among the nobility. Romances delineated a new ceremonious behavior, variously called chivalry, courtliness, or courtly love, which restrained nobles' tempers and passions and upheld the ideals of loyalty, honor, respect for worthy opponents, and protection of the weak, as compared with such warlike values as bravery and physical prowess. Several romances focus on the conflict between old and new values. For ex-

ample, to rescue Queen Guinevere, whom he loves, the knight Lancelot must choose between an honorable but futile appearance on horseback outside the castle in which she is imprisoned or a dishonorable ride in a woodsman's cart that will bring him within the castle's walls. The fact that Guinevere is the wife of his lord, King Arthur, expresses yet another value conflict, in this case between a vassal's love for his lord's wife and the feudal loyalty he owes his lord (usually, as in this case, love wins), but such "affairs" were often more sung about than consummated. Some romances stressed the theme of Christian purity and dedication and urged knights to be holy as well as courteous and loving.

Vernacular Literature for Town Dwellers

In addition to epics, lyrics, and romances for noble audiences, medieval writers produced fables, *fabliaux*, and dramas for town dwellers. Fables were brief stories that taught moral truths; they featured animals that symbolized people and displayed human characteristics. Many of the more popular fables came from France and related the exploits of Reynard the Fox, a wily and unscrupulous character who consistently outwits his moral but stupid adversaries. *Fabliaux* were satirical poems depicting ordinary people in events of everyday life with vigorous and coarse humor while ridiculing conventional morality. In them, all priests and monks are gluttons and lechers, all women are lustful and easily seduced, and praise goes to those who outwit others. Because *fabliaux* were characteristically brief and emphasized plot and climax, they are regarded as forerunners of the modern short story.

Medieval drama developed from brief Latin language performances in church during religious ceremonies, to illustrate events associated with the important holy days of Christmas and Easter. As these performances became more dramatic and attracted larger crowds, they were presented outside the church and used lay actors and vernacular dialogue. In time, new scenes and incidents were invented, stock characterizations and crude scenery developed, and guilds assumed responsibility for presenting these dramas in conjunction with religious festivals. By the thirteenth century,

three distinct types of plays existed: miracle plays recounting events of saints' lives, mystery plays enacting biblical stories, and morality plays teaching correct behavior by personifying virtues and vices. Religious dramas and secular farces employing spoken dialogues, songs and dances, or puppets and pantomimes also contributed to the entertainment of townspeople and the development of European drama.

Although French and German remained the leading vernacular literatures into the thirteenth century, an Italian writer, Dante Alighieri (1265–

Love Scene. The love of lord and lady shown here was the theme of troubadour songs. The ring held by the monkey underscores the love symbolism. The bird does not represent the Holy Spirit, but is a falcon trained by nobles and used for sport hunting. From a fifteenth-century German manuscript collection of lyrics. Universitats Bibliothek, Heidelberg.

1321), produced the greatest medieval literary masterpiece, *The Divine Comedy*. In it, he depicts his journey through hell, purgatory, and paradise, concluding in the awe-full presence of God, which he feels inadequate to describe:

Within the clear profound Light's aureole
  Three circles from its substance now
    appeared
    Of three colors, and each an equal
      whole
One its reflection on the next conferred
  As rainbow upon rainbow, and the
    two
  Breathed equally the fire of the third.
To my conception O how frail and few
  My words! and that, to what I looked
    upon,
  Is such that "little" is more than its
    due.
O Light Eternal, who in thyself alone
  Dwellest and thyself know'st, and self-
    understood,
  Self-understanding, smile upon thine
    own!*

Dante's guides for that journey included Vergil, a spokesperson for classical rationalism, Beatrice, an object of romantic and unconsummated but now spiritualized love, and St. Bernard, the epitome of sanctity. By turns, Dante is a lover of the classics, a love poet, and a mystic, and fills his poem with scientific knowledge, political observations, and psychological insights. In *The Divine Comedy*, he combines those various strands of medieval life with consum-

---

*Paradiso, canto XXXIII, lines 115–126, in Paolo Milano, ed., *The Portable Dante*, Lawrence Binyon, trans. (New York: Viking, 1947).

mate artistry and presents a majestic vision of the entire medieval universe, comparable in scope and stateliness to the *Summa Theologica* of Thomas Aquinas or the Gothic cathedrals.

ART

The artists and artisans of the medieval era created impressive works of architecture, sculpture, and painting that matched the accomplishments of the scholars and writers. As religion was the focal potent force in people's lives and the church was the principal promoter of artistic activity, churches were the primary focus of architectural endeavor. Architecture was the foremost art form of the medieval period; it integrated all the visual arts in coherent and aesthetically satisfying presentations of Christianity's rich symbolic and spiritual values. Other arts were used to decorate churches with sculpture and painting, woodcarving and metalwork, and stained glass. In addition to religious truths and biblical figures and stories, such works of art illustrated literature and legends, philosophical and scientific ideas, and historical facts and everyday events, making the church a veritable encyclopedia. Growing towns displayed their wealth and pride by constructing new churches, and communities of monks and nuns enlarged their existing churches and built new, larger ones. Patrons erected churches in penance for their sins or out of thankfulness for their good fortune. So many churches were built (more than 1,500 in France alone

during the eleventh century) that a writer shortly after 1000 remarked that the Earth was being covered with a white robe of churches.

Romanesque

The architectural style that emerged shortly after 1000 and flourished during the eleventh and twelfth centuries is called Romanesque because builders used Roman-type building materials and architectural features in their work. Special contemporary needs also contributed to the Romanesque style. The destruction caused by invaders and the frequency of fires in wood-roofed churches made Europeans realize the desirability of having churches made entirely of stone. Contemporary Christian rituals emphasizing saints and pilgrimages stimulated a desire for spacious buildings that could accommodate both large congregations and numerous visitors to shrines of saints and relics.

Medieval builders employed the Roman basilica plan as the basis for their structures, but modified and added elements to it. The basilica plan featured a large open rectangular area, called the nave, for accommodating worshipers and a semicircular apse that furnished space for the altar and the conduct of religious services. Aisles were often added alongside the nave and frequently continued around the apse to form an ambulatory (place for walking) from which chapels opened to house images and relics of saints and to permit worshipers to venerate those items. Many Romanesque builders added a transverse aisle called the transept between the apse and the nave, thereby producing a floor plan in the shape of a cross. The walls of

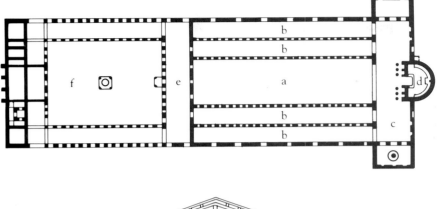

Basilica Floor Plan and Section of Old St. Peter's, Rome. The basilica style remained common for European church architecture until about 1000, but was then superseded by Romanesque buildings.

the nave were usually higher than those of the side aisles.

Romanesque builders adapted the basilica plan to the demand for churches built entirely of stone by covering both nave and aisles with a continuous arched roof, called a barrel vault, and using semicircular arches to support the roof. The stone roof produced a downward and outward thrust that required heavy, thick walls with few openings for windows and doors and massive piers and arches to provide support over those openings. The building consequently was dark and communicated gloom and mystery; it seemed a fortress of the faith similar to contemporary castles, protecting people from a threatening and dangerous world outside.

Sculpture was prominently employed in Romanesque churches. Spaces above the church's entrance doors were favorite places for sculpture, usually of the Last Judgment with Christ sending individuals to heaven or hell. Figures in those scenes were often elongated and depicted in agitated poses and gestures, heightening the horror of the scene. Inside the church, sculptors decorated the capitals of columns with human figures, monsters, or plants.

Painters and other artists decorated the extensive wall spaces of Romanesque churches with scriptural

243

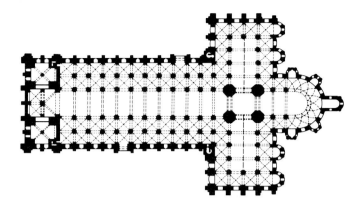

St. Sernin Floor Plan, Toulouse. This Romanesque church was built about 1100. The cruciform shape, employing the basilica plan and apse but adding a transept, is clearly evident.

Tympanum above West Doors, Conques. The Last Judgment, a standard theme of Romanesque sculpture, is shown here. Jesus Christ, on the throne, is approached by a row of pilgrims led by Mary. At lower left, the redeemed are in heaven; at lower right, the dead, shoved through the jaws of hell, are welcomed by the Devil.

scenes, usually expressing Christ's suffering or his judgment of humans. They might paint a large-scale fresco (a painting done while the plaster was still wet or fresh) on a wall or decorate the wall with a mosaic. Such artists used bright colors lavishly, and in the Mediterranean region their work showed much Byzantine influence. Unhappily, little of their work survives. Other painters produced illustrations for manuscripts, known as illuminations because of their bright colors. In their work, the figures were

sharp and angular, like those of Romanesque sculpture.

Romanesque art, so closely associated with Cluniac monasticism, suffered harsh criticism from the great Cistercian leader, Bernard of Clairvaux (1090–1153). Bernard not only disliked the "vast height," "immoderate length," and "superfluous breadth" of Romanesque churches but also rejected "the curious carvings and paintings that attract the worshiper's gaze and hinder his attention." His preference for discipline, simplicity, and austerity would be more adequately realized in the Gothic art that succeeded Romanesque in much of Europe.

Gothic

During the twelfth century, builders brought forth a major innovation in Romanesque architecture, the Gothic style. Introduced in Normandy and England, it developed in and around Paris. The Gothic style was influenced by the emphasis of contemporary writers on light and illumination through prayer and meditation; consequently, Gothic architecture featured space, light, and height. The builders sought to create a unified interior space, rather than the com-

Façade of Cathedral, Rheims. The elaborate decoration of Gothic architecture and sculpture are evident. Note especially the magnificent rose window above the central doorway.

partmentalized interior of the Romanesque style. By replacing the semicircular Romanesque arch with the pointed arch, builders raised arched roofs higher above the floor and directed roof thrust downward rather than outward. They used ribbed vaults to concentrate the roof's thrust at a few points, employing massive supports and external buttresses to bear that thrust; this enabled them to replace the solid and heavy walls of Romanesque churches with large windows, filling the building interior with light.

Later builders explored the structural and decorative possibilities of early Gothic style and made it the dominant form of European architecture. Attempting to build even higher churches, they experimented with the spacing of support piers and buttresses. Despite the use of models, plans, and mathematical calcula-

Charlemagne and Bishop Turpin, Chartres. Stained glass replaced painting in Gothic decoration, and often showed contemporary or historical scenes, as well as biblical ones. Here the Emperor Charlemagne, who warred in Spain on behalf of Christianity, is depicted with Bishop Turpin, a key figure in the *Song of Roland.*

tions, builders making such experiments occasionally discovered when a building collapsed that they had exceeded certain technical limitations. Subsequently, they produced more complex piers and vaults or elaborate stonework decoration and developed regional variations of Gothic styles. The Gothic style remained the dominant European art style into the sixteenth century except in Italy, where a revival of interest in classical artistic forms produced the distinctive art style of the Italian Renaissance.

To fill the window spaces in the Gothic cathedral, artists constructed elaborate stained glass windows, which became characteristic Gothic features corresponding to Byzantine mosaics or Romanesque painted walls. A stained glass window was really a mosaic in glass, composed of pieces of colored glass connected by lead strips, assembled on a large flat table, and fitted into the window opening. Painters and sculptors cooperated in the design, layout, and assembly of these windows, which depicted not only biblical scenes but also many medieval activities. Those large, multicolored windows filled the interior of Gothic churches with light, while impressing worshipers with their visual beauty and inspiring meditative contemplation.

Gothic sculpture was closely linked with church architecture. Sculptors elaborated the external decoration of Gothic churches, deriving subjects from encyclopedias as well as from the Bible and sometimes producing representations of plants and animals. Figures became more realistic, displaying individual facial features that suggested a subject's personality and folding clothing naturally over the figure. Sculptors began to understand

THE CHURCH AS THE BIBLE OF THE LAITY

Pictures and ornaments in churches are the lessons and the scriptures of the laity. For what writing supplies to one who can read, a picture supplies to one who is unlearned and can only look. Those who are uninstructed thus see what they ought to follow, and things are read though letters be unknown. We do not worship images nor regard them as gods, for that would be idolatry; yet we adore them for the memory and remembrance of things done long ago . . .

Paintings appear to move the mind more than descriptions; for deeds are placed before the eyes in paintings, and so appear to be actually occurring. But in description, the deed is done as if by hearsay, which affects the mind less when recalled. Hence in churches we pay less reverence to books than to images and pictures.

Of pictures and images some are above the church, as the cock and the eagle; some without the church, in the air in front of the church, as the ox and the cow; others within, as images, and statues, and various kinds of painting and sculpture, and are represented either in garments, or on walls, or in stained glass. *

Because few people could read, the art of the medieval church served functional as well as decorative purposes and made the church a "Bible for the poor." The thirteenth-century writer quoted here clearly believed that a picture or image was worth a thousand words. Note that he places reverence to images and pictures above that given books, even the Bible. To call paintings, images, and stained glass windows decoration misses the point of the purpose of such art.

*William Durandus, *Rationale divinorum officiorum*, trans. J. M. Neale and B. Webb (Leeds, England: Green, 1843).

body and drapery as separate entities, and their accurate indication of body features beneath the drapery betokens a use of live models.

Because most Gothic churches were cathedrals, bishops ordinarily organized their erection, but town dwellers aided enthusiastically in their construction. Master masons, skilled professionals who moved from one building project to another, exercised general oversight of the construction process. Local carpenters, plasterers, glass makers, and metal workers participated in the enterprise, which eventually used the services of most local craft guilds. Merchant guilds often provided food, drink, or supplies to the work force. In some

churches, guilds contributed windows illustrating their primary activity.

Gothic cathedrals undoubtedly produced a profound impact on their users. The size of the structure and the massive supporting piers communicated a sense of majesty and stability. As worshipers entered, their eyes were drawn upward toward God and forward to the altar. Light flooding through the windows simulated the illumination of the Holy Spirit. The beauty of the window designs and the changing interplay of light and color delighted the eye and soothed the spirit. A sensitive twelfth-century abbot remarked that after spending some time in the church, "I see myself dwelling, as it were, in some strange

Angel of Annunciation, Rheims. In the late Gothic period, sculptors became skilled in depicting figures realistically. Note how the drapery falls naturally over the angel, revealing body contours. The kindly smile suggests a serenely confident faith and betokens considerable artistic ability.

region of the universe . . . and by the grace of God, I can be transported from this inferior to that higher world."

The Gothic cathedral became the town's religious center. Through its combination of the arts, it attempted to teach the religious messages of Christianity and to show humans acting in obedience to God. A Gothic church thus functioned as a school, a theater, and a picture gallery. It was, in both a physical and a spiritual sense, an ordered unity like that of Thomas Aquinas's *Summa Theologica* or Dante's *Divine Comedy*, combining several distinct but related elements into a structurally coherent and spiritually significant whole.

SUMMARY

The growth of universities and the development of various intellectual activities were prominent features of medieval European life. Universities developed from earlier cathedral schools and provided both introductory and advanced studies to prepare individuals for church or government positions. Scholars applied logic and reason to theological study and profited from the new availability of Aristotle's works. Thomas Aquinas synthesized reason and revelation in a coherent scheme of knowledge, but subsequent thinkers elaborated them as mutually independent ways of knowing. Others applied reason to the study of Roman civil law and the development of a systematic body of canon law. Scholars at Oxford promoted scientific study by urging the importance of observation and experimentation.

Medieval Europeans produced important imaginative literature. Latin was used for both sober religious and lustily secular works. Many writers preferred to use vernacular languages and produced notable poetry in epic, lyric, and romance forms for noble audiences. Troubadour lyrics and romances reflected new emphases on ceremonious behavior and courtly love and helped improve the status of women. Fables, *fabliaux,* and dramas were other popular literary forms for townspeople. Dante's *Divine Comedy* uniquely epitomized much of the medieval religious outlook.

Religious architecture was the primary European artistic activity. Most eleventh- and twelfth-century churches were in the Romanesque style, which employed rounded arches and basilica floor plans producing spacious but low buildings. Painters adorned walls of Romanesque churches and decorated manuscripts with illuminations. Later Gothic-style churches used pointed arches and cruciform floor plans and emphasized height and light. Gothic churches prompted the making of mosaic-like stained glass windows. Sculptures were closely linked to the church buildings and became less artificially dramatic and more naturalistically realistic.

The impressive architectural structure of the medieval cathedral constitutes an impressive monument to the creative energy generated by this "age of faith." However, it was rivaled by another noteworthy creation, the medieval state, whose most enduring form was the feudal monarchy. The medieval cultural achievement proved extraordinarily productive of ideas, institutions, and works that influenced future intellectual, literary, and artistic developments.

SELECTED SOURCES

*Adams, Henry. *Mont Saint Michel and Chartes.* 1961. Marvelously presents the "mood" of Gothic churches and medieval life.

*Chaucer, Geoffrey. *The Canterbury Tales.* Translated by Nevill Coghill. 1952. A modern English version of this outstanding literary work, full of information about medieval people, also a film. 1972.

*Crombie, Alistair C. *Medieval and Early Modern Science.* 2d rev. ed. 2 vols. 1959. A convenient presentation of scientific discoveries and progress through the sixteenth century.

*Focillon, Henri. *The Art of the West in the Middle Ages.* 2 vols. 1980. A valuable, full-scale introduction to the topic, with a readable text and quality illustrations.

Jackson, William T. H. *The Literature of the Middle Ages.* 1960. The standard introduction to the subject, with a good guide to additional reading.

*Knowles, David. *The Evolution of Medieval Thought.* 1964. Comprehensive and understandable treatment of this important topic.

The Letters of Abelard and Heloise. Translated by C. K. Scott-Moncrief. 1942. Informative and poignant correspondence of two famous lovers of the twelfth century.

Lewis, Clive S. *The Allegory of Love: A Study in Medieval Tradition.* 1936. Sensitive study of courtly love literature and its significance by a noted scholar and writer.

Morey, Charles R. *Medieval Art.* 1942. Readable survey focusing on sculpture and painting.

*Wieruszowski, Helene. *The Medieval University.* 1966. Provides a brief description of major medieval universities and student life, along with many relevant documents.

*Available in paperback.

FEUDAL MONARCHY IN WESTERN AND CENTRAL EUROPE (900–1300)

Just as the founder of the universe established two great lights in . . . heaven, a greater one to preside over the day and a lesser to preside over the night, so too in . . . the universal church, . . . he instituted two great dignities, a greater one to preside over souls as if over day and a lesser one to preside over bodies as if over night. These are the pontifical [papal] authority and the royal power. Now just as the moon derives its light from the sun and is indeed lower than it in quantity and quality, in position and in power, so too the royal power derives the splendor of its dignity from the pontifical authority.

Although the writer of these words, Pope Innocent III (1198–1216) was the most powerful medieval pope, his "sun and moon" theory coincided only imperfectly with European political reality. Rather than accepting the subordinate position assigned them, medieval kings struggled with popes and also with their nobles for the power to rule their lands. These kings endeavored to restore order in Europe after the anarchy and foreign invasions of the ninth and tenth centuries. Feudal monarchy is the name given to the governmental system of this time, based on the regulation of relationships between the kings and their subjects by established feudal traditions. This chapter examines the development of feudal monarchies in three European areas—Germany, England, and France—and considers why the first failed and the latter two endured.

FEUDAL MONARCHY

During the period 900–1300 European kings managed to replace severely decentralized political order of the ninth and tenth centuries with new political structures known as feudal monarchies by using their still substantial powers and prerogatives. The office of the king was endorsed

Emperor Enthroned. Emperor Otto III is seated on his throne holding the orb and staff, symbols of imperial rule. He is attended by representatives of the nobility and the church. Because Otto III's mother was a Byzantine princess, the Byzantine style of painting was promoted in Germany during the late tenth century. Illumination from the Gospel Book of Otto III.

251

by church and scripture, the person of the king was considered sacred, and kings continued to receive honor and prestige. Their primary functions were to provide justice and maintain peace. They were the accepted leaders of resistance against external foes and the ultimate guardians of justice and order within their realms. Monarchs could raise and lead national armies and preside over national councils. They had the right to enforce the king's peace, and often employed it to extend the scope of their royal jurisdiction.

In addition to these general responsibilities, feudal monarchs were overlords of the greater and lesser nobles within the system of feudal relationships, a system they exploited to extend their controls. The powers that the great nobles and the lesser lords exercised depended, at least in theory, on previous royal grants for the lands they held. Feudal kings had the right to demand the various feudal services and dues owed by their vassals, and they could recover possession of fiefs forfeited by unfaithful vassals or lost by a vassal's failure to produce heirs. They could require lords to verify their claims to special privileges such as immunities from royal jurisdiction or exemption from taxation. They were also the protectors of such nonfeudal elements of society as churches and monasteries, priests and monks, towns and townspeople, traders and foreigners.

Despite many rights and responsibilities, feudal monarchs were limited rulers. The feudal structure ensured that kings had direct contact primarily with their chief vassals and the inhabitants of their own family domains. Between the kings and the remainder of their subjects were various levels of lesser vassals, many of whom exercised such sovereign powers as the rights to wage war, coin money, and dispense justice. Feudal kings were thus suzerains exercising overlordship and sharing power, rather than sovereigns exercising direct and unlimited authority. They ruled as the first among equals, as the following oath sworn by the nobles of Aragon to their king indicates:

We who are as good as you, swear to you who are no better than we, to accept you as our king and sovereign lord, provided you observe our liberties and laws; but if not, not.

Diffused government was another important and distinctive political contribution of feudal monarchy. In the autocratic, centralized Roman and Byzantine empires, the ruler used an extensive military and civilian bureaucracy to perform government services. In contrast, feudal monarchs governed through a series of relationships in which both they and their vassals spent part of their time personally performing the essential public services of administering justice and waging war.

Feudal monarchies lacked the resources to provide more than limited services. The king derived income primarily from the royal domains and estates he personally owned, feudal payments from vassals, fines, and monies paid to him as the patron of certain churches and monasteries. At first, there were no formal governmental departments, no sharply delineated responsibilities for officials, and no clear distinction between family and public aspects of government and finance. Next to the king, the council of the king's great vassals was most important: It formally recognized new kings, furnished the king with advice and counsel, and judged certain important cases in the name of the king. Between meetings, a smaller body of councillors and royal officials carried on council functions. The chancellor had charge of drafting important documents and keeping royal records, the marshal or constable commanded the royal army in the king's absence, and the chamberlain supervised royal finances. The great vassals, who theoretically exercised military, judicial, and police powers, administered local government in the name of the king. In fact, they often acted quite independently of him.

Feudal monarchy had a varied history. It flourished first in the Carolingian lands of Germany and Italy, but it eventually failed there; as a result, national unity in those areas was long postponed. Feudal monarchy developed later in England and France; these two lands became the most successful of the feudal monarchies and later strong national states. The following pages trace both the failure and the success of feudal monarchy during the medieval period.

EMPIRE AND PAPACY

Out of the territories of the former Carolingian Empire two major entities, Germany, or the Holy Roman Empire (Map 32), and France, gradually emerged. Although early German rulers succeeded in creating a strong feudal monarchy, their additional imperial responsibilities complicated the task of their successors. Emperors had duties in both Italy and

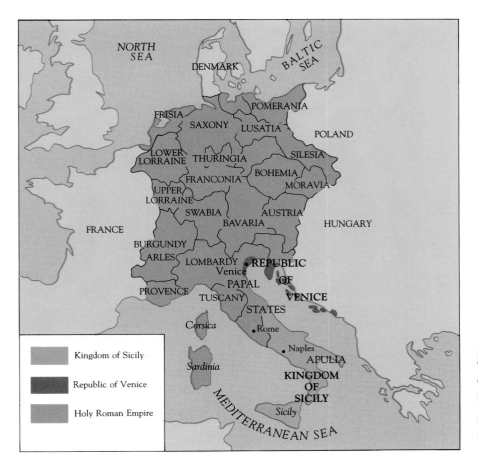

MAP 32
The Holy Roman Empire. Largest of the medieval European states, the empire included all or part of several present-day nations. Its very extent, however, made it difficult to govern. Most of the named areas maintained considerable autonomy, despite imperial efforts to establish strong central government.

Germany, but usually lacked the resources to make their power truly effective in both places. Moreover, as the popes gained power, they came to fear strong emperors and actively to work against them. Consequently, Germany became an example of a feudal monarchy that failed.

Germany Under the Saxons and Salians

During the tenth century, Germany became the first European land to recover from the disorder caused by feudal anarchy and foreign invasions. Under the Carolingians, tribal areas had formed duchies governed by dukes, military commanders who exercised royal powers and performed royal duties. On the death in 911 of the last Carolingian ruler in Germany, the dukes elected one of themselves to be king. The German monarchy thereafter remained elective, despite the efforts of various rulers to make it hereditary. For more than a century, successive dukes of Saxony ruled as kings of Germany, forming the Saxon dynasty (919–1024).

Although the Saxon kings enjoyed prestige and support, the strength of the dukes seriously limited royal power. As few nobles below the dukes held lands directly from the king, the kings lacked a basis for asserting authority over these lesser lords. It quickly became clear to the Saxon kings that feudal relationships presented the chief danger to their rule.

To overcome their "overmighty subjects," the Saxon kings employed a variety of means to augment their authority, as we can see in the career of the foremost Saxon ruler, Otto I (936–973). At his coronation banquet, he made the other dukes act as his servants to symbolize their vassal status. The dukes, alarmed, opposed Otto, who subsequently crushed several ducal rebellions and made the

253

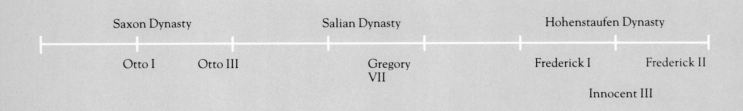

| 900 | 950 | 1000 | 1050 | 1100 | 1150 | 1200 | 1250 |

Saxon Dynasty

Salian Dynasty

Hohenstaufen Dynasty

Otto I   Otto III

Gregory VII

Frederick I   Frederick II

Innocent III

dukes real rather than symbolic vassals. As dukedoms became vacant, he appointed new dukes from his relatives by blood or marriage. He also controlled the appointment of counts, assuring their subordination to him rather than to the dukes.

To avoid depending on the dukes for assistance in governing, Otto and his Saxon successors increasingly relied on churchmen as royal officials. The Saxon kings controlled the appointment of bishops and abbots, both to their royal administrative duties and to their spiritual responsibilities, and regarded them as feudal vassals. These individuals possessed the educational and administrative expertise the rulers needed. They also served as important and strategically placed allies within each duchy, an additional check on ducal power. Because the celibate churchmen produced no heirs, they could be trusted to support royal policies rather than pursuing family interests. By controlling appointments of church officials, the rulers also retained a semblance of control over the church's lands. Churchmen exercised governmental authority on the king's behalf over their territories and provided military contingents from those lands on the king's request.

While consolidating their position inside Germany, the Saxon rulers were also expanding German influence in all directions during the tenth century. To the north, they briefly gained control of Baltic trade routes and introduced both Christianity and their own patterns of political order into the Scandinavian lands of Denmark, Norway, and Sweden. To the east, they conquered several unorganized Slav territories, became overlords of the Slav states of Bohemia and Poland, and aided the conversion of the people of both states, as well as Hungary, to Latin Christianity. To the southwest, Otto made the ruler of Burgundy his vassal and obtained the crown of Italy. The Saxon rulers established control of the Alpine passes, making them safe from bandits, and thereby promoted a revival of commercial activity between Germany and Italy that aided German economic recovery.

Out of gratitude for Otto's propapal intervention in Italian affairs and in recognition of his successes in defeating the Magyars and building royal power in Germany, the pope in 962 crowned Otto emperor. The title of emperor recalled memories of the achievements of Constantine and Charlemagne, and it soon became customary for a newly elected German king to obtain coronation as emperor from the pope. All of Otto's holdings in both Italy and Germany were included in that empire, which a later ruler, Frederick I (1152–1190), designated the Holy Roman Empire. Otto promptly exploited the prominence accorded by his new title, and arranged a marriage of his son to Theophano, the niece of the Eastern Roman or Byzantine emperor. She introduced Byzantine culture to the German imperial court, and until her death in 991 ruled Germany on behalf of her son Otto III (983–1002), while educating him in the Byzantine tradition.

The role of emperor produced significant problems for Otto and his Saxon successors. As German kings, the Saxon monarchs could concentrate their attentions on Germany and strengthen their rule there. As emperors, however, they were required to expend wealth and energy on military expeditions in Italy to help the popes defend the papal territories and interests in central Italy. Imperial involvement in Italy remained an important theme of European history for several centuries.

At the death of a Saxon ruler who had no male heirs, the electors chose another duke as king, bringing the Salian dynasty (1024–1125) to the throne. For the next century, the Salians improved and expanded the governmental apparatus left by the Saxon monarchs. Like the Saxons, they used bishops as advisers and upper-level administrators. However, to further reduce reliance on the aristocracy, the Salians employed *ministeriales,* nonaristocratic laypersons, as lower-level governmental officials. Moreover, they sought to increase monarchical centralization by establishing a compact core of royal domain lands, and used wealth derived from rich silver mines on their domains to pay government officials, thereby reducing the necessity of making land grants to support them.

The Struggle Between Emperor and Pope

The emperors' dependence on control of major ecclesiastical appointments to supply their administrative personnel brought them into bitter and prolonged conflict with a rising European political force, the papal monarchy. As we have seen, reformers had energized and centralized the papal authority, and as one aspect of their reform, they moved to gain control of the selection of church officials. By preventing emperors and Roman laity from interfering in papal elections, they made the selection of reform popes possible and ensured their own continuation in power. They further insisted that other church officials should likewise be chosen by churchmen, not laypersons. Realizing that the imperial administrative structure depended on the emperor's ability to appoint church officials and to invest them with symbols of his authority (thus giving the conflict the name of the Investiture Controversy), the Salian ruler Henry IV (1056–1106) defied the pope and appointed bishops. Pope Gregory VII (1073–1085) responded by excommunicating and threatening to depose the emperor. Henry only avoided this fate by personally appearing in 1077 before the pope as a repentant sinner, at the castle of Canossa in Italy, allegedly standing barefoot in the snow for three days. In 1122, after Henry and Gregory were dead, the dispute was finally settled by an agreement called the Concordat of Worms. The concordat provided that church officials would be elected and established in their positions in accordance with church law and procedure. The pope permitted the emperor to resolve disputed elections and give prelates the symbols of authority over their church lands but not over their spiritual duties. The emperor's loss of control over the appointment of church officials boosted the prestige of papal monarchy by assuring papal rather than imperial control of the church, and forced later German rulers to devise new administrative structures for their territories.

In a larger context, the resolution of the appointment of bishops actually benefited the chief contestants less than it did the German nobles and the Italian towns. As emperors struggled with popes, ambitious German landowners gained power, extended their estates, and usurped royal rights. They forced lesser nobles to become their vassals and enserfed

EMPEROR VERSUS POPE

Henry, King not by usurpation but by the pious ordination of God, to Hildebrand, now not Pope but false monk:

You have deserved such a salutation because of the confusion you have wrought.

You boldly rose up even against the royal power itself, granted to us by God. You dared to threaten to take the kingship away from us—as though we had received the kingship from you, as though kingship and empire were in your hand and not in the hand of God.

I am to be judged by God alone and am not to be deposed for any crime unless I should deviate from the faith. The true pope Saint Peter also exclaims, "Fear God, honor the king." Saint Paul says, "If anyone should preach to you a gospel contrary to that we preached to you, let him be accursed." Descend, therefore, condemned by this saying. Relinquish the Apostolic See which you have arrogated. Let another mount the throne of St. Peter, who will teach the pure doctrine of St. Peter.

I, Henry, King by the grace of God, say to you: Descend! Descend!*

Emperor Henry's view of his conflict with Pope Gregory is clearly stated here. Despite the emperor's use of scripture, his argument was not compelling, so he resorted to name-calling against the pope. The idea that the monarch is to be judged by God alone reappeared later in European history with the absolutist "divine right" kings of the seventeenth and eighteenth centuries.

*Letter of Henry IV to Gregory VII (1076), trans. T. E. Mommsen and K. F. Morrison, *Imperial Lives and Letters of the Eleventh Century* (New York: Columbia University Press, 1962), pp. 150–151.

Emperor Henry IV at Canossa. In this scene, the emperor begs Abbot Hugh of Cluny and Countess Matilda of Tuscany to intercede for him with the pope. Miniature from a twelfth-century manuscript. Vatican Library, Vatican City.

many formerly free peasants. In 1125, when a Salian ruler died without direct heirs, the electors disregarded the claims of his nephew and elected a ruler of a different house, further weakening the monarchy. In Italy, the growth of papal power not only crippled the imperial authority but also diminished the liberty of formerly autonomous bishops. Town dwellers exploited the new situation to make their communities independent of the emperors.

The Failure of Feudal Monarchy Under the Hohenstaufens

Election of a new German ruler in 1138 inaugurated the Hohenstaufen dynasty (1138–1268), whose rulers attempted to rebuild the imperial power but failed because of the determined and effective opposition of German nobles, Italian towns, and the popes. Unable by the terms of the concordat to rule by appointing high churchmen as government officials,

Frederick I sought to exercise authority by other means. He attempted to systematize feudal relationships in Germany and to reassert his overlordship of the German nobles. He required great lords to recognize their feudal obligations to him as suzerain, but left them free to control and make vassals of the lesser lords. He required overriding allegiance to him to be acknowledged in all feudal oaths of allegiance. This was difficult to achieve. Many nobles either refused to accept lands carrying feudal obligations or merged them with their privately owned lands. Nobles created their own dynastic territories, taking advantage of the emperor's involvement in Italy to expand their holdings into areas, primarily in the east, where he lacked authority. The nobles also increased their influence over the German church leaders while Frederick was involved in a lengthy quarrel with the papacy. Hence the rulers could only check the growth of some opponents among the nobility by allying with others, with the unintended conse-

quence of giving the latter wealth and power they might later use to oppose the emperor.

To counter the nobles, Frederick attempted to assert imperial authority over the Lombard cities of northern Italy and claimed the rights Roman law had given to Roman emperors. The fiercely independent cities, however, were unwilling to be ruled by a German emperor and formed a league to resist him. The popes, fearing that a strong emperor might threaten the Papal States, aided the Lombard League. The cities defeated the emperor

in battle and forced him to grant them virtual autonomy in the Peace of Constance (1183).

Following Frederick's death, the principal power in the empire was Pope Innocent III, under whom the authority and prestige of the papal monarchy reached its height. Canon lawyers developed and refined the theory of papal supremacy, and the pope exercised political as well as religious leadership. In the empire, he prolonged a civil war between two candidates for the emperorship and finally designated as emperor his ward,

Pope Innocent III. The pope who brought the papal monarchy to its height is shown here in a thirteenth-century painting.

Frederick I's grandson, Frederick II (1212–1250).

Even at its height, however, papal monarchy had its limitations. Papal authority depended on royal promises of good behavior as well as papal maintenance of spiritual prestige. The promises of kings were notoriously undependable, and to enforce them popes sometimes elected to take political or even military action against these rulers. As popes became involved in secular politics and were themselves selected for their skill as lawyers and diplomats rather than for their qualities of spiritual leadership, papal spiritual prestige eroded, which in turn caused papal political power to decline.

Besides being king of Germany and holy Roman emperor, Frederick II had also inherited the kingdom of Sicily and south Italy. He made that realm his imperial base, establishing his capital at Palermo in Sicily and creating a government bureaucracy and a professional army. He expanded and refined its centralized administration, developed a uniform legal code, and imposed an efficient financial system that levied direct taxes. Moreover, he established a university at Naples to train the scholars and administrators his kingdom needed. From that solid southern base, Frederick attempted to unite Italy under his control, but, as with his grandfather, the Lombard towns and the popes defeated him. The popes, fearing isolation in an Italy ruled by Frederick, organized alliances to thwart him, provoked rebellion in his lands, excommunicated him, and even proclaimed a crusade against him.

Frederick struggled at length against his opponents, but he failed to unite Italy and only weakened the empire further. He regarded Germany primarily as a source of money and soldiers for his Italian campaigns, and therefore surrendered rights and lands in Germany to obtain the support of the German princes for his Italian activities. Towns and princes began to coin money and administer justice independently of the emperor and to build castles to defend and advance their interests.

By the middle of the thirteenth century, it was clear that feudal monarchy had failed in Germany and Italy. The lords and towns of Germany and Italy were the winners in the struggle, gaining an autonomy and independence they retained into the nineteenth century. The popes crusaded against Frederick and warred against his successors until they extinguished the Hohenstaufen line. They transferred Sicily and south Italy to the propapal rule of Charles of Anjou (1266–1282), the brother of the king of France. After Frederick's death, the position of emperor remained vacant more than twenty years.

ENGLAND

By combining features of Anglo-Saxon and Norman society, England became an extremely successful feudal monarchy. During long years of struggle against the Danes, Anglo-Saxon institutions gained strength and maturity, while descendants of Vikings in Normandy developed efficient feudal governing arrangements there. William of Normandy fused the two sets of institutional relationships by conquering England in 1066.

Anglo-Saxon England and the Norman Conquest

By the eleventh century, Anglo-Saxon England had combined strong local government, effective royal authority, and vigorous nobles in an unusually well-balanced political system (see Map 33). Its kings received the direct allegiance of all subjects, commanded the army, and obtained advice from an informal council of nobles, clergy, and officials. Members of the royal household performed administrative duties, such as regulating the royal finances and sending royal commands to local officials. England was divided into regions called shires; each shire had a royal administrative officer, the shire reeve or sheriff, and a system of shire and district courts ordinarily controlled by local lords. Sheriffs collected land taxes and assembled local contingents for the royal army.

The death of the childless Anglo-Saxon king Edward in 1065 enabled the duke of Normandy, a claimant to the throne, to conquer England by defeating and killing his rival in a battle at Hastings in southern England in 1066. Establishing himself as King William I, he introduced Norman political principles and feudal practices to England. First he replaced many Anglo-Saxon nobles with his Norman followers. Royal vassals, known as barons, held English fiefs and supplied the king with mounted knights, as well as performing other typical feudal obligations. The barons in turn gave portions of their land as fiefs to maintain the knights, and with royal permission built castles and established baronial courts.

William deviated from traditional feudal relationships to enhance his

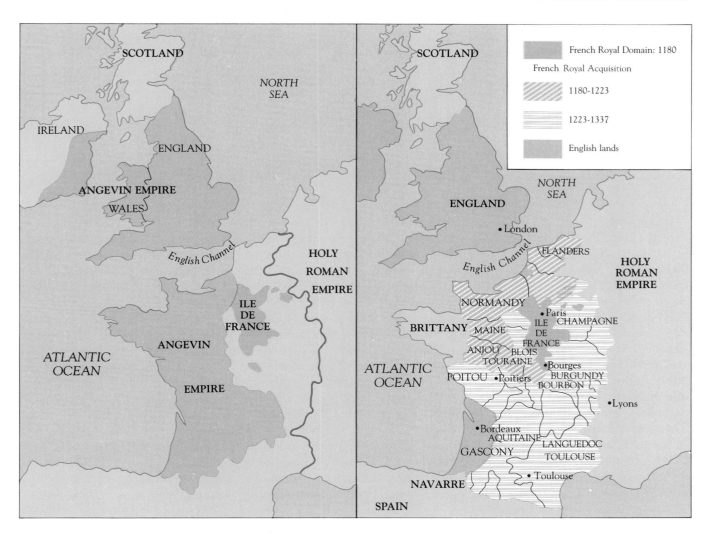

power. Claiming all England as his by right of conquest, he demanded the primary allegiance of all landholders; a knight's allegiance to his lord became of secondary importance. William kept one-fifth of the conquered territory as royal lands. He conducted a thorough survey of the land and its wealth, called the "Domesday Book" which recorded the feudal rearrangements of landholdings and provided a basis for calculating tax levies and making other financial assessments. William retained the prerogatives of coining money and collecting land taxes and also dispensed justice in major criminal cases, such as homicide and robbery or cases involving barons. To consolidate his control of the English church, the king replaced Anglo-Saxons in leadership positions with experienced Norman reformers and worked with them to promote similar religious reform in England.

MAP 33
England and France. These two maps illustrate the rapidly changing fortunes of medieval France. In 1180, as the map on the left shows, the Angevin rulers of England controlled far more territory than did the king of France. But in the subsequent century and a half, French kings acquired many Angevin lands and much of the territory of modern France.

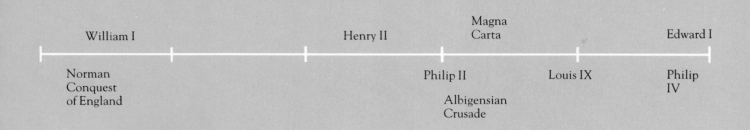

| 1050 | 1100 | 1150 | 1200 | 1250 | 1300 |

William I   Henry II   Magna Carta   Edward I

Norman Conquest of England   Philip II   Louis IX   Philip IV

Albigensian Crusade

The Growth of Royal Centralization

During the twelfth century, England's royal administration became more elaborate and efficient. Financial operations were divided between two government departments: the exchequer, which received payments, and the treasury, which regulated royal expenditures. The monarchs filled administrative and judicial positions with lesser nobles and even nonnobles. Dependent on royal favor and salaries, these appointees increased royal revenues and improved royal administration. Strong government proved profitable: The sheriffs, under close supervision, increased royal receipts, and the royal justices tried more cases and collected more fines for the king. Norman kings extended the scope of royal jurisdiction by sending justices out to travel designated circuits to hear legal cases.

A civil war momentarily slowed the growth of royal government, but Henry II (1154–1189) restored the efficiency of the royal administration and made England Europe's best-governed twelfth-century state. He closely supervised royal officials and established some government departments at a permanent royal capital at Westminster, near London, rather

than requiring them to travel with the king. To enhance royal income, he increased fees and fines, collected payments from royal demesne lands in cash rather than produce, and allowed barons and knights to substitute cash payments for military service. Further consolidating his authority, he destroyed unlicensed castles and halted private warfare.

Henry devoted special attention to extending the scope of royal law. He increased the number of offenses that could be brought to trial in royal courts, transferring their jurisdiction from baronial courts. He established inquest juries (similar to modern-day grand juries), in which inhabitants of a community were gathered together to give information on crimes committed in the area since the last inquest. The king expanded the scope of royal justice by prosecuting criminals as breakers of the king's peace, that is, as offenders against the state rather than merely as offenders against the victim, as had been the old practice. Individuals could transfer cases from other courts to royal courts by purchasing documents known as writs. Because royal courts dispensed quick, fair, and rational justice, they swiftly displaced the district, shire, and baronial courts and made possible a major increase in royal power. Under

Henry, royal law replaced a previous patchwork of local laws and customs with a common law governing all English subjects and made justice uniform as well as equitable throughout England.

Henry's expansion of royal justice, however, engendered conflict with the church's judicial system. Church courts, which could not order the shedding of blood, generally prescribed lesser penalties for offenses than royal courts did. In addition to clerics, whole categories of people, such as university students or workers on church lands, had the right to be tried in church courts, and appeals from church courts went outside England to the papal government in Rome. Henry, disliking this competition with royal justice, labored to bring ecclesiastical courts under royal control. He also sought to limit appeals to Rome and to subject those convicted by church courts to the punishment of royal law. Thomas Becket, Henry's appointee as archbishop of Canterbury, opposed Henry's initiatives as double punishments for individuals and unacceptable infringements on the church's freedom. Although reaction against Becket's murder by overzealous royal servants prevented the king from realizing his major aims, Henry reduced the authority of church

The Murder of Thomas Becket, Archbishop of Canterbury. Overzealous knights, seeking to aid King Henry II, killed the archbishop in the cathedral. To quiet the resulting public hostility, the king did public penance for the crime. Becket was soon made a saint by the church. Carrow Psalter and Hours, Walters Art Gallery, Baltimore.

courts by judicious appointments of church officials and by steady extension of royal justice.

Attempts to Limit the Power of the Monarch

During the thirteenth century, various attempts were made to limit the English monarchy culminating in the establishment of Parliament, but by that century's end the monarchy appeared stronger than ever. After Henry II's death, his widow, Eleanor, became the actual ruler of England for her son Richard I (1189–1199), who was in the land scarcely six months of his ten-year reign, because of crusading in the east, campaigning in France, and enduring imprisonment in the Holy Roman Empire. Thereafter, throughout most of the thirteenth century, Henry's successors exhibited neither his ability nor his interest in government, and royal authority diminished. Popes claimed the right to make ecclesiastical appointments, weakening royal control of the English church.

The barons, angered by heavy taxes

261

Tomb Effigy of Eleanor of Aquitaine. Successively queen of France and England, Eleanor was a noteworthy medieval political figure. She was the actual ruler of England during the crusading and captivity of her son Richard I, and also a prominent patroness of troubadour poetry. Abbey of Fontevrault.

and growing royal centralization, as well as by the king's resort to non-traditional sources of revenue and arbitrary behavior, forced King John (1199–1216) to issue in 1215 a Great Charter (*Magna Carta* in Latin). The Magna Carta committed kings to obtain baronial consent before levying new taxes, to administer justice according to established procedures rather than in an arbitrary and capricious manner, and to recognize and permit subjects to enjoy various rights and liberties. Although primarily intended to limit royal power over nobles, later generations viewed the Magna Carta as a guarantee of fundamental human rights for people of all stations in life.

In the Provisions of Oxford in 1258, barons attempted to impose further limitations on royal power. The provisions required the king to summon a meeting of his chief advisers, the realm's barons, and high ecclesiasti-

cal officials three times a year, and established a small council of barons to share control over the royal administration with the king. King Henry III (1216–1272) refused to accept these restrictions and defeated the barons in a brief civil war.

Edward I (1272–1307) completed the development of royal institutions of government within the British feudal monarchy. By his time, the government had four major agencies: the chancery or secretarial office; the exchequer, a revenue-collecting and accounting agency; the household, made up of governmental officials who traveled with the king, and a council composed of administrators, judges, magnates, and prelates. Chancery and exchequer were located at Westminster, as were the royal courts, which were staffed with trained professionals, primarily accountants and lawyers. In the countryside, sheriffs and traveling justices enforced a comprehensive body of common law based on court decisions that employed custom and reason to resolve disputes. Edward effectively eliminated the private legal jurisdiction of lords; moreover, he further expanded royal involvement in local government by employing additional royal agents, such as coroners to investigate felonies and keepers of the peace to apprehend criminals.

Edward's reign also saw the development of the English Parliament. Edward summoned barons, prelates, royal judges, administrators, shire knights, and members of town governments to those parliaments, or formal conferences, to obtain advice on important issues and to support him in times of crisis. At times, he used them as high courts or to resolve troublesome problems. The knights and town representatives, invited to obtain their assent to royal tax initiatives, gradually began to meet separately from the barons, and thereby laid the basis for dividing later parliaments into a House of Commons and a House of Lords. Through the English common law and the operations of Parliament, English kings and their subjects defined their respective rights and responsibilities and forged elements of a national unity identified by contemporaries as the "community of the realm." Although Parliament at this time was not a major check on royal authority, the groundwork was being laid for major challenges to the power of the monarchy.

FRANCE

In contrast to the rapid growth of feudal monarchy in England, feudal monarchy in France developed slowly, but eventually became a model for other European lands. England's small size, its lack of internal divisions, and the swiftness and thoroughness of William I's conquests made its experience unique. France, by contrast, was a large land of many provinces with widely varying institutions; such conditions more closely resembled those of other European lands than did England's.

The Early Capetian Dynasty

Unable to assert royal power by conquest, as William had done in England, the French kings of the Capetian dynasty (987–1328) built their royal power slowly but steadily. Successors to the last Carolingian king, who died without an heir, the Capetians were chosen by the barons largely to confirm the legal title to their fiefs. As a result, the Capetians were merely feudal lords exercising suzerainty over equals rather than sovereigns ruling over subjects. The Capetians directly ruled only their small state, the Ile de France, whose central town, Paris, played a key economic role in northern France, controlling both water traffic along the Seine River and land traffic crossing it.

Subsequent Capetians were not content to simply maintain their modest heritage, but struggled mightily to augment their power. They secured the throne for their successors by producing a regular sequence of heirs and by crowning new rulers before the reigning king died. Most lived to mature ages, so that regencies were few. The growth of agriculture and trade in their domains supplied them with adequate revenues. They retained the support of the popes and

control of the church in their lands, and used church officials as administrators. Those new administrators worked to extend the king's power and to systematize the royal administration.

By the middle of the twelfth century, the Capetians succeeded in bringing the royal domain of the Ile de France fully under their control. To secure this control, they carefully defined the powers of their officials and closely supervised them. Moreover, they developed Paris as both a trading center and a royal capital. Because the pacified royal domain brought greater revenues to the treasury, by 1200 the Capetians were the wealthiest lords in France.

The Capetians next began to assert their authority over territories outside the Ile de France, a task that was made easier by rivalries among the territories. They convinced lords of those territories to submit disputes to them and to bring legal cases to their courts. As had occurred in Germany two centuries earlier, church officials sought royal aid in their struggles with the nobility. The kings defended their claims and received church lands and fiefs in gratitude for their efforts. The Capetians at the same time enhanced their reputation for defending the Christian faith by aiding the popes against the emperor and by going on crusades.

The Capetians Expand Their Power

On these solid foundations, a series of thirteenth century Capetian rulers developed strong monarchical government, and during the century France surpassed England to become Europe's greatest power. By marriage,

A FEUDAL MONARCH IN ACTION

[King] Louis . . . proved himself an illustrious and courageous defender of his father's realm. He provided for the needs of the Church, and strove to secure peace for those who pray, for those who work, and for the poor . . . .

King Louis spent freely both of money and the sweat of his brow to relieve the sufferings and oppressions of many . . . .

A king, when he takes the royal power, vows to put down with his strong right arm insolent tyrants whensoever he sees them vex the state with endless wars, rejoice in rapine, oppress the poor, destroy the churches, [and] give themselves over to lawlessness.

[King] Louis ordered Burchard [a nobleman] to appear . . . for judgment. Burchard lost his cause, but refused to submit to the judgment. . . . [Louis] laid waste the land of Bur-

chard with fire, famine, and the sword; and overthrew all the defenses and buildings, except the castle itself, and razed them to the ground . . . . By these and other means he . . . satisfactorily adjudicated the dispute . . . .*

These observations on King Louis VI (1108–37) of France highlight the duties of a medieval king. Unlike modern governmental leaders who control an administrative apparatus, a medieval king might on occasion use his own "strong right arm" in battle with his foes. Louis VI spent most of his reign in subduing robber barons such as Burchard, and earned his nicknames of "Wideawake" and "Bruiser."

*Suger, *Life of King Louis* [VI], in *Readings in European History* trans. and ed. James Harvey Robinson, (Boston: Ginn & Company, 1904), Vol. I, pp. 199–200.

exercise of feudal rights, and conquests in both northern and southern France, Philip II (1180–1223), known as Augustus (exalted or majestic) quadrupled the amount of territory under the French king's direct control. His greatest gains in the north resulted from his defeat of England's King John and in the south from his son's military successes against Cathar or Albigensian heretics. To govern those newly acquired lands, Philip, like the Norman conquerors of England a century earlier, centralized royal government. He systematized royal finance, while adapting royal rule to local customs. In accordance with Norman practice, he replaced the he-

reditary high nobles who administered royal territories with salaried officials recruited from lesser nobles and townspeople. He allowed conquered territories to retain most of their indigenous governmental practices, but superimposed on them a new royal bureaucracy of officials who promoted centralization while permitting regional diversity. Those officials performed financial, judicial, and administrative functions that were formerly the prerogative of the local aristocracy, reducing its privileges.

Philip's small, efficient, and loyal court remained unencumbered by local roots and traditions and so aided the development of strong monarchy

by reconciling competing local interests and asserting the king's final authority. The administrative structure in the royal lands came to consist of layers of royal officials at the local, regional, and national level. France in this period has been described as a mosaic state of many territories held together by the cement of the royal bureaucracy.

Philip's successors further advanced the prestige of the French monarchy. Traveling inspectors in the territories under the monarchy's direct control came to hear local grievances and to investigate illegal activities by royal officials. The kings provided justice to all, promoted French commerce, and established a standardized coinage for France. They made France Europe's leading cultural center through encouraging art and education, in particular by founding the University of Paris and stimulating the building of Gothic cathedrals. For his piety, kindly rule at home, and promotion of crusading abroad, one of those kings, Louis IX (1226–1270), widely known as Saint Louis during his lifetime, was formally recognized by the church as a saint soon after his death, thus carrying Capetian prestige to new heights.

Philip IV's Achievements

The reign of Philip IV (1285–1314), called the Fair because of his blond hair and pale complexion, brought the development of the medieval French monarchy to its apex. He brought additional territories, notably Champagne, Navarre, and southern Flanders, under royal control and systematized feudal relationships by demanding direct allegiance and obedience from all vassals. The king consolidated the royal system of justice by placing the court of appeals known as the Parlement of Paris at its center, and he tightened control over royal revenues by developing a special accounting bureau. Philip also regularized the king's right to tax his subjects by obtaining approval of taxes from provincial or regional assemblies. Other means of securing funds were more ruthless. Philip expelled the Jews from France and seized their property, and labeled the Knights Templar as heretics, confiscating their wealth.

Philip IV's move to tax the French clergy produced a convincing demonstration of how powerful and secure the French monarchy had become. Ordinarily, rulers could tax the clergy only when the popes permitted them to do so, and Philip was not given such permission. Instead of abandoning his tax plan, however, Philip responded by prohibiting the export of papal revenues from France in an attempt to force the pope to change his decision. Within France, there was no significant support for the papal position; all major groups supported the king. Philip enjoyed similar widespread support when he subsequently arrested and tried a bishop accused of treason. By their skillful policies, Philip IV and his predecessors accomplished a significant shift of loyalty from local lords and regions to king and state.

Philip's conflict with the papacy also led to the development of two important institutions: the Avignon papacy and the French Estates General. Capitalizing on his demon-

King Philip IV of France in Council. The king's great vassals are present with him to render judgment and give advice. Bishops to the king's left are recognizable by their headgear. Kings as overlords summoned vassals for military service, for advice and counsel, and, as here, to render judgment on other vassals. Bibliothèque Nationale, Paris.

strated strength, Philip influenced the cardinals to select a French pope, who not only repudiated the papacy's opposition to Philip but also transferred the seat of papal government from Rome to Avignon, in the Rhone Valley, on the French border. For the next seventy years, a series of French popes governed the church from Avignon, usually in accord with French royal policy.

The other important institution deriving from Philip's conflict with the papacy was the Estates General, a parliament-like body composed of members of the three great social classes, or estates—clergy, nobles, and townspeople—which Philip summoned to obtain public support for his opposition to the pope. Philip and his successors used the Estates General as a sounding board for royal policy and a means of stirring up support for royal decisions. However, they never permitted the Estates General to gain the authority in financial matters that the English Parliament possessed, preferring to decide those matters in provincial or regional assemblies. The Estates General also differed from the English Parliament by having no judicial powers; instead, the Parlement of Paris handed down royal legal decisions. The Estates General thus had no power base from which to bargain with the king, and consequently never became an integral part of the French government. In contrast to England, where the monarchy transacted its business in Parliament aided by a nobility with a national perspective, in France the crown remained the one great unifying concept, and nobles retained provincial or regional rather than national interests.

SUMMARY

In Germany, France, and England, medieval kings developed monarchies based on feudal relations. The German kings, who became holy Roman emperors, were the first to establish strong monarchy in their territories. Their efforts, however, conflicted with movements for church reform and a developing papal monarchy. To free the church from lay lords' control, reform popes deprived emperors of the ability to appoint church officials and employ them as imperial administrators. Emperors therefore sought alternate ways to rebuild the empire. Frederick I attempted to systematize feudal relationships in Germany and to assert rights based on Roman law in Italy, but the Lombard League and pope combined to thwart him. On the other hand, Pope Innocent III's failure to control the empire revealed the limitations of the papal monarchy's power. Frederick II abandoned imperial rights in Germany and sought to unite Italy by imposing institutions and practices used in his Norman Kingdom of Sicily, but bitter papal opposition wrecked his plans. With Frederick II, the empire effectively died; Italy became free of imperial control, and there and in Germany local princes and towns acquired territory and power for themselves in the absence of strong central government.

To the strong monarchy already existing in Anglo-Saxon England, William I added Norman feudal practices. His successors elaborated the financial and judicial aspects of royal administration. Henry II continued to expand the scope of royal law, but this conflicted with the church's judicial system. Subsequently, barons forced the kings to accept limitations on their power, notably the Magna Carta, and in Edward I's reign, Parliament became part of the English governmental system.

The Capetian kings of France originally held only a small, though strategic, territory, but kept control of the throne and slowly expanded their authority, first over their own domain and later beyond it. Philip II quadrupled the amount of territory under the French kings' control, and Louis IX enhanced the prestige and image of the monarchy. Philip IV advanced the French monarchy's authority and his quarrel with the popes produced both the French Estates General and the Avignon papacy. On the basis of these sound medieval foundations, both England and France developed into powerful national monarchies during the next three centuries.

SUGGESTED SOURCES

*Barraclough, Geoffrey. *The Origins of Modern Germany.* 1984. The best available one-volume treatment of medieval German history.

Becket. 1964. This film focuses on the church-crown controversy in England, and features outstanding acting performances.

*Brooke, Christopher. *From Alfred to Henry III, 871–1272.* 1966. A survey treating economic and social conditions along with political developments.

*De Joinville, Jean. *Life of St. Louis* in *Chronicles of the Crusades.* Translated by Margaret R. Shaw. 1963. An admiring life of France's King Louis IX by a great French noble contemporary.

*Fawtier, Robert. *The Capetian Kings of France.* 1969. Treats the growth of medieval France through biographical sketches of its rulers.

*Haskins, Charles H. *The Normans in European History.* 1966. Emphasizes the Normans as catalysts in medieval European history in France, England, and Italy.

*Kelly, Amy. *Eleanor of Aquitaine and the Four Kings.* 1950. Absorbing biography of this extraordinary woman who was successively queen of France and England.

*Painter, Sidney. *The Rise of the Feudal Monarchies.* 1951. A brief survey which illuminates and illustrates the theory and practice of feudal monarchy.

*Petit-Dutaillis, Charles. *The Feudal Monarchy in France and England.* 1959. Compares and contrasts the constitutional developments in the two lands during the period 1000–1300.

Tellenbach, Gerd. *Church, State, and Christian Society at the Time of the Investiture Struggle.* 1959. Clear, knowledgeable treatment of the conflict between popes and emperors in the Holy Roman Empire.

*Available in paperback.

THE WEST IN TRANSITION

Between 1350 and 1789, Europe saw three crucial cultural and religious developments: the Renaissance, the Reformation, and the age of reason. Important political changes were the rise of royal absolutism and enlightened despotism and the expansion of western civilization outside Europe.

In response to economic and human losses brought by the Black Death, Europeans extended trade activities in Africa and Asia, and discovered the "new world" of the western hemisphere. Wealth derived from these regions promoted Europe's political stability and financed its cultural advances and wars.

Europeans after 1350 capitalized on their rich Graeco-Roman cultural heritage to produce the Renaissance, a rebirth of the classical spirit. Key intellectual values were humanism, an affirmation of human abilities and potentials, and secularism, which stressed the life and values of this world. In the Reformation, persons seeking to renew early Christian values and practices destroyed medieval religious unity and created the major forms of Protestant Christianity.

Such far-reaching changes caused both religious wars and struggles among states to control economic resources and strategic territories. As some European states became powerful, others remained weak or disappeared.

In the seventeenth century, certain kings and queens claimed unprecedented powers over their subjects. Louis XIV, the archetypal absolute monarch, made France Europe's most respected nation. Strong Habsburg and Hohenzollern rulers enhanced the positions of Austria and Prussia in central Europe, and Russia's Peter the Great made his country a great power.

By the eighteenth century, inhabitants of pure or mixed European descent were developing novel forms of western civilization in the Americas. Here, amid testing physical environments and the unfamiliar cultural influences of Amerindians and African slaves, they adapted or jettisoned unsuitable European customs and devised more serviceable strategies.

An emphasis on human reason activated the scientific revolution which had its birth in the heliocentric theory of Copernicus and reached a climax in the work of Isaac Newton. Thinkers of the Enlightenment period, such as Voltaire and Rousseau, grounded radical sociopolitical theories in human reason and gave ideological support to succeeding revolutions.

Enlightenment principles strengthened the political trends of constitutionalism and enlightened despotism. Constitutional guarantees limited the power of monarchs in Great Britain and the Netherlands, while in Austria, Prussia, and Russia, enlightened despots claimed to use their unlimited powers to reform society and benefit their subjects.

Timeline scale: **1300 — 1350 — 1400 — 1450 — 1500**

Politics

1356 Golden Bull (Holy Roman Empire)

1453 Fall of Constantinople to Ottoman Turks

1519–56 Charles V

1532 Spanish conquer Incas

Rise of the Ottoman Turks

1337–1453 The Hundred Years' War

1455–1485 War of the Roses

1519–22 Magellan expedition circles the globe

1521 Spanish conquer Aztecs

Economics & Society

1350–1400 Peasant revolts

1492 Christopher Columbus discovers America

1513 Balboa reaches Pacific

1347 "Black Death" (bubonic plague) begins

Peak of Medici banking family prosperity begins

1494 Treaty of Tordesillas

Science & Technology

First use of steel crossbow in war

1473–1543 Nicholas Copernicus

1313 Europeans discover gunpowder

First record of weaving in England (York)

Leonardo da Vinci invents parachute, horizontal water wheel, etc.

Religion & Thought

1380–1471 Thomas à Kempis' *The Imitation of Christ*

Martin Luther begins Protestant Reformation

1374–1415 John Hus

1309–78 Agivnonese Papacy

1378–1417 The Great Schism; rival popes

1491–1556 Ignatius Loyola's *Spiritual Exercises*

Arts & Literature

1387–1400 Geoffrey Chaucer's *Canterbury Tales*

1452–1519 Leonardo da Vinci's *Mona Lisa, The Last Supper*

1475–1564 Michaelangelo Buonarotti's *Pietà, The Last Judgement*

1313–75 Giovanni Boccaccio's *Decameron*

1386–1466 Donatello's *David*

1466–1536 Desiderius Erasmus' *Praise of Folly*

1550	1600	1650	1700	1750	1800

1533–1584
Ivan IV
"the Terrible"

1618–1648
The Thirty
Years' War

1660–1685
Stuart
Restoration
(England)

1740–1786
Frederick
the
Great
of Prussia

Russia
expands
to Pacific

1643–1715
Louis XIV

1682–1725
Peter the
Great of Russia

1607
First
English
colonies

1619–83
Jean Colbert,
mercantilism

Development
of a
global/colonial
economy

Introduction of
black slavery
into the
Western
Hemisphere

1663
Dutch gain
control of
East Indian
trade

1687
Isaac Newton's
*Mathematical
Principles of
Natural Philosophy*

1718
First
observation of
smallpox
inoculation

1564–1642
Galileo
Galilei

1628
First
crude
steam engine

1561–1626
Francis
Bacon

1571–1630
Johannes
Kepler

1683
Anton
von Leeuwenhoek
discovers
bacteria

1709
First
production
of industrial
coke

1651
Thomas
Hobbes'
Leviathan

1754
Voltaire's
Candide

1555
Peace of
Augsburg

1545–63
Council
of Trent

1509–64
John Calvin

1596–1650
René
Descartes

1690
John Locke's
*Two Treatises
of Civil
Government*

1547–1616
Miguel de
Cervantes'
Don Quixote

1564–1616
William
Shakespeare

1665
Bernini's
High Altar,
St. Peter's
Basilica, Rome

1685–1750
Johann
Sebastian
Bach

1548–1614
El Greco's
*The Burial
of Count Orgaz*

1562–1635
Lope
de Vega

1667–74
John Milton's
*Paradise
Lost*

NATIONAL MONARCHIES AND PLURALISTIC EMPIRES (1340–1600)

No distinction is attached to birth among the Turks; the deference to be paid to a man is measured by the position he holds in the public service . . . In making his appointments the Sultan pays no regard to any pretensions on the score of wealth or rank, . . . he considers each case on its own merits, and examines carefully into the character, ability, and disposition of the man whose promotion is in question. It is by merit that men rise in the service, a system which ensures that posts should only be assigned to the competent . . . .

This is the reason that they are successful in their undertakings, that they lord it over others, and are daily extending the bounds of their empire. These are not our ideas, with us there is no opening left for merit; birth is the standard for everything; the prestige of birth is the sole key to advancement in the public service.

The Turkish "meritocracy," praised here by the holy Roman emperor's ambassador to Turkey, was an ideal that fifteenth- and sixteenth-century monarchs in western Europe and autocrats in the east sought to realize. Such rulers also labored to establish more centralized governments, and where they succeeded, they produced strong states in two quite different patterns. In western Europe, powerful states became national monarchies; beyond central Europe to the east and southeast, pluralistic empires arose. The present chapter examines these two types of states and discusses the prominent European examples of each type.

EMERGING NATIONAL MONARCHIES

During the period 1300–1600 in western Europe certain states developed into national monarchies. Instead of being haphazard collections of fiefs, as feudal monarchies were, such states were organized around a

Queen Elizabeth I. The Dillon Portrait, painted in honor of the queen's visit to Ditchley in 1592. One of the mightiest sixteenth century rulers was Queen Elizabeth I of England. Both politically shrewd and appealingly human, she aroused zealous devotion among her subjects. In this portrait of the queen standing on the map of England, the gems, padded sleeves, farthingale, and long, narrow waist of her courtly costume produce a striking impression of stateliness. National Portrait Gallery, London.

MAP 34
The Hundred Years' War and the Growth of Burgundy. In the fifteenth century, France weathered two serious threats to its existence. The English in 1429 seemed poised to conquer all of France until Joan of Arc rallied French opposition to them. Later efforts of England's Burgundian allies to weld numerous scattered territories into a consolidated state northeast of France collapsed when Duke Charles the Bold was killed in battle in 1477.

basic core of lands and people. The core population of a national state shared common customs and a common language, and thought of itself as a distinctly national group. Rather than relying on feudal lords for governmental services, rulers of national monarchies developed permanent institutions staffed by professional administrators for conducting financial and judicial affairs. National states were also sovereign in that they were independent of any outside power and their rulers possessed final authority over those living within the state. Through their direct provision of services to the people, monarchical authorities promoted loyalty to the state,

which became stronger than any other loyalty and made the monarchies truly national as well as sovereign.

By the sixteenth century, national monarchies had become well established in England, France, and the Iberian Peninsula through the efforts of rulers often termed "new monarchs," although actually little they did was new. They built on the achievements of their predecessors, benefiting from economic recovery after the fourteenth century depression and a desire for peace after destructive civil and foreign wars. As a result, they had time, money, and energy to devote to strengthening their governments. They also possessed the

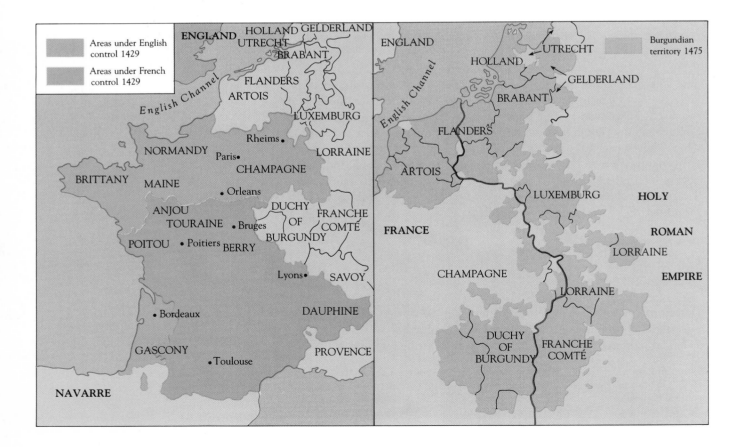

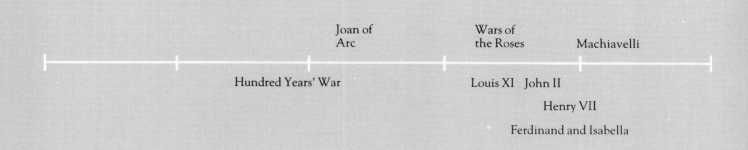

| 1300 | 1350 | 1400 | 1450 | 1500 | 1550 |

Joan of
Arc

Wars of
the Roses

Machiavelli

Hundred Years' War

Louis XI   John II

Henry VII

Ferdinand and Isabella

intelligence to make wise use of resources and the skill to develop increased cooperation between rulers and subjects. However, the expanding powers of the crown came into conflict with the privileges of nobles, prompting the latter to assert their privileges against the monarch. The emergence of strong monarchies therefore required the suppression of the political role of the nobility.

By 1500, several factors favored kings in their conflict with the nobility. Crusades and civil wars had diverted and often eliminated feudal nobles. The church supported the kings' desire to check private warfare and to control feudal lords, and found royal control preferable to local interference. Economic expansion aided the growth of a middle class, which supplied the kings with soldiers for their armies and clerks for government offices. The middle class also provided tax money and loans for the growing expenses of central government in return for exemption from traditional feudal obligations imposed on them by the nobility. Access to the wealth of an entire nation gave kings greater resources than any noble possessed and enabled them to monopolize the new technology of gunpowder and firearms and thereby

gain decisive military advantages in warfare.

Political theorists also favored royal rule. They identified the king with the state, speaking of the king's "two bodies"—his physical and mortal one and his institutional and immortal one—and giving rise to the expression "The king is dead; long live the king [state]!" Students of Roman law replaced feudal contract theory with the idea that the will of the king is law. Niccolo Machiavelli (1469–1527) argued powerfully on behalf of national monarchy and suggested that a national monarch should be unhampered by religious or moral considerations. All these factors promoted the growth of powerful and independent national states that were in existence in Europe by the sixteenth century.

ENGLAND AND FRANCE

England and France were, and remained throughout most of this period, Europe's leading monarchies. However they developed in different directions as a result of their involvement in a mutual conflict, the Hundred Years' War (Map 34).

The Hundred Years' War

The Hundred Years' War (1337–1453) between England and France, which significantly shaped the political organization of each state, had both political and economic causes. In England, barons had forced a king to abdicate; in France, the last Capetian king had died without heirs; hence both new kings sought to consolidate insecure positions by military successes against an outside power. Moreover, the English king Edward III (1327–1377) claimed the French throne as the only grandson of Philip IV of France, whose sons had all died without heirs. Economically, the French sought control of the rich wine trade of Gascony, a territory held by the English king as a fief of the king of France, whereas the English sought to keep Flanders and its valuable wool trade and manufacturing free of French control.

The war was fought in France as a succession of isolated campaigns punctuated by several long truces, and the English generally dominated the campaigning. In the early phases, the English won a naval victory at Sluys (1340), giving them control of the Channel; and at Crécy (1346) their longbows and dismounted, armored

275

horsemen were superior to the French mounted cavalry and crossbowmen. Ten years later, Edward's son, the Black Prince, won a battle at Poitiers and captured the French king. The French paid a large sum for his ransom and signed a treaty ceding two-fifths of their country to England.

Fifty-five years later, England's Henry V (1413–1422) revived the war to try to unify his rebellious nobles. His conduct of the war was successful, thanks partly to an alliance with the Duke of Burgundy, and he won a notable victory at Agincourt in 1415. By the Treaty of Troyes in 1420, Henry was designated regent of France; it appeared that the two countries might become permanently united.

At this dark moment for the French, a young Frenchwoman, subsequently known as Joan of Arc (1412–1431), changed the course of events. Responding to what she understood as divine guidance, she urged Prince Charles, the heir to the French throne, to appoint her as a military leader, promising to obtain for him his coronation as Charles VII (1422–1461). She inspired the French soldiers with confidence, and they defeated the British in several engagements. Aided by those victories, the newly crowned king slowly gained support. Joan's subsequent capture and execution made her a martyr and a symbol of

Joan of Arc. Pictured here with banner and in battle dress, this peasant girl rallied French opposition to England in the Hundred Years' War. The English captured her, tried and condemned her as heretic in an attempt to diminish her influence, and executed her. In the twentieth century, the Roman Catholic church designated Joan a saint. Archives Nationales, Paris.

French national spirit. The English-Burgundian alliance soon dissolved, and the French finally drove the English out of France.

England

In England, the Hundred Years' War contributed significantly to the growth of Parliament, which obtained important political concessions from the kings in exchange for granting funds to fight the war. Parliament secured the right to approve or disapprove new taxes and to have its requests granted before providing funds. It gained control of customs duties and the right to supervise royal expenditures and began to develop a procedure for initiating legislation. Furthermore, members of Parliament began to insist that the king's ministers and the great offices of state were responsible to them, as well as to the king, and impeached several ministers for improper acts. Parliament even on occasion (in 1327 and 1399) forced kings to abdicate and selected new ones, whereas its members were exempted from arrest during parliamentary sessions or while going to or from them.

Parliament thus became established as an integral part of England's governmental machinery and during these centuries took on its modern configuration. The Commons designated a representative, the speaker, to express their views in debate before the king. The Lords became recognized as the supreme court of the realm.

Landed nobility continued to dominate both houses of Parliament, but their power diminished in the Hundred Years' War and in subsequent civil wars from 1455 to 1485, collectively known as the Wars of the Roses, from the legendary emblems later ascribed to the principal rival families.

The Wars of the Roses were essentially a feudal struggle between two powerful families of royal lineage, as the reigning house of Lancaster was challenged by the rival house of York. The Yorkists were victorious in 1461 and the duke of York became Edward IV (1461–1483). Fighting broke out again after Edward's death. Henry Tudor, a step-relation to the house of Lancaster, killed Edward's brother Richard III (1483–1485) at the Battle of Bosworth Field. He took the crown as Henry VII (1485–1509), inaugurating the Tudor dynasty. William Shakespeare made this phase of English history, and many events that preceded and followed it, the subject of several absorbing, if often inaccurate history plays.

The Tudor dynasty (1485–1603) reasserted royal authority after the Wars of the Roses, exploiting the weakened position of the nobility and the widespread desire for peace and checking the growth of parliamentary power. The Tudors created a new group of loyal peers, primarily from the ranks of lesser gentry and wealthy townsmen, and later enriched those new nobles with lands confiscated from the Roman Catholic church during the Protestant Reformation.

The Tudors also developed effective techniques for the control of Parliament. They seated many of their councillors in the Commons, and when royal programs were presented, those individuals directed the deliberations and guided the ruler's program through the chamber. Much legislation was initiated by the crown rather than by Parliament.

Henry VII, the first Tudor mon-

Henry VII of England. This "new monarch" seized the throne in 1485 and founded the Tudor dynasty. He is depicted here toward the end of his reign. National Portrait Gallery, London.

arch, set the pattern for Tudor authority. He and his successors preferred to govern through councils that they appointed and controlled and from which the great nobles were excluded. Henry used one council as a court (called, from the decor of its meeting room, the Court of Star Chamber) functioning under his direct control, and without the procedure of common law. The Court of Star Chamber was especially diligent in stripping nobles of their private armies and preventing them from disturbing the peace. The king also destroyed illegal castles and fortifications and confiscated the lands and wealth of "overmighty subjects." He promoted commercial activity by negotiating favorable treaties, but otherwise kept England free of foreign entanglements, winning for the Tudors the support of the merchants. Henry received such ample revenues from customs duties on increased trade and through fines from active law enforcement that he summoned Parliament only once in the last twelve years of his reign.

Henry VIII (1508–47) inherited from his father a full treasury and a stable government, but squandered the former on foreign wars and endangered the latter by his difficulties in producing an heir. The young king sought fame and glory in war with France, but gained no territory and ran short of funds. More popular and productive was his coordinating of England's opposition to the papacy and his assuming, with parliament's concurrence, headship of the church in England. By abolishing monasteries in England, the king gained wealth which he used to avoid unpopular taxation and to purchase the loyalty of the landed gentry. Moreover, church officials he appointed an-

nulled his first marriage, thus permitting him to remarry in hopes of siring a son. Henry VIII carried royal power to new heights by using arbitrary executions and by obtaining from Parliament an expanded definition of treason and permission to make valid laws by proclamation. However, the prominence of Parliament also grew, and its ties with the king were strengthened by the requirement that royal councillors must be elected in order to vote in the Commons.

Elizabeth I (1558–1603), Henry VIII's popular daughter, concluded the Tudor dynasty and guided England to prominence abroad and prosperity at home. Restoration of religious peace and defeat of the Spanish Armada (see chapters 20 and 21) created possibilities for expansion overseas and permitted greater royal management of economic and social affairs. The queen restored a sound currency following the debasement practiced by her predecessors, sought to maintain a balanced budget, and encouraged economic development by granting individuals monopolies of the sale of particular articles for a specified period of years. To aid English merchants in recovering old markets and obtaining new ones, Elizabeth I chartered joint stock companies (notably the East India Company, 1600) able to protect English merchants and to deal with foreign governments. Such economic development widened the scope of central government responsibility as local efforts to regulate economic activities or to assist the needy proved inadequate. The Statute of Artisans (1563) regulated their working conditions by mandating a seven-year apprenticeship and requiring justices of the peace to set wages and hours of labor annually according to local conditions. A particularly press-

ing problem was poverty, worsened by sheepraising landlords' evictions of tenant farmers and by the closing of monasteries which provided the era's social services. The Poor Law of 1601 appointed overseers of the poor in each parish and authorized them to provide work for the able-bodied unemployed and to raise funds for poor relief by levying a tax on local property owners. Members of all levels of English society had ample reason to mourn the passing of "Good Queen Bess."

France

In France, as in England, the Hundred Years' War and succeeding civil wars discredited the nobles and contributed to the development of a stronger monarchy supported by significant popular sentiment. Like their English counterparts, the French kings needed money to make war, but the Estates General, unlike the English Parliament, failed to exploit the king's needs and did not establish control over royal finance. Meetings of the Estates General were costly, and some areas wished to avoid the expense of sending delegates. Moreover, the Estates General represented the northern provinces rather than the whole kingdom; the southern provinces had their own regional assembly. The kings easily dominated the feeble financial machinery the Estates General had established, and in general obtained assent for royal policies and taxes from provincial rather than national assemblies. Two of the most important taxes collected by the king were the *gabelle*, a tax on salt, and the *taille*, a national tax on households. Nobles and clergy, who were the wealthiest groups in France, were exempt from those taxes, but on occasion made

NATIONAL MONARCHIES AND PLURALISTIC EMPIRES

special gifts and contributions. In time, the kings imposed taxes without seeking special authorization, and the increased revenues thus gathered gradually made them independent of the assemblies.

The rulers of France used their independent income to consolidate and extend their power. Middle-class professional bureaucrats who were dependent on the crown were appointed to set up a rudimentary central administration. The French kings also organized a paid standing army of professional soldiers, equipped with artillery and supported by permanent taxation. They sought advisers from the ranks of non-nobles rather than using the cumbersome Estates General, and extended the operations of the royal bureaucracy and judiciary increasingly into local affairs.

It fell to Louis XI (1461–1483) to rebuild France after the Hundred Years' War and advance monarchical centralization, a task he performed with signal success. He attracted the loyalty of the lesser nobility and prevented the nobles from acquiring new fiefs and building new fortifications. He promoted national prosperity by supporting French fairs in competition with those held outside France and established state commercial monopolies. Through negotiations with the papacy, Louis placed the national church under firm royal control. Royal control was also tightened over the populace as he steadily reduced urban liberties and town autonomy, and began to curb the administrative independence of the provinces. By continuing to collect the taxes established by his forerunners and managing that income frugally, Louis enjoyed a substantial revenue. He summoned only one Estates General during his reign, and that

assembly requested that he rule without them in the future.

Louis advanced France's territorial consolidation by absorbing the great royal dukedoms known as *appanages,* granted by earlier kings to their children. The Hundred Years' War had demonstrated the dangers of the *appanage* system when some *appanage* nobles claimed the French crown or tried to turn their lands into independent kingdoms. Louis adroitly used money, warfare, litigation, and intricate webs of diplomacy (which won him the nickname "The Universal Spider") to acquire the *appanages* for the crown or otherwise eliminate them.

Burgundy, the most impressive of those *appanages,* presented Louis with the greatest problems. Burgundy had grown by a series of advantageous marriages and territorial acquisitions into a leading state consisting of many scattered territories in both France and the Holy Roman Empire. Louis bought off the English from allying with the Burgundian dukes and paid the Swiss to oppose them. The marriage in 1477 of the surviving female heir of the house of Burgundy to the son of the Habsburg holy Roman emperor laid the foundation for centuries of French-Habsburg hostility. Nevertheless, at Louis's death in 1483, France was Europe's strongest state.

THE IBERIAN STATES

During the late fifteenth century, the Iberian kingdoms of Portugal and Spain also became strong national monarchies. By the sixteenth century, Spain, thanks to an amazing sequence of events, had become Europe's strongest state (Map 35).

Portugal

Enlarged by territory reconquered by the Muslims, Portugal experienced consistent monarchical development during the fourteenth century. During the reconquest, Portuguese kings had encouraged immigration, promoted agriculture, and established many towns. But military orders of knighthood, clergy, and nobility challenged royal power, and the Cortes, a parliament-like body that included town dwellers as well as nobles and clergy, became politically prominent.

The Avis dynasty (1385–1580), inaugurated through election by the Cortes after the previous line of kings died without heirs, maintained internal stability and promoted economic prosperity while asserting strong monarchical rule. Nobles, church, and townspeople all supported the monarchy against a Castilian attempt to annex Portugal. In 1385, the Portuguese decisively defeated the Castilians and safeguarded their independence in the following year by negotiating a treaty of permanent alliance with England.

During the fifteenth century, Portugal's energies were devoted to overseas explorations and conquests. Contemporary with the strong rulers of England, France, and Spain, John II (1481–1495) strengthened royal power in Portugal by establishing royal administration of justice in feudal territories and by crushing the power of the nobles, suppressing a revolt and executing many of their leaders. Wealth from confiscated estates and the profits of the Portuguese empire furthered the growth of royal power and enabled the kings to rule without the Cortes, which ceased to meet regularly after 1521.

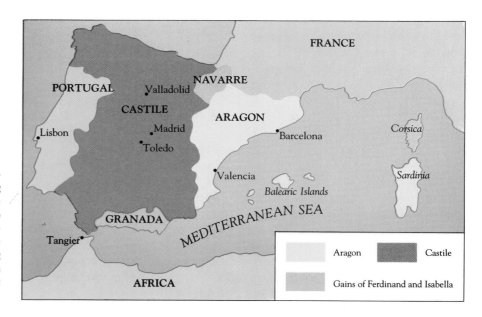

MAP 35
Iberian Peninsula. In 1479 Ferdinand of Aragon and Isabella of Castile married, joining their territories and forming the basis for Spanish unity and greatness. Thereafter the two rulers conquered Granada and acquired Navarre. In Spain's overseas empire, the combination of Aragon's bold and enterprising commercial spirit with Castilian institutions developed during centuries of warfare against Muslims proved remarkably effective.

Spain

The kingdom of Spain made its appearance in the late fifteenth century, formed by the union of two older kingdoms by the 1469 marriage of Ferdinand of Aragon (1479–1516) and Isabella of Castile (1474–1504). Castile's leadership in *reconquista* activities played an important role in shaping its political development. Warrior nobles led the fight against the Muslims and in the process obtained numerous privileges and concessions from the monarchs, notably exemption from taxes and the right to raise private armies. The *reconquista* disrupted agriculture and drove many people to reside in towns, which became influential in Castilian life. Towns often received charters of self-government from rulers wishing to counterbalance the power of the nobles. The urban brotherhoods provided important military forces that generally supported the kings in times of crisis. The Church also had gained land,

wealth, and power in the course of the *reconquista*. The Cortes, a parliamentary body, gave advice and presented requests to the kings, but did not achieve legislative power or become a supreme court. It did, however, restrain royal actions by restricting funds, and remained a symbol of unity.

In Aragon, in contrast to Castile, the trend of government was toward royal centralization. Aragon's nobles had gained privileges through constitutional opposition rather than through *reconquista* activity. Among those privileges were exemption from overseas military service, the right to be deprived of their fiefs only by due process of law, and the promise of annual meetings of the Cortes. But by the mid-fourteenth century, the crown had crushed the nobles in battle and annulled those privileges.

Equally important to the history of Aragon were the kingdom's overseas interests. During the thirteenth century, kings of Aragon conquered the

Balearic Islands and Sardinia, obtained the throne of Sicily, and attempted to establish overlordship over portions of Islamic north Africa. Aragon's involvement in Italian affairs intensified in the fifteenth century, but the crown's interest in Italy provoked unrest among Aragonese nobles, who lacked sympathy for overseas expansion.

Although the union of Castile and Aragon was only in the royal marriage, with each kingdom retaining its own offices, laws, institutions, courts, financial organization, and armed forces, the monarchs used their combined resources to follow united policy in many areas. They enforced both religious orthodoxy and political authority by controlling the appointment of church officials, by expelling Jews and Muslims from Spain, and by employing the judicial process of the Inquisition to eliminate dissent.

The opposition to the Jews and Muslims who dominated Spanish commerce was ethnic, religious, and cultural as well as economic. Ending this friction by forcing them to join the Roman church or leave Spain left the monarchs free to support other projects such as the explorations of Columbus. They concluded the reconquest of the peninsula by capturing the last Muslim stronghold, Granada, in 1492. The two rulers continued to expand their territories, acquiring Navarre and other lands in the Pyrenees and directing Spanish crusading energies overseas to Italy, north Africa, and the Americas.

To strengthen their royal control, Ferdinand and Isabella established new institutions of royal authority. Many functions of the Cortes were transferred to royal officials, who were educated administrators and trained lawyers of non-noble origin. The monarchs ruled through a council of twelve or thirteen members, of whom only three were nobles. They appointed royal officials to sit as members of every town's governing council, and saw to it that town representatives who supported monarchical policies were elected to the Cortes. The Cortes, however, lost independence and importance and ceased to meet regularly; for fifteen years (1483–1497) it was not summoned at all.

Isabella of Castile and Ferdinand of Aragon, who promoted Spanish unity by their marriage, are shown here at the Surrender of Granada in 1492, which ended the *reconquista.* Because of their deep religious devotion they were called *Los Reyes Católicos* (the Catholic Sovereigns). Ruling jointly, they cooperated closely in governing their lands, and made Spain a great power in sixteenth-century Europe.

PLURALISTIC EMPIRES

In contrast to the national monarchies forming in western Europe, two pluralistic empires, the Russian and the Ottoman, became dominant in eastern and southeastern Europe after 1300. Unlike national monarchies with their unified core populations, these pluralistic empires included diverse populations with varied customs and numerous languages. Their rulers relied on military force to control their lands and peoples and to conquer additional territories, and often exploited their subjects. The Turks, for example, referred to their non-Turkish subjects by the term *reaya*, (the flock) meaning herds of animals that were repeatedly milked and sheared.

Both the Russian and Ottoman empires appeared in the wake of the Mongol conquest of Asia and owed much to the Mongol model and influence. Both expanded rapidly by conquering adjacent land areas and incorporating Asiatic and European populations within a single state. In both, strong rulers with highly centralized authority emerged, relying on cavalry as the heart of their military forces. A bureaucratically managed agricultural economy was also a common characteristic, with a tax system designed to exploit that agricultural resource base. Ruling elites controlled agricultural revenues and discouraged the growth of large-scale commerce and a middle class. Class status was regulated by law to ensure social stability. Religious systems, Christianity in Russia and Islam (despite millions of Slavic and Greek Christians) in the Ottoman Empire,

supported the rulers and promoted ideological unity.

Between them, the Ottoman and Russian empires controlled almost all former Eastern Orthodox Christian territories. That faith remained potent among the Greek and Slavic subjects of those empires and kept ethnic identities and national heritages alive. But the pluralistic empires also insulated those regions from the western European movements of Renaissance and Reformation, and turned them in a direction of development quite different from that of western Europe. Both empires were aggressive toward their central European neighbors, and their influence on that region was great.

THE RISE OF THE OTTOMAN EMPIRE

Between 1300 and 1600, southeastern Europe underwent a significant transformation. The Byzantine Empire, which had persisted for more than a millennium, disintegrated and finally disappeared, to be replaced during the fifteenth century by a new, non-Christian power, the Ottoman Turks, who maintained the Byzantine tradition of absolute rule.

Byzantine Disintegration

In southeastern Europe, the Byzantine Empire declined rapidly from its twelfth-century apogee. The Comneni dynasty (1081–1185) of Byzantine emperors had vigorously asserted imperial authority, increased commercial connections with Italian cities, and restored Constantinople as a

leading cultural center. But thereafter, a rapid succession of short-lived rulers weakened the empire. By 1200, rebellions in Serbia and Bulgaria established independent states. In 1204, Latin crusaders sacked the capital of Constantinople and made most of the Byzantine Empire a Latin Empire until 1261. During this period, Roman Catholic church leaders attempted unsuccessfully to force Catholicism on Orthodox Christians, and Latin nobles transplanted French culture and institutions to Greece.

Although the Paleologi dynasty (1261–1453) destroyed the Latin Empire and recovered Constantinople and much of northern Greece, the Byzantine Empire was weaker and greatly reduced in size from the days of the Comneni. Southeastern Europe became, like central Europe, a politically fragmented region. Two Italian cities, Genoa and Venice, dominated the empire's trade and reaped its profits. Nobles enlarged their landholdings and reduced farmers to serfdom. The southern portion of Greece remained under Latin control, and Bulgaria retained its independence. The Serbs extended their territories during the fourteenth century, especially under Stephen IV Dushan (1331–1355), medieval Serbia's greatest ruler, who conquered Bulgaria and Macedonia. Stephen also intervened in the Byzantine Empire's civil wars, hoping to obtain the Byzantine throne and to unite the Balkans under his rule against the Ottoman Turks, but his death precluded that event. Contests for succession to the Byzantine throne and the absence of adequate resources rendered strong rule impossible and offered interested parties ample opportunities to intervene in the empire's affairs.

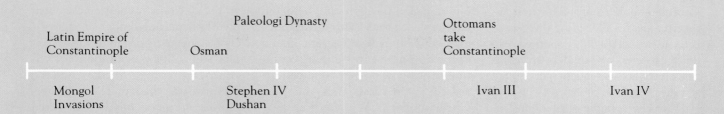

| 1200 | 1250 | 1300 | 1350 | 1400 | 1450 | 1500 | 1550 | 1600 |

Paleologi Dynasty

Latin Empire of
Constantinople
Osman

Ottomans
take
Constantinople

Mongol
Invasions

Stephen IV
Dushan

Ivan III

Ivan IV

Ottoman Rise to Power

In contrast to Byzantine disunity and fragmentation, the rising power of the Ottoman Turks brought unity and stability amidst territorial expansion. Named for the early leader Osman (1290–1326), the Ottomans com- bined both nomadic and urban Turks into a militaristic state dedicated to warfare with enemies of the Islamic faith. They began conducting regular raids against the Byzantines about 1300 from a strategic location in the An- atolian Peninsula next to the Byzan- tine frontier (Map 36). They soon

MAP 36
Southeastern Europe. Following the thir- teenth century, Christian-Muslim encounter dominated the history of this region. Between 1180 and 1400 the Christian Byzantine Em- pire shrank from the large area indicated by the broken lines to a few small territorial en- claves. Meanwhile, the Islamic Ottoman Em- pire expanded rapidly, winning control of many Balkan lands in the battle of Kossovo and de- feating later Christian reconquest attempts.

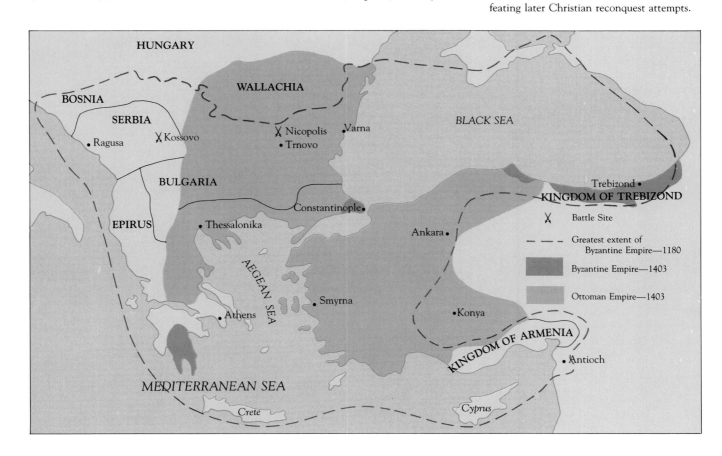

subjected all of Anatolia to their authority, meanwhile aiding the Byzantines in warfare against southeastern European foes. Contenders in Byzantine civil wars also sought Turkish aid at times.

With the collapse of Stephen Dushan's Serbian Empire, the Ottoman Turks exploited Byzantine weakness and Balkan disunity to acquire territory and influence in southeastern Europe. They warred against the Serbs and Bulgars, and their victory at Kossovo in 1389 gave the Ottomans control of the areas of present-day Greece, Serbia, and Bulgaria. At first, they established vassal dynasties there, but later replaced those with direct Ottoman control. Balkan peasants found Ottoman rule no worse than Byzantine control; also, they were permitted to retain their lands and their Christian faith. Western European crusade efforts against the Ottomans in 1396 and 1444 were unsuccessful, but warfare with central Asian Mongols halted Ottoman expansion for several decades. By the mid-fifteenth century, however, the Ottomans resumed their conquests, took Constantinople in 1453, and brought the Byzantine Empire to an end.

The Ottoman Empire resembled the old Byzantine Empire at its sixth-century height, both in territorial extent and political institutions. North Africa, Egypt, Syria, Turkey, and the Balkans were the empire's major territories. It was a highly centralized state governed by autocratic rulers called sultans and boasting a well-organized and efficient government. The Ottomans conducted detailed statistical surveys of their newly conquered territories and made these the basis for future fiscal exploitation. Rather than substituting a wholly new governing class, the Ottomans al-

MAP 37

Growth of Russia. Rulers of the small but centrally located principality of Moscow made it dominant in the emerging state of Russia. Laborious acquisition of lands to 1462 prepared the way for dramatic gains during the next one hundred and twenty years. Venturesome bands of settlers called Cossacks advanced Russia's frontier against its Muslim neighbors.

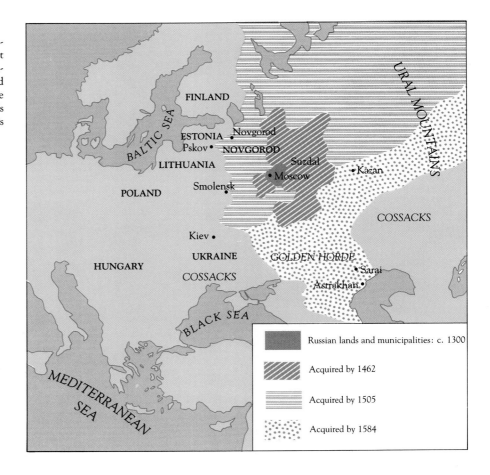

lowed Christian nobles to retain their feudal rank and estates. But they conscripted children from conquered Christian lands, raised them as Muslims and as the Sultan's slaves, and trained them to serve as administrators and soldiers. The sultans controlled the government's administrative machinery by placing slaves personally loyal to them in bureaucratic positions. The Ottoman armies consisted of a cavalry supplied by feudal lords and an infantry whose core, the Janissaries, was composed of these trained slaves.

RUSSIA

Like the Byzantine Empire, Russia passed through periods of disintegration and foreign rule before achieving unity, stability, and expansion. Russia emerged from a disorganized welter of petty territories thanks to the vigorous leadership of strong princes, and became one of Europe's strongest states by 1600 (Map 37).

From Kievan State to Mongol Domination

Russia's transformation in this period came about through a transfer of power and leadership to new regions. The earlier Kievan state, Eastern Orthodox Christian in religion and Byzantine in civilization, disintegrated during the late eleventh century, and was succeeded in prominence by Novgorod and Suzdal by the thirteenth century. Novgorod controlled a vast northern territory rich in furs and forest products, traded actively with northern Europe, and defeated

---

AN ENGLISH VIEW OF THE MONGOLS

An immense horde of that detestable race of Satan, like demons loosed from Tartarus (so that they are well called Tartars, as it were inhabitants of Tartarus [Hell]); . . . ravaged the eastern countries, spreading fires and slaughter wherever they went. . . . They razed cities to the ground, burnt woods, pulled down castles, tore up the vine-trees, destroyed gardens, and massacred the citizens and husbandmen. . . .

The men are inhuman and of the nature of beasts, rather to be called monsters than men, thirsting after and drinking blood, and tearing and devouring the flesh of dogs and human beings; they clothe themselves in the skins of bulls, and are armed with iron lances; they are short in stature and thickset, compact in their bodies, and of great strength; invincible in battle, indefatigable in labour. . . .

They have no human laws, know no mercy, and are more cruel than lions or bears. . . They take their herds with them, as also their wives, who are brought up to war, the same as the men; and they come with the force of lightning into the terror of the Christians, laying waste the country, committing great slaughter, and striking inexpressible terror and alarm into everyone.[*]

This example of propaganda against Mongols was compiled in England where few people saw or knew Mongols but instead relied on rumors and reports about their activities. Because the Mongols were few in number, they did employ the psychological warfare tactic of destroying cities that resisted them, and sometimes massacred the resisters. They had a well-developed tribal law, of which the author knew nothing. The Mongols' ability to move rapidly over long distances and to coordinate the movements of several armies precisely was undoubtedly alarming to Europeans accustomed to the slowness and disorganization of the typical feudal military campaign.

[*]Matthew Paris, English History, trans. J. A. Giles (London: H. G. Bohn, 1852), vol. 1, pp. 312–313.

---

thirteenth century Swedish and German attempts at invasion. In Novgorod, a popular assembly and elected officials shared power with the prince. Princely-ruled Suzdal, an insignificant central Russian territory that had acquired Kiev, came under Novgorod's control in the thirteenth century. Suzdal became the nucleus of future Russian development after the coming of the Mongols, a band of Asiatic conquerors who detached it from Novgorod's rule.

The thirteenth-century Mongol conquests, which extended throughout Asia, exercised a decisive influence on future Russian developments. United by an able chief, Temujin (1162–1227), who assumed the title Jinghiz Khan (very mighty ruler), the Mongols formed a confederation of nomadic tribes living north of China and thereafter rapidly expanded. Fast-moving Mongol armies conquered north China, central Asia, and northern Persia and raided the Russian steppes. After the conqueror's death, his grandson, Batu (1224–

TWO VIEWS OF RUSSIA

The Church of Old Rome fell because of its heresy [adopting Roman Catholic rather than Eastern Orthodox Christianity]; the church of the Second Rome, Constantinople, has been cut down by the axes of the infidel Turks; but the Church of the third new Rome, [Moscow] shines brighter than the Sun in the whole universe. . . . Two Romes have fallen, but the third stands fast; a fourth there will not be.[*]

. . .

The cold is rare, the people rude, the prince so full of pride,
The realm so stored with monks and nuns, and priests on every side,
The manners are so Turkey like, the men so full of guile,
The women wanton, Temples stuft with idols that defile
The seats that sacred ought to be, the customs are so quaint,
As if I would describe the whole, I fear my pen would faint,
Wild Irish are as civil as the Russies in their kind
Hard choice which is the best of both, each bloody, rude and blind.[*]

Then as now, Russians saw their country differently than did outside observers. In the first quotation, a sixteenth-century monk sees Moscow's acquisition of the Byzantine heritage making it the "third Rome" and the guardian of Orthodoxy. In the second, an English visitor considers the Russians barbarians and unflatteringly equates them with the Irish and the Turks.

[*]Letter from Abbot Philotheus of Pskov to Basil III, adapted from Thorton Anderson, *Russian Political Thought* (Ithaca, N.Y.: Cornell University Press, 1967), p. 72. Poem cited without additional information in Richard S. Dunn, *The Age of Religious Wars, 1559–1715*, 2d ed. (New York, W. W. Norton, 1971), p. 69.

1256) inherited the western Mongol lands and sought to enlarge them. He mounted a westward expedition during 1236–1241 that produced widespread destruction throughout Russia, Poland, Hungary, and Bulgaria. Their skillfully planned, long-distance troop movements, swift horses, and unfamiliar tactics gave the Mongols decisive victories; they also employed smoke screens and gunpowder against their European foes.

Batu's followers, known from the color of his tent as the Golden Horde, settled on the lower Volga River and dominated Russia for two centuries. The Horde exercised suzerainty over Russian lands, collected tribute, and levied military contingents. The Mongols allowed Russian princes autonomy, however, and permitted them to retain control of their territories. By embracing Islam soon after 1300, the Golden Horde separated itself from the Christian Russians, but granted toleration, privileges, and protection to the Russian church. The Mongol domination had the important effect of reducing Russian contacts with Byzantine civilization and isolating Russia from the Renaissance, thus assuring a distinctive development.

From Moscow Princes to Russian Tsars

The autocratic princes of Moscow, an important Suzdal market town and trading center, adroitly used Mongol policies to become the founders of a new Russian state. By serving as peace enforcers and tribute collectors for Russia's Mongol rulers, they gained authority over nearby Russian states and wealth for themselves. The metropolitan bishops of the Russian church made Moscow their headquarters shortly after 1300 and supported the Moscow princes' efforts to establish control. The church promoted unity among Slavic Christians and hoped that a strong Moscow might overthrow the Mongol domination. Moscow's victory over the Mongols in the Battle of Kulikovo in 1380 started a period of power intrigues and civil wars that split the Golden Horde into three states and freed Russian from the "Tartar yoke."

During the fifteenth century, Moscow continued to expand in every direction. Building on the achievements of his predecessors, Moscow's Prince Ivan III (1462–1505) subjected other Russian princes to his rule and transformed the principality of Moscow into the Russian state. He repudiated Mongol authority and stopped tribute payments. Moreover, he tripled the territory under his control by annexing several Russian principalities and conquering Novgorod and various Lithuanian-held lands.

Ivan also identified Russia as the cultural heir of the recently conquered Byzantine Empire. He made the Russian church independent of

Constantinople and established it as the defender of the true Orthodox faith. His marriage to Zoe, niece of the last Byzantine emperor, and adoption of the Byzantine imperial emblem, the double-headed eagle, and Byzantine court ceremonial helped consolidate this identification. Ivan added Byzantine political prestige to his military-based state and termed himself tsar (caesar or emperor) of all the Russians. He saw himself as the successor of the Byzantine emperors and regarded Moscow as the new center of Orthodox civilization, replacing Constantinople.

During the sixteenth century, Russian territorial expansion continued. Ivan III's grandson Ivan IV (1533–1584), the Terrible, the first Russian ruler to be crowned tsar, defeated two

St. Basil's Cathedral, Moscow. Built by Ivan IV to celebrate his victories, the cathedral displays traditional Russian and Byzantine architectural styles. Its contrast with contemporary Renaissance architecture is apparent, especially in the exotic domes, which are painted in brilliant and sharply contrasting colors.

of the Golden Horde successor states and won control of the entire Volga River. He also gained an outlet on the Baltic Sea and launched Russian penetration into Siberia.

Because the Russian state was created by conquest, the Russian princes imposed the laws and institutions of Moscow on the entire empire and endeavored to eliminate local variations. The state was viewed as the tsar's personal patrimony rather than a national community. Like western monarchs, the tsars sought consent for their important decisions from a council of nobles, and to broaden support for his program Ivan IV introduced a national assembly composed of clergy, great nobles, lesser nobles, and townsmen. Governors were appointed to administer individual provinces, but they often escaped from the control of the central government. Local government worked through assemblies that dealt

with judicial, financial, and administrative matters and elected local officials.

To weaken the power of the hereditary nobility, Ivan granted newly conquered lands as nonhereditary military fiefs and produced a lesser, service nobility that became the most powerful class in the state. To ensure a supply of workers for those lands and steady revenues for the tsars, owners and tsars together imposed a rigorous serfdom on the formerly free Russian peasants.

Russian literature and art during these centuries were dominated by Eastern Orthodox Christianity, and an overpowering reverence for tradition and form crushed creative efforts in arts and learning. Christian literature consisted primarily of translations in a formal written language known as Old Church Slavonic, featuring sermons and saints' lives. The only important example of secular lit-

erature from the period is the lively *Tale of the Host of Igor*, a poetic account of a prince's unsuccessful campaign against a foe. Church building followed established Byzantine architectural patterns until the end of the fifteenth century, when Ivan III imported Italian architects who combined Italian Renaissance design with features borrowed from Russian wooden churches. The new style produced impressive sixteenth-century buildings, but was stifled as a result of strong protests from church leaders and government officials. Painting became free from Byzantine influence earlier and gradually produced figures with more movement and a greater inner warmth. Individual icon painters, such as Andrei Rublev, (c. 1360–1430) became both skillful and famous. But in painting as in architecture, strong reactions among the powerful in church and state halted this pattern of artistic development.

SUMMARY

During the fifteenth and sixteenth centuries national monarchies developed in the west and pluralistic empires in the east of Europe. National monarchies established territorial unity and centralized governmental functions, and overcame the opposition of the nobles by allying with towns and relying on non-noble advisers and bureaucrats.

Strong national monarchies in England and France were shaped by the Hundred Years' War. In England, Parliament gained prominence and became part of the governmental ma-

chinery, but Tudor monarchs, beginning with Henry VII, controlled it to royal advantage as they reasserted royal power. In France, the Estates General remained unimportant as kings relied on local assemblies, and Louis XI advanced France's territorial consolidation by absorbing the *appanages* and eliminating Burgundy.

In the Iberian Peninsula, Portugal and Spain became strong national monarchies. Kings in Portugal crushed the power of nobles and used wealth from their overseas empire to rule without the Cortes. Spain was cre-

ated by the marriage of Ferdinand and Isabella and the joining of their kingdoms in a personal union, in which Castile was the senior partner. They curbed the nobles' power, controlled the church, and received the support of the towns.

The pluralistic empires of the Ottoman Turks and Russia were not national but incorporated both European and Asiatic populations. The Ottoman Turks profited from the disintegration of the Byzantine Empire to conquer it and the Balkan states, and modeled their governmental structure on Byzantine autocracy. Russia emerged after the breakup of the Kievan state and the Mongol invasions. Princes of Moscow asserted their authority and expanded their territory, claiming to be the heirs of the Byzantine Empire and the leaders of Orthodox civilization. The tsars established a powerful lesser nobility and a rigorous serfdom.

Not all European areas possessed the unity achieved by national monarchies and pluralistic empires. Many still lived in lands that were parts of some dynast's personal holdings or in other territories that failed to become national states during this period.

SELECTED SOURCES

*Coles, Paul. *The Ottoman Impact on Europe.* 1968. Well-illustrated, easy to read account of this important but neglected topic.

Commynes, Philip de. *Memoirs.* edited by Samuel Kinser. Translated by Isabelle Cazeaux. 1969. Best contemporary source for Louis XI's policies and Burgundy's rise and fall; gossipy and opinionated.

Costain, Thomas B. *The Moneyman.* 1947. Historical novel based on the life of noted fifteenth-century French merchant Jacques Coeur.

*Davies, R. Trevor. *The Golden Century of Spain, 1501–1621.* 1961. Clear and convincing account of this age of Spanish greatness.

Fennell, John L. I. *Ivan the Great of Moscow.* 1961. Focuses on diplomatic and military events in the rapid rise of Moscow under Ivan III.

Grey, Ian. *Ivan the Terrible.* 1964. Readable, sympathetic biography of this often misunderstood ruler; also the title of a 1944 film by Sergei Eisenstein correlating Ivan's career with Stalin's.

Inalcik, Halil. *The Ottoman Empire: The Classical Age, 1300–1600.* 2d ed. 1983. Comprehensive study of the central centuries of the empire by a noted Turkish historian; treats structures and institutions as well as events.

*Pernoud, Régine. *Joan of Arc, by Herself and Her Witnesses.* Translated by Edward Hyams. 1969. A powerful biography, drawn from Joan's trial testimony and other contemporary accounts; the film *Joan of Arc* (1948) adapts Maxwell Anderson's play and stars Ingrid Bergman.

*Perroy, Edouard. *The Hundred Years' War.* 1965. Best book on this topic, excellently combines social and political history with military events.

*Read, Conyers. *The Tudors: Personalities and Practical Politics in the Sixteenth Century.* 1969. Biographical sketches of each of the Tudor rulers, showing both their personalities and their political skills.

*Available in paperback.

DYNASTIC STATES AND THE QUEST FOR NATIONAL MONARCHY (1350–1600)

You acknowledge the emperor as your king and lord, but he seems only to rule on sufferance, and his power amounts to nothing. You obey him only so far as you wish, and this is very little indeed. Liberty is pleasing to everyone and neither cities nor princes render to the emperor what is due to him; he has no revenue and no treasury. Everyone wishes to be the manager and arbiter of his own affairs, hence the constant quarrels and perpetual wars which rage in your midst, from whence there arise pillage, slaughter, conflagration and a thousand other kinds of evil.

In this passage, the future Pope Pius II (1458–1464) clearly analyzed political conditions in fifteenth-century Germany. As discussed earlier, the conflict between popes and emperors had by the mid-thirteenth century destroyed the Holy Roman Empire as a viable political entity. Instead, nobles, prelates, and towns in both Germany and Italy gained political power, rendering the emperor politically insignificant. In that setting, no single ruler could amass enough power to establish a national monarchy in either Germany or Italy, and no emperor could achieve the centralized autocracy of his Ottoman or Russian contemporaries.

Similar problems afflicted Germany's Scandinavian and Slavic neighbors to the north and east. In those lands, attempts to unite several territories into empires proved fragile and temporary, and efforts to create national monarchies foundered on the opposition of the nobles. Invasions and warfare between rulers of those lands kept them dependent on the nobles; thus the nobles gained and retained political power. The nobles kept monarchies elective rather than hereditary, and often chose foreign princes as kings to control them more easily. Unlike the western monarchs, Scandinavian and Slavic kings lacked a middle class to counter the nobles' power, because the modest commercial activity and urban life in those

Emperor Charles V. Although he needed to spend much time administering his far-flung lands, the emperor was frequently on the move to counter his numerous foes. Titian has captured here that militant aspect of Charles's activity. Prado Museum, Madrid.

lands were controlled by German traders who retained much autonomy. Hence the quest for national monarchy, and even national unity, was generally unsuccessful in Germany and Italy and in Scandinavian and Slavic lands.

DYNASTIC STATES

In the Germanic, Italian, Scandinavian, and Slavic areas of central Europe, politically ambitious rulers created neither national monarchies nor pluralistic empires but dynastic states. Unlike the well-developed governmental institutions of the national monarchy, the focus of government and the basis for political organization in the dynastic state was allegiance to an individual ruler or to a dynasty. Instead of sharing a common language and customs, a dynastic state might comprise a varied collection of territories, resembling a pluralistic empire. But unlike the centralized empires, dynastic states were typically very decentralized. The various territories owing allegiance to a ruler ordinarily retained their own institutions, laws, and customs. Hence a dynastic state was frequently weaker than its extensive territories might indicate.

Dynastic rulers concentrated both their foreign and domestic policies on making desirable marriages for themselves and their children to increase the wealth and prestige of their families, while trying to prevent others from doing the same. By means of marriage, they attempted to gain additional territories for themselves or their descendants and often fought wars to confirm their claims to inherit lands. The accidents of birth and death frequently produced startling changes in dynastic arrangements, leading to astonishing successes as well as distressing failures.

Although dynasts attempted to employ the successful practices of national monarchies to integrate their territories, dynastic states tended to remain unstable. The three most important centralizing institutions of national monarchies, the church, the bureaucracy, and the military, each presented problems for dynastic rulers. Religious reform movements in the fifteenth and sixteenth centuries often placed subjects in opposition to their rulers and made the ruler's control of church appointments and revenues an uncertain means of promoting unity. The number of royal officials in bureaucracies was small in proportion to the population, and kings could not always control their officials effectively. Royal armies likewise were relatively small; often they were effectively opposed by armed nobles and town militias. Moreover, the nobles and lower classes who composed the royal armies often proved disloyal, and foreign mercenaries obeyed the officers who paid them rather than the king.

In the absence of strong armies or institutions, rulers depended heavily on attaining and maintaining popular support. One way of doing so was to restore order after periods of warfare. Another was to travel widely to remain in close contact with the inhabitants of their various territories. Ceremonial displays impressed subjects with royal power and splendor. In spite of uncertain effects, rulers controlled appointments to high positions in church and government and awarded those offices, as well as many other privileges and favors, to loyal and faithful supporters. Rulers might also win popular support by using representative institutions to explain their policies and to affirm their authority.

Dynastic states might, of course, become national monarchies under favorable circumstances. England became a national state as its rulers lost personal possessions in France by a series of wars. Earlier marriage alliances had failed to produce Spanish national unity, but the union of Ferdinand and Isabella did so, although resistance to that union remained strong for some time. Although dynastic connections between scattered territories did at times prove long-lasting, national monarchies backed by the homogeneous populations and compact territories supportive of monarchical governments were generally more successful. The successes of dynasticism and its failures to achieve national monarchies in central Europe would be very important for the future.

GERMANY AND BURGUNDY

Germany and Burgundy were two examples of territories that seemed likely to become strong states but failed to do so. The destruction of the Hohenstaufen family brought both the significance of the imperial office and the hope of uniting Germany to an end—600 years would pass before German unification and the German Empire became realities. Burgundy briefly appeared likely to become western Europe's strongest state in the fifteenth century; instead, it gained a prominent place on the list of history's might-have-beens.

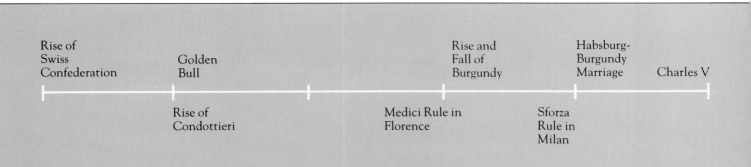

1300	1350	1400	1450	1500	1550

Rise of Swiss Confederation

Golden Bull

Rise and Fall of Burgundy

Habsburg-Burgundy Marriage

Charles V

Rise of Condottieri

Medici Rule in Florence

Sforza Rule in Milan

The Decline of Imperial Power

During the century following the death of Frederick II, strength drained from the emperor and flowed to the German princes. After the death of Frederick II's son in 1254, the imperial throne remained vacant for twenty years. Thereafter, emperors were elected because of their weakness and their willingness to pay for the electors' votes. The princes of the empire shifted the imperial office from one family to another until their own power was firmly established. The transfer of rule to new families destroyed continuity in imperial administration, as each time a new family assumed the title, new officials were installed. The triumph of the princes was confirmed in the 1356 Golden Bull (an imperial edict bearing a golden seal). The Golden Bull clarified the election process and eliminated papal interference in imperial elections by specifying seven lay and ecclesiastical princes, now designated "electors," as the only ones who could elect an emperor. It also confirmed the territorial integrity of the electors' lands and made them almost completely independent of imperial control. Other lay and ecclesiastical lords within the empire promptly assumed similar privileges and immunities; cities and knights also became more independent. Lacking authority within the empire, the emperors devoted their efforts to increasing their own domains, usually inside and beyond Germany's eastern borders, and to advancing the fortunes of their families.

The Growth of Princely States

After 1356, the history of Germany becomes the history of its principalities. For another century, virtual anarchy existed as princes warred with one another and divided their inheritances into ever smaller states. Towns and knights sought to free themselves from princely rule, but were hampered by economic difficulties, princely usurpation of authority, and the growing use of mercenaries. Economic problems forced many lesser nobles to become robber barons, and leagues of towns were formed to protect against them. Many imperial territories passed into the control of other powers or became partly or completely independent. Noteworthy in this latter category were the previously mentioned German Hansa and the Swiss Confederation, a group of Alpine regions and communities that emerged as a mutual defense league in 1291 but subsequently threw off the suzerainty of its princely overlords and gained eventual independence.

Many Germans moved eastward during this troubled period. German knights crusaded against non-Christian, mostly Slavic peoples living east of the Oder River and introduced Christianity there. The Teutonic Knights, a German military crusading order, and later German nobles acquired lands and established feudal lordships in territories stretching along the Baltic coast from Brandenburg to the Gulf of Finland. Their eastward advance was halted by the Russians under Alexander Nevsky in 1242, when he defeated them in a winter battle on the ice of frozen Lake Peipus, west of Novgorod.

German peasants and merchants quickly settled in the conquered lands along the Baltic, producing a network of villages and towns that soon became trading centers and joined the German Hansa. German settlers also pushed into other east central European lands, forming towns and providing services for the local agricultural populations. German eastward expansion produced an enduring legacy of hostility between Germans and Slavs.

By the fifteenth century, the balance of power within the Holy Ro-

GERMANS SEEK TO CHRISTIANIZE SLAVS

No people is more distinguished in its hospitality [than] the Slavs, [who] have many forms of idol worship. Some display in the temples fantastically formed images; other deities live in the woods and groves. But they admit that there is one god in the heavens ruling over the others.

[When] the lord bishop exhorted the [Slavs] to give up their idols and worship the one God, to receive baptism and renounce their evil works, [they] said: "Your princes burden us so severely with taxes and labor services that death is better for us than life. How, therefore, shall we be free to build churches for this new religion and to receive baptism?"

The lord bishop replied: "Our princes think it proper to treat harshly those who worship idols and are without God. Indeed, as you alone differ from the

religion of all, so you are subject to the plundering of all." [The Slavs] said: "Grant us German property rights and German tax rates and we shall willingly be Christians, build churches, and pay our tithes."*

These selections from the account of a twelfth-century German chronicler indicate German views of Slavs, Slav experiences of Germans, and German missionary methods. The Germans persistently treated the Slavs as subjects to be exploited, rather than as equals. Hence German expansion into Slav territories remained a disruptive force in east central European areas into the twentieth century.

*Helmold, *Chronicle of the Slavs*, trans. F. J. Tschan (New York: Columbia University Press, 1935).

man Empire was shifting eastward to Austria, Bohemia, and Brandenburg. Here strong princes ruled substantial territories and managed to establish firm governments modeled after the strong national monarchies. They used the practice of primogeniture, inheritance by the eldest son, to concentrate power and resources, and enlarged their territories by marriages and warfare. They maintained effective armies and created vigorous councils, specialized bureaucracies, and more efficient taxing systems. These three states had developed active economies, and not only possessed the military strength to resist warlike powers on their frontiers but

also in many cases were able to expand against their neighbors.

Burgundy

The possibilities and limitations of dynastic state building can be seen in the contrasting fortunes of two territories and families in the Holy Roman Empire, the Burgundians and the Habsburgs. Established as an *appanage* for a younger son of the French royal family, Burgundy grew to include Flanders and most provinces of the Netherlands, Burgundies in both France and the Holy Roman Empire, and numerous territories along the Rhine Valley. Fifteenth-century dukes

of Burgundy sought to unite those scattered lands into a compact block of territories from Switzerland to the North Sea and to obtain a royal crown from the emperor.

The Burgundian rulers failed in both ventures, however. Unlike the national monarchies, which had a tradition of loyalty to the crown and to the monarchical principle, political loyalties in Burgundian territories were purely personal, and the dukes were unable to institutionalize that personal power. Consequently, no office could be abstracted from the duke's titles, no name applied to all their territories, and no political self-consciousness developed. When the duke died without male heirs in 1477, the Burgundian state disintegrated.

Charles V and the Habsburg Inheritance

The collapse of the Burgundian state contributed to the astonishingly successful dynastic achievements of the Habsburgs. In the thirteenth century, the Habsburgs, already an illustrious Swabian family, laid the basis for their future prominence by wresting control of Austria and other nearby lands from the king of Bohemia. The next steps in their ascent were classic examples of dynastic marriage. The daughter of the last Burgundian duke married Maximilian, son of the holy Roman emperor and later (1493–1519) emperor himself. The marriage of their son to the daughter of Ferdinand and Isabella of Spain gave their grandson Charles V (1519–1556) an inheritance that included Austria, the Netherlands and other Burgundian lands, Spain, and the Spanish Empire in the Americas (see Map 38). As a result of other Habsburg marriage al-

Duke Philip the Good of Burgundy, Architect of Burgundian Greatness, with His Son and Successor, Charles the Bold. Wealth and luxury abounded at Philip's court, although the duke himself dressed simply. The Burgundian court was a major fifteenth-century center of European literary and artistic achievement. French manuscript drawing, fifteenth century.

Family Tree of Emperor Charles V.

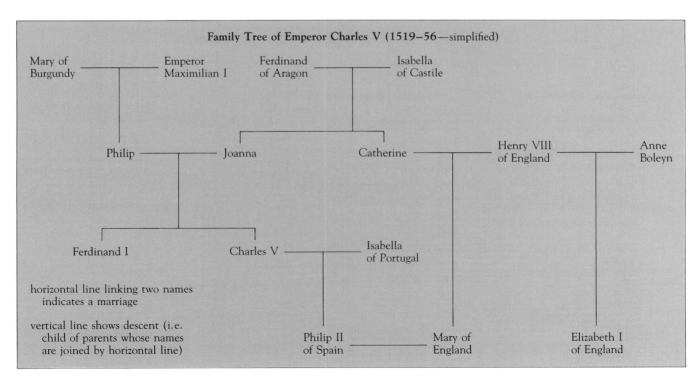

Family Tree of Emperor Charles V (1519–56—simplified)

Mary of Burgundy ——— Emperor Maximilian I

Ferdinand of Aragon ——— Isabella of Castile

Philip ——— Joanna

Catherine ——— Henry VIII of England ——— Anne Boleyn

Ferdinand I

Charles V ——— Isabella of Portugal

horizontal line linking two names indicates a marriage

vertical line shows descent (i.e. child of parents whose names are joined by horizontal line)

Philip II of Spain ——— Mary of England

Elizabeth I of England

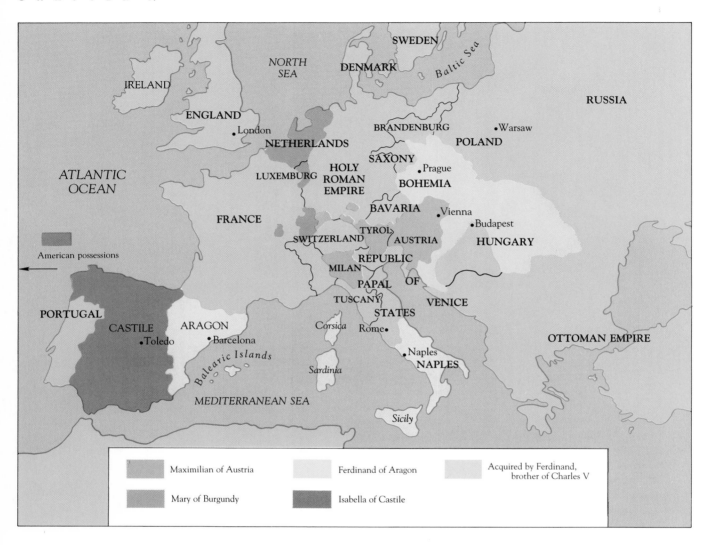

MAP 38
The Holy Roman Empire. A remarkable series of marriages made Charles V Europe's most prominent sixteenth-century ruler. The map shows the territories he acquired from each of his grandparents. It is easy to see why France feared encirclement by the Habsburgs during Charles V's reign.

liances, Charles's brother Ferdinand acquired Bohemia and Hungary when their king died in battle with the Turks. As a contemporary observed, "Others war to acquire territories, you, fortunate Austria, marry."

The vast empire Charles nominally ruled was, in actuality, less than the sum of its parts. He had to deal with a variety of governmental structures, and was continually negotiating with areas of his empire to gain

recognition of his authority over them or to obtain soldiers and support for his campaigns. His territorial princes refused to surrender any of their authority to permit creation of an imperial administrative structure and dominated the imperial parliament and the emperor's governing council. They also thwarted efforts to establish an imperial army and an imperial court system. Charles created no administrative machinery to unify the areas he inherited, nor did he have a central treasury to manage taxes and expenditures. His primary sources of money were gold and silver from Spain's American possessions and the wealth produced by manufacture and trade in the Netherlands.

The many emergencies he faced forced Charles V to travel constantly from one trouble spot to another and prevented him from dealing in a timely and thorough manner with any problem. The Reformation accelerated decentralization: Protestant princes had additional reasons for resisting the emperor, and Catholic princes were reluctant to help the emperor subdue the Protestants lest he subsequently attempt to dominate them.

Exhausted by his efforts to govern his scattered lands, Charles abdicated in 1556 and divided his territories. He left Austria to his brother Ferdinand, who became holy Roman emperor, and Spain and the Burgundian territories to his son, Philip II (1556–1598). Without the Burgundian lands, Austria lacked the resources to maintain the imperial office, and with Burgundian money Philip became involved in a bitter civil and religious war.

ITALY

The failure of Frederick II's unification efforts had left Italy, like Germany, disunited and fragmented. Three blocks of territory emerged from this confusion: a southern kingdom comprising Sicily and south Italy, the Papal States in the center of the peninsula, and the lands stretching north of the Papal States to the Alps, where city-states flourished. Although the unification of Italy was an avowed goal of both thinkers and doers, it was not achieved until the nineteenth century.

South Italy and the Papal States

Although most of Italy passed from imperial control shortly after 1300, the hope or threat of imperial interference in Italy remained, creating pro- and anti-imperial factions in each state. In the Papal States and the south Italian kingdom, political patterns resembled those of western monarchies, with an effort to balance the prerogatives of both monarchs and nobles. Thirteenth-century wars between popes and emperors, however, transformed Sicily from the wealthiest and most cultured land in Europe to a pauperized and divided territory that eventually came under the control of the kings of Aragon. The Aragonese in the fifteenth century also held the southern mainland of Italy as a separate kingdom centering on Naples.

In the center of the peninsula, the Papal States formed a unified block of territory, but the absence of the popes in Avignon during the fourteenth century and their financial concessions in the conciliar movement weakened their rule. Although fifteenth-century popes attempted to strengthen their control by appointing relatives to key administrative posts and raising mercenary armies, the elective nature of their office and their inability to establish hereditary succession was a persistent source of weakness.

North Italian City-States

In northern Italy, an area of manufacturing and trading cities, the breakdown of imperial authority and the removal of the popes to Avignon left Italians free to manage their own affairs, and city-states exhibiting a variety of political forms developed. These city-states removed politics from ecclesiastical control and emphasized civic responsibility and concern for public welfare. Their social structure included four classes: nobles, wealthy merchants, members of craft and shopkeeper guilds, and day laborers. In internal power struggles, the wealthy merchants, supported by members of the lesser guilds, gradually forced the powerful nobles to surrender their lands and powers. However, party strife within the cities and alliances between them frequently produced a sequence of conflicts, conquests, and temporary truces that disrupted commerce and industry.

To overcome party strife, cities experimented with appointed chief magistrates, but soon accepted popularly elected *condottieri* (military commanders), often of noble origin, as despots or absolute rulers. Some of these despots succeeded in making their positions hereditary, legitimizing them by purchasing the titles of vicar or duke from the emperor. They increased wealth in their city-states, promoted trade, and encouraged literature and art. By the fifteenth century, such rulers formed a new class of great nobles, ruling their territorial states as vassals of popes or emperors and arranging marriage and military alliances among themselves.

The three leading Italian cities, Venice, Milan, and Florence, each had a distinctive form of government, and by 1454 had conquered virtually all of the other north Italian cities and towns. Venice, freed from foreign threats and the rule of feudal nobles by its island location, was governed by a merchant oligarchy composed of 200 families, exercising power through a grand council that elected the senate, the cabinet, and the *doge,* or duke. In Florence, Cosimo di Medici (1434–1464), head of a family of merchant bankers who obtained support from lesser guilds and workers, seized control in 1434 of a complex, theoretically republican system that had in fact become dominated by the

wealthy. The Medici made Florence the capital of the Italian Renaissance.

In Milan, the nobles triumphed over the guilds before 1300, and the Visconti family dominated the city almost continuously until 1447. Soon after, Francesco Sforza (1450–1466) a mercenary commander, seized control and became dictator, establishing a dynastic despotism, maintaining a brilliant court, and keeping his position by a vigorous program of public works and military expenditures. Milan's example of a ruler exercising direct personal control that was largely independent of traditional institutions was widely emulated. The 1494

request of Ludovico Sforza (1479–1500) for French aid against Milan's foes, however, began the lengthy Italian wars that brought an end to the city-states.

SCANDINAVIA

In addition to the great states of England, France, and the Holy Roman Empire, lesser European political entities emerged during the medieval period. Monarchies in Scandinavia, for example, sought to emulate their grander neighbors and adopted the

The Gattamelata Monument. The first full-size equestrian statue made in Europe since Roman times, by Donatello, shows an Italian despot ready for war. Piazza del Santo, Padua.

latter's practices to help them do so. Neither feudal nor national monarchies, however, flourished in Scandinavia.

Medieval Developments

During the medieval period, the three Scandinavian lands of Denmark, Norway, and Sweden, now Christian monarchies, were dominated by the nobility. The agricultural economy of the Scandinavian lands, leaving limited scope for trade and towns, favored aristocratic rule. Monarchs generally obtained the support of the church, but relied on nobles to perform military and administrative services. In return, the nobles received tax exemptions, offices, and lands.

Denmark was the strongest Scandinavian state in this period, and a series of able rulers during the twelfth and thirteenth centuries made the monarchy strong enough to conquer territories east of the Baltic. In the thirteenth century, however, civil war between contenders for the throne and struggles between kings and church weakened the Danish monarchy. Thus in 1282, nobles and clergy obtained a royal charter confirming their lands and privileges and establishing a national assembly to control the king. During the fourteenth century, nobles drove a king from the throne.

In Norway and Sweden, the nobles remained strong in relation to the crown, and the rulers of those two lands never attained the power enjoyed by the kings of Denmark. Rugged terrain and frequent dynastic struggles rendered unification difficult in Norway, allowing nobles to gain power and lands. Thirteenth-century Norwegian rulers dissipated

royal strength in unsuccessful wars, and were forced to permit German merchants to trade freely throughout the kingdom. Nobles were similarly dominant in Sweden. Like Denmark, Sweden expanded eastward and acquired Finland in the twelfth century, but was repulsed in its attempts to invade Russia in 1240 by the same Alexander Nevsky who defeated a German attack on Russia two years later. The rule of a child king in Norway and Sweden after 1319 diminished royal power in both lands, enabling Swedish nobles to gain power and authority and to hold their first parliament in 1359.

With the breakdown of imperial authority in the Holy Roman Empire, Germans pursued interests and opportunities outside the empire and intensified their influence in Scandinavia. German nobles obtained control of Scandinavian lands, and German merchants dominated Scandinavian trade, obtaining lucrative commercial privileges. The vigorous king of Denmark Waldemar IV (1340–1375) revived strong monarchic rule in his land by restricting the power of clergy and nobles and by breaking German influence. Through his wars, he gained control of southern Sweden and the key Baltic island of Gotland

---

AN ITALIAN PATRIOT SEEKS NATIONALITY

At present in Italy many things concur to favor a new ruler who may heal her wounds and cure her of those sores which have long been festering. Behold how she prays God to send someone to redeem her from this barbarous cruelty and insolence. Behold her ready and willing to follow any standard if only there be someone to raise it. . . .

This opportunity must not, therefore, be allowed to pass, so that Italy may at length find her liberator. I cannot express the love with which he would be received in all those provinces which have suffered under these foreign invasions, with what thirst for vengeance, with what steadfast faith, with what love, with what grateful tears. . . . What Italian would withhold allegiance? This barbarous domination stinks in the nostrils of everyone! May your illustrious [Medici] house therefore assume this task, so that under its banner our fatherland

may be raised up, and Petrarch's saying be proved true:

Valor against fell wrath
  Will take up arms; and be the
    combat quickly sped!
For, sure, the ancient worth,
That in Italians stirs the heart,
  is not yet dead. *

With this passionate outburst of national sentiment, Niccolo Machiavelli (1469–1529) concluded his little book The Prince. *He hoped that its recipient, the Medici prince Lorenzo, might lead a campaign to oust the foreigners and unite Italy. Machiavelli's dream of Italian unity was not realized until 350 years later.*

*Niccolo Machiavelli, *The Prince,* trans. Luigi Ricci, rev. E. R. P. Vincent (New York, Mentor/New American Library, 1952), pp. 124–27.

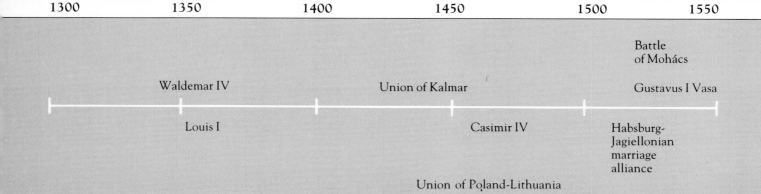

1300	1350	1400	1450	1500	1550

Battle of Mohács

Waldemar IV   Union of Kalmar   Gustavus I Vasa

Louis I   Casimir IV   Habsburg-Jagiellonian marriage alliance

Union of Poland-Lithuania

and threatened the Baltic trade monopoly of the German Hansa. But despite early Danish successes, the German towns triumphed, retained their economic dominance and privileges, and gained the right to intervene in Danish internal affairs.

The Union of Kalmar

The growth of German influence and economic exploitation by the German towns stimulated Scandinavian opposition to the Germans and contributed to a willingness to unite against them. At the same time, however, international marriages among the Scandinavian nobility intensified their pursuit of family interests at the expense of national patriotism. Such nobles readily acquiesced in both Scandinavian union and foreign rule.

Waldemar IV's daughter Margaret (1387–1412) was able to combine the Scandinavian lands in a personal union. Regent of Denmark for her young son since her father's death, she became regent for him in Norway in 1380 on the death of her husband, Norway's king. When the boy died in 1387, she became ruler of both lands, and in the following year Swedish nobles elected her to replace

their recently deposed king. To formalize that union, nobles from the three states met at Kalmar in 1397 and agreed that the states would act jointly for their mutual interests, but would remain separate entities and retain their own institutions and officers.

The dynastic consolidation achieved in the Union of Kalmar proved too weak to establish a permanently united Scandinavian state. It flourished during the early fifteenth century with able leadership from Danish rulers and strong support from Swedish nobles. But Swedish peasants resented the heavy taxes levied by alien rulers, and resistance to Danish dominance grew. Also, Sweden had important mining and industrial interests, and trade and urbanization were more developed there than in Norway, contributing to Sweden's disaffection. During the later fifteenth century, the union grew increasingly uneasy and collapsed when a strong Danish king pursued repressive policies and provoked a revolt (1520–1523) that drove Sweden from the union. Norway and Denmark, however, remained united until 1814, and the Scandinavian lands deepened their mutual affinities by adopting Lutheranism.

Swedish Separation

The Swedish revolt that ended the Union of Kalmar revived the Swedish national monarchy, as one of the nobles who led the revolt against the Danes became King Gustavus I Vasa (1523–1560). By following a successful policy of Baltic expansion, Sweden temporarily gained the status of a great power. The Swedes ended the German Hansa's trade monopoly in the Baltic, and during the sixteenth century conquered Estonia, Livonia, and adjoining territories around the Gulf of Finland (see Map 39). Sweden also gained three small territories from the Holy Roman Empire by the Treaty of Westphalia, which ended the Thirty Years' War in 1648.

Sweden enjoyed an admirable social stability, but even with its extensive territorial holdings it lacked the economic and human resources to remain a great power. Unlike eastern European lands, Sweden had no serfs. Swedish peasants owned half of the nation's farmland and had their own chamber in the national assembly. The nobility were poorer and less privileged than those in other European states, and although they possessed political leadership and large farms, their life-style was not greatly different from that of the peasants. Kings recruited nobles for administrative service, maintained the loyalty of town dwellers and clergy, and financed military operations from port charges and customs duties, thereby keeping taxes low.

EAST CENTRAL EUROPE

In east central Europe, the quest for unity was an important theme of the region's history from early medieval times. Slavic leaders sought some union, usually by conquest or mar-

riage, that would unite all Slavs to resist the relentless pressure of the Germans from the west. German leaders, however, had a vision of Slavic union under German overlordship. Each approach enjoyed success; together they determined the history of this region for many centuries.

Weak Kings and Powerful Nobles

Two major Slav states, Bohemia and Poland, emerged during the tenth century, accepted Christianity, and sought to remain free of German control while uniting the western Slavs. However, eleventh-century holy Ro-

man emperors thwarted Polish efforts to achieve unity and forced their overlordship on Bohemia. During the twelfth and thirteenth centuries, nobles attained political dominance in both lands, elected and deposed kings, and gained lands, privileges, and concessions. Immigrating German settlers and Jews increased agricultural production and restored trade and town life, but instead of counteracting the power of the nobles as the rulers desired, those immigrants created towns that were either virtually autonomous or else controlled by nobles, as in the case of the Jewish *shtetelm* ("little towns").

Hungary, a non-Slav state, suc-

MAP 39
Central and Eastern Europe. Dynastic unions characterized this region for several centuries. In the north, Denmark and Norway were united under one ruling family, while another controlled both Sweden and Finland. The Habsburg monarchy ruled Austria and other territories, and the Poland-Lithuania union formed for a time Europe's largest state.

Seal Hunters. Although Sweden became a national monarchy in the sixteenth century, its level of life hindered it from attaining great power status. An activity in which some Swedes engaged was hunting seals. From an old print.

cessfully rebuffed German expansionism and enlarged its territories during the medieval period. Its rulers recruited German settlers to develop agriculture, trade, and town life; they also admitted nomadic peoples to provide for frontier defense and ex-

panded southward to the Adriatic Sea. But during the thirteenth century, the Hungarian monarchs lost lands, power, and prestige to their nobles. The great nobles and higher clergy obtained large landholdings and exemption from taxes, and gained the

right to hold an annual assembly, whereas lesser nobility, organized in provisional governments, controlled the state's administration.

During the fourteenth century, some dynastic unions occurred in east central Europe. The energetic Bohemian king Ottokar II (1253–1278) nearly united much of that region under his rule but his defeat by the emperor gave the Habsburgs ascendancy there. His son and grandson briefly ruled Poland, Hungary, and Bohemia shortly after 1300, but the latter's early death without heirs ended that hope of unity. The death of a childless Polish ruler in 1370 united Poland and Hungary under one ruler, Louis I (1342–1382); however, on his death the two lands were again separated.

Jagiellonian Prominence

The most noteworthy dynastic state in east-central Europe came about through the union of Poland and Lithuania in the fourteenth century. The marriage of Louis's daughter Jadwiga to Lithuania's prince Jagiello (1377–1434) brought the prince and his people to Christianity and joined Poland and Lithuania in a Jagiellonian dynastic union that formed Europe's largest territorial unit. That union, however, was weak; it had no central government, skilled administrators, or functional political institutions. Moreover, Lithuania retained a separate grand duke, and Poland and Lithuania continued to have separate laws and customs. Nobles wielded political power in both lands and cooperated with the ruler only rarely, usually in military campaigns to expand their territories.

During the reign of Casimir IV (1447–1492) the union seemed strong. He was both king of Poland and grand duke of Lithuania and obtained west Prussia by decisively defeating the Teutonic Knights, while the easing of Mongol pressure permitted Lithuania to expand southeast into the Ukraine. To win the support of the lesser nobles against the great magnates, Casimir agreed to consult them in all matters of legislation or war and peace. He developed a national assembly, divided into a senate composed of magnates, royal officials, and high churchmen and a chamber of deputies representing the lesser nobility. Provincial assemblies of officials and nobles gradually became independent legislative bodies and obtained the right to mobilize the militia and to elect provincial officials, weakening royal power. Such power seemed temporarily enhanced when Casimir established his son as king of both Bohemia and Hungary, extending the Jagiellonian union to embrace all of east central Europe.

Polish Diet in Session. The diet or assembly permitted the nobility to control Poland's affairs. By extorting various concessions from prospective kings before electing them, the nobility seriously weakened the Polish monarchy.

Within a generation, however, the Austrian Habsburgs replaced the Jagiellonians in Bohemia and Hungary. A double marriage between the children of Habsburg and Jagiellonian families was celebrated in 1515. The subsequent death of the young Jagiellonian king of Hungary and Bohemia without heirs in battle against the Ottoman Turks at Mohács in 1526 terminated the separate monarchies of the two lands and delivered what remained of Hungary to the Habsburgs, who retained it into the twentieth century.

Although Poland and Lithuania remained under Jagiellonian rule, in the sixteenth century the lesser nobility emerged as the controllers of power. Polish kings lacked funds to enlarge the administration or develop an adequate army. They relied for defense on the lesser nobility, who extracted concessions in return for giving military assistance. This military class included about 8 percent of the population and controlled most of the land. They exercised central government powers through their provincial assemblies, ruined the towns by inept trade regulations, and reduced the peasants to serfdom. Lithuanian nobles, fearful of Russia, abandoned their autonomy and merged with the Polish nobles in 1569, and the Uniate church—which recognized papal authority but retained Eastern Orthodox rites and practices—created some religious unity. After the last Jagiellonian king died without heirs in 1572, foreigners sought the elective Polish crown, and the lesser nobles required each new ruler to confirm their privileges and to accept limitations on royal control.

During the latter part of the seventeenth century, this extreme insistence by the nobles on their independence produced a practice called the liberum (free) veto, by which any noble who disagreed with a resolution could defeat it by his negative vote and by that same action terminate the current session of the assembly. Such conditions made the Polish state so weak that it invited attack and dismemberment by neighboring powers.

SUMMARY

During the period 1300–1600, many European rulers tried to establish dynastic states. They sought to gain territory for themselves and their descendants by means of marriages and inheritances. Dynastic states were typically decentralized and tended to remain weak.

The collapse of strong imperial rule in the Holy Roman Empire facilitated dynastic state-building by imperial princes. The collection of territories known as Burgundy failed to endure, but fortunate marriages enabled the Habsburgs to build an astonishing dynastic empire, which reached its greatest extent under Charles V. In Italy, family dynasties controlled city-state territories.

In Scandinavia, Denmark was the strongest medieval kingdom, and Margaret of Denmark combined the Scandinavian lands in a personal union. But that union did not produce a permanently united state. Early in the sixteenth century, Sweden broke from the union and established a national monarchy.

In east central Europe, the quest for dynastic unity was an important theme of the region's history. Strong nobles kept kings weak and monarchies elective. Bohemia gradually became part of the Holy Roman Empire, whereas Poland and Hungary were briefly united in both the fourteenth and fifteenth centuries. About 1500, the Jagiellonian dynasty embraced all of east central Europe, but wars and deaths brought Hungary and Bohemia into Habsburg hands, and Jagiellonian rule of Poland and Lithuania ended in 1572. Although the European dynastic states enjoyed few political successes, they proved to be especially fertile soil for the development of the literary, intellectual, and artistic activity of the Renaissance.

SELECTED SOURCES

*Brandi, Karl. *The Emperor Charles V.* 1968. The foremost biography of the emperor, sympathetic and thorough.

Dvornik, Francis. *The Slavs in European History and Civilization.* 1962. Comprehensive treatment of Slavic political and cultural achievements, by a noted Czech scholar.

Halecki, Oscar. *Borderlands of Western Civilization: A History of East Central Europe.* 1952. Fast-paced survey of the region's history, written by a prominent Polish historian.

*Holborn, Hajo. *A History of Modern Germany,* vol. 1: *The Reformation.* 1982. The best history of sixteenth century Germany.

Koenigsberger, Helmut G. *The Habsburgs and Europe, 1516–1660.* 1971. Focuses on the careers of Charles V, Philip II of Spain, and the events of the Thirty Years' War.

*McNeill, William H. *Europe's Steppe Frontier, 1500–1800.* 1975. A stimulating interpretation of historical currents in southeast Europe by a first-rate historian.

Queen Christina. 1933. This film stars Greta Garbo as the seventeenth-century Swedish ruler who renounced the throne for her religion.

Roberts, Michael. *Gustavus Adolphus and the Rise of Sweden.* 1973. Fast-moving, well-informed portrayal of this great Swedish ruler.

Romeo and Juliet. 1968. Shakespeare's play presented in a historically authentic fifteenth-century Italian setting by prominent filmmaker Francesco Zefferelli.

Stavrianos, Leften S. *The Balkans Since 1453.* 1958. The most reliable treatment of the complex history of this European area.

*Available in paperback.

THE RENAISSANCE ERA
(1350–1600)

If then we are to call any age golden, it is beyond doubt that age which brings forth golden talents in different places. That such is true of our age, he who wishes to consider the illustrious discoveries of this century will hardly doubt. For this century, like a golden age, has restored to light the liberal arts, which were almost extinct: grammar, poetry, rhetoric, painting, sculpture, architecture, music . . . and all this in Florence. Achieving what had been honored among the ancients, but almost forgotten since, the age has joined wisdom with eloquence, and produce with the military art . . . and in Florence it has recalled the Platonic teaching from darkness into light.

The golden age that Florentine philosopher Marsilio Ficino describes in these words, the age of the Italian Renaissance (literally, rebirth), was, like the age of Pericles in Athens, a period of remarkable intellectual, literary, and artistic activity. Extending over three centuries from 1350 to 1600, the Renaissance drew inspiration from, and sought to emulate the achievements of, classical antiquity. Thinkers, writers, and artists of the Renaissance emphasized the manifold potentialities of human beings and aimed at the full and harmonious development of all the powers of both body and mind. Individualism and the attainment of personal distinction were encouraged. These Renaissance figures believed in the importance and delights of life in this world in contrast to traditional Christian preoccupation with human sinfulness and heavenly existence after this earthly life, and taught, in the words of a contemporary poet:

> Let him be happy who wishes to be so
> For nothing is certain about tomorrow.

In addition to its interest in classical civilization, however, the Renaissance was strongly influenced by contemporary developments. Voyages of exploration provided new information and new stimuli for writers and artists. A growing interest in science directed attention to the natural world and suggested new interpretations of observable phenomena. Capitalistic economic activity supplied the wealth needed to support the

CONTENTS

Cupola or Dome of the Florence Cathedral. This first domed structure in Europe in more than nine hundred years, by Brunelleschi, dominates the city's skyline. Rather than using the cathedral's proper name, local inhabitants often refer to it as "the Dome."

achievements of thinkers and artists. New political conceptions expressed by Italian thinkers like Marsilio of Padua (1290–1343) and Niccolo Machiavelli (1469–1527) removed the pope, the church, and apparently even moral considerations from politics; and rulers laboring to develop nation-states produced a new environment for intellectual and artistic endeavors.

For several reasons, the Renaissance developed first in Italy. Trade remained important in Italy throughout the medieval period, and furnished the material resources for cultural development. Urban life, with its rich variety of experiences, had persisted in Italy throughout the me-

dieval centuries and enjoyed renewed vigor in the wake of the crusades. Prominent commercial cities of north Italy, such as Milan, enjoyed almost complete autonomy and competed with one another in cultural as well as commercial affairs. The presence of the Roman artistic and architectural heritage and the use of Latin as a living language kept memories of classical civilization alive in Italy. Moreover, Italy benefited from the direct influence of both Islamic (via Sicily) and Byzantine cultures. The present chapter traces the growth and development of the Renaissance in Italy, and its subsequent extension to other European lands.

ITALIAN RENAISSANCE LITERATURE AND THOUGHT

One of the earliest manifestations of the Renaissance in Italy was the development of literature written in Italian. The strength of Latin usage there long inhibited the growth of Italian, and the political disunity of the peninsula produced regional dialects rather than a national language.

Tuscan Efflorescence

During the fourteenth century eloquent writers from Tuscany (the area

MAP 40
Renaissance Italy. The commercial vitality and political disunity of northern Italy stimulated cultural creativity. Prosperous towns patronized and promoted artists and scholars. A remarkable number of Italian cities significantly contributed to Renaissance thought, literature, and art.

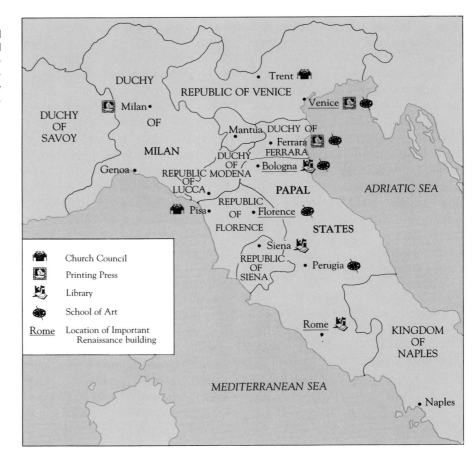

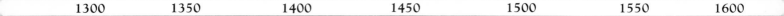

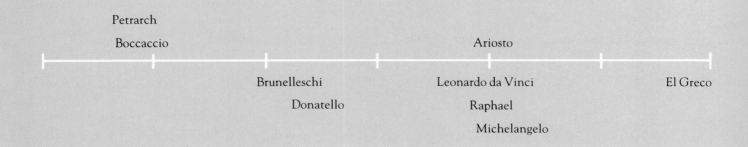

| 1300 | 1350 | 1400 | 1450 | 1500 | 1550 | 1600 |

Petrarch

Boccaccio

Ariosto

Brunelleschi

Leonardo da Vinci

El Greco

Donatello

Raphael

Michelangelo

around Florence) made their dialect the basis of the modern Italian language. Dante Alighieri, whose *Divine Comedy,* was a culmination of medieval thought and outlook, used Italian to express the deepest beliefs and sublimest thoughts of human beings, and did so with consummate poetic skill. He argued passionately for greater use of Italian in a tract entitled *On the Eloquence of the Common Language*. In addition to his masterpiece, he wrote love poems in Italian to one Beatrice, apparently his vision or dream of the ideal woman.

Less scholastic and allegorical and more human and this-worldly than Dante was another Tuscan writer, Francesco Petrarch (1304–1374), who produced outstanding lyric poetry. A keen observer of nature, his works communicated and stimulated interest and delight in the physical world. He wrote tender sonnets and exquisite odes in celebration of his love for Laura, a married woman with whom he became enamored after seeing her at mass, but who died of the plague. Although his poems are reminiscent of troubadour pleas for a lady's love and laments over its unattainability, Petrarch expresses real love for a living woman. He rhapsodizes over her physical features, devoting several poems to praise of her eyes or hands,

and imagines her in a variety of forms from water nymph to angelic being. Although his love is inspired by her physical beauty, he offers her only spiritual devotion, and the conflict between body and mind, emotion and reason, underlies his poems. Petrarch placed little value on his sonnets, but others found them appealingly passionate expressions of feeling.

As Petrarch perfected the sonnet, his friend Giovanni Boccaccio (1313–1375), the first great Italian prose writer, developed the short story form. His *Decameron* is a collection of 100 tales taken from other sources, marvelously recast as stories told by a group of ten young people who are passing the time in a rural estate while plague ravages Florence. The satires are concerned with everyday life and commonplace events and portray a variety of people from all social classes. With Boccaccio, the lustfulness and earthy wit of the lower classes enters sophisticated literature. The *Decameron* celebrates physical life and revels in carnal love, but breathes a spirit of love for humans and tolerance for their failures and weaknesses. It continues to delight readers by its literary skill, its satirical reflection of Italian life of the time, and its overall sense of humor. In contrast to Dante's *Divine Comedy*, it is some-

times termed the "Human Comedy." Boccaccio also wrote poems and romances based upon the triumphs and disasters of his very physical love for Maria; *Fiammetta*, which recounts his experiences with her, is a forerunner of the modern psychological novel.

Humanism in Literature and Thought

Despite their outstanding contributions to Italian literature, Petrarch and Boccaccio maintained that Latin was superior to Italian as a literary language and promoted a literary and cultural outlook known as humanism, which emphasized the study of literature, primarily from classical antiquity. They and other writers found in classical literature a style, form, and eloquence absent from most medieval literature, and they argued that to speak and write correctly one should imitate the ancients.

Petrarch, who developed the finest Latin style of his age, insisted that writers should imitate not only the literary style and form of the classical writers but also their language. He persuaded Boccaccio to write works on classical antiquity in Latin to teach both moral lessons and superior style, and other Renaissance writers followed Boccaccio's lead. Those suc-

A Humanist Finds a Manuscript

I truly believe that, if we had not come to the rescue, he [Quintilian] must speedily have perished; for it cannot be imagined that a man magnificent, polished, elegant, urbane, and witty could much longer have endured the squalor of the prison-house in which I found him. . . He was indeed right sad to look upon, and ragged, like a condemned criminal. . . . Hard indeed it was for him to bear, that he who had preserved the lives of many by his eloquence and aid, should now find no redresser of his wrongs, no savior from the unjust punishment awaiting him. [But by good fortune] in the middle of a well-stocked [monastery] library . . . we discovered Quintilian, safe as yet and sound, though covered with dust and filthy with neglect and age. The books, you must know, were not housed according to their worth, but were lying in a most foul and obscure dungeon at the very bottom of a tower, a place into which condemned criminals would hardly have been thrust. . . *

In these words, a leading humanist, Poggio Bracciolini (1380–1459), shared his delight on discovering a manuscript of the Institutions *of Quintilian, a noted Roman rhetorician and educator. His treatment of the manuscript as a person and his numerous word pictures are characteristic of humanist writing. Quintilian was a primary source of guidance for the well-rounded program of training humanists promoted to develop the full range of human qualities.*

*Letter from Bracciolini to a friend, quoted in John Addington Symonds, *Renaissance in Italy: The Revival of Learning* (New York: H. Holt and Company, 1888), pp. 135–136.

---

cessors, stimulated by the migration of Byzantine scholars to Italy after 1400, promoted the study of Greek as well as Latin language and literature.

An important aspect of humanist activity was the recovery of manuscripts of classical works. Rich merchants and patrons of learning competed with one another to acquire manuscripts and establish libraries. Searchers discovered many Latin manuscripts in European monasteries and churches. They obtained copies of Greek manuscripts through contacts with Byzantine scholars, and by translating them into Latin, they made Greek history and literature available to western scholars. The recently developed process of printing books with movable type, usually attributed to Johannes Gutenberg of Mainz about 1450, enormously aided their activity, enabling them to turn their energies from copying manuscripts to editing them.

Humanists studied the subjects the ancients emphasized and found in them a secular and individualistic attitude that shaped their own conception of how people should act. According to humanist teaching, one ruled one's own life, and success and failure depended on one's own abilities and accomplishments, particularly such qualities as talent, imagination, intelligence, ambition, and self-reliance. The humanist ideal was the "universal man," one who excels in many different fields.

Most humanists found employment as teachers in Italian cities, and their activities reshaped educational theory and practice. Although they taught grammar (which included poetry) and rhetoric (which included prose writing and public speaking), they also became teachers and writers of history and moral philosophy. The goal of education, they believed, was to produce persons whose actions expressed their individuality and who would lead good and useful lives in whatever careers they followed. They revised the Italian educational system to make classical training a principal ingredient of elementary and secondary education and established curricula that included classical literature, mathematics, music, and science. Those studies would develop the students' intellectual discipline, stimulate their imagination, and guide their moral conduct. Athletics and outdoor activity were added to encourage harmonious development of body and mind. Students trained in classical studies contributed humanistic dimensions to law and theology; other Italian humanists combined their interest in classical scholarship with careers as secretaries for princes, prelates, and town councils.

Renaissance historians modeled their work on the classical historians, producing histories of their city or states, rather than universal histories or annalistic accounts commonly composed by medieval Christian historians. These works combined an objectivity derived from their study of classical writings with their deeply felt patriotism toward their own cities. Although they stressed politics and ignored economic and social matters, they explained all events as a result of human motives and actions rather than divine intervention, critically evaluated the materials they used, and sought history's political, moral, and ethical lessons.

Leonardo Bruni (1374–1444) wrote a history of Florence that was modeled on Livy, used sources critically, but at the same time livened his accounts by introducing imaginary speeches into the narrative. The best known Italian historian of the six-

teenth century was Francesco Guicciardini (1483–1540), whose works included *History of Florence* (to 1509) and *History of Italy* covering the period 1494–1534. His treatment of the relations between geographical units and the connections between the external and internal political situation of a country was especially noteworthy, as was his psychological insight into the aims and motives of the human actors in those historical events.

From their careful study of classical

The School of Athens. In this work, the Renaissance master Raphael painted his version of the classical antiquity beloved by humanists. Numerous Greek and Roman cultural heroes are depicted as sixteenth-century Italians in a setting of Renaissance architecture and sculpture. At the center, framed by the arch, are Plato and Aristotle, deep in discussion. Vatican Palace, Vatican City.

manuscripts, humanists developed skill in textual criticism. They learned how to examine sources for genuineness, stimulating the disciplines of archeology and philology (the critical study of written texts). Lorenzo Valla (1406–1457) demonstrated how a critical spirit developed by humanistic study could operate on historical problems by proving that the document termed the Donation of Constantine, used by popes to claim territorial sovereignty and generally assumed to be a fourth-century composition, was actually written in the eighth century.

Philosophically inclined humanists reasserted the conflict between Aristotle's materialism and Plato's idealism, but preferred Plato over Aristotle because of the superiority of his literary style and the more idealistic and mystical nature of his thought. Marsilio Ficino (1433–1499) became the foremost exponent of Italian Renaissance Neoplatonism. He had studied philosophy and Greek as a youth, and translated into Latin all the works of Plato as well as many Neoplatonic writings. Because the Platonic ideas and ideals were considered in medieval times to be part of God, contemplation of those ideas gained a religious significance. Ficino held that love of physical beauty in this world was the first in a series of steps leading to the love of the spiritual beauty of God, a doctrine that artists found especially attractive. Plato's fascination with numbers and harmonies was used by Neoplatonists to promote interest in geometry and mathematics. Ficino and his disciples also held that humans were spiritual individuals, who had social responsibilities and whose dignity derived from their position midway between the material world and the spiritual

God. People had complete free will and the capacity to make of themselves what they would.

Italian humanism declined in the early sixteenth century. As printed editions of Greek and Latin works made knowledge of classical civilization more widely available, demand for humanist educators dwindled. International warfare in Italy diverted the interests of patrons and scattered the practitioners of humanism. Thereafter, humanism flourished in areas outside Italy.

Sixteenth-Century Synthesis

Sixteenth-century Italian writers sought to incorporate the trends of preceding centuries in their work, with interesting results. They abandoned the humanist penchant for using Italian, but applied the lessons on style and form learned from humanist studies. Like writers of the Hellenistic period, they exhibited disenchantment with urban life and composed pastoral romances that glorified the simple life and unspoiled rustic pleasures or filled their stories and plays with skillful descriptions of nature. Others wrote comedies, especially of the satirical variety; one such, Machiavelli's *Mandragola*, wittily criticized Florentine life. Ludovico Ariosto (1474–1533) included classiclike descriptions of natural splendor and bits of information from various classical sources in his *Orlando Furioso*, an epic tale about Charlemagne's heroic general Roland, done in the form of the medieval chivalric romance. Baldassare Castiglione (1478–1529), in his *Book of the Courtier*, transformed the humanist ideal of the fully developed man into the perfect gentleman, who combined social graces and soldierly

skills, eloquent and witty speech, appreciation of art, and learning in literature (including knowledge of Greek and Latin). The work became a handbook of manners, and Castiglione's standards of social and intellectual accomplishment guided the nobility whose lives were more concerned with courtly ceremonial than political and military functions. His perfect gentleman also became a model for later authors.

RENAISSANCE ART IN ITALY

During the fourteenth century, Italian painters and sculptors, like Italian writers, obtained inspiration from classical models. Roman buildings and ruins were numerous and near at hand and therefore easily studied. Moreover, Gothic art, so prominent elsewhere in Europe, had penetrated only slightly into Italy. The Italian ground was fertile for a rebirth of classical art.

The Resurgence of Naturalism

A primary influence on Italian artists was the close observation of nature. In accord with Thomas Aquinas's dictum that "Art is imitation of nature; works of art are successful to the extent that they achieve a likeness of nature," painters and sculptors began to observe the world around them and to depict what they saw. As artists became more aware of the beauty of the natural world, they developed more naturalistic forms of art. This naturalistic trend, already evident in late Gothic art, was reinforced by the Franciscan preaching that all things in nature were divine creations for human happiness.

Lamentation. In this painting, Giotto broke sharply from previous Byzantine-influenced painting. The slanting rock directs the viewer to the dead Christ, who is mourned by angels above and humans below. By daringly depicting two figures with their backs to the viewer, Giotto gives the scene depth and perspective. Arena Chapel, Padua.

Artists abandoned old traditions and developed new techniques. To depict objective realities rather than mystical abstractions they substituted landscapes for blank backgrounds and chose subjects in which movement and the expression of emotion were paramount. Because the artists often painted in quick-drying tempera (a process using a medium such as egg white to carry the pigment) or on fresh plaster, they had to paint rapidly with little attention to detail.

Painters seeking to imitate nature in a two-dimensional medium confronted a formidable problem when they tried to create the illusions of movement and depth on a flat surface. The Florentine painter Giotto di Bondone (1266–1337) was per-

haps the first to successfully discard the flat forms, aloof figures, and formal compositions of the Byzantine style that had dominated Italian painting. Allegedly able to draw a fly so realistic that viewers attempted to brush it away, he made his human figures look round and solid. By using foreshortening, carefully modeling the body and its parts, and skillfully employing light and shadow, he created an illusion of depth on the flat surface. Giotto portrayed action by depicting gestures and suggesting movement, and he pioneered in representing emotions such as grief and astonishment in the faces and postures of his figures. Giotto envisioned how an event probably looked and how people in it moved and acted;

he then used the new techniques to make the event appear to be happening before the viewer's eyes.

During the fifteenth century, Florentine painters mastered the art of depicting nature. Thomas Guidi, nicknamed Masaccio (1401–1428) employed the mathematical laws of perspective, discovered by his architect friend Filippo Brunelleschi (1377–1446), to show objects receding into the background of a painting and to make his figures appear truly three-dimensional. He enhanced the naturalness of his art by the skillful use of light and shadow and the elimination of unnecessary detail. Other artists conducted further experiments with light and color, composition and perspective, to present nature more

David. This young, supple figure, sculpted in bronze by Donatello, shows the Renaissance ability to produce freestanding statues and conveys the age's interest in the grace and beauty of the human body. Rather than emphasizing the spiritual values of David's destruction of the giant Goliath, Donatello directs the viewer to the human achievement. Museo Nazionale, Florence.

realistically and to delight the viewer.

What Masaccio was to painting, his contemporary Donato di Niccolo di Betto Bardi, known as Donatello (1386?–1466) was to sculpture. In sculpture, a three-dimensional medium, the task of imitating nature offered few technical difficulties. Sculptors, like writers, studied the sculptural forms of classical antiquity and gained information and inspiration from them. From Florence, Donatello traveled with Brunelleschi to Rome to study ancient art remains, gaining a thorough knowledge of classical form. His studies included anatomy and the human body, and he employed models. His figures are solid, but possess a lively energy with an easy poise and muscular litheness. Donatello's *David* is the first nude statue of the Renaissance and the first figure in the round independent of architectural surroundings produced for centuries; it is graceful, well-proportioned, and superbly balanced. The same is true for his *Gattamelata*, the first monumental equestrian statue produced since Roman times.

Architects, less dependent than other artists on observing the natural world, were slower in exploring new directions, but were more strongly influenced by the study of classical models. Not until Brunelleschi was there much innovation. Brunelleschi was eclectic, and used both Roman and Romanesque elements. He executed many secular commissions, including residences such as the palace of the Pitti family in Florence. In his churches, he employed the Romanesque cruciform floor plan, but used classical decorative features such as columns, rounded windows, and arches. His greatest triumph was the cupola (or dome) atop the Florence

cathedral, which echoes both the Pantheon of Rome and Constantinople's Hagia Sophia.

Sixteenth-Century Greatness

With the technical problems of portraying nature mastered and the insights of the classical heritage assimilated, artists of the late fifteenth and early sixteenth centuries attempted to improve upon and idealize nature. Following Ficino's assertion, derived from Plato, that love of the world's physical beauty is the first of a series of steps leading to love of God's spiritual beauty, they sought to make figures more beautiful, and thus more godlike, and studied anatomy to assist their efforts. Through such study, the Italian artists developed theories of proportion, the mathematical relation between the size of one part of the body and another in various circumstances, which enabled them to beautify and idealize the human form. Especially noteworthy in this connection was Sandro Botticelli (1444–1510) who vividly embodied that artistic Platonism and painted figures of a mystical beauty. His *Birth of Venus* is a tribute to love and beauty, using watery hues and airy spaciousness to achieve its other-worldly impact. He employed his knowledge of anatomy to distort the human figure for the purpose of achieving a satisfying composition.

Three outstanding sixteenth-century Italian artists, Leonardo, Raphael, and Michelangelo, sought in various ways to express the divine essence of humanity. Leonardo da Vinci (1452–1519), a scientist as well as an artist, was a keen observer of the natural world and a master portrayer of human psychology and personality.

His *Virgin of the Rocks* displays remarkable technical skill in its detailed and accurate presentation of rocks and plants. The *Last Supper* is a careful study of the emotions that each of Jesus's disciples was likely to have expressed on that occasion. In the *Mona Lisa,* he skillfully employed light and shadow and perspective to make the figure fully human, enigmatic and mysterious, and forever fascinating.

Raphael Sanzio's (1483–1520) subjects were idealized, ennobled, and spiritualized humans. His painting, *School of Athens,* is a symbolic and allegorical portrayal of the classical philosophers Plato and Aristotle with their students. But he won his fame and popularity for his numerous madonnas (paintings of Mary with the baby Jesus), which are warm and sweet, pious and graceful. He achieved beautiful, perfectly balanced paintings that, rather than trying to represent nature, made nature represent his idea of beauty.

Michelangelo Buonarotti (1475–1564), who excelled as a poet as well as a painter and a sculptor, made the muscular male figure his ideal of beauty. In his zeal to develop his ability to depict the human body accurately, he researched anatomy, dissected cadavers, and used models. He presented his figures, whether standing like *David* or seated like *Moses,* in dramatic and emotional postures and expressions. A master of sculptural technique, he powerfully exhibits the Renaissance glorification of man. Many of Michelangelo's sculptures were intended to decorate tombs and represent his own deep preoccupation with death. Especially moving is the *Pietà* exquisitely depicting a sorrowing Mary holding Jesus's dead body. His greatest painting was the ceiling of the Sistine Chapel in Rome. Covering about 10,000 square feet and including over 340 figures, Michelangelo spent more than four years (1508–1512) completing it. By skillfully eliminating unnecessary details, he enabled viewers to focus on the powerful figures, which are well described as painted sculpture.

Not all Italian artists, however, shared the Florentine concern with philosophical idealization. Artists in Venice obtained inspiration from the pageantry and picturesqueness of Venetian life. They chose to explore the possibilities of color, especially in oil painting, and achieved a remarkable splendor in its use. Their emphasis on color and elegance owes much to the prominence of Byzantine and Islamic influences in that commercial city. Venetian artists typically painted individual portraits or idyllic landscapes, and even their madonnas and saints represent real human life rather than spiritual ideals.

Tiziano Vecelli (1477–1576), commonly called Titian, was the foremost Venetian painter. He was unexcelled in his use of color, and skillfully painted textures, such as those of skin and hair. A distinctive reddish-gold hair color, frequently used in his paintings, is called by his name. He depicted a wide variety of subjects with vitality and an exuberant joy of life. His religious paintings convey a sense of high spirituality, and his portraits reveal not only the outward appearance but also the inner feelings of the subjects.

The Mannerist Revolt

The impressive achievements of the High Renaissance masters left little

Mona Lisa. Leonardo da Vinci's achievement, considered by many to be the greatest painting of all time, shows a consummate mastery. By adroit techniques, such as shadow at the corners of eyes and mouth, and the use of two different perspectives in the background, Leonardo makes the woman seem alive. Louvre Museum, Paris.

315

Alba Madonna. Raphael's figures of Mary with the child Jesus were the painter's specialty and earned him a comfortable living. Here, mother and child are depicted in a landscape featuring meticulously painted plant life. National Gallery of Art, Washington, D.C.

for later artists to do in representing real nature or idealized humanity. Wars ravaged Italy after 1520, causing widespread destruction and diverting wealth from support of the arts. Religious reform replaced Renaissance secularism with greater attention to human suffering and doubt and uncertainty about human life. Artists sought to express the changing spirit of the sixteenth century by ignoring beauty, rules of proportion, and attention to three-dimensionality and presenting twisted and elongated figures in emotional scenes that stressed the unusual and the bizarre in a movement known as mannerism.

Michelangelo's later works demonstrate these changes. In place of the balance, proportion, and beauty he sought earlier, his later sculptures show an exaggeration, elongation, and distortion that heightens their emotional and religious qualities. In a later portrayal of Jesus's descent from the cross, he disregards scale and proportion to convey the tortured agony of that sacrificial death. His crowded *Last Judgment* painting on the Sistine Chapel's end wall is full of violence, tragedy, and horror, in contrast to the ceiling, which shows the proportion, harmony, and restraint of classical Greek sculpture. Artists in Italy and elsewhere who followed these tendencies became known as mannerists because they worked "in the manner" of Michelangelo, painting allegories full of contorted figures and juxtaposing elements in unconventional ways.

The most prominent mannerist was the Cretan-born, Italian-trained, Spanish-lived Domenico Theotocopuli (1548?–1614), known as El Greco (the Greek). He used severe colors and elongated features to express Spanish religious zeal in his powerful and emotional paintings. Although capable of producing impressions of horror or flights into mysticism, his greatest work, *The Burial of Count Orgaz,* conveys the Catholic spirit of communion among God, saints, and humans.

RENAISSANCE LITERATURE OUTSIDE ITALY

In areas of Europe outside Italy, vernacular literatures, already developing in the thirteenth century, began, like Italian, to register remarkable achievements. Many writers continued to produce conventional religious literature of sermons and saints' lives or wrote chivalric romances for a dwindling courtly audience. Others began to write on secular topics for the increasingly numerous and literate merchant and artisan class in towns and cities.

Fourteenth-Century Accomplishments

Spain and England were early leaders in Renaissance literature outside It-

aly. Castilian literature became well established by two outstanding fourteenth-century works. Alfonso X's nephew, Don Juan Manuel (1282–1349) brought Castilian prose to maturity in *Count Lucanor,* a collection of moral tales and fables written with delicate humor and irony and with careful attention to style. Juan Ruiz (1283–1351) produced an outstanding Castilian poetic achievement in his *Book of Good Love.* In form a satiric autobiography, Ruiz's work included examples of all contemporary poetic forms and themes. Although he incorporated existing ideas and stylistic devices in his work, Ruiz observed real life keenly and humorously and fully expressed his own individuality.

In England, Geoffrey Chaucer (1340–1400) made the East Midland dialect the ancestor of modern English. He borrowed freely from Boccaccio in writing both *Troilus and Cressida,* a story of noble but ill-fated

The Creation. By the simple device of the two fingers nearly touching, Michelangelo dramatically rendered the transmission of the spark of life. The woman and child behind God represent Eve, the first woman, and Christ, the second Adam. Sistine Chapel, Vatican City.

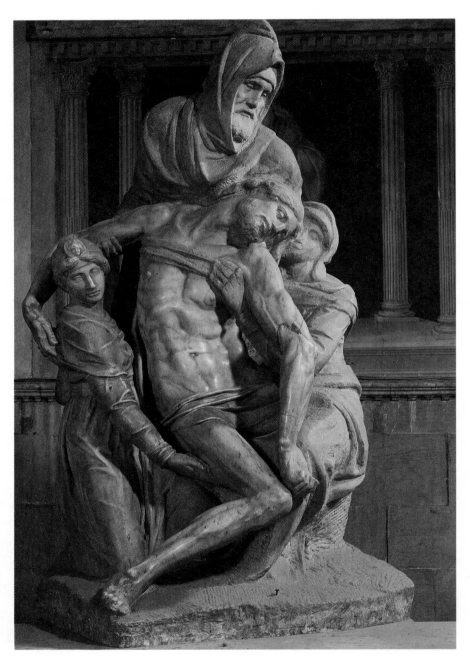

The Deposition. Michelangelo's long career was extremely stormy and emotion filled. *The Deposition* dates from his later period, and shows the sculptor as Joseph of Arimathea assisting in the sorrowful task of removing the body of Jesus from the cross. The twisted, elongated bodies and the powerful emotion depicted characterized the subsequent art style of mannerism. Duomo, Florence.

love set in Homeric Troy, and the *Canterbury Tales,* which carefully delineated individuals from various English social groups with realism and humor.

Northern Humanism

Between 1490 and 1530, humanism became the leading intellectual movement throughout western Europe, in part because communications between Italy and the north were fast improving. Italians accepted positions as secretaries and diplomats with northern kings and princes.

Scholars from the north studied in Italy, returning to write and teach humanism. Universities incorporated humanist studies into their curricula, and humanist historians were invited to employ their critical skills in writing the histories of northern lands. Because books were central to humanist activity, the development of printing contributed significantly to the spread of humanism by reducing their cost.

Northern humanism was distinguished from Italian humanism by several qualities. In contrast to the secular outlook of Italian humanists, northern humanists held a deeply religious world view. Their humanism was more conservative, placed less emphasis on the enjoyment of life, and attended more closely to the teachings of the church. They attempted to integrate new humanist learning with Christian heritage and are therefore known as Christian humanists. Although they stressed the study of the Bible more than the study of classical writings, northern humanists believed that by combining the literatures of classical and Christian antiquity, they could achieve a new synthesis of wisdom that would improve the moral lives of individuals and revitalize and purify contemporary social and religious life. In its emphasis on morality and social conduct, northern humanism was more practical than its Italian counterpart.

By applying humanist techniques of textual criticism, humanists outside Italy hoped to remove obscurities and errors from Christian thought and

The Burial of Count Orgaz. In this manneristic masterpiece, El Greco conveys the emotions associated with the count's death, but also vividly depicts Roman Catholic faith, specifically the close correspondence between human beings on Earth and the heavenly host. Santo Tomé, Toledo, Spain.

MAP 41
The Renaissance Outside Italy. Outside Italy, the Renaissance was a western European phenomenon. Many centers of cultural activity were located on or near important trade routes to and from Italy. Note the concentration of buildings, primarily residences for great nobles, in central France.

teachings and make known the purest forms of Christianity, giving the church new strength and vitality. Generally, northern humanists used philology to improve their understanding of the Bible and the writings of the early church fathers and to produce more accurate editions and translations.

Northern humanists thought their studies would enable individuals to use reason to live better and more pious lives. They believed, as Thomas More stated, that education in Latin and Greek "doth train the soul in virtue." Among the more notable humanists in northern European lands were Jacques Lefèvre d'Étaples (1450–1536) and Thomas More (1478–1535). Lefèvre stressed religion rather than reason in his writings and produced primarily Bible commentaries and works on religious philosophy. He also accomplished an influential

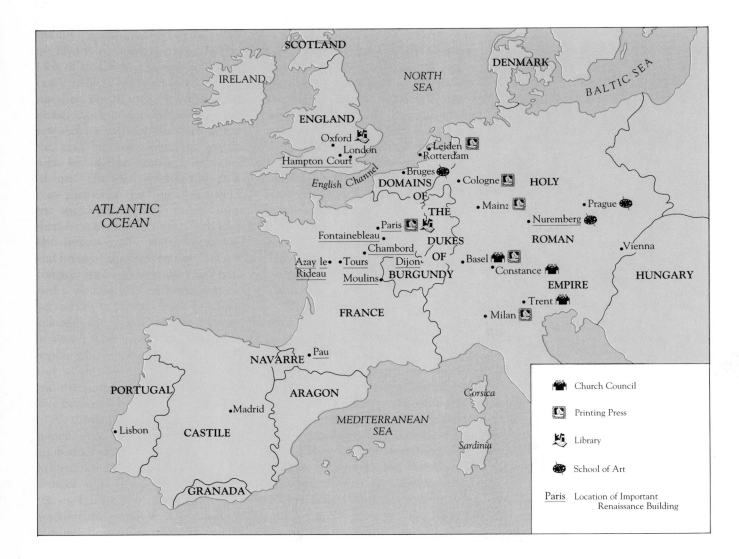

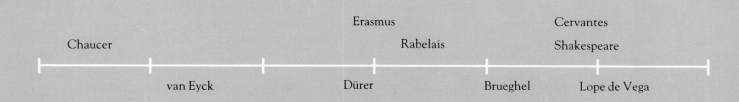

Erasmus

Cervantes

Chaucer

Rabelais

Shakespeare

van Eyck

Dürer

Brueghel

Lope de Vega

French translation of the Bible. More, unlike most humanists, never studied in Italy and was neither a scholar nor a teacher. A lawyer and diplomat, he advanced by his brilliance to become lord chancellor of England. He wrote numerous sober devotional works, but is best known for his *Utopia,* a criticism of contemporary life that presented an ideal society living in peace and prosperity according to Christian ideals and reason, holding property communally, and satisfying all its members' needs.

The foremost northern humanist was Desiderius Erasmus (1466–1536). His wit, the quality and superb style of his writings, and his extensive travels gave him international importance. He loved learning for its own sake, and his works were the first "best sellers" in the history of printing. From the classics Erasmus derived a humanist religion of simple piety and noble conduct based on a belief in human dignity and free will. People, he claimed, could live morally good lives with proper education and guidance, rather than relying on scholastic philosophy, medieval theology, or religious rituals and observances. He embraced the ideas of naturalism, tolerance, and humanitarianism that he found in classical writings, and used

his formidable powers of irony and satire to oppose war, violence, ignorance, and irrationality. His *Adages* collected apt sayings from classical Latin writers, and the *Praise of Folly* attacked the pedantry and dogmatism of scholars and the ignorance and credulity of the masses. In the *Handbook of a Christian Soldier,* he condemned the formalism of Christian religious observances and urged a return to the simple teachings of Jesus, praising Christian ideals such as simplicity of heart and love of others. Erasmus' fresh edition of the New Testament in Greek was another significant work and became the basis of various translations into the vernacular languages.

The Flowering of National Literatures

The humanist stimulus to non-Italian literature was soon apparent in several lands, among them France. Francois Villon (1431–1463) movingly and vigorously expressed his lusty appetite for life and preoccupation with death in verse noted for its subjectivity, frank portrayals of himself and others, and colorful, reliable pictures of his times. Francois Rabelais (1490–1553) was perhaps the dominant French prose

writer of the age. He glorified the human and the natural, rejected Christian doctrine and morality, and satirized scholasticism, bigotry, and church practices. His *Gargantua and Pantagruel* shows people as essentially good and able to fulfill themselves by a vigorous life of action. At the abbey where many of the book's episodes occur, the only rule is "do what you will."

Most of Spanish literature's golden age came somewhat later than that of France and Germany. Fernando de Rojas (1465–1530?) created in *La Celestina* a vivid and voluble, willing and witty, old woman, Celestina, who serves as an intermediary to help a pair of noble lovers advance their relationship. Although she lives by and for sexual love, and is wicked and unscrupulous, she wins the reader's sympathy by her frankness, intelligence, and utter humanness.

Miguel de Cervantes's (1547–1616) *Don Quixote* is sometimes regarded as the greatest novel ever written, a complete image of human nobility and folly. Cervantes laughs at the pretensions of nobles as champions of honor and morality by recounting the adventures of a Spanish gentleman who, after reading numerous chivalric romances, becomes a wandering knight.

A RENAISSANCE VIEW OF HUMANITY

What a piece of work is man! how noble in reason! how infinite in faculty! in form and moving how express and admirable! in action how like an angel! in apprehension how like a god! the beauty of the world! the paragon of animals!

In these words, spoken by Hamlet, prince of Denmark, English playwright William Shakespeare expressed the exalted Renaissance view of man (Hamlet, Act 2, Scene 2), praising both the mental and physical abilities of people. Notice that the language raises humanity close to nearly divine status (infinite, like a god). This view contrasted sharply with the contemporary assessments of human worth delivered by religious leaders in the Reformation.

Imagining windmills to be giants and inns to be castles, the hero (mis)behaves in accord with those (mis)perceptions. His squire, Sancho Panza, is, by contrast, a practical man untroubled by romantic dreams and content with the simple physical pleasures of eating, drinking, and sleeping. *Don Quixote* satirizes both the literature of Cervantes's day, which featured chivalric romances and sentimental pastoral novels, and the lingering vestiges of the feudal codes of behavior.

Spanish drama developed rapidly during the sixteenth century. In Seville, Lope de Rueda (1510–1565) presented plays of ordinary life on makeshift stages, alternating verse passages and prose interludes. Lope de Vega (1562–1635), Spain's greatest dramatist, wrote nearly 2,000 plays. His secular dramas depict violent intrigues and exaggerated ideas of honor among the upper classes or celebrate the gaiety and flavor of Spanish country life; he also wrote numerous religious allegories. Lope perfected the *comedia,* a three-act play blending comedy and tragedy, written in verse in a variety of metrical patterns. Most of his plays use historical subject matter, rural settings, and conflicts involving the assertion of personal dignity.

England's great literary developments are contemporary with those of Spain. Edmund Spenser's (1552–1599) colorful epic, *The Faerie Queene,* celebrates England's greatness during the reign of Elizabeth I. Spenser exalted bold individualism and strong national pride, proclaimed joy in conquest, and expressed nostalgia for the virtues of chivalry. Following the contemporary English conception of the poet as the revealer of morally perfect actions in an aesthetically ideal world, the work describes the marriage of Arthur, who combines all the virtues and resembles Castiglione's ideal courtier with Gloriana, who symbolizes ideal womanhood and represents Elizabeth I.

Even more impressive were England's achievements in drama. William Shakespeare (1564–1616) knew the stories of Greek and Roman literature and borrowed them freely; he also wrote plays extolling English history. Extremely adept in the use of language and the analysis of character, he showed an intense love of humanity and earthly things. His heroes create their own tragic dilemmas and fall through their own sins and mistakes. Although Shakespeare's earlier dramas are largely adaptations and versions of existing plays, the middle group of his plays expresses bitterness, overwhelming pathos, and troubled searching into life's mysteries. Those written during his last years, however, present the overall plan of the universe as benevolent and just despite individual tragedy and grief. Ben Jonson (1573–1637), who shaped the course of English drama after Shakespeare, wrote carefully plotted comedies in a sober style and satirized departures from the norm of good sense and moderation.

RENAISSANCE ART OUTSIDE ITALY

During the fourteenth century, artists outside Italy also devoted their attention to the accurate portrayal of nature. Around 1400, painters began to apply a mastery in rendering detail derived from the painting of manuscript illuminations to larger and highly visible works called altarpieces, wooden panels intended for placement behind altars. At the same time, sculptors were making free-standing lifelike statues for private chapels.

The first flowering of this northern art occurred at the court of the dukes of Burgundy, where both painters and sculptors sought to represent physical and emotional reality by use of detail, careful observation and study of nature, and the skilled application of the technique of foreshortening. The painter Jan van Eyck (1370–1440) pioneered in the employment of oil paints, which dried more slowly than the egg-based paints commonly in use, and thus was able to produce smoother color transitions, finer shadings, and much greater accuracy. By attention to detail, van Eyck excelled as a portrait painter. The subjects of his portraits seem alive, and every blade of grass or hair of a dog is meticulously rendered.

Later fifteenth-century artists applied realism in various ways. Some turned to delineating the pageantry of courtly life in tapestries or to designing carefully sculpted or carved altarpieces. Others attempted to combine those technical innovations with traditional ways of doing art. Still others produced paintings and sculptures with an emotional and religious intensity.

Artists developed new techniques for making closely detailed representations. One such form is the woodcut, made by cutting away from a wood block what should not appear, then inking the block and pressing it on paper to produce a print. Another form is the engraving, made by cutting the design into copper plate, inking the cuts, and then pressing plate to paper to produce the print.

After 1500, Italian influences upon northern European art became more direct. Northern artists went to Italy to study or otherwise to learn of the Italian artistic techniques. Italian mathematical perspective provided a unity sometimes lacking in excessive northern attention to detail, and Italian study of anatomy produced mathematical proportions for the relative size of body parts, which facilitated the creation of beautiful and idealized human forms. But unlike Italian High Renaissance artists, who sought to

The Prophets. In this work by Claus Sluter, carved around 1400, the individuality of the figures and their realistic portrayal show an advance over gothic sculpture. Abbey of Chartreux, Dijon.

The Betrothal. Jan van Eyck's work was apparently intended to attest the engagement of the wealthy townsman Jan Arnolfini and his bride-to-be. The meticulous attention to detail characteristic of north European painters is evident in the hairs of the dog, the wood grain of the floorboards, and the mirrored reflection of the couple. The National Gallery, London.

render idealized human beauty, the goal of northern artists was to stimulate piety and religious feeling in their viewers, and so they adopted and assimilated only those Italian techniques that suited their purposes.

Several early sixteenth-century artists demonstrate both Italian influ-

ences and and northern aspirations. Albrecht Dürer (1471–1528) studied the human form carefully and gave attention to both detail and harmonious composition in woodcuts, engravings, and paintings. He admired Luther and often chose biblical themes for his work. Many of his pieces have

a pervasive somber and often gloomy quality. Matthias Grunewald (ca. 1475–1528) painted a crucified Christ in painful, tortured agony to stimulate religious reflection. Hieronymous Bosch (1450–1516) contrasted good and evil and sought to stimulate attention to the former by dwelling on the latter, depicting Christ's tormentors with exaggerated features and a hell abounding in grotesqueries. Pieter Brueghel (1525–1569) produced richly detailed and ingeniously composed scenes of peasants at work and play. Hans Holbein the Younger (1497–1543) of Augsburg, a skillful maker of sketches and woodcuts, was an eminent portraitist, demonstrating characteristic Renaissance interest in this-worldly things and persons.

Architects outside Italy continued to use Gothic techniques in building both churches and secular structures, but as they reached the structural and decorative limits of the Gothic, they began to employ instead the classical Greco-Roman style revived by fifteenth-century Italians. Those Italian influences are especially evident in central France's Loire Valley chateaux, country houses for French kings, nobles, and wealthy townspeople.

Melancolia I. The melancholy figure by Albrecht Dürer sits amid symbols representing the new learning of the sixteenth century, suggesting that greater knowledge has not produced happiness. Perhaps the figure represents Dürer himself; if so, it may be the first depiction of the "tormented artist" familiar in modern times. The work shows the fine detail that engraving could portray when employed by a master. Victoria and Albert Museum, London.

Erasmus. Hans Holbein turned his artistic skills to the task of earning a living by painting portraits. Although he painted other continental figures besides Erasmus, he is especially known for his representations of English royalty and nobility. Louvre Museum, Paris.

Summary

The Renaissance was a period of remarkable intellectual, literary, and artistic activity, and one of its earliest manifestations was in Italian literature. The vernacular writings of Petrarch and Boccaccio developed Italian poetry and prose. Humanists recovered ancient manuscripts and obtained inspiration from the works of classical Greece and Rome. They also produced quality work in history, philosophy, and philology. However, Italian literary production became less important in the sixteenth century.

Italian Renaissance art achieved greatness by seeking inspiration from nature. Painters at first employed techniques of color, light and shadow, and perspective to create the illusion of three-dimensional realism, but later labored to idealize nature. Sculptors studied anatomy and used models to produce realistic works. By the later sixteenth century, however, artists produced the physically distorted and emotionally charged works of mannerism.

Outside of Italy, vernacular literature flourished early in Spain and England. By 1500, humanism was a strong force in most lands, and Erasmus was its foremost exponent. During the sixteenth and seventeenth centuries, several French writers attained prominence, and England and Spain enjoyed golden ages of literary productivity, particularly in drama.

Painters outside Italy elected to represent nature by meticulous attention to detail, and developed the techniques of oil painting, woodcuts, and engraving. Sixteenth-century artists introduced aspects of Italian artistic achievement to the north in painting and in architecture. The religious tendencies present in the Renaissance would find a fuller outlet in the religious movement known as the Reformation.

SELECTED SOURCES

Burckhardt, J. *The Civilization of the Renaissance in Italy.* 2 vols. 1958. A masterpiece of synthesis which dominated Renaissance studies for nearly a century after its appearance in 1860.

Benesch, Otto. *The Art of the Renaissance in Northern Europe.* 1965. Well-illustrated presentation relating northern European art to contemporary trends in thought and religion.

*Castiglione, Baldessare. *The Book of the Courtier.* translated by C. S. Singleton. 1959. Provides interesting insights into sixteenth-century manners and morals.

*Cellini, Benvenuto. *Autobiography.* 1927. Cellini, a noted artist of the period, vividly depicts both art and life in Renaissance Italy.

Dunn, Esther C. *The Literature of Shakespeare's England.* 1936. Thoughtful treatment of the outstanding period of English writing.

Fletcher, Jefferson B. *Literature of the Italian Renaissance.* 1934. Skillful discussion of the most important works; treats each writer in a separate chapter.

*Harbison, E. Harris. *The Christian Scholar in the Age of the Reformation.* 1956. Examines Christian scholarship and analyzes the Christian humanism characteristic of the Renaissance outside Italy.

Phillips, Margaret M. *Erasmus and the Northern Renaissance.* 1950. Valuable introduction to the Renaissance outside Italy through a biography of its most famous figure.

Reade, Charles. *The Cloister and the Hearth.* 1937. Action-packed historical novel based on the lives of Erasmus' parents and vividly depicting fifteenth-century European life.

*Stone, Irving. *The Agony and the Ecstasy.* 1961. Historical novel based on Michelangelo's life; also the basis for a movie of the same title.

Wolfflin, Heinrich. *Classic Art, an Introduction to the Italian Renaissance.* 3rd ed. 1968. Brief, comprehensive, well-illustrated introduction to this large topic.

*Available in paperback.

THE EXPANSION OF WESTERN CIVILIZATION
(1400–1650)

. . . before we had reached the second bridge an infinite number of the enemy were upon us, attacking us from all sides both from the land and from the water . . . I collected all those who were still alive and sent them on ahead while I, with three or four horsemen and twenty foot soldiers . . . took the rear guard and fought with those Indians until we reached . . . the end of the causeway. God alone knows how dangerous and how difficult it was, for each time I turned on the enemy I came back full of arrows and bruised by stones.

This is the voice of Spanish *conquistador* Hernán Cortés as he and his men fought for their lives in 1520 on an expedition to find gold in the highlands of Mexico. Such an adventure, relatively commonplace in the sixteenth century, would have been difficult for Europeans living one hundred years earlier to imagine. In the beginning of the fifteenth century, at the opening of the era of European overseas expansion, Europe was a relatively isolated extension of the Eurasian land mass. A frozen wasteland lay to the north, and to the west there were stormy seas that most Europeans believed to be too large to sail across. To the east and south Europeans faced Islamic power and vast stretches of barren forests, steppes, and deserts. Although Europeans possessed some information about distant lands in Asia and Africa and received some goods from these places, on the whole Europeans had confined their interests to Europe and to the coasts of Asia and Africa immediately across the Mediterranean Sea. This chapter will discuss how the Europeans, led by the Portuguese and Spanish and followed later by the Dutch, English, and French, broke out of this provincial outlook and created a world-wide system of oceanic trade and colonial empires.

CONTENTS

Sixteenth-century Portuguese Carracks. These vessels were small and slow by later standards of sail, but they were versatile, durable, and manned by experienced officers and crews. With such ships, the Portuguese launched the era of discovery and built a colonial empire on three continents. Attributed to Cornelius Anthonizoon; National Maritime Museum, Greenwich.

Dias rounds Cape of Good Hope

DaGama arrives in India

Magellan-DelCano circum-navigate the Earth

Pizarro conquers Inca empire

Columbus discovers Western Hemisphere

Portuguese move into Asian waters

Cortés conquers Mexico

Portuguese settle Brazil

PORTUGUESE EXPEDITIONS AND CONQUESTS TO THE SOUTHEAST

By the opening of the fifteenth century the long-distance trading enterprises that Europeans had maintained with Asia were in jeopardy. Over the centuries Europeans, mostly through the enterprise of non-Europeans, had become accustomed to importing Asian and African condiments, precious commodities, and textiles. Already costly, Asian commodities were becoming even more expensive by 1400. The Black Death had killed many merchants, and the Ming Dynasty in China discouraged trade outside its borders. In addition, strife in southwest Asia and Muslim advances across south and southeast Asia further disrupted commerce. In 1400, setting out a Christmas wassail bowl containing spiced ale, accompanied by cinnamon bread and ham garnished with cloves, marked an English family as wealthy indeed.

In the fifteenth century the Portuguese led the way in launching an era of discovery, trade, and colonization. At this time Portugal was the most unified nation in Europe; its *reconquista* was completed and it was free from the internal strife plaguing other European lands. The members of the Portuguese royal house were interested in overseas opportunities and were willing to provide money and direction to encourage exploration and conquest abroad. Portugal merchants were interested in expanding their commercial opportunities, and Portuguese seamen were experienced navigators. In addition, the fifteenth century saw advances in cargo-hauling capacity, sail and rigging combinations, navigation aids, and naval armaments. It was now possible for fast, well-armed caravels to make long voyages out of sight of land.

The era of European expansion began in 1415 when the Portuguese seized the Muslim city of Ceuta in Morocco. The capture was made for traditional reasons: to continue the crusade against the Muslims, to win knightly glory for the Portuguese royalty and nobility, and to tap the valuable trans-Sahara trade in gold, salt, and slaves. Once in control of Ceuta, the members of the Portuguese royal house entertained a new idea: to sail down the African coast and deal directly with the blacks in west Africa for gold dust and slaves. Curiosity was also involved: What lay down the African coast? Traditional ideas ac-

companied these innovative plans: by sailing south and perhaps east, the Portuguese might link up with the legendary Christian kingdom of Prester John believed to be somewhere in Africa or southwest Asia. The Portuguese could combine with this kingdom to encircle the Muslims and attack them from the rear. Whether or not Prester John was found, there would be ample opportunity to convert Africans to Christianity.

The Early Voyages

Europeans of the early fifteenth century had inherited incomplete and contradictory geographical knowledge about what lay outside European and the Mediterranean. This was a key barrier to venturing far from Europe. The geographers of classical antiquity, the authorities for Europeans of the fifteenth century, were sharply divided about whether water connected the Atlantic and Indian oceans and therefore whether it was possible to sail south and east from Europe around Africa to Asia. Added to these scholarly disputes were more commonplace fears, especially among seamen, about venturing into tropical waters that were boiling hot or that turned white men black. Some also

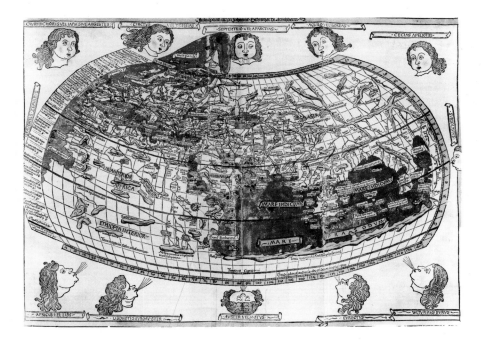

A Fifteenth-century European View of the World. Taken from Ptolemy's second-century *Geographica*, this map indicates the general state of geographic knowledge as the age of discovery got under way. A land mass blocks any sailing route from the Atlantic Ocean to Asia. Ulm, 1482.

feared that hell existed on the face of the Earth to the south.

To gather geographical information, rather than rely on classical theory, Prince Henry (1394–1460) of the royal house of Portugal established a research center at a villa overlooking the sea at the southern tip of Portugal. Here he gathered navigators, astronomers, cartographers, instrument makers, and anyone else who might help him accumulate information and insights.

Shortly after the fall of Ceuta Prince Henry sent out a series of regular expeditions, each one exploring a section of the African coast and returning with information that would help the next venture proceed farther (see Map 42). By the time of Henry's death in 1460 Portuguese ships had arrived at Guinea, some 2,000 miles south and then east around the bulge of Africa. As they went along the coast the Portuguese set up fortified posts, traded for gold dust and slaves and undertook the conversion of Africans.

By the 1470s, as their ships turned southward again and crossed the equator, the Portuguese were now concentrating on finding a route that would divert the Asian spice and silk trade to Portugal. In 1488, an expedition commanded by Bartholomew Dias passed the southern tip of the African coast, and before being forced to turn back by a mutiny, saw the coast stretching away to the northeast. The Portuguese government was now convinced that ships could sail around Africa to India and open up a direct trade in Asiatic commodities. In 1493, however, the Portuguese were unsettled by the news that a Spanish expedition sent westward across the Atlantic under the command of Christopher Columbus had, in a single lucky voyage, apparently discovered Asia by a much shorter route than the long voyage around Africa

Prince Henry of Portugal. The English later called him "the Navigator." He and his brothers and nephews, the kings of the ruling house of Aviz, sponsored the opening of the new age of discovery and exploration. Zurara *Chronicle*, Museu Nacional de Arte Antiga, Lisbon.

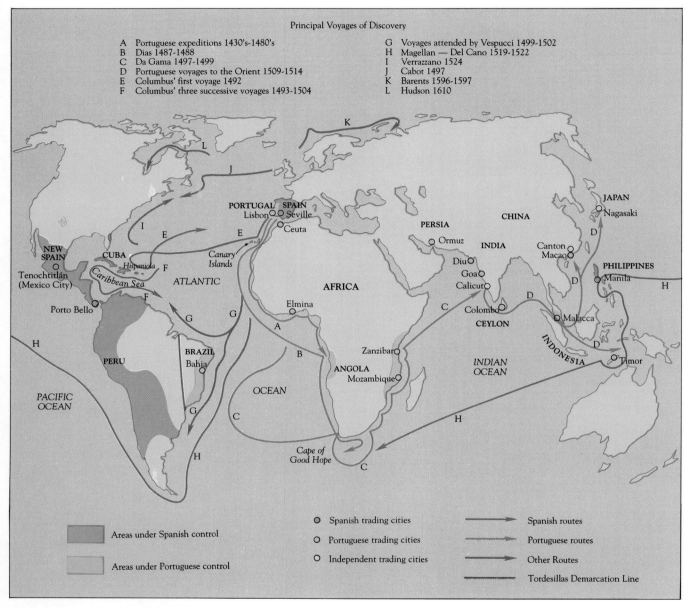

Principal Voyages of Discovery

A	Portuguese expeditions 1430's-1480's
B	Dias 1487-1488
C	Da Gama 1497-1499
D	Portuguese voyages to the Orient 1509-1514
E	Columbus' first voyage 1492
F	Columbus' three successive voyages 1493-1504

G	Voyages attended by Vespucci 1499-1502
H	Magellan — Del Cano 1519-1522
I	Verrazzano 1524
J	Cabot 1497
K	Barents 1596-1597
L	Hudson 1610

Areas under Spanish control

Areas under Portuguese control

- ◎ Spanish trading cities
- ◎ Portuguese trading cities
- ○ Independent trading cities

Spanish routes

Portuguese routes

Other Routes

Tordesillas Demarcation Line

MAP 42

Portuguese and Spanish Overseas Possessions, 1600; Principal Voyages of Discovery. After 100 years of overseas conquest, the difference between the two empires is apparent: the Portuguese possessions are a collection of trading posts stretching halfway around the globe, while Spanish holdings are primarily a huge but compact land mass. European explorers have traversed the globe via the southern route, but have made little headway in the frozen north.

that the Portuguese were contemplating.

By 1496, now suspecting that Columbus had not found Asia, the Portuguese resumed their efforts. By the papal bull (proclamation) of 1493 and the Treaty of Tordesillas in 1494, the Portuguese and the Spanish had agreed to respect each other's routes to Asia:

The Spanish would have the western route across the Atlantic and the Portuguese the route to the southeast around Africa. In 1497, Vasco da Gama set out from Portugal for Asia with a small fleet of trading vessels. After courageously voyaging through the Atlantic ninety-six days out of sight of land, da Gama swung around the southern tip of Africa and stopped at ports on the east coast of Africa. Da Gama then sailed eastward across the Indian Ocean, landing at Calicut, India. Asked by the Indians why he had come, he allegedly replied, "Christians and spices." He made trading arrangements with the Hindu ruler of the area, and, loaded with cinnamon and pepper, returned to Portugal in 1499. An era of European ocean-based commerce—and conquest—had begun.

Building an Empire in Africa and Asia

Once they had found their way to Asia, the Portuguese acted with calculated policy and energy to seize control of as much of the waterborne spice trade as possible. By 1557, they had defeated Asian fleets and established naval control of the Indian Ocean. With this naval power, the Portuguese acquired islands such as Zanzibar, Goa, and Malacca, lying immediately off the coasts of strategic areas in the Indian Ocean. The Portuguese turned them into fortified naval bases and then secured a number of satellite trading stations on the mainland, protecting them with ships cruising out of the naval bases. The Portuguese were unable to acquire fortified posts in the Indonesian spice islands east of Singapore, but they were permitted to build trading posts in the clove-producing Moluccas, on the south China coast at Macao, and at Nagasaki in southwestern Japan. As a result of these conquests and arrangements, a fleet left Asia annually for Portugal loaded with spices and textiles. It returned from Portugal with gold, silver, and weapons to pay for the Asian products and with

soldiers and administrators to replace those lost to disease and combat. The voyage to "the Indies" took six to eight months, and many travelers, sometimes half, perished along the way.

The Portuguese presence in Africa and Asia constituted the first of several types of colonial arrangements that Europeans fashioned in the first two centuries of overseas activities. The Portuguese did not aspire, nor did they have the manpower, to control vast stretches of territory and masses of subject peoples. They wished to set up an overseas trading empire that would monopolize the valuable Asian sea trade routes, while if possible converting many Asians and Africans to Christianity. Portugal, a small nation, could only maintain about 10,000 men in Africa and Asia. Although possessing superior arms it lacked the interest, manpower, and overall resources to conquer Asian states and hold extensive colonial areas. In Africa, the Portuguese were much more powerful than any of the tribes, but seeing no valuable resources concentrated at any one spot, they were satisfied for the most part to stay on the coast and trade for slaves and local products.

SPANISH EXPEDITIONS AND CONQUESTS TO THE WEST

While the Portuguese were setting up an empire in Africa and Asia, the Spanish were trying to make sense—and profit—out of what they were finding across the Atlantic. Before exploration had begun, many edu-

cated Europeans knew that the earth was round, and knowing Erastosthenes' calculations of the earth's circumference, had correctly estimated that Asian lands lay some 10,000 miles across the sea to the west. Unaware of previous Viking discoveries indicating the presence of an intervening land mass, and unconvinced that legendary western lands such as Atlantis really existed, they believed 10,000 miles was too far for the ships of that day to sail without being able to re-provision.

The Early Voyages

Some Europeans, however, were convinced that the earth was much smaller in circumference; one of these men, the experienced sea captain Christopher Columbus, computed that Japan was about 2,400 miles west of the Canary Islands (off the African coast), within range of the sailing ships of that day. In 1492, with the backing of Queen Isabella of Castile, Columbus sailed westward 33 days from the Canaries and landed in the Bahamas, approximately where he had calculated Asia to be. Assuming that he was off the coast of Asia and using a term that Europeans often employed to indicate the farther reaches of Asia, he called the islands the "Indies" and their inhabitants "Indians" (in this text, Amerindians). In 1493, Columbus returned to Spain in triumph.

The successful voyage of Columbus spurred the Spanish to set up trade routes westward to Asia. Columbus made three more voyages, the last in 1502. During that time Columbus and other explorers discovered many islands, an undeveloped mainland, a little gold, a few pearls, and a local subsistence culture. By 1507, the suspicion was widespread that this area was not Asia, but a disappointing barrier to Asia that appeared to contain little of value. At this time Amerigo Vespucci, a navigator–geographer who accompanied several expeditions to this area, sent Europeans streams of interesting information about the lands across the Atlantic. His publishers, virtually convinced the area was not Asia, named the area "America" in his honor.

Between 1506 and 1520, other Spanish expeditions looking for a "Passage to India," a water route through or around the American barrier to Asia, brought back the discouraging information that the main-land extended well northward from the Caribbean and southward to the stormy and icy waters of the far southern Atlantic. On the other hand, in 1513, Vasco Núñez de Balboa, crossing the Isthmus of Panama, discovered on the other side of the barrier a "western ocean" that might take ships all the way to Asia. In 1519, the Spanish government dispatched an expedition under Ferdinand Magellan to search for a passage to the Pacific at the southern end of the American land mass, and if he found one, to go on to Asia. Magellan fought his way for thirty-eight days through a stormy water passage (later the Strait of Magellan) at the tip of South America. Afterwards, on the enormous stretches of the calm (pacific) western ocean, his men died from lack of water and were reduced to eating rats. Undaunted, Magellan headed northwest, but was killed in a skirmish in the present-day Philippines. His navigator, Sebastian del Cano, and his surviving crew pushed on across the Indian Ocean. They arrived in Spain in 1522, having circumnavigated the earth, perhaps the greatest feat of exploration in history. Although the voyage confirmed the basic dimensions of the earth, the discoveries of Magellan and del Cano also demonstrated to the Spanish that Asia was too far away, around a huge

The Conquest of Mexico. This Amerindian painting depicts several of the techniques by which the Spaniards triumphed. Although the painting does not show the firearms of the Spanish, it pictures their horses, wardogs, and numerous Amerindian allies. The Amerindians on both sides are equipped with swords edged with black, razor-sharp obsidian, whose lethal effects are apparent.

land barrier and across two enormous oceans, for a successful western trade route to Asia. The Spanish did take over the Philippine Islands and use it later as an exchange point for Chinese products and American bullion, but other than persistent missionary activity they did not play a major role in Asia.

Building an Empire in the Americas

At the same time that Magellan and del Cano were dashing the hopes of the Spanish for easy access to the wealth of Asia, the New World proved to have enormous riches of its own. Spaniards who had begun to settle some of the islands of the Caribbean heard stories that powerful Amerindian empires in the highlands of present-day Mexico and Peru controlled tremendous wealth in silver and gold. Hernán Cortés led several hundred Spaniards into the Mexican highlands to confront the Aztec empire ruled by Montezuma. Although heavily outnumbered, the determined Spaniards exploited divisions among the Indians and manipulated their religion (see box). In addition, Cortés's men, assisted by several thousand Indian allies, also possessed the advantages of iron armor and weapons, muskets and cannon, and men mounted on horses; in contrast, the Aztecs employed Stone Age weapons and fought on foot. Consequently, after some initial failures, Cortés defeated the Aztecs and seized and destroyed the imposing Aztec capital of Tenochtitlán, on the site of present-day Mexico City, in 1521.

After eliminating the Aztec leaders, the Spanish possessed a vast territory on the American mainland

---

MONTEZUMA HEARS ABOUT THE SPANISH

. . . strange people have come to the shores of the great sea . . . Their trappings and arms are all made of iron; they dress in iron and wear iron casques on their heads. Their swords are made of iron; their shields are iron; their spears are iron. Their deer carry them on their backs wherever they wish to go. Those deer, our lord, are as tall as the roof of a house. . . . The stranger's bodies are completely covered, so that only their faces can be seen. Their skin is white, as if it were made of lime. They have yellow hair, though some of them are black. Their dogs are enormous, with flat ears and long dangling tongues . . . their eyes flash fire. [referring to a gun:] A thing like a ball of stone comes out of its entrails; it comes out shooting sparks and rain-ing fire. The smoke that comes out has a pestilent odor, like rotten mud. . . . If the cannon is aimed against a mountain, the mountain splits and cracks open.[*]

This is an example of messages depicting the Spanish reportedly sent by Amerindian observers to the Aztec emperor Montezuma. Such information was undoubtedly unsettling, and in conjunction with the Aztec belief that Cortés might be the returning god Quetzelcoatl, weakened the Aztecs' will to resist.

[*]Miguel León-Portilla, ed., *The Broken Spears: The Aztec Account of the Conquest of Mexico.* trans. A. M. Garibay and Lysander Kemp, (Boston: Beacon Press, 1969), pp. 30–31.

---

populated by a settled native work force already accustomed to taking orders. Shortly thereafter the Spanish discovered enormous quantities of silver in the Mexican highlands and put the Amerindians to work in mines. They also found the area, which they named New Spain, suitable to stock raising and, in some areas, plantation agriculture. The Spaniards dispatched several expeditions to the north, such as those under Francisco de Coronado and Hernán DeSoto, seeking rumored Cibola, the seven cities of gold, but finding nothing they valued. Consequently, they did not extend their power into the rest of North America until the eighteenth century, except to build a fort on the Florida peninsula at St. Augustine (1568) to guard the northern approaches to the Caribbean.

In 1532, the Mexican story was repeated in Peru when Francisco Pizarro led a force of 170 men into the Andes, looking for the riches of the Inca empire. Finding this highly structured and powerful civilization divided by civil war, Pizarro destroyed each element of the Inca leadership in turn, and by 1533 had gained control over a tract of territory extending from present-day Ecuador to Bolivia. As in Mexico, the Spanish found themselves in possession of large quantities of silver ore and a ready-made Amerindian work force. From their base in the old Inca empire the Spanish fanned out northward and southward along the mountain and

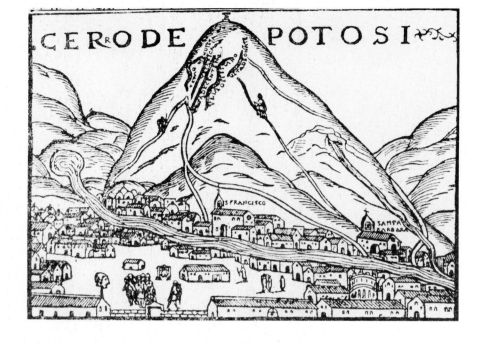

The Mountain of Silver at Potosí. Shown here in a 1553 woodcut, this was the main fruit of Pizarro's conquest of the Inca Empire. The silver mines and smelteries at Potosí (in present-day Bolivia) produced about $1 billion worth of silver for the Spanish during the colonial period. The woodcut glosses over one grim fact about Potosí: the death of tens of thousands of Amerindian workers. Chronica del Peru.

valley chains of western America, conquering what are now Colombia and Venezuela to the north and Chile to the south. The Spanish did not penetrate the Amazon jungles to the east, but they did move into the plains of southeastern South America, establishing a ranching economy in present-day Paraguay and Argentina.

By the middle of the sixteenth century, unlike the Portuguese, who had established a collection of fortified coastal towns and trading depots, the Spanish had created a second and more ambitious form of European colonial holding. On the mainland of the new world, Spanish were in control of territory many times larger than Spain itself, while holding in subjugation some twenty million of another race. In the middle of the sixteenth century the Amerindians were proclaimed subjects of the crown. As

such they could not be legally enslaved, as formerly, but in fact many were still worked to death in the mines, businesses, and fields of their Spanish overlords. Over time, miscegenation created many mixed-race individuals called mestizos, who eventually formed a major element in the population of Latin America.

Based on the toil of this Amerindian work force, annual fleets carried an enormous wealth of silver, hides, gold, dyes, cacao, and quinine from the mainland of the New World to Seville, whose merchants had been given the monopoly of the overseas trade. The Spanish monarchy, from its share of the precious metals and taxes, received 40 percent of the value of the shipments, building up an enormous treasury that could be used to finance dynastic adventures in Europe. Two annual fleets, one bound for Vera Cruz and one for Panama,

returned from Spain carrying food, clothing, wine, tools, an assortment of household goods, and some settlers. As time passed, however, the Spanish economy fell further and further short of sending over enough goods to meet the needs of its colonists.

BLACK SLAVERY IN THE NEW WORLD

At the same time that the Portuguese were active in Asia and the Spanish were establishing huge mainland colonies in the Americas, Europeans were creating a third type of colonial arrangement. The Spanish had found that tobacco, a new drug craze in Europe, and sugar, traditionally in demand, could both be grown in the

Caribbean. After 1534, the Portuguese had begun to occupy Brazil, on the eastern coast of South America, and found that area also suitable for growing sugar and tobacco. Both crops required year-round labor, but European-imported diseases and enslavement had taken their toll; too few Amerindians remained alive in the Caribbean and Brazil to do the work. Whereas some Spaniards and Portuguese had settled in these areas, none were willing to die working in the tropical sugar and tobacco fields. However, the Portuguese had for a century shipped black slaves from Africa to their sugar plantations on the Azores and Madeira islands in the Atlantic Ocean. Blacks were regarded as subjects of African kings, and could be made prisoners in war; according to the understanding of Europeans of the time, non-Christian prisoners of war could be legally enslaved.

By the end of the sixteenth century the Portuguese were shipping thousands of African slaves—some caught by European-led raiding parties and others supplied by Africans—to the sugar plantations of Brazil. Many blacks died in route, succumbing to the horrors of weeks of being packed in the holds of the slave ships. Except for a lucky few, the survivors of the voyage were sent into the sugar cane fields, where they were worked, starved, and beaten to death. The average life for a slave in Brazil was seven to ten years; many thousands of replacements were brought in annually, not only to replace the dead, but those who had revolted and escaped into the interior. Controlling no source of black slaves, the Spanish government gave the Portuguese an *asiento* (agreement) to bring in slaves to the Spanish holdings in the Caribbean.

THE ENTRY OF THE NORTH ATLANTIC NATIONS

While the Spanish and Portuguese exploited the rich lands overseas during the sixteenth century, their potential competitors, the states in northern Europe with access to the Atlantic, remained relatively inactive. The French and English were only intermittently interested in overseas projects, and in any case were distracted by secular and religious civil wars. The Dutch were fighting to gain

A Seventeenth-Century Sugar Mill. This engraving is from the early sixteenth-century; the work is being carried out by Amerindian slaves, before masses of blacks were imported to do the labor. Large-scale sugar production entailed high labor costs because of heavy slave mortality, and required heavy, expensive, cane-grinding machinery. It was nonetheless a very profitable enterprise.

Black Slavery in the Americas. In 1619, at Jamestown, England's Virginia colony, a Dutch slave ship has landed the first blacks offered for sale. The Virginians stare at the strange people, trying to gauge the economic and social consequences of purchasing them. Their decision to buy the blacks contributed to the radical transformation of the racial composition of the New World.

their independence from Spain, the Germans were preoccupied with political and religious divisions, and the Scandinavian nations were caught up in Baltic wars.

A Growing Interest in Overseas Expansion

While the northern European states were too weak to interfere with the established Portuguese and Spanish colonies to the south, many northerners hoped that a water route to Asia might yet be found somewhere to the north. From 1497 into the early seventeenth century English, French, and Dutch expeditions probed for a "Northwest Passage" through or around North America and a "Northeast Passage" around Siberia. To their dismay, they found the northern seas clogged with impenetrable ice. However, the explorers did learn that northern North America contained valuable timber and furs, and the North Atlantic teemed with fish.

By late in the sixteenth century, 100 years after the Portuguese and Spanish had begun building empires in America, Africa, and Asia, the states of northern Europe were sufficiently united at home to be able to challenge Portuguese and Spanish power abroad (see Map 43). The rising merchant classes in these states were becoming increasingly interested in developing profitable projects overseas. Population pressures and nationalistic rivalries were also factors in stimulating interest in expansion, as was the desire of the Dutch and English Protestants to compete with the Catholics in missionary activities.

In their contest with Spain and Portugal the northern nations developed a flexible and efficient economic weapon. The Spanish and Portuguese had allowed a small percentage of their business community to monopolize opportunities abroad, thus excluding additional investment resources that might have been available for overseas expansion. The English, French,

and Dutch governments, however, amassed a larger investment pool from their merchants and bankers by fostering a new departure in business organization—granting charters to "joint stock" companies specializing in trading and colonization. Participants in joint stock companies had their risks

MAP 43

European Overseas Possessions, 1658; Slave Trade. In only sixty years, the North European states have made a substantial impact overseas. They have established themselves in Asia, the Caribbean, and the east coast of North America, in the first two areas at the expense of the Portuguese and the Spanish. The slave trade, now 150 years old, has become a monumental international enterprise.

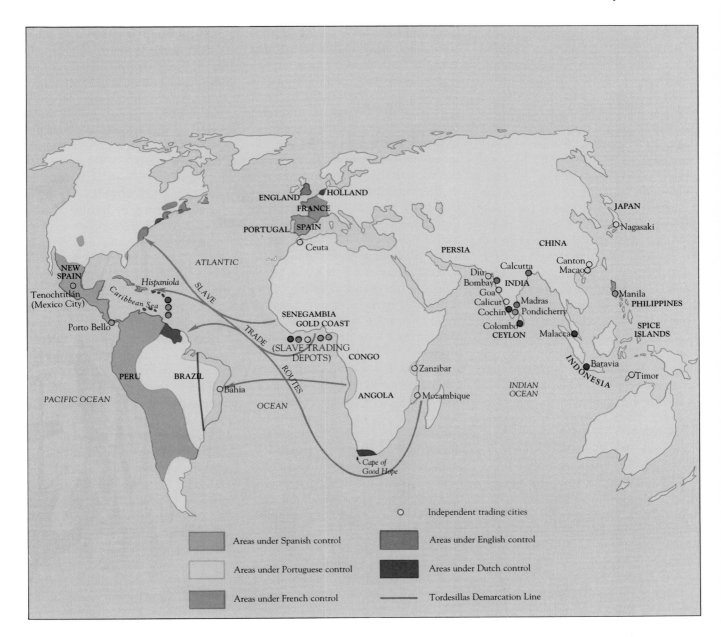

Independent trading cities

Areas under Spanish control

Areas under English control

Areas under Portuguese control

Areas under Dutch control

Areas under French control

Tordesillas Demarcation Line

limited to the proportion of their investment; this limited liability encouraged those who had modest sums available to put their money in these new overseas companies. Investment was further encouraged by easier access to marine insurance. Some of these organizations, such as the Dutch East India Company, were in effect mini-nations, huge conglomerates complete with armies and navies. Others, such as the New England Company, were quite modest affairs. Each of these new companies received a monopoly to develop a particular area; profits were paid off in dividends to the shareholders. The government received its share through customs duties, taxes, and in some cases either a percentage of or a monopoly on certain products. The English and Dutch companies were essentially privately managed organizations, whereas the French companies were state-directed enterprises; but the goal was identical—to gain profits, by whatever means.

The quickest path of wealth for the northerners was to both trade and raid in Spanish America. By the late sixteenth century the Dutch in particular were smuggling goods to the Spanish colonists, who were starved for European goods and slaves but forbidden to trade with foreigners. Meanwhile, pirate "buccaneers" and some marauders secretly outfitted by northern governments pillaged the "Spanish Main," raiding the Spanish silver fleets and attacking ports in the Caribbean. A number of Englishmen such as John Hawkins and Francis Drake won renown in the Caribbean, bringing substantial amounts of Spanish silver to Queen Elizabeth I (1558–1603). In 1577 Drake launched the most spectacular raiding expedi-

tion of that era, attacking the west coast of Spanish America, exploring the west coast of North America, and returning to England in 1579, having circumnavigated the globe.

Creating New Colonial Empires

In the seventeenth century northern European states moved beyond mere raiding and began to capture colonies from the Spanish and Portuguese. The Dutch, as an offshoot of their struggle for independence from Spain, took the lead; since Portugal was now ruled by Spain, they had sufficient pretext to attack the weaker of the two colonial empires. Now possessed of the most powerful merchant marine/navy in the world, the Dutch East India Company methodically conquered Portuguese possessions in Asia, and by 1663 only Goa and Diu in India, Timor in Indonesia, and Macao remained. These the Portuguese would hold into the twentieth century. The Dutch East India Company now controlled the spice traffic of Asia, administering it from their headquarters at Batavia in Indonesia. The enterprising Dutch also built up trade specialties in Javanese coffee and Chinese tea, creating new consumer habits in Europe. To ensure an ample supply of coffee and spices, the Dutch began to take over control of Java and Moluccas, subjecting increasing numbers of Indonesians to forced labor.

Meanwhile, a resurgence of Muslim power drove the Portuguese from the Persian Gulf and from much of east Africa, leaving them with a few trading posts and a few mixed-blood settlers in Mozambique. Needing a spot to provision and water ship's crews on the long voyage to Asia, the Dutch

attempted to dislodge the Portuguese from Mozambique. Failing, the Dutch created a settlement of farmers (boers) at the Cape of Good Hope in 1652, the first substantial European settlement in Africa. Following the Dutch, the French, English, and Danes obtained a few trading posts in India and China and some slaving posts on the west African coast.

At the same time they were active in Asia and the Indian Ocean, the Dutch seized most of the Portuguese slave-trading depots in west Africa and Angola and annexed part of Brazil. By the 1650s, however, the Portuguese had regained Angola and Brazil, and from then on, the remaining Portuguese empire was centered on the sugar plantations of Brazil, supplied with Angolan slaves. Despite the loss of Angola, the Dutch now dominated the Atlantic slave trade. Except for the growing Dutch control in the "East Indies" (Indonesia) the northerners, like the Portuguese before them, were at that time interested in a commercial empire in Asia and Africa rather than in acquiring blocks of territory, and kept their involvement in these areas limited to trading posts backed by sea power.

The northern European states also increased their activity in the Caribbean. The Dutch, English, French, and Danes snatched up a number of small islands in the "West Indies," most of them not under Spanish control. They intended to use them as bases to intensify their raiding and trading enterprises, but later they saw better possibilities in using the islands for sugar and tobacco production. To work the crops, these nations shipped in slaves from their trading posts in west Africa and bought more from the Dutch. Virtually every European nation with overseas possessions was now involved in plantation agriculture and the importation and exploitation of black slaves. In so doing, Europeans had for the first time in history moved masses of people from one continent to another. As a result, they transformed the racial composition of the eastern fringe of the Western Hemisphere from southern North America to Brazil, replacing the original Amerindian population with a few Europeans and masses of Black slaves.

Northern European states also began to establish colonies on the east coast of North America in the seventeenth century. The Dutch, Swedes, and French were primarily interested in developing a lucrative fur trade with the Amerindians, but their colonies proved to be only modestly profitable, considering the cost of maintenance and defense. To cut down on costs, they brought over a few farmers to provide food.

In 1607, the English inaugurated a fourth type of colony, "New Europes," on the east coast of North America. In such colonies, masses of European settlers killed off or drove out the original Amerindian inhabitants and attempted to set up replicas of European society. The founding companies had originally hoped to trade with the Amerindians for skins and furs and failing that, to find or grow the products that had made the Spanish and Portuguese rich: gold, silver, silk, spices, and tea. They had other motives as well: outflanking the Spanish; converting Amerindians to Christianity; and removing criminals, paupers, religious dissenters, political unreliables and the unemployed from England. English leaders believed that the work of these people would be profitable to the merchant trading companies. More than 100,000 settlers, with varying degrees of encouragement or pressure by the

government and the trading companies, came to English North America by the middle of the seventeenth century.

To the disappointment of the English investors, many colonies produced little in the way of Asian and Latin American wealth. North of Chesapeake Bay, the natural products were timber, fish, grain, and meat, of which only the first was wanted in England. The foodstuffs, however, could be sent to the Caribbean, allowing the planters there to keep their slaves at work growing sugar and tobacco. From the Chesapeake southward, the English had more luck: Here settlers could grow tobacco and (later) rice, indigo, and cotton, all valuable products. Slave traders brought in black slaves from the Caribbean and from Africa to raise these products, and some areas took on many of the brutal economic and social characteristics of the Caribbean and Brazil.

The Early Fur Trade. Furs were the lucrative product sought by Europeans in the circumpolar regions from Siberia to North America. As depicted here in bartering with the Amerindians, the trade started out on a relatively equal footing. In time, however, Europeans took over the trapping enterprise, often reducing the indigenous peoples to dependence on European blankets, clothing, firearms, and alcohol.

A PLEA TO ENGLISHMEN TO BEGIN COLONIZATION

1. The soil yields . . . all the several commodities of Europe . . . that England trades with . . . .

3. . . . a safe passage, and not easy to be annoyed by prince or potentate whatsoever.

6. . . . This enterprise may keep the Spanish King from flowing over all the face of America, if we seat and plant there in time. . . . And England possessing the proposed place of planting, her Majesty [Queen Elizabeth I] may . . . have plenty of excellent trees for masts, of good timber to build ships and to make great navies. . . . How easy a matter may yet be to this realm . . . having . . . the best and most cunning shipwrights of the world, to be lords of all these seas, and to spoil Philip's [King Philip II of Spain] . . . navy and to deprive him of yearly passage of his treasure into Europe and consequently to abate the pride of Spain and of the supporter of the great An-

tichrist in Rome and pull him down in equality to his neighbor princes, and consequently to cut off the common mischief that comes to all Europe by the peculiar abundance of his Indian treasure. . . .

12. By the great plenty of those regions . . . shall be rich . . . [and] shall be able to afford the commodities for cheap prices to all subjects of the realm.

13. By making of ships and . . . by making of cables and cordage, by planting of vines and olive trees, and by making of wine and oil, by husbandry, and by thousands of things there to be done, infinite numbers of the English nation may be put to work, to the unburdening of the realm with many that now lie chargeable to the state at home.

14. . . . salt . . . wine, oils, oranges, lemons, figs, . . . iron, all with much more is hoped. . . .

16. We shall by planting there enlarge the glory of the gospel, and from England plant sincere religion, and provide a safe and a sure place to receive people from all parts of the world that are forced to flee for the truth of God's word. *

Richard Hakluyt's words in 1584 represent the mixture of economic, political, strategic and religious arguments for colonization that were increasingly advanced in England in the late sixteenth century. Shortly after, Sir Walter Raleigh and others attempted, unsuccessfully, a settlement at Roanoke Island in present-day North Carolina.

* Richard Hakluyt, "A Discourse Concerning Western Planting," Maine Historical Collections, 2nd Series, *Documentary History of the State of Maine,* (Portland, Maine: n. p., 1869–1916), Vol. 2, 36–41.

RUSSIAN CONQUESTS TO THE EAST

While western Europeans were concentrating on overseas development, Russians were moving eastward across Asia. In the late sixteenth century the domains of Russia lay almost entirely to the west of the Ural Mountains, the dividing line between Europe and Asia. To the east of the Urals lay the immense expanse of Siberia, thousands of miles of cold northern forests thinly populated with scattered Asiatic tribes, but thickly inhabited by fur-bearing animals, in particular by sable, whose fur was the "golden fleece" of that era. Like the thirst of western Europeans for gold, silver, and spices, a lust for furs lured Russians eastward.

The Cossacks, a military caste that defended the frontiers in return for land, led the way into Siberia. In 1582, the Cossack hero Yermak crossed the Urals and defeated the tribes immediately to the east, gathering booty for himself and exacting tribute in furs for the tsar. Adventurers like Yermak were followed by traders, soldiers, and administrators, who set up fortified posts and collected pelts from the natives by purchase or force to send back to Russia. The pattern was now set for further Russian expansion. Heavily armed Cossack bands pushed eastward in a zigzag pattern, boating up and down the river systems of Siberia. In 1639 the Cossacks stood on the shores of the Pacific at Okhotsk, 5,000 river and portage miles from the point of Yermak's departure eastward. Soon a string of fortified posts stretched across Siberia to the Pacific. Russia now possessed vast north Asian domains and would prosper for generations from an immense fur trade.

1580	1600	1620	1640	1660

Russians
penetrate
Siberia

English,
French,
Dutch
settle
N. America

English
settle
New
England

Russians
reach
Pacific

Dutch
settle
Cape of
Good Hope

Dutch conquer Portuguese possessions in Asia

North Europeans seize islands in the Caribbean

Black slavery continues to spread through the Western Hemisphere

The movement of Russians across Siberia brought them to the northern borders of the Chinese Empire, ruled after 1644 by the Manchu dynasty. The cossacks and Chinese troops clashed in the Amur River Valley, but in 1679 at the Treaty of Nerchinsk Russia acknowledged Chinese claims to the area. Peace followed, accompanied by limited trade and a Russian diplomatic post in Peking. The Chinese, already dealing with European "barbarians," as they considered them, in their southern ports, now had to face them in the north as well.

The Impact of Discovery and Colonization on Europe

In the two and a half centuries after the Portuguese had taken Ceuta, a remarkable transformation had taken place. Europeans of the fourteenth century, beset by plague, economic dislocation, and Muslim power, had focused their attention on their limited area of the world and on the secular and religious events of the past. Europeans of the seventeenth century were at home around much of the globe; they had traversed the great oceans and established themselves on four other continents, defeating most of the people they found abroad and seizing their wealth. The strange plants, animals, and humans from other lands fired the curiosity of European scientists and captured the imagination of many European artists and writers. Much of the world still remained unknown to Europeans, but with their new outlook they believed it would be only a matter of time before the rest of the world opened to them. The present was exciting and the future beckoned.

The daily lives of Europeans were greatly affected by their overseas activities. Over succeeding generations many European peasants would gradually change their diet and their farming practices, growing, eating, and using for fodder potatoes and maize, which produced more nutrition per acre than traditional grains. More and more Europeans were consuming spices, sugar, tobacco, tea, and coffee, although the mass of laborers could not as yet afford most of these products. Upper-class Europeans increasingly indulged themselves in furs, silks, and fine cottons, jeweled gold and silver ornaments, and porcelain ("china") table settings.

As Europe drew on the agricultural and mineral resources of Asia, Africa, and the Americas, the wealth so derived was not equally shared throughout Europe. Most European states did not have colonial holdings. Of those that did, Portugal, a small nation, spent much of its resources preserving the remnant of its empire from attacks. France's holdings were still comparatively small, and the costs of defending its colonies while pursuing wars in Europe ate up most of the profits the French derived from colonial products. For Spain, creating a vast colonial empire led to massive problems. Despite harassment from its competitors, Spain derived great wealth from abroad during the sixteenth century, but it dissipated its colonial income and borrowed more to pay for its European adventures. In addition, the early flood of wealth contributed to a ruinous inflation. These factors, plus a banking and mercantile system weakened by the expulsion of the Jews and Muslims, put Spain into an economic, political, and military decline during the seventeenth century.

England and the Netherlands, two latecomers in colonial affairs, gained the most from the new era; consequently, the center of economic power in Europe shifted from the Mediterranean to the North Sea nations. Having sufficient power and economic stability, these nations were able to create, enlarge, and protect their colonial empires. Becoming increasingly efficient in mercantile and banking affairs, they augmented the profits obtained from their colonies and avoided dissipating their wealth in European wars. Many English and Dutch families became wealthy from overseas trade, and company investors plowed profits from colonial enterprises into new trading ventures and also into banking, mining, merchandising, transportation, and manufacturing projects in Europe.

SUMMARY

In 1400, except for some sketchy information derived from trade with Asia and Africa, Europeans knew little about the world except their own continent and its immediate surrounding waters. After 1415, the Portuguese began to explore the west coast of Africa, establishing a trade in gold and slaves. By 1497 they had passed the southern tip of Africa and crossed the Indian Ocean to India. The Portuguese established a collection of fortified trading posts along the African coast and throughout south and southeast Asia, diverting much of the spice trade to Portugal. The Spanish explored westward across the Atlantic and discovered a new land stretching north-south across the globe, which effectively barred them from trade with Asia. By 1540, they had discovered that the highlands in Mexico and in South America were rich in silver, which could be extracted by the forced labor of conquered Amerindians. Later, the Spanish and Portuguese transformed the Caribbean and Brazil into sugar and tobacco plantations worked by black slaves imported from the west coast of Africa, who lived and died under brutal conditions.

In the seventeenth century, the French, Dutch, and English became active overseas. They raided the Spanish Caribbean, eventually seizing several islands, where they created sugar plantations and brought in black slaves. The English, French, and Dutch also established trading posts in Asia, the Dutch in particular seizing most of the possessions of Portugal and assuming control of most of the spice and slave trades.

Although they failed to find passages to Asia through the Arctic ice, the northern states did establish fur trading colonies in North America. The English in particular established a number of colonies on the Atlantic seaboard of North America; here thousands of Europeans settled, displacing the Amerindians. By the middle of the seventeenth century, several European nations possessed extensive overseas dominions, and the European life styles began to reflect the presence of products from around the world. However, the great wealth already absorbed from abroad would only whet the appetites of the colonial powers for further conquest of the nonwestern world, and, at times, for fiercer struggles among themselves.

SELECTED SOURCES

*Boxer, Charles R. *The Dutch Seaborne Empire, 1600–1800.* 1977. This work gives excellent insights into life in the Dutch Colonies.

*Bradford, William. *Of Plymouth Plantation, 1620–47.* 1983. The first-hand account of the Mayflower crossing and the settlement of Plymouth, by the leader of the Pilgrims.

*Clavell, James. *Shogun: A Novel of Japan.* 1976. The economic, political, and religious influence of the Portuguese in sixteenth century Japan, from the point of view of an English opponent. (Also a television series.)

Davis, David Brion. *The Problem of Slavery in Western Culture.* 1966. A brilliant discussion of one of the most important phenomena in western history.

*Haring, Clarence H. *The Spanish Empire in America.* 1975. An authoritative study that is more sympathetic to the Spanish than some accounts.

Innes, Hammond. *The Conquistadors.* 1969. A lively, beautifully illustrated account.

Kerner, Robert J. *The Urge to the Sea: The Course of Russian History.* 1971. Contains an interesting account of the Russian advance across Siberia.

*Morison, Samuel E. *Christopher Columbus, Mariner.* 1983. A lively introduction to a remarkable man and his remarkable feat.

*Nowell, Charles E. *The Great Discoveries and the First Colonial Empires.* 1982. Brief, readable introduction to this broad topic.

Shaffer, Peter. *The Royal Hunt of the Sun.* 1981. A play depicting the story of the capture, imprisonment, and execution of the Inca emperor Atahualpa by Pizarro.

*Available in paperback.

THE REFORMATION ERA

Since then Your Majesty and your lordships desire a simple reply, I will answer without any eloquent flourishes. Unless I am convinced by Scripture and plain reason—I do not accept the authority of popes and councils, for they have contradicted each other—my conscience is captive to the word of God. I cannot and I will not recant anything, for to go against conscience is neither right nor safe. Here I stand, I cannot do otherwise. God help me. Amen.

With these bold words, delivered before the holy Roman emperor and an assembly of German princes meeting in the city of Worms in 1521, Martin Luther (1483–1546) defied authorities of both church and state and turned an already well-advanced reformation in the church in a new direction. The movement unleashed by Luther, known as the Reformation, was a recurrence of the reform impulse that had characterized medieval Christianity. Although the Reformation was in part shaped by contemporary political developments and economic and social changes, it was basically a movement concerned with change in religious belief and practice. It resembled the Renaissance in its use of the idea of individualism and classical sources, but it differed by emphasizing faith, the spiritual life, and human wickedness instead of reason, worldliness, and human goodness. The present chapter begins by outlining the religious developments and conditions that precipitated the Reformation, examines four patterns of Protestant reform, and concludes by considering the Reformation inside the Roman Catholic Church.

CONTENTS

CAUSES OF THE REFORMATION

The Reformation had many causes. Powerful rulers of national states clashed with the leaders of an international church. These monarchs opposed papal claims to authority over their subjects, and sought reforms that would enable them to control the church in their lands and use its wealth for royal purposes. Impoverished free peasants and expansionist-minded nobles coveted the church's vast and wealthy lands. Members of

Luther and the Wittenberg Reformers. In this painting by Lucas Cranach the Younger in 1543, Luther is at the far left; his close associate Philip Melanchthon is at the far right in the front row. The large figure in the center foreground is Elector John Frederick of Saxony, who gave Luther crucial protection and significant support. Toledo Museum of Art.

347

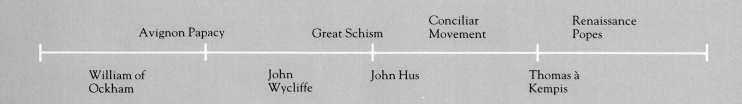

Avignon Papacy · Great Schism · Conciliar Movement · Renaissance Popes

William of Ockham · John Wycliffe · John Hus · Thomas à Kempis

the growing business and commercial classes disliked both the church's economic policies (notably its opposition to loaning money at interest) and its close ties with the landed aristocracy. The Reformation was a religious movement, however, and its most important causes were religious.

The Decline of Papal Power and Prestige

One important impetus to the Reformation was a decline in papal power and prestige during the fourteenth and fifteenth centuries. Following his humiliation of Pope Boniface VIII, King Philip IV of France had influenced the cardinals to elect a Frenchman as pope and persuaded him to move his residence to Avignon, a city separated from France only by the Rhone River. For more than seventy years (1305–1378) a series of French popes resided there, in what contemporaries, alluding to the exile of Jewish leaders following the capture of Judah in 586 B.C., called the "Babylonian Captivity" of the church. These popes, dominated by the French king, were regarded skeptically by many, who noted that the popes' power was based on their being successors of Peter as bishop of Rome, not Avignon.

France's political foes, notably the English, opposed papal control over church affairs in their lands and viewed payments to the Avignon popes as subsidies to an enemy. Bishops and abbots seeking escape from papal control found protection, at a price, available from their kings.

The Avignon popes responded by increasing their control over the organization and resources of the church. They enlarged the papal bureaucracy, and the cost of maintaining it, by creating new church offices and controlling appointments to them. They increased both the number of judicial cases which required appeal to the pope and the revenues derived from such legal activity. To defend their lands in the Papal States and to combat rebellions there, the Avignon popes required expensive armed forces, for which they devised new fund-raising measures. They sold church offices and *expectancies,* which entitled a buyer to the next vacant position. Appointees paid the papacy *annates,* the first year's income from the position, and heavy income taxes in subsequent years. Laypeople were required to pay an annual levy to the pope, tithes (10 percent of income) to support the parish church, and fees for almost every religious service or

benefit. Not surprisingly, many Europeans came to resent wealth leaving their lands to benefit the popes and echoed the contemporary observation that the pope "was ordered to lead the Lord's sheep to the pasture, not to fleece them." Bribery, corruption, and luxurious living became common in the papal government and further discredited it, and the popes were unable or unwilling to correct those conditions.

The return of Pope Gregory XI (1370–1378) to Rome in 1377 ended the Babylonian Captivity, but his death the following year inaugurated a more serious problem for the papacy, the Great Schism (division). Responding to popular demand, the cardinals first elected an Italian pope, Urban VI (1378–1389) who publicly scolded them for their worldliness and attempted to reduce their revenues. The cardinals thereupon left Rome, elected a Frenchman as Pope Clement VII (1378–1394), and settled with him at Avignon while Urban VI appointed a new group of cardinals to reside at Rome. The rival popes created competing systems of church administration, courts, and taxation, and corruption and financial abuses became worsened. The nations of Europe divided almost evenly in their allegiance to the two popes, who by avidly seeking the support of rulers appeared more like secular politicians than spiritual leaders. The two-pope situation persisted for more than thirty years and prompted the calling of a general church council at Pisa in 1409 in an attempt to resolve it. The council deposed both popes and authorized the cardinals to elect a new one, which they did; but as the incumbents disregarded their depositions, there were now three popes. The subsequent Council of Constance (1414–1418) finally ended the schism by deposing two popes and persuading the third to abdicate, making possible the election of a new pope whom all could accept.

Recourse to councils to resolve church problems further challenged papal authority. Theorists such as Marsilio of Padua (1290–1343) proposed that an elective council should govern the church and make the papacy a limited monarchy. Attracted by the idea, a number of lay and religious leaders formed the conciliar movement, which advocated reform and governing of the church through regular councils. Between 1409 and 1449, four such councils were held, but although the second, at Constance, ended the Great Schism, they accomplished little else. Popes, fearing the conciliar challenge to their authority, exploited disagreements among clergy from different lands to manipulate the councils and render them ineffective.

Although the popes eventually scuttled the conciliar movement and maintained papal supremacy, they obtained that victory at the cost of allowing secular monarchs more control of church appointments and revenues in their own countries. Hence

both papal revenues and papal power declined. By challenging the position and power of the papacy, yet failing to adopt a practical program of church reform, the conciliar movement contributed substantially to the sixteenth-century Reformation.

A series of Renaissance popes in the last half of the fifteenth century dissipated what little papal influence remained. Unable to assert their authority throughout Europe, they became merely Italian princes. Rather than providing religious leadership, they devoted their energies to ruling the Papal States, warring with their Italian neighbors, and sponsoring literature and art. Alexander VI (1492–1503) used the papacy to promote the interests of his family, particularly his notorious son Cesare Borgia, and was considered so depraved that a council was proposed to depose him as being "not a Christian." Thus, although the popes remained wealthy and politically powerful, they had lost the moral authority that was their chief source of influence.

Developments in Religious Thought

The decline in papal power and prestige between 1300 and 1520 was paralleled by an transformation of religious thought, which was also significant in precipitating the sixteenth-century Reformation. Up to 1300, church leaders were teaching that the truth revealed by God agreed with the truth discovered by human reason, that the sacraments transmitted God's grace, and that priests in cooperation with God could forgive sin. Pious living consisted of regular church attendance, reception of the sacraments, and obedience to the clergy. But after

1300, many individuals, dissatisfied with that formulation, looked for new ways to lead a religious life and took religious thought in new directions.

One intellectual change with important consequences for the Reformation was the revival of nominalism in the fourteenth century. Nominalists taught that only individual or "particular" things have real existence. In opposition to realists, who insisted on the objective reality of important "universals" such as society, state, church, and Christendom, the nominalists contended these "universals" were mere words (nomina, names), not realities. The nominalists also taught that knowledge is based on concrete experience and is obtained only through sense perception. The outcome of this line of reasoning, as William of Ockham (1300–1349) argued, was that the existence of God and other matters of faith could not be known by reason, but only by intuition. Instead of leading to a single truth, as Thomas Aquinas had taught, faith and reason now became two unrelated types of intellectual activity. According to nominalism, God was best understood as omnipotent will, arbitrary and irrational, and human faith was unquestioning obedience to that will. It was therefore no longer possible to buttress faith with philosophy or science.

From their emphasis on particulars, nominalists developed a literal interpretation of the Bible, and jettisoned medieval allegorical interpretations that supported the traditional Catholic theology and hierarchy. By vitiating such ideas as original sin, universal church, and Christendom, nominalists prepared the way for Protestantism. Although most nominalists continued to accept on faith what they formerly considered reasonable, the logical conclusion of their thinking was a complete rejection of human reason as a means of attaining religious truth and the total bankruptcy of attempts to rationalize religion.

Contemporary mysticism similarly rejected reason and emphasized a direct intuitive experience of God for which priests and sacraments were unessential. An especially prominent mystic was Catherine of Siena (1347–1380). As a youth, she vowed to remain unmarried to serve Christ, and devoted herself to prayer and self-denial. Later she energetically sought to aid the poor and the sick. She also promoted church reform and was influential in securing the papacy's return to Rome from Avignon. At her death, she was widely regarded as a saint possessing healing powers.

Mystics and those they influenced rejected the subtleties of scholastic theology and pursued lives of simple piety, often in group movements. Notable among these were the Brethren, and the Sisters, of the Common Life, whose lives were based on prayer, love, and direct communion with God. They established communities, pooled their earnings, engaged in group prayer, and cared for the needy. The Brethren of the Common Life were especially noted for their schools and for their devotional writings, of which the most significant was *The Imitation of Christ*, compiled and partially written by Thomas à Kempis (1380–1471). The book said little about rituals and dogmas but contained prayers and meditations to help the faithful lead lives of morality and piety; it was immensely popular and became the most widely read book ever written in Europe.

Although most reformers stayed within the bounds of orthodoxy, some carried their criticisms of the church or their opposition to ecclesiastical authority so far that they were adjudged heretics. John Wycliffe (1320?–1384) of England, an Oxford scholar and teacher, urged the state to undertake religious reform by stripping the church of its property. He subsequently argued for the destruction of the whole clerical hierarchy, claiming that forgiveness of sin depended on God alone. The Bible was the only source of God's law, he taught, and a morally unworthy priest could not administer a valid sacrament. He attacked such religious practices as pilgrimages, prayers to saints, and veneration of relics. Wycliffe also argued against transubstantiation, the belief that the bread and wine were transformed during the Mass into the body and blood of Jesus Christ. Protected by his king, Wycliffe died peaceably, but his followers, known as Lollards, were cruelly destroyed by the Lancastrian rulers of the fifteenth century. The Bohemian reformer John Hus (1374–1415) who shared most of Wycliffe's ideas, was executed for heresy by the schism-settling Council of Constance in 1415. His Bohemian followers, however, combined support for his teachings with passionate patriotic opposition to the Germans who dominated the country's religious and political life, and his death triggered a vigorous rebellion. Papally supported and imperially led crusades failed to crush the Hussites and led instead to the formation of a Hussite church in which laity received both bread and wine in the Eucharist, rather than the bread alone, as was standard Roman Catholic practice.

Humanists helped to promote reform by studying the Bible and the writings of early Christian leaders. Some pointed to a contrast between the early church and that of their own times. Critical of scholastic thought, some humanists rejected, sometimes with biting satire, Catholic dogma and ritual. Preferring the practice of simple piety, they taught a moral code common to both Christianity and classical antiquity that emphasized human dignity. Although most humanists preferred to remain within the Roman Catholic church, their thoughts and writings helped to prepare the way for religious reform.

Abuses in Religious Practice

A more immediate cause of the Reformation was widespread abuses in religious practice. Reformers complained of ignorant clergy who could not understand the Latin of the Mass and of immoral clerics who lived in luxury and disregarded vows of chastity and celibacy. They sought to eliminate simony (the buying and selling of church offices), pluralism (the holding of several church offices by one individual), nepotism (the appointing of relatives to church positions), and absenteeism (the failure of church officials to perform their religious duties). Reformers also opposed the collecting of fees for the performance of religious services and other forms of ecclesiastical money-raising. Perhaps most widely criticized was the promotion of veneration of relics. Clerics sold what purported to be pieces of, say, Christ's cross to those who believed that objects used by Christ, Mary, or the saints possessed miraculous powers of healing or protection. Another troublesome abuse was the sale of indulgences, remissions of temporal punishment in purgatory owing to sin. Originally, indulgences were issued

Issuing of Letters of Indulgence at a German Country Fair. Sixteenth-century. Although indulgences, which shortened the length of an individual's stay in purgatory, were supposed to be linked to the sacrament of pennance, churchmen sometimes issued them merely on payment of money. Here, clerics and financial agents collect money in exchange for indulgences, varying the price according to the social class of the purchaser.

for charitable works or extraordinary religious activities such as fasting or crusading and only as part of a sincerely performed sacrament of penance. As popes became more desperate for revenue, however, they contracted with agents to sell indulgences on a commission basis. Such peddlers dispensed with bothersome religious requirements and made great profits by proclaiming that "as soon as the coin in the coffer rings, the soul from purgatory springs." The disregard of church teaching by indulgence peddlers distressed many, including an obscure university professor named Martin Luther.

MAINSTREAM PROTESTANT REFORM

Unlike earlier reform efforts, which had remained within the Roman Catholic church, the sixteenth-century activities broke from it and created a new branch of Christianity called Protestantism. This name was first applied to followers of Martin Luther, who protested attempts in 1529 by Roman Catholic leaders in the Holy Roman Empire to prevent further changes in religious practice; it was later applied to other religious groups that disagreed with Roman Catholicism. The most prominent forms of Protestantism developed in Germany and Switzerland, and are here labeled mainstream Protestantism to distinguish them from other forms described later.

Luther and German Reformation

The power of his thought and his compelling personality made Martin Luther the leader of the Reformation in Germany. Educated first in a school of the Brethren of the Common Life and later at the University of Erfurt, he abruptly renounced plans to study law, joined a congregation of Augustinian hermit friars, and was ordained a priest. Rigorous practice of the Augustinian discipline did not give Luther spiritual satisfaction. In preparing for his teaching responsibilities at the University of Wittenberg, however, he was impressed by Paul's statement that "the just shall live by faith" (Romans 1:17), and came to see simple faith, rather than sacraments, works, and rituals, as the path to right relationship with God—a position known as "justification by faith."

At that juncture, Luther became embroiled in religious controversy by publicly posting a list of theses (debate topics) on indulgences. Expecting to engender a scholarly debate, Luther was astonished to discover himself a German celebrity. Because he expressed the thoughts and feelings of many Germans on contemporary religious issues, opposition to religious abuses and papal exactions promptly crystallized around him.

351

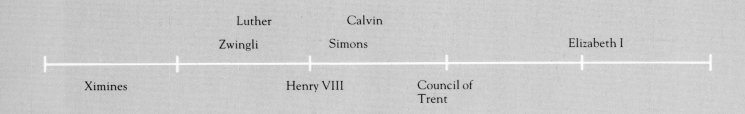

Luther

Calvin

Zwingli

Simons

Elizabeth I

Ximines

Henry VIII

Council of Trent

Within two years, Luther realized his position was hopelessly opposed to that of the church. In a series of pamphlets, he denounced the pope and the church organization and urged the German princes to seize church lands and assume control of the German church. His teachings were condemned, and he was soon excommunicated by the pope and outlawed by the emperor in the 1521 imperial assembly at Worms, where he made his famous "Here I stand" speech.

Reformers with other interests promptly attempted to link their causes with Luther, forcing him to delineate his position more precisely. He repudiated religious zealots who preached doctrines of individualism and extremism in his name, and broke with humanists who upheld free will by writing a pamphlet entitled *On the Bondage of the Human Will.*

Luther also had to define his stand on political and social issues. South German peasants, resentful of nobles who deprived them of customary rights while increasing rents and financial exactions, revolted against their oppressors and sought Luther's support. Luther, although sympathetic, believed that only duly constituted authorities should use force. He harshly denounced the peasants' recourse to violence, and opposed the rebels' at-

tempts to link their economic and social demands with religious reform.

In that context of conflict, Luther's own religious views were clarified. He saw God's forgiveness of sin as a miracle that could not be understood by reason and therefore had to be taken on faith. Luther advocated replacing the authority of the pope and the rulings of church councils in the determination of church doctrine and practice with the Bible as the sole source of religious authority, translating it into German to make it more accessible. The church, he believed, consisted of all believers, rather than any particular organization. Therefore he rejected the Roman Catholic hierarchy, and approved of the secular rulers as heads of the church in their territories, which allowed them to appropriate church lands. According to Luther, monasticism and clerical celibacy should be abolished (he married a former nun) and priestly functions diminished. Moreover, he taught the "priesthood of all believers"; because individuals receive God's forgiveness directly, they are priests to themselves and others. Luther encouraged lay participation in worship activities and promoted congregational singing by writing numerous hymns. He rejected most of the Catholic sacramental system, retaining only

baptism and the Lord's Supper as valid sacraments. In place of the Catholic doctrine of transubstantiation, Luther taught Christ's "real presence" in the bread and wine.

After Luther's death in 1546, Lutheranism continued to spread, fracturing the religious unity of Latin Christendom. A nine-year war between Catholics and Protestants in the Holy Roman Empire (1546–1555) ended with the 1555 Peace of Augsburg, which allowed princes and cities to determine whether their subjects would be Lutherans or Catholics and permitted those who objected to their ruler's choice to emigrate elsewhere. Although south German peasants, embittered by Luther's opposition to the Peasant Revolt, remained staunchly Roman Catholic, most north German and all the Scandinavian states soon embraced Lutheranism.

Calvin and Swiss Reformation

Interest in reform was strong in Switzerland as well as in Germany. Ulrich Zwingli (1484–1531), a priest in the city of Zurich and the first important Swiss reformer, pursued political and moral changes there even before Luther posted his theses. He accepted most of Luther's teachings, incorporated them into the reforms he had launched, and spread those doctrines to other nearby cantons (Swiss political divisions similar to city-states). However, he disagreed with Luther's interpretation of the Lord's Supper, holding Jesus Christ to be spiritually but not physically present and the bread and wine to be merely symbols of Christ's body and blood. This disagreement proved unresolvable, and

Swiss Protestantism thereafter developed independently from Lutheranism. Zwingli's attempts to spread reform into other cantons produced civil war, which ended with an agreement that a canton's government could decide the religion of its inhabitants.

After Zwingli's death, Swiss reform leadership passed to John Calvin (1509–1564) of Geneva. Born in France and thoroughly trained in

the humanities and law, he showed promise of becoming a first-rate humanist. But a conversion to Protestant Christianity, probably influenced by his reading of Luther's works, directed his attention to religious reform.

Governmental hostility soon forced Calvin to flee France for Switzerland, where he published an outstanding exposition of Protestant principles,

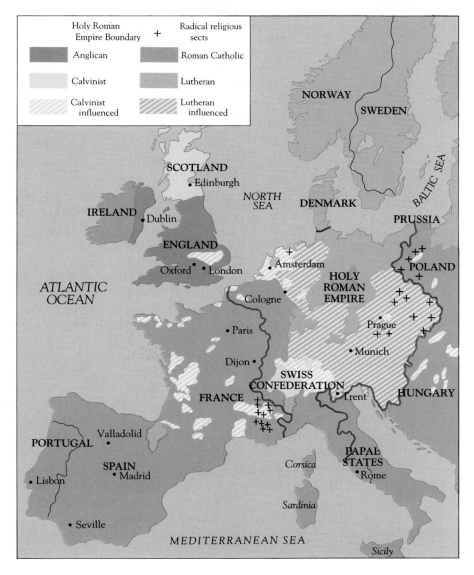

MAP 44

Reformation Europe. Like the Renaissance, the Reformation was a western European occurrence. However, rather than uniting Europe, it disrupted and divided it. Protestant forms of Christianity proved especially congenial to northern and central Europeans.

CALVIN ON DIVINE PREDESTINATION

When we attribute foreknowledge to God, we mean that all things always were, and perpetually remain, under His eyes, so that to His knowledge there is nothing future or past, but all things are present . . . And this foreknowledge is extended throughout the universe to every creature. We call predestination God's eternal decree, by which He determined with Himself what He wished to become of each man. For all are not created in equal condition; rather, eternal life is foreordained for some, eternal damnation for others. Therefore, as any man has been created to one or the other of these ends, we speak of him as predestined to life or to death.*

In these few words, John Calvin stated the doctrine of predestination, which became a distinguishing characteristic of Calvinist churches. The doctrine of predestination stimulated Calvinists to do God's work. Although none could know who were the elect, indications of election were a desire to live rightly, practice pious conduct, and affirm a personal profession of faith.

*John Calvin, *The Institutes of the Christian Religion*, ed. John T. McNeill (Philadelphia: Westminster Press, 1960), book 3, chap. 21, p. 5.

The Institutes of the Christian Religion (1536). He was invited to settle in Geneva. Under Calvin's leadership Geneva became the focus of Swiss reform activity. Already a banking and commercial center, Geneva had recently ousted its feudal lords and es-

tablished a free republic governed by a council. Calvin and his followers soon gained decisive authority in the city's affairs by means of a seventeen-member consistory (a councillike body) composed of clergy and laity, which regulated church discipline and religious life and whose members sat on and influenced the decisions of town councils.

Calvin drew heavily on Augustine's writings to formulate his teachings, which were very similar to Luther's. He accepted Luther's doctrine of justification by faith, but his own central religious principle was the absolute sovereignty of God, whom Calvin viewed as the arbitrary deity of the Old Testament. Coupled with God's sovereignty was the sovereignty of law, incorporated in the Bible, a body of rules to be followed precisely. The universe was totally dependent on God's will, which was also the highest rule of justice. Although owing to Adam's sin, all humans were sinners by nature, God had predestined or elected some to be saved and others to be damned.

All members of the Christian commonwealth were to exhibit lives of piety and morality, to help fulfill God's purposes, and to strive for God's glory. Whereas the elect performed God's will by the gift of God's grace, the damned should honor God by conforming so far as possible to the Christian way of life. To make Geneva a true city of God and to enable its citizens to live according to God's word, detailed regulations governing all aspects of life were enacted and enforced. Geneva's regulations required residents to attend sermons and forbade them to criticize ministers and to work or play on Sunday. Regulations also outlawed dancing, card

playing, and theater attendance at any time.

Calvinist patterns of worship and church government differed sharply from those of the Roman Catholic church. Elaborate rituals, instrumental music, stained glass windows, and images were eliminated from Calvinist churches; and prayers, preaching, and psalm singing characterized the worship service. Calvin, like Luther, recognized only baptism and the Lord's Supper as valid sacraments, but asserted against Luther's "real presence" teaching that Christ was only spiritually present in the bread and wine. Dispensing with the Roman Catholic church's hierarchy, Calvinist congregations governed themselves through councils of elected elders. Above the individual congregation, a series of local, regional, and national councils, called synods, in which elders and clergy shared control, governed the Calvinist church.

Calvin's teachings had important social implications, particularly in stimulating capitalism and opposing political tyranny. Calvinism supported and sanctified the work of merchants and moneylenders, and its ethics emphasized the virtues of thrift and industry. Individuals frequently interpreted the business success that often resulted from those practices as a sign of God's grace. Calvin's rejection of the traditional Christian prohibition against collecting interest on loaned money encouraged investment and commercial activity. In political matters, Calvin taught that although people should obey secular authority, they should passively disobey commands contrary to God's will, and he allowed that duly constituted authorities could resist tyrannical rulers. Later, Calvinism supported revolts against despots in England and France and Spanish tyrants in the Netherlands. Calvinist church government, with its use of election and representation, powerfully contributed to the growth of democracy.

After Luther's death, Calvinism was the main force in the spread of Protestantism. Missionaries from Germany traveled throughout Europe, and many persons in France, the Netherlands, Germany, Poland, and Hungary adopted Calvinism. In Switzerland, most of Zwingli's followers joined the Calvinists, and John Knox (1505–1572), after a visit to Geneva, made Calvinism the dominant religion in his native Scotland.

John Calvin Preaching. Sixteenth-century woodcut. Opposing appeals to the senses, Calvinists eliminated statues, paintings, and stained glass from their churches. Because the sermon rather than the sacrament was central to Calvinist worship, the pulpit was often the central focus of the church.

OTHER PROTESTANT GROUPS

Although Luther and Calvin represent the mainstream of Protestant reform, other reformers with alternative notions of religious change soon appeared. Some attempted to recreate primitive Christianity and to reconstruct society along early Christian lines. These radical reformers proposed far-reaching changes in existing social and religious institutions. On the other hand, religious changes in England under the new Anglican church were at first very conservative.

The Radicals

The radical reformers that emerged during the Reformation emphasized a thoroughgoing individualism in religion. They embraced Luther's teaching that each individual should follow the guidance of his or her conscience or, as some phrased it, the "inner light." Although, like other Protestants, they stressed a literal interpretation of the Bible and believed people could and should interpret the Bible for themselves, they also believed that God's revelation continued and God spoke directly to chosen followers.

The radicals regarded the church as a community of saints. They admitted only persons who had experienced spiritual regeneration. Grace, in their belief, was not imparted to a person by a sacramental system, but was a direct gift from God that took the form of an inner, partly mystical, experience. Therefore, unlike other Christian groups that practiced infant baptism, they baptized only believers who could testify to such an experience, the sign of spiritual regeneration. The original radicals had been raised as Catholics and had received infant baptism in the Catholic church; they were now rebaptized as adults as a testament to their new faith. Contemporaries therefore called them Anabaptists, or rebaptizers.

The Anabaptists departed further from Roman Catholic ritual and dogma than the mainstream Protestants. They interpreted communion as merely a commemorative service; in a strict sense clergymen were therefore unnecessary. All members of congregations participated in making decisions. Congregations also elected their pastors, who wore no distinctive garments and often lacked formal education, but gave evidence of special gifts received from God's Holy Spirit. Others who were not pastors helped fellow believers and also served as missionaries to nonbelievers.

To radical reformers, other evidence of spiritual regeneration was the practice of what they called discipleship. Beyond practicing a strict moral code, they insisted that a person's relationship with God should go beyond acceptance of doctrines and inner experience, to produce a transformed style of life. They denounced accumulation of wealth and taught that Christians should share their goods with one another. Most seditious of all to their contemporaries, radicals also refused to recognize distinctions of rank or class, holding that all humans were equal in God's sight.

Unlike Catholics and other Protestants, who attempted to work closely with rulers and governments, radicals insisted on a complete separation of church and state. Most refused to hold political office and abstained from political life. Many refused to perform military service, take oaths, or pay taxes to governments engaged in war. Because of their own stress on freedom of conscience, they condemned religious persecution and refused to attempt to compel others to believe as they did.

Radical reformers were widely feared and hated, not only because of the extreme nature of their religious positions but also because a few espoused social revolution. Most followers of radical reform came from lower social and economic classes and were attracted by its emotional strength and democratic practices. Many radicals anticipated the early destruction of this world and the establishment of God's kingdom of justice and peace, but some sought to use force to establish that kingdom. Radicals of the latter persuasion briefly (1534–1535) seized control of the German city of Munster, expelled Lutherans and Calvinists from the city, and, with appropriate biblical justification, established such practices as polygamy and community ownership of property. That episode served to discredit the Anabaptist movement.

Both Catholics and mainstream Protestants harshly persecuted radicals for their pursuit of a thoroughgoing Christian perfection, their real and implied threat to the existing social order, and their practice of rebaptizing persons previously baptized as infants (a practice illegal since the fifth century); consequently, many radicals met early and violent deaths. Radical reformers were almost completely eliminated in Germany, but some managed to survive under tolerant Polish rulers and in the loose

Execution of Anabaptist Reformers. Sixteenth-century woodcut. Religious radicals, who alienated Catholics and Protestants alike, were frequently hunted down and executed as heretics. To mock their beliefs regarding baptism, their persecutors often put Anabaptists to death by drowning rather than burning. In some parts of Europe, however, they found tolerant rulers and survived.

political organization of the Netherlands. Survivors abandoned extreme dogmas and adopted a posture of religious quietism. Many radicals in the Netherlands were organized by Menno Simons (1496–1561) into the Mennonite church, which subsequently influenced English-speaking Quakers, Baptists, and independents.

Anglicanism

In England, Protestantism proceeded from dynastic difficulties. When Catherine of Aragon (1485–1536), the wife of King Henry VIII (1509–47) reached the end of her childbearing years without producing a son, the king, in 1527, sought to annul their marriage so he might remarry and produce a male heir. However, because of a papal dispensation that had allowed them to marry in the first place, and because Emperor

Charles V, the queen's nephew, controlled Rome, the pope refused to grant an annulment. Henry thereupon took independent action. First, he summoned an assembly of the English clergy, which in 1532 recognized him as head of the English church. Next, Parliament agreed to abolish payments to the pope and to place the church in England under royal authority. Henry promptly appointed a compliant archbishop of Canterbury, Thomas Cranmer, who granted the desired annulment, enabling the king to remarry (altogether, he married six times). Although the king disbanded the monasteries and confiscated their wealth, using their lands to purchase the support of nobles, he had Parliament reaffirm Roman Catholic doctrine in the Six Articles in 1539.

During the short reign of Henry's young son, Edward VI (1547–1553), however, continental reformers gained

control of the Anglican church and made it Protestant. Priests were allowed to marry, English replaced Latin in religious services, images were eliminated, and new articles of doctrine affirmed the Lutheran concept of justification by faith and recognized only baptism and the Lord's Supper as sacraments. The reformers promulgated the decidedly Calvinistic Forty-two Articles of Faith and published *The Book of Common Prayer* (1549, revised in 1552), which all English clergy were required by law to use.

On Edward's death without heirs, Mary (1553–1558), the daughter of Henry VIII and Catherine, succeeded him and attempted to restore Roman Catholicism in England, returning England to papal obedience and restoring the rule of clerical celibacy. However, she encountered much opposition. Although most

Henry VIII Transfers Power to His Son Edward VI. Contemporary painting. The Reformation in England was closely linked with political events. Although Henry VIII made himself head of the English church, he kept it Roman Catholic. The transfer of power to young Edward, however, gave Edward's Protestant advisers an opportunity to protestantize the English church. The figure collapsed at Edward's feet is the pope. The printed words draw a Protestant propaganda contrast between the enduring quality of God's word and the brevity of human, even papal, life. National Portrait Gallery, London.

people in England still preferred Roman Catholicism, they resented papal interference, and beneficiaries of the confiscation of monastic lands feared the loss of their new wealth. Moreover, Mary's marriage to Philip II of Spain caused many in England to fear either foreign complications or actual Spanish domination. In her efforts to hasten religious change, she executed many prominent Protestants, thus earning the nickname "Bloody Mary." Hence, despite her efforts to promote Roman Catholicism, Mary actually helped to reduce enthusiasm for it in England.

Mary's successor, her half-sister Elizabeth I (1558–1603), followed a moderate religious policy. Attracted

to Catholic pomp and ceremony in religious services, but depending on Protestants for political support, Elizabeth separated England from Rome soon after her accession. Parliament acted to make her supreme governor, rather than head, of the Anglican church, and adopted a new statement of faith. The Thirty-Nine Articles, which embodied Protestant dogma in somewhat ambiguous terms, was intended to appeal to many types of Protestants as well as to Roman Catholics. The liturgy, although in English, resembled that of Catholicism, and the episcopal form of church organization was retained. Many lower clergy and most English laity found the Anglican church acceptable; they appreciated the ceremony it preserved and concerned themselves little with subtleties of dogma.

Although many people in England were content with the Elizabethan Anglican compromise, two groups remained dissatisfied. Among Roman Catholics, some supported the efforts of Mary Stuart (1542–1587), the Roman Catholic queen of Scotland, to overthrow Elizabeth or the attempts of Philip II of Spain to conquer England. Some extreme Calvinist Protestants, desirous of returning to the simple rituals of early Christianity, strove to "purify" the Anglican church of its ecclesiastical hierarchy and its "Romish" rites, becoming known as Puritans. The Puritans gained strength and in the seventeenth century briefly gained control of England.

ROMAN CATHOLIC REFORMATION

Although many reformers became Protestants, others remained within the Roman Catholic church to work to correct abuses and through their efforts produced important changes. Many humanists also, like Erasmus, despite their criticism of scholastic thought and deemphasis on Roman Catholic dogma and ritual, remained Roman Catholic and rejected Protestantism.

Beginnings

In some lands, Roman Catholic reform predated Protestantism. In Spain, Cardinal Ximenes (1436–1517) inaugurated a religious revival with royal approval; he eliminated abuses from monasteries, established schools for the training of clergy, and improved the quality of priests. In Italy, earnest clergy such as the friar Savonarola (1452–1498) in Florence worked to make priests more worthy of their calling and to upgrade the moral life of laypeople. New religious orders dedicated to high ideals of piety and social service developed, such as the Oratory of Divine Love, in which clergy and laity sought personal holiness through private devotion and charitable deeds, or the Capuchins, an order of friars dedicated to strict self-discipline and religious observance.

Roman Catholic reform was not easily accomplished. Because of the church's hierarchical structure, reformers had to attain high positions to make significant changes, but the popes and kings who controlled such appointments rarely granted them to reformers. Even if appointed, a bishop rarely controlled the monasteries or even all the clergy in his diocese. If reformers wished to correct financial abuses, they would have to find alternative sources of revenue, and if they were to defend the faithful against heresy, they would have to carefully define Roman Catholic dogmas. The spread of Protestantism strengthened the position of the reformers, however, and the election of Pope Paul III (1534–1549) made reform a churchwide priority.

The Council of Trent

An important event in the promotion of Roman Catholic reform was a general council that met in several sessions between 1545 and 1563 in the north Italian town of Trent. High hopes were held for the council. Secular rulers sought to use it to facilitate a compromise with the Protestants,

The Council of Trent. School of Titian. During a period of almost twenty years, the council upheld Roman Catholic doctrines against Protestant challenges, while introducing reforms in Roman Catholic practice. Louvre Museum, Paris.

LOYOLA ON JESUIT OBEDIENCE

Although I wish all of you perfection in every virtue and spiritual gift it is . . . in obedience more than in any other virtue that I desire to see you excel. And that is because, as St. Gregory says, obedience is the virtue which plants all the other virtues in the mind . . . We may allow ourselves to be surpassed by other religious orders in fasts, watchings and other austerities, . . . but in the purity and perfection of obedience, and the true resignation of our wills and abnegation of our own judgment, I am very desirous . . . that . . . this Society be conspicuous, so that by this virtue its true sons may be recognized as men who regard not the person whom they obey, but in him Christ our Lord, for whose sake, they obey. For your superior is to be obeyed not because he is prudent, or good, or qualified by any other gift of God, but because he holds the place and the authority of God. *

For Loyola, absolute obedience was to be the hallmark of the Jesuit order. In this letter to Portuguese Jesuits dissatisfied with a new leader, Loyola extolled its importance. His followers consequently became remarkable for their obedience, dedication and zeal for service; they closely resembled the Calvinists.

*Letters of St. Ignatius of Loyola, ed. and trans. William J. Young, S. J. (Chicago: Loyola University Press 1959), pp. 287–288.

and religious reformers anticipated it would develop further checks on papal authority.

In its discussion of Catholic doctrine, the Council of Trent reaffirmed traditional Roman Catholic dogmas and rejected any concessions to Protestant beliefs. It upheld the doctrines of purgatory, transubstantiation, the sacraments as indispensable means of grace, clerical celibacy, and all other Catholic beliefs. The council emphasized the tradition of apostolic teaching—derived from the writings of church fathers and the decisions of church councils—as equal in authority to the Bible. It also reaffirmed the monarchical government of the church, holding that papal authority transcended that of a church council.

Regarding religious practice, the Council of Trent sought to eliminate abuses and restore church discipline. It prohibited pluralism and the sale of indulgences, ordered the establishment of seminaries in every diocese to combat priestly ignorance, and gave bishops greater authority within their dioceses. To protect the laity from harmful or heretical ideas, the council established an Index of Prohibited Books and established an agency to revise that list periodically. To eliminate heresy where it already flourished, the council revived and reorganized the Inquisition and encouraged rulers to establish it in their lands.

The Society of Jesus

A new order, the Society of Jesus, became a prominent agency for the promotion of Roman Catholic reform. Founded by a Basque noble, Ignatius Loyola (1491–1556), in conjunction with a group of fellow students at the University of Paris, its members, called Jesuits, took monastic vows and labored for religious reform. From his own religious explorations, Loyola wrote a devotional guide entitled *Spiritual Exercises* (1523), which led individuals through a contemplation of sin and Christ's life to renounce their own desires and follow God's will. The Society of Jesus was a highly centralized, strictly disciplined organization constructed on a military model, whose members took special vows of obedience to the pope. They also became effective preachers and zealous missionaries, halting or reversing the growth of Protestantism in much of Europe and spreading Christianity in the Americas, Africa, and Asia.

SUMMARY

The religious reformation of the sixteenth century had several antecedents. Avaricious Avignon popes and a period of multiple popes lowered papal prestige, and papal concessions to secular rulers to defeat the conciliar movement and involvement in Italian politics diminished papal influence. Many abuses in religious practice stirred reformers to action. A resurgence of Pauline-Augustinian ideas and a revival of nominalism stimulated reform, and both mystics and heretics challenged the Catholic church.

During the sixteenth century, reformers broke with the Catholic church and established Protestant Christianity. Luther and Calvin were the major mainstream Protestant reformers. Luther's teaching of justification by faith made the Catholic apparatus for earning salvation unnecessary. He recognized the Bible as the sole source of religious authority, and emphasized the role of laity in the church. Calvin stressed God's arbitrary sovereignty, and his doctrine of predestination stimulated Calvinists to extensive activity. Geneva became a city of God on earth, and Calvinist churches were purified of all Catholic features.

Other forms of Protestantism developed. Radical reformers emphasized individualism in religion and granted baptism only to adults. They regarded the church as a community of saints, allowed congregations to govern their own affairs, and insisted on complete separation of church and state. Protestantism in England began as a result of dynastic difficulties and, as the Anglican church, became established under Elizabeth I. Although Protestant in its doctrines, the Anglican church retained Roman Catholic features in organization and ritual.

Within the Roman Catholic church, humanists and clergy in several lands conducted reform activities, and Pope Paul III made reform a churchwide priority. The Council of Trent reaffirmed traditional Roman Catholic doctrines and sought to eliminate abuses, the Society of Jesus became a prominent agency for Roman Catholic reform. Religious tensions persisted, however, and contributed significantly to civil wars and international conflicts within Europe.

SELECTED SOURCES

*Bainton, Roland H. *Here I Stand: A Life of Martin Luther.* 1950. Readable, scholarly presentation of Luther's life and work.

*Bainton, Roland H. *The Reformation of the Sixteenth Century.* 1952. Brief account by a Protestant writer; neglects the Roman Catholic Reformation.

*Dickens, Arthur G. *The Counter Reformation.* 1969. Presents Roman Catholic activities often neglected in Protestant histories of the Reformation.

Dickens, Arthur G. *The English Reformation.* 1964. Treats the personalities and the issues with sympathy and insight.

Erikson, Erik H. *Young Man Luther.* 1958. An insightful account of Luther's early years by a noted child psychologist.

*Harkness, Georgia. *John Calvin: The Man and His Ethics.* 1958. Brief but insightful biography of Calvin, coupled with extensive discussion of his ethical teachings.

*Ignatius Loyola. *The Spiritual Exercises of St. Ignatius.* translated by Anthony Mottola. 1964. A vital expression of sixteenth century spirituality.

*Littell, Franklin H. *The Origins of Sectarian Protestantism.* 1964. A spirited presentation of the radical Reformation outlook by an heir of that tradition.

Luther. 1974. Stirring film interpretation of Luther's reforming activity.

McNeill, John T. *The History and Character of Calvinism.* 1954. The standard treatment, focusing on the movement rather than the man.

*Neale, John E. *Queen Elizabeth I.* 1957. Sympathetic biography of this outstanding English ruler.

*Tawney, R. H. *Religion and the Rise of Capitalism.* 1926. A classic study which stimulated extensive controversy concerning its topic.

*Available in paperback.

INTERNATIONAL CONFLICTS AND RELIGIOUS STRUGGLES (1450–1660)

For a prince . . . it is very necessary . . . to seem merciful, faithful, humane, sincere, and religious and also to be so; but you must have the mind so trained that, when occasion requires it, you may be able to change to the opposite qualities. And it must be understood that a prince . . . cannot observe all those things which are considered good in man [and must often] in order to maintain the state, act against faith, against charity, against humanity, and against religion. . . .

Let a prince therefore aim at conquering and maintaining the state, and the means will always be judged honorable, and praised by everyone, for the common people are always taken by appearances and by results.

Niccolo Machiavelli (1469–1527) is famous for his teachings on the irrelevance of morality in international affairs and the paramount value of survival and self-interest in conducting state policy. He derived his principles from his study of history and observations of Italian politics and the international conflicts fought out in Italy. His amoral approach to politics, especially his contention that rulers might act against religion for the sake of the state, aroused much opposition both then and later. But Machiavelli's views guided many leaders involved in the international conflicts and the religious wars this chapter examines. His ideas are at least partly responsible for the development of diplomatic techniques in the Italian wars, and, ironically, contributed to the rise of religious toleration amid the religious wars of sixteenth- and seventeenth-century Europe.

CONTENTS

WARFARE AND DIPLOMACY

The rapid development of Europe's strong national monarchies, dynastic states, and autocratic, pluralistic empires during the sixteenth century led to significant international conflicts as those states attempted to expand

Marauding Army in the Thirty Years' War. Detail. Jan Brueghel and Sebastian Waux. Seventeenth-century armies frequently lived off the land, and foraging for food was a necessity. Such activity brought war home to many civilians, especially when accompanied by bitter religious hatred. Kunsthistorisches Museum, Vienna.

at the expense of weaker neighbors. In those struggles, religious loyalties were sometimes abandoned for political expediency; thus Catholic France allied with the Muslim Turks against the Catholic Holy Roman Empire and Protestants might find themselves joined with, as well as opposing, Catholics. Although these wars often produced only modest shifts of territory, they established patterns for both conflict and diplomacy and were highly significant for future European development.

Europe and the Turks

One area of continual conflict comprised the Danube basin the Balkans, where Christian states struggled to resist the Ottoman Turks. The Ottoman rulers, after taking Constantinople in 1453 and eliminating the Byzantine Empire, continued to ad-

MAP 45
Mediterranean Europe in the Sixteenth Century. At this time, continuing Ottoman expansion seemed likely to make most of the Mediterranean a Turkish lake. France's invasion of Italy triggered over sixty years of warfare, weakening resistance to the Turks. However, Ottoman attacks on Otranto and Vienna, although alarming to European Christians, marked the limits of Turkish power.

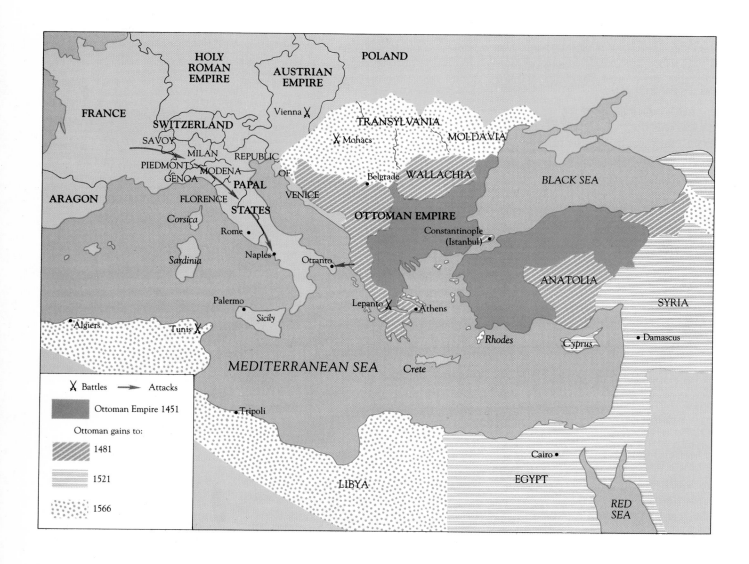

Turks take
Constantinople

Turks take
Belgrade

Turks
defeated   Spanish
at Lepanto   Armada

French
invade
Italy

French
defeated
at Pavia

French religious wars

Spanish-Dutch
religious wars

vance toward central Europe. The Turks sought to complete their conquest of the rich, grain-growing area of the Balkans, where they were long established and the Christians were weak and divided (Map 45).

The Christians, however, were strong enough to hold back the Turks until the sixteenth century. In the rugged mountains of the western Balkans, Albanians maintained vigorous guerrilla resistance, and in the peninsula's center, Hungary was an effective buffer state deterring Ottoman advance. In the east, the Ottomans pushed beyond the Danube to take the Rumanian territory of Wallachia in 1476, but were checked further east by the hard-fighting warriors of Moldavia.

As local leaders proved able to halt the Turkish advance, Ottoman forces posed little threat to other European lands. Repeated papal calls for crusades against the Turks produced no significant response. European states in fact established accommodations with the Turks, negotiating military alliances and commercial agreements with them. The Ottomans were drawn into the European state system.

Europeans gained a respite from Ottoman advances for nearly forty years, (1480–1520) while the Turks devoted their energies to a bitter succession struggle and conquests of their eastern neighbors. Taking northern Mesopotamia, Syria, and Egypt, they secured their eastern frontiers. They also established the caliph, the titular head of Islam, at Constantinople, thus assuming the religious leadership of all Muslims.

Under Suleiman I (1520–1566), the Ottomans turned their attention again to Europe. In 1521, they took Belgrade, the key bastion of the middle Danube. In the following year, they occupied the island of Rhodes, off Asia Minor, which had been a base for Christian attacks on Islamic commerce. The sultan conquered Hungary in 1526 and defeated Habsburg attempts to retake it. He also twice besieged Vienna, but failed to take the Habsburg capital.

Meanwhile, the Ottomans extended their influence into the western Mediterranean. Here, at the beginning of the sixteenth century, Islamic fortunes were in decline. To extend the Spanish successes against the Muslims and to safeguard communications with Italy, Ferdinand of Spain had seized several Islamic ports in north Africa. The Spanish had also

expelled Muslims from the Iberian Peninsula, and many of those exiles settled in north African Islamic lands, subsequently engaging in piracy against Christian commerce. The Islamic pirates ousted the Spanish from their African strongholds and became Ottoman vassals. The Emperor Charles V, acting as protector of Christendom and seeking to eliminate the Islamic pirates from the Mediterranean, took Tunis temporarily in 1535, but his effort to seize Algiers failed. The Islamic pirates continued to harass Mediterranean shipping and to ravage Christian coastal areas.

By the 1560s, however, Ottoman power began to reach its limits. The Turks failed to take Malta in 1565, and a temporary alliance of Italian cities and Habsburg states destroyed a large Turkish fleet at the Gulf of Lepanto in 1571, weakening the Turkish naval presence in the Mediterranean. To the northeast, the Turks attempted to dig a canal between the Volga and Don rivers in southern Russia to counter Ivan IV's successes against the Volga Islamic states and to protect their Crimean Tartar allies, but in 1568 they abandoned the project.

Italian Wars and the French-Habsburg Conflict

Italy was another important focus of European international conflict in the sixteenth century. Although Portugal and Spain had partly satisfied their expansionist impulses by undertaking aggressive adventures overseas to the Americas, Africa, and Asia, other states sought to conquer weaker territories in Europe. Italy's combination of commercial prosperity and political disunity and its proximity to the strong monarchies of France and Spain as well as to the Ottoman Empire made it a tempting target for such expansionist efforts.

Several factors kept Italy disunited. The popes opposed unification, which would eliminate their temporal power. Commercial rivalry among Italian cities remained intense. Each city-state sought to further its own interest by taking as much territory as possible and keeping others from doing likewise. There were almost constant wars conducted by professional mercenaries commanded by captains who sold their services to the highest bidder. However, these wars were limited and produced little bloodshed, as mercenaries wished to live to collect their pay and no state wanted its commerce completely destroyed. Before the French invasion, the Italian states had evolved a "balance of power" policy among themselves, in which a coalition of weaker states joined forces to balance the power of a stronger state to prevent it from achieving dominance. As the power of participating states waxed and waned and interests changed over time, the patterns of alliance changed, often with bewildering rapidity.

The balance-of-power method of controlling conflicts had a long history in European affairs, and its effective maintenance stimulated the development of diplomacy. Rulers calculated the probabilities of a rival state's continued resistance by analyzing its resources and patterns of income and expenditure. States anticipated shifts of alliances and alignments by sizing up personalities and intrigues at a royal court or capital. To obtain such information, Italian states began to maintain at foreign courts a regular and permanent system of envoys, or ambassadors, who sent frequent reports to their home states.

If a state was too weak to oppose its neighbors, however, it invited, or threatened to invite, foreign rulers to assist it. In 1493, the duke of Milan asked Charles VIII (1483–1498) of France to intervene in Italy, an action that inaugurated sixty-five years of French involvement in Italian affairs and a new chapter in European international relations.

The duke's appeal elicited a prompt and positive response. The French kings had historic claims to the throne of Naples, dating from the thirteenth century. Besides ruling the most populous state in western Europe, they possessed, in a strong bureaucracy and army, the means to pursue aggressive policies. Furthermore, a foreign war would engage the energies of French nobles suffering from declining economic conditions and from royal centralization. Charles invaded Italy in 1494 and, meeting little resistance in a march down the peninsula, took Naples.

Although the French invaded Italy repeatedly between 1494 and 1559, Italian resistance and a series of coalitions, usually including the pope, the Spanish king, and the Holy Roman emperor, prevented any permanent French conquest. When the Habsburg Charles V, already king of Spain, became the Holy Roman emperor in 1519, the European balance of power significantly altered and Italy became part of a larger conflict between the French kings of the house of Valois and the Habsburg rulers. The French kings, fearing a potential Habsburg encirclement of their kingdom, attempted to acquire territory in Germany and to retake Navarre from Spain.

Despite struggles in other areas of Europe such as Germany and Navarre, Italy became the main theater of the Habsburg-Valois wars. Charles V's imperial forces shattered the French army at Pavia in 1525 and subsequently, owing to problems of paying imperial troops, sacked Rome, ending its significance as a center of the Renaissance. Charles also defeated a French invasion of Italy in 1529 and incorporated Milan into the empire on the death of its duke in 1535. Another French-Habsburg war followed, but in 1559 the Treaty of Cateau-Cambresis ended the struggle by removing France almost completely from the Italian peninsula. Rivalry between French and Habsburgs would remain a persistent aspect of European international relations into the nineteenth century.

A CENTURY OF RELIGIOUS WARS

During the sixteenth and seventeenth centuries, wars fought for secular reasons increasingly gave way to religious conflicts. Charles V had engaged in religious warfare both with Muslim Turks and with Lutheran Germans, and for a century after his abdication in 1556, warfare over religious issues ravaged western European nations.

France

Religious wars especially troubled France in the latter half of the sixteenth century. Here, perhaps 10 percent of the total population and half of the nobility were Calvinists. Calvinism reinforced the efforts of townspeople to escape the authority of local royal officials and supported efforts of certain nobles to establish control over particular provinces.

The religious wars in France began in 1562 when the French monarchy's increasingly harsh measures against the Protestants drove them to military resistance. Calvinism was stronger in southwestern France while Catholicism prevailed elsewhere. The massacre of some Calvinists worshiping in a supposedly safe barn in Champagne touched off a series of wars in which the French Calvinists gained limited freedom of worship. In 1572, Henry of Navarre, the foremost Protestant leader, married the sister of the Catholic king of France in an effort to end religious conflict. But French Catholics slaughtered many leading Protestant nobles gathered in Paris to celebrate Henry's wedding, in the infamous St. Bartholomew's Day massacre.

Gradually, as the civil war in France persisted, three parties developed among the nobles: Roman Catholics, Protestants, and *politiques*, those who placed the need for national unity and a strong monarchy above religious

---

RELIGIOUS DISUNITY RENDS FRANCE

Into the whole body [of France] there has been introduced the curse of the new sects which has totally confused the religion of the realm, which is the sole means of holding a people united and obedient to its prince . . . [Three principal consequences of religious disunity are,] first, it lessens the fear of God, which should always take precedence over all other considerations, because on that rests the rule of life, the concord of men, the preservation of the state, and all greatness. And how can there be fear of God where there is no observation of divine law, no obedience to magistrates, either ecclesiastical or civil, . . . The second evil consequence of this change in religion is that it destroys the control and order of the government, because from it springs a change in the usual habits and customs of life, contempt for the laws and authority of magistrates, and finally even for the

prince. . . . To these two disorders is added a third, the division of the people, the seditions, and civil wars which always spring from religious confusion.[*]

These observations of a Venetian ambassador to France indicate how seriously the religious conflicts engendered by the Reformation affected sixteenth-century life. The ambassador, like his contemporaries, assumed that fear of God and obedience to civil authorities went together and that religious unity was a prerequisite to political unity. However, France's "religious confusion," which so distressed him, produced new leaders who maintained political unity while permitting religious diversity.

[*]Michele Suriano, trans. James B. Ross, in James B. Ross and Mary M. McLaughlin, eds., *The Portable Renaissance Reader* (New York, Viking, 1953), pp. 319–321.

---

loyalties (Map 46). Called the War of the Three Henries, it was named for King Henry III of France, Henry of Guise who was head of the Catholic League, and Henry of Navarre who was the Protestant cousin and heir-apparent to the childless Valois kings. When the last Valois king died without heirs in 1589, Henry of Navarre, next in succession but a Protestant, succeeded to the throne as Henry IV (1589–1610) with the aid of Protestants and *politiques*. To secure his position, however, he required the support of Paris, which he obtained only after he converted to Roman Catholicism, supposedly remarking, "Paris is worth a Mass." In

1598, Henry issued the Edict of Nantes, which gave legal status to limited religious toleration, allowing French Calvinists (Huguenots) to hold public office and fortify several towns for their protection.

Spain and the Netherlands

While France was being wracked by Catholic-Protestant civil war, Spain also became embroiled in sixteenth-century religious warfare, largely as a consequence of its rigorous religious policies. Spanish rulers between 1492 and 1609 expelled Jews and Muslims from various peninsular territories. To eliminate all forms of heresy, they used

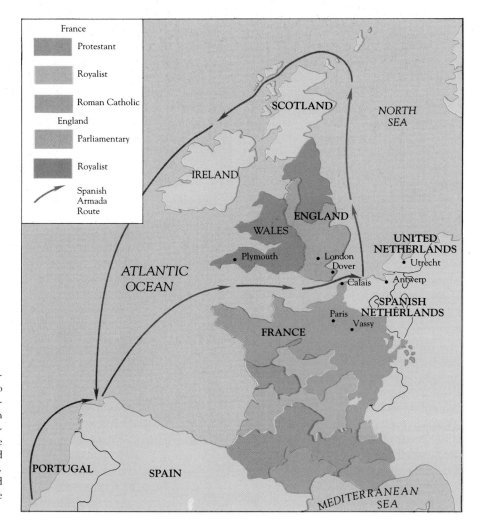

MAP 46
Western Europe in the Sixteenth Century. Political and religious differences contributed to civil wars in both France and England. Hostility between French Protestants and Roman Catholics prompted formation of a party willing to place the state above religion. The Spanish Armada, intended to regain England for Roman Catholicism, failed in its mission. Triumphant parliamentary forces in England executed a king, but soon elected to restore the monarchy.

the Inquisition, which energetically and carefully examined the purity of faith of those Jews and Muslims who had converted to Christianity. Philip II not only sought to extend this religious purification program to his other territories but also devoted his wealth and army to defending Catholicism and eradicating Protestantism throughout Europe. His wife, Mary, queen of England from 1553 to 1558, briefly restored Catholicism

there, and Philip supported the Catholic party in the religious wars in France.

Philip's most troublesome religious problems were in the seventeen provinces known as the Netherlands, a family inheritance from the Burgundians. Here most nobles were Catholic, although Calvinism had spread among town dwellers. Philip, already known for his staunch opposition to Protestantism, pursued a Spanish-

centered policy in the Netherlands that alienated both groups. He offended the nobles by appointing Spaniards to administrative posts, alarmed Protestants by reorganizing ecclesiastical jurisdictions, and frightened both by maintaining a large Spanish army on Dutch soil. Dutch opposition to Philip thus combined both political and religious elements.

Although facing a common enemy, cooperation between Dutch

Catholics and Calvinists was difficult to achieve. Eventually, however, a capable leader, William I (1579–1584), prince of Orange, brought them together. Faced with Spanish oppressions, such as a 10 percent sales tax, imposition of the Inquisition and other harsh measures to suppress Calvinists, and executions of leading nobles, Philip's opponents solidified their resistance. After 1573, a change of governors and a more moderate and conciliatory Spanish policy detached the ten southern, predominantly Catholic, provinces from the anti-Spanish alliance. The seven northern, mainly Protestant, provinces, however, joined to form the United Provinces in 1579 and proclaimed their independence from Spain two years later.

During the 1580s, Philip became seriously concerned about Protestant inroads into Roman Catholic territories north of the Pyrenees and de-

Henry IV of France Makes His Wife Regent for Their Son, the Future Louis XIII. Rubens. Although raised a Protestant, Henry IV adopted Catholicism to unite France. This concern with political unity rather than religious loyalty became common during the seventeenth century. Louvre Museum, Paris.

cided to take dramatic action. In 1587, Elizabeth I executed Mary Stuart (1541–1581), Scotland's Catholic queen; this, and the likelihood of France acquiring a Protestant king, appeared to place Roman Catholicism in great danger. Therefore, besides financially supporting French Catholics, Philip planned a military and naval expedition, the Armada, to contain Protestantism in the Netherlands and to conquer England and return it to Roman Catholicism. English ships, however, decisively defeated the Armada in 1588; most of the surviving Spanish ships were wrecked on rocky coasts by a "Protestant wind." Both England and the Netherlands remained Protestant, though developing distinctive Protestant cultures. Spain subsequently made peace with England in 1604 and instituted a twelve-year truce with the United Provinces in 1609, but refused to recognize their independence.

The United Provinces of the Netherlands flourished both economically and politically following their separation from Spain. Trade and in-

Slaughter of the Innocents. Brueghel. In the Spanish Netherlands, the Spanish government adopted a harsh policy toward Protestants and frequently executed them. The artist uses the biblical story of King Herod's massacre of infants at the time of Jesus's birth to depict such a scene of Spanish brutality. Kunsthistorisches Museum, Vienna.

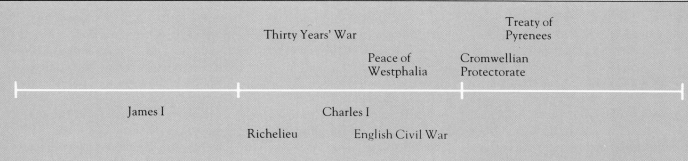

Thirty Years' War

Treaty of
Pyrenees

Peace of
Westphalia

Cromwellian
Protectorate

James I

Charles I

Richelieu

English Civil War

dustry boomed, as Dutch cargo ships hauled large loads at lower costs than other European shippers, and Amsterdam, home to merchants and bankers emigrating from the southern provinces, became Europe's chief trade and banking center. The United Provinces formed a decentralized state, and despite some internal conflicts, able leadership at home and dangers from abroad kept the fledgling republic united and vigorous.

The Thirty Years' War

For several decades, Charles V's successors as Holy Roman emperors directed their energies toward fighting against the Turks in Hungary, but religious conflicts again gained prominence within the empire in the early seventeenth century. Calvinists, who had received no recognition and no privileges from the 1555 Peace of Augsburg, were leaders in the formation of a Protestant Union in 1608. This league was countered by an opposing Catholic League in the following year.

The prospective accession of Ferdinand of Bohemia as Holy Roman emperor intensified religious tensions. Jesuit-educated, Ferdinand hoped to reassert the authority of the emperor in the empire and to reestablish Catholicism as the dominant form of Christianity in central Europe. He was supported by Spain, which also planned to recover the Calvinist Netherlands provinces when the twelve-year truce expired. German Catholic princes were also willing to assist him, provided his efforts did not increase imperial power sufficiently to threaten their independence.

Phases of the Conflict

It was Ferdinand's efforts to eliminate Protestantism in his own lands that started a conflict in Bohemia that grew into the Thirty Years' War. Protestantism was well established in Bohemia, buttressed by a charter permitting Bohemian lords, knights, and royal cities free exercise of religion. Both Protestants and Hussites opposed Habsburg efforts to enforce Catholicism, and Bohemia nobles resisted Habsburg encroachments on their power.

When Catholics damaged and closed Protestant churches and imposed a predominantly Catholic board of governors to administer Bohemia, the Bohemians revolted, dramatizing their opposition to Ferdinand's policies by pitching his representatives out of a second-story window (an event known as the "defenestration of Prague"). In 1618, the rebels quickly seized control of the area, chose the Calvinist elector of the Palatinate (whose father-in-law, Protestant James I of England, never sent his promised army) as their king, and marched on Vienna. By so doing, they disrupted the balance of power in the empire and threatened Ferdinand's ambitions. Bohemia was essential to an emperor because it supplied approximately half of the imperial revenue. Moreover, as three of the seven imperial electors were already Protestant, Bohemia's transfer to a Calvinist elector would permit election of a Protestant emperor rather than the Catholic Ferdinand. Ferdinand therefore quickly allied with Spain and Bavaria, and with their aid soon reconquered Bohemia and ensured his election as Emperor Ferdinand II (1619–1637). He swiftly restored both Catholicism and royal authority in Bohemia and made the formerly elective monarchy a hereditary Habsburg dominion.

Although Ferdinand and his allies

371

now firmly controlled southern Germany, their successes prompted interested neighbors to intervene in imperial affairs and continue the conflict. The French once more perceived prospects of Habsburg encirclement of France, whereas the Lutheran Danes were concerned for the future of their north German coreligionists. Ferdinand's armies handily defeated the Danes and established control of north Germany. But his attempts to restore to the Catholic church lands seized by Protestant princes since 1555 and to deny free exercise of religion to Protestants other than Lutherans frightened the Protestant princes and rendered the establishment of unity and peace impossible.

In 1629, the conflict resumed with the entry of a new Protestant champion, Sweden's King Gustavus II Adolphus (1611–1632) into Germany. Sweden had adopted Lutheranism a century earlier, and the Swedish king intervened partly on behalf of his Lutheran coreligionists. Other motives also played a role in his actions. He wished to assist relatives who had lost their German lands to the emperor's armies. Gustavus also sought to prevent an alliance between the emperor and the king of Poland, who needed the emperor's aid to press his claim to the Swedish throne. Finally, the king hoped to add conquests in north Germany to Sweden's already extensive territories around the Baltic Sea. The French, who were more afraid of Habsburg power than they were of Protestants, willingly financed Gustavus's involvement, and during 1631 and 1632, he led the Swedes to brilliant victories. After his death in battle, however, his successors proved ineffective, and the Swedes suffered a crippling defeat in 1634. The German Protestant princes then sought to make peace with the emperor, who in turn no longer insisted on returning seized church lands to the Roman Catholic church.

With peace nearly assured, the French now chose to intervene directly in the struggle. As in the sixteenth century, they aimed to limit Spanish power, to keep Germany disunited, and to prevent Habsburg encirclement of France. Religion thus became a secondary issue in the war, even for Cardinal Richelieu, chief adviser to the French crown. In 1642, Catholic French and Lutheran Swedish forces marched as allies through different regions of the empire, finally converging in Bavaria and bringing hostilities to a close on a note of victory.

Peace

The Treaty of Westphalia brought the Thirty Years' War to a conclusion in 1648 and extensively reordered European affairs (Map 47). The treaty recognized the independence of the Swiss Confederation and the United Provinces and allowed individual states within the Holy Roman Empire to make war and conclude alliances, making them effectively independent also. It gave Calvinist rulers in the empire the right to determine the religion practiced in their territories, the same right that Catholic and Lutheran princes had enjoyed since 1555. The treaty divided Pomerania and other north German territories between the Protestant states of Sweden and Brandenburg-Prussia, making both of them important northern powers. In south Germany, Catholic Bavaria obtained additional territory, and its ruler became an eighth imperial elector. The Habsburgs, although unsuccessful in increasing their authority and eradicating Protestantism within the empire, obtained firm control of Bohemia and were well positioned to expand to the south and east. By the Treaty of Westphalia and the subsequent Treaty of the Pyrenees (1659), France gained various territories along its frontiers and replaced Spain as the greatest power in Europe.

Germany was the major loser of the Thirty Years' War. Perhaps 300,000 soldiers and civilians were killed during campaigns and battles in Germany, and several times that number had died of malnutrition and disease. The war accelerated a population decline that had begun fifty years earlier as trade routes shifted from central Europe to the Atlantic seaboard. The damage caused by marauding armies, when added to the population decline, wrecked the German economy and intensified a seventeenth-century economic depression. Many Germans migrated to British North America to escape the devastation and poverty. Moreover, the war prevented the territorial unification of Germany and permitted the larger principalities to become virtually autonomous. The empire remained in existence, however, and its institutions continued to function. The imperial army was enlarged, the imperial court more widely used, and the imperial assembly became permanent.

The Thirty Years' War brought the wars of religion to an end. Religious persecution waned. The division of Europe into Protestant, Roman Catholic, and Eastern Orthodox areas became accepted. Europeans proved increasingly willing to obey and to give their allegiance to a ruler of a different faith, and rulers became less insistent on religious unity within their

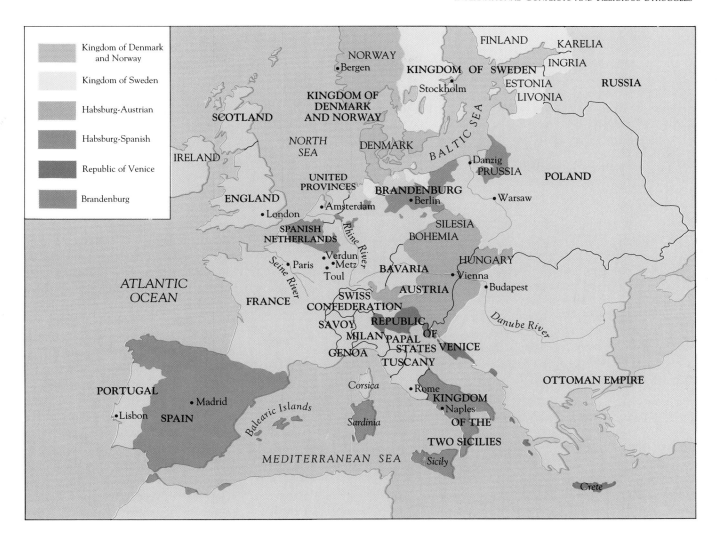

realms. Catholic princes permitted Protestant worship in their lands, and Protestant princes tolerated Catholic worship.

SEVENTEENTH-CENTURY ENGLAND

Whereas the Thirty Years' War dominated continental European affairs, religious conflict, muted under Elizabeth I, flared up in England under the rule of the Stuart kings James I (1603–1625) and Charles I (1625–1649) and became linked with a serious constitutional struggle. Puritans sought to eliminate vestiges of Roman Catholic practice from the Anglican church, while Roman Catholics hoped to reverse the tide of Protestantism in England. Parliament became increasingly restive under royal manipulation, and the merchants and the gentry (the lesser landowning nobility), impatient with high-handed royal actions, sought a larger share in the direction of policy.

MAP 47
Europe in 1648. With the end of the Thirty Years' War, the Peace of Westphalia changed the map of Europe. France and Sweden, as victorious powers, made important territorial gains, and the enlarged state of Brandenburg-Prussia became capable of playing a greater role in European affairs. Spain's economic decline reduced its political significance, and Germany and Italy remained fragmented and disunited.

THE DIVINE RIGHT OF KINGS

The state of monarchy is the supremest thing on earth; for kings are not only God's lieutenants upon earth, and sit upon God's throne, but even by God himself they are called gods . . . .

Kings are justly called gods, for that they exercise a manner or resemblance of divine power upon earth; for if you will consider the powers attributed to God, you shall see how they agree in the person of a king. God hath power to create or destroy, make or unmake at his pleasure, to give life or send death, to judge all things and to be judged nor accountable to none; to raise low things and to make high things low at his pleasure, and to God both are soul and body due. And the like power have kings: they make and unmake their subjects, they have power of raising and casting down, of life and of death, judges over all their subjects and in all causes and yet accountable to none but God only. *

The author of this passage, King James I of England, had already ruled Scotland, where the parliament was weak, for more than twenty years. His fondness for political theorizing and his lack of practical governing skills caused contemporaries to term him "the wisest fool in Christendom." With the exalted view of monarchy revealed in this statement, it is easy to understand how James became involved in bitter quarrels with Parliament that eventually led to civil war.

*The Works of the Most High and Mightie Prince, James . . . King of Great Britaine (London, 1616), p. 529; reprinted in George L. Mosse et al., eds., Europe in Review, rev. ed. (Chicago: Rand McNally, 1957, 1964), p. 44.

Religious and Constitutional Conflicts

The accession of James I inaugurated a long struggle between king and Parliament. He unwisely claimed to hold by divine right powers the Tudors had exercised only by carefully managing parliaments, and by rejecting the Tudor practice of sharing sovereignty gave the impression of defying established law. A growing decentralization of parliamentary activity reduced the crown's ability to control parliamentary business and facilitated the development of effective counterproposals to royal initiatives. Hence conflict between kings and Parliament intensified, especially when rising government costs and Parliament's reluctance to increase royal revenues prompted James to attempt to raise money without parliamentary consent.

James also stirred up religious discontent by staunchly opposing both Presbyterian ideas of democratic church government and Puritan disruption of the state church and promising such dissidents he would "harry them out of the land." Although he sponsored a new English translation of the Bible, known subsequently as the King James version, he removed clergy in both Scotland and England who refused to follow Anglican practices and refused to intervene in the Thirty Years' War on behalf of German Protestants.

James's son and successor, Charles I (1625–1649), rather than improving relations between crown and Parliament, made them worse, and the constitutional clash became acute during his reign. Parliament showed its displeasure by forcing him to levy

The Horrors of War. Callot. The artist produced numerous engravings of scenes from the Thirty Years' War. Here, rough and ready justice has been taken on looters and plunderers.

customs duties only on a yearly basis rather than throughout his reign, as was customary. In 1628, Parliament, in return for a grant of funds, obtained the king's agreement to a statement known as the Petition of Right, which prohibited the billeting of soldiers in private homes, declarations of martial law in peacetime, arbitrary imprisonments, and taxation without parliamentary consent. That parliamentary initiative was, like the Magna Carta, a landmark attempt to limit royal authority.

After 1628, the constitutional struggle intensified. Charles I accepted but failed to respect the Petition of Right. When Parliament protested levying customs duties without its consent, Charles dissolved it, arrested and imprisoned several parliamentary leaders, and for eleven years governed alone. By withdrawing from the continental war and reducing government expenditures and by continuing to levy taxes unsanctioned by Parliament, he raised enough money to keep the government functioning. Especially unpopular was his extension to the whole country of a navy support tax called ship money, formerly levied only on coastal towns because they needed protection from raiding Norsemen. By 1640, Charles I had thoroughly alienated the parliamentarians and many others in England.

Civil War and the Cromwellian Period

Although his political policies produced substantial unrest in England, Charles's religious program provoked civil war and the dissolution of the monarchy. Charles's marriage to the French princess Henrietta Maria introduced Catholic influences at the royal court and raised fears that Charles himself might become Roman Catholic. His efforts to introduce more ritual into the Anglican church and to make it more administratively authoritarian moved it closer to Roman Catholicism and antagonized Puritans. Puritans also resented his attempts to compel all Protestants to conform to Anglican doctrine, liturgy, and church organization.

In 1640, the moment of crisis was reached when Charles tried to impose Anglicanism on Presbyterian Scotland. The Scots rose to oppose him, and to obtain money to suppress them, Charles reluctantly summoned Parliament. The members of Parliament promptly exploited the king's difficulties by requiring, in exchange for its grant of funds, the dismantling of his absolutist apparatus. Parliament passed and forced the king to sign laws impeaching his chief advisers and executed one of them, Archbishop of Canterbury William Laud (1573–1645). Charles was also made to sign legislation abolishing royal prerogative courts, requiring Parliament to meet every three years, and permitting Parliament to control its own dismissal. Charles's subsequent unsuccessful attempt to seize five parliamentary leaders convinced his opponents he could not be trusted and would not obey the laws. In early 1642, Parliament therefore assumed control of the militia and raised its own army. The king responded by seeking to rally forces to his support against the rebellious Parliament.

In the ensuing civil war, merchants and gentry joined with English Puritans against the king and upper nobility. The Presbyterian Scots intervened on the side of Parliament, and an able Puritan commander, Oliver Cromwell (1599–1658), formed a well-trained army composed largely of Puritans. These two forces tipped the balance against the king and enabled the parliamentary armies to defeat royalist forces in 1644 and 1645. Charles attempted to weaken the parliamentary opposition by exploiting differences among his opponents. Presbyterians, who favored a constitutional monarchy and sought to make Presbyterianism the established church of England, clashed with pro-Anglicans and with radical elements who sought to establish a republic and desired religious toleration for all Protestants. When the civil war resumed in 1648, Charles was soon defeated by Cromwell, who promptly purged Parliament of many of its Presbyterian members. Charles was tried, condemned, and executed in 1649. Killing a king was a highly unusual act, and for a group of commoners to do so was revolutionary and unprecedented; nevertheless, the execution of Charles I provided an example for later revolutions in other European lands.

During a decade of ruling England (1649–1658), Cromwell experimented with various alternatives to monarchical government and promoted the Puritan religious program. Under the Commonwealth, which lasted until 1653, he governed through a council of state and the recently purged Parliament. He brutally suppressed an Irish rebellion, dispossessing many Catholic landholders to benefit his Protestant supporters. He also crushed a Scots invasion on behalf of Charles I's son.

When disagreement arose between Parliament and the army over delays in payment of troops, Cromwell dis-

Execution of Charles I. Woodcut from a tract of 1649. Charles was the first western monarch tried, condemned, and executed by his own people. His death concluded the English Civil War. However, his successor, Cromwell, soon adopted many of the same measures that had made Charles unpopular.

solved the Parliament and council of state and established a new governmental structure, the Protectorate, with himself as lord protector. The Protectorate had a written constitution, the Instrument of Government, which allowed Cromwell to govern through a new council of state and to control a standing army, but provided that Parliament alone could levy taxes and grant supplies. Cromwell and his parliaments continued to quarrel until his death, partly because his wars against the Dutch and the Spanish made high taxes necessary. In time, he became virtually a military dictator, dividing England into districts, each administered by a general with an army. Puritanism gained ascendancy under the Protectorate. Anglican clergy were forbidden to teach or preach, theaters were closed and recreation forbidden, and Sunday became a day for prayer alone.

Cromwell's son Richard proved too weak to control the generals and Parliament after his father's death. In 1660, a military commander seized London and summoned a special Parliament that invited Charles I's son to assume the throne as Charles II (1660–1685), presumably to establish a moderate parliamentary regime.

SUMMARY

During the Renaissance and Reformation eras, strong monarchies and pluralistic empires expanded. The Ottoman Turks, blocked in the late fifteenth century, expanded in the Balkans and in the western Mediterranean during the sixteenth century, but reached the limits of their power by the 1560s. The French invaded Italy, which led to French-Habsburg conflict throughout western Europe, but also produced balance-of-power diplomacy and the use of permanent ambassadors.

Following the Reformation, religious struggles afflicted several European lands. In France, Calvinists struggled with Catholics to gain religious toleration. With the religious issue temporarily resolved, a series of capable royal advisers greatly strengthened the French monarchy. In the Netherlands, religious wars split the territory into Catholic and Calvinist states; the latter won independence from Spain and became a major commercial center.

The Thirty Years' War began as a religious war, but eventually included a Swedish quest for Baltic territory and a renewal of the French-Habsburg rivalry. It devastated Germany's population and economy and made the German princes virtually autonomous. It also consolidated the positions of Lutherans, Calvinists, and Catholics in areas where they were dominant. The peace treaties ending the conflict redrew the map of central Europe and created new national powers.

England experienced religious and political conflict during the period. Puritans wished to eliminate the "Romishness" of the Anglican church, and Parliament wished to check Stuart tendencies toward royal absolutism. Civil war resulted, the king was executed, and Oliver Cromwell attained power. Under his rule, Puritanism flourished, but his experiments with alternatives to monarchy were unsatisfactory, and after his death the monarchy was restored. The English experience proved almost unique, however; throughout continental Europe royal absolutism became dominant.

SELECTED SOURCES

*Geyl, Pieter. *The Revolt of the Netherlands, 1555–1609.* 2d ed. 1980. Authoritative treatment of the topic by an outstanding Dutch scholar.

*Mattingly, Garrett. *The Armada.* 1959. Combines readability with sound scholarship to place the Spanish expedition in its European context.

*Neale, John E. *The Age of Catherine de Medici.* 1978. Informatively places the French wars of religion in their European setting.

Palm, Franklin C. *Calvinism and the Religious Wars.* 1932. Brief, authoritative treatment of the religious wars in France.

Salmon, John H. M. *Society in Crisis: France in the Sixteenth Century.* 1975. Readable account of French society in the period, focused on the impact of the wars of religion.

Steinberg, Sigfrid H. *The Thirty Years' War.* 1967. Brief revisionist treatment of the war, which argues its destructiveness has been exaggerated.

*Stone, Lawrence. *The Causes of the English Revolution, 1629–1642.* 1972. A prominent historian assesses and distills current historical scholarship on this much-debated topic.

The War of the Fools. 1964. This Czech film satirizing war, set in the period of the Thirty Years' War, has authentic historical flavor.

*Wedgwood, Cicely V. *Oliver Cromwell.* 2d ed. 1973. Brief, readable biography of England's Puritan leader; also a 1972 film, *Cromwell.*

*Wedgwood, Cicely V. *The Thirty Years' War.* 1956. Detailed, comprehensive presentation of events and personalities of the conflict.

*Available in paperback.

FROM ABSOLUTISM TO REVOLUTION

The seventeenth and eighteenth centuries were an age of intellectual rationalism and revolutionary change in western civilization. Essential elements in these charges included royal absolutism, intellectual enlightenment, and violent revolution.

In the seventeenth century, monarchs such as France's Louis XIV claimed unprecedented powers over their subjects. Strong Habsburg and Hohenzollern rulers enhanced the positions of Austria and Prussia and Russia's Peter the Great made his country one of the great European powers.

By the eighteenth century, in Latin America and British North America, colonists were developing novel forms of western civilization. Under the influence of the cultural variety of Amerindians and African slaves, they adapted European customs and devised more helpful or appropriate ones.

The most significant intellectual current in the seventeenth and eighteenth centuries was the emphasis on human reason that activated the scientific revolution and the Enlightenment. Early modern science, which had its birth in the heliocentric theory of Copernicus, reached a climax in the work of Isaac Newton in the 1600s. Such scientific achievement prompted thinkers of the succeeding Enlightenment period—Voltaire, Rousseau, and others—to ground radical sociopolitical theories in human reason.

Enlightenment principles strengthened the political trends of constitutionalism and enlightened despotism. Governments in which the power of monarchs was limited by constitutional guarantees of subjects' rights emerged in Great Britain and the Netherlands. In Austria, Prussia, and Russia a number of celebrated enlightened despots claimed to use their powers to reform society for the benefit of the governed.

Great changes were also taking place outside Europe, as British, French, and Dutch imperialists joined the Spanish and Portuguese overseas. With the spread of western power across North America, Asia, and Australia, Great Britain attained mastery of the largest empire in the world. Between 1776 and 1830, however, successful rebellions against European overlords added most American colonies to the list of independent western nations.

The greatest revolution of the age occurred in France, Europe's most powerful nation. Between 1789 and 1799, the French shattered the traditional power structures. Domestic turmoil and foreign intervention, however, produced rampant radicalism, a reign of terror, and dictatorship.

Out of the chaos of the French Revolution came Napoleon Bonaparte. This successful revolutionary general not only became emperor of the French but again and again defeated great-power coalitions to impose his will on much of Europe.

1625	1650	1675	1700

Politics

1618–48
The Thirty
Years' War

1660–85
Stuart
Restoration

1682–1725
Peter
the Great
of Russia

1624–43
Cardinal
Richelieu

1643–1715
Louis XIV

1688
The
"Glorious
Revolution"

Economics & Society

Growth of
mercantilism

1670
Hudson's
Bay Company

Development
of a
global/colonial
economy

Colonization
of North
America
underway

1619–83
Jean Colbert

1679
Habeus
Corpus Act
(England)

Science & Technology

1564–1642
Galileo
Galilei

1683
Anton
von Leeuwenhoek
discovers
bacteria

1709
First
production
of industrial
coke

1561–1626
Francis
Bacon

1628
First
crude
steam
engine

1687
Isaac Newton's
*Mathematical
Principles of
Natural Philosophy*

1718
First
observation
of smallpox
inoculation

Religion & Thought

1651
Thomas
Hobbes'
Leviathan

1685
Edict of
Nantes

Growing
religious
toleration
in British
North America

1596–1650
René
Descartes

1646–1716
Gottfried
Wilhelm
von
Leibnitz

1690
John Locke's
*Two Treatises
of Civil
Government*

Arts & Literature

1577–1640
Peter Paul
Rubens

1622–73
Jean
Baptiste
Molière

1667–74
Milton's
*Paradise
Lost*

1719
Daniel
Defoe's
*Robinson
Crusoe*

Age of
Baroque
and
Classicism

1606–69
Rembrandt
van Rijn

1665
Bernini's
High Altar,
St. Peter's
Basilica, Rome

1685–1750
Johann
Sebastian
Bach

1725	1750	1775	1800	1825	1850

1739–63
Colonial struggles
in Western
Hemisphere
and India

1775–83
American
War for
Independence

1799
Napoleon
overthrows
The
Directory

1809–26
Independence
movements
in Latin
America

1740–86
Frederick
the Great

1756–63
Seven
Years'
War

1789
French
Revolution
begins

1815
Waterloo;
Congress
of Vienna

Industrial
Revolution
begins in
Great
Britain

1776
Adam
Smith's
*The Wealth
of Nations*

1789
French
Declaration of
Rights of Man

Increased
importation of
black slaves
to North
America

1764
Cesare
Beccaria's
*Crimes and
Punishments*

1787–91
U.S. Constitution
and Bill of Rights

1740
Development
of crucible
steel-making
process

1769
James Watt
patents
the steam
engine

1803
John Dalton's
table of
atomic
weights

1746–51
Benjamin
Franklin's
experiments
with electricity

1770
James
Hargreaves'
spinning
jenny

John Wilkinson
improves
iron
production
techniques

1739
David Hume's
*Treatise on
Human
Nature*

1754
Voltaire's
Candide

1743–94
Marquis
de Condorcet

1793
Worship
of God
outlawed
in France

1751–72
Diderot's
Encyclopedia

1762
Rousseau's
*The Social
Contract*

1781
Kant's
*Critique
of Pure
Reason*

1801
Concordat
between
Napoleon
and the Pope

1726
Jonathon
Swift's
*Gulliver's
Travels*

1742
George
Handel's
Messiah

1786
Mozart's
*The Marriage
of Figaro*

1770–1827
Ludwig
von Beethoven

Age of
Neoclassicism
and Rococo

1749–1832
Johann
Wolfgang
von Goethe

THE RISE OF
ROYAL ABSOLUTISM
(1648–1725)

*To assign the right of decision to subjects and the duty of deference to sovereigns
is to pervert the order of things. The head [of the state] alone has the right to
deliberate and decide, and the functions of all the other members consist only in
carrying out . . . commands . . . [In a well-run state] all eyes are fixed upon
[the monarch] alone, all respects are paid to him alone, everything is hoped for
from him alone; nothing is undertaken, nothing is expected, nothing is done,
except through him alone. His favor is regarded as the only source of all good
things; men believe that they are rising in the world to the extent that they come
near him or earn his esteem; all else is cringing, all else is powerless. . . .*

In these words, begun for his son and heir around 1661, Louis XIV
expressed the ideal of absolute monarchy. Louis himself was the most
successful embodiment of royal absolutism in government and a model for
the other kings of Europe.

Louis spoke for the dominant political theory of his age when he
condemned a state in which "subjects" have a right to share in political
decision making. Democracy was scarcely more than a glimmer in the eyes
of a few radicals when Louis came to the throne of France in the middle of
the seventeenth century. During his immensely long reign, monarchs who
exercised "absolute sovereignty" over their peoples also came to power in
Austria, Prussia, Russia, and elsewhere. The result was what has been
described as Europe's "splendid century" of kings and queens. This period
of royal magnificence produced some spectacular art; it also, however, saw
some terrible wars and real suffering among the peoples of Europe.

The present chapter recounts the rise to power of these royal absolutists
and outlines the consequences of their strong government for the evolution
of the nation-state in Europe. It also describes the impact of absolutism on
society, art, and international relations in the seventeenth and earlier
eighteenth centuries.

CONTENTS

Louis XIV. This royal portrait by Hyacinthe Rigaud, 1701, shows the king as he looked in his
later years. Pose, costume, and opulent setting all combine to project the splendid image of the
Sun King to which all absolute monarchs aspired. Louvre Museum, Paris.

ABSOLUTIST THEORY

The emergence and widespread acceptance of belief in the absolute power of kings and queens was rooted in two conflicting circumstances. In the broadest perspective, absolute monarchy was part of a long-term trend toward more efficient central government in the nation-states of Europe. The strong kings of the medieval era and the new monarchies of the Renaissance represented earlier stages of this political evolution. The absolute monarchies that rose in the seventeenth century and became "enlightened" in the eighteenth were the next stage in the growth of governmental power. The powerfully centralized governments of the nineteenth and twentieth centuries would be the climax of this trend.

Origins of Absolutism

During the seventeenth century, however, Europeans embraced strong government as a reaction to the political breakdowns that had beset them during the last hundred years without thinking of themselves a part of a continuing long-term trend toward powerful rulers. The religious wars of the sixteenth century, particularly destructive between the 1560s and the 1590s, had also been civil wars in France and the Netherlands. The Holy Roman Empire had been torn by religious dissent in the mid-1500s and ravaged by the Thirty Years' War between 1618 and 1848. England had experienced decades of domestic strife between Parliament and king in the 1600s, climaxing in the temporary overthrow of the monarchy during the

"kingless decade" of the 1650s. Finally in mid-century, France had fallen once more into anarchy during the upheaval known as the Fronde.

These revolts actually strengthened the appeal of the emerging absolute monarchies of the later 1600s. The widespread bloodshed and destruction that resulted from these civil struggles led many propertied Europeans and long-suffering peasants to long for a return to peace and order. The best guarantee many could imagine for the restoration of order was a strong hand on the tiller—a powerful monarch at the head of state.

Absolute Sovereignty

Supporting this widely felt need for strong government were a number of theoretical arguments drawn from ancient, medieval, and modern political thought. Older arguments drew on scripture, which seemed to assert more than once that God sanctified the authority of secular rulers. Medieval kings had insisted on their "divine right" to rule, a view that absolute monarchs like Louis XIV accepted as gospel. Medieval and early modern lawyers and legal scholars had also drawn on the example of the Roman emperors. Like the Caesars of old, these experts asserted, modern kings had a right to demand loyal obedience from their people.

More recent defenders of royal power went still farther. Thus the sixteenth-century political theorist Jean Bodin rejected the medieval idea that each subdivision of society—church, state, classes, guilds, and other groups—had its own rights and obligations in a balanced society. Bodin urged that the state must have a single, absolute authority that could impose order on all estates, classes, and conditions of men. The English philosopher Thomas Hobbes agreed. In his *Leviathan* (1651), Hobbes insisted that people were naturally selfish, ambitious, and aggressive. To avoid an anarchic "war of all against all," an all-powerful central government was therefore necessary. For Bodin, Hobbes, and other political thinkers of the age, the only available wielders of this absolute sovereignty were the monarchical governments of the great nations of Europe.

Mercantilism and Bullionism

The growing power of Europe's monarchies was especially enhanced by their ability to foster and control the economic development of the nations. The policy of government intervention in the economic affairs of their people was not new in the age of absolutism, but such intervention increased markedly during the seventeenth and eighteenth centuries. For the age of royal absolutism was also the great age of mercantilism in economic life and of the bullionist theory of the wealth of nations.

Mercantilism was a system of economic regulation by the royal government that emphasized commerce and the role of the merchant in society. The first goal of mercantilist policy was to expand production in every area—land and mineral wealth, old and new handicraft industries. The object was to achieve a surplus of production over consumption. This surplus could then be traded with foreign nations—again with the object of achieving a surplus, in this case a favorable balance of trade.

Such a favorable trade balance would mean that the nation exported

more than it imported. The surplus of exported goods would have to be paid for in gold and silver coins—that is, in bullion. Mercantilists were therefore also bullionists, supporters of the theory that the real wealth of any nation is measured in the amount of precious metals it accumulates. To keep this flow of gold coming into the country through expanded productivity and a favorable trade balance thus became the prime goal of European mercantilism.

To achieve these ends, mercantilistic royal governments regulated their economies in many ways. They pro-

vided subsidies and other supports for new industries. They regulated some industries to keep the quality of their products competitive in foreign markets. They granted monopolies to powerful merchant companies to trade in certain areas or in particular products. They established high tariffs to protect local producers from foreign competitors.

Mercantilist administrators also integrated overseas colonies into this system. Colonial producers in the Americas and elsewhere were expected to contribute raw materials and agricultural products otherwise un-

View of Versailles. This painting of 1668 shows Louis XIV's newly rebuilt palace, with the king himself arriving in pomp and circumstance at lower right. Note the geometrical layout of the palace and grounds, as well as the vast extent of both buildings and gardens.

385

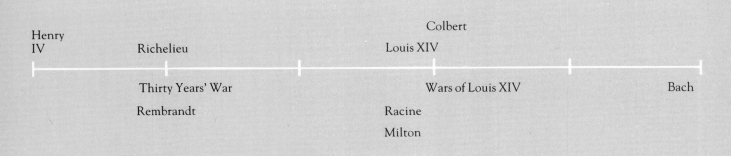

Henry IV

Richelieu

Colbert

Louis XIV

Thirty Years' War

Wars of Louis XIV

Bach

Rembrandt

Racine

Milton

available in Europe. They were to purchase surplus manufactured goods from the European "mother country." Colonials were forbidden to compete with producers at home, and were expected to trade only with the mother country, never with rival imperial powers. Producers in Europe were also, in some cases, prevented from growing agricultural products which were important to colonial economies. Each overseas empire was to be a closed system in economic competition with all others.

ABSOLUTISM IN FRANCE: THE AGE OF LOUIS XIV

Absolutism took different forms in different parts of Europe, but all of them were based in one way or another on that of France.

In the later 1500s, France was ravaged by a succession of wars of religion pitting Catholics against Protestants and rival factions of nobles against one another. The next century, saw two royal minorities: Louis XIII (1610–1643) inherited the throne at the age of nine, Louis XIV (1643–1715) at age five. With children on the throne, greedy or ambitious courtiers and nobles exploited

the country and feuded with one another. Wars took place between the crown on one side and both the rival armies of the nobles and the garrisoned strongholds of the Protestants on the other. At midcentury, finally, came the breakdown of order called the Fronde (1648–1652). This revolt, led by rebellious nobles, also involved peasants and urban poor, who were suffering from famine and the final agonies of the Thirty Years' War.

The Rise of French Absolutism: Richelieu

Through the first decades of the seventeenth century, a series of strong royal ministers labored to strengthen the French monarch to restore order to the nation. As early as the 1590s, Henry IV had ended the wars of religion and brought the house of Bourbon to the throne. He and his first minister, Sully, worked to strengthen the economy and to balance the budget. The breakdown of central authority during the early years of Louis XIII's reign was initially a serious setback. The appointment of the powerful Cardinal Richelieu as chief minister of state, however, gave France a strong political leader for the next two decades, from 1624 to 1643.

Richelieu advanced the cause of royal absolutism, both by weakening

the enemies of central power and by strengthening the royal administration. He fought a series of wars to deprive France's Protestants of the 100 fortified towns they had been granted by Henry IV. Richelieu also compelled the nobles to dismantle their fortified chateaus, another source of potential defiance of royal authority. To advance that authority into the provinces, finally, Cardinal Richelieu greatly expanded the duties of formerly minor officials called *intendants*—officials Louis would also find very useful.

Louis's minority accession in 1643, fortunately, also brought Richelieu's handpicked successor, Cardinal Mazarin, who was able to continue the process of building up the royal bureaucracy. The Sicilian Mazarin had a difficult time keeping ambitious aristocrats in line. Nevertheless, he did carry on the tradition of state building for another decade and a half.

Other motives were involved in these efforts to strengthen the central government. Richelieu and Mazarin were not selfless statesmen, but men as ambitious as those whose divisive ambitions they crushed. Richelieu built a palace in Paris so splendid that it was converted to a royal residence after his death, and Mazarin's greed was notorious. Nevertheless, while advancing their own interests, Richelieu and Mazarin were also constructing a centralized national government eminently suited to an absolute monarch.

Developed Absolutism: Louis XIV and Colbert

In the second half of the century, Louis's France found a king large enough to take charge of the absolute monarchy Richelieu and Mazarin had forged. Louis, who began to rule independently in 1661, was a strong, handsome man, a good Catholic, and a profound believer in his own divine right to rule, He was a hardworking ruler and had considerable tolerance for the endless round of public ceremonies that were required of an absolute sovereign. For most of his reign of more than seventy years, he showed both political shrewdness and an unswerving concern to increase the power of the French monarchy.

Louis, as had Richelieu, undermined rival sources of power and strengthened royal administration. To weaken his rivals, Louis lured the once rebellious aristocracy to his court at the magnificent new palace of Versailles outside Paris. There France's nobility gradually became dependent

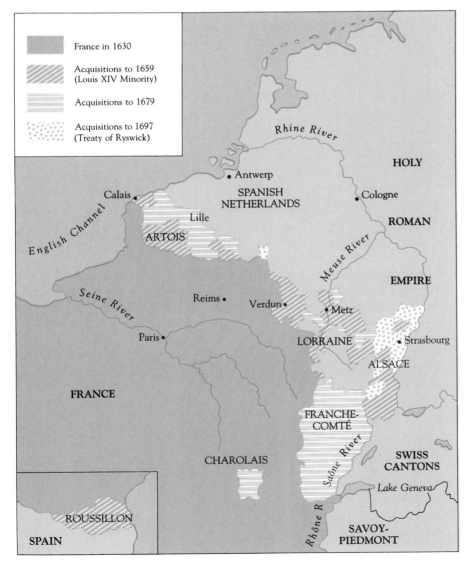

MAP 48

Expansion of France under Louis XIV. Like other absolute monarchs, Louis XIV expanded his domains through war. He focused most of his efforts on the Netherlands and the Rhine Valley. Opposed by strong coalitions, even the Sun King's powerful armies were unable to acquire much new territory. Nevertheless, he succeeded in advancing the French frontier to the southern Rhine.

LOUIS XIV STARTS THE DAY RIGHT

After he had risen, and had been helped into his dressing gown by the Great Chamberlain or the First Gentleman of the Chamber, the other courtiers who had the right to attend the *lever* were gradually admitted, in four successive "waves." Meanwhile, the great noblemen who held posts in the royal Household carried out their functions of aiding the King to dress. The Master of the wardrobe pulled off the King's nightshirt by the right sleeve, and the first Valet of the wardrobe pulled it by the left sleeve. The honor of presenting the King with his shirt belonged to Monsieur (Louis' oldest son), failing him to a *prince du sang*, and failing him to the Great Chamberlain; the first *Valet de chambre* held out the right sleeve, the First Valet of the Wardrobe the left. To the Master of the Wardrobe fell the honor of helping His Majesty to pull on his breeches. And so the ceremony went on.*

This description of a small part of the daily round of ceremony and ritual that attended the life of the Sun King tells us much about life at Versailles and about the central role of the absolute monarch. Every detail of Louis XIV's day was filled with ritual of this sort, performed with a reverence usually reserved for religious ceremonies. The people who performed such menial chores, furthermore, were great noblemen and princes of royal blood (princes du sang). Such idolatry of the royal person further strengthened the godlike royal image of an absolute monarch.

*John Lough, *An Introduction to Seventeenth Century France* (New York: David McKay, 1969), p. 163.

on the king for honors, promotions, and revenues. Louis also bought and sold offices in the formerly independent chartered towns. He compelled the French law courts, called *parlements*, to rubber-stamp all royal decrees; their occasional resistance in earlier centuries was no longer tolerated. Louis also followed the policy of Richelieu and Mazarin in dealing with the Estates General, France's closest approximation of the English Parliament, never convening this body during his three-quarters of a century on the throne.

To impose his own will on the nation, Louis used the *intendants* as his chief agents in the provinces. These bureaucrats, middle-class appointees entirely dependent on the king, had many functions. They kept an eye on the nobles and the provincial cities, provided some police protection for the countryside, and supervised markets. They also collected taxes and recruited soldiers, two crucial functions of the absolutist state.

At the top of this administrative system was a structure of royal councils and powerful royal ministers of state. The two most important ministers were the war minister, the marquis de Louvois, and the minister of finances, Jean Colbert. Louis himself met regularly with his ministers, actively governing Europe's most powerful state.

Colbert was the chief architect of France's elaborate mercantile system. Under his discretion, Louis's government built roads and canals and regulated wages, prices, and the quality of goods. The government protected local industry with high tariffs and granted monopoly rights to powerful combines likely to advance French trade abroad. France's expanding overseas empire was also incorporated into the mercantile system. The government furnished military protection and subsidies for the colonies, but required them to trade exclusively with France and to transport goods only in French ships. Colbert thus became the most persistent and successful practitioner of paternalistic mercantilism.

Louvois, by contrast, encouraged Louis to advance French interests by force of arms. In so doing, he contributed to the four long and costly wars, four massive conflicts fought between 1667 and 1713, that were the reign's least successful ventures. Louis fought the Dutch to punish France's greatest trade rivals and made war on the Holy Roman Empire over territory which both claimed. His most costly military involvements, however, were his struggles to put a Bourbon on the throne of neighboring Spain. Much of the rest of Europe, led by the Dutch and the English, resisted this ploy, which could have made the Bourbon dynasty masters of the continent. After many years of fighting, a Bourbon did gain the Spanish throne, but only by agreeing that the French and Spanish dynasties should remain separate. France, meanwhile, paid dearly in blood and treasure for the king's ambition.

Louis XIV called himself the "Sun King," the center of the political universe, supposedly describing his position as France's absolute sovereign with the famous phrase: *l'état, c'est*

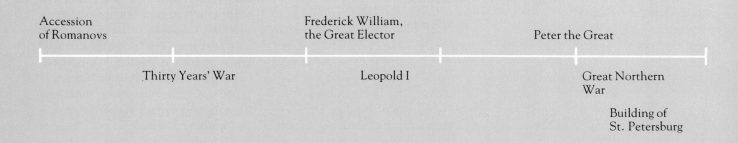

| 1600 | 1625 | 1650 | 1675 | 1700 | 1725 |

Accession of Romanovs

Frederick William, the Great Elector

Peter the Great

Thirty Years' War

Leopold I

Great Northern War

Building of St. Petersburg

moi—"I am the state." His palace at Versailles was a magnificent symbol of this immense power. A third of a mile long, surrounded by vast gardens and housing 10,000 people, Versailles was the embodiment of the grandeur of Europe's most admired ruler.

ABSOLUTISM IN GERMANY

Among the German states of central Europe, two monarchies would dominate the region from the seventeenth through the nineteenth centuries. They would also feud with each other over much of that time. One was the ancient Habsburg Austrian line that ruled the Holy Roman Empire, the other the rapidly rising Hohenzollern dynasty of Prussia.

Both these central European powers moved toward royal absolutism in the seventeenth and early eighteenth centuries. Both sought to follow Louis XIV in strengthening their administrative and military machinery and in building impressive royal courts. Both depended rather more on a powerful and relatively independent aristocracy than Louis did. But the absolutist Habsburg and Hohenzollern dynasties differed strikingly from each other in the degree of success they achieved.

Austrian Absolutism and Habsburg Revival

The Thirty Years' War left the power of the Habsburg dynasty in German-speaking central Europe shattered. The electors of the Holy Roman Empire, now eight, still elected Austrian Habsburgs emperor, but the emperor's actual authority over the separate German states, never great, had been all but destroyed by the war. In the later seventeenth century, however, Habsburg power revived surprisingly, forging a new multinational empire that stretched along the Danube River into the Balkans.

The Habsburg emperor who built this new empire was Leopold I (1658–1705). A contemporary of Louis XIV, Leopold was an unaggressive, extremely religious prince who had none of the Sun King's self-confidence or skill at public relations. Nevertheless, with the help of some of the greatest generals of the age, Leopold built up the Austrian army, with which he was able to turn back the last great Ottoman Turkish invasion of central Europe and to drive the Turks out of Hungary in the 1680s. With these

extensive lands to the east and with its older holdings in Bohemia (modern Czechoslovakia) to the north, Austria had a new empire to rule. Further, this resurgence of Austrian fortunes enabled the Habsburgs to renew their claims to authority in the German States and to great-power status in Europe as a whole.

Under Leopold also, the Habsburg monarchy attempted to strengthen its hold on these non-German speaking lands through centralized absolutist institutions. Leopold and his heir, Charles VI (1705–1740), prepared official documents declaring the unity of all the Austrian Habsburg lands. These included not only Austria, Bohemia, and Hungary but also other territories acquired over centuries, including parts of the Netherlands and Italy.

The Austrian attempt at absolutist centralization, however, was undermined by the fact that Leopold and his successors depended, not so much on the bourgeoisie, as Louis XIV had done, but on the aristocracy, including the non-German nobility of Hungary and Bohemia. To win their support, the Habsburgs allowed these aristocrats to increase their traditional control over their own peasant populations, thus reinforcing their independent power base.

389

Other divisive forces in the Austrian domains included the resistance of the provincial assemblies, or *diets,* and the deep ethnic divisions between the Germans and their Slav, Czech, Magyar, Hungarian, Italian, and other subject peoples. In addition, Charles in his later years allowed the bureaucracy and the army to decline, further weakening the Habsburg monarchy.

Prussian Absolutism and Hohenzollern Power

Royal absolutism in Prussia got off to a stronger start than it did in Austria in the seventeenth century. The architect of early Prussian absolutism was one of the most famous members of the ruling Hohenzollern dynasty, Frederick William (1640–1688), known as the "Great Elector." Frederick William and his successors built an impressive north German power center on an alliance with the Prussian Junker aristocracy and on such basic absolutist institutions as an efficient civil service and a strong army.

The problems the Hohenzollerns faced in the wake of the Thirty Years' War were as great as those confronted by their Habsburg rivals in southern Germany. The Hohenzollern electors—of the Holy Roman Empire—governed a string of territorially scattered lands stretching across northern Germany. These included Prussia, on the Polish frontier in the east, the central territory of Brandenburg, and Cleves in the Rhineland, in western Germany. The dynasty had first to connect these regions by adding new territories between them. At the same time, they had to impose centralized absolutist rule on all these fiercely independent lands. Finally, they had to build an effective army to protect Prussia, which was located on a plain lacking natural frontiers.

Frederick William took great strides toward these goals. He began to build a small but powerful army. This not only enabled him to acquire new territories, but also gave him a weapon with which to suppress resistance to Hohenzollern absolutism in the states thus captured. The Great Elector also encouraged the development of an extremely efficient bureaucracy, another potent tool to use in imposing a single, centralized authority on the Hohenzollern domains.

To run both his army and his administration, Frederick William and his successors depended on the businesslike Prussian aristocracy known as Junkers. In return for increased authority over the peasant population, the Prussian nobility were willing to support the monarchy. Far from resisting royal power, the Junkers thus established a tradition of state service. They would be the backbone of Hohenzollern power from the Great Elector's day to World War I.

Frederick William had established the fact of Prussian power in north Germany. He remained only an elector, however, not a king; and Brandenburg-Prussia, as it was then known,

MAP 49

Expansion of Prussia to 1740. With their original center of power in Brandenburg, the Hohenzollern monarchs expanded their realm across north Germany. By 1740 they had reached the Baltic to the north and east and had aquired possessions in the Rhine valley to the west. They were now in a position to challenge the Austrian Hapsburgs for domination of the German states.

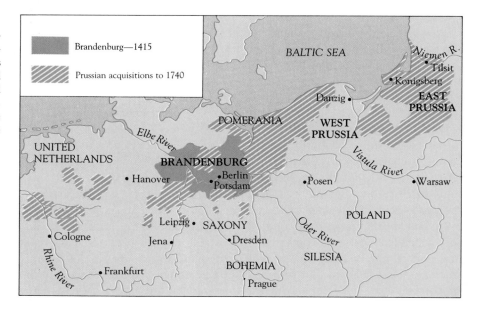

Brandenburg—1415

Prussian acquisitions to 1740

was only a second-class European power. Both these handicaps were overcome by the Hohenzollern rulers who came after him.

Elector Frederick III (1688–1713) earned the title of King Frederick I in 1701 by shrewdly timed military support for the Habsburg emperor. Frederick also began the transformation of Berlin from a provincial city into a great German capital.

King Frederick William I (1713–1740), finally, used the strength of the Prussian army to achieve recognition of Prussia as one of Europe's great powers. As militaristic as Frederick I had been cultured, Frederick William identified wholly with his army. It was easy to laugh at him for his "barracks mentality" and his pleasure in drilling his troops. Nevertheless, Frederick William did cut court expenses drastically and discipline his bureaucrats as he did his soldiers. Perhaps most important, he more than doubled the size of his army, making it the fourth largest and one of the most efficient in Europe.

The disciplined, growing kingdom of Prussia would find brilliant new leadership in the second half of the eighteenth century under Frederick the Great. But the absolutism of the earlier Hohenzollerns, had already transformed a scattering of German principalities into a new European power.

ABSOLUTISM IN RUSSIA: PETER THE GREAT

Strong government was not new to Russia when Peter the Great came to the throne in 1689. Moscovy, as the nation was earlier known, had an autocratic tradition that reached back hundreds of years.

The Romanovs and Russian Autocracy

This autocratic heritage, coupled with a widely felt need for order after a period of anarchy, led to the election of a new royal house early in the seventeenth century. Pretenders to the throne, popular revolts, and foreign invasions by the neighboring states of Poland and Sweden had produced fifteen years of chaos known in Russian history as the "Time of Troubles" (1598–1613). An unstable alliance of aristocrats, townsmen, and cossacks eventually defeated both domestic rebels and foreign invaders. Thereafter, a meeting of the Zemsky Sobor representing all major elements in the population except the serfs selected a new tsar to govern the nation. Their choice, Michael Romanov, was a sickly, pliable young man who was not expected to be a strong ruler. The Romanov dynasty would, however, rule Russia from 1613 down to the revolution of 1917.

The first three Romanov tsars were not strong rulers, but even so they claimed to wield the "full autocracy" of their fifteenth- and sixteenth-century predecessors. They also presided over some expansion of a bureaucracy that was to be a hallmark of Russian government. This period of revival also saw foreign trade grow once more and witnessed the culmination of Russia's great eastward expansion across Siberia to the Pacific.

But the early Romanovs were unable to solve the nation's economic problems, including a decrease in both agricultural production and government revenues. Domestic disorders also continued through the first three-quarters of the seventeenth century, including endless peasant and cossack rebellions and a great schism or split in the Russian Orthodox church.

At the beginning of the 1680s, then, Russia remained a growing but ramshackle autocracy on the eastern edge of Europe. The potential power inherent in its vast size and in autocratic tradition could best be realized by transforming Russian along the political and economic lines already laid down in western Europe. This transformation was finally undertaken by the most famous and controversial of Russian monarchs, Peter the Great.

Peter the Great and the Transformation of Russia

Peter I (1682–1725) came to the Russian throne at the age of ten in 1682 and took control of the country (from an older sister, who had ruled as regent) in 1689. For the next thirty-five years, he was a human whirlwind, shaking up backward, traditional Russia as it had never been shaken up before and would not be again until the twentieth century.

Peter was huge, nearly seven feet tall, ill educated, uncouth, and often brutal. At the same time, he was open to new ideas, practical, and immensely hardworking and energetic. What education he had he gained from Moscow's foreign colony of artisans and advisers who had come to work in backward Russia where their skills were much needed. Peter's orientation toward westerners and western Europe was to be crucial to the direction Russia would take in coming decades.

Like many absolute monarchs, Pe-

Peter the Great. The most powerful of Russian czars, and the first to use the title of emperor, Peter looks every inch a king in this contemporary likeness. Contrast the relative simplicity of Peter's costume with the sumptuous clothing and setting with which Louis XIV surrounded himself. While the Sun King's France was already the arbiter of European fashion, Russia was still a relatively rude and uncultivated place by contemporary standards in Peter's day.

ter was deeply concerned with foreign policy and military matters. Many of his reforms were intended to strengthen his army or improve his international position. He tried to secure the latter by war as well, defeating two powerful rivals, Sweden and Poland. In the long and bloody Great Northern War (1700–1721) with Sweden's dashing King Charles XII, Peter seized territory on the Baltic Sea on which he proceeded to build a new capital for Russia— St. Petersburg. Peter built this "window on the west" on a swamp at a cost of many thousands of lives; but by moving the capital away from isolated Moscow, he opened Russia further to western European trade and cultural influences.

Peter plunged into his domestic reforms with the same drive and determination that he brought to the Great Northern War or to expanding Russian territory. These efforts to transform Russian society are perhaps Peter's main claim to a central place in Russian history. As a dedicated autocrat working within an established Muscovite autocratic tradition, Peter attempted to strengthen his hold on key elements of the population. Russia's ancient hereditary aristocracy thus lost their position to an expanding "service nobility," who earned their ranks by service in the army or the state bureaucracy. The Russian Orthodox church, historically subservient to the tsars, became almost a branch of the government when its traditional head, the patriarch, was replaced by the procurator, a civil servant appointed by the tsar. The peasant masses, including many serfs, were made even more subordinate to

the landowning nobility. In addition, peasants were made liable for high taxes and for forced labor on Peter's major building projects.

Voted emperor for his victory in the Great Northern War, Peter also strengthened his authority in other ways. He created an elaborate system of central bureaus and imposed a structure of provincial and district administration on Russia. To import western European skills and efficiency, he hired more foreign experts and encouraged the new service nobility to study abroad.

In typical absolutist style, Peter's government did its best to foster economic growth. Government initiatives led to increased agricultural and mineral production, encouraged new industries, and improved the status of Russia's small middle class. Peter was particularly eager to improve Russia's primitive transportation network, building many roads, bridges, and major canals.

Some of Peter's reforms—like his insistence on western clothing and shaven faces instead of long robes and beards—outraged traditional Russian mores. Russia's peasantry certainly suffered under his relentless demands. Many of his changes, including much of the new governmental structure, did not long outlive him. Nevertheless, Peter did set his country on a new path. From his time, Russia was recognized as one of Europe's great powers. Equally important, his efforts to transform old Muscovy into a modern state began Russia's long push toward modernization. This drive for modernization and world power would reach its climax only in the present century.

SOCIETY AND STRUGGLE IN THE AGE OF ABSOLUTISM

The society over which Europe's absolute monarchs presided was as undemocratic and hierarchic as any in western history. Society under the absolutists was organized according to a system of estates or social classes based more on social prestige and noble titles than on mere wealth. Each class, institution, and even family or household, furthermore, had its own traditional hierarchy. Hereditary aristocrats and high churchmen usually stood at the top of this structure, though royal officials, successful busi-

nessmen, and professional people also enjoyed high status.

Aristocrats sneered at the very idea of a middle-class gentleman as a contradiction in terms. Yet it was possible in some places to work one's way up the social ladder, either through business or the royal administration. In western Europe, the commercial middle classes often grew richer under the mercantilist economic policies of royal absolutists; and even in Peter's Russia, merchants sometimes benefited from his reforms. An efficient royal administrator could sometimes rise to the top, particularly if he could point to even a recently-acquired noble title or coat of arms.

MAP 50

Expansion of Russia to 1796. Beginning in Muscovy in the northern part of Russia's European heartland, the Tsars extended their authority across Eurasia to the Pacific. In the eighteenth century Peter the Great and Catherine the Great pressed south to the Black Sea and west towards the European heartland. Russia had now emerged as one of the great powers of Europe.

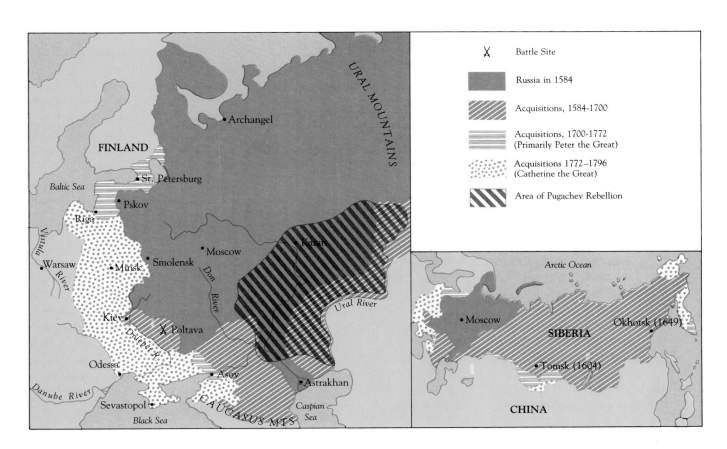

PETER THE GREAT, NATION-BUILDER OR ANTICHRIST?

(1)

This monarch had brought our country to a level with others: he taught us to recognize that we are a people. In brief, everything that we look upon in Russia has its origin in him, and everything which is done in the future will be derived from this source.*

(2)

Ah, this is why he hobnobs with Germans, this is why he . . . robbed Jesus Christ of his primacy and took the title of patriarch. This is why he shaves his beard, why he has donned a short coat . . . this is why he has levied new taxes and assessments upon the Christian world. . . . There have been seven Antichrists. According to the Holy Writ, an eight is to be born. And now he has come in the person of Peter.*

These drastically conflicting evaluations of Peter the Great's place in Russian history reflect two contemporary points of view. For those like Ivan Nepleuv, who shared Peter's vision of a modernized and westernized Russia, the emperor's reign was a great step forward. To those who valued old Russian traditions, particularly Russia's ancient Orthodox Church, the iron-fisted reformer could look like the Antichrist himself.

Whether he was the founder of modern Russia or the destroyer of Russia's soul, Peter's central place in this great debate shows once more how great the impact of an absolute monarch could be.

*Ivan Nepleuv, Memoirs, in Vasili Klyuchevsky, Peter the Great "The Opposition of the Traditionalists," in Marc Raeff, ed. Peter the Great Changes Russia (Lexington, Mass.: D.C. Heath, 1972), pp. 175–176.

The preeminence of the aristocracy, however, remained generally recognized. The nobility failed in efforts to reassert their medieval independence in revolts like the Fronde in France. Nevertheless, hardworking Prussian Junkers, Russian service nobility who served Peter well, and even the courtier nobility of France were rewarded with the highest positions and the greatest social prestige.

The Splendid Century

Life at the top of this society has earned for the seventeenth century its designation as "the splendid century." Court life at Versailles or at the Schonbrunn palace in Vienna or Peter the Great's new capital of St. Petersburg was enormously expensive and often not particularly comfortable, but it was undeniably magnificent. Absolute monarchs moved in splendor, surrounded by extravagant ceremonials and elaborate rules of precedence. Consultations with their ministers of state might be the core of a monarch's day, but there was plenty of time for banquets, balls, hunting, cards, conversation, opera, theatre, and other entertainments. The palaces were the largest and most ornate, the costumes the most expensive, that Europe had ever seen.

There was vanity and self-indulgence in all this, but there was political realism as well. Absolutism required stately magnificence to maintain its public image of glory and splendor, its political claim to supremacy.

The Lower Orders

The lower orders or classes of society lived under much less enviable conditions. The urban poor and the masses of rural peasantry were the ones who benefited least from the royal absolutism.

Most Europeans were peasants, and they suffered from many misfortunes in the seventeenth century. Some of these were natural calamities, including famines, a return of the plague, and the so-called little ice age, a half-century of cold winters and short growing seasons. But other peasant problems were caused by the policies of their absolutist rulers. Rising taxes to pay for royal grandeur, long and bloody wars to advance royal ambitions, and even a resurgence of serfdom in eastern Europe all hurt Europe's country population.

The urban poor, often migrants from the countryside, had their share of miseries. These included the difficulty of finding work in cities still dominated by the guilds, repeated economic depressions, and particular helplessness in the face of famine and plague.

Under such pressures, Europe's lower orders reacted with sometimes irrational violence. Peasant rebellions, in nations as different as Louis XIV's France and Peter the Great's Russia, were one form of social protest. Waves of witch hunting, sweeping from the German states to Britain's New England colonies, were probably in part expressions of social frustration. In the seventeenth century, gin and rum also began to provide a very unhealthy escape from urban wretchedness in particular.

Popular festivals and social organizations still existed for the masses. Western European peasants tended to be better off than eastern Europeans, and free peasants than serfs. Altogether, however, it is hard to see that the masses of Europeans had much reason to be grateful for the age of absolutism.

War in the Age of Absolutism

The tendency of absolute monarchs to advance their interests by force of arms made warfare a common feature of European life under the absolutists. The wealth and power these monarchs brought to military affairs in fact led to the creation of larger and more powerful armies than Europe had ever seen before.

This royal militarism took some odd forms. Prussia's King Frederick William I prided himself particularly on his "giants," a regiment composed entirely of strapping soldiers more than six feet tall, whom the king much enjoyed drilling. As a child, Russia's Peter the Great organized his aristocratic playmates into military units, trained with real weapons—and worked his own way up from the ranks, beginning as a humble private.

The Great Elector Mounts a Siege. This seventeenth-century engraving depicts Prussian artillery in action against the besieged city of Stettin in 1678. Note the elaborate design of the artillery emplacements, the troops marching into position, and Frederick William himself issuing orders at lower right.

But war was a serious business for wielders of absolute sovereignty. Indeed, much of the effort they put into expanding government, revenues, and national wealth seems to have been ultimately intended to strengthen the armies with which monarchs could try to dominate the international stage. Certainly, large portions of the money collected in taxes went to pay for royal armies and royal wars.

Seventeenth-century armies put new emphasis on discipline and training. Supplies, uniforms, and superior artillery were more readily available than ever before. The arts of military fortification and siegecraft were brought to a high level: It was said of Louis XIV's military engineer, Vauban, that no city he defended could ever be taken, no city he attacked would ever stand. Military commanders planned sweeping campaigns across the map of Europe, and

Bernini's Baldachino in St. Peter's. This huge bronze and gilt canopy over the tomb of St. Peter in St. Peter's Cathedral, Rome, well illustrates the splendor at which baroque art aimed. Standing more than ninety feet high, the baldachino features twisted columns and curving shapes, color, and movement, all typical of baroque.

soldiers marched in step from camp to battlefield.

Many of these troops were dragooned into the king's service, and many of their officers were young noblemen who had purchased commissions rather than earning them through military skill. But some were crack troops, like many in the Prussian army, and some ranks in the French army were promoted on a merit basis. In size, the military machines of the absolute monarchs were awesome. Louis XIV had 400,000 men in his later years, far more troops than the Roman Empire had at its height. Emphasis on military engineering, a relatively efficient supply system, and such innovations as the bayonet all contributed to the power of Louis's military machine.

From one point of view, these militaristic policies served Europe's crowned heads well. With his huge armies, Louis XIV rounded out France's frontiers and put a Bourbon on the throne of Spain, even if not on Louis's terms. Leopold of Austria used military force to create a new Habsburg empire on the Danube. The Hohenzollerns manipulated their powerful army to win a place among the great powers for Prussia, and Peter the Great's hard-won victories in the Great Northern War made Russia a major power.

These wars, however, brought immense suffering to the peoples of Europe. Crushing taxes, military conscription, marauding armies, and heavy casualties were all part of their cost. Even the greatest victories of Peter the Great or Louis XIV cost many lives and drained their nations economically.

MAXIMS

(1)

Self-esteem is the greatest of flatterers.

We are never so well off or so badly off as we imagine.

We are all strong enough to bear the misfortunes of others.

In the distress of our best friends we always find something that does not displease us.

Absence destroys small passions, and increases great ones; the wind extinguishes tapers, but kindles fires. *

(2)

Women run to extremes; they are either better or worse than men.

Children are overbearing, supercilious, passionate, envious, inquisitive, egotistical, idle, fickle, timid, intemperate, liars, and dissemblers; they laugh and weep easily . . . they bear no pain but like to inflict it on others; already they are men. *

These brief maxims and pithy sayings reflect the wit of two shrewd literary observers of the seventeenth-century scene: the Duc de la Rochefoucauld and Jean de la Bruyere. Some of them, at least, seem to have that feel of eternal truth at which classicism aimed. Such satirical sayings and cynical worldliness also lent an air of sophistication much admired in some court circles.

*La Rochefoucauld, *Maximes*, ed. Roger Charbonnel (Paris: Larousse, n.d.), pp. 17, 26, 36; Crane Brinton, ed., *The Portable Age of Reason Reader* (New York: Viking, 1956), pp. 537–540.

The Arts: Baroque and Classicism

Europe's artists, often found Europe's absolute rulers generous patrons, and the arts flourished at their courts. Architects, sculptors, painters, composers, poets, and playwrights were in fact essential to absolute monarchy, for artists provided the lavish life style and the magnificent public image that distinguished the splendid century.

Two styles in particular dominated the arts in the seventeenth century: baroque and classicism. Both reflected the larger political, social, and cultural currents of the age.

The baroque style dominated such arts as architecture, painting, sculpture, and music for much of the seventeenth century. *Baroque* derived from the Portuguese *barroco*, meaning a misshapen or deformed pearl, and some critics saw baroque art as a warping of the Renaissance art from which it grew.

Baroque artists did in fact emphasize or exaggerate certain features of Renaissance art. These included size and magnificence in building, color and movement in painting, and the mixing of various forms, as in the mixture of music and drama in the first operas. The huge, colorful, crowded pictures of the Flemish painter Peter Paul Rubens and the melodies of Claudio Monteverdi, the inventor of opera, were masterpieces of baroque art.

This new style in the arts exactly

The Building of St. Petersburg. Seventeenth-century absolutists demonstrated—and further enhanced—their power by building or refurbishing palaces and even capital cities. Here, Peter the Great supervises the construction of his new capital city of St. Petersburg (Leningrad today). Peter, who had worked with his hands in his own youth, was a hard taskmaster, but the city he built is considered by many to be the most beautiful in Russia today.

suited the new era. Counter-Reformation popes seized on the new style for churches in the later sixteenth century. The result was the emotionally moving, even awe-inspiring, grandeur of churches like St. Peter's in Rome. Absolute monarchs, who wanted to impress their subjects with their own grandeur, began to build baroque palaces in the seventeenth century. Louis XIV's palace at Versailles, with its huge gardens, many fountains, great hall of mirrors, and other splendors, used the baroque style very effectively to glorify the Sun King.

Classicism, important in architecture, painting, and literature, was another widely admired style. It was perhaps especially important as an influence on writing in the seventeenth century. Classicism in general stressed classical Greek and Roman models and rules for the arts, especially regularity, balance, and order. An outstanding example was the French classical tragedy that was so popular at the court of Louis XIV. The plays of Jean Racine, for instance, had plots derived from classical mythology and were written in regular, rhythmic verse. Their themes, heroes, and heroines also had a classic nobility: powerful characters torn between such exalted emotions as duty, honor, and love. The aristocrats of that age of courtly magnificence liked to see themselves as just such noble characters.

These styles served some of the greatest writers and artists of the age. The Dutch painter Rembrandt van Rijn used light and sometimes color with baroque effectiveness in emotionally moving canvasses. The English poet John Milton wrote great religious poems like *Paradise Lost* in classically regular verse, but with language filled with baroque color and grandeur. The French comic playwright Jean Moliere used classical dramatic forms to satirize all classes of French society. The baroque grandeur of Versailles and the stately classicism of Racine's noble tragedies had a special appeal to the kings and aristocrats of the age of absolutism.

SUMMARY

The age of royal absolutism in Europe was an important stage in the growth of powerful governments in the western nations. Reacting against a period of civil wars and social upheaval, Europeans accepted autocratic rulers who could bring domestic order in the seventeenth and early eighteenth centuries.

These new state builders claimed absolute sovereignty over their subjects. To carry out their will, they developed larger and sometimes more efficient administrative systems than their predecessors. These bureaucracies particularly imposed the mercantile system of government regulation on production, trade, and other aspects of the economy.

Absolutism reached its height in the France of Louis XIV, the Sun King. Louis's lavish court, administrative system of *intendants,* huge armies, and impressive power were the envy of his royal rivals. In central Europe, the ancient Austrian Habsburg dynasty used absolutist methods to recover from their loss of power in the Thirty Years' War. At the same time, the Prussian Hohenzollerns thrust their way into the front rank of the nations with the help of absolutist techniques and an impressive bureaucracy and army. In east Europe, the heavy-fisted autocrat Peter the Great won great-power status for Russia by a violent exercise of royal will.

The society over which the absolutist monarchs presided was splendid at its top level, among the aristocracy. The middle-class merchant community, though socially excluded from the elite, often benefited economically from mercantilist policies. Much misery existed among peasants and the urban poor, however, and the wars of the absolute rulers were costly in lives and human suffering. Nevertheless, the artists who built the palaces and entertained the upper classes produced baroque and classical masterpieces of great power. The next chapter will look at the spread of modified forms of this highly developed western society to the European colonies beyond the seas.

SELECTED SOURCES

Adam, Antoine. *Grandeur and Illusion: French Literature and Society, 1600–1715.* Translated by Herbert Tint. 1972. Good survey of the intellectual history of the age, particularly useful on classicism.

Carsten, F. L. *The Origins of Prussia.* 1954. Older but still recommended history of the period through the reign of the Great Elector.

*Dumas, Alexandre. *The Three Musketeers.* 1982. Famous novel of swashbuckling seventeenth-century soldiers. There are also film versions.

Goubert, Pierre. *Louis XIV and Twenty Million Frenchmen.* Translated by Ann Carter. 1970. An analysis of French society under the Grand Monarch.

Kitson, Michael. *The Age of Baroque.* 1966. Beautifully illustrated history of art in Europe in the seventeenth and eighteenth centuries.

Lougee, Carolyn C. *Le Paradis des Femmes: Women, Salons, and Social Stratification in Seventeenth Century France.* 1976. Women in the intellectual and social elite.

Massie, Robert. *Peter the Great.* 1980. Highly readable, Pulitzer prize-winning account.

*Rabb, Theodore K. *The Struggle for Stability in Early Modern Europe.* 1975. Brief but sweeping survey of the "crisis of the seventeenth century," to which absolutism provided a partial solution.

*Wolf, John B. *Louis XIV.* 1968. Monumental biography of the Sun King.

Wolf, John B. *Emergence of the Great Powers 1685–1715.* 1951. Older standard history of Europe and European international relations in the age of Louis XIV and Peter the Great.

*Available in paperback.

WESTERN SOCIETY IN THE NEW WORLD IN THE EARLY EIGHTEENTH CENTURY

[British] America is formed for happiness, but not for empire: in a course of 1200 miles I did not see a single object that solicited charity; but I saw insuperable causes of weakness, which will necessarily prevent its being a potent state; . . . it appears to me very doubtful . . . whether it would be possible to keep in due order and government so wide and extended an empire; . . . fire and water are not more heterogeneous than the different colonies in North-America. . . . nothing can exceed the jealousy . . . they possess in regard to each other. . . . In short, such is the difference of character, of manners, of religion, of interest of the different colonies, that . . . were they left to themselves, there would be a civil war, from one end of the continent to the other; while the Indians and Negroes would, with better reason, impatiently watch the opportunity of exterminating them all together. . . . [there] will never take place a permanent union or alliance of all the colonies, . . .

The good Reverend Andrew Burnaby, traveling in British North America in the middle of the eighteenth century, was not the only European who had difficulty reading the future of an area so different from Europe. To a person coming from a more unified culture, the multitudinous diversity of British North American society must have appeared to be a prescription for perpetual disorder. Burnaby would undoubtedly have made the same comments if he had been traveling in Latin America, which had its own diversities and its own divergences from Europe. By the early eighteenth century, western civilization was no longer confined to the continent of Europe and to its immediate environs. Three million inhabitants of European descent and millions of mixed ancestry now lived in Latin America and British North America. Far from Europe and living in the presence of Amerindian cultures and African slaves, they were developing forms of western civilization that departed more and more from those of Europe.

Western Civilization in the New World. The Chiesa de la Merced in Cuzco, Peru represents the establishment of the Catholic church in the Americas by the Spanish and the Portuguese. The Catholic Church was the most monumental European institution transferred to the Western Hemisphere, eventually encompassing millions of people in a huge area. Whether great urban cathedrals, city churches such as this one, or rural mission stations, the Spanish and the Portuguese built thousands of edifaces to express their faith.

European settlers arriving in the western hemisphere naturally expected to live in much the same way as they did in their homelands. However, faced first with fighting for survival in the new environment and later finding unique opportunities for prosperity, they rapidly dropped or modified those European customs that turned out to be inappropriate or obstructive, and evolved more suitable practices. This chapter begins with Latin America, the first western culture to markedly differ from the standards of Europe. It then takes up the more radical version of western culture that evolved later in British North America.

LATIN AMERICA

By 1700, Europeans from the Iberian Peninsula had been living in the western hemisphere for more than two centuries. Coming into control of three quarters of the hemisphere, an area some forty times larger than Iberia, European settlers found extremes of climate from steaming jungles to icy wastes. Isolated in small groups by great distances and often by impassable terrain, they found themselves surrounded and outnumbered by Amerindians and African slaves, whose grudging labor was the foundation of their economy.

The Land of Three Races

The unique multiracial situation that developed in Latin America marked the greatest difference between western civilization in Latin America and in Europe. As a result of economic conditions and religious policies, whites in Latin America were always a distinct minority. Through the years, only a small number of settlers crossed the Atlantic. Ordinary Iberians had little incentive to immigrate, because only a few privileged aristocrats could own land, and the Amerindians and black slaves provided all the labor. In addition, Spain's policy dictated that only "reliable" Catholic Spaniards would go to America. This excluded foreigners, Jews, Jewish converts to Catholicism, and those with some Moorish ancestry. Despite these regulations, other Europeans, including some Protestants and Jews, made their way there. By downplaying their religion and their origin, they sometimes became important landholders, merchants, and officials.

Gender also played a key role. Most of the white immigrants were men; owing to custom and circumstance, few white women migrated to Latin America. The white men, especially those living among the numerous highland Amerindians, took concubines and wives from the subject races. Amerindians remained in the majority in some areas of the former Aztec, Maya, and Inca empires and were the largest single racial group in Latin America as a whole throughout the colonial period. By the eighteenth century, however, mestizo descendants from white-Amerindian unions were the largest racial group in some areas. White males living among the black slaves had also produced an extensive mulatto population throughout the Caribbean and Brazil. Black-Amerindian unions were less common.

The realities of multiracial living brought about a more relaxed attitude about race in Latin America than in Europe or British North America. The status of the large and increasing mestizo population had to be worked out, much of it by a rough color code. A few individuals with some Amerindian ancestry, if they were from wealthy and accomplished families, became accepted members of the white ruling class; others became a part of the small middle class. The great majority, particularly those who were predominantly Amerindian, were part of the laboring masses.

Although American practice to some degree worked in favor of those of mixed ancestry, it worked against the pure Amerindian. After a short period during which some Amerindians were enslaved, the Spanish crown and the Catholic church consistently held that the Amerindians were free subjects of the crown, to be treated as dependent minors. They could be parceled out to work for the benefit of whites, but only on a limited basis, and were to receive religious and vocational instruction. In actuality, white masters, often working through the Amerindian village chiefs, generally neglected their obligations. They forced the Amerindians under their control to work in mines and factories, on ranches and farms, and as porters and construction laborers. Often separated from their families, Amerindians frequently labored under brutal conditions that brought premature death. They sometimes rose in revolt, but the uprisings were always crushed. Some individuals such as Bartolomé de las Casas campaigned for the welfare of the Amerindian, but neither good intentions nor royal decrees from afar made much headway. By the eighteenth century, some of the more brutal systems of forced labor were on the decline, except in the Andes. Instead, the mass of Amerindians and mestizos had become peons. Bound to the land by debts for shelter, food, and clothing that they could never pay off, they and their descendants were forced to work for their masters in perpetuity.

Blacks as a group fared even worse than the Amerindians. Most Amerindians at least lived a family life in their villages, practicing many aspects of their traditional culture. Blacks were shipped to America as individuals, torn away from their native culture, and put to grueling labor in a strange new land. Most of them were males and thus even denied the comfort of family life. Under the law, they held a dual status. They were human beings, and therefore entitled to humane treatment. However, they were also chattel, like livestock. They could own no property, had no right to keep their families together, and had to obey all commands of their master. In practice, most masters treated their slaves as chattel rather than as human beings. Many slaves were simply worked to death or to incapacity and then replaced by new slaves supplied by the efficient slave-trading companies.

There were a few ways out of slavery. Portugal in particular had provided relatively liberal laws for Brazilian slaves to buy their freedom, and masters found few legal obstacles to freeing a slave if they chose to do so. However, few slaves could accumulate the price of freedom, and few masters chose to free them. Those blacks and mulattoes who did gain their freedom legally found that, unlike the situation in British North America, their race was not an ab-

solute barrier to rising in society. In areas where few lower-class Iberians were present, many blacks possessed valuable skills as artisans and mechanics that whites needed. Particularly in Brazil, where in some areas slaves and free blacks overwhelmingly outnumbered whites, even a small amount of white ancestry gave some mulattoes the social status of whites.

Slaves in the Caribbean sporadically rose in revolt, but always unsuccessfully. Running away into unsettled areas was often more effective. Sometimes, such as with the Maroons in the interior of Jamaica, runaways banded together to successfully hold out against whites. Brazilian slaves often fled into the vast interior; there, during the seventeenth century, blacks set up the state of Palmares, which lasted thirty years before it was destroyed.

European Economic Theory and American Reality

In the early eighteenth century, when mercantilism was still the reigning economic theory, the Spanish government continued to closely regulate the Spanish American economy. As earlier, the crown permitted a group of companies, first in Seville and later in Cadiz, to monopolize the commerce with Spanish America. The companies acted under the regulations of the *Casa de Contratación*, the government bureau that managed the details of the economic life of the colonies and collected the crown's share of taxes and monopolies. The *Casa* still sent out two annual convoys under the protection of the royal navy to the colonies. The convoys called only at three Caribbean ports, through

which all trade with Spain had to pass. A single convoy returned to Spain carrying the exports of Spanish America. The Portuguese were not as rigid, allowing merchants from ports other than Lisbon to trade with Brazil and to send their ships directly there instead of joining the convoys passing in and out of Lisbon.

The convoy arrangement, practical when cargoes from Spanish American production were predominantly gold and silver in need of careful protection, was strangling Spanish American commerce by the eighteenth century. In the first place the fleets often did not have the cargo space to carry away all the products awaiting export. Second, continuing to have the convoy ports only in the Caribbean made it extremely difficult for South American producers to get their goods to Spain. To cite an extreme problem, except for a period in the seventeenth century, ranchers in Argentina could not import or export through their Atlantic port of Buenos Aires. Instead, porters and mules had to haul, say, hides, hundreds of miles across the plains and up into the high country of Bolivia, then down through the passes of the Andes to the Pacific coast. Here the hides were loaded into ships and carried to the Isthmus of Panama, then overland by pack train to Portobello on the Caribbean, one of the three convoy ports. Finally, if cargo space was available, they were placed on a ship to Spain.

The problem of imports was perhaps worse. Following mercantilist doctrine, colonists were not supposed to produce items, such as metalware, textiles, and wine, that competed with the products of the mother country. By the eighteenth century production in Spain was in such decline that most of the products destined for America came from elsewhere in Europe, at high prices and in inadequate amounts. From early times, the desperate colonists had welcomed British, Dutch, and French smugglers; in addition, they ignored the prohibitions on competing with Spanish goods. They began to produce their own textiles, metalware, and wine, combining such production with Amerindian skills in weaving, pottery, and basketry. These colonial products were mostly of the cruder make, however, and the upper classes, though small in number, continuously demanded a supply of products that could not be satisfied by the convoy or even by Spain itself.

Spreading the Catholic Faith

The Roman Catholic church, responsible for meeting the spiritual needs of the millions living in the huge area across the ocean, of necessity created a widespread colonial organization. The Spanish monarchy had secured from the papacy the right to nominate all clerical officials in America as high as the rank of archbishop, giving the crown another large arena for patronage. Since the church, like the state, reflected the class structure of the time, nearly all the top ecclesiastical appointments, numbering eventually ten archbishops and thirty-eight bishops, went to Spanish aristocrats. Most of the clergy that served in America were also Spaniards.

The church had many responsibilities in America but its main charge was, as it saw it, to save the souls of multitudes of heathens doomed to hell. The religious orders (the regular clergy) of Franciscans and Dominicans ac-

companied the early conquistadores and converted millions of Amerindians, by persuasion and sometimes with the aid of force. Later, in the more remote areas, the regular clergy, now joined by the Jesuits, replaced the conquistadores as the frontiersmen, setting up missions in previously unconquered territories. With the help of army detachments, they rounded up the nearby Amerindians and brought them in to live around the mission, to work to maintain themselves and the clergy, and to receive Christian instruction and baptism. Once the area had been secured, the orders set up new missions farther in the interior and repeated the process.

Behind the regular clergy came the secular or diocesan clergy and the religious orders of nuns, whose responsibility was to sustain and consolidate the faith in the settled areas. They organized local parishes, built up a system of education from the primary grades through universities, and founded hospitals, orphanages, and poor houses. Bishops, rich laity, and the government erected cathedrals and other religious edifices, many outstanding for their architectural and artistic beauty.

Spain was perhaps the nation in Europe most devoutly loyal to the Catholic church, and religious practice in its American colonies reflected this zeal. As in Spain, Roman Catholicism was the only faith tolerated; under the watchful eye of the Holy Office (the Inquisition), blasphemy was subject to fines and corporal punishment. Unrepentant Protestant, Jewish, and atheist heretics faced exile or burning at the stake, although executions were infrequent compared with Europe, and the Amerindians

were not subject to its jurisdiction. Spanish America became a bastion of Catholicism, in the jungles of the Amazon and the extreme south, where the Amerindians were unconquered.

Despite an impressive record of accomplishment in transplanting a major aspect of western culture to the New World, many abuses and problems bedeviled the Catholic church in America. The church had accumulated enormous wealth by the eighteenth century, and the huge size of the church organization made corruption inevitable. As a result of these and other factors, the American Catholic church was burdened with idle clerics who congregated for luxurious and sometimes debauched living in the cities. Up to one-half of city property was owned by the church, much of it by the religious orders. The orders often used their money to compete with the laity in banking and commerce, taking advantage of their special exemptions from taxation and economic regulation.

Perhaps the greatest problem for the church was in the countryside. Many dedicated clerics served their mestizo and Amerindian parishioners faithfully, devoting themselves to teaching, vocational instruction, and spiritual guidance. On the other hand, rural parishes were often left impoverished by the church hierarchy, so that many had no priests or were staffed by incompetent, uneducated, or avaricious individuals. Many Amerindians and blacks learned only the external, ceremonial aspects of their new faith, which they combined with their traditional religion. Some parish priests exacted high fees for administering the sacraments and saying mass. The clergy at the missions sometimes exploited Amerindian labor as brutally as the secular landlords. Ironically, some orders attempted to protect the Amerindians from enslavement and other forms of mistreatment by exploiting black slaves instead and bidding others to do the same.

Ruling America

The class structure and government of eighteenth century Latin America were as intertwined in the colonies as they were in Iberia and the rest of continental Europe. Like Europe, Latin America was governed by a small class of aristocrats and gentry, separated from the rest of society by hereditary privileges and certain immunities from the operations of the law. Through the years the crown had granted control over property in the New World to adventuresome conquistadores and to certain favored aristocrats. By the eighteenth century Peninsulars (aristocrats from Spain who returned there) and Creoles (aristocrats of Spanish descent born and residing in America), who comprised approximately 2 percent of the population, owned virtually all the property of value—mines, ranches, plantations, and manufacturing establishments. Below the aristocracy, mestizos and lower-class Iberian immigrants filled some of the need for merchants and artisans, occupations largely ignored or scorned by the upper class. More than 90 percent of the population—the blacks, mulattoes, Amerindians, and most of the mestizos—toiled for the few.

The administration of Spanish America, until the Bourbon reforms of the mid-eighteenth century, reflected in general the traditional process of royal government in Spain. In

---

THE WEALTH OF MEXICO CITY

The streets of Christendom must not compare with . . . the richness of the shops which do adorn them. . . . where a man's eyes may behold in less than an hour many millions' worth of gold, silver, pearls and jewels. . . .

[The] churches . . . are the fairest that ever my eyes beheld, the roofs and beams being . . . all daubed in gold, and many altars with sundry marble pillars, and others brazil-wood stays standing above one another with tabernacles for several saints richly wrought with golden colors. . . .

. . . the inward riches belonging to the altars are infinite, . . . such as copes, canopies, hanging altar cloths, candlesticks, jewels belonging to the saints, and crowns of gold and silver, and tabernacles of gold and crystal. . . .

Both men and women are excessive in their appearance, using more silks than stuffs and cloth. Precious stones and pearls further much their vain os-

tentation; a hat-band and rose made of diamonds in a gentleman's hat is common, and a hat-band of pearls is common in a tradesman; [even] a black or a tawny young maid and slave . . . will be in fashion with her neck-chain and bracelets of pearls, and her earbobs of some considerable jewels.*

This seventeenth century account of Mexico City, as seen by an English priest, portrays the world of the elite classes in urban Latin America. In an era where life was short even for the rich, ostentatious display of their wealth for themselves and for their church is understandable. Sudden abundance also caused families to use their wealth to compete for social standing and political power. The slaves referred to are undoubtedly domestic servants, adorned by their masters as another sign of family wealth.

*Thomas Gage, The English-American: A New Survey of the West Indies, (London: R. Coates, 1648), pp. 89–92 passim.

Spain the monarchy was limited to a degree by the traditional privileges of the nobility and churchmen. The core of royal power lay in its control over, and support from, the cabildos, the councils of the municipal city-states into which Spain was divided. Historical circumstances, however, gave the monarchs even greater power in America. The popes had awarded the New World to the Spanish monarchs as their personal possession. Here there would be little competition from aristocrats and clerics. The Spanish crown quickly set up cabildos in Spanish America to underpin royal authority.

The monarchs soon realized that

the Spanish settlements were swallowed up in the huge American landscape and too distant from Spain for regular, effective control. The American cabildos there soon came under the control of the local elites and often ignored royal wishes. The monarchs therefore added a complex system of controls centered in Spain and fanning out over the islands, jungles, plains, and highlands of the sprawling region. Power passed by appointment from the crown to the Council of the Indies, which had the authority to act in the name of the king on matters dealing with broad economic policy, justice, military affairs, and supervi-

Mexico City, 1673. Like Tenochtitlán, conquered 150 years earlier, the city is built in the middle of Lake Texcoco on an artificial earthen base interwoven with canals. The new Mexico City is clearly a Mediterranean city architecturally. The approaches to the causeways are protected by turreted fortifications. Historical Pictures Service.

sion of the Church. Next came the viceroys, who represented the king in New Spain (Mexico and Central America) and Peru (South America). The viceroys, paid well by the crown, had great power over local appointments, administration, finance, and the military forces. Their authority was subject to review, however, by the audiencias, ongoing judicial-consultative bodies in their area of jurisdiction, and by inspectors sent out from Spain.

Below the viceroy were the regional presidents and captains-general, the provincial governors, and finally a network of local officials operating in the rural areas. These local officials supervised the Indian villages, and it was here that extreme abuses often occurred. The local officials were usually either the local landlords or worked with the landlords. They frequently violated Amerindian legal rights, impinged on water rights, seized Amerindian land, exploited labor, and exacted fraudulent taxes.

Whereas the government of Latin America, as in Europe, reflected the class structure, it also divided the white minority in America into factions. The Council of the Indies, immersed in court politics, gave many government positions in America to Peninsulars, thus rebuffing the resident Creoles. Of the 170 viceroys who governed Spanish America during the colonial period, only four were Creoles. Creoles did have some seats in the audiencias and throughout the sixteenth century considered themselves Spanish. By the early eighteenth century, however, some Creoles were beginning to think of themselves as Spanish Americans and resented the political dominance of the Peninsulars. As a group the Creoles had become an idle class without the responsibility or the power that traditionally accompanies an aristocracy.

Class feelings in Latin America were strong: The Creoles were jealous and contemptuous of the lower-class persons arriving from Iberia. They also looked down on the mestizos who were working their way up into the middle class and into some of the lesser offices, especially in the towns.

An Amalgamation of Cultures

Iberian education and culture dominated Latin America in general and was, of course, the exclusive milieu of the ruling elite. The church controlled the classroom from the primary grades through the university curriculum. Education was reserved for the upper and middle classes, who considered it unnecessary and even dangerous for the masses below to be educated. As a result, Latin America, like most of Europe, was 90 percent illiterate. Few women were taught to read and write; most were trained in domestic and social skills.

Advanced study was a strong feature of Spanish American education. By the beginning of the eighteenth century ten major universities of uneven quality were functioning in Spanish America, although the Portuguese colony of Brazil had none. As was traditional, the overwhelming majority of university students studied theology and law, although at the University of Mexico, a person could also study medicine, rhetoric, and certain Amerindian languages.

Intellectual and artistic developments in Latin America closely followed the pattern in Iberia. Latin American scholars worked primarily within the frame of reference of Aquinas and the scholastics. Innovative thought was discouraged by the Inquisition and its index of banned writings. Meanwhile, most Spanish American writers simply added to the stream of standard Spanish chivalric romances, poetry, and devotional literature demanded by the small reading public.

A few writers made unique contributions to the body of western literature. Some writers in Spanish America filled old bottles with new wine, employing traditional epic and romance formats to portray the struggles between the Spaniards and the Amerindians. The most notable was the sixteenth century epic *La Araucana* by Alonso de Ercilla y Zúñiga, which celebrated the heroic resistance of the Araucanian Amerindians of Chile. The greatest poet of Latin America may well have been Sor Juana Inés de la Cruz, a beautiful and highly intelligent young woman with an interest in science, mathematics, and writing. Refused admission to the University of Mexico because she was a woman (although she offered to wear men's clothes) she went into a convent at sixteen and there wrote exquisite drama and love poetry while continuing her studies in other subjects. Her superiors later put a stop to her writing; she sold her enormous library and devoted herself to charity until she died at forty-four.

A great demand both in Europe and America also existed for histories of the conquest, such as that written by one of Cortes's soldiers, Bernal Díaz del Castillo. Perhaps the most intriguing book on the conquest was the *Royal Commentaries of the Incas,* written by the mestizo Garcilaso de la Vega, son of a Spanish father and a princess of the royal line of the Incas. Garcilaso shows the mind of the mestizo caught between two cultures, as he idealizes both the conquering Spanish and the conquered Incas. The European and Latin American publics were also interested in books describing the hemisphere's strange new flora and fauna, such as the *General and Natural History of the Indies,* by Gonzalo Fernández de Oviedo.

The enormous impact of European culture on Latin America by no means meant the elimination of Amerindian and African influence in Latin America. Amerindian culture remained the heart of daily life in many of the rural villages, whereas Amerindian foods, textiles, basketry, metalworking, building materials and techniques, and artistic motifs were integrated into the daily lives of the European immigrants. Black slaves, although cut off from their home culture, nevertheless permanently implanted African foods, music, art forms, and religious practices in the Caribbean and Brazil.

Antonio de Mendoza, Viceroy of New Spain, 1535–1551. The embodiment of the authority of the Spanish crown, the viceroys exercised great power in the New World. Their ability to act, however, was to some degree circumscribed by competing colonial institutions and by inspectors sent out by the crown itself.

BRITISH NORTH AMERICA

Settlers on the Atlantic seaboard of British North America, operating in a different geographical and historical

407

Slavery in British North America. This 1700 woodcut for a tobacco label depicts the results of the 1619 decision at Jamestown. In Virginia, white planters take their ease in the shade, while black slaves toil in the tobacco fields under a hot sun.

context, departed further from European culture than did Latin Americans. British North America east of the Appalachians was more than a century younger than Latin America. It was one-tenth the size, with a temperate climate and relatively fertile soil, and in the early eighteenth century mustered one million compared to ten million Latin Americans.

Races and Racism

As in Latin America, European arrivals in British North America had to come to terms with the presence of the Amerindians, with fundamentally different results. Unlike some sections of Latin America, the Amerindians were too few in numbers in the Atlantic seaboard of North America to provide an instant work force. By the eighteenth century, the Europeans had liquidated them or driven them west, seizing the seaboard for whites. The small number of Amerindians and, until the eighteenth century, of many imported Africans, meant that British North America, unlike Latin America, would be a white offspring of Europe, without a large class of mestizos and mulattoes.

The status of blacks in British North America was both better and worse than in Latin America. Despite the regimentation and brutality inevitable in slave labor, particularly on the rice plantations of South Carolina, slaves in British North America enjoyed a higher standard of living and lived longer than in much of Latin America. Slaves also enjoyed more chance for a family life as the percentage of women rose through generations of natural increase.

As a minority race, however, blacks were in a more difficult position than in Latin America. Northern Europeans who settled in British North America manifested strong attitudes of racism toward the nonwhite minorities under their control. Those few Amerindians who lived among whites were treated contemptuously, facing segregation and other forms of oppression. European settlers did not

want to share their opportunities for property and power with the growing number and percentage of blacks. Whites accordingly made it difficult for slaves to gain their freedom and for free blacks to acquire property, especially land. British America had many white artisans and mechanics, and such avenues to prosperity and status were unavailable to blacks. Most free blacks therefore found themselves faced with a precarious existence, carrying out the most menial tasks. In contrast to Brazil, racial bias was so strong in British North America that a small percentage of black ancestry made an individual legally black.

The Genesis of a New Society

Although British North America more closely resembled Europe racially than did Latin America, the virtual ab-

sence of commodities of great value in British North America led to a more radical departure from the European economic social order than had occurred in Latin America. British North America did not produce the spices and silks of Asia, the precious metals of Spanish America, or the sugar of the Caribbean and Brazil. Trapping fur-bearing animals was a lucrative enterprise in the north, but on the whole British North America produced only food and a few staples of secondary value.

The absence of valuable products soon upset traditional patterns of landholding. As in Iberia, the English monarchs during the seventeenth century had given extensive land grants to their political favorites, as individuals or as incorporated companies. However, those grantees who created companies and sent workers over to produce profitable commodities soon found the ventures unremunerative.

New York Harbor, 1717. This view from Brooklyn across the East River to Manhattan is predominantly rural, with little foretaste of the megalopolis to come. Still, the scene gives an impression of modest prosperity. Shipping was a major component of the versatile economy of the northern colonies of British North America.

Frustrated by the virtual absence of traditional products of great wealth, the English government and the aristocratic grantees rapidly abandoned the company/worker format. In its stead they began to encourage a flow of settlers to make a profit from rents and passage rights. Unlike Spain, the English government, presiding over a religiously fragmented nation, did not restrict settlement to nationals of the state church. The British government, grantees, and colonial officials encouraged continental Protestants to settle, and some colonies even tolerated Catholics and Jews. As this became known in Europe, hundreds of thousands of settlers—individuals, families, and religious groups—migrated to British North America beginning in the eighteenth century, quadrupling the population between 1700 and 1740.

Landholding patterns in British North America quickly developed differently from those of Europe and Latin America. The government and the grantees, and many of the settlers had presumed that European society would be replicated; the aristocrats would own the land, the settlers would rent and work it. Conditions in British America soon changed from this outlook. Absentee landlords found it difficult to collect rent, and there was competition to attract settlers among the grantees and between the grantees and the crown. In many instances, settlers simply seized crown and grantee lands and claimed "squatter's rights"—ownership on the basis that they had not been challenged for years and had improved the property by erecting buildings and tilling the soil. As a result, the crown and the grantees found it easier and more profitable to simply sell the land at prices that most settlers could afford. By the early eighteenth century, most colonists in British North America owned property or paid a nominal rent, and thus for the most part were financially independent. This was a new form of western civilization, for in Europe and Latin America the land was held by a few families and worked by masses of laborers.

British North America also differed sharply from Europe in suffering from a chronic labor shortage, which in turn both raised and depressed the status of labor. Employers on farms and in shops found that neither standard wages nor indentures were sufficient to hold white workers, who could easily obtain their own property. In most of British North America, where production was based on small farms, the labor shortage continued and laborers commanded high wages. Along the coast of the southern colonies, however, the rice, indigo, and tobacco planters solved their shortage of white field hands by importing more and more black slaves.

Although there were many more European women present in British North America than in Latin America, they were still in short supply. This circumstance marginally improved their condition compared with Europe. In the colonies, as in Great Britain, the common law defined a married woman as the subject of her husband, and the property she owned before marriage as his. However, the general scarcity of women in the colonies enabled some of them to insist on prenuptial agreements that gave them some control over their property while married. Because male assistants were scarce, wives often helped their husbands to run small businesses of all kinds and sometimes inherited and operated the businesses when their husbands died.

Compared with the situation in Latin America and Europe, classes were more fluid in British North America. The colonists still retained the strong sense of class that they brought from Europe, with the "middling sort" and "lower sort" deferring to those seen as the "better sort." This attitude, however, was by no means translated into the servility found in Europe, and even the habit of deference was increasingly diluted over time by a sense of individual worth stemming from economic independence. In a land without aristocrats, wealth and merit rather than inherited title rapidly became the chief index of social status.

Unlike both Latin America and Europe, it was possible for large numbers of whites in British North America to move up in social class. No aristocratic class monopolized property and opportunity, so it was relatively easy to obtain property, especially land. Laborers who later acquired their own farms or shops moved into the middle class. Those of the middle class who accumulated extensive land or commercial property—or who rose to distinction as professionals, particularly some lawyers and clergy—became the gentry. This gentry dominated society and politics in British North America, although they were looked on as country bumpkins by European aristocrats.

The Colonial Economy and British Mercantilism

By the eighteenth century, British North America had progressed far beyond a subsistence economy and had developed an extensive international trade shaped by the commandments of mercantilism. The colonists were required to send products on the

"Enumerated Articles" list—furs, lumber, molasses, naval stores (turpentine, pitch, tar, masts, spars), tobacco, rice, and indigo—to Great Britain, or through Great Britain before transshipment to other destinations. The northern colonies had built an extensive merchant marine to carry their grains, meat, and fish to the West Indies and the Mediterranean. New Englanders also engaged in the "carrying trade," hauling cargoes from port to port all over the world. Colonists north and south had begun to produce iron and iron products, but since they competed with British iron, the British government soon regulated their production. Like Latin American colonials, the colonists in British North America often were forced to sell too low and buy too high and as a result turned to smuggling.

Although operating under the principles of mercantilism, the English government placed fewer controls on its colonies than did Spain. It restricted trade with the colonies to English and colonial (after 1707 also Scottish) ships, but it did not limit the trade to a few companies. Fearing no attacks on the colonies' relatively cheap exports, it allowed individual ships to sail in and out of any port in the colonies and in England. The government allowed products not on the Enumerated Articles list to be sold anywhere in the world in peacetime without regulation.

A New Religious Configuration

Religious and ethnic diversity was another characteristic that increasingly distinguished British North America from the states of continental Europe and from Latin America. Not only did the groups from the British Isles

A CHEERLEADER FOR BRITISH NORTH AMERICA

He is an American who leaving all behind him all his ancient prejudices and manners, receives new ones from the new mode of life he has embraced, the new government he obeys, and the new rank he holds . . . Here individuals of all nations are melted into a new race of men, whose labors and posterity will one day cause great changes in the world. Americans are the western pilgrims, who are carrying along with them that great mass of arts, sciences, vigor, industry which began long since in the east; they will finish the great circle . . . Here the rewards of his industry follow with equal steps the progress of his labor; his labor is founded on the basis of nature, self-interest . . . without any part being claimed, either by a despotic prince, a rich abbot, or a mighty lord. Here religion demands but little of him; a small voluntary salary to the minister, and gratitude to God; . . . From involuntary idleness, servile dependence, penury, and useless labor, he has passed to toils of a very different nature, rewarded by ample subsistence.[*]

This enthusiastic comment by Hector St. John de Crevecoeur was typical of the messages he addressed to eighteenth century Europeans concerning the characteristics of the new culture in British North America. Although written later in the century, his remarks quite clearly pertain to a society that had already formed earlier. From an old Norman family, Crevecoeur immigrated to Canada and then settled on a farm in New York in 1765. Although imprisoned and exiled by the rebels during the War for Independence, he remained loyal to his adopted land. Only briefly returning to the United States, he worked throughout the rest of his life, in retirement in France, to explain the North American world to the people of Europe.

[*]Hector S. John de Crevecoeur, *Letters from an American Farmer* (New York: Fox, Duffield, and Company, 1904), pp. 90–91.

populate the colonies, but settlers from the Continent too: Germans, French, Dutch, and Swedes. Before 1750 there were English-speaking Anglicans, Congregationalists, Presbyterians, Catholics, Baptists, and Quakers. From continental Europe came Dutch, German, and French Reformed; German, Dutch and Swedish Lutherans; German Moravians, Mennonites, Dunkers and Schwenkfelders; and Portuguese-speaking Jews.

This religious diversity had not been anticipated in the seventeenth century when most of the British colonies were originally established and initially settled. The traditional idea that a political unit should have a common religion to bind the inhabitants together led the large Congregationalist majorities in New Hampshire, Massachusetts, and Connecticut to set up state churches. The Congregationalists drove out other religionists, in 1656 even hanging four Quakers who dared to return after being banished. The Anglican church was established in some colonies; there the Anglicans had enough supporters to harass dissenters, but not enough to suppress them.

Despite the fact that established churches were in place in most colonies by the eighteenth century, ef-

A New Farm in British North America. This archetypal scene depicts a clearing being hacked out of the forest. Already, there is a comfortable house, an outbuilding, a fence, a well, cattle, and oxen. Despite the rude conditions and the backbreaking labor, farm families like these were often better off than they would have been in Europe.

forts to enforce religious uniformity failed in British North America. The English Act of Toleration in 1689 acknowledged England's religious divisions by giving some religious rights to Congregationalists, Presbyterians, and Baptists. This new law helped these three dissenting groups in the Anglican colonies. About the same time, the English government forced the Congregationalist colonies to allow Anglicans to worship without penalty.

Conditions in the New World did more than English laws to encourage diversity. Most colonies needed settlers and unofficially tolerated thousands of new arrivals fleeing religious persecution, unemployment, and war who were adherents of other religions. Often the new dissenters settled in such numbers that it was impractical for the established churches to control them or drive them away. In the southern backwoods, where the non-Anglicans were in the great majority, colonial officials were often forced to ignore the requirements of

the state church simply to survive. Even in New England, minorities were becoming too large to control: In the 1750s, dissenting Baptists were permitted to contribute to their own churches the money they had been forced to pay to the Congregationalist church.

Some colonies were founded to protect dissenters, further encouraging religious diversity. Catholics, banned in England and most colonies, were tolerated in Maryland through part of its history. Catholics and all Protestant groups had full rights in Pennsylvania. Rhode Island went farther, granting full religious freedom to Christians, Jews, and Muslims. Thus, although complete religious freedom was advocated only by a few reformers in Europe in the early eighteenth century, British North America moved steadily in that direction in practice.

Missionary activity was feeble compared with Latin America. Because Protestants, unlike Catholics, were cool to missionary work in that

era, churches in British North America made only sporadic efforts to convert the Amerindian and African populations. Protestants, unlike Catholics, had no religious orders dedicated to the mission field, so evangelistic work depended at first on the enthusiasm of individuals. Later in the eighteenth century the Anglican missionary organization, The Society for the Propagation of the Gospel, and members of the Moravian Brethren worked among the Amerindians. Still, few Amerindians and only about 1 percent of the Africans would have called themselves Christians in 1750.

Limited Government and a New Political Process

As the Iberian monarchies had imposed their tradition of expensive, centralized government on Latin America, the English government set up its particular brand of frugal, partially decentralized government in their colonies. In England, the lesser gentry had long represented the royal government in local affairs, sparing the crown the expense of a large set of appointed officials. The English government applied this principle to most of its colonies, simply sending over a governor to work with an assembly representing the gentry that controlled local government. The governor of a colony had the power to appoint from the ranks of the colony's gentry a few executive officials and a council, which also served as the upper house of the colonial legislature and performed certain judicial functions. The governor could control the procedures of the assembly and veto its acts. His position was severely weakened, however, because the British government—to save expense—had given the assembly the power to pay his salary from taxes laid by the assembly on the colonists. Unlike Latin America, the colonists paid no tax money or royal "fifths" to the crown. Nevertheless, many colonial gentry, like many Creoles, chafed at what they saw as excessive power wielded by outsiders.

Underneath the traditional governmental apparatus, a new political process, quite unlike anything in Europe, was evolving. Because of the widespread incidence of property holding in British North America, many white males had access not only to social standing but to political power as well. In Great Britain, one of the few nations having some semblance of government by consent, only adult males who owned property that brought in forty shillings annual rent and who belonged to the state church could vote. This requirement restricted political participation to about 5 percent of the adult males. When these requirements were brought over to British North America from England, however, they produced radically different effects in a population where landholding was increasingly widespread. The colonial assemblies frequently translated the "forty shilling freehold" into 50 to 100 acres of unimproved land or half that amount improved, or land valued at forty to fifty pounds. This practice allowed an estimated one-half of the adult white male colonists to vote in the early eighteenth century, and the proportion continued to rise. Many colonists also met the much higher requirements for holding office. However, despite such widespread enfranchisement, only about 10 percent of the eligible voters took advantage of the opportunity. Most of the potential voters had little appreciation for voting practice or its potential. The New England tradition of the local town meeting was a major exception. By and large, however, colonial voters served as no more than a check, occasionally turning out an incompetent gentleman officeholder.

A Young, Raw Culture

By the lights of most of the European elite, British North America was as much of a wasteland in intellectual and cultural matters as it was in geography. The French scientist the Comte de Buffon and his followers at one time claimed that all species, including humans, degenerated in the New World environment. Certainly, it was true that all class levels gave their attention to exploiting the land's resources and correspondingly little time or interest to financing the development of scholarship, arts, or letters.

In fact, however, a significant start toward a popular rather than an elite culture had been made. Impelled by the Protestant belief that it was important to read the Bible, and that education might help a person to advance, many men and women in British North America were interested in learning to read and write. The resources and density of population of the New England towns and the Atlantic seaports facilitated establishing schools. In these locales perhaps two-thirds of the males and one third of the females were literate by early in the eighteenth century, a far higher percentage than anywhere else in the western world. In the rural areas, private academies were beginning to spread literacy. Higher education lagged far behind the great learning centers of Europe and Latin America, but a beginning had been made. By the early eighteenth century, three private colleges, beginning with Harvard in 1636, offered a traditional curriculum designed to train ministers. Seven more colleges would soon be founded.

SUMMARY

By the eighteenth century, the Iberian monarchies had performed the remarkable feat of firmly implanting western civilization throughout an area twice the size of Europe. Because of the divisive geography and the presence of other races and cultures, the impact of western culture varied widely according to region, ranging from strong in Mexico and Peru to nonexistent in the Amazon and the southern tip of South America. The impact also varied widely by class, the upper classes consciously clinging to their Iberian background and the lower orders still strongly influenced by their native Amerindian and African cultures. The Iberians established Roman Catholicism as the only faith throughout the colonies, although many Amerindian converts had only a rudimentary understanding of their new religion. The Iberian languages were somewhat less widespread, although they were spoken by all races in the urban and commercial centers. Three key characteristics of Iberia—paternalistic government, aristocratic social and economic privilege, and mercantilist economics—were substantially replicated in Latin America. Latin Americans also inherited the intellectual, literary, and artistic outlook of Spain and Portugal. While Iberian culture predominated in Latin America, however, its ongoing interaction with Amerindian and African cultures modified its characteristics, creating a new form of western civilization.

By the early eighteenth century the residents of North America had developed another distinct culture inside Western Civilization, one that on the whole departed more substantially from Europe than did Latin America. In a few characteristics British North America did approximate Europe more closely than did Latin America: The area was overwhelmingly European racially and linguistically, and Amerindians and Amerindian culture played an insignificant role. The African impact was also less profound, although it would grow in time. On the other hand, British North America was fast departing from continental European and Latin American standards on a broad spectrum of economic, social, and political characteristics. It exhibited, in a more accelerated form, a trend towards social and political liberalization that was also getting under way in Great Britain.

Europeans visiting British North America were naturally impressed by the differences rather than the similarities. They commented on the strange landscape, the raw look of both cities and farms, and the lack of monuments or any sign of a living, visible past. They were discomfited by the restless moving about of the population and the cacophony of ethnic groups and religious sects. Above all, Europeans were struck by the individualism at all levels of society and by the absence of servility among the middle and lower orders of whites. Europeans attributed these characteristics to the general prosperity of the population, to education, and to the weakness of the class system. Most of these visitors went home dismayed by the brawling confusion and the social dislocation, but a few enthusiasts thought they had seen in this place the future of western civilization.

SELECTED SOURCES

*Bailyn, Bernard. *Origins of American Politics.* 1970. Insightful examination of the colonial roots of American political theory and practice.

*Bannon, John Francis. *The Colonial World of Latin America.* 1982. A useful introduction to Spanish America and Brazil.

Boxer, Charles R. *Four Centuries of Portuguese Expansion, 1415–1825.* 1969. Treats Brazil within the context of the Portuguese Empire.

*Bridenbaugh, Carl. *Myths and Realities: Societies of the Colonial South.* A well-written survey of the British North American colonies that most resembled the Caribbean and Brazil.

*Commager, Henry Steele, and Elmo

Giordanetti. *Was America a Mistake?* 1967. A fascinating collection of eighteenth-century attacks on, and defenses of, the New World.

*Gibson, Charles. *Spain in America.* 1968. An authoritative interpretation by a renowned scholar.

*Hofstadter, Richard. *America at 1750: A Social Portrait.* 1971. Incomplete at Hofstadter's death, an insightful pre-sentation of the society in British North America.

*Leonard, Irving A. *Baroque Times in Old Mexico: Seventeenth-Century Persons, Places, and Practices.* 1959. A colorful insight into the society and culture of Latin America.

*Martin, Luis. *Daughters of the Conquistadores: Women of the Viceroyalty of Peru.* 1983. An informative survey, with applications to all of Latin America.

Williams, Selma. *Demeter's Daughters.* 1976. A survey of the various roles of women in British North America, stressing the stories of individuals.

*Available in paperback.

THE AGE OF REASON

If we limit ourselves to showing the advantages which have been extracted from the sciences . . . the most important of them perhaps is to have destroyed prejudice and reestablished . . . human intelligence formerly compelled to bend to the false directions forced upon it by . . . absurd beliefs . . . the terrors of superstition and the fear of tyranny.

We may observe that the principles of philosophy, the maxims of liberty, the knowledge of the true rights of men and of their real interests have spread in too great a number of nations, and control in each of them the opinions of too many enlightened men, for them ever to be forgotten again.

This optimistic account of "the progress of the human spirit" in the eighteenth century sums up some of the deepest convictions of that age: the liberating impact of science and reason on the human mind, the importance of human rights, and the inevitable triumph of freedom in the world. The author of these impassioned sentiments, the marquis de Condorcet (1743–1794), was an enlightened aristocrat and a disciple of Voltaire, the most famous philosopher of the era. A strong believer in freedom and progress, Condorcet was an admiring student of the American experiment in free government across the Atlantic. Ironically, he died a victim of the political terror that accompanied the struggle for survival of the French Revolution. Yet this tract, written shortly before his tragic death, indicates that Cordorcet died still confident that in the long run, the political promise of that age of intellectual enlightenment would be realized. The following pages discuss the scientific revolution from which the age of reason sprang. Thereafter, they focus on the Enlightenment itself, in Europe and in the European colonies overseas, and conclude with a summary of developments in the arts during this innovative period.

CONTENTS

Voltaire. This is one of many portraits and sculptural representations of the most celebrated intellectual and social critic of the French Enlightenment. As famous for his wit as for his radical critique of society, Voltaire is shown here with the smile that could make even kings nervous.

417

THE SCIENTIFIC REVOLUTION

No current of western thought is more characteristic of the modern period than is the scientific approach to understanding the world around us. Whereas earlier centuries depended on philosophy or religion to explain the universe, the modern age has turned increasingly to science for such explanation. The work of the makers of this scientific revolution is thus of great importance in the history of the shaping of the modern mind.

Origins of the Scientific Revolution

One of the major obstacles to scientific progress was the inherited thought of ancient and medieval times. The theories of Greek scientists like the astronomer Ptolemy and the wide-ranging philosopher Aristotle, although inadequate as explanations of the natural world, were accepted as the final word. This attitude was reinforced by the medieval Christian church, which used fundamentally religious ideas to explain the physical world, setting up formidable roadblocks to scientific analysis. More recently, Renaissance scholars and Reformation religious leaders had focused attention on literary, moral, and spiritual values, dismissing the material world as unimportant.

At the same time, the wisdom of the ancients also helped to stimulate attempts to explain the material world. The rediscovery and translation of some Greek scientists stimulated early modern Europeans to think in new ways about the universe. The new

scientists who had read Archimedes on physics, for example, discovered a purely mechanical explanation for the behavior of the material world, an approach they found strongly appealing. The ancient Greek atomic theory, which asserted that the universe was made of tiny particles of matter, also provided a useful framework for modern scientific thinking. The very fact that the "wise ancients" had disagreed among themselves made it easier for the scientific revolutionaries to challenge their famous predecessors.

More recent trends also encouraged the rise of modern science. Among these, two oddly contrasting developments were particularly important: technology and magic. Technological developments like the printing press, the magnetic compass, and the widespread use of gunpowder increased respect among Europeans for practical knowledge. In fields as diverse as gunnery, metallurgy, ship-building, and surgery, early modern technicians commonly replaced older ideas with new knowledge. The ancients, they pointed out, were not always right, at least about practical matters.

A wide range of sixteenth-century studies that today would be called magical also helped create an exciting intellectual environment in which the scientific revolutionaries flourished. The common belief in astrology, which claimed to explain earthly affairs by the motions of stars and planets, contributed to the interest in astronomy. Alchemy stressed a mystical search for ultimate truth, but it also used laboratory equipment and chemical experiments. Mystical studies of Neoplatonism and of the Jewish religious book called the Kabbala em-

phasized the importance of numbers in understanding the way the world works, a mathematical approach that modern science would follow up with great success.

In this stimulating intellectual world, the scientific revolution was born.

The New Scientists

The most famous makers of the scientific revolution were a group of sixteenth- and seventeenth-century innovators in astronomy and physics. These great names included Copernicus, Kepler, Galileo, and Isaac Newton. Scientists in such fields as biology and chemistry also contributed to the expanding knowledge of the material world.

Nicholas Copernicus (1473–1543), who revealed the basic structure of the solar system to the modern world, is sometimes called the Columbus of the scientific revolution. A Polish churchman with a purely theoretical understanding of astronomy, Copernicus questioned the orthodox view of the ancient Alexandrian astronomer Ptolemy that the Earth stood at the center of the cosmos. Copernicus's book *On the Revolutions of the Heavenly Spheres* (1543) declared that the Sun was the true center, with stars and planets orbiting around it. The Earth, Copernicus dared to suggest, was merely a planet moving around that solar center.

The German astronomer Johannes Kepler (1571–1630), offered a much more detailed and exact account of the laws of planetary motion. In particular, he was able to correct the assumption, made by both Ptolemy and Copernicus, that the planets move

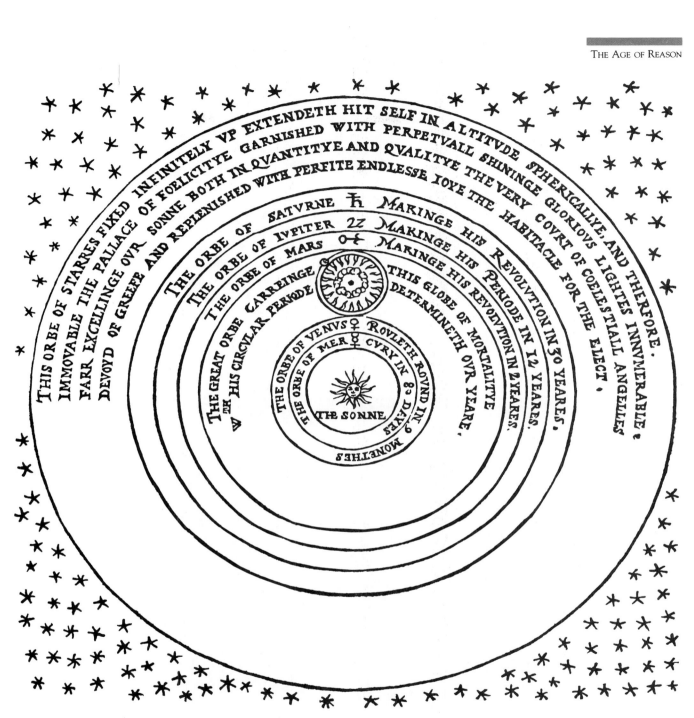

THIS ORBE OF STARRES FIXED INFINITELY VP EXTENDETH HIT SELF IN ALTITVDE SPHERICALLYE, AND THERFORE IMMOVABLE THE PALLACE OF FOELICITYE GARNISHED WITH PERPETVALL SHININGE GLORIOVS LIGHTES INNVMERABLE. FARR EXCELLINGE OVR SONNE BOTH IN QVANTITYE AND QVALITYE THE VERY COVRT OF COELESTIALL ANGELLES DEVOYD OF GREEFE AND REPLENISHED WITH PERFITE ENDLESSE IOYE THE HABITACLE FOR THE ELECT.

THE ORBE OF SATVRNE ♄ MAKINGE HIS REVOLVTION IN 30 YEARES.

THE ORBE OF IVPITER ♃ MAKINGE HIS REVOLVTION IN 12 YEARES.

THE ORBE OF MARS ♂ MAKINGE HIS REVOLVTION IN 2 YEARES.

THE GREAT ORBE CARREINGE ⊕ THIS GLOBE OF MORTALITYE Wᵀᴴ HIS CIRCVLAR PERIODE DETERMINETH OVR YEARE.

THE ORBE OF VENVS ♀ ROVLETH ROVND IN 9 MONETHES

THE ORBE OF MERCVRY ☿ CVRY IN 8 DAYES

THE SONNE

in circles around the Sun, demonstrating that their paths are in fact ellipses, with the Sun at one of the two foci. Kepler's years of precise observation of the night sky as assistant to the Danish astronomer Tycho Brahe and his elaborate mathematical calculations of planetary orbits were a great step forward. In a more general sense, they showed the value of both observation and mathematics for scientific explanations.

The Copernican View of the Universe. This schematic presentation was the work of the Englishman, Thomas Digges, some thirty years after Copernicus's book appeared in 1543. The Sun is shown in the center, the Earth as the third planet out from it, and the Moon revolving around the Earth.

419

Galileo Galilei, (1564–1642) a brilliant Italian student of astronomy and physics, made major contributions to both fields. His researches into the laws of falling bodies challenged Aristotle's views. By experiment, he demonstrated that larger objects did not fall faster than smaller ones as Aristotle had said, and even established the mathematical formula for the accelerating speed at which all bodies fall. Like Kepler, Galileo supported Copernicus's Sun-centered theory of the universe against Ptolemy's Earth-centered model. By using a telescope, recently developed in the Netherlands, for astronomical observations, Galileo discovered sunspots, the moons of Jupiter, and the geography of the Moon. In his later years, the pugnacious Italian was summoned before the Inquisition because of his controversial views, but his ideas long outlived the power of his persecutors.

Finally, Isaac Newton (1642–1727) tied the achievements of his predecessors together with his crucial formulation of the law of gravity. His *Mathematical Principles of Natural Philosophy* (1687) asserted that every particle of matter in the universe attracts every other particle with a force that varies with the size of the objects

The Trial of Galileo. This painting by an unknown artist shows the trial of the scientist Galileo by the religious court of the Inquisition. This was actually a rare case of overt persecution of the scientific revolutionaries by ecclesiastical authority. Nevertheless, Galileo's trial, climaxing in his forced recantation of the Copernican worldview, has become symbolic of resistance to the new scientific understanding of the nature of the physical universe.

and the distance between them. Newton's discovery, a century and a half after Copernicus, of a single force affecting everything from planets in space to falling bodies on Earth made Newton the most honored of all the makers of the scientific revolution.

Newton made many other contributions to the scientific revolution besides his formulation of the law of gravity. He explored the nature of light and the laws of optics empirically, using a prism to show that ordinary sunlight is in fact composed of all the colors of the spectrum. He redefined the general laws of motion in terms of inertia (of motion as well as of position) and of action and reaction (for every action, he asserted, there is an equal and opposite reaction). He was a pioneer explorer of the mysteries of calculus. In his long life of service to science, Newton thus vigorously embodied the range as well as the depth of the scientific revolution.

The new scientists constructed a new, coherent, and increasingly accurate picture of the physical universe. It was the beginning of an unparalleled surge of scientific progress which, with many additions and corrections, has continued to the present day.

The Scientific World View

In the course of the sixteenth and seventeenth centuries, scientists and philosophers of science also evolved both a new method of investigation and a new view of the nature of things. The result was a broadly scientific world view that has become one of the central features of modern western thought.

The best minds of the medieval era

THE FIRST HUMAN EYE TO LOOK UPON THE MOUNTAINS OF THE MOON

About ten months ago, a report reached my ears that a certain Fleming had constructed a spyglass by means of which visible objects, though very distant from the eye of the observer, were distinctly seen as if nearby . . . I succeeded in constructing for myself so excellent an instrument that objects seen by means of it appeared . . . over thirty times closer than when regarded with our natural vision . . .

Now let us review the observations made during the past two months . . . Let us speak first of [the] surface of the moon . . . I distinguish two parts of this surface, a lighter and a darker . . . the darker part discolors the moon's surface like a kind of cloud, and makes it appear covered with spots . . . From observations of these spots repeated many times, I have been led to the opinion and conviction that the surface of the moon is not smooth, uniform, and precisely spherical, as a great number of philosophers believe it (and the other heavenly bodies) to be, but is uneven, rough, and full of cavities and prominences, being not unlike the surface of the earth, relieved by chains of mountains and deep valleys . . .*

Vivid reports like this account of Galileo's discoveries made the new "natural philosophy" an increasingly exciting subject as the scientific revolution proceeded. Such concrete discoveries could also have broader theoretical implications. The discovery of mountains and valleys on the moon, for example, challenged the orthodox belief that all the universe except the Earth was perfect and unblemished by irregularities. This view was harder to defend after Galileo's observation of lunar "geography" and sunspots.

*Galileo Galilei, "The Starry Messenger" in Stillman Drake, ed. and trans. *Discoveries and Opinions of Galileo* (New York: Doubleday, 1957), pp. 28–29, 31.

---

had been religious thinkers like Thomas Aquinas, who had tried to understand the physical world as they did the spiritual one, through revealed truth and abstract reasoning. Typically beginning with some religious authority like the Bible or with the writings of a classical scholar like Aristotle or Ptolemy, they used an elaborate system of logic to demonstrate the truth of explanations of the material world. The result was a vision of the world in which religion had a central place, but that included many factual errors about how the universe actually works.

The new scientific world view took explicit shape in the seventeenth century, the century after Copernicus, especially in the writings of the English philosopher Sir Francis Bacon (1561–1626) and the French thinker René Descartes (1596–1650).

Bacon firmly rejected ancient authority as the infallible source of all truth. He also had no use for the abstract, logical hairsplitting of medieval religious thinkers. Instead of blind acceptance of authority or abstract logic, Bacon urged the use of empirical methods—the direct observation and collection of data. This emphasis on empiricism, beginning with observable data and building general

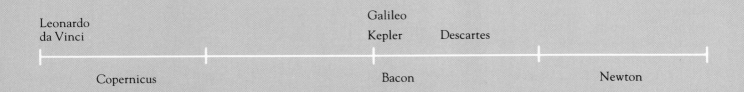

truths on this foundation, became one of the hallmarks of the scientific method.

Descartes also openly expressed his doubt of the authorities, but he offered another road to certainty. Not empirical observation but rational understanding as clear as that of a geometrical theorem was for Descartes the guarantor of truth. The French philosopher's famous assertion "I think, therefore I am," was the first link in a chain of rational proofs that accounted philosophically for the existence, progressively, of humanity, of God, and of God's universe. A medieval religious thinker like Thomas Aquinas, by contrast, would have *begun* with the revealed truth of God's existence and reasoned his way from this to more modest truths about humanity and the individual. Descartes' emphasis on rational processes which he thought were as convincing as mathematical reasoning, like Bacon's stress on empiricism, was fundamental to the scientific world view.

On the basis of empirical observation and mathematical reasoning, seventeenth-century scientists and philosophers constructed a new scientific method to guide the further search for truth. The new approach began with a hypothesis, a scientific guess about the cause or operation of some natural phenomenon. The scientific approach then required investigators to collect data on the actual behavior of the natural objects concerned. This evidence was then used to test and modify the original hypothesis. Scientists then accepted the result as a scientific law of nature— a new truth added to the store of understanding of the way the world works.

The accumulation of such laws of nature led scientific philosophers to a new vision of the world. The universe came to be seen as an immense and intricate machine operating according to mathematically formulated laws. Many believed that all matter was composed of atoms, tiny particles whose mass, motion through space, and encounters with other atoms explained everything that happens in nature.

To expand our understanding of this "world machine," Bacon in particular pleaded for large, state-supported research institutions. By applying the scientific knowledge thus accumulated, he accurately predicted more than three and a half centuries ago, the human race would acquire a greater mastery of the material environment than humanity has ever had before.

THE ENLIGHTENMENT

Bacon's great fame, like that of Newton and the other builders of the scientific world view, came not in the sixteenth or seventeenth century, but in the eighteenth. It was then that the age of reason reached its climax in the great intellectual movement known as the Enlightenment, a ferment of new ideas important in the growth of modern social, economic, and political thought.

Sources of the Enlightenment

The sources of the enlightenment itself included several major cultural trends of the early modern centuries. Among these were Renaissance humanist reverence for the classics, reaction against the religious intolerance of the Reformation, the impact of the age of discovery on the European mind, and above all the influence of the scientific revolution.

Classical education, with its study of the literature of the Greeks and Romans, contributed to the air, rationality, and cool philosophical tone of much of the writing of the Enlightenment. It also provided models and mentors. French radicals and American revolutionaries alike, for instance, could see themselves as heirs to that "republican virtue" which had flourished in Rome before the Caesars rose.

The wars of religion which had climaxed the reformation spawned a bigotry on the part of both Catholics and Protestants which continued into the eighteenth century. The leaders of the Enlightenment reacted strongly against the official persecutions and mob violence produced by these religious prejudices. The new movement demanded not only an end to sectarian intolerance, but a more secular society in general.

Expanded contacts with other cultures resulting from the age of discovery and the establishment of European empires overseas also affected the Enlightenment. Eighteenth-century European thinkers were impressed by a wide range of non-European cultural achievement, from the ancient learning of Confucian China to the native wisdom of pre-literate Amerindian cultures. Enlightenment Europeans did not yet know much about these nonwestern societies: nevertheless, they pioneered a broader form of toleration, a recognition that no single continent or culture had a monopoly on truth.

The new science, with its continuing success and growing popularity, profoundly shaped the thought of the Enlightenment. New discoveries in a broad spectrum of scientific fields—biology and chemistry as well as physics and astronomy—kept the physical sciences in the forefront of western intellectual life. Scientific societies like the British Royal Society were founded to bring scientists and interested laymen together and to further

support the advancement of science. Popular books explained the scientific world view to a larger public. Enlightenment Europeans dabbled in science as Renaissance Europeans had patronized the arts, and faith in the scientific approach grew steadily.

The Enlightenment, although influenced by new thinking about the physical universe, had broader concerns. The intellectual leaders of the new movement began to apply the scientific method, so successful in explaining the natural world, to the social world as well. They used reason as a scalpel to dissect and expose traditional social institutions that had outlived their time. They sought scientific laws governing human society like those Copernicus and Newton had discovered ruling nature.

This application of science to society was the foundation of the great Enlightenment critique of European political, economic, social, and religious institutions, which challenged the inefficiency, injustice, and intolerance of the old regime, as society in this period later came to be called. Some Enlightenment thinkers began to dream of a perfect society of the future, designed according to scientific principles, in which human beings might live a better life. This scientific analysis of society was also crucial in establishing the modern social sciences, including political science and economics.

The Critics: The Philosophes

The critical aspect of the new movement centered in France, and its leaders were known by the French term *philosophes.* The philosophes were not philosophers in the professional or traditional sense—systematic think-

ers about large abstract issues. Rather, they were philosophizers, social critics who depended on rational analysis to suggest solutions for the concrete problems of their times.

The philosophes found an audience for their views in two important social groups: the aristocracy and the bourgeoisie. The influence of Enlightenment popularizers would even reach the lower classes toward the end of the eighteenth century, but it was the educated classes who were first touched by the Enlightenment critique.

A few of Europe's traditional elite, the hereditary aristocracy, were eager to keep up with the latest advanced ideas. These enlightened aristocrats mingled with the philosophes in a distinctive central Enlightenment institution, the salon. At these elegant social gatherings, literary readings, serious talk, and sparkling wit were the main attractions. Discussions of science and art were staples, but some thoroughly subversive social ideas also circulated in the salons. Hostesses like the internationally known Madame Geoffrin (1699–1777) thus played a crucial role in the intellectual life of the time. The middle class—wealthier, better educated, and more self-confident than ever before—was attracted to the new ideas in even larger numbers. Reading pamphlets and books written by the philosophes, its members found in them expressions of some of their own social discontents. Middle class men and women would provide the leadership for the political upheaval that would follow this intellectual assault on the old order of society.

Among the most influential of the philosophes were the French writers Voltaire, Rousseau, and Diderot. All three were ardent spokesmen for reform and expert propagandists for their causes.

Francois Marie Arouet (1694–1778), under the pen name of Voltaire, was the leader of the philosophes and the most famous intellectual of his age. Voltaire's career spanned most of the century and produced many volumes of innovative history, philosophical fiction, drama, poetry, popular science, pamphlets and essays on social questions, and much more. His comic novel *Candide* (1754) exposed to scathing ridicule many groups and attitudes, from snobbish aristocrats and hypocritical churchmen to the military establishment and establishment philosophy. Voltaire particularly attacked organized religion for its intolerance, superstition, and closed-minded attitude to the new ideas.

In contrast to the witty Voltaire, Jean-Jacques Rousseau (1712–1778), was an emotional, deeply serious critic of the social order who insisted on the superiority of pure nature over artificial society. A pioneer of modern educational theory, he opposed rote learning and championed the development of the individual's innate capacities. He was also a passionate spokesman for a more democratic form of government.

Denis Diderot (1713–1784), one of the most aggressive and colorful of the philosophes, achieved his greatest fame as the editor of one book: the multivolume *Encyclopedia* (1751–1772). This vast compendium of knowledge, twenty years in the making, set out not only to inform but also to change people's way of thinking by approaching political and religious institutions in a thoroughly analytical and critical spirit. So critical was Diderot, in fact that his work was condemned as impious, seditious, and immoral, and he himself spent some time in prison. The *Encyclopedia* also disseminated the achieve-

The Salon of Mme Geoffrin. This painting, done after the fact in the early nineteenth-century, shows a gathering of French aristocrats and intellectuals during the reign of Louis XVI, the last Bourbon ruler before the Revolution. Neither Mme Geoffrin, the white-haired lady on the right, nor the elegant room, carpeting, paintings, and costumes of the guests look at all revolutionary. Nevertheless, radical ideas as well as high culture were staples of salon conversation during the later eighteenth century.

ments of eighteenth-century science and technology, printing many pictures of the intricate machines that had been developed by the eve of the Industrial Revolution.

Other issues that agitated enlightened minds in the eighteenth century included organized religion and the position of women in society. Many philosophes became deists or advocates of "natural religion," and some few even drifted into atheism. Deists believed in a rational God who had created the world the scientists studied, had set it working according to natural laws, and had thereafter ceased to intervene or involve himself in human affairs. In addition to the existence of God, believers in natural religion accepted a few other basic religious propositions—human brotherhood, perhaps even the immortality of the soul—but rejected any more detailed sectarian creed. Protestants and Catholics, Muslims and Buddhists, might all have access to God as they understood him. Out-and-out atheism, was rare in the eighteenth century, but by 1800 a famous scientist was able to tell Napoleon that he had no need of the "hypothesis" of God's existence to explain the universe.

Both the seventeenth and eighteenth centuries saw an undercurrent of intellectual debate about the equality of the sexes and the position of women in society. Some of the learned women of the literary salons of the age of Louis XIV had insisted that women were by nature the equals of men, made subservient by artificial laws and institutions. Such eighteenth-century thinkers as Diderot agreed and demanded reforms to give women the same legal rights as men. Perhaps the most eloquent

---

A MEDIEVAL SOLUTION TO THE PROBLEM OF EARTHQUAKES

The University of Coimbra had pronounced that the sight of a few people ceremoniously burned alive before a slow fire was an infallible prescription for preventing earthquakes; so when the earthquake had subsided after destroying three-quarters of Lisbon, the authorities . . . could find no surer means of avoiding total ruin than by giving the people a magnificent auto-da-fe.

They therefore seized a Basque, convicted of marrying his godmother, and two Portuguese Jews who had refused to eat bacon with their chicken; and after dinner Dr. Pangloss and his pupil, Candide, were arrested as well, one for speaking and the other for listening with an air of approval . . . They were then marched in procession . . . to hear a moving sermon followed by beautiful music in counterpoint. Candide was flogged in time with the anthem; the Basque and the two men who refused to eat bacon were burnt; and Pangloss was hanged . . . The same day another earthquake occurred and caused tremendous havoc.[*]

Voltaire seized on the historic Lisbon earthquake of 1755 as a focus for this assault on the medieval views and practices of the Inquisition, lampooned here in a passage from Candide. *The "crimes" mentioned included violation of dietary and marriage laws (though a godmother is, of course, no blood relation) and the too-free speech for which the philosophes themselves were often punished. To the enlightened eighteenth-century mind, much of the organized religion of the time seemed this superstitious and fanatical.*

[*]Voltaire, *Candide or Optimism*, trans. by John Butt (Baltimore: Penguin Books, 1947), pp. 36–37.

---

advocate of female emancipation, however, was Mary Wollstonecraft (1759–1797), whose *Vindication of the Rights of Women* (1792) was a milestone on the road to sexual equality. Writing at the time of the French Revolution, Wollstonecraft dared to demand a revolt against the tyranny of men and the recognition of women as in every way their equals.

The System Builders: Political and Economic Thought

Building on the critical spirit of the Enlightenment, some leading thinkers of the period offered positive insights and prescriptions for a better society. The political and economic theories of the intellectual leaders of the age of reason in fact provided the western world with some of the fundamental social ideas of the next two centuries.

The Enlightenment challenge to the inefficiency and injustice of government under the old regime is well illustrated by the Italian Cesar Beccaria's (1735–1794) pioneering ideas on reforming the prevailing system of justice. Eighteenth-century courts and prisons were notorious for imposing arbitrary and often savage punishments. Beccaria's famous book, *Crimes and Punishments* (1764) emphasized that criminal codes should be clear,

NATURAL RIGHTS AND THE SOCIAL CONTRACT ACCORDING TO JOHN LOCKE

All men are naturally in . . . a state of perfect freedom to order their actions . . . as they think fit, within the bounds of the law of nature . . .

[They are in] a state also of equality . . . there being nothing more evident, than that creatures . . . born to all the same advantages of nature, and the use of the same faculties, should also be equal one amongst another without subordination or subjection. . . .

Men being, as has been said, by nature all free, equal, and independent, no one can be . . . subjected to the political power of another without his own consent . . . by agreeing with other men to join and unite into a community. . . . And all this to be directed to no other end but the peace, safety, and public good of the people.*

Belief in human freedom and equality and in government by "consent of the governed" expressed in a social contract or constitution, voiced by John Locke in the seventeenth century, was taken up enthusiastically by enlightened minds in the eighteenth. In the late 1700s, these doctrines would be enshrined in the "Declaration of the Rights of Man and the Citizen" produced by the French Revolution and in the Bill of Rights appended to the Constitution of the United States.

*John Locke, Two Treatises of Government in T. V. Smith and Marjorie Grene, ed. From Descartes to Locke (Chicago: University of Chicago Press, 1940), pp. 456, 470, 474–475.

---

penalties applied equally to all classes of society, and punishments swift and sure. These views would influence legal and prison reform in a number of countries and remain influential today.

On the political side, the Enlightenment fostered the radical new doctrines of natural rights, constitutional government, and even popular sovereignty. On the economic side, advanced thinkers argued for the existence of natural laws governing the economy and for the freedom of the marketplace.

John Locke (1632–1704), the philosopher of the English revolution of the seventeenth century, was the first influential thinker to claim that all people have inborn natural rights.

These, he said, included freedom, equality, and the right to private property. Locke also insisted that the only legitimate government was one created by a "social contract" or constitution that the people themselves had agreed to. The closest approximation of this ideal in the eighteenth century was the constitutional monarchy of Great Britain. Many continental thinkers admired the British parliamentary system, though they depended on enlightened absolute monarchs to enact social reform on their side of the Channel.

Ideas emphasizing limited governmental power circulated on the continent as well in the eighteenth century. The baron de la Brede et de Montesquieu (1689–1755) thus pro-

posed that government power should be divided among several institutions, rather than concentrated in a single set of hands. This, he said, would create a system of checks and balances that would prevent tyranny. This approach would later be built into the Constitution of the United States.

Jean-Jacques Rousseau's most influential work, The Social Contract, went even farther, urging the principle of popular sovereignty. In this book, Rousseau made an impassioned plea for government by consent of the governed, the "general will" of the people. Rousseau's ideas would be very influential during the time of the French Revolution.

In economic thought also, the Enlightenment produced startling challenges to the autocratic status quo, particularly to the reigning economic theory of mercantilism. In France, a group of economic theorists called physiocrats claimed that land and agriculture were the true sources of national wealth, rather than bullion and trade, as the mercantilists insisted. The physiocrats also urged free trade and opposed government regulation of the economy—the heart of the mercantile system. They thus became early spokesmen for laissez-faire, the belief that economic affairs in general should be allowed to follow natural laws rather than be determined by government decrees.

The most influential spokesman for the free market was the English economic thinker Adam Smith (1723–1790). Smith's extremely influential book The Wealth of Nations (1776) asserted that a natural law of supply and demand underlay all economic processes. If the economy is left free of government regulation, it will re-

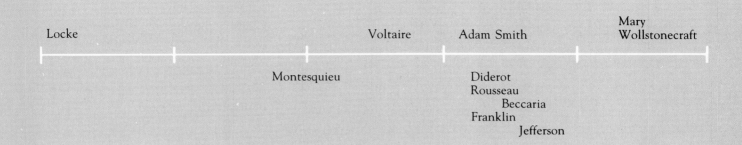

1675	1700	1725	1750	1775	1800

Locke   Voltaire   Adam Smith   Mary Wollstonecraft

Montesquieu   Diderot
Rousseau
Beccaria
Franklin
Jefferson

spond naturally to public demand, supplying what the people want at a price people are willing to pay. The result of such free market policies, Smith believed, would be a steady growth in the wealth of all nations. The free trade and free enterprise systems of a number of western nations would reflect these convictions in later centuries.

<hr />

THE ENLIGHTENMENT OUTSIDE EUROPE

The Enlightenment was an international phenomenon, centered in France but flourishing in other European nations and spreading to those of European heritage living beyond the seas. The new views attracted followers particularly in the British settlements in North America and in the Spanish colonies of Central and South America.

The Enlightenment in British America

Some of the most important ideas of the Enlightenment found a congenial home in the thirteen British colonies of North America, and both scientific and social thought flourished.

Perhaps stimulated by the new environment in which they found themselves, English colonial investigators made significant contributions to the fields of biology, physics, astronomy, and other sciences. Scientific subjects were taught in the colonial universities, from Harvard and Yale in the north to William and Mary in the south. In the New World as in the Old, educated persons dabbled in science. They met in societies dedicated to the study of the natural philosophy, and more than a dozen colonists were elected to the British Royal Society in London.

Colonial enthusiasm for science is perhaps most vividly illustrated in the colorful career of Benjamin Franklin (1706–1790), the many-sided Philadelphia printer who would become one of the founders of the new United States. Franklin's most famous scientific investigations established that lightning "bolts" were really discharges of electrical energy. His technological contributions included such practical inventions as the Franklin stove and the lightning rod. The founder of a philosophical society, a journal, and an academy that subsequently became a major university, Franklin was also elected to the Royal Society.

The political, economic, and social ideas of the Enlightenment also found a natural home in the British colonies. The colonists, with their elected legislative assemblies, had more political freedom than most Europeans. Merchants and farmers who had come to find greater economic opportunity in the New World embraced freedom of enterprise. Even religious toleration, for which French philosophes like Voltaire fought so hard, was relatively widespread in British North America.

Enlightenment ideas in the colonies perhaps had their greatest expression in the colonies in the writings of Thomas Jefferson (1743–1826), a Virginia planter who, like Franklin, was a latter-day Renaissance man. An avid student of the physical sciences and an architect of note, Jefferson corresponded with leaders of the European Enlightenment on subjects ranging from science to economics. He was a strong believer in religious toleration and in greater social equality. He opposed black slavery, though he could conceive of no practicable solution except gradual emancipation and emigration. His broader com-

427

THE DREAM OF FREEDOM SPREADS TO THE AMERICAN COLONIES

We hold these truths to be self-evident: that all men are created equal; that they are endowed by their Creator with certain inalienable rights; that among these are life, liberty, and the pursuit of happiness; that to secure these rights, governments are instituted among men, deriving their just powers from the consent of the governed. . . .*

Compare Thomas Jefferson's statement of the theory of natural rights and constitutional government with the earlier version proposed by John Locke. Compare it also with the ideals expressed in the slogan of the French revolution: Liberty, Equality, Brotherhood. Over the next two centuries, these beliefs would become the basis for new governments all across the western world.

*Thomas Jefferson, The Declaration of Independence in Saul K. Padover, ed. *Thomas Jefferson on Democracy* (New York: New American Library, 1946), p. 13.

mitment to political rights and popular sovereignty still lives in the words of the American Declaration of Independence and Bill of Rights.

The War of Independence itself was in many ways a struggle to realize the ideals advocated by the European Enlightenment, from opposition to mercantilism to government by consent of the governed. The new American nation would incorporate in its Constitution many of these same ideas, including natural rights, checks and balances, and popular sovereignty.

The Enlightenment in Spanish America

The scientific revolution and the Enlightenment reached colonial Latin America also. Particularly with the rule of the enlightened Bourbon dynasty in Spain in the later eighteenth century, the spirit of reform in Spanish America experienced a considerable growth.

The ideas of Copernicus and Newton, Bacon and Descartes were taught in Latin America's two dozen universities, some of which, like those at Mexico City and Lima, Peru, were much older than Harvard and Yale. Some Spanish American colonists, like the British settlers to the north, corresponded with European scientific societies and made important contributions to astronomy, biology, geology, and what amounted to Indian anthropology, as well as to other sciences. The Inquisition was still capable of occasionally persecuting those who advocated the Copernican theory, but in the eighteenth century even the Jesuits were teaching Newton's ideas in the colonies.

Spanish America was strongly influenced by the social theories of the Enlightenment. Colonial newspapers expressed concern over political abuses, voiced demands for economic and social change, and spread the ideas of the philosophes. Similar views were discussed by middle-class mestizo groups in colonial "economic clubs" and by aristocrats in traditional social gatherings called *tertulias*. No representative assemblies existed in the Latin American colonies, but enlightened Bourbon administrators encouraged social reform.

Bourbon reforms would not be enough, however. Enlightenment belief in reason and social progress and willingness to challenge authority and demand political and economic reform would also contribute to the outbreak of the Latin American wars of independence in the early nineteenth century.

ART IN THE AGE OF ENLIGHTENMENT

The arts in the eighteenth century were less innovative than the scientific and social thought of the age. Nevertheless, there were new developments in literature, music, painting, and architecture, including both new styles and new and larger audiences for the arts.

A wider audience was particularly important for the long-term future of the arts. Aristocratic patrons and small, elite groups continued to dominate much of the artistic life of the eighteenth century, and encourage sophisticated traditional styles. But there was a growing middle-class interest in the arts as well, which demanded more contemporary subjects and forms. The music of the period, too, reached larger numbers of people than ever before in opera houses and concert halls.

Aristocratic Art: Neoclassicism and Rococo

Europe's eighteenth-century aristocracy, classically educated and living elegantly, sought art to satisfy both these tastes. Neoclassicism responded to its appreciation of Greek and Roman culture, rococo to its concern for elegance.

Neoclassicism was in essence a refinement of the classical styles of the seventeenth century, which required the artist to adhere to the rules and models of the ancients. The forms of poetry, as in the preceding century, were those used by Greek and Roman poets. Subjects for painting often came from ancient history and myth. Balance and symmetry prevailed in architecture and rationality in neoclassical literature. The sophisticated rhymed couplets of Alexander Pope (1688–1744), and the formally posed portraits of Sir Joshua Reynolds (1723–1792) embodied the neoclassical spirit.

Rococo art, by contrast, was light, elegant, and informal—a decorative style of architecture, sculpture, and painting designed to create a pleasant atmosphere for members of the ruling class to live their lives. Named for the stone and seashell (*rocaille* and *coquille*) motifs used in its room decorations, the rococo style was far less

The Swing. Jean-Honoré Fragonard's famous painting of aristocrats at play is typical of the rococo style. Its subject is frivolous and a bit risqué—the husband pushing the young lady in the swing is presumably unaware of the young man in the bushes. The Wallace Collection, London.

splendid than baroque art, and less stiff and formal than classical design. It offered pleasant paintings of well-dressed ladies and gentlemen, decorations for the walls of aristocratic boudoirs, and sexy china shepherdesses to titillate the fancy of the "beautiful people" of the eighteenth century.

Bourgeois Art and the Novel

The increasing wealth, education and aggressiveness of Europe's rising middle class also exerted an influence on

the art of the century. The bourgeoisie demanded contemporary subjects from everyday life, the expression of sentiment, and often a clear moral message in art and literature.

Interest in the "common people" was expressed in paintings of peasants or working people, who were often depicted in close-knit family groups or in ordinary household occupations. Dignity, piety, and warmth were common themes. The English artist William Hogarth (1697–1764), by contrast, produced satirical printed etchings of lowlife in London, with

subjects like *The Harlot's Progress* or *Gin Lane*, which sold many copies.

It was in prose fiction, however, that bourgeois taste had its most creative impact, producing the first modern novels. *Robinson Crusoe* by Daniel Defoe (1661–1731) showed the middle-class spirit of industry, inventiveness, and piety at work transforming a desert island into a microcosm of the material world Crusoe had left behind. Henry Fielding (1707–1754) wrote a number of broadly humorous novels, including *Tom Jones*, recounting a young man's colorfully ris-

The Kitchen Maid. Jean-Baptiste Chardin's depiction of a humble servant at work reflects a very different attitude than that of Fragonard's picture, above. Paintings like this attributed a dignity and value to the respectable bourgeoisie and even the hard-working lower orders of society that was often lacking among Europe's rulers in the eighteenth-century. National Gallery of Art, Washington, D.C.

Defoe   Pope   Fielding   Fanny Burney

Bach   Haydn

Handel   Mozart

que adventures in a world of hard-drinking country squires and city sharpers. Despite their exaggerated characters and situations, novels like Fielding's dealt with a down-to-earth world that was thoroughly familiar to middle-class readers. Such books pleased the hard-headed, literal-minded citizens who would in the next century displace an effete aristocracy as Europe's new master class.

Another important audience for eighteenth-century fiction was bourgeois women. Not so highly educated as the aristocratic ladies of the salons, respectable, middle-class women nevertheless influenced the evolution of the novel by encouraging fictional expression of their own interests. Samuel Richard's widely popular *Pamela, or Virtue Rewarded* appealed to these interests with a story of a servant girl who resists her master's efforts to seduce her and is finally rewarded by an honest offer of marriage. Fanny Burney (1752–1840), one of many women novelists, made her literary reputation with her first book, *Evalina, or A Young Lady's Entrance into the World* (1778), detailing a girl's discovery of high society with an ironic eye and a shrewd sense of character. Fictional works like these and the shorter stories appearing in many women's magazines stressed feeling and

morality, qualities that would also be important in middle-class fiction—and middle-class character—of the next century.

A Century of Musical Genius

Perhaps the greatest artistic achievements of the eighteenth century came in music. Composers, continuing to develop older forms, including sacred music and opera, created the orchestra and developed new instruments like the piano and new musical forms such as the classical symphony. Eighteenth-century music, like bourgeois literature and Enlightenment thought, reached beyond the patronage of an aristocratic elite to the larger audiences who flocked to opera houses and concert halls.

The German states, particularly Austria, produced a series of brilliant composers who decisively shaped classical music during this period. From Bach to Mozart, it was one of the great ages in the history of music.

Johann Sebastian Bach (1685–1750) spent a quietly brilliant life creating religious music for German church congregations. Yet his baroque compositions are so rationally and intricately constructed that, formally at least, they seem to embody the very spirit of the age of reason.

George Frederick Handel (1685–1759), Bach's contemporary, emigrated to the England of the Hanoverian kings, where he produced huge oratorios, including his famous *Messiah* (1742), and other dramatic combinations of instrumental music and choral song. Handel's music, though commissioned by England's elite, reached large audiences, as it does today. The operas of Christoph Willibald von Gluck (1714–1787), meanwhile, transformed the traditional opera from a baroque showcase for virtuoso performances and musical fireworks into a more structured and coherent form of musical drama. Opera houses also multiplied in European cities during this century as princes and wealthy cities vied for the prestige of sponsoring these spectacular and widely popular entertainments.

Two other Germans dominated the musical scene in the second half of the century. Joseph Haydn (1732–1809) enjoyed the patronage of Austrian royalty throughout his long and immensely productive musical life. He left a huge number of oratorios, operas, symphonies, and other compositions to enrich the classical tradition. Wolfgang Amadeus Mozart (1756–1791), a child prodigy who dazzled courtly audiences with his playing, in later life tried to break the common pattern of dependence on aristocratic patronage. He earned a precarious living composing operas, symphonies, and other works at a feverish rate, and died in debt at the age of thirty-five. Haydn and Mozart between them developed the modern orchestra and gave definitive form to the symphony. Mozart's operas, arguably his greatest achievements, including the often-performed *Marriage of Figaro* (1786), combined comic and tragic themes, intricate composition and lovely melody in works of singular beauty that transcend the age.

SUMMARY

The period in the history of European thought that is sometimes called the age of reason grew out of the scientific revolution of the sixteenth and seventeenth centuries and reached its climax in the eighteenth-century Enlightenment. It was an age in which new theories and discoveries about the natural world inspired new notions about the sort of social world one ought to live in.

The scientific revolution began with Copernicus's theory that the stars and planets revolve, not around the Earth as they seem to, but around the Sun, and climaxed with Newton's formulation of a law of universal gravitation binding the entire cosmos together. Meanwhile, seventeenth-century philosophers like Bacon and Descartes developed the scientific method, emphasizing an empirical and rationalistic approach.

In the eighteenth century, the intellectual leaders of the Enlightenment used rational analysis for another purpose: to criticize existing social institutions and to propose new principles on which to base a new and more just society. French philosophes like Voltaire, Rousseau, and Diderot attacked the abuses of the old regime with shrewdness, satirical wit, and passion. Thinkers like John Locke and Adam Smith urged a new order based on political and economic freedom, natural rights, and the natural laws of human society. The Enlightenment spread beyond Europe to the European colonies in the Americas, where they sowed the seeds of coming revolutions.

The cultural life of Europe in the eighteenth century also included a variety of artistic achievements, in particular, neoclassical and rococo art, which reflected the predominance of an aristocratic elite, and the novel, which catered to the tastes of the rising middle class. In the history of the arts, as in the history of ideas, the western world was on the threshold of great changes as the eighteenth century drew toward a close.

SELECTED SOURCES

*Artz, Frederick B. *The Enlightenment in France.* 1968. A brief survey of the movement in the land of the philosophes.

*Fielding, Henry. *Tom Jones: A Foundling.* Many editions. Panorama of eighteenth-century England, with rousing adventures.

*Franklin, Benjamin. *The Autobiography of Benjamin Franklin.* Many editions. Engaging life of a colonial who made good—and shared in the main currents of Enlightenment life and thought.

*Galilei, Galileo. *Dialogue Concerning the Two Chief World Systems—Ptolemaic and Copernican.* 1967. Readable discussion of the rival views, by a scientist with an eye to the larger audience.

*Kitson, Michael. *The Age of the Baroque.* 1966. An art book with substantial sections on rococo and neoclassicism; excellent illustrations.

*Koyre, Alexander. *From the Closed World to the Infinite Universe.* 1968. Expanding knowledge of the universe, from Copernicus through Newton.

*Roberts, Kenneth. *Northwest Passage.* 1981. Brilliant fictional recreation of an American artist's life, from Indian encampments to the slums of Hogarth's London.

*Rousseau, Jean-Jacques. *Confessions.* 1953. Intriguing autobiography by one of the more emotional spirits of the age of reason.

*Shaffer, Peter. *Amadeus.* 1984. Recent play—and film—about Mozart, exploring larger questions of artistic mediocrity and genius.

*Voltaire, Francois Marie Arouet de. *Candide or Optimism.* Many editions. Satirical novel highlighting foibles and hypocrites of eighteenth-century European and colonial life.

*Available in paperback.

CONSTITUTIONALISM AND ENLIGHTENED DESPOTISM

Impetuous, vain, presumptuous, scornful, restless, but also attentive, kind and easy to get on with. A friend of truth and reason. He prefers great ideas . . . likes glory and reputation but cares not a rap what his people think of him. . . . He knows himself very well but the funny thing is that he is modest about what is good in him and boastful about his shortcomings. Well aware of his faults, but more anxious to conceal than to correct them. Beautiful speaking voice. . . . I think that, both as a matter of principle and character, he is against war. He'll never allow himself to be attacked, as much from vanity as from prudence—he will find out what his enemies are planning and attack them suddenly before they are quite ready. Woe to them if they are not strong, and woe to him if a well-organized league should force him into a sustained effort of great length.

This portrait of Frederick the Great of Prussia by a French contemporary would apply to almost any enlightened despot of the period. Enlightened despotism, the dominant trend in European politics in the second half of the eighteenth century, is a term assigned to absolute monarchs who, encouraged by the philosophes, exercised their power to make basic rationalist reforms. What made these rulers different from their predecessors was the claim that they used their authority for the benefit of their people. Among other activities, enlightened despots reformed judicial procedures, codified and simplified laws, granted religious toleration, supported scientific research, promoted better public health, and extended popular education.

Another movement, one that preceded enlightened despotism by a century, was the appearance of constitutional government. As a forerunner of democracy, seventeenth-century constitutionalism sought to strike a balance between the authority of the state and the rights of its subjects. In an age when absolutism prevailed nearly everywhere in Europe, the Netherlands and England dealt with the question of sovereignty by establishing a constitutional state. This chapter first surveys the development of constitutional rule in the Netherlands and England, then examines three monarchs who espoused enlightened principles and one who did not.

Joseph II of Austria. Joseph was the most radical but least effective of the enlightened despots, lacking the political acumen that marked Frederick the Great's happy blend of idealism and realism. He worked relentlessly to bring social justice and effective government to his land, but he was rejected by his own subjects. Nevertheless, Joseph was a symbol of energetic reform, and therein may lie his chief historical significance.

CONSTITUTIONALISM

A unique feature of the seventeenth century was the emergence of constitutional governments in the Netherlands and in England. Constitutionalism is a doctrine or system in which government authority is limited by enforceable rules of law. Various checks and balances prevent the concentration of power so that basic rights of individuals and groups are protected. A nation's constitution may be written, as would be the case of the United States, or unwritten, that is, based on parliamentary statutes, judicial decisions, and traditional laws and practices, such as in Great Britain. What makes constitutionalism function, whether written or unwritten, is recognition by the various branches of government that they must operate within a legal framework. A constitutional state may take the form of a republic or a monarchy. Early constitutional systems restricted the franchise and the holding of public office to a privileged few who could meet stringent property qualifications. In a modern-day democracy, by contrast, most adults can participate directly or indirectly through their elected representatives in the process of government.

CONSTITUTIONALISM IN THE UNITED PROVINCES OF THE NETHERLANDS

During the sixteenth century, the Dutch created the first major constitutional state. In 1581, the United Provinces of the Netherlands, as the provinces that had become independent of Spain termed themselves, formally renounced their allegiance to the Spanish King, Philip II. They embodied their justification in the Act of Abjuration, often termed "the Dutch Declaration of the Rights of Man," a statement that was the model for declarations during subsequent revolutions and independence movements in other lands. The opening comment read: "The people were not created by God for the sake of the Prince . . . but, on the contrary, the Prince was made for the good of the people." The document argued that when a ruler ignored the law that defined his relationship with his subjects, he could be justly deposed.

When the Dutch threw off the Spanish yoke, they considered electing a ruler, but in the end created a republic. Although the Dutch enjoyed more individual rights than citizens elsewhere, their government in the seventeenth century was dominated by an elite of merchants and bankers. The constitutions of the Dutch Republic, the common name for the United Provinces, set up a political system in which the provinces retained a large measure of sovereignty. Each province had its own army, assembly, and elected stadtholder (governor). The federal assembly, the States-General, which sat at the Hague, was composed of delegates from the seven provinces. Its members could do nothing on their own authority. They had to refer all matters to their respective provinces and await directives on how to vote. Often the opposition of a single province was enough to deter action. If a decision was reached, it was not binding on the member states unless it involved foreign affairs and defense.

Operating under such a slow and inefficient system, the republic would probably have collapsed had it not been for the steadying influence of the leadership of the House of Orange. The descendants of William the Silent were men of exceptional ability, and through the office of stadtholder helped to unite the country. Maurice (1584–1625) was stadtholder of five provinces and his successors became stadtholders in six. Since the days of William the Silent and the wars of independence, they had enjoyed enormous prestige, which enabled them to exercise an authority that exceeded that of the office they held. Gradually, they assumed direction of foreign affairs and general supervision of internal administration and were regarded, both at home and abroad, as the rulers of the Dutch Republic. In 1747, the office of stadtholder, then under William IV (1711–1751) became hereditary and the country ceased to be a republic in fact if not in name. It was formally converted into a kingdom by Napoleon and continued as a monarchy after his overthrow in 1815.

THE DECLINE OF ROYAL ABSOLUTISM IN ENGLAND

In the seventeenth century, England reversed the trend toward absolute monarchy and established a semipopular parliamentary government. The process of change was accompanied by chronic political instability. Puritan resistance to the Elizabethan religious settlement had merged with fierce parliamentary opposition to Stuart absolutism to produce one of the most violent and tumultuous periods England has ever known. Before constitutional rule was achieved, England suffered through a civil war, beheaded one king, experienced a military dictatorship, then restored the monarchy, and finally, in a bloodless revolution, overthrew another king. Since we have already described the earlier events, we begin this narrative with the Restoration of 1660.

The Stuart Restoration, 1660–1688

The Cromwellian experiment having failed, England was ready to restore the monarchy. Living in exile on the continent, Prince Charles, son of Charles I, carefully prepared the way for a Stuart restoration. He promised that if chosen king, he would respect the authority of Parliament and grant a pardon to all rebels, except those lawfully designated to be punished. Proclaimed king by a newly elected Parliament, Charles II (1660–1685) arrived in London on May 29, 1660, amid hysterical jubilation. Charles wanted above all to keep his throne. Patient, shrewd, and manipulative, he operated within the established framework of government, concealing his Catholic bias and desire for absolute authority.

England entered the Restoration period with two major problems unresolved. One was the state's position regarding Catholics and non-Anglican Protestants. Along with the monarchy, the Church of England had been restored as it existed in the reign of Charles I. The Anglican and royalist majority in Parliament, anxious to guard against a revival of Puritan power, enacted a series of repressive

measures between 1661 and 1665 known as the Clarendon Code. The new legislation excluded all but Anglicans to municipal or national office and provided harsh penalties for dissenters who attended services held by non-conforming ministers. Charles was interested less in religious toleration than he was in removing restrictions against Catholics. In 1672, he issued a Declaration of Indulgence, suspending all laws against Catholics and dissenters. Parliament's dread of Catholicism, however, was so intense that Charles was compelled to revoke the declaration. To fortify its victory, Parliament passed the Test Act, which required all officeholders to take communion according to Anglican rites. This forced Charles's brother, James, who had publicly avowed his Catholicism, to resign his admiralship of the navy.

The second problem facing England after 1660 was the relationship between the monarchy and Parliament, which the Restoration settlement had not defined. Charles's ideal political system, an absolute monarchy patterned after the Bourbons, was irreconcilable with the national temper. Treading warily, Charles employed different techniques to increase his power at the expense of Parliament. One way was to become financially independent of Parliament. Parliament had voted the king a grant for life, but this proved insufficient to support his court. As Charles had no wish to become indebted to or involved in strife with Parliament as his father had done, he managed to obtain the necessary funds by other means. He sold Dunkirk to France and married a Portuguese princess who brought a large dowry. For a substantial sum of money, he

entered into the secret Treaty of Dover with Louis XIV, in which he pledged to support the French in a war against the Dutch.

Charles also attempted to influence the actions of Parliament. He appointed members of Parliament as his major advisers, foreshadowing the later cabinet system. The king also sought support for his policies in Parliament through favors and bribes, a practice that led to the development of political parties. Those who were inclined to allow the monarchy relatively broad powers and defended the Anglican church came to be called Tories (Irish robbers) by their opponents. The other faction, derisively nicknamed Whigs (Scottish cattle thieves), favored the subordination of the crown to Parliament and toleration for dissenters. The two groups were not yet true parties, for they lacked organization and discipline.

James II (1685–1688) had little in common with his brother, whom he succeeded in 1685. An arrogant and obstinate man with no sense of political reality, James alienated practically every segment of the population during his brief reign. Having crushed a rebellion shortly after his accession, he kept his army encamped on the outskirts of London and demanded the repeal of the Test Act and Clarendon Code that barred Catholics from office. Parliament, protesting the presence of troops, refused the king's request, whereupon he dismissed it in November 1685. In defiance of the laws, James appointed Catholics to positions in the government, the universities, the army and even the Anglican church. In 1687, James issued a Declaration of Indulgence, which gave religious freedom to all denominations. Because it removed restrictions against the hated Catholics, it thoroughly alienated the Tories while failing to win over the dissenters as he had hoped. He tried seven Anglican bishops for sedition, but they were acquitted by a jury, news of which caused wild public rejoicing. To contemporary English people, it seemed as if James was bent on making Catholicism the estab-lished religion of the country and on reviving the absolutism of his father and grandfather.

The prospect of a Catholic becom-ing the next king of England crystal-lized discontent into an active op-position that ended James's rule. The English people had hitherto tolerated the royal government's tyranny, for James was elderly and without a male heir and it was supposed that on his death the crown would pass to Mary, his eldest daughter by an earlier mar-riage. She was a Protestant and mar-ried to William III of Orange (1672–1702), stadtholder of the Dutch Re-public. In 1688, however, James's second wife, a Catholic, gave birth to a son, apparently assuring a Cath-olic dynasty. To forestall such an

King James II. The narrow-mindedness, rigid temperament, and lack of imagination are not apparent in this portrait of the last Stuart mon-arch. These characteristics, which affected James's mode of governing, dissipated the good will of his subjects and not only brought about his own downfall but also led to permanent changes in the British political system.

United
Provinces declare
their independence
from Spain

Stuart
Restoration

The "Glorious
Revolution"

Act of
Settle-
ment

Maurice of Orange

Bill of
Rights

War of
the Spanish
Succession

Louis XV
of France

event, a group of prominent Tories and Whigs, usually bitter political rivals, united and offered the crown to Mary and her husband, William, to rule jointly. In November 1688, William landed with his army in England and was welcomed as a deliverer by the great majority of people. Deserted even by those he considered loyal, James fled to France. The overthrow of James II, known to history as the Glorious Revolution, had brought about a change of rulers with a minimum of bloodshed. The events of November 1688 marked the final triumph of Parliament over the monarchy. By arrogating to itself the authority both to depose and appoint a monarch, Parliament dealt a powerful blow to the concept of the divine right of kings to govern as they saw fit.

The Triumph of Parliament

The Revolution of 1688 brought in its wake major constitutional changes, in the form of legislative enactments. Early in 1689, William III (1689–1702) and Mary II (1689–1694) accepted the throne from Parliament on terms that were later embodied in a formal statute known as the Bill of Rights. This important document asserted and extended the rights of English people and laid down the principles of parliamentary supremacy. Another law eased restrictions against the dissenters in recognition of their opposition to James II. The Toleration Act of 1689 granted freedom of worship to non-Anglican Protestants, but continued to bar them from civil and military office. It conferred no privileges on Catholics, Unitarians, or Jews. The act, with all its limitations, marks the first step toward religious toleration in England.

Speaker of the House of Lords Offering William III and Mary the Crown. Initially, Parliament wanted Mary as sole sovereign, the successor by hereditary right. Mary, however, refused to reign alone. For his part, William would not accept the subordinate position of a prince consort. He insisted on being king for life; otherwise he would remain in his own land. Thus it was that Parliament proclaimed William and Mary joint sovereigns, the actual administration resting with William alone.

439

THE BILL OF RIGHTS

And thereupon the said lords spiritual and temporal and Commons . . . for the vindication and assertion of their ancient rights and liberties declare:

1. That the pretended power of suspending laws, or the execution of laws, by regal authority, without consent of parliament, is illegal.

2. That the pretended power of dispensing with laws, or the execution of laws, by regal authority, as it hath been assumed and exercised of late, is illegal . . .

4. That levying money for or to the use of the Crown by pretense of prerogative, without grant of parliament, for longer time or in other manner than the same is or shall be granted, is illegal.

5. That it is the right of the subjects to petition the king, and all commitments and prosecutions for such petitioning are illegal.

6. That the raising or keeping a standing army within the kingdom in time of peace, unless it be with consent of parliament, is against law.

7. That the subjects which are Protestants may have arms for their defense suitable to their conditions, and as allowed by law.

8. That election of members of Parliament ought to be free.

9. That the freedom of speech, and debates or proceedings in parliament, ought not to be impeached or questioned in any court or place out of parliament.

10. That excessive bail ought not to be required, nor excessive fines imposed nor cruel and unusual punishments inflicted . . .

13. And that for redress of all grievances, and for the amending, strengthening, and preserving of the laws, parliament ought to be held frequently. . . .

The said lords spiritual and temporal, and commons assembled at Westminster, do resolve that William and Mary, prince and princess of Orange, be, and be declared, king and queen of England, France, and Ireland, and the dominions thereunto belonging, to hold the crown and royal dignity of the said kingdoms and dominions to them the said prince and princess during their lives. [*]

Like the two earlier safeguards of English liberty, the Magna Carta and the Petition of Right, the Bill of Rights was predominantly specific and negative and did not deal in broad generalities of political theory. Nevertheless, the Bill established the essential constitutional principles underlying limited monarchy and remains the closest to a formal constitution that the British possess. The Bill of Rights also served as an inspiration for republican forms of government. The first ten amendments to the U.S. constitution (1791) and much of the French Declaration of the Rights of Man (1789) owe a debt to the English declaration of 1689.

[*]Cited in Edward P. Cheyney, *Readings in English History*, Ginn, (Boston and New York: 1922) pp. 545–547.

Finally, Parliament planned the order of succession to the English throne. In 1694, Mary had died of smallpox, leaving William without an heir to the throne. Mary's younger sister Anne was still alive, but her last surviving child died in 1701. To ensure the exclusion of the Catholic Stuarts, Parliament created the Act of Settlement in 1701. The bill prescribed that if Anne succeeded William and died without an heir, the crown would go to the closest Protestant blood relation, Sophia of Hanover, and then to her Protestant descendants.

William, who ruled alone after Mary's death in 1694, was more interested in defending the Dutch Republic against the attacks of Louis XIV of France than in governing England. He generally followed the dictates of Parliament, as he constantly required English resources and money, and left his ministers in charge of internal administration. William's hostility to France changed the direction of England's foreign policy. Under his leadership, England joined the coalition (League of Augsburg) against France, marking the start of a series of wars between the two nations that was to continue for more than a century. William's skill in directing the war effort frustrated Louis XIV's plans to dominate Europe and in the process made England a great power.

Anne (1702–1714), the last of the Protestant Stuarts, faced serious difficulties abroad. In an unsuccessful attempt to prevent Louis XIV from placing a French Bourbon prince on the Spanish throne, England became involved in the long and bitterly contested War of the Spanish Succession (1701–1713). The most outstanding accomplishment of Anne's reign was the formal union of England and Scotland in 1707. The Act of Union created the United Kingdom of Great Britain, with one ruler, one parliament, and one flag—the "Union Jack" combining the Scottish cross of St. Andrew and the English cross of St. George. At Anne's death, the crown passed to the elector of Hanover, George, son of the deceased Sophia.

Significant as they were, the events of 1688–1689 did not constitute a democratic revolution. An oligarchy of wealthy interests, largely landowning gentry elected by a very limited suffrage, governed the House of Commons. The House of Lords was composed of hereditary peers and high Anglican prelates. Thus from 1689 until at least 1832, when the Great Reform Bill was passed, the aristocracy controlled the government.

The Development of Cabinet Government

The Glorious Revolution had given Parliament predominance in the British government but had not reduced the monarch to a mere figurehead. The king retained strong executive powers. He was commander of the armed forces, directed foreign policy, created peerages, and appointed officials to ecclesiastical positions as well as to posts in the government and royal household. In theory, the monarch could also veto legislation enacted by Parliament, but the last royal veto was in 1707. Through personal loyalties, patronage, and the granting of honors and favors, the crown could and did exert considerable influence over Parliament.

As chief executive, the king was responsible for the day-to-day conduct of state business. Yet final authority rested with Parliament. How could Parliament control the executive branch of government while assuring the smooth and efficient transaction of state affairs?

The solution lay with the evolution of the cabinet system. Its origins dated back to the privy council, a body of officials and dignitaries chosen by the king to advise him on matters of policy. On coming to the throne in 1689, William III, acknowledging that his chief advisers should be acceptable to the legislature, selected them from the two leading parties. He soon realized, however, that the wheels of government operated more smoothly if his cabinet was restricted to men who controlled a majority in the House of Commons. In establishing this precedent, William continued to regard his cabinet ministers as responsible only to the crown. He assumed, as did his successor, Anne, that it was the ruler's role to administer the daily affairs of the state and formulate broad policy. Both regularly presided over cabinet meetings, participated in policy discussions, and occasionally acted without reference to their advisers.

The presence on the throne of the early Hanoverians, George I (1714–1727) and George II (1727–1760), encouraged the trend toward cabinet government. George I could neither speak nor understand English and soon stopped attending cabinet meetings, a practice that reduced the crown's influence in shaping policy. George II was also disinterested in the intricacies of British politics and followed his father's example.

The absence of the first two Hanoverians from cabinet meetings opened the way for one of the most influential ministers, Sir Robert Walpole, to conduct the discussions and serve as intermediary between the king and cabinet. For some twenty years, from 1721 to 1742, he dominated English politics, enjoying the good will of both kings and leading the Whig party in the House of Commons. Walpole is generally recognized as the first "prime" minister, although he persistently disclaimed the title. Thereafter, it became traditional for the king to appoint as head of the cabinet the acknowledged leader of the strongest party in the Commons. In this way, the cabinet exercised executive power in the king's name but in response to the wishes, and subject to the approval, of Parliament. When Walpole was defeated in the House of Commons in 1742, he resigned at once. His action established the principle that a ministry must resign when it ceased to command the confidence of the lower House.

George III (1760–1820) attempted to subvert the growing power of cabinet government during the early decades of his reign. Born and educated in Great Britain, George believed in the supremacy of Parliament. Still, he wanted to be a "patriotic king," making the cabinet responsible to him and ruling above political parties in accordance with his perception of national welfare. By 1770, George had secured control of Parliament after a decade during which he destroyed the power of the Whig opposition and created his own party,

Sir Robert Walpole Presiding over a Cabinet Meeting. A master orator and unrivaled manager of men, Walpole sought to keep the peace, to encourage trade, and to avoid any dispute that might disturb the collaboration of the king and Parliament. Walpole held a low opinion of human nature, believing that most men can be bought. By patronage, bribery, pressure of all kinds, and hard work, he not only controlled his own Whig party but often enticed some Tories into supporting him as well. His tactics, however unsavory, ensured adoption of policies that gave Great Britain twenty years of quiet government.

known as the King's Friends (mostly Tories), with the help of royal favors and pensions. Over the next dozen years George imposed his personal rule through a docile cabinet headed by Lord North. For England his statesmanship was ruinous, resulting in the loss of most of Great Britain's North American colonies and a huge increase of the national debt. The unpopularity of George's policies, coupled with his periodic lapses into insanity, eroded royal influence and enabled the cabinet to regain the initiative. Ever since, the task of governing Great Britain has belonged to the prime minister and his cabinet colleagues, subject to the approval of Parliament.

ENLIGHTENED DESPOTISM

A new form of absolutism, which came to be called enlightened despotism, emerged on the continent after 1740. Enlightened despotism owed its appearance partly to the writings of the Enlightenment philosophes but mostly to the mid-eighteenth-century wars, which drove some of the crowned heads of Europe to reconstruct their states in anticipation of the next conflict. Enlightened despots believed that their own interests could best be served by adopting national reforms. Measures designed to promote the development of the economy increased the wealth of their subjects but also provided the treasury with more revenues to finance larger armies. By curbing the power of the nobility and clergy, building up a trained and salaried officialdom, and remodeling administrative practices, these monarchs strengthened the central government and increased its efficiency. Other reforms, which resulted in religious toleration, more progressive legal and judicial systems, better health services, a higher level of popular education, solidified internal political support for their rule.

Many of these kinds of reforms had been done by kings before. The difference between the new monarchs and the old absolutists was primarily in attitude and style. Enlightened despots said little about divine or hereditary rights to their thrones. However, holding little faith in the ability of the masses to govern themselves, they firmly believed that a paternalistic monarchy was the best form of government. Their duty, so they claimed, was to act in the interest of their subjects, but in reality few measured up to the image they created of themselves. They ignored the philosophes' cry for social equality and individual rights and generally were loathe to effect any social or political change that might sooner or later turn out to be at their expense. They were more enlightened than their predecessors, but they were still despots. Lesser rulers included Leopold of Tuscany (1765–1790), Charles III of Spain (1759–1788) and Gustav III of Sweden (1771–1792). Of the major rulers, the three most often associated with that title, correctly or not, were Frederick the Great of Prussia (1740–1786), Joseph II of Austria (1780–1790), and Catherine the Great of Russia (1762–1796).

Frederick the Great of Prussia

During the second half of the eighteenth century, Frederick II gained the reputation as the ideal enlightened despot. Possessing an excellent mind, he had from boyhood shown a liking for art, literature, music, and philosophy. He wrote poetry and essays and his treatises on government were sought out by monarchs who wished to emulate his rule. He fervently admired the French philosophes and entertained Voltaire at his court.

Frederick's brilliance lay not so much in actual innovation as in mastering the details of the system he inherited. He worked extremely hard at being king, since he believed that "as the first servant of the state" (as he described himself), his duties were proportionate to his rank. Rising before dawn, he labored at his desk until evening, when he turned to cultural pursuits. No aspect of his government escaped his attention. He visited each part of his kingdom annually, studying problems, talking to citizens, and correcting abuses. He kept a close check on his administrators by corresponding frequently with them and by sending out royal agents to report on their activities. During Frederick's reign, the Prussian civil service attained a level of honesty and efficiency that was unsurpassed in Europe.

Frederick's economic and agricultural policies were designed to achieve national self-sufficiency. Wedded to mercantilist principles, he imposed protective tariffs to foster the development of infant industries, opened new mines, and was careful to protect Prussia's natural resources. As the greatest landlord in Prussia, Frederick devoted special attention to agriculture. The state introduced and supervised scientific farming techniques and the cultivation of new crops such as potatoes and turnips, reclaimed vast areas of farmland, and encouraged the immigration of thousands of farmers.

The most enduring of Frederick's contributions to Prussia were probably his improvements in the administration of justice, his codification of the law, and his policy of religious toleration. He reduced bribery by paying judges adequate salaries, established uniform legal fees, simplified court procedures, and abolished the use of torture to extract confessions except in cases of murder and treason. A new legal code, not completed until 1794, eliminated regional differences and made the laws simpler and more equitable. Personally indifferent to religion, Frederick was the most tolerant ruler in Europe, saying, "All religions shall be tolerated in my states; here everyone may seek salvation in his own way." Jews, however, still faced civil disabilities.

On the other hand, Frederick failed to make significant progress in many areas. He talked at length about the value of a strong educational system, but his improvements were few and unimportant. He did little to change the social order as he found it. Believing in the hierarchical concept of society, he rigidly defined the legal status of the different classes. Because he depended on the aristocracy for service in the army and bureaucracy, he refrained from abolishing serfdom, although he recognized that the institution was an abomination. He permitted only limited freedom of speech and of the press.

In foreign affairs, Frederick's use of power politics was inconsistent with the humanitarian and pacific ideals of the philosophes. A considerable part of Frederick's reign was consumed by two major wars. Frederick had inherited from his father, Frederick William I, a well-filled treasury and perhaps the finest army in Eu-

Frederick II and Voltaire in the Study of the Royal Palace of Sans Souci in Potsdam. Having finally attracted the French intellectual to his side after repeated invitations, Frederick appointed him a court chamberlain and gave him a generous pension. But the relationship between the Prussian monarch and Voltaire was always difficult, in large measure because both were too prickly and self-centered. After two years, Voltaire left Prussia, and in his memoirs, published after his death, poured out his wrath in a scurrilous account of the private life of his former patron.

rope. Although Frederick William had been content merely to build and parade the Prussian army, Frederick was ready to use it for a suitable cause.

Frederick II did not have to wait long to try out his army. Five months after he became king, the Habsburg emperor Charles VI (1711–1740) died. Lacking a male heir, Charles succeeded in obtaining the signature of all the states of Europe, except Bavaria, to the Pragmatic Sanction. This document guaranteed that his daughter Maria Theresa would assume the crown with her territories intact.

Charles had barely been laid to rest when Frederick, without a declaration of war and in defiance of the Pragmatic Sanction, seized the rich Austrian province of Silesia.

This act of aggression by the young Prussian king, who ironically had just published a treatise assailing as immoral the principles of Machiavelli, provoked the long and bloody War of the Austrian Succession (1740–1748). France, Spain, Bavaria, and Saxony joined Prussia, lured by the hope of despoiling Habsburg territory. Great Britain took the side of

Maria Theresa, motivated by its bitter colonial rivalry with France and by a desire to see the Austrian (former Spanish) Netherlands, with which it enjoyed a lucrative trade, remain in friendly hands. The fighting broadened into a worldwide conflict, involving the fate of the Habsburg lands in Europe and a colonial struggle in the western hemisphere and India. Habsburg armies fended off Prussia's allies but were unable to eject Frederick from Silesia. The war ended in a stalemate in 1748. The Treaty of Aix-la-Chapelle restored conditions as they had existed before the conflict, except that Prussia retained Silesia. The pact proved to be merely a truce, for Maria Theresa would not reconcile herself to the loss of her province.

During the next eight years of uneasy peace, a "diplomatic revolution" occurred in which the chief antagonists in the first war changed sides in readiness for the second. In 1756, Austria and France buried their agelong enmity and signed a secret treaty, to which Russia, Sweden, and Saxony also subscribed, agreeing to divide most of Frederick's kingdom among themselves. Spain later entered the alliance against Prussia. Only Great Britain, already at war again with France in the colonies, supported Frederick.

Facing a powerful enemy coalition, Frederick struck before France and Russia were ready to take the field, opening the Seven Years' War (1756–1763). Absorbed in the struggle over-

seas, Great Britain furnished Frederick with subsidies but little military help. For five years, Frederick held his badly coordinated enemies at bay as he trampled back and forth across his ravaged kingdom. His rapid night marches, ability to elude a pursuing army and then strike unexpectedly at another, management of battles against heavy odds, and indomitable spirit astounded Europe and earned him the title of "the Great." By 1762, his ever-dwindling army was exhausted, he was short of funds, and much of his territory was under the heel of the invaders. Frederick was rescued from his predicament when the Russian Tsarina Elizabeth (1741–1762) died and was briefly replaced by the erratic Peter III (1762). Peter was a fanatical admirer of Frederick and promptly withdrew from the war. Thereafter, Frederick managed to hold his own until his enemies wearied of the struggle. The Treaty of Hubertusburg made no significant changes

in the prewar boundaries and confirmed Frederick's possession of Silesia.

Frederick participated in no more major wars, although in 1772 he collaborated with Russia and Austria in partially dismembering Poland. He took as his share West Prussia, which linked East Prussia with the main body of the Hohenzollern state. Under Frederick, Prussia had more than doubled in size and population (see Map 51). With its efficient government, sound economy, and superb army, Prussia was the dominant power in central Europe at Frederick's death.

Joseph II of Austria

The most sincere but the least successful of the enlightened despots was Joseph II of Austria, son of Maria Theresa. Joseph became coruler with his mother in 1765, but she retained final authority until her death in 1780. In the eighteenth century, Austria was

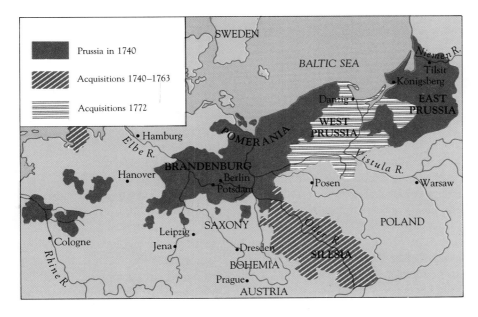

MAP 51
Expansion of Prussia under Frederick II. In two wars against Austria, Frederick secured Silesia and through diplomacy added another large block of land at the expense of Poland, linking Brandenburg and East Prussia. The powerful state created by Frederick was the most striking political achievement of that era.

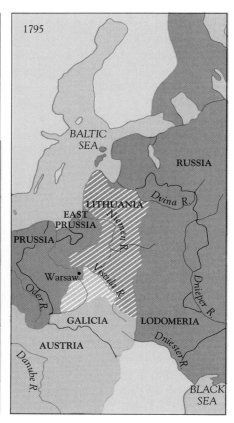

MAP 52

Partitions of Poland. Indefensible borders and internal chaos, largely the result of a highly decentralized government, made Poland easy prey for covetous neighbors. In 1772, Russia, Prussia, and Austria each took a substantial bite, depriving Poland of one-third of its territory and half of its population. In the second partition, in 1793, Russia and Prussia annexed more Polish territory while Austria, preoccupied with a war against revolutionary France, got nothing. Two years later, Russia, Prussia, and Austria divided what remained of Poland. It was not until after World War I that Poland was restored as an independent state.

a loosely-knit empire of diverse peoples and traditions, without a common purpose or will. Although Maria Theresa had enacted some reforms, she was on the whole a cautious monarch, content to follow established practice and careful, whenever possible, not to offend vested interests. Joseph was impatient of custom and less willing to compromise. A disciple of the philosophes, his object was to sweep away archaic institutions and create a new state based on the highest ideals of justice and reason.

Joseph saw that the central administration of the state needed to be tightened if he hoped to enforce his program of reform. To that end, he suppressed provincial assemblies and

other vestiges of local independence, established new administrative districts staffed by his own bureaucrats, and made German the official language.

Joseph's religious policies reflected his tolerance for all faiths and his desire to subordinate the Catholic church to the state. Although a practicing Catholic, Joseph held that "each of my subjects must be reinstated in the possession of his natural rights." One of his first acts was to grant citizenship and religious toleration to Protestants and Orthodox Christians. Jews were granted similar rights and most of the disabilities against them removed. Joseph sought in various ways to eliminate the political influence of the pope and the church. He decreed that no papal bull be published in Austria without the express permission of the government. Bishops were made to swear allegiance to the state, education was freed of church control, and civil marriages were legalized. All monasteries deemed unproductive were dissolved. The wealth of these confiscated properties went to support schools, hospitals, and charitable institutions. Rome naturally protested the assaults on its authority, but in spite of the pope's visit to Vienna, Joseph would concede nothing.

In economic and social matters, Joseph was undoubtedly motivated by the welfare and happiness of his subjects. Joseph was an admirer of the physiocratic theories of economic freedom, but he never completely abandoned the prevailing mercantilist views. He did, however, relax tariff imports, terminate monopolies, and eliminate the power of the guilds to regulate manufacturing.

Joseph expressed his humane concerns by a number of acts. He issued a new penal code that forbade torture and reduced the number of crimes subject to capital punishment. He reorganized the judicial system, making laws more uniform and rational, lessening the influence of local landlords, and establishing equal punishment for the same offenses regardless of the culprit's social standing. Attendance in schools increased but Joseph's hope for universal and compulsory education never materialized. He applied an equitable tax on land, sweeping away the much-cherished exemption previously enjoyed by the privileged classes. Perhaps his most revolutionary move was to abolish serfdom. This legislation entitled the serfs to leave

the land, marry whomever they pleased, and choose their own occupations.

Joseph's rapid efforts to reconstruct Austrian society came to grief. Convinced that he was on the right course, he allowed nothing to stand in his way, riding roughshod over cherished traditions and ingrained prejudices. "Joseph always wishes to take the second step before he has taken the first," was the perceptive judgment of Frederick the Great. The aristocracy chafed at the loss of privileges; the Catholic church resented its diminished status in the state; and Hungary and the Austrian Netherlands revolted against the emperor's plans to make German the official language and to suppress provincial self-government. Joseph died in 1790 at the age of forty-nine, a broken and disillusioned man. Shortly before his death, he summed up his career in an epitaph he composed for himself: "Here lies a prince whose intentions were pure and who had the misfortune to see all his plans miscarry." Indeed, most of his reforms were reversed by his cautious brother and successor, Leopold II (1790–1792). The outcome might have been different if Joseph had enjoyed the support of a large and vigorous middle class such as existed in France.

Catherine the Great of Russia

Catherine II owed her reputation for enlightenment to skillful self-advertising, not to her record of accomplishment. A German princess who went to Russia at the age of fifteen to marry the heir to the throne, she assumed power in 1762 following the murder of her half-demented hus-

band, Peter III. Catherine fancied herself an intellectual. She wrote plays and essays, immersed herself in the literature of the Enlightenment, and corresponded regularly with a number of philosophes, expressing sympathy with many of the ideas they supported. Being a foreigner and a usurper, however, she recognized that she could not afford to alienate the aristocracy who had engineered the palace revolution that deposed Peter. Consequently, her good intentions were rarely translated into deeds.

Catherine did begin her reign auspiciously, summoning a legislative commission to codify the laws of Russia. The 564 deputies, chosen from every class except the serfs, assembled in 1767. Drawing heavily from Montesquieu's *Spirit of Laws*, Catherine prepared a set of *Instructions* to guide their deliberations. The *Instructions* proclaimed equality before the law, denounced capital punishment and torture, and called into question the institution of serfdom. The commission met sporadically for a year and a half, but from the outset it split along class lines. In particular, the peasant deputies clashed with the gentry, who refused to make any concessions for the benefit of the serfs. Catherine used the outbreak of a war against the Ottoman Empire in 1768 as a pretext to disband the commission. The commission failed to accomplish its work, but from Catherine's point of view it had served some purpose. It gave her considerable information about the nation and enhanced her image in the west.

The antagonisms that had simmered in the legislative commission exploded in a great serf uprising in 1773. The lot of the serfs, who comprised about half the peasant population of Russia, had been deteriorating steadily. The landlord's authority over them was practically absolute. Serf owners could transfer them from the land to work in factories or mines, sell them singly or in families, order or forbid their marriage, and punish them at will. Pretending to be Peter III, Emelian Pugachev, an illiterate cossack, sounded the call to arms in September 1773, promising freedom from serfdom, taxation, and military service for the people. Tens of thousands of serfs and servile workers flocked to Pugachev's banner. The rebels threatened Moscow before they were dispersed. Pugachev, betrayed by his own men, was taken to Moscow in an iron cage and publicly executed.

After this outbreak, Catherine dismissed any further thought of rural reform and closed ranks with the nobility. The line that separated serfdom from the chattel slavery, to which blacks in the United States were subjected, became almost indistinguishable. Catherine allowed landlords greater authority over their serfs. Huge grants of land to her favorites converted relatively free crown peasants into serfs. Serfdom was extended into new areas such as the Ukraine. In 1785, Catherine drew up a charter for the nobility, confirming earlier privileges and exemptions and adding certain new ones. Members of the aristocracy were exempt from personal taxes, military service, corporal punishment, and trial by judges whose status was inferior to their own. Under Catherine, the nobility reduced its responsibilities while increasing its privileges.

The Pugachev rebellion also caused Catherine to introduce a new system of local government. Frightened by the collapse of authority under the strain of the revolt, the empress proposed to strengthen provincial government through a process of decentralization. She divided the country into fifty provinces, which in turn were divided into districts. At the provincial level, the governor and his associates were appointed, but in the districts, the officials were mostly elected by the aristocracy.

In other domestic areas, Catherine carried out such reforms as she felt were politically feasible. She founded hospitals and orphanages, assisted artists and writers, and established schools and academies for the upper class. A believer in laissez-faire principles, Catherine abolished internal

A Flattering Portrait of Catherine the Great as an Equestrian. Her awareness that she was not beautiful prompted Catherine to surround herself with young and handsome men. The older she grew, the younger were her favorites. The empress had twenty-one known lovers, the last after she had turned sixty. As each lover dropped from favor, she rewarded him with a title, estate, serfs, and money, which were said to be based on his sexual performance.

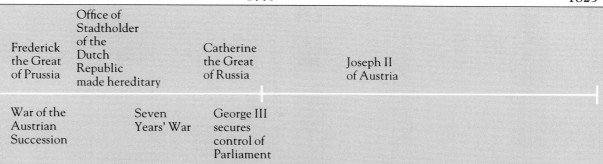

tolls and monopolies and fostered a series of commercial treaties with other countries. Hundreds of new factories sprang up all over Russia. These were built mostly on the estates of the nobility, where serf labor could be used. Some peasants benefited from the new policy by becoming active in cottage industries.

Catherine pursued an expansionist and unscrupulous foreign policy. "If I could live for two hundred years," she remarked to a friend, "all of Europe would be brought under Russian rule." Catherine's drive for warm water ports provoked two wars with the Ottoman Empire. In these wars, she gained the north shore of the Black Sea and vague rights to protect the Christian subjects of the sultan—rights that her successors used as a justification for repeated intervention in Turkey's domestic affairs. Through three partitions of Poland (1772, 1793, and 1795; see Map 52), she acquired about two-thirds of the once huge Polish state, pushing Russia's western boundary deep into central Europe. Catherine's conquests, for which she is called "the Great," made Russia a major European power.

Catherine's Polish acquisitions included a very large Jewish population, which her successors sought both to reduce and assimilate. The resulting oppression accelerated a Jewish drift back to western Europe and in the later nineteenth century, a massive migration to the United States.

Unreformed France

Among the great states, France alone cannot claim to have produced an enlightened ruler. Although raised to believe in the principle of divine right monarchy, Louis XV (1715–1774) was not cast in the same mold as Louis XIV. Indolent, fickle, and devoted to the pleasures of the flesh, Louis lacked the interest or patience to oversee the details of government in the manner of his predecessor. While seeking new ways to alleviate his boredom, he permitted the current woman of his interest to influence state policy. His succession of mistresses, the most prominent of whom were Mme. de Pompadour and Mme. du Barry, encouraged his spendthrift habits and misused their power, rewarding and enriching their friends and wreaking vengeance on their enemies. In thirty years, eighteen foreign secretaries and fourteen controller-generals served in Louis's

administration. Louis's haphazard and irresponsible conduct of policy dragged France into lengthy and unprofitable wars. France did not attain its goals in the War of the Austrian Succession, and not only sustained a shattering defeat in Europe during the Seven Years' War but also lost most of its vast overseas possessions to Great Britain. The immense cost of prosecuting these wars, added to the profligate extravagance at the court, cut deeply into the nation's finances.

In the last decade of his reign, Louis XV was shaken enough by his own unpopularity and by the growing financial crisis of the nation to attempt, in concert with his chief minister, René Maupeou, a few essential reforms. Their most controversial action was to propose shifting some of the national tax burden to the hitherto untaxed nobility and clergy. Louis's edicts were challenged by the regional parlements, or supreme law courts, as an infringement of the natural rights of French people, in particular those of the privileged classes. Because of the weakness of the central government under Louis, the parlements, made up of judges with noble status, had acquired a virtual veto power and frequently used it to hinder royal programs or to interfere with legislation. When Maupeou with the king's support initiated new reforms, the parlements challenged them. Tired of their obstructionism, Louis abolished the parlements and created new law courts with restricted authority. The reforms had barely begun to take effect when Louis died of smallpox in 1774. His successor lacked the strength and determination to continue the struggle against the privileged classes.

SUMMARY

Although absolute monarchy was already established as a dominant trend in early modern Europe, two states, the Dutch Republic and England, evolved in an opposite direction—toward constitutional rule. The Dutch replaced Spanish tyranny with a loose association of provinces, each retaining its individual sovereignty. Although republican in form, the government was in fact controlled by an oligarchy of wealthy merchants and a hereditary succession of powerful stadtholders. In England, the Glorious Revolution destroyed once and for all the Stuart quest for divine right absolutism and laid the foundation for a constitutional monarchy. In the eighteenth century, the development of cabinet government, in which executive power was exercised by ministers responsible to the House of Commons, progressively reduced the king to essentially a ceremonial role.

In the second half of the eighteenth century, Europe produced a new breed of kings—enlightened despots—who were influenced by the ideas of the French philosophes. These monarchs were no more willing than Louis XIV to sacrifice personal power or national glory, but they claimed that they used their authority for the benefit of the people. The three most often cited as enlightened monarchs were Frederick the Great of Prussia, Joseph II of Austria, and Catherine the Great of Russia. To varying degrees, these monarchs rooted out irrational customs and vested interests, made administrative improvements, adopted progressive economic measures, curbed the power of the nobility, and proclaimed religious toleration and equality of all before the law. However, these benevolent monarchs were primarily interested in strengthening the state as a military instrument, and indulged in ruthless territorial aggrandizement.

Equally significant was the absence of enlightened despotism in France. Louis XV was indifferent to affairs of state, and without a firm directing hand the French government moved in fits and starts, pulled in different directions by the passing influence of short-lived advisers. As a consequence, political abuses multiplied and the nation's financial crisis deepened. Few people at the time realized that these danger signals foretold the advent of a cataclysm that would bring down the old regime.

SELECTED SOURCES

*Bernard, Paul P. *Joseph II.* 1968. A concise and balanced treatment of the ill-fated monarch.

*Chimes, Stanley B. *English Constitutional History.* 1967. Succinct account by an eminent scholar, particularly good on seventeenth- and eighteenth-century developments.

*De Madariaga, Isabel. *Russia in the Age of Catherine the Great.* 1981. Meticulously researched biography, sympathetic to Catherine.

*Fraser, Antonia. *Royal Charles: Charles II and the Restoration.* 1979. A lively and thoughtful biography.

*Gagliardo, John G. *Enlightened Despotism.* 1967. A good introduction to the subject.

Gooch, G. P. *Louis XV: The Monarchy in Decline.* 1956. A highly respected study.

*Haley, Kenneth H. D. *The Dutch in the Seventeenth Century.* 1972. A richly illustrated book, emphasizing Dutch accomplishments.

Jones, James R. *Country and Court: England, 1658–1714.* 1978. An excellent treatment of the period.

Miller, J. *James II: A Study in Kingship.* 1977. An even-handed and scholarly volume in which James II is depicted as personally honest but sadly lacking in political acumen.

*Pushkin, Alexander. *The Captain's Daughter.* Various editions. A colorful Russian novel, set against the Pugachev rebellion.

*Plumb, J. H. *England in the Eighteenth Century.* Various editions. A good short account.

*Plumb, J. H. *The First Four Georges.* 1956. Well written and informative.

Ritter, Gerhard. *Frederick the Great.* 1968. A useful assessment by a leading German scholar.

*Thackeray, William M. *The Story of Henry Esmond.* Various editions. A fictional aristocrat caught in intrigue and rebellion during the reign of George II. Also a motion picture.

*Available in paperback.

SOME PRINCIPAL EMPERORS, KINGS, AND POPES

ROMAN EMPIRE

Augustus	27 B.C.–A.D. 14	Commodus	180–193
Tiberius	14– 37	Septimius Severus	193–211
Caligula	37– 41	Caracalla	211–217
Claudius	41– 54	Elagabalus	218–222
Nero	54– 68	Severus Alexander	222–235
Vespasian	69– 79	Philip the Arab	244–249
Titus	79– 81	Decius	249–251
Domitian	81– 96	Valerian	253–260
Trajan	98–117	Gallienus	260–268
Hadrian	117–138	Aurelian	270–275
Antoninus Pius	138–161	Diocletian	284–286
Marcus Aurelius	161–180		

West		East	
Maximian	286–305	Diocletian	284–305
Constantius	305–306	Galerius	305–311
		Maximius	308–313
		Licinius	308–324
Constantine	308–337	Constantine	324–337
Maxentius	307–312		
Constantine II	337–340		
Constans	337–350		
Constantius II	351–361	Constantius II	337–361
Julian	360–363	Julian	361–363
Jovian	363–364	Jovian	363–364
Valentinian	364–375	Valens	364–378
Gratian	375–383		
Valentinian II	383–392		
Theodosius	394–395	Theodosius	379–395

CAROLINGIAN KINGDOM

Pepin, Mayor of the Palace	680–714
Charles Martel, Mayor of the Palace	715–741
Pepin the Short, Mayor of the Palace	741–751
Pepin the Short, King	751–768
Charlemagne and Carloman, Joint Kings	768–771
Charlemagne, King	771–814
Charlemagne, Emperor	800–814
Louis the Pious, Emperor	814–840

West Franks

Charles the Bald	840–877	Charles	855–863
		Lothar II	855–869
Louis II the Stammerer	877–879		
Louis III	879–882	**East Franks**	
Carloman	879–884	Louis the German	840–876
		Carloman	876–880
Lotharingia		Louis	876–882
Lothar	840–855	Charles the Fat	884–887
Louis II	855–875		

ROMAN EMPIRE—CONTINUED

West		East	
Honorius	395–423	Arcadius	393–408
		Theodosius II	408–450
Valentinian III	425–455	Marcian	450–457
		Leo	457–474
Romulus	475–476	Zeno	474–491
		Anastasius	491–518
		Justin	518–527
		Justinian	527–565

HOLY ROMAN EMPIRE

Saxons

Henry the Fowler
919– 936
Otto I   962– 973
Otto II   973– 983
Otto III   983–1002

Salians

Conrad II   1024–1039
Henry III   1039–1056
Henry IV   1056–1106
Henry V   1106–1125
Lothar II   1125–1137

Hohenstaufens

Frederick I Barbarossa
1152–1190
Henry VI   1190–1197
Philip of Swabia
1198–1208
Otto IV (*Welf*)
1198–1215
Frederick II   1215–1250
Conrad IV   1250–1254

Luxemburg, Hapsburg, and Other Dynasties

Rudolf of Hapsburg
1273–1291
Adolph of Nassau
1292–1298
Albert of Austria
1298–1308
Henry VII of
Luxemburg 1308–1313
Ludwig IV of Bavaria
1314–1347
Charles IV   1347–1378

Wenceslas   1378–1400
Rupert   1400–1410
Sigismund   1410–1437

Hapsburgs

Frederick III   1440–1493
Maximilian I   1493–1519
Charles V   1519–1556
Ferdinand I   1556–1564
Maximilian II   1564–1576
Rudolf II   1576–1612
Matthias   1612–1619
Ferdinand II   1619–1637
Ferdinand III   1637–1657
Leopold I   1658–1705
Joseph I   1705–1711
Charles VI   1711–1740
Charles VII   1742–1745
Francis I   1745–1765
Joseph II   1765–1790
Leopold II   1790–1792
Francis II   1792–1806

THE PAPACY

Leo I   440– 461
Gregory I   590– 604
Nicholas I   858– 867
Silvester II   999–1003
Leo IX   1049–1054
Nicholas II   1058–1061
Gregory VII   1073–1085
Urban II   1088–1099
Paschal II   1099–1118
Alexander III   1159–1181
Innocent III   1198–1216
Gregory IX   1227–1241
Boniface VIII   1294–1303
John XXII   1316–1334
Gregory XI   1370–1378
Martin V   1417–1431
Eugenius IV   1431–1447
Nicholas V   1447–1455
Pius II   1458–1464
Alexander VI   1492–1503
Julius II   1503–1513
Leo X   1513–1521
Adrian VI   1522–1523
Clement VII   1523–1534
Paul III   1534–1549
Paul IV   1555–1559
Pius V   1566–1572
Gregory XIII   1572–1585
Pius VII   1800–1823
Gregory XVI   1831–1846
Pius IX   1846–1878
Leo XIII   1878–1903
Pius X   1903–1914
Benedict XV   1914–1922
Pius XI   1922–1939
Pius XII   1939–1958
John XXIII   1958–1963
Paul VI   1963–1978
John Paul I   1978
John Paul II   1978–

ENGLAND

Anglo-Saxons

Alfred the Great	871– 900
Ethelred the Unready	978–1016
Canute (*Danish*)	1016–1035
Harold I	1035–1040
Hardicanute	1040–1042
Edward the Confessor	1042–1066
Harold II	1066

Normans

William the Conqueror	1066–1087
William II	1087–1100
Henry I	1100–1135
Stephen	1135–1154

Angevins

Henry II	1154–1189
Richard I	1189–1199
John	1199–1216
Henry III	1216–1272
Edward I	1272–1307
Edward II	1307–1327
Edward III	1327–1377
Richard II	1377–1399

Houses of Lancaster and York

Henry IV	1399–1413
Henry V	1413–1422
Henry VI	1422–1461
Edward IV	1461–1483
Edward V	1483
Richard III	1483–1485

Tudors

Henry VII	1485–1509
Henry VIII	1509–1547
Edward VI	1547–1553
Mary I	1553–1558
Elizabeth I	1558–1603

Stuarts

James I	1603–1625
Charles I	1625–1649
Charles II	1660–1685
James II	1685–1688
William III and Mary II	1689–1694
William III alone	1694–1702
Anne	1702–1714

Hanoverians (from 1917, Windsors)

George I	1714–1727
George II	1727–1760
George III	1760–1820
George IV	1820–1830
William IV	1830–1837
Victoria	1837–1901
Edward VII	1901–1910
George V	1910–1936
Edward VIII	1936
George VI	1936–1952
Elizabeth II	1952–

FRANCE

Capetians

Hugh Capet	987– 996
Robert II the Pious	996–1031
Henry I	1031–1060
Philip I	1060–1108
Louis VI	1108–1137
Louis VII	1137–1180
Philip II Augustus	1180–1223
Louis VIII	1223–1226
Louis IX	1226–1270
Philip III	1270–1285
Philip IV	1285–1314
Louis X	1314–1316
Philip V	1316–1322
Charles IV	1322–1328

Valois

Philip VI	1328–1350
John	1350–1364
Charles V	1364–1380
Charles VI	1380–1422
Charles VII	1422–1461
Louis XI	1461–1483
Charles VIII	1483–1498
Louis XII	1498–1515
Francis I	1515–1547
Henry II	1547–1559
Francis II	1559–1560
Charles IX	1560–1574
Henry III	1574–1589

Bourbons

Henry IV	1589–1610
Louis XIII	1610–1643
Louis XIV	1643–1715
Louis XV	1715–1774
Louis XVI	1774–1792

Post 1792

Napoleon I, Emperor	1804–1814
Louis XVIII (*Bourbon*)	1814–1824
Charles X (*Bourbon*)	1824–1830
Louis Philippe (*Bourbon-Orléans*)	1830–1848
Napoleon III, Emperor	1851–1870

SPAIN

Ferdinand	1479–1516
and	
Isabella	1479–1504

Hapsburgs

Philip I	1504–1506
Charles I (Holy Roman Emperor as Charles V)	1506–1556
Philip II	1556–1598
Philip III	1598–1621
Philip IV	1621–1665
Charles II	1665–1700

Bourbons

Philip V	1700–1746
Ferdinand VI	1746–1759
Charles III	1759–1788
Charles IV	1788–1808
Ferdinand VII	1808
Joseph Bonaparte	1808–1813
Ferdinand VII (restored)	1814–1833
Isabella II	1833–1868
Amadeo	1870–1873
Alfonso XII	1874–1885
Alfonso XIII	1886–1931
Juan Carlos I	1975–

AUSTRIA AND AUSTRIA-HUNGARY

(Until 1806 all except Maria Theresa were also Holy Roman Emperors.)

Maximilian I, Archduke	1493–1519
Charles I (Emperor as Charles V)	1519–1556
Ferdinand I	1556–1564
Maximilian II	1564–1576
Rudolf II	1576–1612
Matthias	1612–1619
Ferdinand II	1619–1637
Ferdinand III	1637–1657
Leopold I	1658–1705
Joseph I	1705–1711
Charles VI	1711–1740
Maria Theresa	1740–1780
Joseph II	1780–1790
Leopold II	1790–1792
Francis II	1792–1835
Ferdinand I	1835–1848
Francis Joseph	1848–1916
Charles I	1916–1918

PRUSSIA AND GERMANY

Hohenzollerns

Frederick William the Great Elector	1640–1688
Frederick I	1701–1713
Frederick William I	1713–1740
Frederick II the Great	1740–1786
Frederick William II	1786–1797
Frederick William III	1797–1840
Frederick William IV	1840–1861
William I	1861–1888
Frederick III	1888
William II	1888–1918

RUSSIA

Ivan III	1462–1505
Basil III	1505–1533
Ivan IV the Terrible	1533–1584
Theodore I	1584–1598
Boris Godunov	1598–1605
Theodore II	1605
Basil IV	1606–1610

Romanovs

Michael	1613–1645
Alexius	1645–1676
Theodore III	1676–1682
Ivan IV and Peter I	1682–1689
Peter I the Great alone	1689–1725
Catherine I	1725–1727
Peter II	1727–1730
Anna	1730–1740
Ivan VI	1740–1741
Elizabeth	1741–1762
Peter III	1762
Catherine II the Great	1762–1796
Paul	1796–1801
Alexander I	1801–1825
Nicholas I	1825–1855
Alexander II	1855–1881
Alexander III	1881–1894
Nicholas II	1894–1917

ITALY

Victor Emmanuel II	1861–1878
Humbert I	1878–1900
Victor Emmanuel III	1900–1946
Humbert II	1946

INDEX

291 Aeneas Silvius Piccolomini, 1457 letter to Martin Meyr, chancellor of the archbishop of Mainz, entitled *De ritu, situ, moribus et conditione Germaniae,* in the former's *Opera omnia* (Basel: Ex officina Henricpetrina, 1571), p. 1064.

307 Letter of Marsilio Ficino to Paul of Middleburg, translated by M. M. McLaughlin from *Opera omnia* (Basel, 1576) in *The Portable Renaissance Reader* (New York: Viking, 1953), p. 79.

329 Hernán Cortés, *Letters from Mexico,* edited and translated by A. R. Pagden (New York: Grossman Publishers, 1971), p. 138.

342 R. Hakluyt, "A Discourse Concerning Western Planting," Maine Historical Collections, 2nd Series, *Documentary History of the State of Maine,* (Portland, Maine: n.p., 1869–1916), Vol. 2, 36–41. Courtesy Maine Historical Society.

347 Adapted from R. H. Bainton, *Here I Stand: A Life of Martin Luther* (New York: New American Library, 1950), p. 144.

363 Niccolo Machiavelli, *The Prince,* translated by L. Ricci, revised by E. R. P. Vincent (New York: Mentor/New American Library, 1952), pp. 93–94.

383 Louis XIV, "Lessons in Kingship," from his *Memoires,* translated by H. H. Rowen, in *From Absolutism to Revolution* (New York: Macmillan, 1963), pp. 26–27.

401 A. Burnaby, *Travels through the Middle Settlements in North America,* 2nd ed. (Ithaca, N.Y.: Cornell University Press, 1960), pp. 110–114.

417 M. J. de Caritat, Marquis de Condorcet, "Equisse d'un Tableau Historique des Progress de l' Esprit Human," in O. E. Fellows and N. L. Torrey, eds., *The Age of Enlightenment: An Anthology* (New York: Appleton-Century-Crofts, 1942), pp. 623, 626.

435 The Duc de Niverais, cited in N. Mitford, *Frederick the Great* (Harmondsworth: Penguin Books, 1970), pp. 190–193.

A-1–A-4 D. Kagan, S. Ozment, and F. Turner, *The Western Heritage* (New York: Macmillan, 1983), pp. i–iv. Reprinted with permission of Macmillan Publishing Company from *The Western Heritage* by D. Kagan, S. Ozment, and F. Turner. Copyright © 1983 by Macmillan Publishing Company.

PHOTO CREDITS

4 Scala/Art Resource, N.Y.; 10 The Oriental Institute, The University of Chicago; 17 Rene Burri, Magnum Photos; 18 The Metropolitan Museum of Art, New York; 22 Erich Lessing, Magnum Photos; 28 Constantine Manos, Magnum Photos; 29 Giraudon/Art Resource, N.Y.; 31 The Granger Collection; 36 Erich Lessing, Magnum Photos; 37 Ernst Haas, Magnum Photos; 40 Scala/Art Resource, N.Y.; 43 The Oriental Institute, The University of Chicago; 45 The Granger Collection; 56 Scala/Art Resource, N.Y.; 58 Hirmer Fotoarchiv; 63 Constantine Manos, Magnum Photos; 66 Walter S. Clark, Photo Researchers, Inc.; 68 Hirmer Fotoarchiv; 69 (left) Hirmer Fotoarchiv; (right) Hirmer Fotoarchiv; 70 (top left) Hirmer Fotoarchiv; (top right) Alinari/Art Resource, N.Y.; (bottom) Hirmer Fotoarchiv; 74 The Granger Collection; 79 The Bettmann Archive; 85 Giraudon/Art Resource, N.Y.; 87 (top left) Giraudon/Art Resource, N.Y.; (top right) Hirmer Fotoarchiv; (bottom) Giraudon/Art Resource, N.Y.; 90 Scala/Art Resource, N.Y.; 93 Historical Pictures Service, Chicago; 94 Hirmer Fotoarchiv; 95 Scala/Art Resource, N.Y.; 96 Alinari/Art Resource, N.Y.; 100 Musées Nationaux, Paris; 106 Scala/Art Resource, N.Y.; 109 Alinari/Art Resource, N.Y.; 118 (top) Michael Holford; (bottom) Alinari/Art Resource, N.Y.; 119 Alinari/Art Resource, N.Y.; 122 Scala/Art Resource, N.Y.; 129 Alinari/Art Resource, N.Y.; 132 Art Resource, N.Y.; 138 George Holton, Photo Researchers, Inc.; 142 Brian Brake, Photo Researchers, Inc.; 144 Michael Holford; 147 Art Resource, N.Y.; 149 (top) Alinari/Art Resource, N.Y.; (bottom left) Michael Holford; (bottom right) Michael Holford; 150 Courtesy of The Oriental Institute, The University of Chicago; 151 Alinari/Art Resource, N.Y.; 153 Art Resource, N.Y.; 162 Erich Lessing, Magnum Photos; 167 Scala/Art Resource, N.Y.; 170 George Holton, Photo Researchers, Inc.; 172 Art Resource, N.Y.; 174 Bibliothéque Nationale, Paris; 177 Bibliothéque Nationale, Paris; 180 Bibliothéque Nationale, Paris; 185 The Bettmann Archive; 186 Giraudon/Art Resource, N.Y.; 187 The Bettmann Archive; 191 Culver Pictures, Inc.; 196 Scala/Art Resource, N.Y.; 198 The Fotomas Index; 201 The Fotomas Index; 205 Photographie Bulloz; 209 Guy Gillette, Photo Researchers, Inc; 214 Bibliothéque Nationale, Paris; 220 Scala/Art Resource, N.Y.; 222 The Metropolitan Museum of Art, New York; 223 Bibliotéque Nationale, Paris; 228 Scala/ Art Resource, N.Y.; 232 Culver Pictures, Inc.; 238 Scala/Art Resource, N.Y.; 241 Culver Pictures, Inc.; 244 Scala/Art Resource, N.Y.; 245 SEF/Art Resource, N.Y.; 246 Scala/Art Resource, N.Y.; 248 Hirmer Fotoarchiv; 250 Hirmer Fotoarchiv; 256 The Bettmann Archive; 257 Scala/Art Resource, N.Y.; 261 Courtesy of The Walters Art Gallery, Baltimore; 262 Giraudon/Art Resource, N.Y.; 265 Giraudon/Art Resource, N.Y.; 272 The Granger Collection; 276 Photographie Bulloz; 277 National Portrait Gallery, London; 281 Historical Pictures Service, Chicago; 287 John O'Hagan, Photo Researchers, Inc.; 290 Scala/Art Resource, N.Y.; 295 The Granger Collection; 298 Scala/Art Resource, N.Y.; 302 Culver Pictures, Inc.; 303 Historical Pictures Service, Chicago; 306 Scala/Art Resource, N.Y.; 311 Scala/Art Resource, N.Y.; 313 Scala/Art Resource, N.Y.; 314 Scala/Art Resource, N.Y.; 315 Giraudon/Art Resource, N.Y.; 316 National Gallery of Art, Washington, Andrew W. Mellon Collection; 317 Scala/Art Resource, N.Y.; 318 Scala/Art Resource, N.Y.; 319 Art Resource, N.Y.; 323 H. Roger-Voillet, Paris; 324 E. T. Archive; 325 Art Resource, N.Y.; 326 Scala/Art Resource, N.Y.; 328 Michael Holford; 331 (top) The Fotomas Index; (bottom) Michael Holford; 334 Historical Pictures Service, Chicago; 336 Historical Pictures Service, Chicago; 337 The Bettmann Archive; 338 The Bettmann Archive; 341 Brown Brothers; 346 The Toledo Museum of Art; 351 The Granger Collection; 355 The Bettmann Archive; 357 Culver Pictures, Inc.; 358 The Fotomas Index; 359 Photographie Bulloz; 362 Erich Lessing, Magnum Photos; 369 Giraudon/Art Resource, N.Y.; 370 Erich Lessing, Magnum Photos; 374 The Bettmann Archive; 376 The Mansell Collection; 382 Scala/Art Resource, N.Y.; 385 Giraudon/Art Resource, N.Y.; 392 The Bettmann Archive; 395 The Bettmann Archive; 396 Saskia/Art Resource, N.Y.; 398 The Bettmann Archive; 400 SEF/Art Resource, N.Y.; 406 Historical Pictures Service, Chicago; 407 The Granger Collection; 408 The Granger Collection; 409 Brown Brothers; 412 The Granger Collection; 416 The Granger Collection; 419 The Bettmann Archive; 420 Art Resource, N.Y.; 424 Giraudon/Art Resource, N.Y.; 429 The Wallace Collection; 430 National Gallery of Art, Washington, Samuel H. Kress Collection; 434 The Bettmann Archive; 438 Culver Pictures, Inc.; 439 The Bettmann Archive; 442 The Fotomas Index; 444 Photographie Bulloz; 448 Giraudon/Art Resource, N.Y.

ABOUT THE AUTHORS

Richard D. Goff (Ph.D.: Duke) is Professor of History at Eastern Michigan University where he has taught survey courses in Western and World Civilization. In 1983 he received a distinguished faculty service award from the university. Among his publications is *The Twentieth Century: A Brief Global History*, published by Knopf.

George H. Cassar (Ph.D.: McGill) is Professor of History at Eastern Michigan University where he has taught survey courses in Western Civilization, and courses in European and Military History. He is a recent recipient of the Faculty Award for Research and Publication from Eastern Michigan University. His publications include *The French and the Dardanelles, Kitchener: Architect of Victory, The Tragedy of Sir John French,* and *Beyond Courage: The Canadiens at the Second Battle of Ypres.*

Anthony Esler (Ph.D.: Duke) is Professor of History at the College of William and Mary. He has written on a variety of topics, including the history of youth movements and global history. His most recent book is *The Human Venture: A World History*, published by Prentice-Hall.

James P. Holoka (Ph.D.: Michigan) is Professor of Foreign Languages at Eastern Michigan University where he has taught Classics and Humanities for twelve years. He is a recipient of a Rackham Prize Fellowship as well as an excellence in teaching award from Eastern Michigan University. He is the author of numerous publications in such journals as *Classical World, Transactions of the American Philological Association,* and *Classical Philology.*

James C. Waltz (Ph.D.: Michigan State) is Professor and former Chairman of History at Eastern Michigan University where he has taught survey courses in Western Civilization and courses in Ancient, Medieval, Renaissance, and Reformation History. He is a recipient of an N.E.H. Fellowship for residents for college teachers (University of Chicago). He is the author of many articles and book reviews in *The Muslim World* and other publications.